Behind Bars

Readings on Prison Culture

RICHARD TEWKSBURY
University of Louisville

Upper Saddle River, New Jersey 07458

Library of Congress Cataloging-in-Publication Data

Behind bars : readings on prison culture / [edited by] Richard Tewksbury.—1st ed.
p. cm.
Includes bibliographical references and index.
ISBN 0-13-119072-5
1. Prisons. 2. Prisons—United States. 3. Prisoners. 4. Prisoners—United States.
I. Tewksbury, Richard A.

HV8491.B44 2005
365—dc22

2005042958

Senior Editor: *Frank Mortimer, Jr.*
Assistant Editor: *Mayda Bosco*
Director of Production and Manufacturing: *Bruce Johnson*
Managing Editor: *Mary Carnis*
Manufacturing Buyer: *Cathleen Petersen*
Production Liaison: *Brian Hyland*
Production Editor: *Christine Knapp*
Design Director: *Cheryl Asherman*
Senior Design Coordinator: *Miguel Ortiz*
Cover Designer: *Marianne Frasco*
Cover Photographer: *David R. Frazier, Getty Images/STONE*
Compositor: *The GTS Companies*
Printing and Binding: *Courier Stoughton*

Pearson Education LTD.
Pearson Education Singapore Pte. Ltd.
Pearson Education, Canada, Ltd.
Pearson Education–Japan
Pearson Education Australia Pty, Limited
Pearson Education North Asia Ltd.
Pearson Educación de Mexico, S.A. de C.V.
Pearson Education Malaysia, Pte. Ltd.

10 9 8 7 6 5 4 3 2 1
ISBN 0-13-119072-5

Introduction

What is it really like to be a prison inmate? Is the experience similar to what most people assume? Is the life of a prison inmate like what we see on television and in the movies? What is it about serving a period of incarceration that really makes it punishment? Are prison inmates mistreated, as many political activists and "liberals" claim? Are prisons too "soft" on criminals, as "conservatives" often argue? And at the core of the debate, it is necessary to ask, what is the goal of prison? The thirty-two selections in this book address these questions and more and offer answers. However, as readers will quickly see, these answers are not necessarily easy to conclude, nor is there always only one answer to each of these questions. Especially when considering what the ultimate goal of prison is, the answer may more likely be more questions.

This book is designed to give the reader an "insider's" view of the experience of being in prison. The focus is on how prison inmates experience being segregated from society; living in a congregate environment of offenders; and being subject to single-sex environments where sex, drugs, violence, and stresses are common and sometimes dominate one's day-to-day activities and thoughts. It is the intent of this book to leave readers with a thorough understanding of what prison inmates encounter from their first day in prison until after they leave and look back on their experiences. Understanding incarceration from the point of view of those who live it is an important perspective, although not that common in social science. If we are able to understand "what it is really like" to be in prison, we should be better equipped to design prisons, plan their operations, oversee their daily activities, and identify problems in their operation.

When we think about what it is like to serve time in prison, there are many issues we need to consider. First, we need to think about how the experience would affect us individually. How would our thinking (about ourselves, others, society, prisons, and other prisoners) be affected, and how would we react emotionally to being segregated from society? How would we respond to losing the vast majority of our freedoms and having our every movement and activity watched and restricted by someone else? These are the issues addressed in the first section of this book. The five articles in the Psychological Adaptations section examine what inmates experience as they first arrive at prison, how their individual styles of coping affect their experiences, and how different types of criminal sentences and prison structures are experienced.

The second section of the book addresses common and, for many observers, problematic types of relationships inside prisons. Inmates usually have two types of people with whom to interact while incarcerated: other inmates and corrections officials/staff. The four articles in this section look at three basic forms of relationships that any inmate is going to encounter in prison. They are violent relationships, sexual relationships, and interactions with prison staff. Referring to these interactions as "relationships" may be a bit of a stretch, for as these articles show, there are not many close, emotionally intimate, and truly personal types of interactions in an inmate's life. However, these types of interactions are found in every prison, and therefore, it is important that we both recognize and understand how individuals perceive and react to these and other types of events. Only if we know about the types of relationships that develop among inmates will we be able to predict the consequences for those involved and the ways the interactions influence the overall operation of an institution.

In addition to their relationships inside the prison, most inmates maintain some type of relationship with persons beyond the walls of the prison. The third section of this book looks at the most common type of outside relationship for inmates, that of family. As these three articles show, both male and female inmates experience stress and a sense of loss related to having their family ties strained (or completely severed). Large numbers of prison inmates—especially females—are parents, and during their time of incarceration, time and opportunities to maintain contact with one's children are typically drastically reduced. One of the best ways for maintaining a relationship with outsiders is through a prison's visitation program. As the final article of this section shows, however, the opportunity to actually sit and visit with one's loved ones is not always a pleasant or desired experience. As a result, maintaining relationships with others outside the prison can be a very difficult task and one that inmates often see go unfulfilled.

The next two sections of the book look at two of the most frequently encountered aspects of day-to-day life for prison inmates. First, the section on health care and substance abuse examines what has become the most expensive service provided to inmates. It focuses on the challenges inherent in delivering and using health care services in an institutional setting. There are many problems related to health care in prisons, and as these articles point out, some of them are related to the politics, economics, social structure, and desires of providers. Some of the problems are also related to either specific types of inmates or specific types of health problems. Regardless of the specifics, the important issue for corrections is that it is mandatory to provide health care, and this area of institutional operations is fraught with difficulties.

The other frequently encountered aspect of day-to-day life for inmates that is addressed is programming. As the basis for "correcting" inmates, institutional programs are designed to keep inmates busy, provide them with opportunities to rehabilitate themselves, and enhance the likelihood of their returning to society as law-abiding citizens. Programs for inmates are often misunderstood and are [illegible] articles in this section examine common—and frequently misunderstood—prison programs. These articles make it clear that [illegible] programs for inmates and that [illegible] and correctional systems that invest in programs are pursuing many good outcomes at a relatively small cost.

The next set of articles examine what is often thought of as a fairly common, yet perhaps exaggerated, aspect of prison life: violence. A great deal of the attention the public focuses on prisons is centered on issues of violence. Many people assume that American prisons are chaotic, exceptionally dangerous, and experience severe violence on a daily basis. While there is some degree of these present in most prisons, the belief that these are the primary defining aspects of an inmate's life is far from the truth. In the six articles in this section, the authors focus on the role of threats, dangers, consequences, and related anxieties that violence and the possibility for violence in prison introduce. Violence inside prisons comes in a wide range of forms. Some are obvious, such as assaults, rapes, and riots. Other times violence is found in "small" forms and includes psychological and social forms of violence. Individuals may perpetrate some forms of violence, while other forms are committed within an organizational—or gang—culture. Each of these types of violence is examined in the articles presented in this section, with special attention to the ways that violence impacts the experience of living in prison.

The last two sections of this book take a different approach. First, they examine the ways that media portrayals of corrections correspond with political goals for prisons, as well as "common knowledge" and "realities" of prison life. And second, attention is focused on what is involved in an inmate's experience of attempting to get out of prison legally and return to the community. It also addresses how structural aspects of community and criminal justice system actions and agencies can serve as barriers to this.

The three articles in the media portrayal section highlight the issues that are central to media presentations about corrections and the ways that media influences the public's ideas and understandings about prisons. The final section shows that preparing to return to the community can be a highly stressful time for the inmate and may be exceptionally difficult to complete successfully. Just as how first coming to prison introduces a great deal of uncertainties, anxieties, and fears to inmates, so too does the prospect of leaving prison and returning to "freedom." The ways that inmates experience this transition are highlighted in these final two articles, showing the similarities of this period of change to the transition from free society to prison.

Taken as a whole, it is hoped that these articles will highlight for the reader at least some of the complex issues that contribute to the experience of incarceration for inmates. Several themes run throughout the readings in this book. First is the question of how the experience of incarceration, and the structure of prison, is created. The debate between whether culture and behavior are imported to prison from the streets or whether inmates' attitudes and behaviors are a product of the deprivations of incarceration run throughout these discussions. The importation argument says that prison inmates are very similar to how they were on the streets, and the way that life is structured and experienced behind the walls is essentially the product of the characteristics, experiences, attitudes, and values that inmates bring to prison with them. In contrast, the deprivation model argues that prisoners' experiences and activities are the product of living in an environment that deprives them of the things that are part of "normal" life. Because of their feelings of deprivation, inmates respond to stimuli and their environment differently than they would in free society.

In simple terms, living inside prison is very, very different from living in free society. This fact remains for prisoners in all societies, which introduces the second theme of the book. Several of the articles in this book draw on research conducted in other nations, including England and Australia. However, while there are some important differences in how prisons operate and who is incarcerated there, it is clear that many of the experiences of prisoners are universal. As the authors of the articles in this collection make clear, in almost all ways it is a much worse experience to live in prison than outside. This is not to say that life in prison is horrible or hellish, but it does suggest that prison life is very stressful and not necessarily what correctional officials and policy makers intend.

What is it like to live in prison? It differs for every inmate, but there are clearly some general patterns and similarities for most—if not all—inmates. These are the focus of this collection of articles. After reading this collection, one should have a more complete understanding of the experience of incarceration and how the structures, personnel, resources, activities, and constraints of prisons establish possibilities for inmates. As you examine these issues, it is important to keep in mind the larger question: What is the goal of incarceration?

Contents

Part 1: Psychological Adaptations

Living in prison is clearly physically restricting; inmates cannot leave, and their movements within the prison are often carefully controlled, scheduled, and observed. But, as the articles in this section highlight, sometimes the *physical* aspects of incarceration are not the most restrictive. The psychological aspects are believed to be a greater form of punishment, and much more stressful, than the simple physical restrictions that prison imposes on inmates.

When thinking about the psychological punishment of prison, it is important to examine the stresses that the environment creates and imposes on inmates. Inmates are separated from the culture, loved ones, material goods, privacy, and an array of liberties that most Americans are accustomed to having. One should examine how disconnection from these things creates difficulties and suffering for inmates.

The psychological stresses of incarceration begin even before the inmate arrives at prison. As Schmid and Jones point out in the first article, first-time inmates find themselves in a confusing and chaotic world that they struggle to make sense of while also struggling to come to grips with their newfound status and identity. The ways that first-time, short-term inmates cope with their experience varies across the time they are in prison, although they rarely come to fully accept and internalize an identity as an inmate.

The way an individual copes with stressful situations and changes in his life is important for how an inmate adjusts to prison. This is the focus of Gullone, Jones, and Cummings in their article, "Coping Styles and Prison Experience as Predictors of Psychological Well-Being in Male Prisoners." As their research makes clear, there are coping styles and personal characteristics that can facilitate an inmate's successfully navigating the experience of incarceration. However, some are likely to lead to greater levels of stress and suffering.

The ways that inmates' mental health is affected by incarceration and the different structures of the specific prison in which they are housed is the focus of Wooldredge's "Inmate Experiences and Psychological Well-Being." How incarceration is experienced is largely a consequence of what an inmate does to fill his or her time while in prison, and how much contact he or she has with people outside of prison. This research finds that if inmates stay busier while incarcerated and if they are able to maintain frequent contact with loved ones, they are more likely to have positive mental health.

In "Women's Accounts of their Prison Experience," Pogrebin and Dodge look at the ways that incarcerated females perceive and interpret their experiences. Their article makes clear that how women experience prison is different from the ways their male counterparts do. Women in prison experience high levels of anxiety, perhaps feeling punishment to a greater degree than many law and policy makers intended. And, because women constitute such a small portion of American inmates, the options available for programming and administrative structures and responses are more restricted than those for male inmates.

Haney discusses the psychological consequences of one of our nation's newest and more popular forms of incarceration, the supermax prison. This new method of keeping people in prison, in which individuals are locked up alone for at least twenty-three hours of every day, is shown to have serious negative effects on inmates' mental health. Although supermax prisons were designed with the idea of controlling the most incorrigible of inmates, research shows that while they may be effective at controlling behavior in the present, there are serious concerns about long-term consequences.

A couple of factors need to be kept in mind as you read these articles. First, try to think about the experiences and structured worlds of prisons from the perspective of someone who is living this life. Taking the perspective of the inmate is different from how many of us would initially view prison life and experiences. Also, keep in mind that prison and the prison experience differ across cultural and geographic locations. The articles in this section should bring this to light for you, as the research being reported comes from both in the United States and elsewhere.

Finally, as you read these articles, keep this in mind: What is the goal of sending criminals to prison? As you read about the ways that inmates adjust to prison, how they do or do not change while in prison, and how different types of prisons are associated with different outcomes, ask yourself whether our goal for prisons is being achieved.

Discussion Questions

Psychological Adaptations

1. What about the experience of being incarcerated leads to inmates having difficulty adjusting to life in prison?

2. What are the major sources of social and emotional support available to prison inmates? How can these assist inmates in both initially adjusting and maintaining mental health while incarcerated?

3. How is the experience of incarceration in segregation or supermax different for inmates?

1. Ambivalent Actions

Prison Adaptation Strategies of First-Time, Short-Term Inmates

Thomas J. Schmid
Richard S. Jones

A person who is incarcerated for the first time becomes a "prisoner" but does not automatically acquire a meaningful status within the prison world. If the incarceration is short term, the person is unlikely to ever achieve a significant prison status because participation in the prison world will be inhibited by identification with the outside world. This condition of social marginality results in an ambivalence that directly shapes inmates' strategies for survival within the prison world. This article examines the effect of ambivalence on inmates' adaptation strategies. Data for the study were collected through participant observation and focused interviews with inmates at a maximum security prison for men.

"Doing time" in a maximum security prison is not simply a matter of being in prison. It is, rather, a creative process through which inmates must invent or learn a repertoire of adaptation tactics that address the varying problems they confront during particular phases of their prison careers.

There is an extensive literature on the informal organization of prison life and the socialization processes through which inmates come to participate in this informal organization. Clemmer (1958) defines prisonization as "the taking on in greater or lesser degree of the folkways, customs, and general culture of the penitentiary" (p. 279). Prisonization is thus fundamentally a process of cultural accommodation through which inmates are first initiated into and then made a part of the prison social and cultural system. Neither of the two theoretical models developed to account for inmate adaptations to imprisonment—the "deprivation model" (Goffman 1961; Sykes [1959] 1971; Sykes and Messinger 1960) or the "importation model" (Thomas 1973; Thomas and Peterson 1977)—adequately represent the multiple ambiguities faced by the sociologically distinctive category of inmates who have no prior experience with the prison world and whose imprisonment is relatively brief.

When first-time inmates are sentenced to prison they have already lost their status as free adults but have not yet achieved any meaningful status within the prison world; they are, to older inmates, "fish" (see Cardozo-Freeman 1984; Irwin 1980). They can shed this label through their increasing participation in prison life, but if they are short-term inmates as well as first-timers they are unlikely to ever achieve a significant prison status. Their participation in the prison world will continue to be inhibited by their ties to, and identification with, the outside world. Their social marginality, grounded both in place and in time, is thus parallel to that experienced by immigrants who expect to return to their country of origin within a few years' time (see Morawska 1987; Shokeid 1988) or who otherwise manage to maintain a "sojourner orientation" (Gibson 1988). Immigrant sojourners, however, can typically draw on shared symbols or institutions in their transient adaptations to a new culture. New inmates, in contrast, have little in common with one another except their conventionality (Schmid and Jones 1991) and consequently have fewer collective resources available to resist assimilation into the prison culture.

In this article, we examine how first-time, short-term inmates in a maximum security prison make use of their social marginality, and the sociological ambivalence that results from it, to forge highly delimited adaptation strategies to the prison culture. After describing our methodological approach and fieldwork experiences, we briefly summarize our earlier analysis, which demonstrated that the social marginality of the first-time, short-term inmates we studied shaped their experiential orientations toward the prison world. We then analyze the relationship between ambivalence and inmates' prison strategies and discuss the extended sociological implications of our findings.

Method

Ordinarily, one of the most difficult steps in sociological research on prisons is gaining unrestricted access to inmates' day-to-day lives within the prison world. Our study originated with such access, when one of the authors (R. Jones) was serving a year-and-a-day sentence in a maximum security prison for men in the upper midwestern region of the United States. Through negotiations with prison officials, Jones was permitted to enroll in a graduate sociology course in field methods. What began as a directed studies course between professor and former student rapidly evolved, at Jones's suggestion, into a more comprehensive project conducted by co-researchers.

As the "inside observer," Jones had a number of specific advantages. In his interactions with other inmates and with guards, he was not viewed as a sociologist or a student or any other kind of outsider: He was viewed as a prisoner. Moreover, he was not merely assuming the role of a prisoner to learn about the prison world—he *was* a prisoner. He literally shared the experiences of other first-time, short-term inmates, enabling him to contextualize his observations of others with a full measure of sociological introspection (Ellis 1991).

As the "outside" observer for the project, Schmid attempted to guide the direction of the fieldwork by placing Jones's observations in a sociological context, suggesting theoretical concepts that could be useful, additional questions that might be asked, methods that could be used to address these questions, and procedures through which we could test the validity of Jones's initial obser- [illegible] with his own observations at the prison, and took a primary role in data analysis.

Our fieldwork essentially began with a journal that Jones started keeping several days before the beginning of his sentence. [illegible] personal expressions, although they included more traditional ethnographic descriptions as well. Once our research project was formally initiated, Jones restricted his journal entries to personal thoughts and impressions and chronology of his daily experiences. Using a process similar to the "diary-interview" method described by Zimmerman and Wieder (1977), these entries provided a framework for extended conversations between the researchers.

In addition to journal entries, Jones also prepared field notes on his participation in prison activities, his conversations with individual prisoners and groups of inmates, and his general observations of prison life.

We were able to discuss our research progress through letters, occasional telephone calls, and regular meetings arranged with the cooperation of prison officials. Shortly after the beginning of the study, we settled on a communication routine that proved to be quite efficient. Jones prepared one to three field observations each week (averaging 8–10 handwritten pages) and mailed them to Schmid for annotation and suggestions. Every other week Schmid would meet with Jones in an office or testing room provided by the prison's education department. At these meetings, we would review the journal entries and observations, plan our research strategy, and piece together our emerging conceptualization of the prison world.

Following Jones's release from prison, we devoted a year to the analysis of our initial data, and then returned to the prison to conduct focused interviews. Using information provided by prison officials, we were able to identify and interview 20 additional first-time, short-term inmates.

Our analysis of the prison experiences of first-time, short-term inmates thus draws on three primary sources of data. Our principal source is the field notes, representing 10 months of participant observation by a "complete participant" in collaboration with a "complete observer." A second source is Jones's prison journals in which he recorded his own prison experiences. Our subsequent interviews with other inmates constitute our third source of data; these interviews allowed us to pursue a number of topics in greater depth and provided us with an independent source of data to test our initial findings.

Marginality, Prison Imagery, and Prison Adaptations

Our earlier analysis of experiential orientations to prison (Schmid and Jones 1990) demonstrated that, at the beginning of their sentences, first-time, short-term inmates defined prison from the perspective of an outsider, drawing on the shared public meanings that exist in our society about prison. By the midpoint of their sentences they had not lost their outsiders' perspective completely and still had only a marginal status within the prison world, but they nonetheless defined prison principally in terms of shared subcultural meanings learned from other inmates. This "insider's perspective," however, subsequently gave way to concluding images that again expressed an outsider's point of view. (More precisely, their concluding imagery was a reflection of their marginal involvement in both worlds; it was a synthesis of their anticipatory and midcareer images and hence a synthesis of their outsider's and insider's perspectives.)

Inmates' subjective understandings of the prison world are important because they provide a basis for action (Blumer 1969). Our earlier analysis also demonstrated, in a general way, how inmates' adaptation strategies followed their shifting prison imagery. For example, in response to the violence of their initial outsider's imagery, their earliest survival tactics were protective and defensive in nature. As cultural outsiders, however, new inmates also recognized their need for more information about the prison world, and virtually all of their early survival tactics served as information seeking as well as protective measures. Thus territorial caution, impression management, and their partnerships (a friendship with another prisoner recognized by other inmates and guards) guided their ventures into the cafeteria, the yard, the gym, and other unexplored areas of the prison. Selective interaction with other inmates, impression management, and their partnerships helped them confront such prison experiences as parole board hearings, cell transfers, legal and illegal recreational activities, and participation in the prison economy. The barrage of often conflicting information they received through these tactics was the raw material out of which they continuously revised their prison images. Although they continued to view prison with essentially an outsider's perspective, their survival tactics allowed them gradually to acquire an insider's knowledge of the prison and to modify their adaptation tactics accordingly.

A common form of prison adaptation is the creation of a survival "niche" (Seymour 1977) that allows inmates some measure of activity, privacy, safety, emotional feedback, structure, and freedom within the larger, hostile environment of the maximum security prison (Johnson 1987; Toch 1977). Because of their inexperience, first-time inmates were particularly ill-equipped for finding such niches (Johnson 1987, 114), and new short-term inmates were further handicapped by their continuing marginality in the prison world, which restricted their ability to exert personal control (Goodstein, MacKenzie, and Shotland 1984) and inhibited their acceptance by other inmates. But short-term inmates, in contrast to those facing years of imprisonment, needed only to develop a *transient* niche in prison. The problems they faced were similar—understanding the prison status hierarchy and recognizing their place in it, learning whom to trust and whom to avoid, and determining how to evade trouble in a trouble-filled environment—but their solutions did not need to be as enduring. The men we studied were able to achieve such transient "accommodation without assimilation" (Gibson 1988) within a few months' time. To a casual observer, moreover, they soon became indistinguishable from long-term inmates, relying on such adaptive tactics as legal and illegal diversions and conscious efforts to control their thoughts about the outside world. Their relative integration into the prison world [illegible] lived, however, and their marginality within this world again became evident as they prepared for their departure from prison. Like more experienced [illegible] finding a job and a place to live, and existential concerns about how the outside [illegible] time in prison (see Irwin 1970). Faced with these problems, it became increasingly apparent to inmates that most (though not all) of the adaptation tactics associated with their prison orientation were inadequate for dealing with the outside world.

Based on this general pattern, it is tempting to infer that inmates' adaptations strategies change simply because their reference group changes. In this explanation, suggested by Wheeler's (1961) finding of a curvilinear relationship between institutional career phase and conformity to staff expectations, inmates come to abandon the beliefs, values, and norms of the outside world as they acquire more information about and eventually achieve membership in the prison world. In similar fashion, they abandon the beliefs, values, and norms of the prison world when they are about to regain membership in the outside world. Our earlier analysis (Schmid and Jones 1990) challenged this explanation by focusing on inmates' continuous and active work to *interpret* the prison world. This explanation becomes even more unsatisfactory when we introduce into our analysis the ambivalence that inmates experience throughout their entire prison careers.

Ambivalence and Prison Strategies

In its most general sense, ambivalence refers to the experience of being pulled in psychologically different directions; because prison inmates *share* this experience, it becomes sociologically as well as psychologically significant. The ambivalence of first-time, short-term inmates flows directly from their transitional status between the outside social world and the prison's: It is an ambivalence grounded in the marginality of "people who have lived in two or more societies and so have become oriented to differing sets of cultural values . . . [or] of people who accept certain values held by groups of which they are not members" (Merton and Barber 1976, 11–12). Although inmates' ambivalence affects their prison imagery and strategies in various ways, its principal effect is to limit behavioral changes by inhibiting new inmates from becoming fully assimilated into prison culture.

Feelings of ambivalence characterized the thoughts, emotions, and, sometimes, the actions of the inmates throughout their entire prison careers. Their adaptations to prison expressed both the outsider's perspective they preferred and the insider's perspective they provisionally accepted. Because their strategies were guided by their imagery, their outsider's perspective was most apparent in their behavior at the beginning of their sentences, whereas their insider's perspective was most apparent during the middle part of their sentences. Their behavior during the final months of their sentences was a mixture of nonprison forms of interaction and prison adaptive tactics because their concluding imagery was a synthesis of outsider's and insider's perspectives. Yet a closer inspection of inmates' evolving strategies reveals that the simultaneous influence of the outside and inside worlds was not restricted to the end of their sentences. At every stage of their prison careers, their actions were influenced by the underlying ambivalence

TABLE 1 Experiences of Ambivalence During Prison Career

	Career Experiences	*Reported Ambivalence*
Preprison	Conviction and sentencing Detention in county jail Transportation to prison	Desire to postpone sentence versus desire to proceed with sentence
Early months of sentence	Holding cell In-processing First night in cell	Desire to insulate self versus desire for sociability
	Orientation classes (first week) Initial correspondence and visits with outsiders	Desire to proceed with new experiences versus relief at security of close supervision during first weeks of sentence
	Transfer to another cell Assignment to caseworker First contacts with general inmate population Job or program assignment Cellblock transfer	Desire for greater mobility within prison versus fear of greater contact with inmates
Middle portion of sentence	Work/program participation Legal and illegal diversions Correspondence and visits with outsiders	Desire to discontinue outside contacts and "do your own time" versus desire to maintain outside contacts
Conclusion of sentence	Application for transfer to minimum security Transfer to minimum security Outside passes	Desire for greater freedom versus willingness to complete sentence in maximum security
	Home furloughs Transfer to reentry program Release from prison	Desire to put prison in past and return to free world versus desire to avoid existential concerns about return to free world

that resulted from their marginal position in both the outside and prison social worlds. Table 1 presents the various manifestations of this ambivalence that occurred throughout the prison career.

Preprison and Early Career Experiences

Inmates' ambivalence began before they arrived at prison. Like most outsiders, they viewed prison as a world quite different from their own and had difficulty picturing themselves within that world. In the final days of their freedom, they [illegible] They wanted desperately to avoid their [illegible] to proceed because they knew this was inevitable. They retained an outsider's [illegible]

Their ambivalent feelings continued throughout their sentences, although the form and emphasis of their ambivalence changed as they progressed through their prison careers. But even in their earliest days in prison, the dominant form of their ambivalence emerged: Their desire to insulate themselves from the surrounding prison world was countered by their desire for human sociability (see Glaser 1969, 18–21). Throughout their careers, but especially during the first half of their sentences, both sides of this fundamental conflict between an outsider's detachment and an insider's participation in the prison world influenced their behavior. Of importance here is that inmates began to *act*, albeit cautiously, on their desire for contact with others during the first week of their sentences. Their initial contacts with others were quite limited, and they did not appreciably alter their images or strategies, but these contacts did indicate that their isolation did not need to be as extreme as they had anticipated. A 23-year-old inmate, convicted of narcotics sales, described his earliest encounter with another inmate:

> There was one guy that they brought in with me, and we sort of talked off and on. He was sort of scared too, and it was his first time too. He was talking to a guard; I overheard him talking to a guard. I heard him say that he was just basically scared as hell. The guard was trying to calm him down. We were all together in a group; we eat at the same table and everything, and I got talking to him. So I had somebody to talk to. (Interview)

During their first week in prison, in which they were housed together with other incoming inmates but segregated from the general inmate population, they were able to express their desire for contact with others through limited interaction with both guards and inmates. They learned that not all guards fit their initial stereotypes, and many new inmates encountered one or more fellow inmates with backgrounds similar to their own. They were still intimidated by the prison, particularly by those aspects of prison life that they had not yet experienced, but they began to reduce their isolation and expand their knowledge of the prison world.

The first week thus enabled new inmates, through passive observations and direct interaction, to modify (but not radically transform) both their images and their strategies. Their segregation during this week also led to yet another variant of their ambivalence: They were relieved at the protection of close supervision, but because they knew that they could not avoid facing the general inmate population indefinitely they were anxious to move on to the next phase of their sentences. Similar feelings of ambivalence resurfaced with each new experience. When they learned that they would be transferred to a different cell, and later to another cellblock entirely, they looked forward to the greater mobility these moves offered, but they feared the increased inmate contact the moves would necessitate:

> After only 2 days they moved me [to another cell]. . . . With this move came more freedom. . . . I could go out in the yard and to the dining hall for meals. I was a little apprehensive about getting out. I had made friends with one guy, so we went into the yard together. We were out for about an hour when we were approached

> by a black dude. He wanted to get us high. I'm sure that's not all he wanted. . . . It helps to find a friend or two; you feel safer in a crowd. (Field notes)

Their fear mirrored the violence of their prison imagery, whereas their desire to proceed reflected their acceptance that they were now prison inmates.

The evolution of inmates' prison perspectives continued and accelerated through the early months of their sentences. The survival strategies they formulated during these months, like their anticipatory survival strategies, were based on their images of prison. But increasingly their strategies led to modification of these images. This happened because their strategies continued to be influenced by the same motivational factors: (a) their concern for safety but also their recognition that their prison imagery was incomplete and (b) their ambivalence, especially their desire to proceed with new and inevitable prison experiences. The same tactics that gave them new information also reflected the opposing directions of their ambivalence. Their practice of territorial caution and their rudimentary impression management skills expressed their apprehension over contact with other prisoners and their desire for self-insulation, but these tactics also allowed them to initiate or accept limited interaction with others. Their selective interaction with other inmates and their partnership with one other inmate directly expressed their desire for sociability while providing them with a means of maintaining social and emotional distance from the majority of the inmate population.

Midcareer Experiences

Inmates' midcareer adaptation strategies, like their earlier survival strategies, were based on their prison imagery and their ambivalence. Their adaptation strategies differed from their survival strategies because their images changed and because the form and emphasis of their ambivalence changed. Their survival strategies were intended to insulate them from the violence of their anticipatory images but also to allow them to confront new prison experiences and to provide them with new information about the prison world. By midcareer their imagery was dominated by the theme of boredom rather than violence, and they no longer saw a need for more information. But boredom was only one of the problems associated with "doing time" at midcareer: Their relationships with the outside world presented them with other difficulties. As they approached an insider's perspective on the prison world, they came to share the long-term inmate's belief that preoccupation with the outside world could make their sentences more difficult:

> I was talking with [a long-term inmate] and he was telling me that he doesn't usually hang around short-timers because they are so preoccupied with time. He said it took him a long time to get over counting the days, weeks, and months, and that he doesn't really like to be reminded about it. (Field notes; conversation [illegible])

Intimate relationships were likely to be questioned and might even be curtailed [illegible]

> I think it would be almost impossible to carry on a relationship, a real close relationship, being here for 2 years or a year and a half. It's literally impossible. I think that the best thing to do is to just forget about it, and if the relationship can be picked up again once you get out, that's fine. And if it can't, you have to accept that. (Interview)

Similar concerns were raised regarding all outside contacts. A 26-year-old inmate, convicted of the possession and sale of marijuana, told us,

> When they [the inmate's visitors] left I felt depressed. . . . It's a high when they come, and you get depressed when they leave. I was wondering if that's good. Maybe I should just forget that there is an outside world—at times I thought that, maybe as a survival mechanism to forget that there are good people in the world. (Interview)

Within a few months' time, inmates' adoption of an insider's perspective thus resulted in yet another manifestation of their ambivalence: Their desire to maintain their involvement in the outside world was countered by a temptation to discontinue all outside contacts so that they could do their own time without the infringement of a world to which they no longer actively belonged.

In a matter of months, then, inmates' perspectives underwent a substantial transformation: They were now viewing the outside world from the perspective of the prison world rather than the reverse, and their adaptation strategies, accordingly, were designed to help them cope with their insider's problems of "doing time" rather than their outsider's fears. Their viewpoints were only an *approximation* of an insider's perspective, however, and their insider's tactics were equivocal because they never achieved more than a marginal status within the prison world. During the middle portion of their sentences they may have been tempted to sever all outside contacts to make their time pass more easily, but they did not actually follow through on this temptation. And although the relationships they established in prison, especially their partnerships, might have seemed more important than their outside relationships, they knew that they would not have freely chosen to associate with most of these people on the outside, and they knew that they would not continue most of these relationships once they were released from prison. In this respect, the prison relationships of the men we studied were more cautious than those typically formed by long-term inmates (Cordilia 1983, 13–29; Johnson 1987, 62–63): They acknowledged that they did not fully belong to the prison world in the same sense that long-term or multiple-term inmates do, and they recognized that these other inmates did not fully accept them as members of their world. First-time, short-term inmates, in other words, never completely relinquished their outsider's perspective, even in the middle stage of their prison careers when they were most alienated from the outside world.

Concluding Experiences

Inmates' continuing ambivalence was a motivating factor in their decision to apply for a transfer to the minimum security unit in the concluding months of their sentences. Their behavior, once again, embodied both directions of their ambivalence: Their outsider's perspective was apparent in the application itself, which indicated a desire for the greater privileges and outside contacts available in minimum security, whereas their insider's perspective was reflected in their emotional caution about their chances that the transfer would be approved:

> As much as I try to, it is very difficult to keep [minimum security] off my mind. I figure that if I don't think about it, it won't be as agonizing waiting for it to happen. It would be much easier if they would give a date to go, but they won't. (Journal)

If their applications were approved, their ambivalence also influenced their response to the transfer itself:

> I am looking at this transfer a little bit differently from my coming to prison and my transfer to "B" Hall. I don't want to expect too much from [minimum security] because then I won't be disappointed. Also, there is one big difference; if I don't like it out there I can always come back here. (Journal)

They were aware that their transfer marked the final phase of their prison sentences and a first step toward rejoining the outside world, but they were equally aware that they would still be in prison for some time and that they could be returned to maximum security at the whim of prison officials. Consequently, they were reluctant to admit—to themselves or others—that their transfers held great symbolic importance. They armed themselves with an insider's rationalization: If they didn't like minimum security, they could always come back. And if they should be sent back involuntarily, they were now confident of their capabilities to survive the remainder of their sentences in maximum security.

Once inmates were transferred to minimum security, they experienced yet another manifestation of their ambivalence, similar to that reported by long-term inmates after they have been placed in halfway houses (Cordilia 1983, 99–100): They wanted to put their prison experiences behind them and prepare for their return to the free world, but they also wanted to avoid the existential concerns raised by this preparation and to complete their sentences by "doing their own time," just as they did when they were in maximum security:

> Doing time is not as easy as it may sound; actually, it is a rather complicated business. For one thing, you must try to keep yourself busy even though there is very [illegible] You would like to plan for the future, but it seems so far away [illegible] really seem like it is worth thinking [illegible] [illegible] mistake that got you in here. [illegible]

> But then, you don't really want to just think about the prison, because there isn't anything more depressing at all. (Journal)

In the final months and weeks of their sentences they vacillated between directly confronting questions about their futures and avoiding these questions through their continuing tactics of thought control and diversionary activities.

Each of the manifestations of ambivalence itemized in Table 1 reflects inmates' marginality because each involved a conflict between an outsider's and an insider's point of view. At various stages in their careers, inmates might place more emphasis on one or the other viewpoint but they never fully resolved their feelings of ambivalence. During the middle portion of their sentences, for example, they might believe that thoughts about the outside world made their sentences more difficult (an insider's belief) and hence might consciously suppress these thoughts (an insider's tactic), but they did not generally terminate outside contacts and would be severely disappointed if their visitors or letters had ceased to arrive. Thus, even when inmates placed greatest emphasis on an insider's viewpoint, their perspectives (that is, the interdependent relationship between their images and their strategies) expressed their marginality. Similarly, when they placed most emphasis on an outsider's viewpoint, namely, at the beginning and end of their sentences, closer inspection of their perspective again reveals their marginality. Our analysis thus suggests that inmates' changing imagery and strategies did not represent a total conversion to an insider's point of view and a subsequent reversion to a more conventional point of view, as suggested in Wheeler's (1961) cyclical model of prison socialization. Rather, the inmates we studied experienced a subtler transformation in which their movement toward either an insider's or an outsider's perspective was circumscribed by their ambivalence.

Discussion

The ambivalence experienced by the inmates we studied was derived from a very specific set of circumstances: involuntary but relatively brief confinement in a total institution that was both entirely unknown and absolutely feared. Similar, if less extreme, feelings of ambivalence can emerge whenever human beings become fully immersed in highly demanding but time-limited social worlds or social situations. For example, we would expect ambivalence to characterize the behavioral adaptations of new mental patients, military recruits, ethnographic researchers, or students entering college or graduate school. The nature and effects of ambivalence will obviously be influenced by a host of other considerations: how the individuals involved define and evaluate the social world in question, whether their participation is voluntary or involuntary, whether participants share a previous culture, the extent to which they desire to maintain that culture, and so on. Although acknowledging the importance of such situational variations, we nonetheless believe that our analysis of inmates' prison adaptations may help interpret the experiences of others whose ambivalence results from social marginality.

For a new inmate the conflict of value systems was as important, or more important, than the content. The first-time inmates we studied were socially heterogeneous; one of the few characteristics they had in common was their belief that they were different from other inmates and hence did not "belong" in the prison world (Schmid and Jones 1991). To differing degrees they learned (but did not fully accept) the norms and values of the prison world. The prison strategies of new inmates had to acknowledge and deal with the content of prison norms and values, but it was the conflict between this value system and their outside values that resulted in their marginality.

The second connotation noted by Room (1976)—that ambivalence refers to a pervasive social condition—is a temporal one. But time itself was central to the marginality of the inmates we studied: They knew that they would be in prison for a year or two but they hoped (and later expected) to return to the outside world. Although ambivalence pervaded their entire prison careers, their role in prison, as defined by themselves and other inmates, was primarily determined by their status as short-timers. Their ambivalence was thus situational, imposed by the specific circumstances of their imprisonment.

In our analysis, inmates' feelings of ambivalence served sometimes to motivate action (for example, to break through their initial isolation or later to apply for transfer to minimum security) and sometimes to inhibit action (not to break off ties to the outside world during the middle portion of their sentences despite a temptation to do so). At some career points, the inmates' ambivalence offered them no real choice in behavior (after orientation, inmates were transferred to another cellblock regardless of how they felt about it); at other points, they did face choices (decisions about continuing outside contacts). The principal effect of their ambivalence, however, was to circumscribe their behavior, keeping it somewhere between the more extreme perspectives of the prison outsider and the long-term inmate.

The traditional model of prison socialization suggests that inmates enter prison with conventional values, become socialized to the values of an inmate culture, and then subsequently become resocialized to the values of the outside world. Our research suggests an alternative model of the prison experiences of first-time, short-term inmates, in which their social marginality continuously shapes both their subjective understanding of the prison world and their adaptations to it. Specifically, we argue that the ambivalence that results from these inmates' transitional status limits the behavioral adaptations they make in prison and inhibits their assimilation into prison culture.

References

Blumer, H. 1969. *Symbolic interactionism: Perspective and method.* Englewood Cliffs, NJ: Prentice-Hall.

prison. Springfield, IL: Charles C. Thomas.

Cordilia, A. 1983. *The making of an inmate: Prison as a way of life*. Cambridge, MA: Schenkman.

Davis, F. 1973. The Martian and the convert: Ontological polarities in social research. *Urban Life* 2:333–43.

Deising, P. 1971. *Patterns of discovery in the social sciences*. Chicago: Aldine-Atherton.

Ellis, C. 1991. Sociological introspection and emotional experience. *Symbolic Interaction* 14:23–50.

Giallombardo, R. 1966. *Society of women: A study of a women's prison*. New York: Wiley.

Gibson, M. A. 1988. *Accommodation without assimilation: Sikh immigrants in an American high school*. Ithaca, NY: Cornell University Press.

Glaser, D. 1969. *The effectiveness of a prison and parole system*. New York: Bobbs-Merrill.

Gold, R. 1958. Roles in sociological field observations. *Social Forces* 36:217–23.

Goffman, E. 1959. *The presentation of self in everyday life*. Garden City, NY: Doubleday.

———. 1961. *Asylums: Essays on the social situation of mental patients and other inmates*. Garden City, NY: Doubleday.

Goodstein, L., D. L. MacKenzie, and R. L. Shotland. 1984. Personal control and inmate adjustment to prison. *Criminology* 22:343–69.

Hayano, D. 1979. Auto-ethnography: Paradigms, problems, and prospects. *Human Organization* 38:99–104.

———. 1982. *Poker faces: The life and work of professional card players*. Berkeley: University of California Press.

Irwin, J. 1970. *The felon*. Englewood Cliffs, NJ: Prentice-Hall.

———. 1980. *Prisons in turmoil*. Boston: Little, Brown.

Jacobs, J. 1977. *Stateville: The penitentiary in mass society*. Chicago: University of Chicago Press.

Johnson, R. 1987. *Hard time: Understanding and reforming the prison*. Monterey, CA: Brooks/Cole.

Jones, R. S., and T. J. Schmid. 1989. Inmates' conceptions of prison sexual assault. *Prison Journal* 69:53–61.

Merton, R. K., and E. Barber. 1976. Sociological ambivalence. In *Sociological ambivalence and other essays*, by R. K. Merton, 3–31. New York: Free Press.

Morawska, E. 1987. Sociological ambivalence: Peasant immigrant workers in America, 1880s–1930s. *Qualitative Sociology* 10:225–50.

Room, R. 1976. Ambivalence as a sociological explanation: The case of cultural explanations of alcohol problems. *American Sociological Review* 41:1047–65.

Schlenker, R. 1980. *Impression management: The self concept, social identity and interpersonal relations*. Belmont, CA: Wadsworth.

Schmid, T. J., and R. S. Jones. 1990. Experiential orientations to the prison experience: The case of first-time, short-term inmates. In *Perspectives on social problems*, edited by G. Miller and J. A. Holstein, vol. 2, 189–210. Greenwich, CT: JAI.

———. 1991. Suspended identity: Identity transformation in a maximum security prison. *Symbolic Interaction* 14:415–32.

Seymour, J. 1977. Niches in prison. In *Living in prison: The ecology of survival*, by H. Toch, 179–205. New York: Free Press.

Shokeid, M. 1988. *Children of circumstances: Israeli emigrants in New York*. Ithaca, NY: Cornell University Press.

Sykes, G. [1959] 1971. *The society of captives: A study of a maximum security prison*. Reprint. Princeton, NJ: Princeton University Press.

Sykes, G., and S. Messinger. 1960. Inmate social system. In *Theoretical studies in social organization of the prison*, by R. A. Cloward, D. R. Cressey, G. H. Grosser, R. McCleery, L. E. Ohlin, G. M. Sykes, and S. L. Messinger, 5–19. New York: Social Science Research Council.

Thomas, C. C. 1973. Prisonization or resocialization? A study of external factors associated with the impact of imprisonment. *Journal of Research in Crime and Delinquency* 10:13–21.

Thomas, C. C., and D. M. Peterson. 1977. *Prison organization and inmate subcultures*. Indianapolis: Bobbs-Merrill.

Toch, H. 1977. *Living in prison: The ecology of survival*. New York: Free Press.

Turner, R. H. 1978. The role and the person. *American Journal of Sociology* 84:1–23.

Wheeler, S. 1961. Socialization in correctional communities. *American Sociological Review* 26:697–712.

Zimmerman, D., and D. L. Wieder. 1977. The diary: Diary-interview method. *Urban Life* 5:479–98.

2. Inmate Experiences and Psychological Well-Being

John D. Wooldredge

This study examined how inmate psychological well-being is influenced by participation in institutional programs, frequency of visitation with outsiders, and experiences with victimization during incarceration. Participants were 581 adult inmates from three Ohio correctional facilities. Support was found for the hypotheses that healthier attitudes correspond with greater program participation, more frequent visitation, and no experience with victimization.

The ability to mentally cope with confinement in prison has implications for the success of institutional treatment programs as well as for reducing the violence and illness among inmates that result from anxiety and depression (Wright & Goodstein, 1989). These concerns have led psychologists to explore the psychosocial characteristics of prison climates that affect psychological adjustment to prison settings (e.g., MacKenzie & Goodstein, 1986; Porporino & Zamble, 1984; Toch, 1977, 1984; Wright, 1985, 1993).

Researchers have found that social interaction is more difficult for inmates when they feel less safe during incarceration (e.g., Toch, 1977; Wright, 1993). In addition, inmates are more likely to become angry and disagreeable with others when they have limited assistance for self-improvement or they experience lower levels of activity and social stimulation. However, additional research is needed to test these observations more fully. This article examines the influences of victimization experiences during incarceration, frequency of visitation with outsiders, and levels of program participation (education, vocational training, counseling, work, and legitimate recreational activities) on the psychological well-being of male inmates (i.e., their degree of difficulty in relating to others in conjunction with their levels of depression, anger, stress, and neglect).

Institutional Experiences and Psychological Adjustment

Murray (1938) hypothesized that all persons have particular needs that interact with social environments to influence their behavior. Certain attributes of a social environment may influence a person's ability to satisfy his/her particular needs. Needs constitute internal determinants of behavior, whereas the social environment constitutes an external press that may either help or hinder need satisfaction. Pertinent to this study, Lazarus and his colleagues (Lazarus, 1966; Lazarus, Averill, & Opton, 1970; Lazarus & Launier, 1978) found that stress may occur when an individual is unable to satisfy his/her specific needs within particular social contexts (i.e., when the interaction between needs and environment prevents an individual from adapting to the environment). Others have applied these ideas to an understanding of the environmental influences on an inmate's psychological adaptation to incarceration (e.g., MacKenzie & Goodstein, 1986; Porporino & Zamble, 1984; Toch, 1977, 1984; Wright, 1985, 1993).

Particular aspects of prison environments may help to lessen some of the negative psychological effects of confinement (e.g., depression, anxiety, alienation), but their effectiveness may depend on the unique needs of inmates (Toch, 1977). Identifying those needs, therefore, is a necessary step toward the development of strategies to facilitate adjustment to incarceration. In a study of inmate perceptions of life in prison, Toch (1977) sought to identify the concerns (needs) of inmates that are most commonly perceived. He argued that prison environments can be created to meet inmates' needs and facilitate adaptation to confinement.

Toch (1977) identified eight central environmental concerns of prison inmates: privacy, safety, structure, support, emotional feedback, social stimulation, activity, and freedom. Wright (1985) used Toch's typology to conceptualize and measure prison climate, as reflected in Wright's Prison Environment Inventory (PEI). Six of Toch's eight dimensions were clearly identified in Wright's factor analysis of the items contained in the PEI, although emotional feedback and activity each did not appear to load on just one factor (dimension).

Wright (1993) used his PEI to examine the effects of climate on inmate adjustment in 10 New York state prisons for adult males. Wright measured inmate perceptions of their adjustment on three dimensions: external problems (difficulties with actually interacting with others), internal problems (internal feelings of hostility toward others), and physical problems (illness, injury, fear, and being taken advantage of). Although none of his models explained more than 5% of the variation in adjustment, he found many statistically significant relationships between his measures of climate and adjustment. Pertinent to this study, he found that external and internal problems were more likely in environments with fewer opportunities for self-improvement (Toch's "support") and among inmates who received less emotional sustenance. Internal problems were also more likely among inmates who (a) felt less safe (although the overall safety of a facility was not found to be related to adjustment), (b) perceived less privacy, and (c) had fewer opportunities for social interaction.

Although researchers have studied several possible influences on an inmate's psychological well-being, some policy-relevant variables have yet to be examined empirically. Some of these variables include program participation (i.e., the degree to which inmates participate in education, vocational training, [illegible] ing, work, and legitimate recreational activities), the frequency of visitation with [illegible] with victimization during incarceration [illegible] [illegible] to actual levels of program participation and the frequency of visitation, and [illegible] perceptions of safety may be related to actual victimization experiences. Researchers have yet to examine these particular variables directly. If they are related to the psychological well-being of inmates, then efforts to reduce institutional crime and encourage greater participation in available programs could help to lessen some of the negative psychological effects of imprisonment and promote what Johnson and Price (1981) called a "human service orientation" toward prison inmates.

Psychological Well-Being

Psychological well-being is conceptualized here as reflecting inmate perceptions of insecurity, stress, depression, anger, low self-esteem, and loneliness felt during incarceration.

Preventing Spurious Relationships

Obtaining valid estimates of the relationships between the institutional variables of interest and the psychological well-being of inmates requires controlling for variation in the background characteristics of inmates that may correlate with these variables (to prevent spurious relationships). Several researchers have suggested that the demographic and background characteristics of inmates (e.g., age, race, marital status) may also influence psychological adjustment (Carroll, 1974; Irwin, 1970; Irwin & Cressey, 1962; Jacobs, 1974, 1976, 1977). Inmates with atypical characteristics (relative to the mainstream prison population) may be more peripheral to various inmate groups, so their adjustment may be more difficult. Extensive research by Thomas and his colleagues (Thomas, 1970, 1977; Thomas & Foster, 1972; Thomas, Peterson, & Zingraff, 1978) has led to the most popular conclusion that both the environmental deprivations of prisons and the importation of preinstitutional characteristics are important for influencing inmate adjustment. Another observation stemming from this research is that background (imported) characteristics may influence institutional (deprivational) experiences, in turn affecting psychological adjustment (see Wright & Goodstein, 1989, for a review of related research).

The most common demographic and background variables that have been examined in recent studies of inmate adjustment include age, race, marital status, education, prior commitments/time spent during prior prison terms, and offense for which they were incarcerated (for examinations of one or more of these variables, see Edwards & Kemp, 1995; Hancock & Sharp, 1993; Peat & Winfree, 1992; Proctor, 1994; and Van Voorhis, 1993). Psychological adjustment may be more difficult for inmates who are older, White, married, who have higher levels of education, have fewer prior institutional commitments, and/or who have committed sex crimes. These inmates are less similar to the mainstream population and may therefore possess greater social distance between themselves and other inmates. Furthermore, some of these characteristics may actually inhibit an inmate from becoming integrated into an inmate social system. In turn, these types of individuals may be more likely to experience external problems (difficulty in relating to others) as well as internal problems (depression, anger, stress, and/or neglect) during incarceration.

Other institutional variables may also be important to control when examining the relationships of interest. To be specific, an inmate's psychological well-being may be influenced by the time until an inmate's parole hearing (or related variables such as time served or sentence length) (McCorkle, 1992; Proctor, 1994; Van Voorhis, 1993) and the physical environment of a facility (Paulus & Dzindolet, 1993). Adjustment may be more difficult for inmates who have longer to wait until a parole hearing and for those incarcerated in a facility with ranges of cells set perpendicular to long corridors (possibly enhancing perceptions of less personal space). In turn, these variables may be related to levels of program participation (if inmates further along in their sentences are more involved in programs) as well as victimization likelihoods (if inmates with less experience in prison and/or those in facilities with a linear design are more likely to be victimized by other inmates).

Method

Participants

Samples of inmates were selected from three Ohio correctional facilities for adult males. The first facility is high-close security with a linear architectural design (i.e., ranges of cells set perpendicular to long corridors). It held roughly 500 inmates at the time of the study. The second facility is also high-close security but with a podular design. There are three campuses within the second facility, housing up to 384 inmates each (1,150 inmates altogether). The third institution is a medium-security podular facility that held 450 inmates at the time of data collection. Inmates at all three facilities are housed one per cell.

Self-report data were collected for the study. Anonymous surveys were distributed individually to inmates during a single count lasting 30 minutes. At the end of the count, inmates sealed the completed surveys in envelopes and placed them in an enclosed box. The pool of completed surveys (N = 581) consisted of 81% of the inmates targeted at the high-close podular facility (n_1 = 312), 75% of those selected from the linear facility (n_2 = 99), and 76% of those targeted at the medium-security facility (n_3 = 170). This sample excluded all illiterate inmates and those in psychiatric units.

Procedure

TABLE 1 Variables and Univariate Descriptives (N = 581)

Variables	*Descriptives*
Dependent variable	
Inmate adjustment (range: 7–28)	M = 14.69, SD = 4.47
Institutional variables	
Daily activity hours (range: 0–16)	M = 8.51, SD = 4.86
Victim of aggravated assault past 6 months	f = 66
Visits last month (range: 0–20)	M = 1.89, SD = 2.22
Years to parole hearing (range: 0–30)	M = 4.46, SD = 5.50
High-close linear design	f = 99
Medium podular design	f = 170
Demographic/background variables	
Age (range: 16–61)	M = 28.65, SD = 7.18
African American	f = 248
Married	f = 143
More than high school education	f = 215
Prior months served (range: 0–304)	M = 20.51, SD = 40.17
Institutionalized for sex offense	f = 43

NOTE: Dummy variables were coded 0 (no) and 1 (yes). Frequencies for dummy variables reflect the numbers of inmates in category 1 of each variable.

1. It is hard for me to relate to others.
2. I often feel depressed.
3. I feel angry at the people around me quite often.
4. I have problems dealing with stress.
5. I often feel tense.
6. No one seems to care about me.
7. I often feel neglected.

Rather than create a factor that would give some of these perceptions more weight than others, these scores were summed so that each item had equal weight. Larger values on the composite measure reflected poorer well-being (more depressed, angry, tense, etc.).

The victimization variable was a dichotomous measure of whether an inmate was victimized by aggravated assault at least once during the 6 months preceding the survey.

Results

Table 2 presents the results of the analysis. Both institutional and preinstitutional (demographic and background) characteristics of inmates were significantly related to the outcome measure examined, which is consistent with the observations

TABLE 2 Results From the OLS Analysis of Inmate Adjustment

Predictor	B	SE B	*Beta*
Constant	16.804		
Institutional variables			
Daily activity hours	−0.155**	0.055	−0.151
Victim of aggravated assault	1.438**	0.522	0.145
Visits last month	−0.333**	0.109	−0.172
Years to parole hearing	0.095*	0.044	0.120
High-close linear design	0.118	0.631	0.011
Medium podular design	0.910	0.648	0.092
Demographic/background variables			
Age	0.014	0.039	0.022
African American	−1.790**	0.482	−0.196
Married	1.038	0.572	0.103
More than high school education	−1.741**	0.495	−0.190
Prior months served	−0.004	0.006	−0.036
Sex offender	−0.703	0.833	−0.045

NOTE: $R^2 = 0.16$; standard error of regression = 4.23. OLS = ordinary least squares.
$*p < .05$. $**p < .01$.

of Thomas and his colleagues (Thomas, 1970, 1977; Thomas & Foster, 1972; Thomas et al., 1978). Both sets of variables accounted for 16% of the variation in adjustment to incarceration.

The predictors of primary interest (i.e., the number of hours spent daily in structured activities, frequency of visitation with outsiders, and whether an inmate was victimized recently by physical assault) were statistically significant, maintaining relationships in the hypothesized directions. To be specific, inmates tended to be more depressed, anxious, stressed, and so forth when they (a) spent less time in structured activities (Beta = −0.15), (b) received fewer visits each month (Beta = −0.17), and (c) had been victimized recently by aggravated assault (Beta = 0.15).

The results for the remaining institutional variables revealed that the time until an inmate's next parole hearing was a significant predictor of adjustment (Beta = 0.12), but the facility-type variables were not significant. All of the statistically significant institutional variables maintained relationships with the dependent variable that were comparable in strength (i.e., the magnitudes of the beta weights were not significantly different).

The findings for the demographic/background variables revealed that higher levels of depression, anxiety, stress, and so forth were more likely among inmates [illegible] variables (9% vs. 7%, respectively). The difference of 2% is statistically significant ($p < .05$).

Discussion

The results of this study suggest that efforts to influence adjustment to incarceration should recognize the importance of both preinstitutional and institutional characteristics of inmates. This is consistent with results from the prisonization studies of Thomas (1977), Thomas and Foster (1972), and Thomas et al. (1978).

The significant variation in the measure of psychological well-being examined here underscores the need to identify and address the institutional barriers to inmate adjustment. This may help to enhance the feasibility of treatment and to reduce the violence and illness among inmates that result from anxiety and depression. The findings of this study support the hypothesis that variation in the psychological well-being of inmates corresponds in part with differences in their routines and experiences.

The findings are consistent with many of the findings from Wright's (1993) research. To be specific, he found that adjustment to incarceration was more difficult for inmates who (a) were in environments with fewer opportunities for self-improvement (i.e., less activity and support, to use Toch's [1977] terminology), (b) felt less safe, and (c) had fewer opportunities for social interaction (i.e., Toch's [1977] social stimulation). In the study presented here, inmates tended to be more depressed, anxious, stressed, and so forth when they (a) engaged less frequently in activities for self-improvement (less activity and support), (b) had been recently victimized by other inmates (less safe), and (c) received fewer visits each month (less social stimulation). Also interesting to note, Wright's finding that the overall safety of a facility was not related to adjustment is supported here. More specific, this study found that an inmate's psychological well-being did not depend on the level of surveillance or the architectural design of a facility, but rather it depended on individual differences in institutional experiences.

Wright (1993) also found that none of his statistically significant models accounted for more than 5% of the variation in adjustment. The institutional variables examined in this study accounted for 9% of the variation in the outcome measure examined. There are two reasons why these findings may be consistent with Wright's. First, the outcome measure examined in the present study had less variation compared to Wright's measures (because of the smaller number of items used in its construction combined with a smaller sample size—581 vs. 942 inmates). Therefore, it is easier to explain variation in an outcome measure with fewer categories because there is less total variation with which to begin. Second, the fact that both figures are under 10% reinforces Wright's observation that many factors determine how inmates adjust to incarceration. Note that the two statistically significant preinstitutional variables alone accounted for an additional 7% of the variation in adjustment.

The findings that program participation, safe environments, and visitation with outsiders are related to psychological well-being reinforces Toch's (1977) contention that prison environments can be created to meet inmates' needs and facilitate adaptation to confinement. Greater opportunities for self-improvement and activity combined with a greater freedom of choice may help inmates to find an appropriate niche in prison when they can achieve greater control over their environment (Seymour, 1977, 1982; Toch, 1977). These findings have implications for research on personal control and its relevance to an understanding of adaptation to imprisonment.

Personal Control and Psychological Adjustment

The ability to control one's environment and predict personal experiences from day to day is considered by many psychologists and sociologists to be a basic human need (Perlmuter & Monty, 1979; Phares, 1976; Rotter, 1966; Seeman, 1959; White, 1959). Related to Toch's (1977) concept of freedom, this ability is often referred to in the literature as personal control. Goodstein et al. (1984) and MacKenzie et al. (1987) argued that the concept of personal control is highly relevant to a study of inmate adaptation to imprisonment. Less personal control over one's environment during incarceration may lead to more intense feelings of depression, anxiety, and stress (MacKenzie et al., 1987; Porporino & Zamble, 1984; Ruback, Carr, & Hopper, 1986).

Variation in the institutional characteristics examined in the present study might reflect differences in an inmate's ability to control his environment. To be specific, inmates who (choose to) spend more time each day in education, vocational training, job work, and recreational programs are necessarily involved for longer periods of time in more structured activities that probably do not vary much in routine from day to day. Provided that the inmate's routine is not overly structured (because too much structure may lead to perceptions of limited choice), greater involvement could enhance feelings of security among inmates because they are better able to predict their experiences from day to day. Similar to this, more frequent visitation with familiar persons may also enhance feelings of security and control. The number of monthly visits an inmate receives could influence the element of personal control involving the opportunity to make choices (Averill, 1973; Steiner, 1979). Inmates who receive more visits each month may perceive more freedom through the regular maintenance of ties to the outside world. Conversely, inmates who are victimized by violent crime may feel less secure about what to expect from day to day if these experiences serve to enhance an inmate's fear of the unknown.

Even the significant finding regarding the time until an inmate's parole hearing has implications for an inmate's perception of personal control. To be specific, inmates who have shorter periods to wait until their first (or next) parole hearings may perceive that they are closer to their freedom to make choices.

The results of this study could therefore be interpreted as *indirect* support for the idea that routines and experiences that enhance an inmate's ability to control his environment and reduce his fear of the unknown generally correspond with a healthier state of mind.

Conclusions

The results of the study presented here support the significance of program participation, frequency of visitation, and victimization during incarceration for predicting an inmate's psychological well-being. Although these specific predictors have never been examined before, these results are consistent with the findings of other researchers regarding the importance of activity, opportunities for self-advancement, social stimulation, and feelings of safety for facilitating adjustment (Toch, 1977; Wright, 1993). Moreover, the findings support the idea of Thomas and his colleagues that both the characteristics of institutional environments and the characteristics of inmates upon entry into an institution are important for influencing how well inmates adapt to their environment (Thomas, 1970, 1977; Thomas & Foster, 1972; Thomas et al., 1978).

As suggested by Carroll (1974), Porporino and Zamble (1984), and Toch (1984), studies of the effects of interactions between the background characteristics of inmates and institutional characteristics (i.e., contextual effects) on adjustment would be worthwhile to see if such interactions improve our prediction significantly beyond the additive effects of each group of variables.

References

Averill, J. (1973). Personal control over aversive stimuli and its relationship to stress. *Psychology Bulletin, 80*, 286–303.

Carroll, L. (1974). *Hacks, blacks, and cons*. Prospect Heights, IL: Waveland.

Edwards, J., & Kemp, G. (1995). Race, drug of choice, and adjustment to incarceration among male inmates. *Journal of Offender Rehabilitation, 22*, 55–63.

Goodstein, L., MacKenzie, D., & Shotland, R. (1984). Personal control and inmate adjustment to prison. *Criminology, 22*, 343–369.

Goodstein, L., & Wright, K. (1989). Inmate adjustment to imprisonment. In L. Goodstein & D. McKenzie (Eds.), *The American prison* (pp. 229–251). New York: Plenum.

Hancock, B., & Sharp, P. (1993). Educational achievement and self-esteem in a maximum security prison program. *Journal of Offender Rehabilitation, 20*, 21–33.

Irwin, J. (1970). *The felon*. Englewood Cliffs, NJ: Prentice-Hall.

Irwin, J., & Cressey, D. (1962). Thieves, convicts, and the inmate culture. *Social Problems, 10*, 142–155.

Jacobs, J. (1974). Street gangs behind bars. *Social Problems, 21*, [illegible]

Johnson, R., & Price. S. (1981). The complete correctional officer: Human service and the human environment in prison. *Criminal Justice and Behavior, 8*, 343–373.

Lazarus, R. (1966). *Psychological stress and the coping process*. New York: McGraw-Hill.

Lazarus, R., Averill, J., & Opton, E. (1970). Toward a cognitive theory of emotion. In M. Arnold (Ed.), *Feelings and emotions*. New York: Academic Press.

Lazarus, R., & Launier, R. (1978). Stress-related transactions between person and environment. In L. Pervin & M. Lewis (Eds.), *Internal and external determinants of behavior*. New York: Plenum.

MacKenzie, D., & Goodstein, L. (1986). Stress and the control beliefs of prisoners: Inmate adjustment and indigenous correctional personnel. *Criminal Justice and Behavior, 12*, 17–27.

MacKenzie, D., Goodstein, L., & Blouin, D. (1987). Personal control and prisoner adjustment: An empirical test of a proposed model. *Journal of Research in Crime and Delinquency, 24*, 49–68.

McCorkle, R. (1992). Personal precautions to violence in prison. *Criminal Justice and Behavior, 19*, 160–173.

Murray, H. (1938). *Explorations in personality: A clinical and experimental study of fifty men of college age*. New York: Oxford University Press.

Paulus, P., & Dzindolet, M. (1993). Reactions of male and female inmates to prison confinement: Further evidence for a two-component model. *Criminal Justice and Behavior, 20*, 149–166.

Peat, B., & Winfree, L. (1992). Reducing the intra-institutional effects of prisonization: A study of a therapeutic community for drug-using inmates. *Criminal Justice and Behavior, 19*, 206–225.

Perlmuter, L., & Monty, R. (1979). *Choice and perceived control*. Hillsdale, NJ: Lawrence Erlbaum.

Phares, E. (1976). *Locus of control in personality*. Morristown, NJ: General Learning Press.

Porporino, F., & Zamble, E. (1984). Coping with imprisonment. *Canadian Journal of Criminology, 26*, 403–421.

Proctor, J. (1994). Evaluating a modified version of the federal prison system's inmate classification model: An assessment of objectivity and predictive validity. *Criminal Justice and Behavior, 21*, 256–272.

Rotter, J. (1966). Generalized expectancies for internal versus external control of reinforcement. *Psychology Monographs, 80*, 609.

Ruback, R., Carr, T., & Hopper, C. (1986). Perceived control in prison: Its relation to reported crowding, stress, and symptoms. *Journal of Applied Social Psychology, 16*, 375–386.

Seeman, M. (1959). On the meaning of alienation. *American Sociological Review, 24,* 783–791.

Seymour, J. (1977). Niches in prison. In H. Toch (Ed.), *Living in prison: The ecology of survival* (pp. 179–205). New York: Free Press.

Seymour, J. (1982). Environmental sanctuaries for susceptible prisoners. In R. Johnson & H. Toch (Eds.), *The pains of imprisonment* (pp. 267–284). Beverly Hills: Sage.

Steiner, I. (1979). Three kinds of reported choice. In L. Perlmuter & R. Monty (Eds.), *Choice and perceived control.* Hillsdale, NJ: John Wiley.

Thomas, C. (1970). Toward a more inclusive model of inmate contraculture. *Criminology, 8,* 251–262.

Thomas, C. (1977). Theoretical perspectives on prisonization: A comparison of the importation and deprivation models. *Journal of Criminal Law and Criminology, 68,* 135–145.

Thomas, C., & Foster, S. (1972). Prisonization in the inmate contraculture. *Social Problems, 20,* 229–239.

Thomas, C., Peterson, D., & Zingraff, R. (1978). Structural and social psychological correlates of prisonization. *Criminology, 16,* 383–393.

Toch, H. (1977). *Living in prison: The ecology of survival.* New York: Free Press.

Toch, H. (1984). Quo vadis? *Canadian Journal of Criminology, 26,* 511–516.

Van Voorhis, P. (1993). Psychological determinants of the prison experience. *The Prison Journal, 73,* 72–102.

White, R. (1959). Motivation reconsidered: The concept of competence. *Psychology Review, 66,* 297–333.

Wright, K. (1985). Developing the prison environment inventory. *Journal of Research in Crime and Delinquency, 22,* 257–277.

Wright, K. (1993). Prison environment and behavioral outcomes. *Journal of Offender Rehabilitation, 20,* 93–113.

Wright, K. & Goodstein, L. (1989). Correctional environments. In L. Goodstein & D. McKenzie (Eds.), *The American prison* (pp. 253–270). New York: Plenum.

CRIMINAL JUSTICE AND BEHAVIOR, Vol. 26 No. 2, June 1999, 235–250.

3. Women's Accounts of Their Prison Experiences: A Retrospective View of Their Subjective Realities

Mark R. Pogrebin, Mary Dodge

This article examines the subjective experiences of previously imprisoned women. Their retrospective narratives of prison life reveal overt behavioral and underlying structural tensions that create an atmosphere of fear and violence. Furthermore, attitudes of indifference between inmates and correctional staff often contribute to fostering an environment of neglect. The study, based on in-depth interviews with fifty-four female subjects, describes and analyzes several aspects of the socialization process for inmates as related by women on parole. The research shows that the "pains of imprisonment" for women are suffered to a greater degree than previously acknowledged. Prison for these women is a social world filled with anxiety and, perhaps, represents a punishment well beyond what the law intended.

Introduction

The number of women in the criminal justice system has spurred a great deal of recent social inquiry, particularly as prison populations continue to soar. Early studies of women in prison focused on pseudo-family and relationship building (Giallombardo, 1966; Larsen & Nelson, 1984; Leger, 1987; Ward & Kassebaum, 1965). Many recent studies have relied on comparisons of female and male prison populations. According to female–male comparative research, women pose less custodial and security risk (Alexander & Humphrey, 1988; Brennan & Austin, 1997; Burke & Adams, 1991; Pollock-Bryne, 1990); women are less likely to riot and assault each other (Hunter, 1984; Rafter, 1990); and women are less apt to commit serious institutional infractions (Austin, Chan, & Elms, 1993). The focus on a gendered dichotomy, however, appears to diminish the fear and violence that delineate the experience of many incarcerated women. This article gives voice to the concerns and hardships as told by formerly incarcerated women.

An Evolving Subculture

The pains of imprisonment and the development of prison subcultures are closely related. In 1958, Gresham Sykes identified the loss of liberty, goods and services, heterosexual relations, autonomy, and personal security as the basic deprivations associated with prison life. Prison subcultures developed as inmates adapted to life in these isolated and stressful environments. Many inmates strive toward normalcy by creating relationships and mores to supplant outside losses. In fact, early research on women inmates focused on the development of social structures based on family and traditional gender roles (Giallombardo, 1966; Ward & Kassebaum, 1965). According to Giallombardo (1966), women alleviated the pains of imprisonment by developing kinship links with other inmates. Similarly, Heffernan (1972) found that adaptation to prison was facilitated by the creation of a pseudo-family. Owen (1998) also notes that the female subculture is based on personal relationships with other women inmates. Others, however, believe that the subculture in women's prisons is undergoing a gradual shift that more closely resembles that of male prisons. Fox (1982) states, for example, that the cooperative caring prisoner community that has embodied characterizations of female prisons has evolved into a more dangerous and competitive climate. Changes in subcultures may be related to the more pronounced deprivations that women inmates experience.

Inmate Experiences and Socialization

Female prisoners generally report that institutional adjustment is more difficult than their male contemporaries for many reasons. Women tend to value privacy more than men (Pollock-Byrne, 1992), and, consequently, experience greater difficulty adjusting to community living and the degrading nature of body searches (Ward & Kassebaum, 1965). Furthermore, women often worry about being abandoned by family and spouses and are concerned with the loneliness they may experience once released (Dobash, Dobash, & Gutteridge, 1986).

Punishment is compounded for many women inmates when they are separated from their children. The majority of incarcerated women are mothers—estimates range from 60 to 80 percent (Bloom & Steinhart, 1993; Henriques, 1996). Most women inmates were living with their children and provided the sole means of family support prior to incarceration (Baunach, 1985; Chesney-Lind, 1997; Datesman & Cales, 1983; Greenfeld & Minor-Harper, 1991; Henriques, 1996). Imprisoned mothers rank estrangement from children as their primary concern (Henriques, 1996; Stanton, 1980). Rasche (2000) notes that the harshest single aspect of being imprisoned may be the separation of mother and child.

Women in prison experience an unparalleled sense of isolation. Added to the pains of imprisonment for women are the frustration, conflict, and guilt of being both separated from and unable to care for their children (Barry, 1987; Bloom & Chesney-Lind, 2000). According to Crawford (1990), as a result of imprisonment, female parents often experience feelings of despair and depression. Crawford further states that these emotions appear to be prevalent, even on the part of women inmates who believe that they were inadequate as parents when they were living with their children at home. Further anxiety arises over fear of losing custody. In some states, authorities use a prison sentence to deprive women of legal custody (Bloom, 1995; Fletcher, Shaver, & Moon, 1993; Pollock-Byrne, 1990).

The loss of adult status and childlike treatment by custodial officers exacerbates the stress that female inmates experience (Fox, 1982). Misbehavior is seldom overlooked. McClellan (1994), who studied rule violations and punishments throughout the Texas Department of Corrections, found from a comparative study of both men and women prisons that women received many more write-ups for minor rule violations than did their male-counterparts. Furthermore, women inmates were more likely to receive the most severe sanctions for their violations. Dobash et al. (1986), for example, found that women consistently were punished more frequently as compared to male prisoners for offenses against prison rules and regulations. They note that the difference is a result of a greater willingness to write-up women for behavior that often is tolerated in male correctional facilities.

Personal autonomy is threatened in numerous ways, but is particularly insidious when women prisoners become the target of sexual abuse, harassment, and sexual misconduct perpetrated by correctional officers. Reporting incidents of mistreatment often proves to be a futile action. The amount of sexual misconduct by staff toward inmates is difficult to determine. Moss (1999) offers numerous reasons for this situation. First, data or investigations are determined in general categories such as assault rather than sexual assault. Second, women fear reprisal or fear they will not be believed by administrators. Third, sexual relations between staff and inmates are seen as beneficial to both parties involved (e.g., trading sex for goods). Fourth, sexual misconduct is difficult to investigate and corroboration of another party is necessary to substantiate a female prisoner's claim. Fifth, prison culture adheres to the code of silence, both for staff and inmates, particularly if both inmates and staff lack confidence that those who report sexual misconduct will be safe from any type of retaliation. Finally, in prison settings staff who report sexual misconduct with female prisoners may be ostracized by other correctional officers.

The factors discussed thus far are illustrative of some of the conditions experienced by women who are serving time. Although current literature offers profiles of the type of women in prison, there is little data that informs us of just how these women, once released, reflect on their years of incarceration. The research presented here sought to explore the varied dimensions of women's imprisonment and to better understand the significance of their experiences. The major themes that emerged include elements of fear, intimidation, and violence; relationships among inmates; drug-related issues; health and medical concerns; and custodial care problems.

Methods

Data were collected from fifty-four female parolees who were incarcerated at a correctional facility in a western state. With the exception of one former inmate, all the women had served their time at one institution.

Women on parole were contacted at the time they had appointments to see their parole officers. Each person was told the purpose of the study, volunteered to participate, and gave informed consent. A total of fifty-four women agreed to participate and were interviewed over a three-month period. Their ages ranged from twenty-three to fifty-five (median = 36) and their length of incarceration ranged from one to twelve years (median = 4.8) for all classes of offense.

Findings

Initial Impressions

When discussing their initial experiences upon entering prison, most of the women interviewed realized genuine fears in being in such an environment for the first time. One respondent explained:

> I was scared to death. When I went to [the facility], I saw women who looked like men, bigger than me. And they were looking at me and I was like: "Oh No."

When discussing her first few days in the facility, a woman related her feelings about the way correctional officers treated her. This experience was like nothing she had ever encountered before in her life. She stated:

> I try and forget what it was like in prison most of the time. When I just got there they stripped me down and this guard did a full body search. I was shocked, I never had anyone touch me like that, especially with other guards just standing there watching me. Then they threw me these clothes and took me to a cell. While we were walking, some girls were yelling names at me. It was the most scary thing I had ever seen.

Inmates who were new to the system, who did not have extensive histories of serving time in county jail or prison, found being incarcerated quite traumatic. According to one novice inmate:

> Prison was nothing you would believe. I came from a good home. I wasn't prepared. Here I was a middle-class, White female with a drug problem and I was locked up with murderers and gang members and it was bad. You think prison would just be a place where you are locked up, but more stuff goes on there, drugs, sex, and violence. Some of the women knew I was scared and they would harass me. The worst part is the noise.
>
> It is never quiet in there. All night long people are talking from cell to cell, screaming, fighting, and the doors opened continually when guards are doing checks.

For many prisoners adjusting to living in a total institution (Goffman, 1961) for the first time is something no one can prepare for. According to the women in this study, new prisoners, who have had limited criminal backgrounds and had no friends already in prison, had the most difficult time adjusting to this environment. The women had to go through a socialization process for a period of time to survive. The respondents noted that weakness was not a valued attribute among inmates and those who displayed fear and remained nonconfrontational when picked on by more aggressive inmates had to adjust for the sake of survival.

Weaknesses and Harassment

The respondents agreed that women who were threatened by other inmates and did not use aggressive tactics to defend themselves were seen as weak and presented no threat of retaliation. For these respondents, their reputation as weak defined who they were in the eyes of other prisoners. Their passivity to more aggressive women often led to constantly being taken advantage of. One women put this situation in perspective:

> It doesn't matter how tough you might think you are, cause it's all a mind game. But people will be nice to you and I know I was lonely and so like "yeah this isn't so bad," but things happen and then taking it all in and you end up getting shit on. There is a lot of that in there and once you get into a situation like that it is hard to get out and everyone knows they can treat you like that.

An extreme case of an inmate's inability to cope with existing in the prison environment resulted in an attempted suicide. Prisoners who were unable or unwilling to act aggressively and stand up for themselves in circumstances where they were constantly harassed by others might find such an ongoing situation unbearable, and believed that ending their life was the only means of escape. One woman related the following story:

> I saw a girl; she was a real mess. We all knew she wouldn't make it cause she was weak. She cut her wrists real bad and she was lying in her cell and there was blood everywhere. She was real young and she ended up moving somewhere else, but she was a mess and that was hard cause that place ruined her and I know she wouldn't make it cause she was already dead inside.

Instilling fear and intimidation were two strategies that were used by more domineering inmates toward those who showed consistent signs of weakness. That is, there was a utilitarian purpose in instilling fear in weaker prisoners. This is not merely done for reasons of power, but appeared more so for tangible gain. Several former inmates faced this predicament. One subject explained how she resolved her problem with being harassed by other women:

> Other inmates would harass me by trying to intimidate me. Pushing me around, knocking my food over, telling me if I didn't do what they said, they would kill me. I was scared and alone.

Finding herself in an alien world-like prison, this novice inmate turned to a more experienced prisoner, who offered to listen to her problems and befriend her, all for future utilitarian purposes. What occurred because of this so-called empathic relationship happened all too often to those people who had yet to be socialized into the prisonization game. She explained how this friendly relationship turned into one best characterized as exploitative in nature:

> I made the mistake of letting this one girl help me. She had been in for a while and she had a reputation for being tougher. I was new and didn't know much about her. I thought she was just being nice. She told me to stick by her and she would protect me. I was relieved. I couldn't take care of myself, at least I thought I couldn't. Anyway, it started out great, we would take walks together and I would cry about losing my daughter and being locked up. She would just listen and it felt good having someone who seemed to care. After a while she started having me do little things for her, and I didn't mind, we were friends. Then it got bigger and she knew my family had a little money and got me to give [money] to her. It got out of hand and she would be mean if I didn't give it to her and I was kind of scared.

The exploitation of this novice prisoner by the more powerful and experienced inmate lasted for over two years, until the exploiter was transferred to another facility. After she was gone, other prisoners began to demand money from the inmate and her family, but she refused and suffered the consequence for not acquiescing to these demands. The former inmate said:

> Another girl came up to me and threatened me if I didn't give her money, but I wasn't getting into that again and I told her no. She bashed my head one day, I had to get six stitches.

Another respondent reported her experiences of incarceration in a different state prison. It is obvious from her narrative that her time served there was based on fear for her safety. She related her feelings:

> I was in prison in Arizona. It was horrible. I was bullied a lot by other women that were involved in gangs. I was terrified to walk outside my cell, that's how bad it was.

In those instances in which new prisoners were being harassed and threatened by more experienced, aggressive inmates there often was another prisoner willing to intercede on her behalf. One interviewee chose not to play the passive weak role on advice from an older inmate, although she was extremely scared to stand up for herself. She described her experience:

> It was hard cause I was scared, but she came at me one day and I fought back. She beat the crap out of me, but I took it. The guards broke it up and we both [were] sent to isolation for seventy-two hours. After that it got better, she still made smart-ass remarks, but she never really bothered me. I guess Shelly [her friend] was right, well I know she was, no matter how bad it is you need to stand up for

> yourself, cause if you don't everyone will be coming after you and you won't have a chance.

In this instance, her willingness to engage in physical aggression seemed to pay off. The fact that she was beaten-up appeared to be part of the price for gaining a reputation among prisoners that being taken advantage of would not be tolerated. Exploitation, unfortunately, was part of the prisonization process that both male and female prisoners face in a correctional environment.

An important part of becoming socialized to the prison subculture was not using correctional staff to help solve interpersonal conflicts. In short, "snitching" was taboo, although prison administrators encourage and use the information from inmate informants to maintain social control in the institution (Cloward, 1977). The following incident best illustrates the consequences of an inmate snitching to correctional staff about another inmate's threatening behavior:

> You don't really want the guards involved in protecting you because you'll become known as a snitch or an ass-kisser. If someone wants to get you, they will find a way to do it and the guards can't do anything about it even if they know. There was this one chick who was young and scared and this other chick was after her, so she went to one of the guards and they told her they would look into it. It was too late and the girl ended up beating the shit out of her. She was in the hospital a long time.

For those novice inmates the above incident became an integral part of the social process of becoming a prisoner. The fact that one had to quickly learn to handle interpersonal conflicts by not going to the authorities could be an extremely frightening occurrence. Yet, becoming acclimated to such prisonization norms of behavior seems to be a vital part of prison survival skills that all incarcerated persons must follow to avoid as much conflict as possible.

An Atmosphere of Bedlam

Violence and noise were two factors that made institutional living in correctional facilities a difficult adjustment. According to Pollock-Byrne (1992), older women prisoners complain most about the constant noise and violent behavior of younger women. This complaint was heard from the majority of the respondents who claimed that not just older women, but inmates of all ages felt this was a problem. Another former prisoner related a similar experience having been housed with women who were prone to settle disputes in a violent manner:

> Fights happened all the time—yelling and screaming about someone stealing your shit at least once a day. A lot of girls used weapons that they made from eating utensils, anything they could use to hurt someone. It would get bad sometimes and the guards leave to take someone to get stitches. One time this girl hit this other girl's head on a bar and ended up crushing her skull. It happens a lot, a couple girls have been killed, one while I was there.

Two subjects explained what it was like living in prison for the first time. It is obvious from their descriptions that the noise and sporadic violence were new to them and they had to learn to deal with it over time. One woman said:

> There is violence all the time. The first time I saw a fight and the guards came in, I was shocked. After a while you get use to hearing and seeing it, then you just kind of ignore it, or walk away. There is a lot of screaming and fighting. I guess it's just part of the atmosphere.

Another woman described her impressions and feelings:

> It's always loud, with a bunch of girls screaming and yelling and fighting. It's hell. There isn't any privacy. I was so lonely and I cried, I just wanted out. I never felt so bad in my life.

Often fights were due to circumstances that were beyond the inmates' control. For example, when an inmate received bad news, there was little a prisoner could do about it, and this frustration could turn into physical acting out. According to one respondent:

> Some of the girls in there have been in for a long time and when they find out they've been denied parole or they don't hear from their family or their boyfriend cheats on them they get pissed. Then, once you realize there is nothing you can do about it cause you're locked up, it makes it even worse.

The reality of prison life as portrayed by these former prisoners was one that posed a constant threat of danger. According to the narratives in this research, some women were better at avoiding trouble than others. For those prisoners who find the adjustment to prison life extremely difficult, their existence was best described as fearful and distrustful of both fellow inmates and correctional staff. One respondent described the difficulty of living with women inmates who often act out violently:

> Some of them were just plain crazy, they would fly off the handle and go nuts. I tried to stay out of their way. There was one chick who gave me a hard time. She would push me around and give me all kinds of crap. It was getting out of hand. I needed to stand up to her.

Inmate Relationships

This section discusses the relationships among inmates: a subject that has been researched in past studies of women's correctional institutions. Homosexual behavior did exist in the prison where these interview subjects served time and all of those who claimed to have participated in such a relationship were candid and forthcoming in relating their accounts.

Homosexuality in women's correctional facilities tends to be consensual with most of participants engaging in these relationships for purposes of emotional fulfillment (Pollock-Byrne, 1990). Toch (1975) points out that women in prison have a great need for emotional support and this is a high priority for them. The emotional fulfillment for a supportive relationship was an important factor for one former inmate:

> You are locked up with all these girls and you get close with some of them. I had been treated like shit by guys all my life and with women it's just different, it's more of a friendship thing. You get lonely and sad in prison and it is just nice having someone around who understands and cares and knows what you are going through.

According to Bowker (1981), homosexual behavior in women's prison is more in the context of a loving relationship based on interpersonal desire for love as opposed to just sexual activity. One woman related her experiences:

> It's funny how we became friends, cause at first we didn't get along and she's a dyke and I just wasn't into that, but then we started talking and got close. It was like we were really good friends and the fooling around part comes second. For us it was much more, we loved and respected each other and we were just really close.

Pearson (1998) claims that female inmates have a desire to be romantically linked to another inmate for reasons of personal security. Many of the respondents explained that they entered into homosexual relationships, but this activity had little to do with lesbianism as a sexual preference once they return to the community. One woman said:

> Almost everyone is involved with someone so long as nobody is getting hurt. I was not involved with women before I came to prison and it's difficult when you get out. I didn't think I am a lesbian, but when you are locked up you do anything to pass the time, and I had someone I really cared about. But now that I'm out there I don't think I would be with anyone like that now.

There also were respondents who discussed close friendships with other females, but denied that there was anything sexual about the relationship. They claimed that having a close female friend to share their problems with played an important role in meeting their emotional needs. A former inmate described the difficulty of leaving a friend inside the prison:

> I am not a lesbian, but I had a few friends. I mean you need people to talk to or you will go crazy. It's hard to know who to trust, but there was one girl who worked in the library with me. She helped me out a lot. She was real smart and she had been in before and when I would get mad she would calm me down. We would talk and we cried together a lot, but it was cool, we helped each other out. You need someone to be your friend to help you just to make it together.

Another woman related similar feelings on the need to have friends while incarcerated:

> I had a few really good friends I met in prison and the funny thing is these girls would do anything for you. I never had anyone like that when I was out. I probably made the best friends I ever had in prison.

Drug Involvement

Much female crime can be attributed to the use of illegal substances (Chesney-Lind, 1991; Chesney-Lind & Pollock, 1995; Snell & Morton, 1994). Crimes such as forgery, shoplifting, drug sales, prostitution, and a host of other property crimes are directly related to drug use. One former inmate related her perception of the drug problems that many women had before coming to prison. She explained:

> A majority of the people in there had a drug problem. Most of us start using at a young age and we just never got the help we needed to get over it. So you start using pot or something and then you go into bigger stuff and use more and more and you get more addicted. So when you go into a prison, there isn't a lot of help and you keep using there and when you get out.

When addressing the issue of drug availability and use of illegal substances while incarcerated the respondents consistently reported the following type of statement:

> A lot of people use drugs, mostly like acid and pot and things like that. Pot is tricky cause of the stench, so you have to be careful not to get caught, but yeah, there are a lot of drugs. A lot of women used them, that's what most of us were in for anyway, it just kind of continues.

This research can neither attest to the veracity of how many drugs were available in the prison, nor can it show how extensive drug use was among the general population. The vast majority of women, however, did report that drugs were available.

Most women participants claimed that drug treatment services were not available, or if they were, they could not get into a program due to their sentences being in the later stages and this disqualified them from being accepted. Furthermore, there were some drug abusers who were not motivated to enter into any type of substance abuse rehabilitation program. In short, although most of the participants admittedly had some type of substance abuse problem before entering prison, very few were involved in any rehabilitation program during their time inside.

One long-term prisoner disputed the perceptions of most others when she discussed the provision of drug treatment programs. This former inmate served over fifteen years in prison and offered a comparison between the existence of programs in the past and now:

> Things were different fifteen years ago. They didn't have all the treatment programs they have now. They didn't have anyone to help you with drugs or anything.
>
> Now it's different, about the last eight years I was in it got better, there were a lot more things to get involved in, like drug programs, and stuff about sexual and physical abuse. It isn't great, but it's getting better.

Medical Services

The provision of health services in female correctional facilities has long been an issue and is still considered a major problem (Fletcher et al., 1993). The majority of lawsuits involving women inmates deal with problems in attaining professional medical care (Aylward & Thomas, 1984). Furthermore, Dobash et al. (1986) claim that receiving medical services is different for women prisoners and that correctional staff often minimize their need to see a doctor. This dilemma was best illustrated by one woman who related her medical problems while imprisoned and the trouble she had in convincing the staff the urgency of her need for medical attention. According to this former inmate:

> They don't listen and they just don't care. I needed to see a doctor cause I was having a lot of weird vaginal bleeding and I was in pain and I kept telling them this. It took a few weeks for them to let me see a nurse. When she saw me she didn't really check me out too good, and about a week later I passed out and was bleeding real bad so they finally paid attention and took me to a hospital. I was there for about two weeks. I had a prolapsed uterus or something like that. They ended up doing a hysterectomy. They said if they caught it earlier they wouldn't have had to do it, but now I can't have kids cause nobody would listen to me.

After her hysterectomy, the respondent was being transferred from a community hospital back to prison by two correctional officers who apparently were insensitive to her medical condition.

> Those guards are assholes. When I was leaving the hospital, they did a full body search to make sure I wasn't trying to bring anything back with me. The guard rammed her hand up me. I still had stitches and everything hurt like hell. But, that's how it is, none of them care, they just treat us like shit.

The following description of a seriously ill woman points to the inadequate screening of inmate medical complaints by nurses. In one instance, a nurse either misdiagnosed a serious illness or was medically negligent. The respondent relayed the following account:

> They think you're making stuff up when you complain about being sick. But, there are some that really do have something wrong and they have to suffer. My cellmate had a bad cough, it would keep her up at night and it was going on for weeks,

> they told her it was a cold. One night she was bad, she was throwing up blood and she was burning up. She ended up having pneumonia or something. She never fully recovered and was still in when I left. She was always real weak and looked bad. I felt awful for her.

The attitude on the part of many correctional staff toward prisoners who complain of ill health can best be characterized as one of suspicion. Years of hearing inmate complaints about needing medical attention, when ulterior motives may very likely be involved, can lead to a cynical view of medical complaints (Mitchell, 1988). This attitude on the part of medical and custodial staff might lead to negligent behavior when health services need to be provided. Prevailing cynical attitudes toward inmate health needs, coupled with the lack of adequate health care providers, often meant a delay before women received needed medical attention. A former inmate explained:

> It was like everything else, they were so short-handed it took forever to see anyone. I got sick a few times and I had a lump in my breast. My mom died of breast cancer so I was scared. It took about a month for me to see the nurse and she kind of felt it and said it was nothing. I had been doing a lot of reading about mammograms and I knew it could be something so I kept on them. Finally, a few months later I saw a doctor and they did a bunch of tests. They ended up doing a biopsy and everything turned out all right, but it was a hassle getting anyone to listen to me.

Relationship Issues with Correctional Officers

The supervision of members of one sex by another often leads to issues related to privacy for inmates. Currently, there are an increasing number of male officers working in women's correctional facilities because of Title VII of the Civil Rights Act of 1964 (Moss, 1999). Cross-gender supervision presents a unique set of problems regarding issues of privacy, sexual harassment, or just sexual accusations against male staff. Most of the respondents claimed that male officers sexually harassed them and that this behavior took many different forms.

The issue of privacy invariably was raised by the former inmates. Almost all of the women had some exposure with male officers seeing them in some stage of undress. A respondent commented:

> Those of us who were minorities were treated bad. They didn't care how they treated us. They would watch us when we were in the showers. I know that they were getting off watching us.

Another former inmate discussed treatment by custodial officers and noted that both female and male custody staff often acted disrespectfully toward inmates in their interpersonal encounters. Inappropriate sexual behavior was included in her discussion:

I had to have six stitches in my forehead because a guard pushed me into a wall and I fell down. Also, the guards were always watching us while we were taking showers. There was a lot of abuse in prison. Most of the abuse was either sexual abuse or emotional abuse.

The most serious allegation against male correctional officers was that of coercing female inmates into having sexual encounters with them. That is, officers using their position of authority who threaten punishment for those women who refuse to cooperate. Even in those circumstances where reciprocity appeared to exist between a male officer and a female inmate, no consent could exist due to the differential power relationship. Often the officer who initiated the proposition for sex with a woman played on her vulnerability. One prisoner who was sexually involved with a guard related this circumstance:

I got caught up in this ring that one of the guards had going. At first, I had no idea what it was about. Then, one day this guard asked if I would like to earn some extra cigarettes. He knew that I smoked and that was his way of getting me in. He told me that I was going to have to give oral sex to one of the guards. At first, I objected, but then I figured that if I didn't do it I would get in trouble or get beat. So I gave the guard oral sex. Before I knew it I was doing other things too. After a while it wasn't a big deal. I learned to block out the experience.

Those former prisoners who were involved in sexual activities with male officers always pointed to being coerced and then bribed with goods to take part. There was a genuine fear of retaliation by those harassing officers if they did not participate. One woman explained:

I used to do thing for guards all the time to get extra things. I would get cigarettes, extra phone time, magazines. I used to get all that stuff. I also saw women who refused to do things for them begin to get write-ups or would be treated badly. I saw that happen all the time.

Another woman claimed that "guards were always pressuring women to have sex with them." A respondent discussed her experience with a male guard:

They are jerks, they are just doing this job. They just do it badly. They really harass you. I had a lot of trouble with this one guy, he used to follow me around and he made a few threats. I took it for a long time, but it was getting old. I complained a few times, but they just laughed at me. I told my caseworker about it and a formal complaint was written. I guess some other girls had complained in the past, but it was just our words against him and nobody believes a convict. After that it was real bad cause he knew I told on him. I would come back to my cell and stuff would be everywhere and missing and I wouldn't get my mail for a long time. After a while he was transferred and it got a little better, but I did not meet one guard the whole time I was there who really cared or treated us any good.

The low rate of reported sexual misconduct by women is understandable. Apparently, even when inmates report incidents to administrators, the onus of proof is placed upon them. The dilemma for women inmates is really a no-win situation. When they report sexual harassment they are not believed and in those situations where they do make accusations, they suffer from retaliatory acts by the very officers they complained about.

Family Separation

For female inmates in this study, being separated from their children provoked considerable stress, along with threats to their self-esteem. The most difficult aspect of being in prison was voiced by one respondent who seemed to portray a representative opinion for the women who left their children behind. She commented:

> It was so long. I missed my kids. I missed my freedom. I went to bed every night and woke up in a tiny cell. I just wish it was all a bad dream and I would wake up and I would still be there.

Often inmates with children begin to perceive themselves as bad people, as expressed by one parent whose child was growing up not knowing her:

> Being away from my daughter affected me a lot. She is only six, so that means that I have been in the system almost her entire life. I haven't been there for her. I feel like a horrible person because of this.

Another great concern for women inmate-parents in this study was the dependability of the father of their children to be responsible for them during their incarceration. There were some cases in which the husband did take responsibility for their children, but left his imprisoned spouse for another woman. Obviously, these circumstances caused great distress for incarcerated women. Feelings of abandonment become very real. One woman stated:

> My husband chose to go to another woman. He cheated on me. It's so much to go through. You lose your husband, you lose your kids, your kid's gonna always love you, but someone else takes care of your kids, another woman, it's so much to go through. It's tragic.

Mothers who were in prison often saw their children living in foster homes when there were no relatives who would assume responsibility. If multiple children are involved, they frequently were placed in different homes and separated, making it difficult for incarcerated mothers to find out where all the children are living.

Not being able to see your children for long periods of time was a reality for many inmate parents. One respondent explained:

> My children, there isn't much to say, I had three boys and I lost them when I went in. I haven't seen them since I violated my probation; it's been about five years. I get letters from a social worker telling me how they are doing, but I can't see them or talk to them or anything. I talked to someone from social services about it, but I will never get them back. I really miss them.

Most of the women told of extreme difficulties in their attempts to regain custody of their children. A female parent on parole must show that she has sustained employment, can financially support her children, has a permanent and appropriate residence, and is no longer involved in any criminal activity. Obviously, these criteria presented insurmountable obstacles for some women who wished to regain custodial rights.

Discussion

The women in this study raised a variety of issues that related to the pains of imprisonment and the need to provide safer facilities that could meet their needs. The low inmate population in most states limits the number of options available to prison administrators when dealing with female prisoners. Improvements in prison classification systems, rehabilitation, and medical care represent areas that have been long neglected and may go a long way in diminishing the stress that female inmates experience.

The lack of classification was perhaps the most problematic area. Although classification of inmates certainly cannot prevent all violence, such a system could go a long way in providing the separation of inmates by security and psychological needs. Most women's correctional facilities house inmates under one roof and space is unavailable to segregate the more aggressive prisoners from those women who are less prone to initiate violent means for conflict resolution (Pollock, 1995).

Those inmates who have severe psychological problems often are not segregated from the rest of the population (Clear & Cole, 1997; Farr, 2000). Again, this was usually a consequence of housing inmates together without regard for the needs of those who needed treatment and separation from the rest of the offender population. Often, female inmates claim that their fellow prisoners who suffer from serious psychological problems engage in abnormal and dangerous behavior (Pollock-Byrne, 1992). In addition, there is a serious problem with women inmates who attempt suicide and engage in self-mutilation (Pollock-Byrne, 1990). Obviously, these inmates should be classified and placed in separate parts of the correctional facility with programs that provide mental health services.

Adequate rehabilitation and medical services are crucial to improving the conditions of most prisons. Women prisoners who are substance abusers have distinct treatment needs that should be provided during their period of imprisonment (Prendergast, Wellisen, & Falkin, 1995). These treatment services are related to mental and physical health, vocational training, and issues involving family. Additionally, most women come to prison with more of a need for medical services than male inmates. According to Lord (1995), they are sicker, have more recent injuries, and lack previous health care. Women in prison are in need of pre- and postnatal care, yet gynecological and obstetrical services are rare in most institutions (Belknap, 1996; Lord, 1995).

Sexual misconduct by male correctional staff is a serious problem that threatens the autonomy and self-esteem of many female prisoners. According to Human Rights Watch (1996), the grievance or investigatory procedures for threatened and abused women often are ineffectual. Furthermore, correctional employees engage in abuse because they believe that they rarely will be held accountable. Female inmates may not report sexual misconduct by staff because they are afraid of reprisals or fear that they will not be believed, or because sexual activities with staff often offer reciprocity in the way of goods and services (Moss, 1999).

It appeared that being a female imprisoned parent came with a high price. The costs included not seeing your children or, if visits were allowed, having limited contact. In some cases, an inmate parent might suffer the consequences of having the state intercede. The loss of outside personal relationships with husbands or children represented one of the most difficult aspects of imprisonment and was seen by many women as the most painful part of prison life.

This research showed that an important element of prison life for many women was dealing with the fear and violence. While the experiences related by the former inmates in this study might not be representative of all imprisoned women, the overriding focus on the hostility they endured points to the need for a better understanding of their experiences. The narratives suggested that violence in women's prisons was common and that female–male comparisons might depreciate the volatile situations and process of socialization that female inmates undergo.

References

Alexander, J., & Humphrey, E. (1988). *Initial security classification guidelines for females*. New York: State Department of Corrections.

Austin, J., Chan, L., & Elms, W. (1993). *Women classification study—Indiana department of corrections*. San Francisco, CA: National Council on Crime and Delinquency.

Aylward, A., & Thomas, J. (1984). Quiescence in women's prison litigation. *Justice Quarterly, 1*, 253–276.

Barry, E. (1987). Imprisoned mothers face extra hardships. *National Prison Journal, 14*, 1–4.

Baunach, P. J. (1985). *Mothers in prison*. New Brunswick, NJ: Transaction Books.

Belknap, J. (1996). *The invisible woman: gender, crime, and justice*. Belmont, CA: Wadsworth Publishing.

Bloom, B. (1995). Public policy and the children of incarcerated parents. In: K. Gabel, & D. Johnston (Eds.), *Children of incarcerated parents* (pp. 271–284). New York: Lexington Books.

Bloom, B., & Chesney-Lind, M. (2000). Women in prison: vengeful equity. In: R. Muraskin (Ed.), *It's a crime: women and justice* (pp. 183–204). Upper Saddle River, NJ: Prentice Hall.

Bloom, B., & Steinhart, D. (1993). *Why punish the children? A reappraisal of the children of incarcerated mothers in America*. San Francisco, CA: National Council on Crime and Delinquency.

Bowker, L. H. (1981). Gender differences in prisoner subcultures. In: L. H. Bowker (Ed.), *Women and crime in America* (pp. 409–419). New York: Macmillan.

Brennan, T., & Austin, J. (1997). *Women in jail: classification issues*. Washington, DC: National Institute of Corrections, Department of Justice.

Burke, P., & Adams, L. (1991). *Classification of women offenders in state correctional facilities: a handbook for practitioners*. Washington, DC: National Institute of Corrections, Department of Justice.

Chesney-Lind, M. (1991). Patriarchy, prisons and jails: a critical look at trends in women's incarceration. *Prison Journal, 71*, 51–67.

Chesney-Lind, M. (1997). *The female offender: girls, women and crime*. Thousand Oaks, CA: Sage Publications.

Chesney-Lind, M., & Pollock, J. M. (1995). Women's prisons: equality with a vengeance. In: J. M. Pollock-Byrne, & A. V. Merlo (Eds.), *Women, law and social control* (pp. 155–175). Boston: Allyn and Bacon.

Clear, T., & Cole, G. (1997). *American corrections* (4th ed.). Belmont, CA: Wadsworth.

Cloward, R. A. (1977). Social control in the prison. In: R. G. Leger, & J. R. Stratton (Eds.), *The sociology of corrections* (pp. 110–132). New York: Wiley.

Crawford, J. (1990). *The female offender: what does the future hold?* Washington, DC: American Correction Association.

Datesman, S., & Cales, G. (1983). I'm still the same mommy. *Prison Journal, 63*, 142–154.

Dobash, R. P., Dobash, R. E., & Gutteridge, S. (1986). *The imprisonment of women*. New York: Basil Blackwell.

Farr, K. A. (2000). Classification for female inmates: moving forward. *Crime and Delinquency, 46*, 3–17.

Fletcher, B., Shaver, L., & Moon, D. (1993). *Women prisoners: a forgotten population*. Westport, CT: Praeger.

Fox, J. G. (1982). Women in prison: a case study in the social reality of stress. In: R. Johnson, & H. Toch (Eds.), *The pains of imprisonment* (pp. 205–220). Prospect Heights, IL: Waveland Press.

Giallombardo, R. (1966). *Society of women: a study of a women's prison*. New York: Wiley.

Glaser, B. G., & Strauss, A. L. (1967). *The discovery of grounded theory: strategies for qualitative research*. London: Weidenfeld and Nicholson.

Goffman, E. (1961). *Asylums*. Garden City, NY: Anchor.

Greenfeld, L. A., & Minor-Harper, S. (1991). *Women in prison* (Bureau of Justice statistics, special report). Washington, DC: US Department of Justice.

Heffernan, E. (1972). *Making it in prison: the square, the cool, and the life*. New York: Wiley.

Henriques, Z. W. (1996). Imprisoned mothers and their children: separation–reunion syndrome dual impact. *Women and Criminal Justice, 8*, 77–95.

Human Rights Watch (1996). *All too familiar: sexual abuse of women in U.S. state prisons*. New York: HRW.

Hunter, S. M. (1984). Issues and challenges facing women's prisons in the 1980s. *Prison Journal, 64*, 129–135.

Larsen, J., & Nelson, J. (1984). Women, friendship, and adaptation to prison. *Journal of Criminal Justice, 12*, 601–615.

Leger, R. (1987). Lesbianism among women prisoners: participants and non-participants. *Criminal Justice and Behavior, 14*, 463–479.

Linn, R. (1997). Soldier's narratives of selective moral resistance. In: A. Lieblich, & R. Josselson (Eds.), *The narrative study of lives* (pp. 95–112). Thousand Oaks, CA: Sage.

Lord, E. (1995). A prison superintendent's perspective on women in prison. *Prison Journal, 75*, 257–269.

McClellan, D. (1994). Disparity in the discipline of male and female inmates in Texas prisons. *Women and Criminal Justice, 5*, 71–97.

Mitchell, J. (1988). Women, AIDS and public policy. *Law and Public Policy Journal, 3*, 50–51.

Moss, A. (1999). Sexual misconduct among staff and inmates. In: P. Carlson, & J. Garrett (Eds.), *Prison and jail administration* (pp. 189–196). Gaithersburg, MD: Aspen Publishers.

Owen, B. (1998). *In the mix: struggle and survival in a women's prison*. Albany, NY: State University of New York Press.

Pearson, P. (1998). *When she was bad*. New York: Penguin Books.

Pollock, J. M. (1995). Women in corrections: custody and the caring ethic. In: A. V. Merlo, & J. M. Pollock (Eds.), *Women, law, and social control* (pp. 97–116). Boston: Allyn and Bacon.

Pollock-Byrne, J. M. (1990). *Women, prison, and crime*. Pacific Grove, CA: Brooks/Cole.

Pollock-Byrne, J. M. (1992). Women in prison: why are their numbers increasing? In: P. J. Benekes, & A. V. Merlo (Eds.), *Corrections: dilemmas and directions* (pp. 79–95). Cincinnati, OH: Anderson Publishing.

Prendergast, M., Wellisen, J., & Falkin, G. (1995). Assessment of and services for substance-abusing women offenders in community and correctional settings. *Prison Journal, 75*, 240–256.

Rafter, N. H. (1990). *Partial justice: women in state prisons, 1800–1935*. Boston, MA: Northeastern University Press.

Ragin, C. C. (1994). *Constructing social research*. Thousand Oaks, CA: Pine Forge Press.

Rasche, C. (2000). The dislike of female offenders among correctional officers. In: R. Muraskin (Ed.), *It's a crime: women and justice* (pp. 237–252). Upper Saddle River, NJ: Prentice Hall.

Seidman, T. E. (1998). *Interviewing as qualitative research: a guide for researchers in education and the social sciences*. New York: Teachers College Press.

Snell, T., & Morton, D. (1994). *Survey of state inmates: women in prison*. Washington, DC: Bureau of Justice Statistics.

Stanton, A. (1980). *When mothers go to jail*. Lexington, MA: Appleton Crafts.

Sykes, G. M. (1958). *The society of captives: a study of a maximum security prison*. Princeton, NJ: Princeton University Press.

Toch, H. (1975). *Men in crisis*. Chicago: Aldine-Atherton.

Ward, D., & Kassebaum, G. (1965). *Women's prison: sex and social structure*. Chicago: Aldine-Atherton.

Reprinted from JOURNAL OF CRIMINAL JUSTICE, Vol. 29, No. 6, Pogrebin, M. R., and Dodge, M., "Women's Accounts of Their Prison Experiences: A Retrospective View of Their Subjective Realities," pp. 531–541.

4. Mental Health Issues in Long-Term Solitary and "Supermax" Confinement

Craig Haney

This article discusses the recent increase in the use of solitary-like confinement, especially the rise of so-called supermax prisons and the special mental health issues and challenges they pose. After briefly discussing the nature of these specialized and increasingly widespread units and the forces that have given rise to them, the article reviews some of the unique mental-health-related issues they present, including the negative psychological effects of isolation and the unusually high percentage of mentally ill prisoners who are confined there.

The field of corrections is arguably impervious to much truly significant change. Of all of the institutions in our society, prisons retain the greatest similarity to their early 19th century form. Indeed, until relatively recently, more than a few prisoners were housed in facilities that had been constructed a half century or more ago. Although there have been advances in the methods by which correctional regimes approach the task of changing or rehabilitating prisoners, and a number of improvements made in overall conditions of confinement compared to the 19th century (often brought about by litigation compelling prison systems to modernize and improve), many of the basic facts of prison life have remained relatively constant. Notwithstanding increased sophistication in the technology of incarcerative social control, and the waxing and waning in popularity of one or another kind of prison treatment program, the argument that there has been nothing fundamentally new on the correctional landscape for many years would be difficult to refute.

However, in this article, I suggest that the last decade of the 20th century did see the rise of a new penal form—the so-called supermax prison. Increasing numbers of prisoners now are being housed in a new form of solitary or isolated confinement that, although it resembles the kind of punitive segregation that has been in use since the inception of the prison, has a number of unique features. At the start of the 1990s, Human Rights Watch (1991) identified the rise of supermax prisons as "perhaps the most troubling" human rights trend in U.S. corrections and estimated that some 36 states either had completed or were in the process of creating some kind of "super maximum" prison facility. By the end of the decade, the same organization estimated that there were approximately 20,000 prisoners confined to supermax-type units in the United States (Human Rights Watch, 2000) and expressed even more pointed concerns about their human rights implications. Because most experts agree that the use of such units has increased significantly since then, it is likely that the number of persons currently housed in supermax prisons is considerably higher.

There are few if any forms of imprisonment that appear to produce so much psychological trauma and in which so many symptoms of psychopathology are manifested. Thus, the mental health implications of these units are potentially very significant. Despite the slight (and sometimes not so slight) variations in the ways different state prison systems approach this most restrictive form of confinement, supermax prisons have enough in common to permit some generalizations about what they are, why they have come about, what special mental health issues they raise, and how they might be regulated and reformed to minimize some of the special risks they pose. I will try to address each of these issues in turn in the pages that follow.

Supermax Conditions of Confinement

Supermax confinement represents a significant variation in the long-standing practice of placing prisoners in what is known as solitary confinement or punitive segregation. For practical as well as humanitarian reasons, prisoners have rarely been confined in literal or complete solitary confinement. But prisoners in solitary or isolation have always been physically segregated from the rest of the prison population and typically excluded from much of the normal programming, routines, opportunities, and collective activities available in the mainline institution. By the late 19th century, most jurisdictions in the United States had, for the most part, restricted solitary confinement to relatively brief periods of punishment that were imposed in response to specified infractions of prison rules.

In contrast to this traditional form of isolation, supermax differs in several important ways—primarily the totality of the isolation, the intended duration of the confinement, the reasons for which it is imposed, and the technological sophistication with which it is achieved. In particular, supermax prisons house prisoners in virtual isolation and subject them to almost complete idleness for extremely long periods of time. Supermax prisoners rarely leave their cells. In most such units, an hour a day of out-of-cell time is the norm. They eat all of their meals alone in the cells, and typically no group or social activity of any kind is permitted.

When prisoners in these units are escorted outside their cells or beyond their housing units, they typically are first placed in restraints—chained while still inside their cells (through a food port or tray slot on the cell door)—and sometimes tethered to a leash that is held by an escort officer. They are rarely if ever in the presence of another person (including physicians and psychotherapists) without being in multiple forms of physical restraints (e.g., ankle chains, belly or waist chains, handcuffs). Supermax prisoners often incur severe restrictions on the nature and amounts of personal property they may possess and on their access to the prison library, legal materials, and canteen. Their brief periods of outdoor exercise or so-called yard time typically take place in caged-in or cement-walled areas that are so constraining they are often referred to as "dog runs." In some units, prisoners get no more than a glimpse of overhead sky or whatever terrain can be seen through the tight security screens that surround their exercise pens.

Supermax prisoners are often monitored by camera and converse through intercoms rather than through direct contact with correctional officers. In newer facilities, computerized locking and tracking systems allow their movement to be regulated with a minimum of human interaction (or none at all). Some supermax units conduct visits through videoconferencing equipment rather than in person; there is no immediate face-to-face interaction (let alone physical contact), even with loved ones who may have traveled great distances to see them. In addition to "video visits," some facilities employ "tele-medicine" and "tele-psychiatry" procedures in which prisoners' medical and psychological needs are addressed by staff members who "examine" them and "interact" with them over television screens from locations many miles away.

Supermax prisons routinely keep prisoners in this near-total isolation and restraint for periods of time that, until recently, were unprecedented in modern corrections. Unlike more traditional forms of solitary confinement in which prisoners typically are isolated for relatively brief periods of time as punishment for specific disciplinary infractions, supermax prisoners may be kept under these conditions for years on end. Indeed, many correctional systems impose supermax confinement as part of a long-term strategy of correctional management and control rather than as an immediate sanction for discrete rule violations.

In fact, many prisoners are placed in supermax not specifically for what they have done but rather on the basis of who someone in authority has judged them to be (e.g., "dangerous," "a threat," or a member of a "disruptive" group). In many states, the majority of supermax prisoners have been given so-called indeterminate terms, usually on the basis of having been officially labeled by prison officials as gang members. An indeterminate supermax term often means that these prisoners will serve their entire prison term in isolation (unless they debrief by providing incriminating information about other alleged gang members). Prisoners in these units may complete their prison sentence while still confined in supermax and be released directly back into the community. If and when they are returned to prison on a parole violation or subsequent conviction, they are likely to be sent immediately back to supermax because of their previous status as a supermax prisoner.

To summarize: prisoners in these units live almost entirely within the confines of a 60- to 80-square-foot cell, can exist for many years separated from the natural world around them and removed from the natural rhythms of social life, are denied access to vocational or educational training programs or other meaningful activities in which to engage, get out of their cells no more than a few hours a week, are under virtually constant surveillance and monitoring, are rarely if ever in the presence of another person without being heavily chained and restrained, have no opportunities for normal conversation or social interaction, and are denied the opportunity to ever touch another human being with affection or caring or to receive such affection or caring themselves. Because supermax units typically meld sophisticated modern technology with the age-old practice of solitary confinement, prisoners experience levels of isolation and behavioral control that are more total and complete and literally dehumanized than has been possible in the past. The combination of these factors is what makes this extraordinary and extreme form of imprisonment unique in the modern history of corrections. Its emergence in a society that prides itself on abiding "evolving standards of decency" (*Trop v. Dulles*, 1958) to regulate its systems of punishment requires some explanation.

The Origins of the Modern Supermax

Two important trends in modern American corrections help to account for the creation of this new penal form. The first is the unprecedented growth in the prison population that started in the mid-1970s and continued into the early years of the 21st century. The rate of incarceration in the United States (adjusting for any increases in overall population) remained stable over the 50-year period from 1925 to 1975. Remarkably, it then quintupled over the next 25-year period. Most state prison systems doubled in size and then doubled again during this period, with no commensurate increase in the resources devoted to corrections in general or to programming and mental health services in particular (Haney & Zimbardo, 1998).

This dramatic influx of prisoners—and the overcrowding crisis it produced—occurred at approximately the same time that another important change was underway. In the mid-1970s, the United States formally abandoned its commitment to the rehabilitative ideals that had guided its prison policy for decades. Often at the insistence of the politicians who funded their prison systems, correctional administrators embraced a new philosophy built on the notion that incarceration was intended to inflict punishment and little else. The mandate to provide educational, vocational, and therapeutic programming in the name of rehabilitation ended at an especially inopportune time (Haney, 1997). Prisons throughout the country were filled to capacity and beyond, and the prisoners who were crowded inside had few opportunities to engage in productive activities or to receive help for preexisting psychological or other problems.

Under these conditions of unprecedented overcrowding and unheard of levels of idleness, prison administrators lacked positive incentives to manage the inevitable tensions and conflicts that festered behind the walls. In systems whose raison d'être was punishment, it was not surprising that correctional officials turned to punitive mechanisms in the hope of buttressing increasingly tenuous institutional controls. Of course, disciplinary infractions often were met with increasing levels of punishment in the modern American prison, even before these trends were set in motion. But the magnitude of the problem faced by correctional administrators in the 1980s pushed their response to an unprecedented level. Supermax prisons emerged in this context—seized on as a technologically enhanced tightening screw on the pressure cooker-like atmosphere that had been created inside many prison systems in the United States. As the pressure from overcrowding and idleness increased, the screw was turned ever tighter.

Historically, correctional polices often harden in times of prison crisis. But once the problem causing the increased tension or turmoil has been identified and resolved, the punitive response typically de-escalates, sometimes leading to even more hospitable conditions and treatment. Unfortunately, the prison overcrowding problem did not subside during the 1980s and 1990s, and the continued punitive atmosphere that marked this period meant that corrections officials were in no position look "soft" in the face of the crisis.

The politics of the era deprived prison administrators of alternative approaches and guaranteed a one-way ratcheting up of punishment in the face of these tensions. They became increasingly committed to more forcibly subduing prisoners whose behavior was problematic ("a threat to the safety and security of the institution"), taking fewer chances with others whom they suspected might be a problem, and set about intimidating everyone else who might be thinking about causing disruption. Supermax simultaneously provided politicians with another stark symbol to confirm their commitment to tough-on-crime policies (Riveland, 1999) and gave prison officials a way of making essentially the same statement behind the walls.

I belabor this recent correctional history to debunk several myths that surround the rise of the supermax prison form. This new kind of prison did not originate as a necessary or inevitable response or backlash to some sort of "permissive" correctional atmosphere that allegedly prevailed in the 1960s, as some who defend the recent punitive trends in imprisonment have suggested (cf. O'Brien & Jones, 1999). It was not a badly needed corrective to liberal prison policies or to previous capitulations to the prisoners' rights movement. Quite the opposite. Supermaxes began in response to the overcrowded and punitive 1980s and came into fruition in the even more overcrowded and more punitive 1990s. They are in many ways the logical extension of a system founded on the narrow premise that the only appropriate response to misbehavior is increased punishment.

In addition, there is no evidence that the rise of supermax prisons was driven by the threat of some new breed of criminal or prisoner. The natural human tendency to individualize, dispositionalize, and sometimes even to demonize problematic behavior, and to ignore the contextual forces that help create it, is intensified in prison systems as perhaps nowhere else. Thus, when correctional officials faced unprecedented pressures from dramatically increased levels of overcrowding and idleness, they naturally ignored the contextual origins of the problem (over which they had little or no control) and blamed the prisoners (over which they did).

But, even if supermax prisons now contain only "the worst of the worst"—a phrase that is often used to justify the use of these newly designed units but whose accuracy is hotly disputed by their critics—there is no evidence that these allegedly "worst" prisoners are any worse than those who had been adequately managed by less drastic measures in the past. In assessing the benefits and burdens of supermax confinement, it is important to keep in mind that correctional officials have not been given a mandate to engage in such extraordinarily punitive and unprecedented measures because they now confront not only an extraordinarily dangerous but new strain of prisoner that has never before existed. There is no such new breed and no such mandate.

The Psychological Pains of Supermax Confinement

In assessing the mental health concerns raised by supermax prisons, it is important to acknowledge an extensive empirical literature that clearly establishes their potential to inflict psychological pain and emotional damage. Empirical research on solitary and supermax-like confinement has consistently and unequivocally documented the harmful consequences of living in these kinds of environments. Despite some methodological limitations that apply to some of the individual studies, the findings are robust. Evidence of these negative psychological effects comes from personal accounts, descriptive studies, and systematic research on solitary and supermax-type confinement, conducted over a period of four decades, by researchers from several different continents who had diverse backgrounds and a wide range of professional expertise. The harmful psychological consequences of solitary and supermax-type confinement are extremely well documented.

Specifically, in case studies and personal accounts provided by mental health and correctional staff who worked in supermax units, a range of similar adverse symptoms have been observed to occur in prisoners, including appetite and sleep disturbances, anxiety, panic, rage, loss of control, paranoia, hallucinations, and self-mutilations (e.g., Jackson, 1983; Porporino, 1986; Rundle, 1973; Scott, 1969; Slater, 1986). Moreover, direct studies of prison isolation have documented an extremely broad range of harmful psychological reactions.

In addition, among the correlational studies of the relationship between housing type and various incident reports, again, self-mutilation and suicide are more prevalent in isolated housing (e.g., Hayes, 1989; Johnson, 1973; A. Jones, 1986; Porporino, 1986), as are deteriorating mental and physical health (beyond self-injury), other-directed violence, such as stabbings, attacks on staff, and property destruction, and collective violence (e.g., Bidna, 1975; Edwards, 1988; Kratcoski, 1988; Porporino, 1986; Sestoft, Andersen, Lilleback, & Gabrielsen, 1998; Steinke, 1991; Volkart, Rothenfluh, Kobelt, Dittrich, & Ernst, 1983). In fact, many of the negative effects of solitary confinement are analogous to the acute reactions suffered by torture and trauma victims, including post-traumatic stress disorder or PTSD (e.g., Herman, 1992, 1995; Horowitz, 1990; Hougen, 1988; Siegel, 1984) and the kind of psychiatric sequelae that plague victims of what are called "deprivation and constraint" torture techniques (e.g., Somnier & Genefke, 1986).

To summarize, there is not a single published study of solitary or supermax-like confinement in which nonvoluntary confinement lasting for longer than 10 days, where participants were unable to terminate their isolation at will, that failed to result in negative psychological effects. The damaging effects ranged in severity and included such clinically significant symptoms as hypertension, uncontrollable anger, hallucinations, emotional breakdowns, chronic depression, and suicidal thoughts and behavior. Of course, it is important to emphasize that not all supermax prisons are created equal, and not all of them have the same capacity to produce the same number and degree of negative psychological effects. Research on the effects of social contexts and situations in general and institutional settings in particular underscores the way in which specific conditions of confinement do matter. Thus, there is every reason to expect that better-run and relatively more benign supermax prisons will produce comparatively fewer of the preceding negative psychological effects, and the worse run facilities will produce comparatively more.

The Prevalence of Pain and Suffering in Supermax

In addition to the serious nature and wide range of adverse symptoms that have been repeatedly reported in a large number of empirical studies, it is important to estimate their prevalence rates—that is, the extent to which prisoners who are confined in supermax-type conditions suffer its adverse effects. My own research at California's Pelican Bay "security housing unit" (or SHU)—a prototypical supermax prison at the time these data were collected—provides one such estimate. In this section, I describe this research in some detail and situate its findings by comparing them to prevalence rates among several other relevant groups.

In the Pelican Bay study, each prisoner was individually assessed in face-to-face interviews. Because the sample of 100 SHU prisoners was randomly selected, the data are representative of and, within appropriate margins of error, generalizable to the entire group of prisoners at this supermax facility. The following two important areas were explored in each interview. In the first, one series of questions focused on whether the prisoner experienced any of 12 specific indices of psychological trauma or distress. A list of those symptoms regarded as reliable indicators of general psychological distress was employed. In the second, a different series of questions was designed to determine whether the prisoner suffered any of 13 specific psychopathological effects of isolation.

The results of this prevalence study are depicted in Tables 1 and 2. As Table 1 indicates, every symptom of psychological distress but one (fainting spells) was suffered by more than half of the representative sample of supermax prisoners. Two thirds or more of the prisoners reported being bothered by many of these symptoms in the SHU, and some were suffered by nearly everyone. For example, virtually all of the isolated prisoners were plagued by nervousness and anxiety, by chronic lethargy, and a very high percentage (70%) felt themselves on the verge of an emotional breakdown. In addition, a very high number suffered from headaches and troubled sleep, and more than half were bothered by nightmares. Well over half of the supermax prisoners reported a constellation of symptoms—headaches, trembling, sweaty palms, and heart palpitations—that is commonly associated with hypertension.

TABLE 1 Symptoms of Psychological and Emotional Trauma

Symptom	*% Presence Among Pelican Bay SHU Prisoners*
Anxiety, nervousness	91
Headaches	88
Lethargy, chronic tiredness	84
Trouble sleeping	84
Impending nervous breakdown	70
Perspiring hands	68
Heart palpitations	68
Loss of appetite	63
Dizziness	56
Nightmares	55
Hands trembling	51
Tingling sensation[a]	19
Fainting	17

NOTE: SHU = security housing unit.

a. Not necessarily a symptom of psychological trauma. It is included as a control question to provide a baseline against which to measure the significance of the trauma-related responses.

As Table 2 shows, the psychopathological symptoms of isolation were even more prevalent among these prisoners. Almost all of the supermax prisoners reported suffering from ruminations or intrusive thoughts, an oversensitivity to external stimuli, irrational anger and irritability, confused thought processes, difficulties with attention and often with memory, and a tendency to withdraw socially to become introspective and avoid social contact. An only slightly lower percentage of prisoners reported a constellation of symptoms that appeared to be related to developing mood or emotional disorders—concerns over emotional flatness or losing the ability to feel, swings in emotional responding, and feelings of depression or sadness that did not go away. Finally, sizable minorities of supermax prisoners reported symptoms that are typically only associated with more extreme forms of psychopathology—hallucinations, perceptual distortions, and thoughts of suicide.

To put both sets of figures in perspective, it is possible to compare these prevalence rates with those derived from other populations in which similar assessments have been made. For example, Dupuy, Engel, Devine, Scanlon, and Querec (1970) assessed some similar indices of psychological distress with a representative national probability sample of more than 7,000 persons. More recent data focusing on similar indices of psychopathology were collected in Epidemiologic Catchment Area Study (ECAS), a multisite study in which the diagnostic interview schedule (DIS) was used to assess the prevalence of psychiatric symptoms in the population at large (Robins & Regier, 1991). Finally, even more extensive

TABLE 2 Psychopathological Effects of Prolonged Isolation

Symptom	*% Presence Among Pelican Bay SHU Prisoners*
Ruminations	88
Irrational anger	88
Oversensitivity to stimuli	86
Confused thought process	84
Social withdrawal	83
Chronic depression	77
Emotional flatness	73
Mood, emotional swings	71
Overall deterioration	67
Talking to self	63
Violent fantasies	61
Perceptual distortions	44
Hallucinations	41
Suicidal thoughts	27

NOTE: SHU = security housing unit.

comparisons are possible with another systematic study of the effects of living under isolated prison conditions—Brodsky and Scogin's (1988) research on prisoners confined in two maximum security protective custody units.

Table 3 contains a summary of the comparisons between the prevalence rates found in the two studies of nonincarcerated normal populations, Brodsky and Scogin's protective custody prisoners, and the supermax sample from Pelican Bay SHU (of course, along only those dimensions measured in each of the respective studies). The contrasts with the nonincarcerated normal samples are striking. As would be expected, in almost every instance, the prevalence rates for indices of psychological distress and psychopathology in the samples from the general population are quite low. The only exceptions were for anxiety and nervousness, which Dupuy et al. (1970) found in 45% of their normal sample, and depression, which Robins and Regier (1991) found in almost a quarter of the persons they assessed. Otherwise, the indices of distress and symptoms of psychopathology occurred in less than 20% of the nonincarcerated samples. On the other hand, in both of the isolated prisoner populations, the prevalence rates were well above 50% on virtually all of the measured dimensions. For certain symptoms, rates for the prisoner samples were five to ten or more times as high.

In fact, in both comparative and absolute terms, the prevalence rates were extremely high for the supermax prisoner sample and exceeded even those reported for the protective custody prisoners. Conditions of confinement for protective custody prisoners are in many ways similar to those in supermax confinement. That is, they are typically segregated from the rest of the prison

TABLE 3 Comparison of Prevalence Rates Between in Normal, Protective Custody and Supermax Populations

Description	*% Normal Dupuy, Engel, Devine, Scanlon, and Querec's (1970) National Probability Sample of 7,000 Adults*	*% Normal Robins and Regier's (1991) Multisite Assessment of 20,000 Adults*	*% Protective Housing Brodsky and Scogin's (1988) Sample of 31 Prisoners in Protective Housing*	*% Supermax Haney's (1993) Random Sample of 100 Prisoners in Security Housing Unit*
Symptoms of psychological trauma				
Anxiety, nervousness	45		84	91
Headaches	13.7		61	88
Lethargy, chronic tiredness	16.8		65	84
Trouble sleeping	16.8		61	84
Impending breakdown	7.7		48	70
Perspiring hands	17		45	68
Heart palpitations	3.7		39	68
Dizziness	7.1		45	56
Nightmares	7.6		42	55
Hands trembling	7		39	51
Fainting			0	17
Psychopathological effects of isolation				
Ruminations			74	88
Irrational anger		2.9	71	88
Confused thought process		10.8	65	84
Chronic depression		23.5	77	77
Overall deterioration			52	67
Talking to self			68	63
Hallucinations		1.7	42	41

population, restricted or prohibited from participating in prison programs and activities, and often housed indefinitely under what amount to oppressive and isolated conditions. Unlike supermax prisoners per se, however, many have some control over their status as protective custody (PC) prisoners (e.g., many have "volunteered" for this status) and, although they live under the stigma of being PC prisoners, they are technically housed in these units for protection rather than for punishment.

Accordingly, Brodsky and Scogin (1988) found high rates of psychological trauma among their sample of protective custody prisoners, so much so that they worried about the "strong potential for harmful effects" that such confinement represented (p. 279). They also observed, in terms that apply equally well to supermax prisoners, that "when inmates are subjected to extensive cell confinement and deprivation of activities and stimulation, a majority can be expected to report moderate to serious psychological symptoms" (p. 279). Yet, note that on 16 of 18 possible comparisons, the symptom prevalence rate for Pelican Bay SHU prisoners are greater than those reported in the protective custody study. Note also that many of the percentage differences are comparatively large. In fact, the Pelican Bay prevalence rates are, on average, 14.5% greater than those reported for the prisoners in Brodsky and Scogin's study.

The prevalence data collected in the Pelican Bay study partially address another important supermax-related issue. Several mental health experts have written about a distinct set of reactions or a syndrome-like condition that occurs in prisoners who have been subjected to long-term isolation. Canadian psychiatrist George Scott (1969) described what he termed "isolation sickness" as coming from "prolonged solitary confinement" (p. 3). In more recent research, it has been labled "RES" (reduced environmental stimulation) or "SHU" (security housing unit) syndrome. Perhaps the most detailed clinical description of the disorder came from psychiatrist Stuart Grassian (1983), who observed that it included massive free-floating anxiety, hypersensitivity to external stimulation, perceptual distortions or hallucinations, derealization experiences, difficulties with concentration or memory, acute confusional states, aggressive fantasies, paranoia, and motor excitement (that may include violent or self-destructive outbursts).

The Social Pathologies of Supermax

The Pelican Bay prevalence study and the other direct studies of the psychological effects of supermax confinement I cited earlier focused on discrete and measurable consequences of this form of imprisonment. The tools used to provide these measurements are extremely useful and scientifically appropriate methods for documenting specific reactions and symptoms. However, they have some inherent limitations that may mask some of the subtle yet important transformations that are brought about by supermax confinement.

For one, indices of measurable harm generally rely on things that persons must be aware of in order to report. Obviously, prisoners must be consciously pained or in distress over a symptom in order to complain about it; the greater their conscious awareness, the higher the frequency and extent of negative effects. However, in the course of adjusting and adapting to the painful and distressing conditions of confinement, many prisoners will strive to essentially "get used to it," adapting and accommodating to make their day-to-day misery seem more manageable. In addition, some supermax prisoners will undergo forms of psychological deterioration of which they are unaware and, therefore, incapable of reporting. As long as the deterioration is not obvious or disabling, it is likely to escape the attention of mental health staff who, in most units, rarely perform careful psychiatric assessments on a routine basis for prisoners who appear to be otherwise minimally functioning.

Indeed, it is not uncommon to encounter a number of supermax prisoners who, although they voice few specific complaints and are not identified by staff as having any noticeable psychological problems or needs, nonetheless have accommodated so profoundly to the supermax environment that they may be unable to live anywhere else. In some instances, these changes are difficult to measure because prisoners are unaware that they are occurring or because they have blunted their perception that such transformations are underway. In other instances, the changes are too broad, complicated, and subtle to be precisely measured. Yet they appear to have lasting mental health implications.

Thus, a number of significant transformations occur in many long-term supermax prisoners that, although they are more difficult to measure, may be equally if not more problematic for their future health and well-being and the health and well-being of those around them. These come about because in order to survive the rigors of supermax, many prisoners gradually change their patterns of thinking, acting, and feeling. Some of these transformations have the potential to rigidify, to become deeply set ways of being, that are, in varying degrees for different people, more or less permanent changes in who these prisoners are and, once they are released from supermax, what they can become. Because they do not represent clinical syndromes per se, and because they constitute patterns of social behavior that are largely "functional" under conditions of isolation—for the most part becoming increasingly dysfunctional only if they persist on return to more normal social settings—I have termed them "social pathologies."

Several of the social pathologies that can and do develop in prisoners who struggle to adapt to the rigors of supermax confinement are discussed below.

First, the unprecedented totality of control in supermax units forces prisoners to become entirely dependent on the institution to organize their existence. Although this is a potential consequence of institutionalization or "prisonization" in general (e.g., Haney, in press), it occurs to an exaggerated degree in many supermax prisons. Thus, many prisoners gradually lose the ability to initiate or to control their own behavior, or to organize their own lives. The two separate components of this reaction—problems with the self-control and self-initiation of behavior—both stem from the extreme over-control of supermax. That is, all prisoners in these units are forced to adapt to an institutional regime that limits virtually all aspects of their behavior. Indeed, one of the defining characteristics of supermax confinement is the extent to which it accomplishes precisely that. But because almost every aspect of the prisoners' day-to-day existence is so carefully and completely circumscribed in these units, some of them lose the ability to set limits for themselves or to control their own behavior through internal mechanisms. They may become uncomfortable with even small amounts of freedom because they have lost the sense of how to behave in the absence of constantly enforced restrictions, tight external structure, and the ubiquitous physical restraints.

Second, prisoners may also suffer a seemingly opposite reaction that is caused by the same set of circumstances. That is, they may begin to lose the ability to initiate behavior of any kind—to organize their own lives around activity and purpose—because they have been stripped of any opportunity to do so for such prolonged periods of time. Chronic apathy, lethargy, depression, and despair often result. Thus, as their personal initiative erodes, prisoners find themselves unable to begin even mundane tasks or to follow through once they have begun them. Others find it difficult to focus their attention, to concentrate, or to organize activity. In extreme cases, prisoners may literally stop behaving. In either event, it is hard to imagine a set of adaptations more dysfunctional and problematic for persons who will one day be expected to exercise increased self-control and self-initiative in mainline prison settings or in the free world, if and when they are released there.

Third, the absence of regular, normal interpersonal contact and any semblance of a meaningful social context creates a feeling of unreality that pervades one's existence in these places. Because so much of our individual identity is socially constructed and maintained, the virtually complete loss of genuine forms of social contact and the absence of any routine and recurring opportunities to ground one's thoughts and feelings in a recognizable human context leads to an undermining of the sense of self and a disconnection of experience from meaning. Supermax prisoners are literally at risk of losing their grasp on who they are, of how and whether they are connected to a larger social world. Some prisoners act out literally as a way of getting a reaction from their environment, proving to themselves that they are still alive and capable of eliciting a genuine response—however hostile—from other human beings.

Fourth, the experience of total social isolation can lead, paradoxically, to social withdrawal for some supermax prisoners. That is, they recede even more deeply into themselves than the sheer physical isolation of supermax has imposed on them. Some move from, at first, being starved for social contact to, eventually, being disoriented and even frightened by it. As they become increasingly unfamiliar and uncomfortable with social interaction, they are further alienated from others and made anxious in their presence. In extreme cases, another pattern emerges: This environment is so painful, so bizarre and impossible to make sense of, that they create their own reality—they live in a world of fantasy instead.

Fifth, and finally, the deprivations, restrictions, the totality of control, and the prolonged absence of any real opportunity for happiness or joy fills many prisoners with intolerable levels of frustration that, for some, turns to anger and then even to uncontrollable and sudden outbursts of rage. Others channel their supermax-created anger in more premeditated ways. Many supermax prisoners ruminate in the course of the countless empty hours of uninterrupted time during which they are allowed to do little else. Some occupy this idle time by committing themselves to fighting against the system and the people that surround, provoke, deny, thwart, and oppress them. There are supermax prisoners who become consumed by the fantasy of revenge, and others lash out against those who have treated them in ways they regard as inhumane. Sadly, there are some supermax prisoners who are driven by these deprived and oppressive conditions to pursue courses of action that further ensure their continued deprivation and oppression.

Although I have described these social pathologies as separate and distinct adaptations, they are not mutually exclusive. Thus, prisoners may move through one or another adaptation to their extraordinarily stressful life in supermax, or engage in several at once in an attempt to reduce the pains of their confinement and to achieve a tolerable equilibrium in this otherwise psychologically hostile environment. In fact, in extreme cases and over a long period of time, a combination of seemingly adaptive responses may coalesce into a more or less permanent lifestyle, one lived so exclusively and with such commitment that the prisoner's very being seems to be transformed. For example, some supermax prisoners whose opportunities for self-definition and self-expression have been effectively suppressed for extended periods of time—who have been denied conventional outlets through which to use their intellect or to express their heightened sense of injustice—come increasingly to define themselves in opposition to the prison administration. They begin to gradually fashion an identity that is anchored primarily by the goal of thwarting and resisting the control mechanisms that are increasingly directed at them. The material out of which their social reality is constructed increasingly consists of the only events to which they are exposed and the only experiences they are allowed to have—the minutiae of the supermax itself and all of the nuance with which it can be infused.

Just as the social pathologies of supermax are the creations of a socially pathological environment, taking prisoners out of these places often goes a long way in reducing or eliminating the negative effects. But there is good reason to believe that some prisoners—we do not yet know how many or, in advance, precisely who—cannot and will not overcome these social pathologies; their extreme adaptations to supermax confinement become too ingrained to relinquish. Those who are not blessed with special personal resiliency and significant social and professional support needed to recover from such atypical and traumatic experiences may never return to the free world and resume normal, healthy, productive social lives. These are extraordinary—I believe often needless and indefensible—risks to take with the human psyche and spirit. Such extreme, ultimately dysfunctional, but often psychologically necessary adaptations to supermax confinement underscore the importance of continuing to critically analyze, modify, and reform the extremely harsh conditions that produce them. Understanding how and why they occur also brings some real urgency to the development of effective programs by which prisoners can be assisted in unlearning problematic habits of thinking, feeling, and acting on which their psychological survival in supermax often depends.

But they also highlight another issue. In what is one of the core irrationalities in the logic on which supermax regimes are premised, these units make the ability to withstand the psychological assault of extreme isolation a prerequisite for allowing prisoners to return to the intensely social world of mainline prison or free society. In this way, prisoners who cannot "handle" the profound isolation of supermax confinement are almost always doomed to be retained in it. And those who have adapted all too well to the deprivation, restriction, and pervasive control are prime candidates for release to a social world to which they may be incapable of ever fully readjusting.

Additional Mental Health Issues in Supermax

In addition to the negative psychological effects of solitary and supermax-like confinement reviewed above, there are several other important mental health issues raised by the nature of these conditions and the policies by which prisoners are placed in them. One such issue involves the number of mentally ill prisoners who are housed in supermax. Prisoners often describe their experience in supermax environments as a form of psychological torture; most of them are in varying degrees of psychic pain, and many of them struggle to cope with the daily stress of their confinement. Although in my experience, virtually everyone in these units suffers, prisoners with preexisting mental illnesses are at greater risk of having this suffering deepen into something more permanent and disabling. Those at greatest risk include, certainly, persons who are emotionally unstable, who suffer from clinical depression or other mood disorders, who are developmentally disabled, and those whose contact with reality is already tenuous. There is good reason to believe that many of these prisoners in particular will be unable to withstand the psychic assault of dehumanized isolation, the lack of caring human contact, the profound idleness and inactivity, and the otherwise extraordinarily stressful nature of supermax confinement without significant deterioration and decompensation.

How many such persons are there? Research conducted over the past several decades suggests that somewhere between 10% to 20% of mainline prisoners in general in the United States suffer from some form of major mental illness (e.g., Jamelka, Trupin, & Chiles, 1989; Veneziano & Veneziano, 1996). The percentages in supermax appear to be much higher. Although too few studies have been done to settle on precise estimates of mentally ill supermax prisoners, and the numbers undoubtedly vary some from prison system to prison system, the percentages may be as much as twice as high as in the general prisoner population.

Why this overrepresentation? Unproblematic adjustment to prison requires conformity to rigidly enforced rules and highly regimented procedures. Many mentally ill prisoners lack the capacity to comply with these demands and they may end up in trouble as a result. If they are not treated for their problems, the pattern is likely to be repeated and eventually can lead to confinement in a supermax unit. As Toch and Adams (2002) have succinctly put it, "an unknown proportion of people who are problems (prove troublesome to settings in which they function) also have problems (demonstrate psychological and social deficits when they are subjected to closer scrutiny)" (p. 13). Prison systems that fail to realize this basic fact will end up blaming—and punishing—prisoners for manifesting psychological conditions for which they should have been treated. Especially for prison systems that lack sufficient resources to adequately address the needs of their mentally ill mainline prisoners, disciplinary isolation and supermax confinement seems to offer a neat solution to an otherwise difficult dilemma. In such systems, supermax becomes the default placement for disruptive, troublesome, or inconvenient mentally ill prisoners. Thus the presence of a disproportionately high number of mentally ill prisoners in supermax often reflects a failure of system-wide proportions.

A number of supermax prisons fail to adequately screen out prisoners with preexisting mental illness, and fail to remove those whose mental health problems worsen under the stress of the extreme isolation, deprivation, and forceful control they confront inside. In addition, many of the units fail to appreciate the potential for these kinds of conditions of confinement to produce psychopathology in previously healthy prisoners. These problems are exacerbated by the fact that even if mental health staff members manage to identify those prisoners with serious psychological and psychiatric needs, many supermaxes are uniquely ill-suited to address them. Not only are they likely to be staffed with too few treatment personnel and plagued by high turnover, but the extraordinary and unyielding security procedures that characterize these kinds of prisons often preclude meaningful and appropriate therapeutic contact.

Thus, supermax prisoners who are in acute distress typically have the option of receiving what is euphemistically called "cell front therapy" in which they can discuss intimate, personal problems with mental health staff who cannot easily see or hear them through the cell doors (unless they speak so loudly that other prisoners in the housing unit also can listen in). Or they can choose to undergo strip searches, be placed in multiple restraints (which are typically left on throughout the therapy session), and taken either to a counselor's office (where correctional officer escorts are often stationed close enough to overhear what is being said) or special rooms fitted with security cages in which the prisoner is placed to be counseled by a therapist who speaks to them through wire screening of the cage. Or, in some places they can submit to "tele-psychiatry" sessions in which disembodied images attempt to assess and address their problems from distant locations. Not surprisingly, under these circumstances many prisoners fail to ask for help or reject it when it is offered.

A separate but related problem pertains to the group of prisoners who, although they do not suffer from preexisting mental illness, nonetheless are psychologically damaged by the extreme situational stress to which they are subjected in supermax. There is much reason to believe that supermax confinement may produce psychopathology in certain persons who otherwise would not have suffered it.

Finally, as I earlier alluded, many of the psychological and psychiatric reactions created or exacerbated by supermax confinement may persist long after a prisoner has been released into the mainline population or freed from incarceration altogether. In addition, even among prisoners who suffer no readily identifiable set of psychological symptoms, the social pathologies of supermax confinement may significantly interfere with long-term adjustment. To date, most supermax prisons appear oblivious to these persistent problems and many offer no meaningful counseling or transitional programs at all to prisoners who are attempting to make the daunting adjustment from near total isolation to an intensely social existence.

These interrelated problems—that prisoners suffering from preexisting mental illnesses are overrepresented in supermax, that the pains of supermax confinement are too severe for many prisoners to withstand, and that many of the psycho- and social pathologies of supermax confinement have disabling long-term consequences—have several important correctional policy implications. In particular, procedures must be implemented for screening prisoners in advance of their transfer to supermax (so that mentally ill and otherwise vulnerable persons are never placed there in the first place). In addition, because the mental health needs of any supermax prisoner can become acute and substantial at any time, prison systems need to be fully prepared to adequately address them (setting aside the obvious question of whether anyone can and should, in a humane system, be housed in such environments in the first place).

This also means that supermax prisons must implement careful psychiatric monitoring of all prisoners during their confinement and have readily accessible procedures in place for the removal of any prisoner at the first sign of deterioration. Given the fact that supermax prisoners behave so little—they are not permitted to actually do much of anything—the opportunities for disturbed behavior to be observed by staff are extremely limited. If monitoring is done passively, as it often is, only the most flagrant cases are likely to come to anyone's attention. Mental health staff who walk through supermax housing units, pausing briefly at each cell to ask prisoners how they are doing or to pose some other equally superficial, pro forma inquiry are not engaging in careful psychiatric screening. In light of the psychological risks posed by this environment and the widely shared reluctance of these prisoners to admit vulnerability, the regular and in-depth evaluation of supermax prisoners should be regarded as the only acceptable and truly effective form of monitoring.

Finally, supermax units should be required to provide extensive mental health resources that are specifically targeted to ease the psychological pains of this kind of confinement and the extremely difficult transitions that typically follow it. Supermax prisoners must enter so-called de-escalation or step-down programs well in advance of their release, and the programs themselves must grapple seriously and forthrightly with the negative psychological changes that supermax confinement often brings about. This will require prison systems that are in denial about the issues reviewed in the preceding pages to overcome it, and to acknowledge and confront the psychological consequences of housing prisoners under conditions that pose such significant mental health risks. Attempts to provide these kinds of transitional services through programs that are delivered without genuine interpersonal interaction and social contact—some systems actually use videotapes that supermax prisoners watch alone in their cells, supposedly to reacquaint them with the social world they are about to reenter—will prove to be painfully inadequate. Moreover, like all meaningful mental health and counseling services, these transitional programs must be made available to prisoners under genuinely therapeutic conditions that foster some degree of privacy, trust, and supportive social interaction.

Conclusion

Supermax prisons inflict varying amounts of psychological pain and emotional trauma on prisoners confined in them. The range of psychopathological reactions to this form of confinement is broad, many of the reactions are serious, and the existing evidence on the prevalence of trauma and symptomatology indicates that they are widespread. The mental health risks posed by this new form of imprisonment are clear and direct, exacerbated by the tendency of correctional systems to place a disproportionate number of previously mentally ill prisoners in supermax confinement, to ignore emerging signs of mental illness among the supermax prison population, and to fail to provide fully adequate therapeutic assistance to those prisoners who are in psychic pain and emotional distress.

It is important to reflect on whether the psychologically destructive conditions to which prisoners in supermax prisons are exposed would be countenanced for any other group in our society. Indeed, revelations that mental patients or elderly nursing home residents have been subjected to punitive isolation are understandably followed by widespread public outcry. Similarly, when typically more psychologically resilient populations have been taken as prisoners of war or as hostages subsequently held in isolation, recognition of the adverse psychological consequences is immediate and generates broad concern. Support for providing psychiatric counseling to the victims of these kinds of traumatic experiences is unquestioned.

The fact that no such recognition and concern is typically extended to prisoners in supermax confinement whose experiences in captivity may be comparable or worse, and of longer duration, raises disturbing questions: Do we allow what we believe to be their blameworthiness for this kind of mistreatment—that they earned it, they deserve it, they asked for it—to blur our understanding of the consequences of the mistreatment itself? That is, has devaluing the prisoners' claim to be free from such harm led to the erroneous perception that the harm is not real? If so, the empirical evidence suggests that we have made a grievous mistake.

I believe that the overwhelming evidence of the negative psychological effects of many forms of long-term supermax confinement provides a strong argument for placing enhanced correctional and legal limits on the use of this new prison form and carefully scrutinizing all aspects of its operation and effect (e.g., Haney & Lynch, 1997, pp. 558–566). As I noted earlier, there are better and worse supermax prisons, and we should take steps to ensure that all such facilities implement the best and most humane of the available practices. In general, far more careful screening, monitoring, and removal policies should be implemented to ensure that psychologically vulnerable—not just mentally ill—prisoners do not end up in supermax in the first place, and that those who deteriorate once there are immediately identified and transferred to less psychologically stressful environments. In addition, prison disciplinary committees should ensure that no prisoner is sent to supermax for infractions that were the result of preexisting psychiatric disorders or mental illness.

Moreover, harsh supermax conditions of confinement themselves must be modified to lessen their harmful effects. That is, it is important to recognize that placing people in conditions of confinement that we know in advance are likely to psychologically harm and endanger them cannot be morally justified merely through assurances that, if and when they do deteriorate, the prison system will make a good faith effort to identify the damage and work reasonably diligently to repair it. Thus, meaningful activities and programming—including access to therapy, work, education, and recreation—should be afforded all supermax prisoners to prevent deterioration, and out-of-cell time should be maximized within the limits of correctional resources. To prevent the total atrophy of social skills and the deterioration of social identities, supermax prisoners should be afforded some form of meaningful collective activity and opportunities for normal social interaction (that includes contact visiting).

Finally, strict time limits should be placed on the length of time that prisoners are housed in supermax. No prisoner should be subjected continuously to even these modified conditions of supermax-like confinement for longer than a period of 2 years, no prisoner should ever be subjected to indeterminate supermax terms for any reason, and no prisoner should be sent to supermax solely on the basis of alleged gang membership in the complete absence of other overt behavioral infractions. Indeed, the units themselves should be organized around the goal of rapid return and reintegration and judged on the basis of their ability to release rather than retain prisoners. Once prisoners are about to be released from supermax confinement, they should be afforded transitional or step-down programming to accustom them to the kind of environment to which they will be sent (mainline prison housing or the free world). Moreover, given the likely long-term effects of such confinement, these transitional programs and services should be continued after the prisoner has been transferred from supermax.

Correctional administrators, politicians, legal decision makers, and members of the public eventually may decide that the harm that supermax prisons inflict is worth the benefit that they arguably beget and that the pains of such confinement are the regrettable but unavoidable price of an otherwise justified policy. However, there are very serious psychological, correctional, legal, and even moral issues at the core of this calculation that are worthy of serious, continued debate. This debate has hardly begun and, in most instances, it has hardly been informed by the empirical record that I have cited in the preceding pages.

Many scholars who have studied supermax prisons—myself included—doubt the validity of the claims that are made on their behalf, and believe that in any event many of the publicly asserted goals of this new form of imprisonment can be achieved through less psychologically onerous and invasive alternatives. Yet, whatever one concludes about the value of supermax prisons in achieving these goals, it represents only one term in a more complex equation. The important determination of what, if any, legitimate role this kind of imprisonment should have in an effective and humane prison system can only be made with its psychological effects clearly in mind. The best available evidence indicates very clearly that many supermax-like conditions of confinement inflict extraordinary levels of psychological pain and create substantial mental health risks. We should not continue to ignore, overlook, or minimize these data in this continuing and important debate.

References

Andersen, H., Sestoft, D., Lillebaek, T., Gabrielsen, G., Hemmingsen, R., & Kramp, P. (2000). A longitudinal study of prisoners on remand: Psychiatric prevalence, incidence and psychopathology in solitary vs. non-solitary confinement. *Acta Psychiatrica Scandinavica, 102*, 19–25.

Austin v. Wilkinson, 189 F. Sup. 2d 719 (2002).

Bauer, M., Priebe, S., Haring, B., & Adamczak, K. (1993). Long-term mental sequelae of political imprisonment in East Germany. *Journal of Nervous & Mental Disease, 181*, 257–262.

Benjamin, T., & Lux, K. (1975). Constitutional and psychological implications of the use of solitary confinement: Experience at the Maine prison. *Clearinghouse Review, 9*, 83–90.

Bidna, H. (1975). Effects of increased security on prison violence. *Journal of Criminal Justice, 3*, 33–46.

Brodsky, S., & Scogin, F. (1988). Inmates in protective custody: First data on emotional effects. *Forensic Reports, 1*, 267–280.

Chappell, N., & Badger, M. (1989). Social isolation and well-being. *Journal of Gerontology, 44*, 169–176.

Cooke, M., & Goldstein, J. (1989). Social isolation and violent behavior. *Forensic Reports, 2*, 287–294.

Cooper v. Casey, 97 F.3d 914 (1996).

Cormier, B., & Williams, P. (1966). Excessive deprivation of liberty. *Canadian Psychiatric Association Journal, 11*, 470–484.

Deaton, J., Burge, S., Richlin, M., & Latrownik, A. (1977). Coping activities in solitary confinement of U.S. Navy POWs in Vietnam. *Journal of Applied Social Psychology, 7*, 239–257.

DeMaio, J. (2001). If you build it, they will come: The threat of overclassification in Wisconsin's supermax prison. *Wisconsin Law Review, 2001*, 207–248.

Dupuy, H., Engel, A., Devine, B., Scanlon, J., & Querec, L. (1970). *Selected symptoms of psychological distress*. Washington, DC: Government Printing Office.

Edwards, K. (1988). Some characteristics of inmates transferred from prison to a state mental hospital. *Behavioral Sciences and the Law, 6*, 131–137.

Fisher, W. (1994). Restraint and seclusion: A review of the literature. *American Journal of Psychiatry, 151*, 1584–1591.

Foster, D. (1987). *Detention & torture in South Africa: Psychological, legal & historical studies*. Cape Town, South Africa: David Philip.

Grassian, S. (1983). Psychopathological effects of solitary confinement. *American Journal of Psychiatry, 140*, 1450–1454.

Haney, C. (1993). Infamous punishment: The psychological effects of isolation. *National Prison Project Journal, 8*, 3–21.

Haney, C. (1997). Psychology and the limits to prison pain: Confronting the coming crisis in Eighth Amendment law. *Psychology, Public Policy, and Law, 3*, 499–588.

Haney, C. (in press). The psychological impact of incarceration: Implications for post-prison adjustment. In J. Travis (Ed.), *From prison to home*. Washington, DC: Urban Institute Press.

Haney, C., & Lynch, M. (1997). Regulating prisons of the future: The psychological consequences of solitary and supermax confinement. *New York University Review of Law and Social Change, 23*, 477–570.

Haney, C., & Zimbardo, P. (1998). The past and future of U.S. prison policy: Twenty-five years after the Stanford Prison Experiment. *American Psychologist, 53*, 709–727.

Harrison, A., Clearwater, Y., & McKay, C. (1989). The human experience in Antarctica: Applications to life in space. *Behavioral Science, 34*, 253–271.

Hayes, L. (1989). National study of jail suicides: Seven years later. Special Issue: Jail suicide: A comprehensive approach to a continuing national problem. *Psychiatric Quarterly, 60*, 7–15.

Herman, J. (1992). A new diagnosis. In J. Herman (Ed.), *Trauma and recovery*. New York: Basic Books.

Herman, J. (1995). Complex PTSD: A syndrome in survivors of prolonged and repeated trauma. In G. Everly & J. Lating, (Eds.), *Psychotraumatology: Key papers and core concepts in post-traumatic stress* (pp. 87–100). New York: Plenum.

Hershberger, G. (1998). To the max: Supermax facilities provide prison administrators with more security options. *Corrections Today, 60*(1), 54–57.

Hilliard, T. (1976). The Black psychologist in action: A psychological evaluation of the Adjustment Center environment at San Quentin Prison. *Journal of Black Psychology, 2*, 75–82.

Hinkle, L., & Wolff, H. (1956). Communist interrogation and indoctrination of "enemies of the states." *Archives of Neurology and Psychiatry, 76*, 115–174.

Hocking, F. (1970). Extreme environmental stress and its significance for psychopathology. *American Journal of Psychotherapy, 24*, 4–26.

Hodgins, S., & Cote, G. (1991). The mental health of penitentiary inmates in isolation. *Canadian Journal of Criminology, 33*, 177–182.

Horowitz, M. (1990). Post-traumatic stress disorders: Psychosocial aspects of the diagnosis. *International Journal of Mental Health, 19*, 21–36.

Hougen, H. (1988). Physical and psychological sequelae to torture: A controlled clinical study of exiled asylum applicants. *Forensic Sciences International, 39*, 5–11.

Human Rights Watch. (1991, November). *Prison conditions in the United States: A Human Rights Watch Report*. New York: Author.

Human Rights Watch. (2000, February). Out of sight: Super-maximum security confinement in the United States. *Human Rights Watch, 12*(1), 1–9.

Jackson, M. (1983). *Prisoners of isolation: Solitary confinement in Canada*. Toronto, Canada: University of Toronto Press.

Jamelka, R., Trupin, E., & Chiles, J. (1989). The mentally ill in prison. *Hospital and Community Psychiatry, 40*, 481–491.

Johnson, E. (1973). Felon self-mutilation: Correlate of stress in prison. In B. Dant (Ed.) *Jail House Blues*. Michigan: Epic.

Jones, A. (1986). Self-mutilation in prison: A comparison of mutilators and non-mutilators. *Criminal Justice and Behavior, 13*, 286–296.

Jones, D. (1976). *The health risks of imprisonment*. Lexington, MA: D. C. Heath.

Jones 'El v. Berge, 164 F. Supp. 1096 (2001).

King, R. (2000). The rise and rise of supermax: An American solution in search of problem? *Punishment and Society, 1*, 163–186.

Koch, I. (1986). Mental and social sequelae of isolation: The evidence of deprivation experiments and of pretrial detention in Denmark. In B. Rolston & M. Tomlinson (Eds.), *The expansion of European prison systems* (Working Papers in European Criminology No. 7, p. 119–129). Belfast, U.K.: Print Workshop.

Korn, R. (1988a). The effects of confinement in the High Security Unit at Lexington. *Social Justice, 15*, 8–19.

Korn, R. (1988b). Follow-up report on the effects of confinement in the High Security Unit at Lexington. *Social Justice, 15*, 20–29.

Kratcoski, P. (1988). The implications of research explaining prison violence and disruption. *Federal Probation, 52*, 27–32.

Kurki, L., & Morris, N. (2001). The purposes, practices, and problems of supermax prisons. *Crime and Justice, 28*, 385–424.

Leiderman, H. (1962). Man alone: Sensory deprivation and behavioral change. *Corrective Psychiatry and Journal of Social Therapy, 8*, 64–74.

Lovell, D., Cloyes, K., Allen, D., & Rhodes, L. (2000). Who lives in super-maximum custody? A Washington State study. *Federal Probation, 64*(2), 33–38.

Madrid v. Gomez, 889 F. Supp. 1146 (1995).

Mason, T. (1993). Seclusion theory reviewed—A benevolent or malevolent intervention? *Medical Science Law, 33*, 95–102.

Miller, H., & Young, G. (1997). Prison segregation: Administrative detention remedy or mental health problem? *Criminal Behaviour and Mental Health, 7*, 85–94.

O'Brien, T., & Jones, D. (1999). A balanced approach for corrections policy needed. *American Psychologist, 54*, 784–785.

Porporino, F. (1986). Managing violent individuals in correctional settings, *Journal of Interpersonal Violence, 1*, 213–237.

Rathbone-McCuan, E., & Hashimi, J. (1982). *Isolated elders: Health and social intervention*. Rockville, MD: Aspen Systems.

Re Medley, 134 U.S. 160 (1890).

Riekert, J. (1985). The DDD syndrome: Solitary confinement and a South African Security Law trial. In A. Bell & R. Mackie (Eds.) *Detention and security legislation in South Africa* (pp. 121–147). Durban, South Africa: University of Natal.

Riveland, C. (1999). *Supermax prisons: Overview and general considerations*. Washington, DC: U.S. Department of Justice.

Robins, L., & Regier, D. (Eds.) (1991). *Psychiatric disorders in America: The epidemiologic catchment area study*. New York: Free Press.

Ruiz v. Estelle, 503 F. Supp. 1265 (1980).

Ruiz v. Johnson, 37 F. Supp. 855 (1999).

Rundle, F. (1973). The roots of violence at Soledad. In E. O. Wright (Ed.), *The politics of punishment: A critical analysis of prisons in America* (pp. 163–172). New York: Harper.

Scott, G. (1969). The prisoner of society: Psychiatric syndromes in captive society. *Correctional Psychologist, 3*(7), 3–5.

Scott, G., & Gendreau, P. (1969). Psychiatric implications of sensory deprivation in a maximum security prison. *Canadian Psychiatric Association Journal, 12*, 337–341.

Sestoft, D., Andersen, H., Lilleback, T., & Gabrielsen, G. (1998). Impact of solitary confinement on hospitalization among Danish prisoners in custody. *International Journal of Law and Psychiatry, 21*, 99–108.

Shallice, T. (1974). The Ulster interrogation techniques and their relation to sensory deprivation research. *Cognition, 1*, 385–405.

Siegel, R. (1984). Hostage hallucinations: Visual imagery induced by isolation and life-threatening stress. *Journal of Nervous and Mental Disease, 172*, 264–272.

Slater, R. (1986). Psychiatric intervention in an atmosphere of terror. *American Journal of Forensic Psychiatry, 7*(1), 5–12.

Somnier, F., & Genefke, I. (1986). Psychotherapy for victims of torture. *British Journal of Psychiatry, 149*, 323–329.

Steinke, P. (1991). Using situational factors to predict types of prison violence. *Journal of Offender Rehabilitation, 17*, 119–132.

Suedfeld, P., Ramirez, C., Deaton, J., & Baker-Brown, G. (1982). Reactions and attributions of prisoners in solitary confinement. *Criminal Justice and Behavior, 9*, 303–340.

Suedfeld, P., & Roy, C. (1975). Using social isolation to change the behavior of disruptive inmates. *International Journal of Offender Therapy and Comparative Criminology, 19*, 90–99.

Tachiki, S. (1995). Indeterminate sentences in supermax prisons based upon alleged gang affiliations: A reexamination of procedural protection and a proposal for greater procedural requirements. *California Law Review, 83*, 1117–1149.

Toch, H. (1975). *Men in crisis: Human breakdowns in prisons*. Chicago: Aldine.

Toch, H. (in press). The future of supermax confinement. *The Prison Journal*.

Toch, H., & Adams, K. (2002). *Acting out: Maladaptive behavior in confinement*. Washington, DC: American Psychological Association.

Trop v. Dulles, 356 U.S. 86 (1958).

Veneziano, L., & Veneziano, C. (1996). Disabled inmates. In M. McShane & F. Williams (Eds.), *Encyclopedia of American prisons* (pp. 157–161). New York: Garland.

Volkart, R., Dittrich, A., Rothenfluh, T., & Werner, P. (1983). Eine kontrollierte untersuchung über psychopathologische effekte der einzelhaft [A controlled investigation on psychopathological effects of solitary confinement]. *Psychologie—Schweizerische Zeitschrift für Psychologie und ihre Anwendungen, 42*, 25–46.

Volkart, R., Rothenfluh, T., Kobelt, W., Dittrich, A., & Ernst, K. (1983). Einselhaft als Risikofactor für psychiatrische Hospitalisierung [Solitary confinement as a risk factor for psychiatric hospitalization]. *Psychiatria Clinica, 16*, 365–377.

Vrca, A., Bozikov, V., Brzovic, Z., Fuchs, R., & Malinar, M. (1996). Visual evoked potentials in relation to factors of imprisonment in detention camps. *International Journal of Legal Medicine, 109*, 114–117.

Waligora, B. (1974). Funkcjonowanie Czlowieka W Warunkach Izolacji Wieziennej [How men function in conditions of penitentiary isolation]. *Seria Psychologia I Pedagogika* NR 34, Poland.

Walters, R., Callagan, J., & Newman, A. (1963). Effect of solitary confinement on prisoners. *American Journal of Psychiatry, 119,* 771–773.

West, L. (1985). Effects of isolation on the evidence of detainees. In A. Bell & R. Mackie (Eds.) *Detention and security legislation in South Africa* (pp. 69–80). Durban, South Africa: University of Natal.

CRIME & DELINQUENCY, Vol. 49 No. 1, January 2003, 124–156.

Part 2: Relationships inside Prison

The number and type of relationships that prison inmates have are much more restricted than what those of us in free society experience. Basically, there are only two groups of *others* with whom inmates can interact. Inmates can interact with and "know" other inmates and prison staff. The prison world is one that is clearly structured, and relatively simple in its structure. These two groups of individuals are sometimes referred to as an "us versus them" setup.

Inmates' relationships with one another are often built on some type of exchange. Whether this is a truly voluntary and "fair" exchange at the core of the relationship is open to debate; although, most scholars would suggest that these are not equal relationships, where all parties involved give and get equally from the relationship. Of course, some people (scholars and laypersons alike) would argue that most of the relationships any of us have are unequal and built on power differentials. Among prison inmates, it is common for exchange relationships to have some degree of coercion and exploitation built into them.

In the first article, Faulkner and Faulkner report on research examining the ways that inmates establish status in a prison setting and what factors play significant roles in that process. Interestingly, they report that the decades-old view of an inmate code largely remains in place, and that adherence to this code of conduct is among the most important factors by which inmates establish status within the prison world. However, they also point out that the influence of these and other factors may be diminishing; their research found that major administrative and structural changes in the way prisons are operated has had some very powerful effects on the types of factors that influence an inmate's status and influence among his peers.

The second article in this section, Ireland and Ireland's analysis of bullying in prison, shows very clearly that inmate culture is based on a hierarchy of power differentials in which the "strong" dominate the "weak." This is not surprising, especially considering the findings reported in the Faulkner and Faulkner article. In this type of a structure, there are clearly differences in experiences for inmates, based upon where the inmate is in the power hierarchy. However, these researchers also argue that bullying has negative effects for everyone involved, including those who at first glance would appear to be controlling others and the environment.

The third article in this section looks at sexual relationships in prison. The article presented here focused on consensual sexual relationships among male inmates (sexual assault and coercive sexual relationships are addressed in section 7). Hensley reports in this article that large numbers of inmates are involved in same-sex sexual relationships. The number of inmates who engage in sexual activities with other inmates is higher than the number of male inmates who report having same-sex sexual relationships prior to coming to prison. Consensual sex in prison, however, is a concept that some argue is not possible. Remembering that relationships in prison are based on exchanges and power differentials, is it possible to have a truly "voluntary" sexual relationship in prison?

Greer's article on women's relationships in prison highlights two important findings. First, this research suggests that traditional understandings of women's prisons, wherein relationships were based on a structure of "pseudo-families" that inmates constructed, is outdated and does not apply to contemporary women's prisons. Second, this research highlights the exchange nature of relationships between female inmates. Friendships and intimate relationships may appear to be present in women's prisons, but the women in Greer's research suggest that these are not authentic relationships. What this points to is a closing of the gap between the culture and inmates of women's and men's prisons.

As you read the articles in this section, keep our central question in mind: What is the goal of prison? How do the relationships inmates have while incarcerated contribute to or impede the pursuit of this goal? You might choose to think of the issue this way: What is positive and negative about the relationships that prison inmates have? Why do inmates not have "better" relationships?

Discussion Questions

Relationships inside Prison

1. In what ways are the relationships prison inmates have with one another similar and different from relationships between persons in free society?
2. Based on the readings, what would be some ways for prison inmates to go about establishing productive and healthy relationships while incarcerated?
3. What are the major obstacles prison inmates face in establishing and maintaining close personal relationships with other inmates, and with staff?

5. Effects of Organizational Change on Inmate Status and the Inmate Code of Conduct

Paula L. Faulkner
William R. Faulkner

This case study describes the process of status assignment among inmates in a maximum security penitentiary. The research involved analysis of both qualitative and quantitative data from semi-structured interviews with a random sample of inmates and selected prison officials. Results show that inmate status is largely dependent upon adherence to an inmate code of conduct. Participants in this study identified components of an inmate code which mirrors almost exactly the code described by previous researchers. This code includes "loyalty" (don't be a snitch), "doing your own time," "standing up" for one's self and "smartness." In addition to these factors, the type of offense for which the individual was serving time was reported to have a significant effect on status. Other factors, including preprison status and gang affiliation, were also discussed. The data also yielded serendipitous findings which indicate that historical changes in the structure and organization of this penitentiary have diluted the inmate culture through which status assignment is determined.

Introduction

This study begins with an investigation of the process of status assignment in a population of male inmates residing in a maximum security state penitentiary. It ends with a description of the weakening of the traditional inmate culture and social organization on which status assignment is based.

Status and Lifestyle in the Prison Literature

The culture or lifestyle of prisoners has been discussed largely in terms of conformity to an inmate code of conduct. The idea of an inmate code is implicit in Clemmer's original concept of "prisonization" first described in 1940 from data collected at the Illinois State Penitentiary at Menard. According to Clemmer, prisonization is defined as the "... taking on, in greater or lesser degree, the folkways, mores, customs, and general culture of the penitentiary."

Over the period of the next 30 years, a number of sociologists and criminologists (Sykes, 1958; McCleery, 1960; Wheeler, 1961; Atcheley and McCabe, 1968; Glaser, 1969) addressed various aspects of prisonization and the inmate code. Perhaps most significant is a short paper by Sykes and Messinger (1960) who described the elements of the code as including: loyalty to the inmate system (don't squeal), doing your own time (don't interfere in others' business), toughness, sharpness and honesty in dealing with other inmates. According to Sykes and Messenger (1960), conformity to or deviation from the inmate code is the major basis for classifying and describing the social relations of prisoners. An inmate who violates the norms prescribing loyalty by betrayal of fellow inmates is labeled a "rat" or "squealer" and this inmate's deviance from the norms elicits the other inmates' scorn and hatred. Aggressive prisoners who quarrel and fight without reason are referred to as "toughs." An inmate who deliberately uses violence as a means to gain his ends is a "gorilla" (breaks the norm which prohibits exploitation by force). The term "merchant" or "peddler" is descriptive of the inmate who exploits others by manipulation or trickery by selling or trading goods in short supply. The weak inmates are referred to as "weak sisters" or "weaklings." Depending on the role played by inmates engaging in homosexual behavior and activities, they are designated "wolves," "punks," or "fags." Inmates who continue to assert their innocence and appeal their cases are "rapos." "Square Johns" are inmates who ally themselves with officials. The "right guy," "real man," or "real con" follows inmate norms. Sykes and Messinger (Sykes and Messinger 1960:11) state in summary,

> . . . two facts emerge: (1) Inmates give strong verbal support to a system of values that has group cohesion or inmate solidarity as its basic theme. Directly or indirectly, prisoners uphold the ideal of a social system of social interaction in which individuals are bound together by ties of mutual aid, loyalty, affection, and respect and are united firmly in their opposition to the enemy out-group; the man who exemplifies this ideal is accorded high prestige; the opposite of a cohesive inmate social system—a state in which each individual who seeks his own advantage without reference to the claims of solidarity—is vociferously condemned; (2) the actual behavior of prisoners ranges from full adherence to the norms of the inmate world to deviance of various types; these behavioral patterns, recognized and labeled by prisoners in the pungent argot of the dispossessed, form a collection of social roles which, with their interrelationships, constitute the inmate social system.

Methods

This study originally sought to update the work of the authors cited above. Both qualitative and quantitative data were thus collected on the process of status assignment and its relationship to an inmate code of conduct.

The data were collected at a maximum security state penitentiary in the midwest. At the time of the research, the institution housed approximately five-hundred and fifty inmates.

As the only maximum security unit in the state, the penitentiary is designed to house problem inmates and those with special needs who cannot be accommodated by other state institutions.

A systematic random sample of 67 inmates was selected. Thirty-four agreed to participate. One of the participants was transferred leaving 33 participants who were actually interviewed. The response rate was thus approximately 50%. Demographic characteristics of inmates who agreed to participate were contrasted with characteristics of non participants and no substantial differences were found.

Findings

When asked to volunteer criteria upon which they felt inmate status was based, participants tended to cite the kinds of things which Sykes and Messinger (1960) list as components of the code. With the exception of "offense type" participants essentially described the elements of an inmate code originally outlined by Sykes and Messinger (1960).

Snitching

The topic of snitching was clearly a dominant theme throughout the interviews. In fact, snitching was mentioned 111 times by the 33 informants. However, although snitching was found to be the most strongly disapproved form of behavior, the enforcement of norms against snitching appears to have weakened in recent years. According to one informant,

> "A real inmate doesn't exist in this prison since the riot (1981); before the riot an inmate had to follow certain standards if he wanted to be able to walk the yard. Then a snitch would have never walked the yard. A snitch (today) still has little respect but they can walk the yard."

While snitching is strongly condemned verbally, it appears that it is tolerated to a greater extent today than in the past.

Doing Your Own Time

"Doing your own time" is a phrase that was frequently used by the participants throughout the interviews. It is generally defined as doing your time without complaining, not associating with staff more than necessary, and never interfering in another inmate's business. One participant supplied the following example:

> "I remember when I was in Kansas and this guy never showered and no one ever said anything about it to him. He got a new cell mate and he came back to his cell and the new guy had cleaned his cell and he killed the guy for it. All the inmates respected him . . ."

In order to maintain his integrity and to "be a man" he killed the inmate who threatened his identity and interfered with his lifestyle. He was respected because he stood up for his rights.

Toughness

In prison, a person must stand up for himself to be respected. Yet, the degree to which a person must "stand up" in today's prisons is somewhat unclear. According to writings by inmate authors from the late 1970's and early 80's, if an individual is to be respected he must resist violent attempts at sexual or other exploitation again and again until he establishes a reputation based on a combination of fear and respect (Rideaux 1992). Jack Henry Abbott (1981:94) observes similarly,

> "This is the way it is done. If you are a man, you must either kill or turn the tables on anyone who propositions you with threats of force. It is the *custom* among young prisoners. In doing so, it becomes known to all that you are a man regardless of your youth."

Most participants in this study, however, described toughness in much less dramatic terms. One participant stated simply, "Inmates who are big and tough are high status, inmates who are young, small, and weak are low status." For most participants, one must be willing to fight, but none stated that one must be willing to die. One was simply required to "stand up." And "standing up" for one's self does not necessarily require physical toughness. One participant stated,

> "It's how you carry yourself, not your size that's important. How you carry yourself is the most important factor in determining status in prison. To be high status you have to act smart, not tough."

While toughness continues to be an important component of the inmate code, it is defined more broadly and in less dramatic terms by participants in the present study than it has been in earlier prison literature.

Smartness or Intelligence

The definition of smartness or intelligence appears to encompass a fairly broad range of skills and behaviors. Persons described as intelligent include those who possess legal expertise or who have the ability to articulate inmate issues. Generally, those who also have the ability to speak or write well can become inmate leaders if they use their talents for the benefit of other inmates.

It thus appears that the code of conduct described in earlier prison literature continues to exist, at least in the sense that most inmates give some lip service to several of its components. Yet, while the validity of various inmate norms is acknowledged, they are often defined in fairly broad terms and enforced with much less vigor than the previous prison literature implies.

Other Factors Affecting Status

The participants were also asked to respond to a listing of factors found in the review of literature or developed through the pretest of the interview schedule. Responses to these factors are described below:

Type of Offense

Offense type was the second most frequently mentioned factor cited in response to the open ended question about status criteria. Thirteen (39%) of the sample mentioned this factor. When asked specifically about the importance of this offense type, thirty-one, (93.9 percent) of the participants agreed that the offense for which an inmate was serving time for was an important factor in determining status. While there are not really any high status crimes, the thirty-one participants who felt offense affected status, thirty (90.9%) were in agreement that child molesters were the lowest status inmates, followed by twenty-one participants (63.6%) who also felt rape or other sex crimes were very low status.

Preprison Status

Seventeen participants, (51.5 percent) felt preprison status did affect status in prison. However, the meaning assigned to the term "preprison status" differed from that of the researchers. Although the interviewer emphasized that status referred to their job or other conventional status prior to incarceration, participants did not answer in terms of status based on traditional lifestyles or employment. Instead, they made reference to criminal ties or legal knowledge that would be useful to other inmates.

This may be the result of the prisonization process that Clemmer (1940) states affects every inmate. The data also suggest the existence of a fairly strong counterculture in which conventional values have little importance and are, in fact reversed. For example, some informants stated that drug dealers and murderers may be highly respected among their peers.

Gang Affiliation

The participants were first asked if gangs do exist in the penitentiary. If they replied in the affirmative, they were then asked if gangs affect status. Twenty-four (72.7%) said that gangs do exist in the penitentiary. Of these twenty-four, eleven, (45.8%) stated that gang affiliation does affect status, but usually in a negative way because most inmates view the gangs as a type of protection for the weak. Others said the gangs were just cliques or family substitutes.

Comments concerning gangs varied. One inmate said, "Being accepted by a clique is somewhat important to having higher status, but there are no real gangs around here anymore." Another said, "Belonging to a gang can help an individual's status or hurt it depending on the individual." Another stated, "Gangs operate down racial lines and they operate for protection, belonging to a gang could decrease status, because it looks like the guy is afraid to stand on his own; belonging to a gang does not increase status." Yet another said, "Gangs are only a status thing among younger inmates and then it is about race not power. Older inmates don't respect gangs."

One participant who was serving time for a marijuana conviction and who had been convicted prior to his twenty-first birthday related the following incident:

> "They thought I was in a gang because I was from Des Moines and I was black, I only sold a little weed to make a few bucks and I got 10 years and I had never been in jail before. They labeled me as a gang member just because I guess I had the wrong tennis shoes. Hell, they was just shoes to me, but look at me now, I am doing lock time because I am a supposed threat to the prison and a big gang member, all because I'm from Des Moines, I'm black, and I wore the wrong shoes."

Even the one participant in the sample who was identified by prison administration as a CRIPS member did not feel that gang membership affected status.

The replies to these questions were interesting because, if taken at face value, it appears that gang affiliation is not really an important status determinant in this penitentiary. However, there is good reason to suspect that some inmates may have lied about the role of gangs in the penitentiary. Being associated with gang activity can have serious consequences for an inmate. This was confirmed by several inmate informants as well as administration sources. One prison administrator who had worked at the penitentiary for over twenty years stated that gangs definitely do exist, but that many of the inmates try to deny the existence of gangs. According to this source, they downplay the importance of gangs because of the negative impact it can have for an inmate who is identified as a gang member. If an inmate is associated with a gang he may be separated from the general inmate population or lose various privileges.

Access to Money

Unlike the outside world, it appears that in prison money doesn't lead to high status. Money may buy protection for the weak and companionship for those who are lonely, but it does not buy the respect it can in free society.

Personal Connections

The general thinking was that anyone doing time couldn't have very important connections or they wouldn't be in prison. Fifteen (45.5%) participants stated connections could improve status but only if these connections were willing to do favors for you or your fellow inmates.

Time Served

For the average inmate time served is comparable to seniority, but if an inmate is a snitch or is incarcerated for sex crimes his status is not likely to improve over time.

Prison Job Assignment

Most jobs were found to have minimal effect on status. However, jobs that require an inmate to work closely with staff, particularly administration, are often associated with snitching. Inmates in these jobs are often rumored to be snitches and come to be seen as snitches even if they remain loyal to the inmates.

Consensus on Ranking

The participants were asked to give the names of those they felt were high in rank. The purpose was to identify if a consensus existed among the inmates. The reply to this request was almost a unanimous "No." The participants courteously refused to answer, giving reasons such as the following for their refusal: "I couldn't mention anyone's name because it wouldn't be right. You don't talk about anyone in here it just isn't respected." Thirty-one participants (93.9%) refused to name any one. This was significant because it reaffirms the importance of minding your own business and doing your own time and possibly not being a snitch. It is interesting that they would not name anyone even though the information being asked was not of a negative nature.

Status Assignment from a Non-Inmate Perspective

As a check of the validity of inmate descriptions of status assignment, data were also collected from several staff members on their views of this process. One individual who had been an employee at this institution for more than twenty years provided particularly useful insights. By reputation, he was generally considered to be the person with the most thorough knowledge of individual inmates.

When questioned about characteristics that made an inmate high in status in the prison, he stated that the most important traits were physical size, the way one carries himself, and the fear he can instill in others. "Carrying oneself" is defined as being tough, not backing down from other inmates and having "heart." He also said that, although size is important, a small inmate can have high status if they have "heart," which basically means that they will stand up for themselves, that they don't show fear, and that they aren't snitches. The characteristics of low status inmates were essentially the opposite of the high status inmate: having no heart, being a snitch, and having an offense such as child molesting.

According to this informant, inmates could be divided into three groups: *convicts, inmates, and residents. Convicts* are the highest status inmates and follow the inmate code. *Inmates* are average status and are considered "middle of the road" because they follow some tenets of the code and disregard others. The *residents* are the lowest status inmates because they don't follow the inmate code or rules, and they are often snitches, and they don't stand up for themselves. In his view, the code was still accepted at the institution, but that it was not as strong as it once was.

The Effects of Historical Changes on Inmate Culture

Throughout the interview process both inmates and prison officials frequently made references to conditions before and after the 1981 riot. It became obvious that structural and organizational changes that occurred following the riot had a major effect on inmate culture in general and the system of status assignment in particular. Interviews were therefore conducted with both administrative staff and inmates who had been at the institution prior to and during the period in which the major changes occurred.

An Administrative Perspective

We spoke with a longtime administrator at the institution to gain some idea of the structural and organizational changes that have taken place. This individual had been employed in various positions at the penitentiary since the 1960's. He stated that during the period from the 1960's through 1981 there was a much larger inmate population within the prison walls and that the lives of inmates were much less structured than they are today. During this time period inmates held many key jobs at the prison. Inmate clerks kept records, inmates did accounting tasks, inmates handled the inmate payroll, and some inmates even did inmate "counts" in their respectively assigned areas. A canteen existed at this time and an inmate clerk would deduct purchases from the other inmates' personal accounts. The administrator explained what a problem this could be because the clerk had knowledge of all of the inmates' financial situations. The clerk might reveal an individual's financial information to another inmate, who could force him to make canteen purchases for him.

The administrator also discussed an incident involving an inmate who had been his clerk in charge of inmate payroll. This inmate had been responsible for securing the signature of the acting warden on the inmates' work hours so that they could be paid. Yet, after they were signed, he would change the hours and the rate of pay. The clerk managed to successfully continue this practice for six months. In this time he was overpaid approximately four-hundred dollars and had overpaid his fellow workers as well. This shows the kinds of control and power certain inmate positions could provide. Inmate jobs seem an effective basis for gaining high status through the power and access to resources they could produce.

Gangs were also very visible during this period when up to a thousand inmates could be on the yard at one time. Various gangs could be viewed assembled in different areas of the yard. These gangs had a great deal of power at the time. Inmate control over various activities was relatively strong during this period. A strong inmate code existed, and those who violated the code were punished. On the other hand, in contrast to the situation today, administrative control was relatively loose. Discipline for a physical fight at this time was typically no more than fifteen days in the hole.

After the riot in 1981 a new warden was brought in and a court order limiting the population to five-hundred and fifty inmates inside the walls was enacted. Inmate jobs of any importance were eliminated, and inmates no longer had access to other inmates' records. Inmate jobs are now supervised by prison staff and consist primarily of janitorial, cooking, and maintenance. The elimination of these inmate positions has eroded the status and importance of inmate jobs as well as decreased inmate knowledge of prison operations.

Discipline was drastically changed. This involved primarily the increased use of lock-up. A physical fight could now result in one to two years lock-up time. These changes altered the enforcement of the code. Freedom of inmate movement became greatly restricted, weakening the communication system among inmates. At the time of this study, over half of the inmate population was typically in lock-up at any given time. These inmates are locked in their cells twenty-three out of twenty-four hours a day. The canteen has been eliminated and the inmates must order their personal items from their cells. These items are then delivered to their cells by staff. This has reduced inmate exploitation and theft, as well as the inmates' ability to trade these items for personal favors. Few inmates are allowed on the yard at any one time. This further reduces the ability to communicate with other inmates. These changes have resulted in weakening inmate communication and power and have increased staff control over the inmate population.

An Inmate Perspective

An interview was also conducted with an inmate who was sentenced to death row in 1956. This sentence was commuted to a life sentence by the governor one year later. We first asked him what made an inmate high in status before the riot in 1981. He stated that "doing your own time" and staying out of others' business was very important. He said being tough and standing up for yourself was especially important. He related the following incident:

> "A guy who became a good friend of mine told me that when he first came in one of the black gangs kept looking at him on the yard. This guy, he got scared because he knew sooner or later they would approach him and he couldn't take on all of them, so he got a shank (knife) and he started carrying it on him. He was in the yard one day and seven or eight of the guys in this gang cornered him and he just stepped back and pulled out the shank and started swinging and yelling that they might get him but not without a fight. They respected this and let him go and he never had any more problems because he stood up for himself."

The informant also stated that playing sports made your status higher before the riot. He said that before the riot, the prison had outsiders come in for sporting events. He also stated that snitching and stealing were very low status and not accepted by the inmate population. Homosexuals were low status, and gang rapes frequently occurred before the riot. Raping another inmate was not viewed as a homosexual act but as an act of power. The inmate being raped was viewed as the homosexual because he could not protect his manhood.

When asked about other changes, he said the yard is set up much differently since the riot. Prior to 1981, the yard was open for the evenings and anybody who wasn't in the hole could go to yard from 4:00 to 8:00 p.m. and on the weekends the yard was open all day. There could be a thousand inmates on the yard at a time. Now the yard is restricted and each cell house has an assigned time for the yard. The lockup inmates, who comprise over half of the inmate population, have a special yard. When the yard was unrestricted there was more open communication between the inmates. The yard was a more dangerous place for new inmates, and acts of violence were more frequent at this time.

Experienced inmates, before the riot and the consequent changes, helped new inmates learn the ropes of the prison. Inmates used be allowed to go to the orientation unit where the new inmates were housed and take a new inmate on a tour of the institution. The experienced inmates would share their knowledge with the new inmates on survival techniques. The informant said,

> "Lifers would help other lifers. Like if a new guy moved into my cell house. And with me being a long timer, I might go down and talk to him and ask him if he is getting along O.K. and ask him if there is anything he needs, like tobacco or something. If I did that now administration kind of looks down on that, and I'd probably get written up for bartering or something."

The informant also reiterated much of what had been said by the administrator about the importance of inmate jobs. He stated that inmates used have meaningful jobs and that they knew everything; if you wanted to know something or get something done you would just go to the right inmate. If you wanted a new job or if you had a friend coming to the prison and wanted him to cell next to you, you could have it arranged in exchange for cigarettes or other favors. Since the riot these jobs are no longer done by inmates.

The Effects of Institutional Change

The organizational and structural changes that have had effects on the inmate status hierarchy can be grouped into three areas: 1) communication, 2) inmate control and power, and 3) the increased use of lockup as a disciplinary tool.

The changes in communication can be attributed to several factors. One of the most important is the change in inmate living arrangements. Before the riot, an inmate knew the cell and the cell house to which he would be assigned for the duration of his incarceration. If he was moved for disciplinary or health reasons he could count on eventually returning to his assigned cell house. The inmate knew his neighbors. The only way he would get a new neighbor was if one of his old cellmates left, and there was a vacant cell. This allowed the inmate to have a familiar, rather than constantly changing, environment. This restriction of communication has resulted in the loss of inmate community and power.

The use of discipline in the form of lockup has weakened enforcement of the code. Before the riot, an inmate might be willing to fight another inmate who violated the code's norms. If an inmate snitched or violated some other norm, a fight would probably result. If an inmate was caught fighting he would probably get fifteen days in the hole, a short enough time period that it was worth the punishment. Now if an inmate gets caught fighting he gets up to two years of lockup. For many inmates this might be too long of a sentence to be worth getting in a fight. There are inmates currently sentenced to thirteen years of lockup time who only have a ten year sentence. These inmates will leave the prison directly from lockup (a place they are locked up twenty-three hours a day) to free society.

Conclusions

One would be foolish to attempt to generalize very much from this study to other penitentiaries. Several of the characteristics of this institution and the state in which it is located make this research setting unique in many respects. Nevertheless, as a descriptive case study, this research fills in a gap in the existing literature. The world of the inmate described here differs substantially from that described in the classic prison literature. Even more recent descriptions of prison life, such as Pete Early's (1992) *The Hothouse* fail to explicitly account for the data described in this study.

The structural factors cited in the literature (such as loss of liberty, enforcement of institutional regulations, and threats to individual identity) which originally produced the inmate code, continue to exist. In fact, in the institution described in this study, these conditions appear to have been greatly exaggerated since the riot in 1981. Yet, ironically, these same structural conditions when carried to an extreme appear to have actually weakened the very system that they originally created. The interruption of communication between inmates, reducing or leveling inmate access to power through job assignment, and the increased use of lockup has severely weakened belief in, and especially enforcement of, the inmate code of conduct.

The changes observed in this case study reveal both benefits and costs. The expansion of staff control over inmate communication, access to power, and the increased use of discipline, coupled with a reduction in the size of the inmate population, have tended to increase inmate and staff safety and reduce the probability of violent disruptions. One might argue that changes of this sort are indeed appropriate in prisons that house violent offenders.

However, the benefits of these changes come at a cost to inmate culture and the informal support system that has traditionally operated in American penal institutions. This may be viewed as a positive or negative effect, depending on one's perspective. Prison culture may mediate the process of "stripping" described by Goffman (1961) and decrease the inmates' loss of identity and sense of isolation. At the same time, the literature implies that it also may contribute to "prisonization" (Clemmer, 1940). Yet, data from this study suggest that the process of "prisonization" continued to operate concurrently with some degree of breakdown in inmate social organization and culture.

Social disorganization often produces personal disorganization. To the extent that incarceration produces loss of identity and an increased sense of isolation, chances for rehabilitation are lessened. Persons released from serving ten years in lockup are not good candidates for survival in conventional society. Therefore, implementation of the kinds of controls described in this case study should be undertaken with caution and a thorough consideration of their consequences.

References

Abbott, J. H. (1981). *In the Belly of the Beast*. New York: Vintage Books.

Atchley, R. and P. McCabe (1968). "Socialization in Correctional Communities: A Replication." *American Sociological Review* 33:774–85.

Clemmer, D. (1965). *The Prison Community*. New York: Holt, Rinehart and Winston.

Cohen, A. (1955). *Delinquent Boys*. New York: Free Press.

Drake, S. and H. R. Cayton (1945). *Black Metropolis*. New York: Harcourt, Brace and Co.

Early, P. (1992). *The Hot House: Life Inside Leavenworth Prison*. New York: Bantam Books.

Glaser, D. (1969). *The Effectiveness of a Prison and Parole System*. Indianapolis: Bobbs-Merrill.

Goffman, E. (1961). *Asylums*. New York: Doubleday Anchor.

Hollingshead, A. B. (1961). *Elmtown's Youth*. New York: Science Editions Inc.

Lloyd, W. W. and L. Srole (1945). *The Status System of a Modern Community*. New Haven: Yale University Press.

McCleery, R. (1960). "Communication Patterns as Basis of Systems of Authority and Power." In *Theoretical Studies in Social Organization of the Prison*. R. A. Cloward et al. (eds.). Washington, DC: Social Science Research Council.

Rideau, W. (1992). "The Sexual Jungle." In *Rage and Survival Behind Bars*. W. Rideau and R. Wikberg (eds.). New York: Times Books.

Roethlisberger, F. J. and W. J. Dickson (1939). *Management and the Worker*. Cambridge, Mass.: Harvard University Press.

Sykes. G. (1958). *The Society of Captives*. Princeton: Princeton University Press.

Sykes, G. and S. Messinger (1960). "The Inmate Social System." In *Theoretical Studies in Social Organization of the Prison*. R. A. Cloward et al. (eds.). Washington, DC: Social Science Research Council.

Warner, W. L. and P. S. Lunt (1941). *The Status System of a Modern Community (Yankee City Series, Vol. I)* New Haven: Yale University Press.

Warner, W. L. (1949). *Democracy in Jonesville*. New York: Harper.

Weber, M. (1946). "Class, Status and Party." In *Class, Status and Power*. R. Bendix and S. Lipset (eds.). New York: The Free Press.

Wheeler, S. (1961). "Socialization in Correctional Communities." *American Sociological Review* 26:697–712.

---

6. Descriptive Analysis of the Nature and Extent of Bullying Behavior in a Maximum-Security Prison

Carol A. Ireland
Jane L. Ireland

This aim of this study was to investigate the nature and extent of direct and indirect bullying in a maximum-security prison and to assess prisoners' attitudes toward victims of bullying. The results showed that more than half of the prisoners sampled had been bullied in the past week. Only a small number of prisoners could be classified as either a pure bully or a pure victim, with almost half classified as both a bully and a victim. The most frequent types of bullying used were psychological/verbal and indirect forms. No significant differences were found between pure bullies, bully/victims, pure victims, and the not involved groups' attitudes toward the victims of bullying.

Introduction

Bullying is a complex behavior that can be difficult to identify (Edgar and O'Donnell, 1997) and define. Slee (1995) states how it relates to the "oppression of one individual by another individual or group of persons, where the behavior is typically repetitive and deliberate." Bullying includes both direct and indirect aggressive behaviors. Direct bullying represents an overt form of aggression in which the aggressor interacts directly with the victim. In a prison environment this has been found to include name-calling, intimidation, physical attack, baroning (borrowing from others and paying back with extortionate interest), sexual assault, and harassment (Ireland and Archer, 1996). Indirect bullying is a more covert form of aggression and was first acknowledged as a form of aggression in the late 1980s (Lagerspetz et al., 1988). It involves social isolation and intentional exclusion of the victim by a single individual or a group (Olweus, 1994). It has been found to occur among prisoners and includes behaviors such as gossiping, spreading rumors, playing practical jokes, and deliberately lying about another individual (Ireland, 1997). Research suggests that indirect aggression is more prevalent among adult than adolescent populations (Björkqvist et al., 1994). Björkqvist et al. (1994) argues that adults utilize indirect aggression in an attempt to conceal their actions in order to avoid detection for fear of social retribution. In a prison environment, indirect bullying may be favored as it is harder to recognize and detect, and thus the risk of punishment is reduced (Ireland, 1997). Indeed, McGurk and McDougall (1991) report that in a prison environment, direct bullying was most likely to occur when detection and surveillance were minimal.

Bullies and victims do not represent two distinct groups; individuals can be both bullies and victims. Bowker (1980) described the bully-victim relationship as "a macabre version of the game of musical chairs in which today's aggressor (bully) may become tomorrow's victim." Research suggests that an individual can fall into one of four groups (Ireland, 1999a): "pure bullies" (those who report bullying others but not victimization), "bully/victims" (those who report bullying others and being victimized themselves), "pure victims" (those who report only being victimized), and "not involved" (those who report no bullying or victimization).

Most research into bullying behavior has focused on schools (Olweus, 1994). Research into bullying in prisons had been greatly neglected until recently. Of the research which has been conducted, most has examined young male offenders (e.g., Beck, 1994; Connell and Farrington, 1996), with a limited amount on adult male offenders (e.g., Brookes and Pratt, 1997; Ireland and Archer, 1996). To the authors' knowledge, no research into bullying has been conducted in a maximum-security prison that houses high-risk offenders.

Of the work that has been conducted in prisons, the reported extent of bullying has been high. Ireland (1996) examined bullying among young male offenders using a self-report behavioral checklist, which addressed direct and indirect bullying behavior with a reference period of 1 week. To avoid problems in defining bullying in a prison environment, the checklist did not include the term "bullying," instead describing discrete bullying behaviors. Of all participants, 45.5% reported at least one interaction defined by the researcher as "being bullied" (39.4% reported direct bullying and 27.2% indirect bullying) and 75.8% of participants reported at least one interaction defined by the researcher as "bullying others" (69.7% reported direct bullying and 57.6% indirect bullying). Beck (1994), in a sample of young male offenders, found that 2 in 10 reported to having been bullied at their current prison, with 1 in 10 reported to have bullied others. With regard to adult male prisoners, Edgar and O'Donnell (1997) addressed victimization as opposed to bullying per se and reported that one fifth of the adults surveyed had been assaulted in the first month, and one quarter had been threatened with violence. One in three of the adults had suffered cell theft. They also report that the aggressor/victim group was represented in both adult and young offender samples.

Only a limited amount of research has examined the true characteristics of those involved in bullying. Most research has concentrated on prisoners' perceptions of the characteristics that bullies and victims possess. For example, Brookes (1993) reports that prisoners new to the prison system, sex offenders, and prisoners serving short sentences are perceived by both prisoners and staff to be potential targets for bullies. Although examining inmate aggressors as opposed to bullies specifically, Shields and Simourd (1991) found that aggressors tended to have more extensive criminal histories and higher levels of substance abuse and psychological problems than their victims. Some research has attempted to look at the true characteristics that victims and bullies possess, but this has been limited. For example, Beck (1996) reported that young male offenders who were on remand were more than twice as likely to bully others than were convicted prisoners, and Beck (1992) reported that victims were most likely offenders with little prison experience.

The role of the social group in bullying is of particular interest when studying that which occurs within a prison environment. Prisoners do categorize themselves into "in-groups" and "out-groups," an example of which could be bullies and victims, respectively (Ireland, 1999). Prisoners who bully are afforded a certain degree of status in a prison environment (Connell and Farrington, 1996). Victims of bullying are not afforded the same status, and being labeled as a victim is seen as more stigmatizing (Ireland and Archer, 1996), with derogatory terms such as "Muppet" and "Fraggle" used to describe them (Beck, 1992). This can lead to negative attitudes toward the victims of bullying and an overall approval of bullies themselves (Ireland, 1999b).

The aim of the present study was to provide a descriptive analysis of the nature and extent of bullying in an adult male maximum-security prison and to assess attitudes toward the victims of bullying.

Method

Sample

One hundred ninety-four adult male offenders participated from a single maximum-security prison. The average age of the participants was 36 years. All participants were sentenced, with an average sentence length (excluding lifer prisoners) of 11 years. A total of 23.3% of the inmates were serving life sentences; 29.8% of the sample were serving sentences for robbery, 14.6% for murder, 12.9% for rape, and 10.7% for drugs, with the remainder sentenced for other indictable offenses.

Questionnaires

The DIPC (Ireland, 1998, 1999a) was used, which represented a modified version of a checklist originally devised by Beck and Smith (1995). The DIPC examines both direct and indirect forms of bullying over a 1-week period. It describes discrete behaviors that represent either being bullied or bullying others. Examples of bully items include "I have encouraged others to turn against another prisoner" and "I have hit or kicked another prisoner." Examples of victim items include "I was called names about my race or color" and "I have been deliberately ignored." The DIPC also includes behaviors described as possible "reactions" to being bullied. The term *bullying* is not used, and no context of bullying is offered.

A modified version of the Rigby and Slee (1991) provictim scale was used to assess attitudes toward the victims of bullying. Reliability and internal consistency of this scale are reported to be good (Ireland, 1999b; Rigby and Slee, 1991). It represents a 24-item scale, modified by Ireland (1997) for use within a prison population. The higher the score on this scale the more positive the attitudes toward the victims of bullying and less supportive the attitude toward bullies.

Procedure

Questionnaires were administered during prison lock downs. This allowed for a more representative sample and also meant that each prisoner could complete the questionaire while in isolation from others as each cell was single occupancy.

Group Descriptions

The sample was split into four main groups: pure bullies, bully/victims, pure victims, and not involved. Prisoners were classified as pure bullies if they admitted to one or more bullying behaviors in the previous week but no victim items. Pure victims represented prisoners who reported one or more behaviors in the previous week representative of being bullied. A participant was classified as a bully/victim if both behaviors indicative of being bullied and bullying others were reported. Participants who reported no bully or victim items were classified as not involved.

In the sample, 11.9% were classified as pure bullies, 43.4% as bully/victims, 13.9% as pure victims, and 30.9% as not involved. A description of each group based on age, length of sentence, length of time spent in prison throughout their lifetime, status (life sentenced prisoner or not), and offense (violent vs. nonviolent) is displayed in Table 1.

Multiple logistic regressions were employed on the above characteristics to assess which significantly predicted the probability of belonging to any of the four groups. The dependent variables represented the bully status groups, i.e., bully, etc.; the continuous independent variables represented length of time spent in prison throughout lifetime (LENGTH), age (AGE), and length of present sentence (SERVE). The categorical independent variables represented violent offenses (VIOLENT—nonviolent and violent) and status (LIFER—life-sentenced prisoners

TABLE 1 Mean Demographic Variables of the Four Different Groups

Variables	*Pure bully (n = 24)*	*Bully/victim (n = 83)*	*Pure victim (n = 24)*	*Not involved (n = 63)*
Age, y	34.7	35	28.6	19.4
Lifers, %	20.8	26.6	28.6	19.4
Average length of sentence (excluding lifers), mo	134	142	130	121
Estimated length of time spent in prisons throughout their lifetime, mo	72	80	86	65
Serving for a violent/aggressive offence, %	91.3	82.9	86.4	71.9

and non–life-sentenced prisoners). Regressions were conducted separately for each of the four groups. The results are presented below.

Bully Group: No significant predictors emerged, with the residual chi square nonsignificant ($\chi^2 = 1.46, P < .83$, ns)
Bully/Victim Group: No significant predictors emerged, with the residual chi square nonsignificant ($\chi^2 = 5.77, P < .22$, ns)
Pure Victim Group: No significant predictors emerged, with the residual chi square nonsignificant ($\chi^2 = .87, P < .93$, ns)
Not Involved Group: No significant predictors emerged, with the residual chi square nonsignificant ($\chi^2 = 6.9, P < .14$, ns)

Self-Reported Victimization

Of the sample, 57.2% reported at least one incident defined as being bullied in the previous week. Of these, 15.3% reported 2 incidents, 9.9% reported 5 incidents, and 0.9% reported 16 incidents. A breakdown of the type of bullying that the victims experienced is presented below.

Direct victimization. Of the sample, 36.1% reported at least one incident defined as being bullied directly in the previous week. Of these, 14.9% reported three incidents and 12.2% reported nine incidents. Of those reporting direct victimization, 80% reported being the victims of psychological/verbal abuse, 44.3% reported physical abuse, 21.4% reported theft-related abuse, and 8.6% reported sexual abuse.

Indirect victimization. Of the sample, 46.4% reported at least one incident defined as being bullied indirectly in the previous week. Of these, 17.8% reported two incidents, 13.3% reported four incidents, and 1.1% reported seven incidents. Of those reporting indirect victimization, the most frequently reported forms were being gossiped about (49%), having had a practical joke played on them (42.2%), having had rumors spread about them (30%), and being deliberately ignored (29%).

Self-Reported Bullying Behavior

Of the sample, 55.2% reported at least one incident defined as bullying others during the previous week. Of these, 12.1% reported 3 incidents and 0.9% reported 15 incidents. A breakdown of the different types of bullying is presented below.

Direct bullying behavior. Of the sample, 26.3% reported at least one incident defined as bullying others directly in the previous week, with 20% of these reporting two incidents and 2% reporting seven incidents. Of those reporting direct bullying, 96.1% of incidences related to psychological/verbal bullying, 2.0% to physical abuse, 2.0% to theft-related bullying, and 2.0% to sexual bullying.

Indirect bullying behavior. Of the sample, 48.9% reported at least one incident defined as bullying others indirectly in the previous week, with 23.2% of

TABLE 2 Percentage of Victims and Nonvictims Who Had Demonstrated the Following Behaviors During the Past Week

Behavior	*Victims, % (n = 107)*	*Nonvictims, % (n = 87)*
Defended themselves against another prisoner	15.0	2.3
Cried	24.3	12.6
Tried to get moved	22.4	8.0
Stayed in their cell when they could be out	41.1	18.4
Threatened to harm themselves	5.6	0.0
Cut themselves	2.8	0.0

these reporting two incidents and 1.1% reporting eight incidents. Of those reporting indirect bullying, the most frequently reported forms were deliberately ignoring someone (64.2%), playing a practical joke on someone (38.0%), gossiping about another prisoner (26.3%), and making fun of another prisoner (20.0%).

Victims' Reactions Toward Being Bullied

The DIPC also examined various behaviors indicative of reactions toward being bullied. For the purpose of this analysis, victims of bullying were classified as such if they had experienced at least one instance of being bullied during the previous week. The reactions exhibited by victims of bullying are compared with those of nonvictims and are presented in Table 2.

Discussion

More than half of the sample reported at least one behavior indicative of being bullied during the previous week, with just less than half of those reporting to be both a bully and a victim. The presence of a bully/victim group is consistent with previous research (e.g., Edgar and O'Donnell, 1997; Ireland, 1999a), as is the finding that the bully/victim group is the most reported of all. More than one third of the sample reported at least one behavior indicative of being bullied directly, with the most frequently reported form being psychological/verbal abuse. Approximately half the sample reported at least one behavior indicative of being bullied indirectly. More than half of the sample admitted at least one behavior indicative of bullying others during the previous week. Of these, one quarter admitted behaviors indicative of bullying someone directly, with the most predominant form involving psychological/verbal abuse. Approximately half of the sample reported behaviors indicative of bullying someone indirectly in the previous week.

The finding that bullying and victimization is predominantly indirect may be a result of indirect aggression representing a more desirable form of bullying for

TABLE 3 Mean Provictim Scores Overall and Across the Different Groups Involved in Bullying/Victimization

Provictim score	*Pure bully (n = 17; 7 missing)*	*Bully/victim (n = 67; 16 missing)*	*Pure victim (n = 23; 1 missing)*	*Not involved (n = 42; 21 missing)*	*Overall (n = 149; 45 missing)*
Mean	65.5	63.5	58.2	67.5	64.0
(s.d.)	(18.9)	(20.5)	(14.2)	(23.3)	(20.4)

adults as they attempt to conceal their aggression (Björkqvist et al., 1994). Similarly, of the direct bullying and victimization described, the majority seems to be of a psychological/verbal nature. This could be described as the subtlest form of *direct* aggression. The surreptitious nature of indirect forms of aggression, and to some extent psychological/verbal forms, may make them harder to detect within a prison environment, and consequently more desirable. As security and supervision of prisoners is very high in a maximum-security prison (with higher staffing ratios and closer staff-prisoner contact), the chances of using the more direct and physical forms of bullying undetected by staff may be much more difficult and, as a result, less favorable. The more indirect and subtle forms of bullying can still have a detrimental impact on the victim, yet the bully can remain hidden.

The most predominant reactions by the victims of bullying were to stay in their cells when they could be out, crying, and trying to get moved to another location. Also reported were defending themselves against another prisoner, threatening to harm themselves, and cutting themselves. A higher percentage of victims reported all of the reaction items than did nonvictims, suggesting that they may be reliable indicators of victimization.

Regarding characteristics of the different groups, the not involved group and the bully group seemed to contain the largest proportion of violent prisoners. The not involved group also included the youngest prisoners, followed by the pure victim group. However, the logistic regressions conducted across each group did not produce any significant predictors of group membership.

There were no differences between each group regarding provictim attitudes. This is inconsistent with previous research that suggests that those who display bullying behavior have significantly lower provictim attitudes than those who do not (Ireland, 1999b). Thus, all prisoners, regardless of group status, seem to hold similar attitudes toward the victims of bullying.

The absence of any significant differences between the groups regarding provictim attitudes could be a result of the nature of the prison and type of prisoners who participated in the research. The mean provictim score reported in the present research (i.e., 64) is considerably lower than that reported in the Ireland (1999) study (i.e., overall mean score, 124.9). Although the Ireland (1999b) study addressed a varied sample (males and females, adults and young offenders) from a number of establishments, none were high-risk prisoners taken from a maximum-security prison. It could be argued that as a whole the prisoners examined in the present study show much more negative attitudes toward the victims of bullying and are more approving of bullies and their behavior than has been found in previous research. In the present study, victims seem to be very much part of the out-group, whereas bullies, who seem to be supported by the peer group as a whole, form part of the in-group (Ireland, 1999b).

The findings of the present study have a number of implications for the development of anti-bullying policies and interventions within prisons. The results demonstrate that bullies and victims are not distinct groups and that there is a third group, namely, the bully/victim group. Interestingly, this latter group is the most prevalent. The high incidence of indirect bullying must also be acknowledged, along with the distress that such forms of bullying may create. As a consequence, anti-bullying programs need to concentrate on educating both prisoners and staff on the different types of bullying, notably, the distinction between direct and indirect forms of bullying. There seem to be a number of behaviors that could indicate that an individual is being bullied, i.e., remaining in their cells when they could be out, crying, and trying to get moved to another location. Recognizing how victims react to being victimized may prove important in identifying the victims of bullying behavior.

Of particular importance in the present study are the findings regarding provictim attitudes. Intervention programs need to make clear reference to the importance of attitudes in bullying. In a maximum-security prison, the negative attitudes toward victims and positive attitudes toward bullies may be helping to maintain bullying behavior. If the peer group as a whole accepts and supports bullies, but not victims, then bullying will continue. Future research needs to address in more detail the specific nature of these attitudes and what is helping to maintain them.

References

Ahmad Y., Smith P. K. 1990. Behavioral measures review, 1: bullying in schools. *Newslett Assoc Child Psychol Psychiatry* 12:26–27.

Beck G. 1992. Bullying amongst incarcerated young offenders. Unpublished MSc thesis. Birbeck College: University of London, UK.

Beck G. 1994. Self reported bullying among imprisoned young offenders. *Inside Psychol* 2:16–21.

Beck G. 1996. Bullying information report: initial report. Unpublished report. Psychology Department, HMYOI Lancaster Farms, UK.

Beck G., Ireland J. 1997. Measuring bullying in prisons. *Inside Psychol* 3:71–77.

Beck G., Smith P. K. 1995. An alternative assessment of the prevalence of bullying among young offenders. In: Beck G., Ireland J. Measuring bullying in prisons. *Inside Psychol* 3:71–77.

Björkqvist K., Osterman K., Lagerspetz K. M. J. 1994. Sex differences in covert aggression amongst adults. *Aggr Behav* 20:27–33.

Bowker L. 1980. Prison victimization. New York: Elsevier North Holland.

Brookes M. 1993. Reducing bullying at HMP Ranby. UK: East Midlands. Psychology Research Report No. 8.

Brookes M., Pratt M. 1997. Bullying: an anti-bullying strategy in a Category C prison. *Inside Psychol* 3:65–70.

Connell A., Farrington D. P. 1996. Bullying among incarcerated young offenders: developing an interview schedule and some preliminary results. *J Adolesc* 19:75–93.

Edgar K., O'Donnell I. 1997. Responding to victimization: victimization and safety in prisons and young offender institutions. *Prison Service J* 109:15–19.

Ireland J. L. 1997. Bullying amongst prisoners: a study of gender differences, provictim attitudes and empathy. MSc dissertation. The Manchester Metropolitan University: Manchester, UK.

Ireland J. L. 1998. Direct and Indirect Prisoner Behavior Checklist (DIPC). Lancashire, UK: University of Central Lancashire.

Ireland J. L. 1999a. Bullying behaviors among male and female prisoners: a study of adult and young offenders. *Aggr Behav* 25:162–178.

Ireland J. L. 1999b. Provictim attitudes and empathy in relation to bullying behavior among prisoners. *J Legal Criminol Psychol* 4:51–66.

Ireland J., Archer J. 1996. Descriptive analysis of bullying in male and female adult prisoners. *J Community Appl Soc Psychol* 6:35–47.

Lagerspetz K. M. J., Björkqvist K., Peltonen T. 1988. Is indirect aggression typical of females? gender differences in aggressiveness in 11–12 year old children. *Aggr Behav* 14:403–414.

McGurk B. J., McDougall C. 1991. The prevention of bullying among incarcerated delinquents. *Inside Psychol* 1:18–23.

Mooney A., Creeser R., Blatchford P. 1991. Children's views on teasing and fighting in junior schools. *Educ Res* 33:103–112.

Olweus D. 1994. Annotation: bullying at school: basic facts and effects of a school based intervention program. *J Child Psychol Psychiatry* 35:1171–1190.

Olweus D. 1996. Bully/victim problems in school. *Prospects* 16:331–359.

Randall P. 1997. Adult bullying: perpetrators and victims. London: Routledge.

Rigby K., Slee P. T. 1991. Bullying among Australian school children: reported behavior and attitudes towards victims. *J Soc Psychol* 131:615–627.

Rigby K., Slee P. T. 1993. Children's attitudes towards victims. In: Tattum D., editor. Understanding and managing bullying. Oxford, UK: Heinemann Educational Books Ltd. p 119–135.

Shields I. W., Simourd D. J. 1991. Predicting predatory behavior in a population of incarcerated young offenders. *Criminal Justice Behav* 18:180–194.

Slee P. T. 1995. Bullying: health concerns of Australian secondary school children. *Int J Adolesc Youth* 5:215–224.

7. Exploring the Dynamics of Masturbation and Consensual Same-Sex Activity Within a Male Maximum Security Prison

Christopher Hensley
Richard Tewksbury
Jeremy Wright

The purpose of the present study was to examine the prevalence, amount, and frequency of masturbation and consensual homosexual activity among male inmates. Surveys were administered to 142 inmates in a male Southern correctional facility. The most salient variable associated with the frequency of male inmate masturbation was education. Educated inmates were more likely to be frequent masturbators in prison than less educated inmates. Race and religion had significant effects on same-sex activities within male prisons. White inmates were more likely to engage in consensual homosexual behavior than non-whites. In addition, non-Protestants were more likely than Protestants to engage in same-sex sexual activities while incarcerated. The present study finds support for both the deprivation and importation models.

The study of consensual sex in male prisons has largely been neglected by researchers and has lacked the attention it deserves. Social scientists have historically focused academic attention and deliberation on sexual coercion instead of consensual homosexual activity in prison (see for example, Bowker, 1980; Lockwood, 1980; Nacci & Kane, 1983; Sagarin, 1976; Saum, Surratt, Inciardi, & Bennett, 1995; Scacco, 1975; Struckman-Johnson, Struckman-Johnson, Rucker, Bumby, & Donaldson, 1996; Tewksbury, 1989b; Wooden & Parker, 1982). According to Saum et al. (1995), this may be due to the nature of the homosexual acts. Saum et al. argue that "consensual sex is seen as less of a threat to inmate or institutional security than rape and thus does not demand the attention of more violent behavior" (p. 415). The purpose of this study is to assess the frequencies and characteristics of male practitioners of autoerotic and consensual homosexual behavior in a male maximum-security prison.

Homosexuality can be defined "as the feeling of sexual desire for members of the same sex, or the experience of having sex with persons of the same sex, or a combination of both feeling and the experience" (Cass, 1979, p. 219). It is more difficult to define what a homosexual is. As the renowned sex researcher Alfred Kinsey worte in 1948:

> People do not represent two discrete populations, heterosexual and homosexual. The world is not to be divided into sheep and goats. Not all things are black or all things white. It is a fundamental taxonomy that nature rarely deals with discrete categories. Only the human mind invents categories and tries to force facts into separate pigeonholes. The living world is a continuum in each and every one of its aspects. The sooner we learn this concerning human sexual behavior the sooner we shall reach a sound understanding of the realities of sex. (p. 639)

Thus, Kinsey assigned people varying positions on a continuum from one extreme being exclusively heterosexual (a score of 0) to the other extreme of being exclusively homosexual (a score of 6). In 1948 and 1953, Kinsey found that 29% of Americans—37% of men and 20% of women—have had some homosexual experience to the point of orgasm between adolescence and old age. These people were plotted from 1 through 6 on the Kinsey scale. Those who were 4, 5, or 6, whom Kinsey referred to as predominantly or more or less exclusively homosexual, consisted of 10% of the American population—13% of males and 7% of females. Those who were exclusively homosexual represented 2.5% of Americans—4% of males and 1% of females.

None of those numbers accurately reflect the true number of homosexuals. Each reflects only the overt or physical aspect of homosexuality, namely, the experience of having sex with members of the same sex. Kinsey ignored the other, covert or mental aspects of homosexuality—the erotic feeling, desire, fantasy, or attraction for members of the same sex. Thus, many people who had homosexual feelings, but had not acted on them, were not included in his estimates. If Kinsey had asked his subjects about both their sexual desire and experience rather than experience alone, he would have perhaps found even higher percentages of Americans being homosexual in one way or another.

Strangely enough, even today, more than 40 years after Kinsey's studies, most sex researchers continue to focus on sexual acts alone to find evidence of homosexuality, although there are conflicting studies. For example, the Janus report found that 5% of women and 9% of men were engaged in an ongoing homosexual relationship (Janus & Janus, 1993); while other studies have found about the same proportion of Americans being exclusively homosexual as Kinsey did, namely, between 2% and 3% (Laumann, Gagnon, Michael, & Michaels, 1994; Michael, Gagnon, Laumann, & Kolata, 1994). However, most research on sexual orientations and identities has suggested this figure to be significantly higher.

There are individuals who engage in homosexual activity but do not consider themselves homosexuals. Individuals' sexual behavior is frequently in contrast with their identity as a sexual person. To have sexual relations with an individual of a particular genital construction does not necessarily make one heterosexual or homosexual. This distinction between identity and behavior has been widely recognized within both social science and human service arenas. Perhaps most notably, public health officials have embraced this distinction in their efforts to combat sexually transmitted diseases and HIV. No longer are prevention/intervention programs directed at "gay men," but instead are targeted on "men who have sex with men."

The idea of focusing on behavior is not a wholly new idea. "Situational homosexuality" has been recognized for decades (Sagarin, 1976). Men immersed in single-sex environments, such as boarding schools, the military, remote work sites, and correctional institutions, have long been known to engage in sexual activities with one another, yet staunchly maintain a heterosexual identity. Sexual activities with other men are defined as simply a response to the deprivation or a lack of mixed-sex interactions. General belief holds that most men engaged in situational same-sex sexual activities would return to heterosexual sexual activities once removed from the segregated environment.

Despite the significant portion of the population that either in the past or in the present engage in same-sex sexual activities, the popular perceptions and definitions of such remain focused on "deviance." Studies of deviance, while a major emphasis in the social sciences, may have the consequence of reinforcing negative definitions and stereotypes. With regard to the study of same-sex sexual activities in controlled environments (such as prison), this is a common concern. This is one reason that only a small body of literature is available addressing consensual sex in male prisons.

It is important, however, to understand the contexts and conditions that give rise to situational homosexuality. The most notable early researcher to do so for the prison environment was Ibrahim (1974), who argued that same-sex sexual activities in prison are most often the result of environmental influences, not inmates' actual social identities. He presented six factors related to the social structure of a prison that produced and promoted homosexual behavior within prison walls.

First, the prison environment is a sex-segregated community. The lack of females sometimes induces men to achieve their sexual gratification with other men. Second, deviant sexual behavior, while typically officially regulated, is often tolerated by other inmates and prison officials. The reasons for these tolerant attitudes are fourfold: (1) status roles are created through the deviant behavior that enable stronger inmates to intimidate weaker ones; (2) under this system, inmates are forced to be either a "man" or a "girl-boy"; (3) prison officials view the behavior as a necessary means of control (i.e., inmates release tension); and (4) authorities do not address such issues for fear of provoking negative public sentiment.

Insufficient work opportunities in prisons are yet another factor that leads to deviant sexual activity. Ibrahim points out that many men are left idle for long periods of time, thus enhancing their likeliness to engage in such behavior. As long as men are working and kept busy, they are less likely to engage in "deviant" sexual behavior (Ibrahim, 1974). According to Flanagan and Maguire (1993), most inmates (as many as 90%) are in fact unemployed while incarcerated.

A fourth factor facilitating prison homosexuality is overcrowding. In many prisons, men are crowded into cells with one another, often resulting in a lack of privacy. Inmates are able to watch other inmates change clothes, use the bathroom, and take showers. Situations like this create an impossible environment for officials to control. Older, more experienced inmates use the overcrowded situation to their advantage by exploiting the younger, more naive inmates.

A fifth factor in deviant sexual behavior in male prisons is the lack of an efficient classification system. Without a solid, scientific, and reliable system of classifying inmates, sex offenders and homosexuals are housed and work with the general population. This environment is inviting for sexual deviants to continue their sexual practices within the prison walls. However, in present prison systems, classification systems do exist.

The final and most practical factor is the complete isolation from the outside world. Some prisons forbid any pornographic magazines and hand drawn illustrations that depict nudity or sex. Pornography can act as a release method for prisoners to achieve their sexual desires through masturbation and fantasy, for instance. This isolation can lead inmates to disregard the norms of society and engage in deviant sexual behavior with other inmates (Ibrahim, 1974). It is important to point out that only five states allow conjugal visits in their correctional facilities (Hensley, Rutland, & Gray-Ray, 2000c). It has been argued that these visits would lower the amount of same-sex sexual activity in prisons (Hopper, 1969, 1989).

The study of consensual sex in prisons is also important in regard to HIV and other sexually transmitted diseases. Saum et al. (1995) stress the need for research on the topic due to the threat of transmitting HIV and other diseases through unprotected sexual activity. By educating inmates on the dangers of unprotected sex, institutions can feasibly prevent or at least slow the spread of sexually transmitted diseases. Saum et al. found the two most common practices reported by inmates to have changed due to the threat of HIV/AIDS are less sex altogether and more protected sex when available. Currently, only five correctional systems allow distribution of condoms within their facilities: Mississippi, New York City, San Francisco, Vermont, and Washington, D.C. (Hensley, 2000b). The need for condoms is obvious in correctional facilities throughout the United States, but administrators cannot seem to escape the contradiction of supplying condoms to inmates when sex is not permitted (Saum et al., 1995).

Unfortunately, researchers have largely neglected the study of sexual behavior in male prisons. For the few studies that do exist, the topic of coerced sexual aggression receives much more attention than consensual sex. This lack of research is perhaps a result of the ideology that little violence exists with consensual sex. Rape is seen to be much more of a threat to institutional security and therefore demands significantly more attention (Saum et al., 1995). To date, five studies exist on consensual homosexual activity within United States male prisons (Hensley, 2000a; Nacci & Kane, 1983; Saum et al., 1995; Tewksbury, 1989a; Wooden & Parker, 1982).

In one of the most in-depth studies of sexual behavior among men in prison. Wooden and Parker (1982) found that 65% of a random sample of 200 inmates in a California prison participated in one or more homosexual acts while incarcerated. Of those who admitted engaging in homosexual activity, 52% reported receiving oral sex, while 20% performed oral sex. Thirty-eight percent had performed anal sex on another inmate and 20% had been anally penetrated while incarcerated. The data also revealed that all inmates in the sample had masturbated while incarcerated. Fourteen percent reported masturbating daily, 46% reported masturbating three to five times per week, 30.5% reported at least one to two instances weekly, 5.5% reported masturbating one to three times per month, and 4% reported masturbating less than once a month.

In 1983, Nacci and Kane conducted a two-part research project documenting sexual aggression and homosexual activity among inmates in response to a violent outbreak at the United States Penitentiary at Lewisburg, Pennsylvania. Within a 26-month period, Lewisburg—a previously non-violent institution—experienced eight inmate murders and numerous inmate-on-inmate assaults. It was determined that five of the eight murders were sexually motivated. Therefore, face-to-face interviews and surveys were designed and distributed to a random sample of 330 male inmates from 17 federal prison facilities. The results revealed that 12% of the inmates had participated in homosexual activity in their current prison. The percentages were higher in penitentiaries with more dangerous offenders who were serving longer sentences. When an inmate admitted to engaging in homosexual activity, he was then asked about his role in the sexual acts. According to their reports, a majority of inmates were "inserters" rather than "insertees." The masculine role (inserter) was associated with being heterosexual, while the feminine role (insertee) was associated with being a homosexual or bisexual.

In 1989, Tewksbury conducted a study that investigated "sexual activities, fantasies, and orientations of prison inmates" (p. 34). Drawing on a sample of 150 inmates in an Ohio prison, the results revealed that 75% of the inmates considered themselves to be exclusively heterosexual. Furthermore, 20% of the inmates reported involvement in homosexual activity during the prior year. Only 7.4% of the respondents were involved in a lasting same-sex relationship. As an additional way of assessing inmates' sexual orientation—and attempting to address identity as well as behavior—Tewksbury also inquired about inmates' masturbation fantasies. Similar to the results concerning behavior, a majority of the inmates (72.1%) reported that they always fantasized about the opposite sex during masturbation.

Saum et al. (1995) also conducted a study focusing on male sexual behavior in correctional facilities. Of the 101 inmates interviewed in a medium security prison in Delaware, only 2% reported engaging in sexual activity with another inmate during the previous year. However, 11% of the inmates contended that they had been in sexual contact with females while incarcerated that could account for the low percentage of inmates that admitted homosexual activity. Having women available for sexual contact would not force men to turn to other men for their needs. The females involved in the sexual relations were visitors, female inmates in classes in the male prison, and correctional officers.

In the most recent study of consensual sexual activity within male prisons. Hensley (2000a) embarked on a study "to explore the amount of consensual homosexual activity in male prisons" (p. 1). Face-to-face interviews were conducted with 174 male inmates in multiple security levels in Oklahoma prisons. The results revealed that 80% of the inmates interviewed considered themselves heterosexual, 8% homosexual, and 13% bisexual. The study also revealed that 8% of the inmates interviewed had kissed another inmate while incarcerated. Twenty-three percent had allowed another inmate to rub his body against him in a sexual manner or rubbed a body part against another inmate in a sexual manner. Twenty-four percent had touched another's penis or allowed another man to touch their penis while incarcerated. Twenty-three percent of the inmates had received or given oral sex to another inmate while incarcerated. Twenty percent of those inmates reported engaging in anal intercourse with another inmate. At the time of the interviews, 18% of the respondents had a male sex partner.

Theoretical Perspective

The two competing theoretical perspectives that attempt to explain why consensual homosexual activity occurs within prisons are the deprivation and importation models. The deprivation model contends that the inmate subculture is a direct result of certain deprivations inflicted by life in prison (Sykes, 1958). One of the pains of imprisonment according to Sykes (1958) is "the deprivation of heterosexual relationships" (p. 70). This deprivation forces inmates to turn to alternative methods of achieving sexual gratification including masturbation and homosexual activity. The lack of heterosexual intercourse is frustrating for inmates and continues to weigh heavily on their minds throughout the duration of their sentence, creating a high level of stress. The stress that they feel pressures them into giving into the surrounding same-sex environment; thus, they engage in homosexual activity in order to satisfy their desires.

The importation model contends that the inmate subculture is imported into the prison from the outside (Irwin & Cressey, 1962). Using this explanation, inmate behavior is a result of values and criminal roles that were acquired in free society (Akers, Hayner, & Grununger, 1974). In other words, prisoners establish an identity in free society subcultures prior to incarceration, bringing it into the prison with them. Under the importation model, inmates who engage in consensual sex do so because the behavior was brought in from the outside. The norms and values that an individual obeys on the outside will ultimately effect how he acts on the inside. If an individual feels it is acceptable to engage in homosexual activity before incarceration, he will more than likely feel it is acceptable to engage in it during incarceration.

Method

Participants

In March 2000, all inmates housed in a maximum security Southern correctional facility for men were requested to participate in the current study. Inmates were assembled in the main area of their respective units by correctional staff in order that the researchers could explain the contents of the surveys. Correctional counselors then distributed self-administered questionnaires to each inmate for completion at a later time. Inmates were asked to return their completed questionnaires in a stamped, self-addressed envelope within two weeks of distribution. Of the 800 inmates incarcerated at that time, a total of 142 agreed to participate in the study, yielding a response rate of 18%.

Results

Of the 142 male inmates that responded, 99.3% had masturbated while incarcerated. Of the 141 who reported masturbating, 3% had not masturbated during the last year. Four percent of the respondents masturbated once or a few times in the last year and 1% masturbated every other month. Approximately 2% masturbated once a month or two to three times a month, while 6% of the respondents masturbated once a week. An additional 30.5% masturbated two to three times per week. Twenty percent of the male inmates reported masturbating once a day. Finally, 22.7% reported masturbating more than once a day.

When asked about their sexual orientation before incarceration, 79% reported they identified as straight, 15% reported they were bisexual, and 6% identified as homosexual prior to incarceration. However, when asked about their sexual orientation during incarceration, 69% identified as straight with an additional 23% reporting they were bisexual and 7% revealing they were homosexual. Table 1 displays the amount of same-sex sexual behavior reported by the respondents both prior to and during incarceration. More inmates reported engaging in homosexual behavior during incarceration than they did prior to incarceration, lending support to the deprivation model.

Because the dependent variables are dichotomous, a series of logistic regression analyses were performed to test if the predictor variables had an effect on the dependent variables (both autoerotic and same-sex sexual activities).

TABLE 1 Inmates Engaging in Homosexual Activities Prior to and During Incarceration

	Prior to Incarceration	*During Incarceration*
Participation in Homosexual Behavior	33.1%	40.1%
Kissed Another Male	19.0%	29.6%
Touched Another Male	30.3%	38.0%
Performed Oral Sex on Another Male	16.9%	16.9%
Received Oral Sex by Another Male	28.2%	35.9%
Performed Anal Sex on Another Male	16.2%	32.4%
Received Anal Sex by Another Male	13.4%	17.6%

The most salient and only statistically significant variable in the frequency of masturbation model was education. Table 2 indicates inmates with some college or more are more likely to be frequent masturbators than inmates with a high school education or less. In other words, more educated inmates were more likely to be frequent masturbators than less educated inmates while in prison.

The most salient variables in the models predicting the set of homosexual behaviors while incarcerated were religion and race. Non-Protestants were more likely than Protestants to kiss, touch, receive oral sex, perform oral sex, and perform anal sex while incarcerated. White inmates were more likely than non-whites to touch, receive oral sex, perform oral sex, and perform anal sex during incarceration. Age, education, amount of time served, and type of offense had no statistically significant effect on the sexual behaviors of the inmates during incarceration.

Discussion

Until recently, the topic of prison sex has received only scattered attention among sociologists and penologists. It has typically only delved into the topics of coerced sex among male inmates and the formation of pseudo-families among female inmates (see for example, Bowker, 1980; Giallombardo, 1966; Halleck & Hersko, 1962; Lockwood, 1980; Nacci & Kane, 1983; Nelson, 1974; Otis, 1913; Propper, 1976, 1978, 1981, 1982; Sagarin, 1976; Saum, Surratt, Inciardi, & Bennett, 1995; Scacco, 1975; Selling, 1931; Struckman-Johnson, Struckman-Johnson, Rucker, Bumby, & Donaldson, 1996; Tewksbury, 1989b; Ward & Kassebaum, 1965; Wooden & Parker, 1982). Free society sex research on masturbation and homosexual behavior, on the other hand, is more common, yet plagued with definitional ambiguity.

Prison sex studies have also neglected the topic of masturbation in prison. We found that 99% of the inmates in our exploratory study reported they had masturbated. This is consistent with the rates of masturbation found by Wooden and Parker (1982). However, it is imperative that future researchers delve deeper into this "forbidden" topic.

Free society studies of homosexuality have consistently reported that 2% to 3% of all Americans are exclusively homosexual. In addition, the most famous sex study (i.e., Kinsey et al., 1948) found that 37% of all men had engaged in homosexual activity to the point of orgasm. Because of the situational nature of prisons themselves, the few studies of homosexual behavior in male prisons have found rates of consensual same-sex activity to be between 2% and 65%. The present study found that 38% of the sample had touched another male in a sexual way while incarcerated. In addition, 36% of the inmates had received oral sex from another male inmate.

Unfortunately, prison sex studies have not explored what factors affect an inmate's decision to engage in same-sex activity. According to the present study, two factors (race and religion) significantly affected an inmate's decision to engage in these sexual behaviors. As we know, race is an importation factor since it is brought into prison and shaped by outside influences. Thus, one might expect

TABLE 2 Summary of Logistic Regression Beta Weights ($N = 130$)

	Frequency of Masturbation[1]	*Kissing*	*Touching*	*Performed Oral Sex*	*Received Oral Sex*	*Performed Anal Sex*	*Received Anal Sex*
Age	−0.72	−0.03	−0.50	−0.35	−0.00	0.42	0.08
Race	0.86	0.59	1.15*	1.19*	1.17*	1.26*	0.75
Religion	−0.07	0.91*	0.76*	1.16*	0.77*	1.29*	0.59
Education	1.58*	0.71	0.40	0.29	0.13	0.21	0.48
Amount of Time Served	0.22	−0.02	−0.06	0.11	−0.13	0.12	−0.05
Type of Offense	0.08	−0.19	−0.14	−0.29	−0.26	−0.12	−0.11
Homosexual Behavior	0.62	N/A	N/A	N/A	N/A	N/A	N/A
Pseudo R^2	0.23	0.10	0.12	0.13	0.11	0.15	0.07

Notes: [1]($N = 141$); *Denotes statistical significance at the .05 level; Coding: Age (0 = Younger than 34, 1 = 34 or older); Race (0 = Nonwhite; 1 = White); Religion (0 = Protestant; 1 = non-Protestant); Education (0 = High School or Less, 1 = Some College or More); Amount of Time Served (0 = Less than 1 Year, 1 = 1–5 Years, 2 = 5–10 Years, 3 = More than 10 Years); Type of Offense (0 = Personal Crime, 1 = Other Crime); Homosexual Behavior (0 = No. 1 = Yes).

nonwhite and white inmates to react and adapt to prison life differently. White inmates in our sample were more likely than non-whites to engage in same-sex activity with other inmates. It is possible that non-white inmates see homosexual behavior as a threat to their toughness and masculinity. Or, as shown by Tewksbury (1989b), white inmates are more likely to be targeted for sexual approaches by other inmates. In addition, Carroll (1974) and Lockwood (1980) found that white inmates often became targets of sexual assaults by black inmates while incarcerated.

It is unclear if religion is an importation factor in prisons. Many inmates "find God" while incarcerated. Others may change their religious preference in prison. The present study found that non-Protestants were more likely than Protestants to engage in consensual homosexual behavior while incarcerated. Since most of the non-Protestants in the sample were Roman Catholic, it may be that they are less fearful of engaging in consensual same-sex activity because there are different aspects associated with the afterlife. Catholics, for example, are taught they any sin will be forgiven through the sacrament of confession and through the penitence of prayer. However, most Protestants are more conservative and fundamental. In addition, the topic of homosexuality has received more public attention in Protestant churches than non-Protestant churches. Furthermore, some of the inmates in the sample indicated that they had no religious preference, which placed them in the Non-Protestant group. Therefore, these inmates would probably not be concerned with engaging in "sinful" behaviors. Additionally, some data (Tewksbury, 1989b) suggest that less religious inmates and non-Protestants are more likely to be sexually approached by other inmates.

It must not be overlooked that the amount of consensual homosexual behavior increased after the inmates were incarcerated. Seventy-nine percent of the respondents reported being heterosexual prior to incarceration. However, that number dropped to 69% once they were incarcerated. In other words, at least some inmates, because of the single-sex environment, engaged in situational homosexuality. This lends support to Sykes' (1958) argument that inmates are deprived of heterosexual outlets, thus increasing their "pains of imprisonment." However, the findings of this research only find weak support for both the deprivation and importation models.

Institutions must be willing to allow inmates to engage in autoerotic behavior without fear of reprisal. Masturbation provides an alternative outlet so that inmates may release pent-up tension and stress. Allowing inmates to masturbate and engage in consensual homosexual activity may reduce the amount sexual coercion in correctional facilities.

Finally, correctional administrators across the U.S. must provide married inmates a "normal" outlet for sexual release. In other words, prison systems should allow married inmates to engage in conjugal visitation with their spouses. Hensley et al. (2000c) found that 74% of conjugal visit participants felt that conjugal visits did relieve homosexuality. Correctional administrators and researchers have a long way to go battling sexual coercion.

It should be noted, however, that our study does have two major limitations. First, the response rate is quite low, which calls into question the representativeness of the sample. Second, the study was conducted at only one correctional facility in a Southern state. It is important that future prison sex researchers continue to investigate masturbation and consensual sex in both male and female prisons.

References

Akers, R., Hayner, N., & Grununger, W. (1974). Homosexual and drug behavior in prison: A test of the functional and importation models of the inmate system. *Social Problems, 21*(3), 410–422.

Bowker, L. (1980). *Prison victimization.* New York: Elsevier North Holland.

Carroll, L. (1974). *Hacks, blacks and cons.* Lexington, MA: D. C. Heath.

Cass, V. (1979). Homosexual identity formation: A theoretical model. *Journal of Homosexuality, 4*(3), 219–235.

Correctional Service of Canada. (1994). *HIV/AIDS in prisons: Final report of the expert committee on AIDS in prisons.* Ontario: Author.

Flanagan, T., & Maguire, K. (1993). A full employment policy for prison in the United States: Some arguments, estimates, and implications. *Journal of Criminal Justice, 21*(2), 117–130.

Gillombardo, R. (1966). *Society of women: A study of a woman's prison.* New York: Wiley.

Halleck, S., & Hersko, M. (1962). Homosexual behavior in a correctional institution for adolescent girls. *American Journal of Orthopsychiatry*, 32, 911–917.

Hensley, C. (2000a). Consensual homosexual activity in male prisons. *Corrections Compendium, 26*(1), 1–4.

Hensley, C. (2000b). What we have learned from studying prison sex. *Humanity and Society, 24*(4), 348–360.

Hensley, C., Rutland, S., & Gray-Ray, P. (2000c). The effects of the conjugal visitation program on Mississippi inmates. *Corrections Compendium, 25*(4):1–3, 20–21.

Hopper, C. (1969). *Sex in prison.* Baton Rouge, LA: Louisiana State University Press.

Hopper, C. (1989). The evolution of conjugal visiting in Mississippi. *The Prison Journal, 69*(1), 103–109.

Ibrahim, A. I. (1974). Deviant sexual behavior in men's prisons. *Crime and Delinquency, 20*(1), 38–44.

Irwin, J., & Cressey, D. (1962). Thieves, convicts and the inmate culture. *Social Problems, 10*(1), 42–55.

Janus, S., & Janus, C. (1993). *The Janus report on sexual behavior.* New York, NY: Wiley.

Kinsey, A., Martin, C., Pomeroy, W., & Gebhard, P. (1948). *Sexual behavior in the human male.* Philadelphia: W. B. Saunders.

Laumann, E., Gagnon, J., Michael, R., & Michaels, S. (1994). *The social organization of sexuality: Sexual practices in the United States.* Chicago: The University of Chicago Press.

Lockwood, I. (1980). *Prison sexual violence.* New York: Elsevier Press.

Michael, R., Gagnon, J., Laumann, E., & Kolata, G. (1994). *Sex in America: A definitive survey.* Boston: Little, Brown and Company.

Nacci, P., & Kane, T. R. (1983). Sex and sexual aggression in federal prisons. *Federal Probation, 47*(4), 31–36.

Otis, M. (1913). A perversion not commonly noted. *Journal of Abnormal Psychology*, 8, 113–116.

Propper, A. M. (1976). *Importation and deprivation perspectives on homosexuality in correctional institutions: An empirical test of their relative efficacy.* Ph.D. Dissertation, University of Michigan, Ann Arbor.

Propper, A. M. (1978). Lesbianism in female and coed correctional institutions. *Journal of Homosexuality, 3*(3), 265–274.

Propper, A. M. (1981). *Prison homosexuality: Myth and reality.* Lexington, MA: Lexington Books.

Propper, A. M. (1982). Make-believe families and homosexuality among imprisoned girls. *Criminology, 20*(1), 127–138.

Sagarin, E. (1976). Prison homosexuality and its effect on post-prison sexual behavior. *Psychiatry, 39*, 245–257.

Saum, C., H., Surratt, J., Inciardi, & Bennett, R. (1995). Sex in prison: Exploring the myths and realities. *The Prison Journal, 75*(4), 413–430.

Scacco, A. (1975). *Rape in prison.* Springfield, IL: Charles C. Thomas.

Selling, L. (1931). The pseudo-family. *American Journal of Sociology, 37*:247–253.

Struckman-Johnson, C., Struckman-Johnson, D., Rucker, L., Bumby, K., & Donaldson, S. (1996). Sexual coercion reported by men and women in prisons. *The Journal of Sex Research, 33*(1), 67–76.

Sykes, G. (1958). *The society of captives: A study of a maximum-security prison.* Princeton, NJ: Princeton University Press.

Tewksbury, R. (1989a). Measures of sexual behavior in an Ohio prison. *Sociology and Social Research, 74*(1), 34–39.

Tewksbury, R. (1989b). Fear of sexual assault in prison inmates. *The Prison Journal, 69*(1), 62–71.

Ward, D., & Kassebaum, G. (1965). *Women's prison: Sex and social structure.* Chicago: Aldine Publishing Company.

Wooden, W., & Parker, J. (1982). *Men behind bars: Sexual exploitation in prison.* New York: Plenum.

THE JOURNAL OF MEN'S STUDIES, Volume 10, Number 1, Fall 2001, pp. 59–71.

8. The Changing Nature of Interpersonal Relationships in a Women's Prison

Kimberly R. Greer

It is generally assumed that the subcultures experienced by men and women in prison are diametrically opposed. Previous research indicates that incarcerated women create more stable interpersonal relationships. Thirty-five women imprisoned in the Midwest were interviewed, and their comments suggest the subculture found in women's prisons might be changing. While their observations support the notion that prisons for women are generally less violent, involve less gang activity, and do not facilitate the racial tensions evident in men's prisons, the respondents indicated their interpersonal relationships may be less stable and less familial than in the past. Specifically, participants discussed the high degree of mistrust inherent in their friendships with other female inmates. In addition, they reported numerous reasons women engage in sexual relationships; however, they believe the primary motivation involves economic manipulation. Finally, respondents did not report a significant or formal enactment of familial networks. Factors which might influence such changes are considered.

Currently, women represent about 6% of the total prison population (Bureau of Justice Statistics, 1999). Upward trends in the incarceration rates of women are attributed to a combination of the new mandatory sentencing guidelines and the country's policy regarding intensified sanctions for drug charges (Bloom, Chesney-Lind, & Owen, 1994; Nagel & Johnson, 1994). Women in prison are more likely than their male counterparts to be incarcerated for offenses involving drugs.

Female and male inmates differ not only in terms of the crimes they commit but also in the backgrounds and personal histories they bring to the institution. Women are three times more likely to have suffered some type of abuse than male inmates; almost 60% of incarcerated women report prior physical and sexual abuse (U.S. Department of Justice, 1997). Female offenders are more likely than male prisoners to have had members of their families imprisoned (Pollock, 1998). In addition, women in prison more often had primary caretaking responsibilities for their children than male inmates. Approximately 7 in 10 women in prison have children under the age of 18 years (Bureau of Justice Statistics, 1999). Therefore, approximately 1.3 million minor children have mothers who are incarcerated in a correctional setting (Bureau of Justice Statistics, 1999). When men are incarcerated, approximately 90% report that their children are in the custody of the mother (U.S. Department of Justice, 1991). On the other hand, when women are confined in prison, only 25% indicate that their children are living with their fathers. Instead, children of incarcerated mothers are more likely to be placed in the custody of grandparents. Furthermore, about 6% of the female inmates enter correctional institutions pregnant (U.S. Department of Justice, 1991).

Although prior research has explored the effect of incarceration on prison inmates, most examinations have focused on male offenders. Female offenders now are receiving increased scholarly consideration, but a thorough understanding of the perceptions and experiences of these women is still lacking.

Previous research provides a wealth of information related to the description of typical female inmates and treatment issues related to their incarceration. Although there have been several excellent ethnographic examinations of prisons for women, there still seems to be a void in understanding the personal experiences of female inmates and how their perceptions shape their interactions within the prison subculture.

Research Questions

The questions this research seeks to answer are as follows:

1. How do women construct the social culture in this particular institution?
2. In what ways might perceptions influence social interactions in the prison?
3. What factors influence relationships in prison?

Our Previous Understanding of Relationships in Women's Prisons

Women prisoners are still frequently referred to as forgotten offenders (Chesney-Lind, 1986; Feinman, 1983; Fletcher, Shaver, & Moon, 1993; Goetting & Howsen, 1983; Morash et al., 1994; Pollock-Byrne, 1990; Simon & Landis, 1991). The typical female inmate has never been married, is a woman of color, is 25 to 29 years of age, and is a single parent with one to three children being cared for by her mother or grandparent (Fletcher et al., 1993; Goetting & Howsen, 1983; Merlo & Pollock, 1995).

In addition, these offenders typically have been easily manipulated by their peers, runaways from home, sexually abused as children, high school dropouts, and arrested multiple times for property crimes (Chesney-Lind & Rodriguez, 1983; Fletcher et al., 1993; Goetting & Howsen, 1983; Owen, 1998). Approximately half of the women in prison are African American, even though only one in eight women in the United States is African American (Pollock, 1998).

Despite the recent advocacy for gender-responsive services for adolescent girls and adult women offenders, institutional policy regarding the treatment of female offenders has not followed a well-studied or consistent plan. A review of the literature suggests women offenders receive less appropriate programs and services than male inmates (Chesney-Lind & Rodriguez, 1983; Culbertson & Fortune, 1984; Genders & Player, 1991; Goetting & Howsen, 1983; McCarthy, 1980). Bell (1976) noted that confinement in prison may be a more difficult experience for women than men because they are more likely to find the social isolation insufferable.

Similarly, women do not as readily become part of an inmate subculture and do not adhere as rigidly to an inmate code (Bell, 1976).

Whether women adopt prison subcultural roles is a question somewhat open for debate. Giallombardo (1966) and Ward and Kassebaum (1965) were some of the first researchers to study subcultures in prisons for women. However, until recently, there have been very few studies examining the subcultures in prisons for either men or women. Early research (Giallombardo, 1966; Larsen & Nelson, 1984; Leger, 1987; Propper, 1982, Ward & Kassebaum, 1965) identified the existence of "pseudofamilies" that were kinship networks established by women to fulfill lost familial roles such as daughter, wife, father, cousin, and grandmother. Homosexual relationships were also discussed by these prior studies and were found to form a significant aspect of the prison subculture for women. Intimate relationships brought with them social structure demonstrated by marriages and divorces as well as jealousy and power struggles (Pollock, 1998).

Although women do "form affectional ties that have some similarity to familial relationships," questions remain as to how pervasive and extensively defined these kinship networks might be (Pollock, 1998, p. 38). There has been some speculation that these types of prison relationships have diminished in recent years (Pollock, 1998). Those women who are alleged to be involved in the prison subculture are described as "being less inclined to introspection and continue to involve themselves in relationships, drugs, and other distractions to divert their attention away from looking at their own behavior" (Pollock, 1998, p. 39).

Barbara Owen (1998) discusses relationships formed by women in prison. Her interviews and observations revealed that female offenders still participate in "play family" and form dyadic sexual relationships (p. 134). Obviously, relationships formed in prison, whether they are friendships among inmates, sexual encounters, or interactions with correctional officers, are quite complex (Owen). Girshick (1999) found mixed reactions; some women still engage in forming kinship networks, but other individuals strongly disapproved of such relationships. Therefore, respected scholars writing as late as 1998 report somewhat contradictory findings (see Owen, 1998; Pollock, 1998).

Method

A total of 35 female inmates from a midwestern state correctional institution participated in an in-depth, semistructured interview. At the time this study was being conducted, a total of 238 women were incarcerated at this midwestern state correctional facility.

The Changing Nature of Social Environments in a Women's Prison

During interviews, respondents painted a picture of the interpersonal environment inside the walls of the institution that can best be described as one based on manipulation and mistrust. The women discussed several different types of relationships: (a) friendships among female offenders, (b) sexual relationships among inmates, and (c) lack of kinship networks. All aspects of their interpersonal environment are tainted with perceptions of dishonesty, paranoia, and hostility. Most of the respondents preferred to view themselves as "loners"; however, as the interviews revealed, avoiding any type of interactions with other inmates or correctional officers is nearly impossible in a closed environment.

Friendships among Female Offenders

One type of relationship discussed by female inmates involved friendships with other inmates. There were several different aspects of the friendships described by the women at this correctional facility. However, the pervasive attitude held by the respondents regarding prison friendships was that any individual who engaged in this type of interaction did so at her own risk. Most of the women I talked with wanted to demonstrate a rather rigid stance against prison friendships. Twenty-one respondents voluntarily described themselves as "loners" at some point during our conversations. Conversely, there were those individuals who talked about forming intense friendships with other women incarcerated at this and other facilities. Phyllis made the following statement while discussing the differences between friends "on the street" and friendships formed in prison: "It is based purely on feelings in here. Out there, you know you run into each other, you are friends, you talk. In here it just, you get dependent upon each other emotionally."

Many respondents believed they had not formed close relationships with any of the other women who were also incarcerated at this institution. They indicated that this lack of friendship was the result of conscious decisions and behaviors on their part. Repeatedly, women referred to "associates" when asked whether they had formed any friendships in prison. One respondent after another appeared to use the distinction between *friend* and *associate* to distinguish the important difference they perceived between "real" friends and people with whom they simply interacted. For example, Kimberly had this response to a question about friendships:

> I have no friends; I have associates . . . even my MOOR [religion] sisters . . . or my Islam sister . . . even them are not my friends and that is sad to say . . . it is very conscious on my part because I am conscious of the other moves, snake moves. . . . I feel deprived because I know that somewhere you can have a good friend. But at the same time it is okay with me because I know where I am at. I know my surrounding. And I know that I can't really trust anybody here fully.

Explaining why she so strongly distrusts the other women who are incarcerated with her, Kimberly continued,

> You deal with a bunch of people every day with different attitudes and different thoughts. You don't know how they going to be today, you don't know how they going to be tomorrow. Today they're fine, tomorrow they're not. . . . You're really

> taking a chance on whether you can have a relationship with someone here and I don't want to take that chance.

Preoccupation with the motives and intentions of other women prisoners caused respondents to forego establishing close relationships with others. Although they might express regret for this forced sense of isolation, they nonetheless thought abstaining was the wisest choice.

Besides the element of mistrust, an additional factor that influenced hesitation at forming friendships had to do with the transitory nature of relationships developed in prison. Respondents indicated that forming friendships takes time, and after an individual leaves the correctional institution, often interpersonal contact is severed.

Because these relationships are perceived as being temporary, respondents may attempt to avoid close friendships in an effort to avoid negative feelings associated with those times in which one person or the other is released. Many respondents mentioned the sadness evoked when a friend was either released or transferred to another institution. Also acknowledging the temporary nature of these alliances during her interview, Brenda commented,

> I don't think friendships inside could compare with friendships outside . . . if you want to be an acquaintance or whatever, you might as well do it now because once you walk out them gates . . . you have to get your life back on track again. Maybe you might call this person once or twice but eventually it just fades out.

Although the experiences these women share in prison could possibly serve to form tight bonds, the mutual problems that bring them to this facility can also contribute to complicated relationships. As Paula noted in the following remark, women prisoners often share similar backgrounds and perceptions, which logically might forge a strong bond. However, those common experiences can prove simultaneously problematic to healthy, sustained relationships in the real world. While discussing this precarious bond, Paula stated,

> I am okay with them [friendships] to a certain extent because I have formed relationships before in prison with women and like I say, most of us that are in prison are some type of users, or addicted to something and when we depart and go back on the street, if I am doing good, they are not doing good. If they are doing good, I'm not doing good . . . it really hurts to see that when the other one is doing good and you aren't.

A few respondents indicated that although they were very selective about the individuals with whom they chose to develop friendships, they nonetheless did allow one or more people in their lives they felt were good, trustworthy companions.

An even smaller number of women discussed relationships in which the friends were portrayed as extremely significant persons in their lives. On the basis of the rather positive interpretation of her friendship, Molly proceeded to reflect on how forming a relationship in prison made her feel:

> Everybody has to have someone that they can trust to talk to about certain things in here and well, you know as well as I do that you can't talk to one person about everything. You have one friend that you can talk to about this and you have another friend that you can talk to about that; you just can't talk to one friend about everything because they probably wouldn't understand. You have different friends who fulfill different roles for you definitely, and that makes me feel pretty good in here.

A few women disagreed with popular institutional wisdom regarding a need for remoteness in interpersonal relationships. Barbara was one respondent who seemed to have a fairly strong resistance toward the majority's perception about the negative repercussions that prison friendships can create for an individual. However, she seemed to find this attitude difficult to accept based more on pragmatism rather than some more complicated interpersonal need. While discussing the predominant attitude toward prison friendships, Barbara reported,

> A lot of people say you don't have friends in the penitentiary . . . you don't come here to make friends. Well, I didn't come here to make friends but it is inevitable. You are living with 300 and some women, it is not easy being alone. So you cannot tell me that you will go and spend your whole day not having one friend in this whole institution. I can't see it.

The primary theme that emerged from the conversations about friendships in prison focused on the women's distrust of close interpersonal relationships with other female offenders. Whether their misgivings were based on personal experiences or observations of other interactions is unknown.

Although these women appeared to perceive their peers as being manipulative and self-serving, the majority nonetheless reported having at least one person whom they considered a friend. Those who did not develop friendships had what they described as associates or individuals with whom they interacted with on a superficial basis. Based on the remarks of respondents, it seems doubtful that very many of these friendships survive transfer to other institutions or release from custody altogether. However, comments made by the women often appeared contradictory in that they discussed the apprehension they have about forming friendships, yet they appeared to establish some form of relationship with at least one other female inmate.

Sexual Relationships among Inmates

All but three women either described their attitudes toward and participation (or lack thereof) in sexual relationships with other female prisoners. This was a subject that most women felt strongly about, either positively or negatively. However, 28% of respondents reported experiencing relatively neutral feelings toward participation in sexual relationships by other women. These respondents indicated that although they did not wish to become involved in intimate relationships with other women, they did not judge harshly those individuals who did choose to engage in such activity. Interestingly, although most respondents described sexual relationships among women as being extremely prevalent (one woman even guessed the participation level as being as high as 90% of all female inmates), only 10 of 35 women admitted ever having been involved in a sexual relationship in prison. At the time interviews were conducted, 5 respondents reported currently being sexually involved with another inmate. In addition, 2 women identified themselves as lesbians, and 1 woman reported she was bisexual. Of these 3 women, 2 indicated they chose not to participate in sexual relationships in prison because of the manipulative nature of the relationships.

Information provided by these respondents suggests that the nature of sexual relationships in prison may be slowly changing. Burkhart (1973), Giallombardo (1966), Hawkins (1995), and Ward and Kassebaum (1965) concluded that incarcerated women chose to form homosexual relationships with other inmates as one technique for lessening the pains of imprisonment. According to Giallombardo (1966), "The vast majority of inmates adjust to the prison world by establishing a homosexual alliance with a compatible partner as a marriage partner" (p. 136). According to responses made by women in this study, homosexual relationships are a fairly significant aspect (both for those who do participate and those who do not approve of such behavior) of the prison culture, but there were a number of respondents who indicated that they have chosen not to participate. Therefore, involvement in these relationships may not be as pervasive as previously discovered and when formed, may be initiated for different reasons. Findings from this study also suggest that these respondents believe sexual relationships are based primarily on manipulation rather than on any perception of compatibility or genuine attraction between partners.

The reactions toward homosexual relationships fell along a continuum, from attitudes that were very accepting to comments indicative of very intolerant perceptions. For instance, Elaine volunteered, "After my divorce . . . I was in a relationship with a female on the street and I have been in one since I was here and it was for 13½ months." Conversely, an example of intolerance was provided by Joan, who stated:

> It makes me sick. In the bathrooms, you might be going to take a shower and you . . . open the curtain and you get shocked . . . if you happen to be in the room . . . like a ten-man room and it goes on at night time . . . so you kind of stop up your ears and face the wall . . . and pray that you don't hear it.

Throughout the course of this study, these women discussed a number of motivations they considered possible impetuses for participation in sexual relationships. On the basis of their comments, seven categories of motivations emerged from the data: economic motivation, sincere relationship, loneliness, curiosity, sexual identity, peer pressure, and other (sexual release and diversion from the boredom).

Economic Manipulation. One element of homosexual relationships that may have changed since the earlier examinations of women's prisons is related to the issue of clearly delineated sex roles. Earlier research (Burkhart, 1973; Giallombardo, 1966, p. 136; Ward & Kassebaum, 1965) strongly suggested that women who became involved in sexual relationships did so by adopting "overtly assumed" sex roles. Such roles have commonly been referred to as *femme* and *stud broad*. Previous scholarly works (Burkhart, 1973; Giallombardo, 1966; Hawkins, 1995; Ward & Kassebaum, 1965) note that inmates even conform their physical appearance to stereotypical assumptions about sex roles. Although I did not specifically ask women whether they played these types of roles, responses did not reflect that these were commonly assumed ways of behaving.

Most respondents did not seem to be trying to portray overly feminine or masculine qualities. During their reflections about the nature of homosexual relationships and the impact these associations have on institutional life, only a couple of women ever referred to other inmates according to clearly defined roles (i.e., "bulldagging"). If anything, these women reported being focused on not forming any close, long-lasting relationships within the institution walls.

My respondents would adamantly disagree with the thought that "mate selection is based upon romantic love" (Giallombardo, 1966, p. 141), as it relates to sexual relationships in prison. Based on the comments obtained by these incarcerated women, the notion that women become involved with each other in prison on the basis of some concept of romance is erroneous in today's correctional institutions for women. Similarly, opinions furnished by respondents would not support the assertion made by Ward and Kassebaum (1965) when they reported, "The process of turning out thus seems to represent socialization of the new inmates into practices which provide support, guidance, and emotional satisfaction during a period when these are lacking" (p. 78).

Although respondents observed that there are numerous motivations for beginning and maintaining a sexual relationship, 25 women (71%) speculated that the primary reason involved what they described as economic manipulation. Repeatedly, female inmates described the element of dishonesty as being pervasive in all prison relationships, but most especially those that involved sexual intimacy. Many women could think of several different reasons why women would pursue or participate in these intimate activities, but foremost in their minds was the issue of unequal access to money and material goods.

Women consistently referred to "canteen whores" or "commissary whores" when describing those inmates who participated in sexual relationships simply to improve their economic standing. All inmates are required to work if they are not in school, but this does not necessarily result in an equal distribution of income. Different job assignments receive varying amounts of financial compensation. The least amount of money an inmate could receive each month was $7.50, and the most was approximately $20.00. This money is credited to an inmate account and can be used by the women to purchase items from the commissary (canteen) or materials can be ordered from approved catalogs. In addition, some inmates have family and friends who send money to their inmate accounts; this money can also be spent by the inmate at the commissary, on catalog orders, or electronic possessions such as televisions and radios that can only be purchased from the state.

As in free society, the inequalities in economic status contributed to power differentials. Women prisoners who have more money are perceived as being more influential in the correctional facility than those individuals who have less monetary support. For example, while discussing possible positive and negative results of sexual relationships between inmates, Joan described how prisoners look for outward signs of financial status before selecting a possible partner. She stated,

> It is canteen for women who don't have money. . . . They always find someone that has got money. . . . Everybody knows when someone has money, and they will sit and watch who has the big bags that comes from the store and who goes to the store every week.

Inmates who receive financial support from significant others may find themselves having more discretion as to whether they become involved in sexual relationships with other women. Sarafina credited her family's economic support with allowing her to not become sexually involved when she commented,

> I am not rich; I am not wealthy, but I'm well looked out [for]. Certain people do certain things around here, that get their little hustle along, have their little cigarettes or buy soap, whatever, because they don't have people looking out for them, and that is hard.

Echoing the consistent concern that these relationships are inherently dishonest and manipulative, Barbara, who had been involved sexually with another inmate, described the majority of women's motivations as being related to this inherent economic inequality when she said,

> A lot of people do it for money. Here it is a money thing. It is not about people's feelings or it is all [a] game really and so, people when you are broke and only get $7.50 a month and somebody may get $250.00 a week or month . . . it begins to be attractive to you.

The fact that money plays a significant role in the perpetuation of at least the more temporary and manipulative sexual relationships did not seem to come as a surprise to any of the women. Although none of these respondents admitted ever being involved in a sexual relationship because of money, they certainly had no compunction about pointing their fingers at their peers. Women who participated in the research indicated that this focus on the exchange of material goods is not a well-kept secret, yet this knowledge evidently does not deter the deceptive behavior. Nor does it prohibit individuals from being taken advantage of during their involvement with others.

Respondents indicated that often women take advantage of each other on more than one occasion. They described instances where one woman will indicate a desire to be with someone else sexually only around the time when canteen orders can be placed. After she has provided the material items, the woman with the money may not see nor hear from her friend until the next time she can place an order at the canteen.

Loneliness and Companionship. The economic factor may explain why some women engage in sexual relationships with other inmates, but it surely cannot explain all the possible reasons for such relationships. Eighteen respondents (51%) perceived that loneliness and the need for companionship provided an incentive for some women to participate in sexual activities. For one respondent, it was important that she make it clear that she did not need anyone and preferred not to be involved with anyone; however, she did recognize that some women initiate or succumb to relationships because they need the companionship of others to survive incarceration. Sarafina, who advised me that her prior employment involved stripping and running an escort service, concluded,

> I'm not looking for a relationship. Some people they do look for relationships and they want, they need someone to spend time with. I'm not saying that I have never been with a woman because when I was, it was business and not pleasure. They get into relationships because they have people that have more time and they need to do their time with somebody.

Indicating that individuals may engage in sexual relationships because of a profound need for belonging, Kimberly noted that the desire these women are acting on may have developed prior to their imprisonment. While discussing why women become sexually involved with other female inmates, Kimberly reflected, "Love, they didn't have that when they was coming up [growing up] and they try to find it here. It be false love, but to them it's basically all they've ever had, so they hold on to it."

Somewhat related to the issue of loneliness is the idea, consistent with previous research (Burkhart, 1973; Giallombardo, 1966; Girshick, 1999; Ward & Kassebaum, 1965), that sexual relationships assist women in serving their prison time with the least amount of psychological discomfort. Phyllis stated,

> Women [who] have never done it out on the streets and will never do it again, they usually do it in here and it is a lonely thing and it is also that little dance you do when you fall in love with somebody . . . that good feeling that you get over somebody pursuing or whatever. They get that charge and they miss that.

Thus, the excitement one may experience when initiating a new love affair can serve to distract one's attention away from the harsh realities of the correctional facility and provide a rationale for engaging in a homosexual relationship. Pressure to conform exists inside a prison as well. Several respondents listed curiosity and the desire to "fit in" as other possible explanations for women's sexual involvement with other inmates. The idea of wanting to fit in suggests a normative aspect to sexual relationships in this prison and many women did suggest that these types of interactions are prevalent.

Sincere Couples versus Dibbling and Dabbling. For most of these respondents, the nature of prison relationships revolves around deceit, deception, distrust, and manipulation. These qualities were also evident in their thoughts on sexual relationships in the correctional facility. However, there were relationships, including their own, that they could describe more positively.

Women who were perceived as being involved in sincere, long-lasting, committed relationships were accorded a special status by respondents. In the eyes of these women, there was a tremendous difference between those individuals who "play games" with each other for canteen privileges and female inmates who nurture stable, monogamous, and caring relationships with each other. Only 9 of the 35 women (26%) interviewed mentioned genuine affection as being a possible explanation for sexual relationships. While discussing these rare but more respected relationships, Brenda reflected, "There is some that they are in a relationship because they care . . . probably five or six couples on this grounds that have been in a relationship for some years." Several respondents noted specifically that lesbians (those who identified themselves as such before they were imprisoned) sometimes formed the most stable relationships in prison or chose not to participate whatsoever for the duration of their imprisonment. Ashley, who identified herself as bisexual, believed there was a noticeable difference in the behaviors of women who had homosexual experience prior to incarceration and those individuals whose first encounters occur in prison. She commented,

> With a lot of them, they come in . . . and they start participating and . . . they don't really know what they are doing anyway so they really get used because they go from individual to individual to individual. But the ones that have been doing it for awhile or had did it before they came to the penitentiary, you can tell it because they might be with one woman for the next six years. You can tell the difference.

While contemplating the nature of relationships among women, Jade reflected on the difference between temporary and long-lasting interactions. After informing me that she was not a lesbian or homophobic, Jade reported,

> There are some women here who have been together almost 10 years. To me, they are real and they are going to do 10 or longer together. They have got 30, they have got life, and if I was in that position, I would probably do the same thing and I would find a companion.

Inmates who are able to maintain caring, sincere interactions are accorded a certain degree of respect. Paula, who indicates she has nothing against individuals who participate in sexual relationships, reported that she can see both positive and negative aspects to their involvement:

> I see both sides . . . because I see the ones that are real about it, that don't play, it is not just a prison game thing. It is a person that is truly a lesbian that truly has a real lover . . . and there is no dibbling and dabbling, you know it is just them two. Now the negative [side], them are the ones that move from one to the other, playing all kind of games in prison.

One of the unfortunate outcomes of intimate relationships mentioned by several women reflected the importation of domestic violence into the correctional facility. Although none of them reported having experienced violence at the hands of intimate others in prison, several women commented on having seen abuse within the prison walls. Some respondents explained that attempts to control others serve as an incentive not to become involved in intimate prison relationships. While describing the downfalls of sexual relationships that often revolve around jealousy and mistrust, Jade asserted,

> They fight . . . and it is jealous like . . . hollering at her, "you don't do this, you don't talk to her, you don't give her nothing, you don't take nothing, you do what I say, I am here for you." I don't think so. You know, I mean personally, I ate enough shit off men [not] to have a woman check [control] me. It is not going to happen.

Throughout the course of these interviews, none of the respondents seemed surprised or offended by the inclusion of questions related to sexual behavior. Obviously, some women were more eager to explore and explain the nature of these relationships than were others. On the basis of their comments, I gathered that intimate personal relationships still are a significant aspect of the interpersonal prison environment. However, rather than being generally neutral or positive strategies to address the harshness of confinement, these relationships are perceived as being interpersonally risky behavior. The unease with which women view these relationships may help explain why there appeared to be a lack of what has previously been described as pseudofamilies in women's prisons.

Lack of Kinship Networks

Observations made by the respondents in this study suggested that changes in the experiences of female inmates have obviously occurred during the past 34 years (since Giallombardo's early research). For instance, although previous research, as well as these respondents, noted that one of the goals of those imprisoned is to do "easy time" rather than focusing on the experiences of friends and family members in the real world, they differ in how that time may be completed with the least amount of psychological grief possible. According to Giallombardo (1966),

> The inmates' psychological transition of self from civil society to the prison world may be considered complete when the individual reacts neutrally to events in the outside world, even when these events concern crucial matters pertaining to close family members. (p. 135)

There may exist a misconception that very few inmates actually maintain contact with their friends and family members once incarcerated. However, respondents indicated through their interview comments that they do perpetuate fairly consistent interaction with family members. Very few women reported consistent visitation with children and family for various reasons. However, through mail and telephone contact, they do remain current on what is taking place with significant others.

Contrary to much of the early research examining the experiences of women in correctional institutions, these respondents described an individualistic approach to doing time rather than a kinship structure that developed in other facilities. Whereas Burkhart (1973), Giallombardo (1966), Hawkins (1995), Owen (1998), and Ward and Kassebaum (1965) discussed the existence of family kinship networks and same-sex relationships, the findings from this research suggest some subtle changes in the manner in which women in prison go about doing their time.

In her classic study of a women's prison, Giallombardo (1966) explained that women experience similar "pains of imprisonment" (Sykes, 1958, p. 63) as encountered by male prisoners. However, she concluded that women create a "separate universe" (Giallombardo, 1966, p. 103) from which they can maintain an identity or sense of self that is relevant to the outside world. This perception led Giallombardo to recognize that women in prison established relationships with other prisoners that were consistent with, as well as familiar to, relationships they had with significant others outside of prison. In essence, female inmates recreate familial and sexual relationships based on the same cultural expectations of women in the larger society.

Kinship networks might also help provide a larger group of individuals from whom the inmate could receive emotional support and socialization into the role of prison inmate (Giallombardo, 1966). In explaining the existence of pseudo-family relationships, Giallombardo (1966) stated, "The family group in the female prison is singularly suited to meet the internalized cultural expectations of the female role. It serves the social, psychological, and physiological needs of the female inmates" (p. 185). Giallombardo elaborated that these needs may arise from several different sources, such as the prison environment itself (deprivation model), women's personalities, and a sense of dependence based on the cultural expectations of women. In other words, women experience a need to form relatively close familial relationships, even in a correctional facility, because of previous socialization experiences and gender expectations.

The 35 women interviewed for this research did not relate examples of similar types of prison relationships. In a few occasions, respondents discussed very loosely established familial acknowledgments, but none of these relationships approximated the rather structured and stable kinship networks described by Burkhart (1973) and Giallombardo (1966). Most women either did not refer to these types of relationships based on their experiences and observations or, when asked, responded directly that those kinds of interpersonal interactions really did not occur at this institution. However, a few women discussed knowing women in the prison whom they referred to by some term of endearment such as "Mom," "Grandma," "Sister," or "Cousin." For example, Destiny commented,

> I do that myself [referring to playing family roles]. The trouble is, it's kinda funny because there is this one Black lady, she is like in her 50s and I call her mom. And she, I go "mom" and she comes up to me and gives me a hug and all that stuff. I mean, everybody looked at me, like that ain't your mom is it? I said, "sure." And I got them to believing it and started laughing, and I said, "No, she is just, she is like a mother role in my life here.

This respondent was one of the youngest women interviewed, and she looked even younger than her chronological age. Therefore, the fact that she would want to be mothered was not surprising. During her interactions with correctional officers, she also conducted herself in a rather childlike manner. While she was describing the nature of what she perceives to be a family-like relationship, her remarks indicated that other women found her calling another woman "Mom" confusing. If the establishment of kinship networks were widespread and pervasive within the institution, others would not be surprised at the use of such titles. Respondents suggested that structured or formal family roles were not performed in this prison even though some older women might be perceived as behaving in a motherly fashion.

Rather than being highly structured and important responses to the pains of imprisonment, family roles do not appear to play a significant part in the day-to-day lives of respondents. Even for those women who admit referring to others as, or considering someone, a family member, the expressions they make toward each other are more representative of respectful terms of endearment rather than acknowledgment of more formal kinship roles. Respondents do not perceive clearly defined family relationships as part of their interpersonal environment.

Discussion

Themes that emerged during analysis of these data were similar to findings reported previously in literature related to contemporary men's prisons (Irwin, 1980; Irwin & Austin, 1997; Johnson, 1996). Because of changes in the diversity of persons being committed to correctional institutions, as well as the move away from rehabilitation toward a more custodial function for prisons, there no longer exists a singular inmate code or subculture (Irwin, 1980; Irwin & Austin, 1997; Johnson, 1996). Instead, male prisons have become much more volatile and less cohesive institutions than those represented during the 1950s (Irwin, 1980; Irwin & Austin, 1997). Responses provided by these women suggest that similarly, changes in female prison subcultures may also be occurring. Rather than forming pseudofamilies and relatively caring dyadic relationships, these women demonstrate through their comments a fear of forming close relationships with other female prisoners. "Doing time" was perceived as being a solitary process, especially if one wanted to avoid as many problems as possible. Therefore, respondents really were hesitant about developing friendships with other prisoners. The prison subculture encountered by these women certainly appears different from the one experienced by women incarcerated in the 1960s, 1970s, and 1980s.

In some ways, the reactions of respondents were comparable with the experiences of their male counterparts. Like these women, Irwin (1980) noted that withdrawal also was one technique employed by some male inmates wishing to avoid conflicts in their unstable prison environments. Male prisoners increasingly choose to avoid the more communal areas of the correctional institution and limit their personal interactions to a few trusted friends in an effort to survive their confinement (Irwin, 1980).

These findings suggest that in some ways the experiences of women in prison coincide with those of their male counterparts. Specifically, the diversified and stratified contemporary prison subcultures present frightening, unstable living environments for both groups of offenders.

In summary, comments made by respondents suggest changes in the interpersonal environment of women's prisons. Because this study involves a small sample derived from a single correctional institution, the findings may not be generalizable to other prisons for women. The overall interpersonal environment was depicted by respondents as being one that is manipulative and distrustful. Intimate sexual relationships are formed primarily on the basis of game playing and economic manipulation. Strong kinship networks previously observed in women's prisons were essentially nonexistent in this facility.

There may be several possible explanations for why the experiences of these respondents differed from those reported by earlier researchers (Burkhart, 1973; Giallombardo, 1966; Ward & Kassebaum, 1965). One factor that may account for the lack of cohesiveness among inmates is the change in the physical environment of women's prisons. Early studies were conducted in the 1960s and 1970s when many women's facilities were built around the cottage system, wherein women were assigned to homelike dwellings. Giallombardo (1966) noted that cottages were remnants of the reform movement during which time the emphasis was placed on rehabilitating fallen women. Reformers believed these women might be more easily rehabilitated if they were incarcerated in facilities that were reminiscent of home. Perhaps living in a cottage setting facilitated the formation of dyadic homosexual relationships based on more positive motives than economic manipulation.

Likewise, a homelike environment might be more conducive to the formation of family networks than cells or dormitory settings. Individual living rooms, kitchens, and dining rooms would be more conducive to facilitating a family-like environment than more institutional contexts. The prison where this research was conducted used a series of dormitories to house the inmates, with one centralized kitchen and dining room used by all the women. Some of these dormitory rooms held up to 10 women, and the smallest rooms had at least 4 women per room. Perhaps this kind of living arrangement is not conducive for the development of intimate relationships or kinship networks.

Another plausible explanation for the change is related to the passage of time itself. Early research suggested that the reason for the formation of sexual and kinship relationships was a cultural expectation regarding women. Giallombardo (1966) speculated that by forming these kinds of relationships in prison, female inmates were simply responding to these cultural expectations about gender roles. Perhaps female inmates incarcerated in the 1990s are responding to different cultural expectations for women in general. Perhaps female inmates bring with them alternative perceptions about acceptable roles for women. On the basis of the comments of respondents, one might question whether these individuals additionally are not as strongly tied to their various social roles as might be expected. These respondents did not seem to be strongly invested in any particular social roles, including those related to gender.

Perhaps the most promising explanations involve the changing nature of prisons in general. As noted previously, the social environment described by the women in this prison is similar in nature to that portrayed in literature pertaining to male correctional institutions. Contemporary prisons are more open systems rather than the stereotypical "total" institution considered representative of all correctional facilities in the past. Inmates are no longer completely closed off from the rest of society. Male and female prisoners can maintain contact with significant others and continue to be influenced by the larger culture through television, radio, movies, correspondence, literature, and visits with family members.

Moreover, the inmate culture has become more complex and complicated due to the importation of various lifestyles and backgrounds by a divergent inmate population. The influences male and female prisoners bring with them to the correctional institution are now considered to be more significant than the indigenous deprivations associated with prisons. Such social influences have contributed to the demise of a singular prison subculture. Both male and female inmates may come to perceive withdrawal and social isolation as the best techniques for adjusting to prison life. Obviously, such a modification in the subculture of women's prisons would not necessarily be viewed as a positive change. Although feminist criminologists have been advocating equality in services for women offenders, creating male-based programs and environments has not been the goal. Supporters of gender-responsive services for adolescent girls and adult women offenders recognize the neccessity of designing institutional programs and environments that address the unique gender and cultural needs of the women confined therein.

References

Alarid, L. F. (1997). Female inmate subcultures. In J. W. Marquart & J. R. Sorensen (Eds.), *Correctional contexts: Contemporary and classical readings* (pp. 134–139). Los Angeles: Roxbury.

Bell, R. R. (1976). *Social deviance*. Homewood, IL: Dorsey.

Bloom, B., Chesney-Lind, M., & Owen, B. (1994). *Women in California prisons: Hidden victims of the war on drugs*. San Francisco: Center on Juvenile and Criminal Justice.

Bogdan, R. C., & Biklen, S. K. (1992). *Qualitative research for education* (2nd ed.). Boston: Allyn & Bacon.

Boritch, H. (1992). Gender and criminal court outcomes: An historic analysis. *Criminology, 30*, 293–321.

Bureau of Justice Statistics. (1999). *Prison statistics*. Retrieved July 27, 2000, from the World Wide Web: http://www.ojp.usdoj.gov/bjs/prisons.htm

Burkhart, K. W. (1973). *Women in prison*. New York: Popular Library.

Chesney-Lind, M. (1986). Women and crime: The female offender. *Signs, 12*, 78–96.

Chesney-Lind, M. (1991). Patriarchy, prisons, and jails: A critical look at trends in women's incarceration. *The Prison Journal, 71*, 51–67.

Chesney-Lind, M., & Rodriguez, N. (1983). Women under lock and key: A view from the inside. *The Prison Journal, 62*, 47–65.

Culbertson, R. G., & Fortune, E. P. (1984). Women in crime and prison. In R. G. Culbertson (Ed.), *Order under law* (2nd ed., pp. 240–254). Prospect Heights, IL: Waveland.

Faith, K. (1993). *Unruly women: The politics of confinement and resistance*. Vancouver: Press Gang.

Feinman, C. (1983). An historical overview of the treatment of incarcerated women: Myths and realities of rehabilitation. *The Prison Journal, 62*, 12–24.

Fletcher, B. R., Shaver, L. D., & Moon, D. G. (1993). *Women prisoners: A forgotten population*. Westport, CT: Praeger.

Fogel, C. I. (1993). Hard time: The stressful nature of incarceration for women. *Issues in Mental Health Nursing, 14*, 367–377.

Genders, E., & Player, E. (1991). Women lifers: Assessing the experience. *The Prison Journal, 70*, 46–57.

Giallombardo, R. (1966). *Society of women: A study of a women's prison*. New York: John Wiley.

Girshick, L. B. (1999). *No safe haven: Stories of women in prison*. Boston: Northeastern University Press.

Goetting, A., & Howsen, R. M. (1983). Women in prison: A profile. *The Prison Journal, 62*, 27–45.

Hassine, V. (1996). *Life without parole: Living in prison today*. Los Angeles: Roxbury.

Hawkins, R. (1995). Inmate adjustments in women's prisons. In K. C. Haas & G. P. Alpert (Eds.), *The dilemmas of corrections: Contemporary readings* (3rd ed., pp. 103–122). Prospect Heights, IL: Waveland.

Irwin, J. (1980). *Prisons in turmoil*. Boston: Little, Brown.

Irwin, J., & Austin, J. (1997). *It's about time: America's imprisonment binge* (2nd ed.). Belmont, CA: Wadsworth.

Johnson, R. (1996). *Hard time: Understanding and reforming the prison* (2nd ed.). Belmont, CA: Wadsworth.

Larsen, J., & Nelson, J. (1984). Women, friendship, and adaptation to prison. *Journal of Criminal Justice, 12*, 601–615.

Leger, R. (1987). Lesbianism among women prisoners: Participants and nonparticipants. *Criminal Justice and Behavior, 14*, 463–479.

Lofland, J., & Lofland, L. H. (1995). *Analyzing social settings: A guide to qualitative observation and analysis* (3rd ed.). Belmont, CA: Wadsworth.

MacKenzie, D. L., Robinson, J. W., & Campbell, C. S. (1989). Long-term incarceration of female offenders: Prison adjustment and coping. *Criminal Justice and Behavior, 16*, 223–238.

Maher, L., & Daly, K. (1996). Women in the street-level drug economy: Continuity or change? *Criminology, 34*, 465–491.

Maxwell, J. A. (1996). *Qualitative research design: An interactive approach*. Thousand Oaks, CA: Sage.

McCarthy, B. R. (1980). Inmate mothers: The problems of separation and reintegration. *Journal of Offender Counseling, Services, and Rehabilitation, 4*, 199–212.

Merlo, A. V., & Pollock, J. M., (1995). *Women, law, and social control*. Needham Heights, MA: Allyn & Bacon.

Miles, M. B., & Huberman, A. M. (1994). *Qualitative data analysis: An expanded sourcebook* (2nd ed.). Thousand Oaks, CA: Sage.

Morash, M., Haarr, R. N., & Rucker, L. (1994). A comparison of programming for women and men in U. S. prisons in the 1980s. *Crime & Delinquency, 40*, 197–221.

Nagel, I. H., & Johnson, B. L. (1994). The role of gender in a structured sentencing system: Equal treatment, policy choices, and the sentencing of female offenders under the United States sentencing guidelines. *Journal of Criminal Law and Criminology, 85*, 181–221.

Owen, B. (1998). *In the mix: Struggle and survival in a women's prison*. Albany: State University of New York Press.

Patton, M. Q. (1990). *Qualitative evaluation and research methods* (2nd ed.). Newbury Park, CA: Sage.

Pollock, J. M. (1998). *Counseling women in prison*. Thousand Oaks, CA: Sage.

Pollock-Byrne, J. (1990). *Women, prison, and crime*. Pacific Grove, CA: Brooks/Cole.

Propper, A. (1982). Make-believe families and homosexuality among imprisoned girls. *Criminology, 20*, 127–139.

Rafter, N. H. (1990). *Partial justice* (2nd ed.). New Brunswick, NJ: Transaction Publishers.

Simon, R. J., & Landis, J. (1991). *The crimes women commit, the punishments they receive*. Lexington, MA: Lexington Books.

Steffensmeier, D. (1993). National trends in female arrests, 1960–1990: Assessment and recommendation for research. *Journal of Quantitative Criminology, 9*, 411–439.

Strauss, A. (1987). *Qualitative analysis for social scientists*. New York: Cambridge University Press.

Strauss, A., & Corbin, J. (1990). *Basics of qualitative research: Grounded theory procedures and techniques*. Newbury Park, CA: Sage.

Sykes, G. M. (1958). *The society of captives: A study of a maximum security prison*. Princeton, NJ: Princeton University Press.

U.S. Department of Justice. (1991). *Women in prison: Survey of state prison inmates*. Washington, DC: Government Printing Office.

U.S. Department of Justice. (1997). *News release*. Washington, DC: Author (http://www.ojp.usdoj.gov).

Ward, D. A., & Kassebaum, G. G. (1965). *Women's prison: Sex and social structure*. Chicago: Aldine.

THE PRISON JOURNAL, Vol. 80 No. 4, December 2000, 442–468.

Part 3: Relationships outside Prison

When offenders are sentenced to prison, not only are their abilities to do what they want restricted, but so too are the abilities of their friends and family members. When we talk about the relationships that prison inmates have with others outside of the prison, the discussion is restricted to thinking only about family members and close friends. In almost all instances, these (and not all of these) are the only persons with whom inmates have opportunities for interactions. One of the problems in looking at these relationships for prisoners, however, is that there simply is not very much research on this issue. This is due, in part, to the difficulties of carrying out such research, and may also be due to our beliefs that inmates do not—and should not—be allowed to maintain contacts outside the prison. Loved ones' opportunities for contacting and interacting with offenders are restricted and, in a practical sense, often eliminated. Because of the location of prisons, visiting may not be possible. The financial costs, time restrictions, and lack of telephone privileges may mean that speaking with loved ones is impossible. Illiteracy can make even the simple solution of writing and receiving letters an unrealistic option for many inmates. As a result, many of the relationships that prison inmates have with individuals outside of prison can be seriously harmed, if not terminated completely.

The most important relationship for many adults is their relationship with their children. This can be the most painful to lose. For prison inmates, this is no exception. A majority of prison inmates are parents, many of whom have minor children. The first two articles in this section discuss the effects of inmates' losing their opportunities to live with, see, and sometimes even maintain communications with their children.

In the first article, Sharp and Marcus-Mendoza report on their research with female inmates, centering their discussion on how these women perceive their incarceration to have affected their family structures and members. What this research reveals is that when mothers are sent to prison, their children are typically raised in foster homes, in state-run institutions, or by other family members. However, many of the family members who take in female inmates' children have histories of abuse. This means that when a woman is incarcerated, her children may be put into a dangerous position where they are susceptible to abuse and victimization.

The second article in this section reports the findings of Lanier's research concerning the experiences of male inmates who are incarcerated and separated from their children. Whereas Sharp and Marcus-Mendoza report that it is highly uncommon for a female inmate to have her children raised by their father, Lanier indicates that it is the norm for male inmates' children to be raised by their mother. Men's experience of losing their role as a parent is decidedly different from the experience of incarcerated mothers. However, this does not mean that men do not suffer from the loss of this relationship, even if they had limited contact and interactions with their children prior to their incarceration.

The last article in this section looks at one of the primary ways that inmates have to maintain their relationships with loved ones, including their children, outside of prison. Casey-Acevedo and Bakken examine the dynamics of female inmates' visits from family members and how inmates perceive and respond to those visits. While most inmates say that they highly value and look forward to visits with loved ones, many inmates also eventually ask their families not to come visit. There are two reasons inmates may request their families not visit. First, inmates often find it too emotionally stressful and difficult to visit, especially at the end of and immediately following a visit. Second, many inmates feel, especially when their loved ones live significant distances from the prison, that visits are too difficult and expensive for family members. As a result, many inmates, including those with young children, have few, if any, visits and see their relationships with loved ones outside of prison deteriorate and often simply fade away.

Is this one of the things that prisons are supposed to achieve? How does the loss of one's family fit with the goals of the criminal justice system? Where do these types of punishments fit into an inmate's sentence? How do one's relationships, or lack thereof, contribute to the punishment and/or rehabilitation of inmates? Keep these questions in mind as you read the articles in this section.

Discussion Questions

Relationships outside Prison

1. How are an inmate's relationships with family members positively and negatively affected by the experience of going to prison?
2. Do male or female inmates have more difficulties maintaining relationships with their family members, especially their children? Support your answer with specifics.
3. How likely is the visitation process to promote solid and lasting relationships for inmates and their families?

9. It's a Family Affair: Incarcerated Women and Their Families

Susan F. Sharp
Susan T. Marcus-Mendoza

In the United States, incarceration rates are increasing at an alarming rate. In particular, the incarceration of women is increasing. Oklahoma has the highest rate of female incarceration in the nation, and drug offenders comprise a significant proportion of these female inmates. Placing large numbers of women in prison may have serious implications not only for the women but also for their families, particularly their children. We surveyed 144 incarcerated female drug offenders in Oklahoma, 96 of whom reported dependent children living with them prior to incarceration. The data included the women's perceptions of the effect of their incarceration on their families as well as an examination of the potential for serious problems due to placement of the children. The study indicates that many children are placed with families that have a history of abuse, which suggests that failure to consider the implications of incarcerating large numbers of women likely contributes to serious abuse risks for their children.

Introduction

Incarceration rates in the United States have increased dramatically over the past two decades, leading to a related increase in research into the causes and consequences of this increase. Until recently, most research has focused on male inmates (Belknap, 1996a; Belknap, 1996b; Girshick, 1999). However, the incarceration rate of females is increasing even more rapidly than that of males, making the study of female inmates of paramount importance (Snell & Morton, 1994; Wellisch, Prendergast & Anglin, 1994; Mumola & Beck, 1997; Chesney-Lind, 1998; Girshick, 1998; Morash, Bynum & Koons, 1998; Steffensmeier & Allan, 1998; Girshick, 1999).

As the number of inmates has increased, researchers have begun examining the benefits versus the costs of massive incarceration programs (Clear, 1996; Watts & Nightingale, 1996). In particular, researchers have become interested in the effects of incarceration on the families of inmates. There is still an implicit assumption that "inmate" and "male" are irrevocably linked and that "family" means "wives and children" (cf., Daniel & Barrett, 1981; Hairston & Lockett, 1985; Hairston & Lockett, 1987; Fishman, 1990; Hairston, 1990; King, 1993; Hagan, 1996). However, recent research has indicated that the impact on inmates and their families varies by sex of the inmate (Sharp et al., 1999). Specifically, female inmates are often sole caretakers of minor children, and it is these children who are most impacted by the women's incarceration (Harris, 1993; Belknap,

1996b; Chesney-Lind, 1997; Girshick, 1998; Girshick, 1999; Sharp et al., 1999; Zaplin & Dougherty, 1998).

In the current study, we explore from the inmates' perspectives the effects of incarceration on female drug offenders and their children. First, we explore whether the amount and source of support for the families of these inmates have significantly changed since the inmates' incarceration. We also examine the placement of children of these women, focusing on children who were living with the inmates just prior to incarceration. We then explore the potential for abuse of these children by juxtaposing the inmates' self-reported abuse histories with the current placement of the children. Finally, we examine negative emotional and behavioral outcomes among the children.

We administered a survey to 144 incarcerated drug offenders, asking about their childhood, their drug use histories, their lives immediately prior to incarceration, and their perceptions of the effects of their incarceration on their children. The focus of this paper is on the effects of incarceration on their children, and we have limited most of our analyses to the 96 women who reported having children with them immediately prior to incarceration.

Female Inmates in the United States: An Overview

To understand the effects of incarceration on women and their families, we must first understand who the inmates are and what their experiences have been. Incarcerated women in state prisons tend to be non-white, and over the age of twenty-five. Although almost half have never been married, at least three-fourths have children. Most of those who are mothers report living with a minor child prior to incarceration (Snell & Morton, 1994; Belknap, 1996b; Girshick, 1999). Almost half the women serving time in state prisons have never been convicted of a violent offense. However, despite the strong link between drugs and women's crimes, less than thirty percent have received any drug treatment prior to incarceration (Snell & Morton, 1994; see also Belknap, 1996b).

The increase in the rate of female incarceration is not necessarily due to an increase in female criminality as has been suggested by some (Adler, 1975; Simon, 1975). In fact, the data suggest that female crime today is not that different from in the past. The feminization of poverty is one potential explanation for the increase in female crime. Larceny, fraud, and drug offenses have increased among women, crimes frequently linked to economic position (Steffensmeier, 1980; Chilton & Datesman, 1987; Belknap, 1996a; Belknap, 1996b; Chesney-Lind, 1997; Girshick, 1998, 1999). However, it may be that female criminality is not the primary explanation for the increased incarceration rates for women. The drive for gender equality has contributed to the increased incarceration of women in an indirect way. Parity in sentencing and "get tough on drugs" policies have replaced past "chivalrous" policies (Chesney-Lind, 1997).

Feminist critics have become concerned that the American criminal justice system is particularly punitive toward women. Chesney-Lind suggests that "'the war on drugs' has become a war on women," pointing out that over one-third of the women incarcerated for drug offenses are convicted of possession only (Chesney-Lind, 1997, p. 147). However, this is not necessarily the public's perception. A recent study in Oklahoma indicated that fewer than 6% of judges believed that women were treated harshly by the criminal justice system. These judges instead attributed the growth in incarceration to an increase in the aggressiveness of female felons (Ochie & Ngenge, 1996). However, other research in the state suggests that this perception is not necessarily accurate. Drug offenses account for over one-third of new incarcerations, with almost half of the female inmates imprisoned for drug offenses convicted of possession only (Sandhu, Al-Mosleh & Chown, 1994). In a society that values female chastity and submissiveness, the poor, single drug-using mother represents an affront to conventional morals (Schur, 1984; Belknap, 1996a; Chesney-Lind, 1997; Girshick, 1999). Thus, "African American and other women of color tend to receive more severe responses by the system" and "poorer women receive more severe responses than wealthier women" (Belknap, 1996a, p. 73).

Incarcerated Women and Histories of Trauma and Abuse

When women are incarcerated, they experience trauma from the disruption of their pre-prison lives. Separation from their children can produce stress (Belknap, 1996b; Boudin, 1998). This is particularly true because female inmates are often placed in institutions far away from family members, thus limiting visitation (Sobel, 1982; Owen, 1998). Potential loss of custody and the motherhood role may also be demoralizing (Sobel, 1982; Koban, 1983; Hairston, 1991; Harris, 1993), and reunification with their children often becomes a primary goal of incarcerated mothers (Owen, 1998). Separation from children can have serious long-term consequences for both women and their children. Indeed, some research suggests that the destruction of family relationships may be linked to higher rates of recidivism among inmates (Light, 1993) and higher rates of delinquency among their children (Clear, 1996).

For many of these women, disruption and trauma are already familiar aspects of life. Many experienced instability during childhood. About one-third of the female inmates in state prisons have reported histories of abuse (physical, sexual or both) before age 18 (Marcus-Mendoza, Sargent & Ho, 1994; Snell & Morton, 1994; Chesney-Lind, 1997; Marcus-Mendoza, Klein-Saffran & Lutze, 1998). Furthermore, over half have reported growing up in homes lacking two parents, and 17% have reported spending time in either a foster home or an institution. Almost half have immediate family members that have been incarcerated, and a third reported that while they were growing up, a parent or guardian abused alcohol or drugs (Snell & Morton, 1994). Similarly, violence and instability have characterized the adult lives of these women. Almost one-fourth of the women have experienced physical abuse after reaching age 18 (Snell & Morton, 1994; Owen & Bloom, 1995; Belknap, 1996b; Chesney-Lind, 1997).

Families of Female Prisoners

There is considerable evidence that family structure and relationships are linked to delinquency and criminality. However, there is a tendency to assume that the family/criminality association is a static one, focusing on how ineffective parenting (Gottfredson & Hirschi, 1990), family power relations (Hagan, Gillis & Simpson, 1988), or differential socialization (Sutherland & Cressey, 1978) contribute to delinquency. The basic assumption in these approaches is that family has some consistent effect on the tendency to become criminal. While there is merit in this approach, it fails to take into account the fact that a child's trajectory may be affected by stressors and events (Agnew, 1992). Indeed, there is a growing body of research that suggests that "shocks" occurring during childhood may result in sharp changes in both achievement and behavior (Menaghan et al., 1997; Kowaleski-Jones & Duncan, 1999). Incarceration of a parent causes suffering, and children may experience financial hardship, decreased quality of care, weakening of family bonds, and multiple placements (Hagan, 1996; Beatty, 1997). Parental incarceration has also been linked to poor school performance, aggressive behavior, teen pregnancy, and emotional problems (Beatty, 1997; Hairston, 1991; Johnston, 1995a; Johnston, 1995b; Kampfer, 1995; Moses, 1995).

Maternal incarceration causes specific problems. The majority of incarcerated mothers are the primary, and often sole, caretakers of minor children. Unlike children of male inmates, the children of incarcerated females may not live with the other parent during the incarceration period (Snell & Morton, 1994). The placement of these children is thus a matter of concern. Many of these children may have to move in with non-parental caretakers, including grandparents, aunts or uncles, and older siblings. In other cases, the children may be placed in institutions or with foster families (Harris, 1993; Snell & Morton, 1994). Placement of children can create additional problems. Unfamiliar surroundings and people (Sobel, 1982) as well as less than optimal parental substitutes (Bloom & Steinhart, 1993) may contribute to insecurity and emotional problems. Even when placed with grandparents, the living arrangements may create problems for the children, depending on the caregiver's age, financial resources, and stamina (Phillips & Harm, 1998). Furthermore, as described above, female inmates' families of origin are often characterized by alcoholism, addiction, and abuse. Thus, children may be placed in unstable and potentially harmful situations. Finally, children of incarcerated mothers are often separated from each other as well as from their mothers, leading to additional strain (Johnston, 1995b; Johnston, 1995c; Belknap, 1996b).

On the other hand, it is important to acknowledge that incarceration of a parent may sometimes have beneficial effects. In some cases, the parent's behavior may have endangered the child (Gabel & Johnston, 1995). Drug use in the home and association with other criminals can place children in unsafe circumstances. Obviously, the immediate safety of the children must be a primary consideration. Still, the trauma involved in parental incarceration often outweighs the benefits (Bloom & Steinhart, 1993; Clear, 1996; Gabel & Johnston, 1995).

Clearly, there is a need to collect detailed information concerning the families of female inmates. With the high rates of incarceration of females in Oklahoma, this state is particularly useful to assess the impact on families and children. In summary, in this study we examine several potential effects of women's incarceration on their children. First, we examine changes in sources of financial support for the families. Next, we focus on where the children who had lived with the inmate are currently living. We then examine the risk for abuse of these children. Finally, we examine negative emotional and behavioral outcomes for children of imprisoned women reported by the incarcerated mothers.

Findings

Demographics of Female Inmates in Oklahoma

Since we focus on the effects of maternal incarceration on children, most of the analyses are based on the subsample of women who reported that one or more of their children were living with them prior to incarceration. Examination of the data indicated that 66.7% (n = 96) of the women reported living with their minor children just prior to incarceration. These women reported 195 minor children who had been living with them, with a mean of 2.01 children in the home reported.

Overall, the women who reported having children in the home were little different from those who did not have children in the home. As might be expected, women reporting children in the home were slightly younger than those without children at home. The mean reported age of women with children in the home was 33.7 years, while the mean age of those without children was 37.8 ($t = 3.091, p \leq .01$). Racial composition was similar for the two groups of women. The modal category for self-reported race was White. However, African Americans and Native Americans were overrepresented. Indeed, previous research suggests that the African American incarceration rates in Oklahoma are more disproportionate than nationally (Sandhu, Al-Mosleh & Chown, 1994). Overall, the women reported similar educational achievement as well. The modal educational category was "high school graduation or GED" for both groups, but 37.6% (n = 36) of those with children in the home and 43.7% (n = 21) of those without children in the home did not complete high school.

We also examined the women's marital status as well as contemplated or actual divorce proceedings. Among women with children in the home, 21.9% (n = 21) were married, and divorce had been discussed in 57.1% (n = 12) of those marriages, and proceedings had been filed in 52.4% (n = 11). Among women without children, a similar pattern was noted, with 27.1% (n = 13) of the women without children reporting legal marriage, although fewer reported contemplated divorce or actual divorce proceedings (6.3% and 4.2% respectively). However, this does not present a completely accurate picture due to being restricted to legal marriages. More women reported common-law marriages than legal ones, with 33.3% (32) of those with children in the home and 27.1% (13) of those without children describing themselves as being in a common-law marriage. However, we did not determine the number of common-law marriages that have terminated since incarceration.

The women with children in the home did differ from those without children in the home across a number of legal dimensions. Notably, almost two-thirds of those without children (62.5%, n = 30) reported prior felony convictions, compared to about half (51.0%, n = 49) of the women with children in the home ($\chi^2 = 4.570$, $p \leq .05$). However, the two groups did not differ in terms of prior incarcerations, with around one-third of each group reporting prior incarcerations. It is also noteworthy that the women with children were more likely to report sentence lengths greater than four years (79.2%, n = 76) than the women without children at home at the time of incarceration (66.7%, n = 32) ($\chi^2 = 17.926$, $p \leq .001$). It may be that this difference is due to more serious crimes, such as possession of larger amounts of drugs. However, it may also be that the punitive attitude identified in earlier research is a factor (Sandhu, Al-Mosleh & Chown, 1994). Finally, women with children in the home (60.4%, n = 58) were significantly more likely than those without children (47.9%, n = 23) to report previous incarceration of a family member ($\chi^2 = 15.123$, $p \leq .001$).

Alcohol and Drug Use Histories

The two groups of women differed little in their alcohol and drug use histories. Those who had a child in the home at the time of incarceration reported that their first drink occurred on average at 16.0 years. Their first drug use occurred at 18.7 years on average, and 44.8% (n = 43) had received treatment. Those without a child in the home took their first drink on average at 14.6 years, their first drug at 17.4 years, and 43.8% (n = 21) had received treatment.

Effects of Incarceration on Family Income

In the remaining analyses, we focus solely on the women who reported living with children at the time of incarceration. Family income was affected by the subjects' incarceration. Only half of the sample responded to questions about prior family income, and about one-fourth provided estimates of family income subsequent to incarceration. Thus, the figures must be interpreted with caution. It may be that the women did not know actual income for either period, particularly for the period subsequent to incarceration. Nonetheless, the reported figures suggested that income was drastically reduced. Mean family income prior to incarceration was $29,402. In comparison, current estimates of family income were $10,693. To investigate this decrease, we asked the subjects about the sources of family income both prior to and subsequent to incarceration.

The inmates' own jobs represented the largest category of reported family income *prior* to incarceration (37.5%). In contrast, help from others was the most frequently reported *current* source of support for their families (33.3%). It is noteworthy that help from others had almost tripled since the subject's incarceration.

Indeed, all other reported sources of income appear to have decreased. Furthermore, it is also noteworthy that prior to incarceration 10.4% (n = 10) of the women reported child support as a source of income. At the time of the study, only 2.1% (n = 2) reported the family was receiving child support ($p \leq .01$). It may be that these women are simply unaware of whether child support continues to be paid. Nonetheless, this represents an 80% decrease of families reported to be receiving child support and thus a matter for concern and further investigation. The implications of these changes in source of income are somewhat alarming. When a mother is incarcerated, it appears that her children may lose not only her income but also virtually every other type of income. The families of who frequently take care of the inmates' children thus assume the brunt of the burden, despite the likelihood that they often can ill afford the additional expense.

Inmates' Perceptions and Concerns: Financial Impact

An open-ended question asked the women to describe their greatest concerns about the effect of their incarceration on their families. Some inmates focused on financial issues and living arrangements of their families. These inmates expressed concern about the disruption and hardships faced by their parents, spouses and children. Several were concerned about deprivations faced by their families, while others indicated they had been contributing to their family members' support, and thus the family was suffering. The following comments illustrate these concerns:

> My oldest daughter has custody of her brothers. It is very hard on them emotionally, mentally and financially. (37-year-old Native American)
>
> The stress and worry, not to mention the money my parents send me every month. (30-year-old white female)
>
> Not being able to take care of my elderly parent who is ill. (47-year-old black female)

Effects of Incarceration on Living Arrangements of Children

Subjects were also asked where children who had been with them prior to incarceration were currently living. The survey provided a range of possible answers, including the child's other parent, several relatives, relatives of the child's other parent, agencies, and foster placement. In Table 1, we present the women's responses. Unfortunately, the data do not allow us to determine the living situation for each dependent child. The women were asked to identify each living situation in which there was now a child who had been living with the subjects at the time of incarceration. Thus, we report the percentage of the 96 women reporting a child in each category of living arrangements, resulting in 133 reported placements. Obviously, some children are placed together. However, it is also apparent that in some cases siblings are separated into different placements.

TABLE 1 Current Living Arrangements of Children as Reported by Women with Dependent Children at the Time of Incarceration

Where is (are) the child(ren) who lived with you at the time of your incarceration?	*No. of inmates responding**
Child now with his/her other parent.	30.2% (29)
Child now with inmate's mother and/or father.	51.0% (49)
Child now with inmate's grandparent/other relative.	10.4% (10)
Child now with inmate's sibling.	15.6% (15)
Child with other parent's family.	8.3% (8)
Child with friends.	2.1% (2)
Child in foster home or agency.	7.3% (7)
Child in other setting.	11.5% (11)
Don't know where child is.	2.1% (2)

*The percentages are based on the 96 women who had children living with them at the time they were incarcerated. These women had 195 children living with them that had to be placed, resulting in 133 different placements. The data did not allow us to determine the total number of children living in each situation.

Only 30.2% (n = 29) of the women reported that a dependent child currently lived with the child's other parent. The majority (51.9%, n = 49) indicated that children now lived with the respondent's family, primarily with one or both parents of the inmate or with the inmate's sibling. In a number of cases, women had children who were not currently living together. Almost one-fifth of the women (19.8%, n = 19) reported children in two or more places, indicating that incarceration had resulted in separation of siblings, although we were unable to determine the number of children experiencing sibling separation. One woman described her concerns about this type of situation:

> My parents keep my 2 Boys I am fine with that but my 2 mo old is living with a Christian Organized Housing program and though I trust them with her I wish it didnt have to be. (33-year-old white female)

This woman went on to express concern about reuniting the family after her release:

> My boy's are going to need counseling as a family unit . . . and my 2 mo. old I fear will not have a bonding prosses with me.

Placement of Children in Potentially Abusive Situations

Since slightly more than half the women reported their children were now living with one or both of the inmates' parents, we next explored the parental situation when the inmate was growing up. First, we asked about parental substance abuse. Many subjects reported family histories of alcohol or drug abuse. In response to a question about whether certain family members had ever experienced a problem with alcohol or drug abuse, 48.9% (n = 47) of the women reported that their own father had a problem with alcohol or drugs. An additional 20.8% (n = 20) identified their mothers as having alcohol or drug problems. These figures demonstrate that a large number of the children of incarcerated women are living in homes that have been affected by alcoholism, whether an active alcoholic or addict remains in the home or not. Thus, the living situations of these children may likely be no more stable than prior to their mothers' incarceration.

We also explored the degree to which the inmates had experienced childhood abuse. Almost two-fifths (37.5%, n = 36) of the sample reported sexual abuse prior to age 18, and 42.7% (n = 41) reported physical abuse, 26.0% (n = 25) of the women reported experiencing both types of abuse. While the abuse experienced by all of these women was distressing, we were particularly concerned about whether the children of the inmates were currently placed in homes with histories of child abuse and violence. The survey included questions regarding whether either or both parents had been violent toward the subject or another family member during her childhood.

Table 2 presents the number of subjects reporting their children currently lived with the subject's mother or father, cross-tabulated with responses to whether either the mother or father had been violent toward family members while the subject was growing up. It is readily apparent that at least some children are placed in a home that was violent during the inmate's childhood. It is disturbing that a child would be placed with any individual with a history of abusive and violent behavior. However, it is even more alarming that abusive parents appear as likely as non-abusive parents to become primary caretakers of their grandchildren. The data in Table 2 indicate that abusive and non-abusive families are equally likely to be the reported caretakers of the women's children (χ^2 = .040, not significant). Although not reported in Table 2 we also examined whether the children were actually living with the individual with the history of violence. The results are disturbing, with 8.3% (n = 8) of the women reporting their child or children are now living with an inmate's mother who was violent, and 3.1% (n = 3) reporting children living with a violent father. Even when the child is not living with the violent individual, there is still reason for concern. An additional 6.3% are living with an inmate's sibling who quite likely experienced violence as a child and thus is at increased risk to be violent himself or herself.

TABLE 2 Cross-Tabulation of Reported Living Situations: Dependent Children Living with Subject's Mother and/or Father by Whether Subject's Parent Was Violent[a]

	Inmate's Mother or Father Violent Toward Inmate or Her Family Members When Inmate Was a Child		
Inmate Reports Child/Children Live(s) with Inmate's Parent(s)	Yes	No	Total
Yes	24.0% (23)	25.0% (24)	49.0% (47)
No	26.0% (25)	25.0% (24)	51.0% (49)
Total	50.0% (48)	50.0% (48)	100.0% (96)
	$\chi^2 = .040$		

[a]The *ns* and percentages based on the 96 women who reported that their child or children lived with them prior to incarceration.

In the open-ended questions, however, the women did not discuss the issue of abusive families. When asked to share their feelings about their children's current living situation, the subjects' responses fell into two broad categories. Some subjects indicated that they felt good about the situation. Generally, these responses focused on how family members were providing good care. A few of these reported that their children were with the other parent, who was providing good care to them. Their answers tended to be short and to the point.

> I'm very comfortable with my son living with his Father. I not at all pleased with where they are living but I know his Father takes very good care of him. (44-year-old black female)

In most cases, family members besides the child's other parent were providing care. As described above, the most common "other" caretakers reported were the inmates' parents and siblings. Inmates tended to report positive feelings about their children's situation in these cases, often expressing relief that the children were safe and receive good care.

> I feel good about it. She with my mother. (28-year-old black female)

> I'm very lucky that my mother and step-brother take very good care of my son. (27-year-old white female)

Other inmates, however, reported mixed feelings. While acknowledging that the children's physical and safety needs were largely met, these inmates also expressed concern about the children's emotional needs. These inmates tended to focus on the mother-child bond, expressing concern that their children were unhappy due to their absence.

> They Love their grandparents, but it is hurting them terribly Bad, we have never been away from each other till now. They want me home. (31-year-old white female)

> I need to be home with her. She will be a year old this month. I haven't gotten to bond. My Mother takes good care of her and so does the organization A Touch of Love. (25-year-old black female)

In a few cases, children were not with family members. In the quote immediately above, the woman reports separated children, with one living in an institutionalized setting. This woman went on to say:

> My baby is not able to experience a bonding prosses with me or really know me. (33-year-old white female)

The last two comments illustrated a special concern for some inmates. Inmates who are pregnant when they enter the criminal justice system are faced with a difficult situation. The woman and her child are often separated shortly after birth, excluding any opportunity for bonding. Oklahoma Department of Corrections policy requires movement to a hospital for the actual birth, followed by return of the inmate to her correction facility within 24 to 48 hours. Virtually no time with the newborn infant is allowed these mothers. The administrator responsible for overseeing these births reported that the infants are placed in a number of different situations. In some cases, the mother's family takes the child and gets temporary custody. In other cases, the child becomes a ward of the state and may be placed in a foster home, an institution, or put up for adoption. In the cases where the mother does not permanently lose custody, upon her release she may wish to regain custody of the child. However, the adjustment period may be quite difficult due to the lack of maternal-child bonding.

Emotional and Behavioral Problems Experienced by Children

Changes in family income, separation of siblings, new living arrangements, and the possibility of being placed in a home with a history of violence are problematic in and of themselves. However, we also wanted to explore the degree to which these factors and separation from the mother might be affecting the children. The final close-ended question addressed the inmates' perceptions of problems that their children had experienced. Inmates were asked if any of their minor children had experienced a number of problems. Answer choices include "no," "yes, but it was a problem before I was incarcerated," "yes, and has only been a problem since I was incarcerated," "was a problem before I was incarcerated but is not now," and "don't know." Percentages of inmates indicating the problem had only incurred *since* their incarceration are presented in Table 3.

TABLE 3 Inmate Perceptions of the Effects of Incarceration on Their Children

	Preschool (*n* = 41)	*Age 6–11* (*n* = 40)	*Age 12–18* (*n* = 34)	*TOTAL* (*N* = 94)
Yes, it is a problem but only since I was incarcerated				
Bad grades?	n/a	27.5% (11)	23.5% (8)	20.2% (19)
Dropped out of school?	n/a	0.0% (0)	20.6% (7)	7.5% (7)
Trouble with guardian?	0.0% (0)	17.5% (7)	26.5% (9)	17.0% (16)
Running away?	0.0% (0)	7.5% (3)	11.8% (4)	7.5% (7)
Child arrested?	0.0% (0)	0.0% (0)	5.9% (2)	2.1% (2)
Problems with alcohol?	0.0% (0)	5.0% (2)	14.7% (5)	7.5% (7)
Problems with other drugs?	0.0% (0)	2.5% (1)	8.8% (3)	4.3% (4)
Depression of child?	24.4% (10)	37.5% (15)	41.2% (14)	41.5% (39)
Child became pregnant or got somebody pregnant?	n/a	0.0% (0)	8.8% (3)	3.2% (3)

*Numbers are reported as a percentage of the number of women indicating a child in each age group lived with her prior to incarceration. The total percentages are based on the 94 women who answered these questions.

The data indicate that bad grades, expulsion, and dropping out of school were perceived problems, as were problems with guardians, and that these problems varied by age of the child. Parents perceived their preschool children as depressed 24.4% (n = 10) of the time. In addition to 37.5% (n = 15) of the subjects reporting problems with depression in children ages 6 through 11, children in this age group were also perceived as having problems with bad grades (23.5%, n = 11), guardians (17.5%, n = 7), and running away (7.5%, n = 3). Finally, the subjects reported that their adolescent children (ages 12–18) had difficulties with school, with 23.5% (n = 8) reporting their children now had bad grades and 20.6% (n = 7) reporting their children had dropped out. Additionally, 26.5% (n = 9) of the women reported their adolescent children had problems with guardians, 5.9% (2) reported arrests, 14.7% (5) reported adolescent children having problems with alcohol, 8.8% reported problems with drugs, and 41.2% (14) reported problems with depression. It is noteworthy that the most often reported problem was depression in all age categories. Indeed, 41.5% of the 94

The women seemed to be very aware of the negative emotional effects of their incarceration on their children. Their responses to open-ended questions reflected concern about emotional damage to family members, especially to their children. For the inmates, concern was less about the damage to their relationships with family members and more about harm suffered by family members.

> My children are missing out on everything a healthy home environment offers. I'm afraid they have deep abandonment fears. (38-year-old white female)
>
> I don't want my son to be lonely missing me and worrying about me which take away from his happiness and his ability to concentrate on his school work. (44-year-old-black female)
>
> They are depress. (39-year-old black female)

The survey also included questions about ways that they believed their families were better or worse off. In general, inmates appeared to believe that the effects were primarily negative, although there were some notable exceptions, which we will examine. The women expressed feelings that their families had grown apart, family members were angry, and that children had gotten into trouble. Others expressed concern about the supervision their children were receiving.

> My Children have no supervision—No Guidance—No Love. (39-year-old black female)
>
> My oldest daughter just running crazy out there. (36-year-old black female)

One female inmate, reflecting on the ways in which her family was affected, may have had a moment of clarity, however. This woman reported her children's grandmother was no longer in the home, suggesting:

> They might miss her more then they miss me. (37-year-old black female)

As mentioned above, a few subjects indicated that their families were better off as a result of their incarceration. The most frequently mentioned issues had to do with placing the family in danger, having drugs around the children, and poor parenting skills. These concerns were realistic, as 64.6% (n = 62) of the women with children in the home indicated they had kept drugs in the home while the children were there, and 4.9% of the entire sample (n = 7) said they had used with their child. The women's comments indicated that their own involvement with drugs and crime had created unsafe conditions and worry for family members that were alleviated by their incarceration.

> I was involved with gang members. (37-year-old black female)
>
> They don't have to worry about where I am and what I'm doing. (36-year-old white female)

Discussion and Conclusions

The primary purpose of this research has been to explore the unintended effects of incarceration on female drug-offenders and their children. By examining their pre-incarceration situations as well as the inmates' current perceptions, we have started to explore how incarceration may have changed the families' situations. Our study of incarcerated female drug offenders reveals that many of the same devastating effects of imprisoning women found in other parts of the United States are apparent in Oklahoma. According to the women in our study, incarceration has a negative impact on the family structure and on children. This is consistent with other studies that suggest that incarceration weakens families (Gabel & Johnston, 1995; Clear, 1996). Furthermore, our study indicates that incarceration is contributing to increases in family instability. Women in our study cite tenuous marital relationships. Less than one-fourth of the women were legally married. However, over half of the married women reported that divorce proceedings had been initiated since incarceration. If this trend is similar for common-law marriages, the implications are depressing. Almost half of the families that are intact at the time of incarceration could be expected to end, leading to even larger numbers of children living in single-parent households following the mothers' release.

Children may be affected in many ways when the mother is incarcerated. Like Belknap (1996b), we found that frequently, siblings are separated from each other as well as from the parent. This is particularly disturbing, as it can represent even more uncertainty and loss to the children. The women in our study also describe negative effects on parent-child relationships, which may disappear or diminish in quality. Many express in their own words the lost of their parental status and identity, and that, in consequence, their children are suffering. According to these mothers, their children experience difficulties at school and may have problems with alcohol, drugs, and depression. Depression was extremely common among the children of all ages, and this could lead to long-term problems such as addiction.

Furthermore, incarceration has economic repercussions for families, who may face not only reduced income but also loss of their home (Phillips & Harm, 1998). Inmates are distressed when they are no longer able to provide financial support, further harming their families and their own parental identity. As found in earlier studies, the children of the subjects frequently move in with the inmate's mother or siblings (Harris, 1993; Snell & Morton, 1994). Yet, little information is available on the income and assets of these new caretakers. The addition of children to an existing household could increase the financial burdens of these families. Bloom and Steinhart (1993) found that frequently children had to move in with family members or others who lacked resources needed to be effective parental substitutes. The data from the current study indicate that not only do these individuals lack adequate resources, but that many of the resources available to the families of female inmates prior to incarceration are no longer available.

Prior research indicates that many female inmates have experienced either sexual or physical abuse as a child (Chesney-Lind, 1997). This has important implications in terms of future problems that both the inmates and their families may experience. Inmates may need counseling or therapy to resolve prior trauma in order to increase their likelihood of remaining drug-free upon parole (Marcus-Mendoza, Sargent & Ho, 1994; Snell & Morton, 1994; Belknap, 1996a; Belknap, 1996b; Chesney-Lind, 1997). Without intervention, the cycle of abuse and chemical dependency may continue, and the children of these inmates may themselves become victims of parental abuse. The trauma of imprisonment may exacerbate the problems of inmates with histories of abuse, in turn affecting their ability to function and be productive upon release (Belknap, 1996a; Belknap, 1996b; Heney & Kristiansen, 1997). Currently, there is little trauma counseling available to them, and chemical dependency treatment is also limited. Thus, it is likely they will return to society at best with no resolution of their problems and in many cases with still greater emotional damage (Belknap, 1996b).

One of the most striking implications of our study is the potential effect on children of the inmates. Inmates' experiences of abuse have implications for their children during their separation and point to the importance of gaining additional information about the abuse histories of the inmates. We need to know who their perpetrators were, as well as whether the caretakers of inmates' children are in fact past abusers. We have shown that substantial numbers of female inmates report histories of physical or sexual abuse while growing up, and that many report parental alcohol and drug problems. We have also demonstrated that the children of female inmates are often living with the inmate's family. Indeed, several women in our study who reported that a parent abused them now report a child living with that parent. Other children are living in homes where violence is part of their family background and therefore may potentially be abusive. This is one of the most alarming aspects of our findings. The women in this study, however, did not address this possibility when asked to voice their concerns. One possible explanation is that it is simply too painful to discuss. Another is related to women's concerns about regaining custody of their children after they are released. Having their children placed with family members increases the likelihood of regaining custody. Children who have become wards of the state are less likely to be returned to the inmate's custody. Thus, some of these women may see placing their children with their own past abusers as simply the lesser of two evils.

References

Adler, F. (1975). *Sisters in crime.* New York: McGraw-Hill.

Agnew, R. (1992). Foundation for a general strain theory of crime and delinquency. *Criminology,* 30:47–87.

Beatty, C. (1997). *Parents in prison: Children in crisis.* Washington, DC: Child Welfare League.

Belknap, J. (1996a). *The Invisible Woman: Gender, Crime and Justice.* Belmont: Wadsworth.

——— (1996b). "Access to Programs and Health Care for Incarcerated Women." *Federal Probation*, 60:34–39.

Bloom, B. & Steinhart, D. (1993). *Why Punish the Children?: A Reappraisal of the Children of Incarcerated Mothers in America.* San Francisco: National Council on Crime and Delinquency.

Boudin, K. (1998), Lessons from a mother's program in prison: A psychosocial approach supports women and their children. *Women & Therapy,* 21: 103–125.

Chesney-Lind, M. (1997). *The female offender: Girls, women, and crime.* Thousand Oaks: Sage.

——— (1998). Foreword. In R. T. Zaplin (ed.), *Female offenders: Critical perspectives and effective interventions* (pp. xiii–xv). Gaithersburg, MD: Aspen.

Chilton, R. & Datesman, S. K. (1987). Gender, race, and crime: An analysis of urban trends. *Gender & Society,* 1:152–171.

Clear, T. (1996). Backfire: When incarceration increases crime. *Journal of the Oklahoma Criminal Justice Research Consortium,* 3:7–17.

Covington, S. S. (1998). Women in prison: Approaches in the treatment of our most invisible population. *Women & Therapy,* 21:141–155.

Daniel, S. W. & Barrett, C. J. (1981). The needs of prisoners' wives: A challenge for the mental health professions. *Community Mental Health Journal,* 17:310–322.

Elliott, D. (1983). *National youth survey (United States): Wave VI,* 1983. Boulder, CO: Behavioral Research Institute [producer]. Ann Arbor, MI: Inter-university Consortium for Political and Social Research [distributor].

Fishman, L. T. (1990). *Women at the wall: A study of prisoners' wives doing time on the outside.* Albany: SUNY Press.

Gabel, S. & Johnston, D. (1995). *Children of incarcerated parents.* New York: Lexington Books.

Girshick, L. B. (1998). The importance of using a gendered analysis to understand women in prison. *Journal of the Oklahoma Criminal Justice Research Consortium,* 4, [On-line]. http://204.62.19.52/docs/OCJRC/1997/ganalys.pdf.

——— (1999). *No safe haven.* Boston: Northeastern University Press.

Gottfredson, M. & Hirschi, T. (1990). *A general theory of crime.* Palo Alto, CA: Stanford University Press.

Hagan, J. (1996). The next generation: Children of prisoners. *Journal of the Oklahoma Criminal Justice Research Consortium,* 3:19–28.

Hagan, J., Gillis, A. R. & Simpson, J. (1988). The class structure of gender and delinquency: Toward a power-control theory of common delinquent behavior. *American Journal of Sociology*, 90:1151–1178.

Hairston, C. F. (1990). Men in prison: Family characteristics and parenting views. *Journal of Offender Counseling, Services and Rehabilitation*, 14:23–31.

——— (1991). Family ties during imprisonment: important to whom and for what? *Journal of Sociology and Social Welfare*, 18:87–104.

Hairston, C. F. & Lockett, P. (1985). Parents in prison: A child abuse and neglect prevention strategy. *Child Abuse and Neglect*, 9:471–477.

——— (1987). Parents in prison: new directions for social services. *Social Work:* 162–164.

Harris, J. W. (1993). Comparison of stressors among female vs. male inmates. *Journal of Offender Counseling, Services, and Rehabilitation* 19:43–56.

Heney, J. & Kristiansen, C. M. (1997). An analysis of the impact of prison on women survivors of childhood sexual abuse. *Women & Therapy*, 20:29–44.

Holley, P. D. & Brewster, D. (1996). The women at Eddie Warrior Correctional Center: Descriptions from a data set. *Journal of the Oklahoma Criminal Justice Research Consortium*, 3:107–114.

Johnston, D. (1995a). Effects of parental incarceration. In K. Gabel & D. Johnston, (eds.), *Children of incarcerated parents* (pp. 59–88). New York: Lexington Books.

——— (1995b). The care and placement of prisoners' children. In K. Gabel & D. Johnston (eds.), *Children of incarcerated parents* (103–123). New York: Lexington.

——— (1995c). Child custody issues of women prisoners: A preliminary report from the CHICAS project. *The Prison Journal*, 75:222–239.

Kampfer, C. (1995). Post-traumatic stress reactions in children of imprisoned mothers. In K. Gabel & D. Johnston (eds.), *Children of incarcerated parents* (pp. 89–100). New York: Lexington.

King, A. E. O. (1993). Helping inmates cope with family separation and role strain: A group work approach. *Social Work with Groups*, 16:43–55.

Koban, L. A. (1983). Parents in prison: A comparative analysis of the effects of incarceration on the families of men and women. *Research in Law, Deviance, and Social Control*, 5:171–183.

Kowaleski-Jones, L. & Duncan, G. (forthcoming). The structure of achievement and behavior across middle childhood. *Child Development*.

Light, R. (1993). Why support prisoners' family-tie groups? *The Howard Journal*, 32:322–329.

Marcus-Mendoza, S. & Briody, R. (1996). Female inmates in Oklahoma: An updated profile and programming assessment. *Journal of the Oklahoma Criminal Justice Research Consortium,* 3:85–105.

Marcus-Mendoza, S. T., Klein-Saffran, J. & Lutze, F. (1998). A feminist examination of boot camp prison programs for women. *Women & Therapy,* 21:173–185.

Marcus-Mendoza, S., Sargent, S. & Ho, Y. C. (1994). Changing perceptions of the etiology of crime: The relationship between abuse and female criminality. *Journal of the Oklahoma Criminal Justice Research Consortium* 1:132–3.

Menaghan, E. G., Kowaleski-Jones, L. & Mott, F. L. (1997). The intergenerational costs of parental social stressors: Academic and social difficulties in early adolescence for children of young mothers. *Journal of Health and Social Behavior,* 38:72–86.

Morash, M., Bynum, T. S. & Koons, B. A. (1998). Women offenders: Programming needs and promising approaches. *National Institute of Justice: Research in brief.* Washington, DC: Office of Justice Programs.

Moses, M. C. (1995). *Keeping incarcerated mothers and their daughters together: Girl Scouts beyond bars.* Washington, DC: U. S. Department of Justice/Office of Justice Programs.

Mumola, C. J. & Beck, A. J. (1997). Prisoners in 1996. *Bureau of Justice statistics bulletin.* Washington, DC: U. S. Dept. of Justice.

National Institute on Drug Abuse (1993). *National AIDS demonstration research project public use data.* Rockville, MD: Author.

Ochie, C. O., Sr., & Ngenge, T. T. (1996). Judicial attitudes on feminist ideas and female felons: The impact on female crime patterns. *Journal of the Oklahoma Criminal Justice Research Consortium,* 3:135–145.

Oklahoma Department of Corrections (1998). *Oklahoma Department of Corrections 1998 Annual Report.* Oklahoma City: Author.

Owen, B. (1998). *"In the mix": Struggle and survival in a women's prison.* Albany: SUNY Press.

Owen, B. & Bloom, B. (1995). Profiling women prisoners: Findings from national surveys and a California sample. *The Prison Journal,* 75:165–185.

Phillips, S. D. & Harm, N. J. (1998). Women prisoners: A contextual framework. In J. Harden and M. Hill (Eds.). *Breaking the rules: Women in prison and feminist therapy.* Binghamton, NY: The Haworth Press, Inc.

Reiman, J. (1998). *The rich get richer and the poor get prison* (5th ed.). Boston: Allyn and Bacon.

Sandhu, H. S., Al-Mosleh, H. S., & Chown, B. (1994). Why does Oklahoma have the highest female incarceration rate in the in U. S.? A preliminary investigation. *Journal of the Oklahoma Criminal Justice Research Consortium,* 1:25–33.

Schur, E. (1984). *Labeling Women Deviant.* New York: McGraw-Hill.

Sharp, S. F., Marcus-Mendoza, S. T., Bentley, R. G., Simpson, D. B. & Love, S. R. (1999). Gender differences in the impact of incarceration on children and spouses of drug offenders. In M. Corsianos & K. Train (eds.), *Interrogating social justice: Politics, culture and identity* (217–246). Toronto: Canadian Scholar's Press.

Simon, R. (1975). *Women and Crime.* Lexington, MA: Lexington Books.

Snell, T. & Morton, D. (1994). *Bureau of Justice Statistics Special Report: Women in Prison.* Washington, DC: Office of Justice Programs.

Sobel, S. B. (1982). Difficulties experienced by women in prison. *Psychology of Women Quarterly,* 7:107–117.

Steffensmeier, D. J. (1980). Sex differences in patterns of adult crime, 1965–1977. *Social Forces,* 58:1080–1108.

Steffensmeier, D. & Allan, E. (1998). The nature of female offending: Patterns and explanation. In R. T. Zaplin (ed.), *Female offenders: Critical perspectives and effective interventions* (pp. 5–29). Gaithersburg, MD: Aspen.

Sutherland, E. & Donald Cressey, D. (1978). *Principles of Criminology.* Philadelphia: Lippincott.

Umberson, D. (1995). *Men's Relationship Project Survey Instrument.*

Watts, H. & Nightingale, D. S. (1996). Adding it up: The economic impact of incarceration on individuals, families, and communities. *Journal of the Oklahoma Criminal Justice Research Consortium,* 3:55–62.

Wellisch, J., Prendergast, M. J., & Anglin, J. D. (1994). Drug abusing women offenders: survey series. *National Institute of Justice: Research in Brief.* Washington, DC: Office of Justice Programs.

Zaplin, R. T. & Dougherty, J. (1998). Programs that work: Mothers. In R. T. Zaplin (ed.), *Female offenders: Critical perspectives and effective interventions* (pp. 331–347). Gaithersburg, MD: Aspen.

WOMEN & CRIMINAL JUSTICE, Vol. 12(4), 2001.

10. Affective States of Fathers in Prison

C.S. Lanier

This study profiles incarcerated fathers, a previously neglected subgroup of the prison population. The study also examines the current status of father-child relationships among prisoners, and how those relationships are related to anxiety, depression, somatic complaints, and fathers' concerns. The data were gathered by interviewing 302 incarcerated fathers in a New York State maximum-security prison. The findings show that some men with poor father-child relationships are more likely to be depressed and to experience an elevated level of concern about the father-child relationship.

Growing numbers of authors have documented and examined the importance of the father-child relationship (Appleton 1981; Biller and Meredith 1974; Derdeyn 1976; Hamilton 1977; Levine 1976; Mackey 1985; Yablonsky 1982). Separation of fathers and children has both emotional and physical concomitants (Ahrons 1983; Greif 1979; Jacobs 1982, 1983; Koch and Lowery 1984; Wallerstein and Kelly 1980a, 1980b). However, the literature is noticeably deficient in cases in which fathers and their children are separated by the walls of a prison.

In an effort to address this omission, the present study provides demographic information on fathers in prison and on their relationships with their children. Moreover, I investigate the father-child relationship and its associations with anxiety, depression, and somatic complaints among male prisoners in a New York State maximum-security prison. I hypothesize that fathers who have poor relationships with their children are more likely than other fathers to experience negative psychological consequences.

Background

Inspired by the importance attached to the role of the family in society (Parsons and Bales 1955), numerous authors have advanced diverse theories as a basis for studying the family (Burr et al. 1979). According to one approach, the family is conceptualized as a "system" and is described as "a complex of elements or components directly or indirectly related in a causal network, such that each component is related to at least some others in a more or less stable way within any particular period of time" (Buckley 1967:41). Systems theory thus offers an appropriate expository framework because it embraces the interactive complexity of the family rather than only the characteristics of individual family members (Broderick and Smith 1979; Compton and Galaway 1979; Kantor and Lehr 1975).

Systems theory posits that families possess penetrable boundaries which serve to regulate stimuli from the surrounding environment (Broderick and

Smith 1979; Compton and Galaway 1979). If hostile forces external to the system violate its boundaries, both the interrelationships and the overall integrity of the family can be upset (Broderick and Smith 1979; Holman 1983; Jacob and Tennenbaum 1988). If a parent is removed involuntarily from the family system (by being sent to prison, for example), the behavior of family members can be expected to change in an effort to cope with the unanticipated imbalance in relationships.

Underpinning this conceptual framework is literature which suggests that mothers, fathers, and children all play essential roles in maintaining the health and vibrancy of the family unit (Berry 1981; Bowlby 1965; Derdeyn 1976; Hamilton 1977; Lamb 1978; Roman and Haddad 1978; Weinraub 1978). In keeping with the systems approach, then, it can be expected that the destruction of the family as a unified entity will have profound effects on each family member involved (Greif 1979; Hetherington and Camara 1984; Hetherington, Cox, and Cox 1978; Mitchell 1985; Wallerstein and Kelly 1980a, 1980b).

However, the breakup of the family unit often isolates the father, who typically lives apart from his children, in contrast to the mother, who usually maintains physical custody. Moreover, it would seem that the potential for negative effects on the father is compounded when he resides behind prison walls. Accordingly it would be prudent to review the literature on fathers in order to fully grasp the foundation for this premise.

Societal dynamics of the late twentieth century provided impetus for a transformation in parental roles. As a result of life choices precipitated by the social acceptability of birth control, the success and proliferation of women in the work force, the disintegration of the nuclear family as a result of spiraling divorce rates, a thaw in sexual stereotypes which allowed fathers to nurture their children, and the increase in work-at-home industries, fathers became more able to serve as caregivers to their children (Levine 1976; Pruett 1987; Thompson 1983; Yablonsky 1982).

Paralleling the expanded role of men as caregivers has been an acknowledgment of the importance of the father and his contribution to the healthy development of his child (Hamilton 1977; Lamb 1978; Weinraub 1978). The father's influence is complex and can be either direct or indirect (Radin and Russell 1983). Various authors hold that fathers are important in their children's sex-role development (Biller 1981; Radin and Russell 1983; Thompson 1983), achievement orientation (Lamb 1986), and intellectual development (Radin 1981; Radin and Russell 1983; Thompson 1983). Fathers also are believed to be important contributors to their children's psychological adjustment and social competence (Lamb 1981; Radin and Russell 1983).

It appears that the father's exclusion from the household can increase the negative effects as his role shifts from that of economic provider to that of an interdependent and nurturing caregiver. Fathers deprived of parental involvement frequently suffer anxiety and depression due to their elimination from the child's developmental matrix (Ahrons 1983; Berry 1981; Dominic and Schlesinger 1980; Greif 1979; Hetherington et al. 1976, 1978; Hetherington and Hagan 1986:

Jacobs 1982, 1983, 1986; Keshet and Rosenthal 1978; Wallerstein and Kelly 1980b; Williams 1986). Some authors also note the presence of somatic complaints among noncustodial, excluded fathers (Greif 1979; Jacobs 1982, 1983). One author further acknowledged the importance of the excluded father's negative affective state by identifying the entire constellation of symptoms as "involuntary child absence syndrome" (Jacobs 1986).

Clearly, then, the breakup of the household has adverse effects on the noncustodial father. Negative affective states in the father seem to stem from an inability to maintain frequent and healthy contact with his children. Also, in most cases the maintenance of the parent-child relationship is subject only to the inclinations of the various family members involved. If a noncustodial parent wants to interact with the child, and if both parents agree to this arrangement, little stands in the way.

Yet when a parent is incarcerated, an additional dimension of difficulty appears. The noncustodial parent is no longer simply subject to the dictates of the visitation agreement. This parent now is severely handicapped by an inability to fulfill the visitation accord. For example, if a family member, such as an ex-spouse or a grandparent, is unwilling or unable to bring the child to visit the imprisoned parent, the parent-child interaction is thwarted.

Most studies about incarcerated men deal only tangentially at best with father-child relationships. The primary focus is typically the prisoner's relationship with his family as a holistic unit and how that association is linked with his institutional adjustment (Bauhofer 1985; Burstein 1977; Davis 1985; Holt and Miller 1972; Howser, Grossman, and Macdonald 1983) or with his eventual rehabilitation (Adams and Fischer 1976; Brodsky 1975; Clemmer 1940; Glaser 1964; Holt and Miller 1972; Howser and Macdonald 1982; Ohlin 1954). In short, the father-child bond among prisoners has not been studied specifically.

Several studies represent notable exceptions to the lack of focus on fathers in prison. These studies deal with father-child interaction (Lanier 1991), family characteristics and parenting experiences (Hairston 1989; Morris 1967), and parenting programs for imprisoned fathers (Hairston and Lockett 1985, 1987; Lanier and Fisher 1989, 1990). Even so, reliable quantitative data on fathers in prison are largely absent from the literature.

The present study attempted to meet the lack of research on incarcerated fathers in two ways. First, survey data yielded a descriptive profile of fathers incarcerated in a single New York State maximum-security prison. Second, the study examined whether fathers in prison who cannot maintain healthy relationships with their children suffer at least the same psychological ailments as do their free-world, noncustodial counterparts.

Method

Sample

I conducted this project in a New York State maximum-security prison for men.

The survey comprised a random sample of 376 men from an alphabetical roster of all 990 men. I obtained a total of 302 questionnaires for a response rate of 80 percent.

Measures

Independent Variables. There were two independent variables: 1) the status of the father-child relationship as it existed before the father was imprisoned and 2) the status of this relationship as it existed at the time of assessment.

Dependent Variables. Four dependent variables—anxiety, depression, somatic complaints, and fathers' concerns—were used in this study. The A-State version of the State-Trait Anxiety Inventory (STAI) measured anxiety (range = 22–78; $\overline{X}$ = 48.02; sd = 10.73). The Beck Depression Inventory (BDI) in its abridged form measured depression (range = 0–28; $\overline{X}$ = 5.13; sd = 4.67), although I omitted the item measuring self-harm at the request of the prison administration at Eastern. The somaticism subscale from the Hopkins Symptom Checklist (HSCL–90) measured somatic complaints (range = 0–29; $\overline{X}$ = 6.16; sd = 5.87).

I constructed an instrument specifically for the present research to measure the fourth dependent variable, fathers' concerns (range = 10–40; $\overline{X}$ = 23.03; sd = 8.73). I added this variable in an attempt to measure the psychological state that lies in the gray area between normal sadness and clinical depression. This condition, which some psychologists call dysphoria, can be regarded as a milder, less clinically obvious form of depression.

Procedure

The data were gathered via interview. I used this method of eliciting information rather than a self-administered questionnaire in order to avoid problems that might arise from a low literacy level in the prison population. A Spanish version of the instrument was available for men unfamiliar or uncomfortable with English.

Graduate students in sociology from the prison population at Eastern were trained and served as interviewers. Sixteen interviewers in all were trained for the survey.

Results

One of the most striking shortcomings in the literature on prisoners is the absence of any comprehensive statistical data on incarcerated fathers and their progeny. Table 1 thus reports the demographic characteristics of the fathers in the sample. Of the entire sample of 302 prisoners, approximately two-thirds of the respondents (188 men) said they were fathers. Of this number, almost the entire group (95.7%) reported that they were the biological fathers of their children.

The 188 fathers had a collective total of 482 children, or a mean of 2.6 children per respondent. Most of the children were between the ages of 7 and 18; almost 40 percent were between 7 and 12. Yet because we collected date of birth only for each man's six eldest children, these estimates are undercounts in each age group, particularly in the younger ages. Moreover, in some cases date of birth was simply unobtainable.

TABLE 1 Demographic Characteristics of Fathers (1987)

	Frequency	*Percentage*	
Number of Fathers	188	62.3	(N = 302)
Biological parent	178	95.7	(N = 186)
Stepfather	8	4.3	
	186	100.0%	
Size of Family			
1 child	55	29.2	(N = 188)
2 children	60	31.9	
3 children	30	16.0	
4+ children	43	22.9	
	188	100.0%	
Children's Ages (Range = 0–43)			
0–6	79	20.4	(N = 388)
7–12	155	39.9	
13–18	81	20.9	
19 or older	73	18.8	
	388	100.0%	
Father's Legal Relationship to Mother of His Children			
Married	56	30.4	(N = 184)
Legally separated/divorced	37	20.1	
Widowed	5	2.7	
Common law	24	13.0	
Never married	62	33.8	
	184	100.0%	
(Divorced or separated respondents)			
Court-ordered visitation rights			
Yes	11	32.4	(N = 34)
No	23	67.6	
	34	100.0%	
Fatherhood Experience			
Live with children before imprisonment			
Yes	134	76.1	(N = 176)
No	42	23.9	
	176	100.0%	
Time spent with children before imprisonment			
A lot	132	75.0	(N = 176)
Some	28	15.9	
A little	6	3.4	
None	10	5.7	
	176	100.0%	

Some Ns vary because of nonresponse on specific items.

TABLE 2 Mean Scores of Indicators of the Father-Child Relationship and Their Change since Incarceration (1987)

	Before	*Current*	*Change*
Closeness	3.684	1.914	1.770*
(N = 174)	(0.789)	(1.111)	(1.574)
Involvement	3.661	2.187	1.474*
(N = 171)	(0.827)	(1.168)	(1.706)
Contact	3.779	2.366	1.413*
(N = 172)	(0.656)	(1.076)	(1.367)
Global FCR	11.117	6.462	4.655*
(N = 171)	(2.075)	(2.870)	(4.173)

*$p < .001$

Table 1 also shows the marital status of the incarcerated fathers in the sample. Approximately the same percentage of men (30.4%) reported being married to their children's mothers as reported never being married to the mothers (33.8%). Moreover, about one-fifth of the sample stated that they were either legally separated or divorced from their children's mothers. Of the men whose marriages had been ended legally, fewer than one-third reported having court-ordered legal rights to see their children. In short, more than two-thirds of the men legally separated or divorced had no legal basis for visitation with their children.

Table 1 also shows the respondents' pre-imprisonment fatherhood experience. Slightly more than three-quarters (76.1%) of the respondents said that they had lived with their children before they came to prison. Approximately the same percentage (75.0%) reported that they had spent a lot of time with their children before serving time in prison. Only a small percentage said they had spent little (3.4%) or no (5.7%) time with their children before they were sent to prison.

Perhaps of more immediate concern is the current overall status of the relationship between the incarcerated father and his children, and how it changed (if at all) during the prison term. As shown clearly by the mean scores in Table 2, most of the men reported high levels of closeness, involvement, and contact with their children in the period before going to prison. In contrast, current levels were statistically significantly lower than pre-imprisonment levels on all three of these dimensions of the father-child relationship. The global measure of the father-child relationship also was statistically significant. As might be expected, most fathers reported significant decay in the relationships with their children.

These findings are especially relevant if prisoners with poor father-child relationships are affected adversely. As noted above, the crux of this research is whether the incarcerated father is affected psychologically by the status of his relationship with his children. I used two independent variables in each of four regression equations, the results of which are reported in Table 3.

TABLE 3 Regression Analyses for the Dependent Variables (1987)

Standardized Regression Coefficients	*Anxiety (N = 122)*	*Depression (N = 122)*	*Somaticism (N = 122)*	*Father's Concerns (N = 121)*
Control Variables				
African-American	0.089	0.099	−0.028	0.008
Hispanic	0.149	0.250*	0.078	0.197
Religious affiliation	0.025	0.072	0.044	0.006
Education	−0.044	−0.231*	−0.061	−0.134
Age	−0.373***	0.124	−0.047	−0.118
Number of children	−0.055	−0.089	−0.016	0.031
Lived with children before imprisonment	−0.023	−0.087	0.085	−0.095
Time with children before imprisonment	−0.132	−0.100	−0.066	0.107
Length of time confined	0.091	−0.176	−0.055	0.012
Independent Variables				
Status now	−0.062	−0.228*	−0.030	−0.469***
Status before	−0.037	−0.020	−0.138	0.008
Adjusted R^2	.114**	.112**	.000	.268***

*= $p < .05$; **= $p < .01$; ***= $p < .001$;

The first independent variable was the status of the father-child relationship as it existed at the time of assessment. The second independent variable measured the status of the relationship as it existed before the father was imprisoned. I created each of these variables by summing scores on closeness, involvement, and contact for the appropriate period. Preliminary testing for the effect of change, measured as the interaction between these variables, demonstrated that change between the variables did not explain additional variance and thus could be discounted.

In addition to the two independent variables, I included eight control variables in each regression equation. These variables were the respondent's race, religious affiliation, level of education at the time of commitment, age, number of children, pre-imprisonment residential status with the children, amount of time spent with the children before imprisonment, and length of time confined. I modeled other variables, such as the respondent's marital status, children's ages, and the number of months before the next parole board appearance, but these yielded nothing to further the analysis.

Table 3 shows that the status of the father-child relationship "now" was related inversely to anxiety, but not significantly so. Among the control variables, only age was related significantly and inversely to anxiety ($p < .001$).

Table 3 also shows the results of the regression analysis for depression. The independent variable STATUS NOW was significantly related negatively to depression ($p < .05$). Thus the worse the perceived current status of the father-child relationship, the more likely that the respondent experienced depression. The father's level of education before commitment likewise was significantly related negatively to depression ($p < .05$). Race was related to depression as well; Hispanics were most likely to be depressed ($p < .05$).

For somaticism, the third dependent variable, both of the independent variables obtained nonsignificant regression coefficients, an indication that no relationships exist between status of the father-child relationship and somaticism. Moreover, somatic complaints do not appear to be predicted by any of the control variables employed here.

Table 3 also shows the results of the regression equation for the summary scale of a father's concerns about the relationship with his children. The independent variable STATUS NOW was related both significantly and inversely to the concerns of the incarcerated father ($p < .001$). The amount of variance explained by the independent variables ($R^2 = .268$) was statistically significant as well ($p < .001$). Overall the regression equation demonstrates that a relationship exists in the hypothesized direction between the father's concerns and his perception of the current father-child relationship.

Discussion

As stated earlier, this research used data from a maximum-security men's prison in an attempt to fill the void of knowledge about incarcerated fathers. The regression analyses suggest that fathers who perceive themselves as detached from their children are more likely to register an elevated level of concern about the father-child relationship. Moreover, this group of men is more likely to suffer from depression.

There are several possible reasons why anxiety and somaticism, the other two dependent variables, showed no statistically significant relationships with the independent variables, contrary to the original hypotheses. The anxiety scores for fathers are clustered at the low end of the scale; therefore this measure shows little variance. Consequently the measure used here may not have been sensitive enough to accurately distinguish the level of anxiety felt by fathers. As for somatic complaints, the subscale used in this study may have been reconstructed inefficiently. Another possibility with regard to both variables is that the measures accurately reflected a prisoner's strategy of denying anxiety and somatic complaints; such denial, one might argue, is adaptive in prison.

One of the most intriguing findings was that change in the status of the father-child relationship itself exerted no statistically significant influence on the dependent variables. Likewise, the status of the father-child relationship before the father's imprisonment appeared to have no effect on the dependent variables. Essentially, then, the only independent variable that demonstrated any influence on the father's affective state was how he perceives the father-child relationship as it exists today.

Also noteworthy was the finding that the length of time in confinement had no statistically significant effect on the incarcerated father's affective state. It would seem that the longer a father was separated forcibly from his children, the more likely that he would experience the anguish and pain associated with a loss of the father-child relationship. This does not appear to be the case, however. Possibly in an attempt to negotiate the prison environment, the father may learn over time to live with the painful separation. In short, the imprisoned father may seek consciously to numb himself emotionally as a matter of survival.

This study also highlighted the importance of being a parent for some incarcerated fathers by identifying the association between the status of the father-child relationship and two of the dependent variables. The importance of this relationship for the father may have remained consistent throughout his children's life. It also is possible that father-child relationships of incarcerated men, who are cut off from other caring human relationships, might increase in importance for the fathers during the period of imprisonment. This increase might be the product of a genuine concern for the parent-child relationship, a temporary method by which to cope better with life behind bars, or a combination of the two.

This research suggests that in incarcerated fathers the potential for negative psychological consequences (depression and concerns about the father-child relationship) are greater among men with poor father-child relationships. In addition to the unwanted effects on the father's psychological state, the deterioration of this relationship may impair his institutional adjustment as well as his capacity for postrelease success. Because many prisoners experience such decay in the relationships with their children, prudence dictates that solutions to the problems arising in these areas should be contemplated.

Providing additional impetus to a search for solutions is the constantly expanding population of imprisoned fathers. Yet in most men's prisons, problems taxing the father-child relationship have not been recognized fully, much less addressed systematically. Several recommendations for dealing with these problems and for improving father-child interaction are in order.

First, programs supported by the prison administration should be implemented for incarcerated fathers. Ideally these programs should include both educational and therapeutic components. The educational component could consist of classes, lectures, and periodic seminars or workshops dealing with all aspects of parenting. Because discussing these issues will be painful for some and perhaps may intensify an already emotionally debilitating situation, a therapeutic component also is warranted.

Parenting programs for imprisoned fathers also could function as a useful means of encouraging prisoners to confront various social issues related to their incarceration. Many prisoners are afflicted with substance abuse problems, low levels of education, no history of legal employment, and family problems such as growing up as an abused child or coming from a broken home. Prisoners might begin to assume responsibility for their lives with assistance from professional counselors who are trained to capitalize on the incarcerated father's parental role.

Second, a Legal Services for Imprisoned Parents could be instituted, whose primary purpose would be to help prisoners maintain a healthy, constructive relationship with their children. Competent legal assistance should be available when interaction with the imprisoned parent would be in the child's best interests.

A third recommendation concerns the uncooperative mother or surrogate caregiver who chooses either to severely restrict or to entirely prevent contact between the incarcerated father and his children. Before legal representation is considered, a cadre of trained mediators could be made available to meet with the children's parents in order to resolve visitation difficulties amicably. The mediators also would be authorized to arrange the intervention of social services if their assistance could facilitate regular, high-quality visitation with the father. Productive mediation also might lead to the involvement of both parents in parenting education programs, as well as in other counseling and therapeutic opportunities. Again, the child's best interests should be the criterion for this type of intervention.

In these various ways, then, we can understand more clearly and address more equitably the problems confronting the incarcerated father and their ramifications for him, his children, the institution, and society. One goal of this research is to contribute to a growing body of literature on the incarcerated father. I also hope that such research will raise the consciousness of imprisoned parents, their non-incarcerated parental partners, their children, prison employees, mental health practitioners, legislators, family court personnel, and (finally) researchers about the issues surrounding the incarcerated father and his children.

References

Adams, D. and J. Fischer (1976) "The Effects of Prison Residents' Community Contacts on Recidivism Rates." *Corrective and Social Psychiatry and Journal of Behavior Technology Methods and Therapy* 22:21–27.

Ahrons, C. R. (1983) "Predictors of Paternal Involvement Postdivorce: Mothers' and Fathers' Perceptions." *Journal of Divorce* 6(3):55–69.

Appleton, W. S. (1981) *Fathers and Daughters*. Garden City, NY: Doubleday.

Bauhofer, V. S. (1985) "Policy Formulation, Policy Modification and Perception of the Application: A Correctional Case Study." Doctoral dissertation, Cornell University.

Berry, K. H. (1981) "The Male Single Parent." In I. R. Stuart and L. E. Abt (eds.), *Children of Separation and Divorce: Management and Treatment*, pp. 34–52. New York: Van Nostrand Reinhold.

Biller, H. (1981) "The Father and Sex Role Development." In M. E. Lamb (ed.), *The Role of the Father in Child Development*, 2nd ed., pp. 319–58. New York: Wiley.

Biller, H. and D. Meredith (1974) *Father Power*. New York: David McKay.

Bowlby, J. (1965) *Child Care and the Growth of Love*. 2nd ed. Baltimore: Penguin.

Broderick, C. and J. Smith (1979) "The General Systems Approach to the Family." In W. R. Burr, R. Hill, F. I. Nye, and I. L. Reiss (eds.), *Contemporary Theories about the Family: General Theories/Theoretical Orientations*, vol. 2, pp. 112–29. New York: Free Press.

Brodsky, S. L. (1975) *Families and Friends of Men in Prison*. Lexington, MA: Lexington Books.

Buckley, W. (1967) *Sociology and Modern Systems Theory*. Englewood Cliffs, NJ: Prentice-Hall.

Burr, W. R., R. Hill, F. I. Nye, and I. L. Reiss, eds. (1979) *Contemporary Theories about the Family: General Theories/Theoretical Orientations*. New York: Free Press.

Burstein, J. Q. (1977) *Conjugal Visits in Prison*. Lexington, MA: Lexington Books.

Clemmer, D. (1940) *The Prison Community*. New York: Rinehart.

Compton, B. R. and B. Galaway (1979) *Social Work Processes*. Revised ed. Homewood, IL: Dorsey.

Davis, R. (1985) "The Effects of Family Reunion Programs on Prison Inmates." Unpublished master's thesis, State University of New York at New Paltz.

Derdeyn, A. P. (1976) "Child Custody Contests in Historical Perspective." *American Journal of Psychiatry* 133(12):1369–76.

Dominic, K. T. and B. Schlesinger (1980) "Weekend Fathers: Family Shadows." *Journal of Divorce* 3(3):241–47.

Glaser, D. (1964) *The Effectiveness of a Prison and Parole System*. New York: Bobbs-Merrill.

Greif, J. B. (1979) "Fathers, Children, and Joint Custody." *American Journal of Orthopsychiatry* 49(2):311–19.

Hairston, C. F. (1989) "Men in Prison: Family Characteristics and Parenting Views." *Journal of Offender Counseling, Services, and Rehabilitation* 14(1):23–30.

Hairston, C. F. and P. Lockett (1985) "Parents in Prison: A Child Abuse and Neglect Prevention Strategy." *Child Abuse and Neglect* 9:471–77.

——— (1987) "Parents in Prison: New Directions for Social Services." *Social Work* (March–April): 162–64.

Hamilton, M. L. (1977) *Father's Influence on Children*. Chicago: Nelson-Hall.

Hetherington, E. M. and K. Camara (1984) "Families in Transition: The Processes of Dissolution and Reconstitution." In R. D. Parke (ed.), *Review of Child Development Research*, pp. 398–439. Chicago: University of Chicago Press.

Hetherington, E. M., M. Cox, and R. Cox (1976) "Divorced Fathers." *Family Coordinator* 25:417–28.

——— (1978) "The Aftermath of Divorce." In J. H. Stevens Jr. and M. Mathews (eds.), *Mother/Child Father/Child Relationships*, pp. 149–76. Washington, DC: National Association for the Education of Young Children.

Hetherington, E. M. and M. S. Hagan (1986) "Divorced Fathers: Stress, Coping, and Adjustment." In M. E. Lamb (ed.), *The Father's Role: Applied Perspectives*, pp. 103–34. New York: Wiley.

Holman, A. M. (1983) *Family Assessment: Tools for Understanding and Intervention.* Beverly Hills: Sage.

Holt, N. and D. Miller (1972) "Explorations in Inmate-Family Relationships." Sacramento, California: Research Division, California Department of Corrections. Research Report No. 46.

Howser, J., J. Grossman, and D. Macdonald (1983) "Impact of Family Reunion Program on Institutional Discipline." *Journal of Offender Counseling, Services, and Rehabilitation* 8(1/2):27–36.

Howser, J. F. and D. Macdonald (1982) "Maintaining Family Ties." *Corrections Today* 44:96–98.

Jacob, T. and D. L. Tennenbaum (1988) *Family Assessment.* New York: Plenum.

Jacobs, J. W. (1982) "The Effect of Divorce on Fathers: An Overview of the Literature." *American Journal of Psychiatry* 139(10):1235–41.

——— (1983) "Treatment of Divorcing Fathers: Social and Psychotherapeutic Considerations." *American Journal of Psychiatry* 140(10):1294–99.

——— (1986) "Involuntary Child Absence Syndrome: An Affliction of Divorcing Fathers." In J. W. Jacobs (ed.), *Divorce and Fatherhood: The Struggle for Parental Identity*, pp. 37–51. Washington, DC: American Psychiatric Press.

Kantor, D. and W. Lehr (1975) *Inside the Family.* San Francisco: Jossey-Bass.

Keshet, H. F. and K. M. Rosenthal (1978) "Fathering after Marital Separation." *Social Work* 23:11–18.

Koch, M. A. P. and C. R. Lowery (1984) "Visitation and the Noncustodial Father." *Journal of Divorce* 8(2):47–65.

Lamb, M. E. (1978) "The Father's Role in the Infant's Social World." In J. H. Stevens Jr. and M. Mathews (eds.), *Mother/Child Father/Child Relationships*, pp. 87–108. Washington, DC: National Association for the Education of Young Children.

——— (1981) "Fathers and Child Development: An Integrative Overview." In M.E. Lamb (ed.). *The Role of the Father in Child Development*, 2nd ed., pp. 1–70. New York: Wiley.

——— ed. (1986) *The Father's Role: Applied Perspectives.* New York: Wiley.

Lanier, C. S. (1991) "Dimensions of Father-Child Interaction in a New York State Prison Population." *Journal of Offender Rehabilitation* 16(3/4):27–42.

Lanier, C. S. and G. Fisher (1989) "The Eastern Fathers' Group: An Educational and Mutual Support Program for Incarcerated Fathers." In S. Duguid (ed.),

Yearbook of Correctional Education: 1989, pp. 155–73. Simon Fraser University: Institute for the Humanities.

——— (1990) "A Prisoners' Parenting Center (PPC): A Promising Resource Strategy for Incarcerated Fathers." *Journal of Correctional Education* 44(4):158–65.

Levine, J. A. (1976) *Who Will Raise the Children?* New York: Lippincott.

Mackey, W. C. (1985) *Fathering Behaviors: The Dynamics of the Man-Child Bond.* New York: Plenum.

Mitchell, A. (1985) *Children in the Middle.* New York: Tavistock.

Morris, P. (1967) "Fathers in Prison." *British Journal of Criminology* 7:424–30.

Ohlin, L. (1954) "The Stability and Validity of Parole Experience Tables." Doctoral dissertation, University of Chicago.

Parsons, T. and R. F. Bales (1955) *Family, Socialization and Interaction Process.* Glencoe, IL: Free Press.

Pruett, K. D. (1987) *The Nurturing Father.* New York: Warner.

Radin, N. (1981) "The Role of the Father in Cognitive, Academic, and Intellectual Development." In M. E. Lamb (ed.), *The Role of the Father in Child Development,* 2nd ed., pp. 379–427. New York: Wiley.

Radin, N. and G. Russell (1983) "Increased Father Participation and Child Development Outcomes." In M.E. Lamb and A. Sagi (eds.), *Fatherhood and Family Policy,* pp. 191–218. Hillsdale, NJ: Erlbaum.

Roman, M. and W. Haddad (1978) *The Disposable Parent.* New York: Holt, Rinehart and Winston.

Rosenkrantz, L. and V. Joshua (1982) "Children of Incarcerated Parents: A Hidden Population." *Children Today* 11:2–6.

Sack, W. H. and J. Seidler (1978) "Should Children Visit Their Parents in Prison?" *Law and Human Behavior* 2(3):261–66.

Sack, W. H., J. Seidler, and S. Thomas (1976) "The Children of Imprisoned Parents: A Psychosocial Exploration." *American Journal of Orthopsychiatry* 46(4):618–28.

Thompson, R. A. (1983) "The Father's Case in Child Custody Disputes: The Contributions of Psychological Research." In M. E. Lamb and A. Sagi (eds.), *Fatherhood and Family Policy,* pp. 53–100. Hillsdale, NJ: Erlbaum.

U. S. Department of Justice (1989) *Correctional Populations in the United States, 1986.* Washington, DC: Bureau of Justice Statistics.

Wallerstein, J. S. and J. B. Kelly (1980a) "Effects of Divorce on the Visiting Father-Child Relationship." *American Journal of Psychiatry* 137(12):1534–39.

——— (1980b) *Surviving the Breakup.* New York: Basic Books.

Weinraub, M. (1978) "Fatherhood: The Myth of the Second-Class Parent." In J. H. Stevens Jr. and M. Mathews (eds.), *Mother/Child Father/Child Relationships,* pp. 109–33. Washington, DC: National Association for the Education of Young Children.

Williams, F. S. (1986) "A Father's Post-Divorce Struggle for Parental Identity." In J. W. Jacobs (ed.), *Divorce and Fatherhood: The Struggle for Parental Identity,* pp. 25–35. Washington, DC: American Psychiatric Press.

Yablonsky, L. (1982) *Fathers and Sons.* New York: Simon and Schuster.

JUSTICE QUARTERLY, Vol. 10 No. 1, March 1993.

11. Visiting Women in Prison: Who Visits and Who Cares?

Karen Casey-Acevedo
Tim Bakken

This article provides a descriptive analysis of visitation at a maximum security prison for women. Women inmates, including those in this study, are young, single, unemployed, and undereducated. This study collected and examined visitation data on 222 women who averaged 22 months of incarceration. During their incarceration, 79% of the women received at least one visit from a friend or family member. Of the women who received visits, the most frequent visitors were friends (evenly divided among males and females), not family members. For all visitors, the major impediment to visitation was the distance that they, especially children, had to travel to reach the prison. Perhaps as a result, 61% of the women who were mothers did not receive any visits from their children. The study concluded that visitation and the separation that ensues when visits are terminated can be a harrowing experience for women inmates, especially those who are separated from their children. Nonetheless, visitation can help foster prison adjustment and lead to better societal adjustment after prison. Thus, if there is to be prison visitation, as is the trend throughout the nation, then prisons and states will have to expend resources to facilitate it, because families and friends of inmates do not have the means to visit.

Researchers have estimated that 55% to 80% of female inmates are mothers of minor children (Banauch, 1985; Henriquez, 1982; Lapoint, 1977; McGowan & Blumenthal, 1978; Stanton, 1980; Bloom & Steinhart, 1993). Indeed, one of the most devastating aspects of imprisonment for women is separation from family and friends, and especially their children. While many women do remain connected to their families through phone calls and letters, they have an extremely difficult time maintaining contact with loved ones through visitation (Banauch, 1985; Henriquez, 1982; Lapoint, 1977; McGowan & Blumenthal, 1978; Stanton, 1980).

Thus, the purpose of the study discussed in this article was to determine how visitation affects the adjustment of women at a maximum security prison so that correctional and state officials can develop programs and plans that will help integrate women into prison and prepare them for life after their incarceration. In analyzing the data resulting from this study and determining how to best assist women inmates in their adjustment, this article explores several questions. First, do women receive visits and, if so, how often? Second, who visits women in prison? For instance, do young children visit and, if so, how often? Third, is the prison adjustment of women affected by visitation, or the absence of visitation?

The Challenges Inherent in Prison Visitation

Historically, prison officials did not permit inmates to receive visits from family members. When men and women were incarcerated, all their ties to their families and friends were severed, and prison officials attempted to keep news of outside events from prisoners. This concept of "separation" was central to all policies and practices of prisons in the early years (Rothman, 1971). Prison officials believed that separation would be beneficial to inmates in their quest for reformation. However, the theories behind isolation and separation gradually evolved into an understanding of the importance of family and friends in rehabilitation.

Consequently, despite a renewed societal focus on punishment models and incarceration rather than rehabilitation (Merlo & Benekos, 1997), there has been a revival of interest in inmates' families and the benefits of maintaining familial ties during incarceration. Indeed, correctional policies across the nation reflect the changes in attitudes toward family contact. The creation of family visiting programs, parenting and child development classes for inmates, and family furloughs are evident in prisons for both men and women (Bloom & Steinhart, 1993; Boudouris, 1985; McGowan & Blumenthal, 1978). There are many reasons that family visitation is seen as important to inmates, especially women. Contact with family members allows an inmate to remain connected to and informed about the activities in the world beyond prison. Such awareness in turn can increase the chances of success on parole (Holt & Miller, 1972; Glaser, 1964). Evidence suggests that visitation from family and friends may also have a positive impact on inmates' behavior inside the institution as well (Ellis, 1974).

Visitation can also affect the family and friends of inmates. Visiting allows outsiders to see that inmates are being treated fairly and that they are in good health, a reality that is especially important to the children of inmates. The absence of a parent can leave a child imagining that something horrible has happened. Although often an intimidating experience, a child's prison visit can result in an acknowledgement that the child's mother is alive and in good health. Also, children's prison visits are important because most incarcerated women plan to reunite with their children upon release (Banauch, 1985; Henriquez, 1982; McGowan & Blumenthal 1978; Stanton, 1980; Zalba, 1964). Continued visitation can help maintain the parent-child relationship and prepare both mother and child for eventual reunification.

However, inmates and families who want to see each other face many obstacles. The most difficult obstacles are the time, cost, and emotional and practical difficulties that friends and family members face in traveling to and actually entering a prison. Many prisons are in remote areas (Pollock-Byme, 1990). Families must travel long distances to prisons, which often limits their ability to visit regularly. Furthermore, prison rules and regulations concerning visitation are often burdensome and restrictive. For example, some prisons might limit visitation to weekends and maintain minimal hours of visitation (Hairston, 1990).

Prison visitation raises complex emotional issues for inmates and their children and families. Visitation is especially harrowing when young children are involved. The separation of mothers from their children, concerns about children's placement or psychological or physical well-being, and mothers' lack of control over children's lives cause hardship and pain for mothers, children, and caretakers. The incarceration of mothers severs significant bonds with children, siblings, and friends and can also cause immense emotional distress for inmates and their families and friends. (Banauch, 1985; Henriquez, 1982; Lapoint, 1977; McGowan & Blumenthal, 1978; Stanton, 1980). Maintaining contact through visitation can alleviate some of the distress caused by separation, although visitation itself can be an extremely emotional experience.

Regrettably, the current research on visitation in women's prisons is very limited. Bloom and Steinhart's (1993) survey of 439 inmates in eight states and the District of Columbia did reveal that 54% of inmates' children did not visit them in prison. Bloom and Steinhart (1993) found that the main barriers to visitation were the distance a visitor had to travel to the prison and the caretaker's resistance to bringing children to prison. Fuller (1993) interviewed a sample of 99 visitors to three California prisons and found that the visitors consisted primarily of friends and family members. As barriers to visitation, the visitors cited the cost of travel, the distance from their homes to the prison, and their job responsibilities.

The following study involves a descriptive analysis of visitation at a maximum security prison for women located in a Northeastern state. To provide an illustration of the nature of prison visiting, the study included an analysis of institutional records, observations of visiting situations, unstructured interviews with inmates, and the perspectives of volunteers and prison staff. Visitation records were collected for all women released (a total of 222) over a two year period. So that the entire sentence of an inmate could be examined, the sample consisted of released inmates. The data on visitation could be collected, because the prison required every person who visited an inmate to complete a visitation pass. The pass indicated the date of the visit and each visitor's name, address, and relationship to the inmate.

Methods

Visitation was measured through two methods. First, a monthly rate of visitors was calculated using the total number of visitors an inmate received divided by the number of months the inmate was incarcerated. Every visitor who visited an inmate was counted. Second, to examine each inmate's varied and diverse circumstances, the data were analyzed to determine the diversity of the visitors. That is, while one woman may receive five visits per month from only one person, another inmate may receive five visits a month from five different people.

During the study, the prison provided the opportunity to observe and interact with women and children in a special visiting area at the prison. The data collection strategy utilized was participant observation, or more specifically "participant as observer" (Burgess, 1984).

Researcher observations spanned approximately one month during the summer. The researcher spent the majority of time in the visiting room with the inmates and their children.

The purpose of observing visits was to ascertain the nature of prison visitation, especially children's visitation. The researcher's interaction with inmates consisted of "conversations with a purpose" (Burgess, 1984). That is, the researcher solicited responses from inmates about whether they maintained contact with families, how they felt about visitation, how often they received visits, and who was caring for their children. Unstructured interviews were also conducted with various staff, inmates, and volunteers. At the time of the study, the prison had very liberal visiting policies. Visiting was allowed everyday from 8:30 a.m. to 3:00 p.m. There were several programs that focused on maintaining bonds between mothers and their children, and the prison provided subsidized transportation for families who could not otherwise visit.

Results

As indicated in Table 1, 80% of the women in the sample were mothers. About half the women in the sample were black and about a quarter were Hispanic and another quarter were white. The women ranged in age from 17 to 60; the average age of all the women in the sample was 29.7. The overwhelming majority of women were not married, and almost two-thirds of the sample had less than a high school education. Twenty percent of those sampled were employed at the time of their arrest. The profile provided by this sample of women is consistent with national statistics.

An examination of the legal data indicated that 42% of the inmates were incarcerated for violent offenses, with the most frequent offense being robbery (24% of the inmates). Larceny-theft represented the second most frequent offense category. Drug offenses accounted for 22% of the incarceration offenses. On average, the inmates served 22.7 months in prison and had 8.3 previous arrests.

When comparing mothers and non-mothers, three factors were considered: the age of the inmate, the crime that was the basis of incarceration, and the county from which the inmate was committed to prison. Non-mothers were considerably younger than mothers. Non-mothers were on average 25.8 years old, while mothers were on average 38.4 years old. Non-mothers were also more violent than mothers. A substantial 66% of the non-mothers were incarcerated for violent offenses compared to 37% of the mothers. Mothers were much more likely to be incarcerated for drug offenses. Twenty-six percent of the mothers were incarcerated for having committed drug offenses, compared with only 5% of the non-mothers. There were also significant differences between the groups in the counties of commitment. Ninety-eight percent of the non-mothers were committed from the surrounding metropolitan area; 87% of the mothers came from this area.

TABLE 1 Demographic Characteristics by Parental Status

	Total Sample (N = 222)	*Mothers (N = 178)*	*Non-Mothers (N = 44)*
	Race (N = 222)	(N = 173)	(N = 44)
Black	52%	51%	52%
White	24	22	34
Hispanic	24	27	14
	100	100	100
	Age*(N = 222)	(N = 178)	(N = 44)
17 or younger	1%	0%	2%
18–24	31	25	55
25–34	48	51	36
35–44	14	16	4
45–54	5	6	2
55–64	1	2	0
	100	100	100
	Average Age* 29.7	38.4	25.8
Marital Status	(N = 222)	(N = 171)	(N = 41)
Single	53%	49%	71%
Married	18	21	7
Div/Sep/Wid	22	23	17
Common Law	7	7	5
	100	100	100
	Education (N = 200)	(N = 164)	(N = 36)
Less 8th gr	7%	9%	3%
Some high sch	46	50	56
HS/GED	25	27	36
College/more	12	15	5
	100	100	100
	Employ (N = 207)	(N = 166)	(N = 42)
Yes	18%	19%	15%
No	82	81	85
	100	100	100
	Commitment County (N = 222)	(N = 178)	(N = 44)
Metro Area[1]	89%	87%	98%
Outside metro area[2]	11	13	2
	100	100	100

Crime Type	Total Sample (N = 222)	Mothers (N = 178)	Non-Mothers (N = 44)
Violent	(42%)	(37%)	(66%)
Homicide	8	7	7
Child Homicide	4	3	4
Robbery*	24	20	41
Assault	4	3	2
Kidnapping	1	0	5
Other Violent	2	1	7
Property	(36%)	(37%)	(29%)
Burglary	6	6	7
Larceny/Theft	14	15	11
Forgery	6	7	2
Arson	1	2	0
Stolen Prop	7	7	7
Other Prop	1	1	2
Drug Offenses*	(22%)	(26%)	(5%)
	100	100	100
Average Number of Months Served	22.7	22.3	24.4
Number of Previous Arrests	8.3	8.5	7.2

[1]Includes counties within a radius of 120 miles from the prison.
[2]Includes all remaining counties in the state.
*$p < .05$

The Frequency of Visitation and a Profile of Visitors

Visitation data were collected for 180 women. One hundred and forty three women (79%) received visits from either family or friends, while 37 of the women (21%) did not receive visits. For nearly a third of the sample, inmates' friends were the most frequent visitors and were evenly distributed between males and females. For 15% of the women, male friends were the most frequent visitors, while for another 15% female friends were the most frequent visitors. One would assume that relationships between inmates and friends who visit are significant, given the burden visitors face traveling to the prison. Also, family members may feel obligated to visit, whereas friends may visit based on friendship alone. Mothers of the inmates were the most frequent visitors for 14% of the inmates, while minor children were the most frequent visitors for 12% of the inmates. Other relatives were the most frequent visitors for 11% of the women, followed by the husband or fiancé for 10% of the women and a sibling for 9% of the women.

A bivariate analysis was conducted to determine whether there were any significant differences between women who received visits and women who did not. The variables examined were parental status, race, marital status, crime type, prison transfers during sentences, age, number of children, average number of months served, and the number of previous arrests and county of commitment. For the county of commitment $X_2 = 3.45037$, $p = .06324$, which was significant. Although not statistically significant at the 0.05 level, it appears that the women who were committed to prison from counties outside the metropolitan area were less likely to receive visits. As mentioned previously, the distance from visitors' homes to the prison is often the greatest burden visitors face when attempting to maintain contact with inmates.

A monthly rate of visitors was calculated to allow for more meaningful comparisons among the women who had visits. An analysis of variance was then conducted using race to determine whether there were any significant differences between racial/ethnic groups in average number of visitors per month. There were significant differences between racial/ethnic groups. White inmates had a higher rate of visitors per month (4.0) than did Hispanic (3.1) or black (2.0) inmates. An analysis was also conducted on the number of different visitors inmates received over the course of their sentences. The average number of different visitors for the total sample was 9.7. An analysis of variance was again conducted using race to determine whether there were differences in the groups in terms of diversity of visitors. The average number of different visitors was 8.9 for black inmates, 11.4 for Hispanic inmates, and 9.4 for white inmates. The differences were not significant.

Children's Visitation

The study included an analysis of children's visitation. There were 158 inmates who were mothers of minor children; they had a total of 285 children. As Table 2 illustrates, much of the data on children's placement during their mothers' incarceration was missing. This finding is consistent with previous data that suggest that women often do not reveal the whereabouts of their children or

TABLE 2 Selected Demographic Characteristics of Inmates' Children

	n	*Percentage*
Placement of Minors	285	100
Grandparents	137	48
Social Services	52	18
Father	33	12
Friends/Relatives	32	11
Geographic Residence of Minors	201	100
Out of Country	20	10
Out of State	32	16
Outside Metropolitan	29	14
Metropolitan Area	89	44
Resided with Mother Prior to Incarceration	219	100
Yes	117	53
No	102	47

Average age of minor children 7.5
Average number of children per inmate 2.1

even the existence of children for fear that authorities will intervene and take custody (McCarthy, 1980). The remaining data revealed that the majority of children are sent to live with relatives and friends. This finding is consistent with previous research, which has indicated that minor children are most frequently placed informally in the homes of family and friends (Banauch, 1985; Henriquez, 1982; Lapoint, 1977; McGowan & Blumenthal, 1978; Stanton, 1980). A somewhat surprising finding is the percentage of children that are in the custody of social services. Other studies have estimated the number of women whose children are in foster care to be approximately 7% to 12% (Beckerman, 1989). However, the prison in this study estimated that approximately 20% of the mothers had children in foster care.

Slightly more than half the children lived with their mothers prior to the present incarceration. This finding is somewhat surprising, because it was anticipated that a greater percentage of children would have lived with their mothers prior to incarceration. Indeed, the bulk of the research on inmate mothers has suggested that many women live with their children prior to incarceration (Bloom & Steinhart, 1993; McCarthy, 1980; McGowen & Blumenthal, 1978). However, previous studies on incarcerated mothers have focused on inmates at minimum and medium security prisons or in county jails. Women in this study (in a maximum security prison) are more likely to have experienced family disruption prior to their current term of imprisonment, because a prior criminal lifestyle led them to a longer term of imprisonment for their most recent crime, which, as recidivists, they might usually serve in a maximum security prison.

The sample of mothers was divided into those who received visits from minor children and those who did not. Thirty-nine percent of the mothers received visits from their children, while 61% did not. A bivariate analysis was conducted to ascertain whether there were any differences between women who received visits from their children and women who did not. As shown in Table 3, an inmate's age is related to visitation of her minor children. Younger women are more likely to receive visits from their minor children; women over 33 are less likely to receive visits from minor children. Perhaps, minor children of older women are in their teens and are less likely to want to visit because of other interests. Several prison staff members believed that upon reaching the age of nine or ten children develop negative attitudes about visiting a prison. Children are more likely to be angry with their mothers, because they have some understanding that their mothers' behavior is responsible for the predicament of mothers and children.

The inmates' county of commitment was also related to the visitation of minor children. Women who were committed to prison from counties outside the metropolitan area were much less likely to receive visits from their children. Consistent with Bloom and Steinhart's (1993) findings, the visitors' distance from their homes to the prison was a barrier to visitation. For the women who had visits from minor children, an annual rate of visits was calculated. With 12.9 visits per year, Hispanic inmates received the most visits from their children. Black inmates received 10.8 visits per year, and whites inmates received 7.4 visits per year, but the differences were not significant.

Discussion

The findings of the study indicate that women do receive visits from family and friends, but not necessarily from their children. There are several reasons why women might not receive visits. One of the most important determinants of visitation may be the inmates' desire to have visitors. Many women may prefer to be isolated from the outside world. Also, given the burden of visiting prison, especially the financial burden, visitors must have a strong desire to remain connected to the women who are incarcerated. In addition, the financial resources of family and friends affect their ability to visit. Also, the relationship between the inmates and their children's caregivers may determine whether children visit the prison. Many women have strained relationships with their children's caregivers, and caregivers may be reluctant to bring children to the institution (Bloom & Steinhart, 1993). Financial concerns of the caregiver may also influence whether children visit.

Although maintaining visitation is difficult, it appears that correctional officials should encourage it. At the prison in this study, the inmates, staff, and correctional officers all believed that visits helped inmates cope with separation. Inmates look forward to visits, especially from their children (Kitzinger, 1997). Although inmates were usually sad after a visit, everyone involved believed visitation was a positive experience. Inmates craved knowledge about their children's lives and were especially grateful to have an opportunity to visit with them (see Boudin, 1998, for an inmate's perspective of a mother's program).

Moreover, visiting provides an opportunity for communication that may not be possible through telephone calls and letters. Such was the case of C.C., a

TABLE 3 Inmate Mothers Receiving Visits from Minor Children by Selected Demographic Characteristics

	Total Mothers	*Mothers Receiving Visits*	*Percent*	X^2	*Significant*
Race	153			3.50249	.17356
White	32	8	25		
Black	83	35	42		
Hispanic	38	17	48		
Marital Status	150			2.69054	.44184
Single	79	35	44		
Married	30	11	37		
Divorced	32	9	28		
Common-Law	9	4	44		
Crime Type	158			1.34678	.50998
Violent	60	27	45		
Property	59	21	36		
Drugs	39	14	36		
Transfer	158			.56705	.45143
Yes	62	14	45		
No	96	48	38		
Age of Admission	157			8.45303	.01460*
24 yrs. or less	44	22	50		
25 to 32 yrs.	77	33	43		
33 yrs. or more	36	7	19		
Number of Children	157			1.57464	.45506*
1–3	132	52	39		
4 or more	25	10	40		
Commitment County	158			7.4682	.00628*
Metro Area[1]	139	60	43		
Outside Metro[2]	19	2	10		
Months Served	158			4.02661	.13355
18 or less	94	31	33		
19 to 36	41	19	46		
Over 36	23	12	52		
Number of Arrests	156			3.76111	.28844
0	28	7	25		
1–4	46	18	39		
5–9	31	15	48		
Over 9	51	22	43		

[1]Includes counties within a 120 mile radius of the prison.
[2]Includes all remaining counties in the state.
*p < .01

four-year-old child who was visiting her mother. During the visit, she revealed to her mother that her father had abused her sexually. It is unlikely that such a revelation would happen without her mother being present to provide feedback and reassurance. Visitation also allows for the possibility of physical touching between mother and child, which can provide a youngster with a sense of security and comfort.

The superintendent at the prison in this study also noted that visitation allows children to see that correctional authorities are not necessarily enemies. They can see that their mothers are not being hurt and that many of the officers are friendly and helpful people. Children's interactions with correctional officials can give children a more realistic view of criminal justice authorities and help dispel threatening perceptions. Such interactions can be especially significant if a child has witnessed her or his mother being arrested and removed from the home by the police. It was apparent that many children had been exposed to police and correctional officials frequently in their young lives. There were several children who spoke of fathers, uncles, aunts, and grandmothers being arrested or in jail.

Conclusion

This study indicated that the distance from the prison may be the major barrier to visitation. Correctional administrators might work with community volunteers, church groups, and other civic organizations to arrange transportation for families. Also, prisons can establish child centered visiting rooms so that when families do visit there is an atmosphere that encourages interaction between the inmates and their children. Of course, many of the barriers to visiting could be eliminated simply if state legislators authorized the building of prisons in urban areas, from which the vast majority of inmates hail, rather than in remote, rural areas.

Several issues require additional study. First, it is important to determine the effects of visitation on reunification between inmates and their family members, especially their children. For example, does visitation help prepare inmates for family commitments upon release? Second, does visitation reduce recidivism? Holt and Miller's study (1972) indicated that parole success might be enhanced by an inmate's contact with family members while incarcerated. Third, do inmates feel that their visitation with families and friends helps them to cope with the pains of imprisonment?

The reality is that women will leave prison and often return home to their children. It is imperative that correctional and social service agencies work together to address the needs of inmate mothers and their children. The lack of resources for this population has been documented (Banauch, 1985; Henriquez, 1982; McGowan & Blumenthal, 1978; Haley, 1977; Stanton, 1980). Thus, maintaining family ties through visitation programs can help strengthen these relationships. Visitation will probably increase the possibility of successful prison adjustment, parole, and reunification with friends and families, and perhaps most importantly with children.

References

Banauch, P. J. (1985). *Mothers in Prison*. New Brunswick: Transaction Books.

Bennett, L. A. (1989). Correctional administrators' attitudes towards private family visiting. *Prison Journal*, 69, 110–114.

Bloom, B., & Steinhart, D. (1993). *Why Punish the Children: A Reappraisal of Incarcerated Mothers in America*. San Francisco: National Council on Crime and Delinquency.

Boudouris, J. (1985). *Prisons and Kids*. College Park: American Correctional Association.

Boudin, K. (1998). Lessons from a mother's program in prison: a psychosocial approach supports women and their children. *Women & Therapy*, 21 (1), 103.

Bureau of Justice Statistics (1998). *Sourcebook of Criminal Justice Statistics*. Washington, DC: United States Department of Justice.

Bureau of Justice Statistics (2000). Prison statistics [On-line]. Available: Washington, DC: United States Department of Justice.

Geotting, A., & Howsen, R. M. (1986). Correlates of prisoner misconduct. *Journal of Quantitative Criminology*, 2, 49–67.

Giallombardo, R. (1966). *Society of women: a study of women's prison*. New York: Wiley.

Hairston, C. F. (1991). Mothers in jail: parent-child separation and jail visitation. *Affilia*, 6, 9–27.

Heffernan, E. (1972). *Making it in prison: the square, the cool and the life*. New York: John Wiley.

Henriquez, Z. (1982). *Imprisoned mothers and their children: a descriptive and analytical study*. Washington: University Press of America.

Holt, N., & Miller, D. (1972). *Explorations in inmate-family relationships*. Sacramento: California Department of Corrections.

Kaplan, A. G., & Surrey, J. L. (1984). The relational self in women: development theory and public policy. In L. E. Walker (ed.), *Women and Mental Health Policy*. Beverly Hills, CA: Sage.

Kitzinger, S. (1997). Sheila Kitzinger's letter from Europe: how can we help pregnant women and mothers in prison? *Birth*, 24 (3), 197.

Kruttschnitt, C., & Krmpotich, S. (1990). Aggressive behavior among female inmates: an exploratory study. *Justice Quarterly*, 7, 371–389.

LaPoint, V. (1977). Mothers inside, children outside: some issues surrounding imprisoned mothers and their children. *107th Congress of Correctional Proceedings*. American Correctional Association. Lanham, Maryland.

LeFlore, L., & Holston, M. A. (1989). Perceived importance of parenting behaviors as reported by inmate mothers: an exploratory study. *Journal of Offender Counseling, Services & Rehabilitation*, 14 (1), 5–21.

McGowan, B. G., & Blumenthal, K. L. (1978). *Why Punish the Children?* Hackensack, NJ: National Council on Crime and Delinquency.

Merlo, A. V., & Benekos, P. J. (1997). Adapting conservative correctional policies to the economic realities of the 1990s. In B. W. Hancock & P. M. Sharp (Eds.), *Public Policy, Crime, and Criminal Justice* (287–99). Upper Saddle River, NJ: Prentice Hall.

Pollock-Byrne, J. (1990). *Women, prison and crime*. Pacific Grove: Brooks/Cole.

Rothman, D. J. (1971). *The discovery of the asylum: Social Order and Disorder in the New Republic*. Boston: Little, Brown.

Schafer, N. E. (1991). Prison visiting policies and practices. *International Journal of Offender Therapy and Comparative Criminology*, 35, 263–75.

Stanton, A. (1980). *When mothers go to jail*. Lexington, KY: Lexington Books.

Ward, K. D., & Kassebaum, G. (1965). *Women's Prison*. Chicago: Aldine.

Young, D. S. (1999). Ethnicity and health service use in a women's prison. *Journal of Multicultural Social Work*, 7, (3–4), 69.

JOURNAL OF OFFENDER REHABILITATION, Vol. 34(3), 2002. Pp. 67–83.

Part 4: Health Care and Substance Abuse

Providing health care to prison inmates is a legal requirement. As a result of a series of United States Supreme Court cases starting in the 1960s, corrections officials are required to provide medical care to inmates for their serious medical needs. Doing this, however, is an extremely expensive and sometimes very difficult task. In recent years, as the American prison population has increased in size and inmates remain in prison for longer periods of time, so too has the number and range of health problems experienced by inmates increased and become more serious. As a result, the challenges and difficulties for correctional officials, health care professionals, and inmates themselves have become more serious and problematic.

The legal issues involved in providing health care to inmates serve as the basis for the analysis presented by Vaughn and Smith. In the first article in this section, the authors draw on official records and letters written by inmates to a monitor appointed by the federal court to oversee the provision of health care services in a large jail facility. As their analysis of the types and range of issues points out, there are a number of serious problems in the delivery of health care in correctional settings. Some of these problems are a result of the focus on security; some are the consequence of structural elements of institutional settings; and some may be the result of inadequately trained, unprofessional, and unethical persons working in correctional health care. The result, as seen very clearly in the words of the inmates providing Vaughn and Smith's data, is suffering and an assortment of harms brought upon inmates.

The next four articles in this section each look at a specific population or type of health care need in depth. The issues at the centers of these four articles are major concerns in correctional health care for financial, safety, and political reasons. In the first special-focus article, Young and Reviere report on the availability of health care services for female inmates. They explain that not only is the population of female inmates growing rapidly, but women present with different and unique health care needs when they arrive at prison. However, there are a number of services for women's health care needs that are not universally (and sometimes not even frequently) available in prisons. While basic health care services are available (due at least in part to legal requirements), some needs are likely to be missed by correctional officials or addressed through inadequate services. This is likely to mean that female inmates may see deteriorating health conditions, which in turn will lead to both administrative and financial problems for correctional institutions and systems.

The second of these specifically focused articles is Morton's discussion of the increasingly large population of elderly inmates. As she outlines, as they become a larger portion of our inmate population, so too do the special needs they present become an increasingly large challenge for administrators. Among these special needs is medical care. Elderly inmates use health care services more often, and in more expensive ways, than do younger inmates. As our incarcerated offender population continues to grow, there will continue to be larger obstacles and challenges that are more difficult to manage facing correctional administrators and policy makers.

The third health care focus presented in this section is HIV. This is probably the best known, yet perhaps the least understood, health care problem in corrections. There is widespread recognition that HIV infection rates are significantly higher among prison inmates than the general population. However, understanding the risks that this presents for correctional staff and other inmates is a vastly misunderstood issue. Krebs's article, "High Risk HIV Transmission Behavior in Prison and the Prison Subculture," addresses this misunderstanding and shows that while sizable proportions of male inmates do engage in sex, intravenous drug use, and tattooing while in prison, their risks of becoming infected with HIV are not perceived as especially high. Inmates have their own ways (which may or may not truly be effective) to manage their risk of infection, and they do recognize that there are risks involved in many of their activities. However, administrators and policy makers may take satisfaction in this research in that there does not appear to be rampant transmission of HIV, nor inmates attempting to transmit it.

The next article in this section focuses on a less frequently addressed, yet very serious, health problem in prisons: suicide. Medlicott, drawing on research in British correctional institutions, looks at the issue of inmate suicide and the ways that prisoners cope with the time, both on a day-to-day basis and in the long run, while incarcerated. She finds that how time is perceived and how inmates find ways to pass time while in prison differs significantly for inmates who are and are not suicidal. Few researchers or observers have given much thought to the idea of passing time while incarcerated, yet as this article shows very clearly, this is a daily concern and perhaps one of the biggest influences on inmates' physical and mental health.

One thing that is well known about prison inmates is that a great many have a history of alcohol and/or illicit drug abuse. Prior to coming to prison, some estimates suggest that three-quarters or more of offenders have abused drugs or alcohol. As a result, once they arrive in prison, many of these individuals continue to desire alcohol and drugs, and some find ways to continue to use. The last two articles in this section discuss inmates' drug use activities and how drugs occupy a position at the center of many prisons' underground economy and sources of institutional violence.

The sixth article changes focus slightly to look at the health issue of drug use in prison. In this discussion Cope draws on interviews with young inmates to discuss how inmates' drug use is similar to the period before incarceration. What is interesting about this article is that inmates explain how their drug use is a very rational activity that is often based on logical and well-thought-out reasons and compatibility between drugs of choice and the situational context of imprisonment. Inmates do not simply use drugs because they are available, and they may choose not to use particular drugs that are available because they know that drug would not produce a desirable effect for them. The situational context of drug use is highlighted in this discussion. However, this article also focuses on how drug use and distribution inside prison is based on rational and carefully thought-out networks of friendships and "trust." It argues that drug use is not necessarily an irresponsible, spontaneous, or uncontrolled behavior, but instead is a rational, planned, and controlled activity pattern.

The last article in this section looks at one of the most popular drugs in our society, one around which large-scale changes are occurring in correctional operations, and a "drug" that most people do not recognize as a "drug": tobacco. As Lankenau reports in "Smoke 'Em if You Got 'Em," as many correctional institutions and systems have moved to restrict or eliminate tobacco products in their prisons (largely due to health care and associated financial costs), there has developed a very organized and expensive underground economy based on cigarettes. Prices have gone up dramatically, and the economic organization has been created out of both demand and individuals looking to profit from providing a supply. The result of smoking bans and restrictions in many institutions is an increase in contraband, increases in corruption and attempts to smuggle, and establishment of a new form of powerful inmate. In the end, such new policies may cause more harm than good.

Addressing inmates' health care needs, including use of drugs and other substances, is a complex, very large, and very expensive aspect of corrections. For administrators, funding and managing health care services is a major challenge. Health care can also be a major management challenge for inmates, despite being a necessity. The health care issues that inmates present to providers run the full range that would be found in any population. However, inmates have special issues they are likely to present with. These special needs present the greatest challenges for administrators and policy makers. And, as the articles in this section make clear, sometimes the ways in which we address health care issues are less than ideal, and sometimes inmates are less-than-ideal patients.

Discussion Questions

Health Care and Substance Abuse

1. What are the major health care problems experienced by prison inmates? What are the factors that contribute to these problems? Why are these problems more acute among inmates than the general population?
2. What could prison officials do to improve the health of inmates? How might these changes be helped or hindered by the need to maintain security?
3. How do health problems of inmates impact their relationships with other inmates and the level of violence in an institution?

12. Practicing Penal Harm Medicine in the United States: Prisoners' Voices from Jail

Michael S. Vaughn
Linda G. Smith

This article explores how the implementation of the penal harm movement within a correctional health care system can lead to the ill-treatment and torture of prisoners. Through an interpretive/inductive analysis of reports written by a federal court monitor and 103 letters written by prisoners to a federal court monitor overseeing a consent decree of a county mega jail located in the United States, we identify six areas of ill-treatment and torture at the jail's medical facilities: (1) using medical care to humiliate prisoners; (2) withholding medical care from HIV-positive prisoners and those with AIDS; (3) withholding medical care from other prisoners; (4) exposing prisoners to temperature extremes and sleep deprivation; (5) using dental care as a means of ill-treatment and torture; and (6) falsifying prisoners' medical records. Because correctional medical personnel work in a system that subordinates their professional canons to the efficiency-based rationality of the new penology and the ethical relativism of the penal harm movement, we conclude that some correctional health providers sympathetic to the custodial subculture abdicate their ethical obligations, and that the result is ill-treatment and torture of prisoners.

From the "deprivation of liberty" perspective of punishment, the sole purpose of incarceration is to restrict the freedoms of those incarcerated (Council of Europe 1987, 1995; Reynaud 1986; Wilson 1993). That is, the "prisoner's punishment is being sent to prison"; "punishing prisoners once they're inside is not the point" (Peters 1992:250). Advocating the deprivation of liberty perspective, Penal Reform International (1990:5) argues that prison managers must be "concerned with ensuring prisoners' personal dignity, their physical and mental well-being, education and recreational facilities, religious provisions, and standards of hygiene and medical and psychiatric care." The Council of Europe (1987:34) contends that the "philosophy and management of any [correctional] system [must be] based on . . . principles of humanity, morality, justice, and respect for human dignity that are essential to a modern civilized society." This perspective is "aimed principally at the re-education and re-socialization of the offender" in which "prisons must show respect for the fundamental rights of individuals" (Neale 1991:207).

Opposed to the deprivation of liberty model is the "penal harm" movement, an emerging alternative perspective in American penology (see Clear 1994;

Cullen 1995). Penal harm advocates contend that the incarceration experience should inflict pain and make conditions of confinement as harsh as possible (see Allen and Abril 1997; Bright 1996, 1997). Because "criminals are commonly associated with slime, darkness, and foul odors, their places of punishment must reflect these qualities" (see Duncan 1996:144). Proponents of penal harm call for a system of punishment that embraces imprisonment because it embodies conscious infliction of pain (see Christie 1981, 1993) and recognizes that the "essence of the penal sanction is to harm" (Clear 1994:4). From this perspective, incarceration is a "planned government act, whereby a citizen" is harmed intentionally. This justifies the purpose of incarceration: offender suffering (Clear 1994:4). Correctional facilities serve as "factories for the manufacture of psycho-physical handicaps," providing the conditions of confinement that harm, damage, and debilitate those confined (Gallo and Ruggiero 1991:278). In recent years, the penal harm movement has gained currency, making the conditions of correctional confinement harsh and punitive, whereas the human rights-oriented "deprivation of liberty" model has been deemphasized (McCoy 1997).

For many years, the workplace culture of corrections was said to be divided into two irreconcilable camps. On one side were custodial personnel who identified with the penal harm movement and wished to inflict pain on prisoners (Fogel 1979). On the other side were the health-oriented medical staff members who focused on the prisoners' welfare and treated them with compassion, dignity, and humanity (Kratcoski 1989). Once correctional systems are committed to implementing the mandates of penal harm, the line between acceptable punishment and ill-treatment becomes blurred. When applied to correctional health care, the implementation of mandates for penal harm challenges the existence of the dichotomy between custody and treatment.

In this article we explore how the implementation of the penal harm movement within a correctional health care system can lead to the ill-treatment and torture of prisoners. Our thesis is that the reported philosophical breach between custodians and some medical staff members is more imagined than real. Because correctional medical personnel work in a system that subordinates their professional canons to the utilitarian rationality of the new penology and the ethical relativism of the penal harm movement, we conclude that some correctional health providers sympathetic to the custodial subculture abdicate their ethical obligations, and that the result is the ill-treatment and torture of prisoners.

Background

Ethical Relativism in Correctional Health Care

Despite the imperative to separate the administration of medical care from custodial and security concerns (Alderslade 1995; British Medical Association Working Party (BMAWP) 1992; Rynerson 1989), some correctional medical personnel emphasize custody and security (Brewer and Derrickson 1992:627; Fleisher and Rison 1997:330; Nightingale and Chill 1994; Reyes 1995). This orientation is fostered by correctional systems' training health care workers in custodial and security arrangements.

The United States Federal Bureau of Prisons trains all physicians, nurses, and physician assistants at the Federal Law Enforcement Training Center in Glynco, Georgia. These medical personnel attend an "intense 3-week course in primary correctional techniques" comprising "Bureau policies and procedures, firearms qualification, self-defense (aikido), legal issues, and custodial techniques. Experienced professional instructors use lectures, live range firing, hand-to-hand self-defense training, and situational simulation in the training process" (Vause, Beeler, and Miller-Blanks 1997:62). Socializing correctional medical personnel in an occupational subculture that embraces the custodial/security mission of the institution may diminish their commitment to treatment, healing, and rehabilitation.

Ethical relativism occurs when "no clear distinction is made between the custodial function of [security] personnel and the caring function of personnel who have been trained to provide health care" (van Heerden 1995:345). When correctional medical personnel engage in ethical relativism—the belief that ethical standards are not universal but are malleable depending on the context—(Buchanan 1996; Tomasevski 1992:194; Wessner 1996)—they find themselves in "extreme, morally ambiguous situations." In this role conflict, health care personnel may function "as state-supporting victimizers rather than as patient-protecting healers" (Brown 1987:156; Hornblum 1997; Nightingale et al. 1990:2100). Divided loyalties and ethical relativism allow medical officials to affiliate with the custodial subculture while casting off their allegiance to the Hippocratic Oath (Breed 1998; Rosalki 1993; Trevelyan 1988), the creed of the medical profession, which states *primum non nocerc*: "Above all, do no harm" (Jacobs and White 1996:49; Laing 1996; Nightingale 1990; Savage et al. 1997; Scroggy 1993). "Caught in this situation, the [correctional health care worker] may find forces of economics, career, and loyalty to the organization stronger than the moral compulsion to protest" the machinery of penal harm (Browde 1989; DuBose 1996; Meyer-Lie 1986; Sagan and Jonsen 1976:1428).

A similar utilitarian logic guided Nazi doctors' participation in genocide during World War II (Lifton 1982, 1986; White 1996). The prisoners' medical interests were subordinated to the Third Reich; thus it became morally acceptable to harm Jewish, gypsy, and mentally ill prisoners to preserve the Nazi state. Under this ethic it was assumed "that benefits and harms should be distributed among individuals so as to maximize the [perceived] aggregate" good for society (Veatch 1987:22). Nazi "doctors and others spoke only about how to do things most efficiently, about what worked best" (Lifton 1982:294); this view resembled the new penal managerialism spearheading today's correctional reform.

Ill-Treatment and Torture of Prisoners

In the 1960s, correctional medical personnel in the United States were implicated in the torture of prisoners. The infamous "Tucker Telephone" was invented by Dr. A.E. Rollins, the physician at the Tucker State Prison Farm in Arkansas. At this facility, prisoners "designated for 'elimination' often were committed to the hospital, where the prison physician allegedly would 'put them to sleep'; . . . death certificates then were falsified to indicate 'natural causes.'" In addition, medical care was sold to prisoners, and indigent prisoners in "need of medical help . . . had . . . to submit to homosexual activities in return for medication." (Murton 1971:25).

In the 1990s, after court-ordered change (*Estelle v. Gamble* 1976), most correctional facilities in the United States reportedly reformed their medical facilities to remove punitive and pain-inflicting mandates; recently, however, the emergence of the penal harm movement has raised questions about the use of correctional medical care for punitive purposes (Vaughn 1995; Vaughn and Carroll 1998). At the 1992 International Conference on Penal Reform in Former Totalitarian Societies, Al Bronstein of the American Civil Liberties Union said "Western prisons too were often dirty, dangerous, unsanitary, overcrowded, and were by no means immune from breaches of international norms regarding human rights," including the use of medical care as a means of ill-treatment and torture (Hornblum 1997; King 1994:62; Paden 1984).

Despite these concerns, "criminologists and penologists have been remiss in their treatment of [ill-treatment and torture], largely ignoring it; and it has been mainly human rights and prison reform organizations that, in the last decade or so, have heightened the awareness of the public to the prevalence of torture in modern police and prison settings" (Sheleff 1987:286). In correctional health care, researchers suggest that "most [prisoners] experience no change in their health status during incarceration" (Marquart et al. 1996:345, 1997:199) or that "prisoners leave prison healthier than when they entered" (Bonta and Gendreau 1990:357; Fleisher and Rison 1997:328). Although some observers argue that prisoners' poor pre-incarceration health accounts for the poor state of their health while incarcerated (Marquart et al. 1996, 1997), this view ignores the role and practice of penal harm medicine as a factor contributing to the deterioration of prisoners' health conditions.

Some observers argue that the word *torture* should be reserved for extreme government-sanctioned actions in the context of organized violence (Turner and Gorst-Unsworth 1990; Van Willigen 1992), including state-sponsored physical acts of depravity such as burning flesh, breaking bones, and other types of permanent disfigurement (Asad 1996). Yet groups that work with torture survivors in the torture rehabilitation movement (Genefke 1993; Jaranson 1995) believe that the physical and the psychological effects of torture are not separated so easily; they argue that "trauma's impact on the psyche is as real as a bullet tearing through flesh" (Engdahl and Eberly 1990; Rosenberg 1997:34). These treatment professionals recognize that "while the physical consequences of torture can be severe, the psychological sequelae usually have the most profound and debilitating impact on the lives of the survivors" (Jaranson 1995:268; Melamed, Melamed, and Bouhoutsos 1990; Petersen and Rasmussen 1992).

Most agree that the purpose of torture is the infliction of physical pain, psychological degradation, and dehumanizing humiliation of prisoners (Punamaki 1988; Turner and Gorst-Unsworth 1990), but the "distinction between [ill-treatment and torture] is a matter of degree: torture and other forms of ill-treatment represent different points along a continuum" (Morgan and Evans 1994:143). According to this conceptualization, the word *torture* is not used exclusively (Asad 1996); the term *ill-treatment* is preferred because it encompasses the full range of activities associated with deplorable correctional practices (Morgan and Evans 1994:146; Sheleff 1987:312). Ill-treatment focuses on "deliberately squalid material or psychological conditions, brutal acts. . . . [and] disciplinary rules designed to break the spirit" (Morgan and Evans 1994:146).

Although it is difficult to specify the practices and conditions that constitute ill-treatment and torture of prisoners because these are manifested in various forms (Downie 1993; Tindale 1996), Amnesty International (1975, 1984b) has identified four essential elements. First, two individuals are involved: the victim and the torturer. Second, the "victim is under the physical control of the torturer" (Sagan and Jonsen 1976:1427). Third, the torturer inflicts mental or psychological pain, seeks to harm the victim emotionally, and is "both purposeful and systematic" (Bendfeldt-Zachrisson 1985; Nightingale 1990:132; Shue 1978). Fourth, the torturer attempts "to break the will of the victim, to destroy his/her humanity" (Sagan and Jonsen 1976:1427; also see Haritos-Fatouros 1988) "in an attempt to perpetrate a determined order of power relationships" (Bendfeldt-Zachrisson 1985:339). Simply put, "torture is the deliberate infliction of pain by one person on another" (Nightingale 1990:132). Just as the goal of the penal harm movement is the "violation of a [prisoner's] well-being" (Clear 1994:16), torture "is intended to destroy and wipe out the victim's personality," identity, and soul (Kooijmans 1995:15; Parmentier 1992:571), to cause the "destruction of [the victim's] mind, body, and spirit" (Laurence 1992:301), and "to break [prisoners] as individuals and change them into docile masses" (Tindale 1996:351).

Methodology

Research Site

The jail is classified as a mega jail and is located in a large metropolitan area.

The jail complex consists of several buildings that house maximum-, medium-, and minimum-security male and female prisoners, both pretrial detainees and sentenced inmates. Although a high-rise building serves as the maximum-security facility for male prisoners, it also contains booking and holding cells for males and females, the primary medical unit, the kitchen, several housing units for males, and administrative offices. Another building houses maximum-security female prisoners; this facility contains a small medical clinic for women prisoners. A separate building houses medium-security male prisoners, and two barrack-style buildings houses minimum-security males and females. Work-release centers are located in two separate buildings; one temporarily houses minimum-security females, and the other holds minimum-security male work-release prisoners. Separate buildings hold additional administrative offices, a visitors' center, a kitchen and dining area for staff and prisoners, and the laundry.

The primary medical unit is located in the high-rise maximum-security facility, where a wing is dedicated for male prisoners under suicide watch and those requiring constant medical supervision. Because of growing demand for medical services, some of the regular housing units have been designated as medical housing units; thus some prisoners are remote from the nurses' stations located in the primary medical unit. In the primary medical unit, prisoners report for sick call, dental services, and psychiatric evaluation. Prisoners who suffer minor medical mishaps are treated in the jail's medical unit, but those with major emergencies are transported to local hospitals that have contracted with the jail to accept these individuals. Some prisoners requiring special medical care such as ophthalmology, dermatology, or oncology, are transported to external medical providers for treatment.

The jail has a history of failing to maintain the facility in accordance with constitutional standards and consent decree requirements. In November 1979 the county entered into a consent decree to remedy unconstitutional conditions of confinement, including unacceptable medical facilities and health care at the jail (see appendix). From November 1979 to January 1998, when the consent decree was terminated, the jail's medical facilities were never in full compliance with the consent decree's mandates, although the jail remained accredited by the NCCHC (Federal Court Monitor 1992–1996).

As part of the 1979 agreement, the supervising federal court appointed a "court monitor" to assess the jail's compliance with the consent decree. The consent decree mandated that a copy of the agreement be "continuously posted in each prebooking or holding cell and in each cell block" ("Final Proposal" 1979:14). Ten copies of the consent decree were also to be placed in the jail library, and all prisoners were to be "advised in writing of the availability of [the] consent decree and the method to be used in securing a copy" ("Final Proposal" 1979:14). Moreover, the consent decree stated that the federal court monitor's "name and address shall be provided to all [prisoners] upon entering the . . . jail and they shall be advised that [the court monitor] may be contacted in regard to any violation of this agreement" ("Final Proposal" 1979:14). A mailbox was established in each housing unit so that prisoners could drop off letters written to the court monitor. Prisoners who wished to communicate with the court monitor were provided with writing materials to compose letters. Prisoners who did not write a letter but who desired to communicate with the court monitor received the opportunity to do so during quarterly jail inspections.

Data Collection and Analysis

The primary units of analysis were letters written by prisoners to the jail monitor to complain about medical facilities and health care personnel. Although prisoners raised many other constitutional and consent decree-related issues in their letters, we focus here on the medical concerns because the court monitor believed that "medical services were the most problematic area of concern under the consent decree" (Federal Court Monitor 1994). Allegations in prisoners' letters were corroborated by independent information gathered from several sources including the federal court monitor (Federal Court Monitor 1992–1996), medical and legal documents (*Nelson v. Prison Health Services* 1997), medical and custodial personnel who worked in the jail, and individuals with detailed knowledge of the consent decree.

In addition to analyzing prisoners' letters, we became familiar with the jail's delivery of medical services by reading sick call slips submitted by prisoners seeking medical treatment, grievance forms filed by prisoners claiming inadequate treatment, reports filed by the jail monitor to the federal judge overseeing the consent decree, internal policies promulgated by the medical provider, and memoranda written by jail staff in response to sick call requests and medical grievances filed by prisoners. We reviewed prisoners' medical records, toured the facility, and interviewed the prisoners' attorney. He brought the original suit that resulted in the consent decree and remained the plaintiffs' attorney for the 18-year life of the case. We also interviewed staff members who worked for the federal judge overseeing the consent decree, prisoners at the jail, the sheriff charged with maintaining the jail, the lieutenant who acted as a liaison between the jail and the federal court monitor, the medical care contract monitor who worked for the sheriff's office, and numerous other custodial staff members at the jail. In addition, we interviewed jail physicians, nurses, physician's assistants, and medical technicians responsible for delivering health care. In all, we spent more than 1,000 hours evaluating the health care system at the jail.

Over the life of the consent decree, three separate federal court monitors were assigned to watch over the jail's compliance with the consent decree. In this article we focus on letters written to the third monitor, whose appointment began in October 1992. The letters were organized chronologically and numbered sequentially by date of postmark. The length and quality of the letters varied markedly. Some prisoners submitted handwritten letters of only two or three sentences; others crafted typed, single-spaced, multiple-page narratives that painted a vivid picture of medical practices at the jail. Several prisoners wrote rambling, stream-of-consciousness diatribes. A few, however, wrote sophisticated, highly developed, well-organized letters consistent with a college education.

Reliability and Validity

Determining the veracity of prisoners' allegations was a problem. Prisoners generally tend to use circular reasoning, make false statements, and reach erroneous conclusions (Shields and de Moya 1997:54). Although not all of the allegations in the prisoners' letters could be sustained to a medical certainty, the jail monitor believed that their complaints had enough merit to warrant further investigation, which required an administrative response to the allegations.

In many cases, the administrative reaction from jail medical personnel was nonresponsive, inadequate, and defensive. The jail monitor frequently determined that medical providers at the jail engaged in practices of ill-treatment and torture (Federal Court Monitor 1992–1996). In these ways, allegations in the prisoners' letters were corroborated consistently during the court monitor's jail inspections, and claims raised in the letters routinely implicated problems with the delivery of medical care that were addressed specifically in the consent decree.

On the basis of the themes in the prisoners' letters, the court monitor's reports, the interviews, the observations made during more than 20 site visits, medical and legal documentation, internal jail memoranda, and depositions from a civil lawsuit for inadequate medical care at the jail, we used an interpretive/inductive process to create six categories: (1) using medical care to humiliate prisoners; (2) withholding medical care from HIV-positive prisoners and those with AIDS; (3) withholding medical care from other prisoners; (4) exposing prisoners to temperature extremes and sleep deprivation; (5) using dental care as a means of ill-treatment and torture; and (6) falsifying prisoners' medical records.

Findings and Discussion

From October 1992 to September 1997, prisoners wrote more than 250 letters to the federal court monitor; 103 of these letters pertained to medical care. During this time, the jail incarcerated approximately 2,400 prisoners per day.

Table 1 shows the specific medical provisions of the consent decree that were addressed in the prisoners' letters (see appendix). Table 2 displays the number of letters pertaining to various practices of ill-treatment and torture of prisoners at the jail. Although the number of cases was small, these practices are difficult to document and represent the most egregious violations of medical ethics.

TABLE 1 Provisions in the Consent Degree Pertaining to Medical Care Addressed in Prisoners' Letters Written to the Federal Court Monitor

Provision of the Consent Decree	*N*	%
Access to Physicians	18	17.5
Evaluation of Prisoners' Complaints	10	9.7
Emergency Medical Service	2	1.9
Treatment within 24 Hours	39	37.9
Medical Diet	3	2.9
Hospitalize Infections/Contagious	13	12.6
Custodial Personnel Handling Medication	0	.0
Dental Care	15	14.6
Health Screening	3	2.9
Total	103	100.0

TABLE 2 Practices of Medical Ill-Treatment and Torture Identified in Prisoners' Letters to the Federal Court Monitor

Categories of Ill-Treatment and Torture	N	%
Using Medical Care to Humiliate Prisoners	21	20.4
Withholding Medical Care from HIV-Positive/AIDS Prisoners	15	14.6
Withholding Medical Care from Other Prisoners	36	34.9
Exposing Prisoners to Temperature Extremes and Sleep Deprivation	5	4.8
Using Dental Care as an Instrument of Ill-Treatment and Torture	15	14.6
Falsifying Prisoners' Medical Records	8	7.8
Other Unethical Medical Practices	3	2.9
Total	103	100.0

Using Medical Care to Humiliate Prisoners

When prisoners enter correctional systems, they frequently experience degradation ceremonies designed to transform them from being complete persons to "discredited ones" (Goffman 1962, 1963; Irwin 1985; Toch 1992a). Because "there is no confidentiality between prisoner and doctor" (Hudson 1987:958), medical conditions of HIV-positive prisoners and those with AIDS are used as an instrument to label, stigmatize, and cast them out of the general prisoner population (Gostin and Lazzarini 1997:111; Greenspan 1996:115; Turnbull, Dolan, and Stimson 1993:204).

Letters written to the jail monitor and the monitor's subsequent inspections showed an extensive process of degradation, humiliation, and subjugation of prisoners by medical personnel (Federal Court Monitor 1992, 1996). Some jail medical officials disclosed prisoners' HIV-positive/AIDS status to everyone in the facility, including custodial staff, noncustodial staff, and other prisoners (Letter 028).

In one instance a correctional officer, in the presence of three prisoners, ordered the jail barber to wear rubber gloves while cutting the hair of an HIV-positive prisoner (Letter 021), even though the barber did not routinely wear rubber gloves while cutting prisoners' hair. When the prisoner told the officer that he wanted to file a grievance because the officer had divulged his confidential medical history to nonmedical and noncustodial personnel, the officer refused to provide the prisoner with a grievance form, remarking "to another [prisoner] that those AIDS-infected motherfuckers want to file a grievance against me" (Letter 021).

According to the court monitor, HIV-positive/AIDS prisoners were identified by a large blue dot placed above their cells (Federal Court Monitor 1992). This symbol revealed who was HIV-positive to everyone in the jail. A detainee with AIDS (Letter 041) complained that "detainees' medical conditions and privacy rights are violated every day [at] the jail. All known HIV-positive/AIDS detainees are separated and isolated from other detainees, even if they are completely healthy." HIV-positive/AIDS prisoners, both pretrial detainees and convicted inmates, have segregated recreation and exercise times; their food trays are specially marked and are used only for HIV-positive/AIDS offenders. As a result, "HIV-positive/AIDS detainees have been humiliated, threatened, discriminated, isolated, teased, and constantly asked, 'Are you dying from AIDS?"' (Letter 041). Letters to the jail monitor and the monitor's jail inspections confirmed that custodial staff members and some medical personnel identified HIV-positive prisoners to noncustodial staff members, security personnel, and other prisoners by leaking confidential information contained in health care records.

This idea was expressed in Letter 179, where a prisoner told the jail mental health counselor that the custodial staff used excessive force against him; the counselor assured the prisoner confidentiality and promised to investigate the matter. After the prisoner talked with the counselor, custodial officers "knew every thing [the prisoner] told the counselor." Thereafter the officers harassed, threatened, and taunted the prisoner, attempting to provoke him to violence. In a letter to the court monitor, the prisoner lamented "I'm in fear of my life from these officers," who are "trying to get me to loose [sic] control so [they can] retaliate and be justified in what they will do to me."

Using medical care to break prisoners' will and to exploit known weaknesses was a theme in letters written to the jail monitor. In Letter 098, a Vietnam veteran who suffered from posttraumatic stress disorder (PTSD), manifested in insomnia, combat flashbacks, and anxiety attacks, was diagnosed as 100% disabled by the Department of Veterans Affairs (VA) and was under medical supervision and treatment by VA physicians. When the vet was incarcerated at the jail on a probation violation, his VA-prescribed medication was discontinued. Although the inmate was classified, where he fully disclosed his medical condition and his ongoing treatment, and made repeated requests to continue his Lithium (to control mania) and Xanax (to control anxiety), he never saw a physician during his 16 days of incarceration.

Eleven days into his incarceration, the inmate was examined by a psychiatric nurse, who said "We don't give your type of medication here" and reminded the inmate that jails are "very stressful places and [to] just get use[d] to" being without the medication. When the inmate asked the nurse "why it took so long to see medical" personnel at the jail, the nurse replied, "I've been on vacation." The inmate suffered medication withdrawal, nightmares, and combat flashbacks, saying "[E]very time a helicopter landed. . . , I felt I was in combat back in Vietnam."

In a system of medical depravity, prisoners are made to wallow in their own excrement (Cockburn 1997) in an attempt to humiliate them and break their will (La Forte, Marcello, and Himmel 1994:177–88; Roth et al. 1987; Silver et al. 1986). One pregnant prisoner, who suffered a miscarriage at the jail, waited "six or seven hours before [medical personnel] sent [her] to the hospital even though [she] was bleeding profusely" (*Nelson v. Prison Health Services* 1997:1456). According to the court monitor, another female detainee was booked at the jail under the influence of alcohol and/or drugs. Because health care personnel failed to provide proper supervision, the detainee experienced alcohol/drug withdrawal, suffered from hallucinations, removed all of her clothes, and ate her own menstrual flow in view of other prisoners. "Despite the fact that she should have been placed in a medical unit because she was at high risk of withdrawal (D.T.'s), she was left unattended for five days by medical staff" (Federal Court Monitor 1994). The detainee received medical attention only after it was requested by the court monitor, in violation of the consent decree.

Wallowing in excrement is profoundly "humiliating because contact typically demonstrates powerlessness" and lack of environmental control, from which humans draw comfort (Silver et al. 1986:272). These emotions were expressed by another female prisoner; she was under treatment by free-world physicians for a disease known as "short bowel syndrome," from which she suffered "chronic diarrhea 10 to 20 times a day" (Letter 225). Because of the prisoner's condition, she was unable to eat solid food; consequently, free-world physicians had surgically inserted a feeding tube into her stomach, where specially prepared food was pumped into her digestive system.

When the prisoner entered the jail, the medical department threw her "infusion pump . . . and bag of supplies . . . out with the garbage." As her diarrhea worsened, she "was housed in maximum security, not because of [her] behavior, but because" of the foul odor that accompanied her illness. The illness, a "form of cancer, is not contagious, but some staff said she had AIDS, . . . treating her like she had the plague." Although many medical personnel were "rude and very crude, one [counselor] in particular [was] exceptionally offensive." The counselor "threatened to quit her job because of the odor, [and] claimed the smell made her so sick that she had to miss days from work" (Letter 225). As a result, the prisoner was never placed in the jail's medical dormitory but was "moved . . . many times throughout the jail for the convenience of the other prisoners with no regards to [her] own feelings or sickness." Clearly at the breaking point, the prisoner concluded her letter, "[I'm] so sick and tired of being tossed around."

Another tactic used by jail medical staff members to humiliate prisoners and break their will involved the misrepresentation of treatment options available to prisoners; seriously ill prisoners were forced to plead for health care (Federal Court Monitor 1995). Letter 085 was written by a pregnant prisoner who had not been examined by a physician after several weeks of incarceration. The prisoner, who had a history of pregnancy problems, said that the medical staff told her they did not treat pregnant prisoners. She suffered "pain so much at times [she couldn't] even eat and keep food down." Moreover, the prisoner reported that she was "scared of loosing [sic] the baby, depressed, and crying most of the time." She concluded "[W]e are human beings, not animals, and . . . animals get better treatment than what we have been receiving. Please, help me with this problem, as I'm going to be here for at least 3 more months."

A similar scenario was reported in Letter 190, in which a pregnant prisoner, jailed for two months, received no treatment for a vaginal discharge that "looks and feels like chlamydia" (Federal Court Monitor 1995). According to the prisoner, the "discharge feels awful and has a terrible odor—everyone can tell, [which is] embarrassing. I go through over 10 pads a day." The prisoner reported that she saw an obstetrician one month into her incarceration, but remained untreated one month after being examined. At sick call, the jail physician refused to see the prisoner. Humiliated and exasperated, the prisoner wrote "[N]ow I sit going on 2 months with this 'mystery illness,' untreated, getting worse everyday. . . . I'm constantly having headaches, stomach cramps, and can't sleep . . . I'm very scared for my baby and myself . . . This medical condition is awful . . . I'm going crazy with this medical problem . . . I'm at the verge of tears everyday over it, and the medical staff treat me as a pain-in-the-ass! Please help me!! Help my baby!" The degrading and humiliating medical practices that these pregnant prisoners described in their letters to the jail monitor have been reported in the historical (Butler 1997:163–68) as well as the contemporary literature as a common "correctional response to the health needs of pregnant women" (Acoca 1998:55).

Letters to the jail monitor illustrated how prisoners with serious medical needs were humiliated and forced to grovel before health care was forthcoming. In the jail, medical care was used to "break prisoners' spirits," and the prisoners in Letters 085, 098, 190, and 225 appeared to be at the breaking point. Prisoners' letters and the jail monitor's inspections (Federal Court Monitor 1992–1996) also indicated that some jail medical personnel violated a basic provision of the consent decree, which mandated that "all [prisoners'] complaints shall result in treatment within 24 hours of the complaint." Reflecting the effects of a total institution, the letters show prisoners' helplessness and dependence; prisoners no longer believed that they were in control of their lives or medical conditions.

Withholding Medical Care from HIV-Positive Prisoners and Those with AIDS

Although torture involves physicians overtly punishing prisoners, more subtle forms of ill-treatment include the withholding of medical treatment from suffering prisoners (Burkhalter 1995; MacPherson 1989; Nightingale et al. 1990; Sagan and Jonsen 1976). Belknap (1996:36) reported that prisoners in the United States were denied access to a physician for as long as eight months. In these circumstances, it is not the application of medical care but the omission of care that inflicts pain, (Laborde 1989).

Indeed, because "mankind's most fundamental beliefs are those that concern life, suffering, and death" (Bankowski 1996:147), perhaps the cruelest example, in the jail, of the custodial-medical implementation of penal harm involved lack of care for prisoners who were dying and near death. Letters to the jail monitor showed a disregard for the health condition of HIV-positive prisoners: They were made to wait to see a physician, which caused their health to deteriorate rapidly. Research in the United States (Committee on the Judiciary 1991:86; Griffin et al. 1996) and in Great Britain (Turnbull, Dolan, and Stimson 1993) also shows that HIV-positive prisoners and those with AIDS experience more rapid declines in health than do free-world outpatients because they receive little high-quality health care.

When prisoners are admitted to correctional facilities, health care received before admittance is stopped until correctional medical personnel can assess their medical needs (Anno 1997). Prisoners in our sample reported that this technique was adapted somewhat by some jail physicians: They promised HIV-positive/AIDS prisoners treatment from free-world medical providers, but ordered all in-jail medical treatment to stop before the free-world health care was available. As a result, some severely ill AIDS prisoners went months without medical care.

One extremely ill prisoner with AIDS, who suffered from Kaposi's sarcoma, received medical care and medication for HIV/AIDS at the jail (Letter 028). Because of his advanced AIDS and his deteriorating health, the prisoner requested and received permission from jail medical officials for medical treatment in the free-world community. After the external referral was approved but before the prisoner received any treatment by a nonjail physician, the jail medical staff discontinued all of his medical treatment and medication for two months, which caused his condition to deteriorate rapidly. The Federal Court Monitor (1994) confirmed that "orders for outside consultation continues to be a problem with failure by the [jail's] medical staff to follow-up on these [free-world] consultations."

Letter 041 revealed a similar situation. A pretrial detainee wrote the court monitor in February 1993, describing his rapidly declining health status. A long-term AIDS survivor (since 1981), the detainee had Kaposi's sarcoma and was slowly going blind. He had been able to control HIV/AIDS in the free world for more than a decade, but was near death after six months in the jail. Even though he was never examined by an external medical provider, the detainee was told for four months that he would be examined by a free-world physician. The detainee lamented "I haven't been found guilty of anything, but it seems like I have already been sentenced to die in the jail."

In one letter the writer reported that even when jail medical personnel possessed medication to treat seriously ill prisoners with AIDS, they refused to distribute it. A prisoner with end-stage AIDS (Letter 147; Letter 148) did not receive the medication prescribed by his free-world physician during his seven weeks of incarceration at the jail, even though jail officials possessed the 18 medications prescribed by physicians at the Veterans Affairs Hospital. A month into the prisoner's incarceration, the supervisor at the jail medical unit wrote him a letter saying "I received today your 107 bottles of pills at the sheriff's office, and I will ask [the doctor] to review this list with you . . . when he returns from his vacation." When the prisoner urged jail medical officials to distribute the medication, staff members told the prisoner that AIDS medication was too much trouble, and commented "[Y]ou are in jail not a hotel; if you don't like it bond out."

HIV-positive individuals are susceptible to opportunistic infections that weaken their immune system, leaving them more vulnerable to the virus that causes AIDS (Blumberg and Mahaffey-Sapp 1997; Stein and Headley 1996; Tesoriero and McCullough 1996). According to Gostin and Lazzarini (1997:139), HIV-positive prisoners possess immunocompromising conditions and "are more susceptible to . . . infection and substantially more likely to develop active disease than persons with normal immune systems." Because fever is one manifestation of infection, it is important to treat fever in HIV-positive individuals aggressively to decrease risk of severe illness and death (Blumberg 1990). Letters to the jail monitor and the monitor's investigations (Federal Court Monitor 1992, 1996), however, revealed that some HIV-positive prisoners waited weeks or days before receiving treatment for fever and infections.

On the morning of June 16, 1994, for example, an HIV-positive prisoner sought immediate medical care for a fever (Letter 140). The nurse making medication rounds told the prisoner that "she was in a hurry and didn't have time to set the medication tray down to sign the medical request form." Without examining the prisoner, she told him that his request for medical treatment was no emergency, but encouraged him to submit the request during her 9:00 p.m. rounds. The prisoner did so, but "no doctor, nurse, or anyone contacted [the prisoner] about the medical problems" cited in the complaint.

After the prisoner submitted another request for medical care and after his family called the jail to protest the denial of health care, the prisoner was examined on June 20, 1994 by a physician, who discovered a 102.9-degree fever. Treatment began on June 21, 1994, 6 days after the original request. This delay violated the consent decree, which mandated that "all [prisoner] complaints shall result in treatment within 24 hours of the complaint" ("Final Proposal" 1979:9).

Withholding medical care from HIV-positive/AIDS prisoners is an example of a jail health care system's implementation of penal harm mandates. A health care system operating under the principles of the penal harm movement would withdraw treatment from prisoners with symptoms of advanced AIDS.

Withholding Medical Care from Other Prisoners

HIV-positive/AIDS prisoners were not the only inmates at the jail who suffered from the effects of the withdrawal of medical care. Some prisoners in severe pain also were denied medication (Letter 199; Letter 209). In some cases, jail medical staff members delayed implementation of a health care regimen, hoping to stall long enough to allow the prisoner to be released from jail or transferred to another facility before any health care was delivered in the jail (Federal Court Monitor 1992, 1996; Letter 183; Letter 190).

Letter 110 was written by a prisoner with leukemia, who lost all sensation in the left side of his body and the right side of his face but was denied all medical care during his three months in jail. When the prisoner repeatedly asked for treatment, medical personnel told him that they were still evaluating his records. Another prisoner, who suffered from a painful hernia, waited three weeks to see a physician (Letter 168). When he finally was examined, medical staff members told him that hernias "could be all right for a year or so"; therefore no treatment would be provided for the hernia while he was incarcerated at the jail. The medical literature suggests that this cavalier attitude toward prisoners with hernias may be dangerous because early treatment reduces morbidity, mortality, and life-threatening complications (Chung et al. 1997; Naude and Bongard 1997; Witherington 1987).

A third prisoner was denied medical care for four months despite bleeding sores in his mouth (Letter 054). Jail medical personnel told him that he was not receiving health care because "you will be moved soon and not [our] problem anymore." Although he filed numerous requests for treatment with medical personnel, the physician responded "I was told you were gone up the road." A fourth prisoner informed health staff members at intake that she suffered from rectal bleeding and blood in her stool (Federal Court Monitor 1996). Three months later, medical personnel told the prisoner to "see a doctor when [you get] out." Finally, in a lawsuit involving a pretrial detainee, a jail nurse admitted that she had said the jail's medical unit saves "money because we skip the ambulance and bring them right to the morgue" (*Nelson v. Prison Health Services* 1997:1458).

A form of "selection bias" (Glazier 1997; Light 1997), the practice of releasing prisoners to avoid medical expenditures, has also been reported. One jail in the United States housed a prisoner with a "grapefruit-sized hernia that was definitely incarcerated and perhaps strangulated." Although the prisoner was in "obvious need of immediate surgical evaluation," he was released so that the health care costs did not "come out of the detention center's budget" (Saunders 1993:132).

In the United States, some correctional medical personnel either provide inadequate pain medication to prisoners or place a prisoner suffering intense pain on a mild over-the-counter analgesic and then deny him or her stronger pain medication when it is requested (Vaughn 1995, 1997). Such practices were confirmed in the court monitor's investigations (Federal Court Monitor 1996) and were reported in Letter 115, in which a prisoner, who injured his back falling in the jail shower, was examined by the jail physician and placed on pain medication. After two weeks, he reported severe pain and sought alternative therapies for pain relief. When the prisoner asked for stronger pain medication, the doctor removed him from all medication and refused to prescribe further treatment.

Another detainee (Letter 125) was brought to the hospital, where he was diagnosed with a fractured neck vertebra. At the jail, the physician prescribed aspirin; a few weeks later, however, despite the detainee's protests, he was denied all medical care, including the aspirin. He remained in jail for 90 days with no medical care, medication, or therapy for the fractured neck vertebra.

Mutual respect between medical provider and patient is a necessary condition for high-quality medical care (Maeve 1997). This reciprocity includes dialogue in which the health care provider communicates openly with patients to fully document their medical conditions (Anno 1991). In a medical environment predicated on ill-treatment and torture, however, health officials portray prisoners as "vicious, scheming, manipulating individuals with little or no concern for others" (Maeve 1997:504). In this environment, health providers "become cynical and distrusting of [prisoners] and may withhold sick call" requests in order to inflict pain on suffering prisoners (Drob 1992:169; Moore 1986:533).

This distrust was confirmed by letters to the jail monitor and by the monitor's subsequent investigations, which showed that some jail health care providers did not communicate well with prisoners (Federal Court Monitor 1992–1996) and relied on the custodial staff to confirm medical emergencies. In a lawsuit brought by the family of a pretrial detainee who died in jail from lack of medical care, nurses admitted that they frequently relied on custodial personnel to let them know if prisoners were experiencing "acute [medical] problems."

Even when health care workers were notified of medical complaints, their suspicions of the prisoners were so intense that some medical staff members refused to believe these complaints. When a female pretrial detainee with a history of heart trouble and previous heart attacks told the nurse that she had not received her physician-prescribed medication for 36 hours, that she was sweating profusely, and that she was experiencing chest pain, clammy skin, and shortness of breath, the nurse said "[I]f there was something really wrong with you, your doctor would have called by now" (*Nelson v. Prison Health Services* 1997:1458). The nurse further testified that she believed the detainee was "faking" and was not in a "cardiac emergency," even though the detainee suffered from "chest pains in conjunction with shooting pains down the left arm" (p. 1459). After the detainee had a heart attack (which proved fatal) in front of a nurse, the nurse responded "[H]ere we go again . . . I am really getting tired of this phoney bullshit—I don't have time for it . . . Stop the theatrics and get up on the chair" (p. 1459). The United States District Court for the Middle District of Florida characterized the nurse's care as expressing a "positive antipathy toward her patients" (p. 1464).

In some cases, medical personnel simply did not believe that prisoners suffered medical problems. Such was the case in Letter 022, in which the prisoner's jaw was broken in an assault by another prisoner. Although the prisoner could not eat solid food and was in considerable pain, the jail physician and nurse did not believe that the injury was serious enough to warrant referal to a dentist. After the prisoner's sixth request for dental treatment, it became clear that more invasive treatment was needed. The prisoner was referred to a dentist, who performed surgery. Even so, he had to endure at least five weeks without medical treatment because jail health care personnel refused to believe that he was injured.

A similar situation arose in Letter 031, in which a prisoner asked to see a physician. When no medical care was forthcoming, he stated his intent to file a grievance for lack of medical care. Upon hearing this, the on-duty nurse appeared at the prisoner's cell, asking "[W]hat's your problem now?"

In correctional health care systems, acute critical care of severely ill prisoners is occasionally provided by free-world physicians; these prisoners thus must be transferred to free-world health care facilities. When they are released, the free-world physicians customarily provide detailed instructions and orders for the prisoner's treatment upon reincarceration (Bernheim 1993). Prisoners' letters to the jail monitor, however, indicated that some medical officials ignored the free-world physicians' treatment recommendations, thus inflicting undue pain and suffering upon prisoners. The writer of Letter 048, for example, suffered a stroke and was transferred to an external hospital to be treated. When he was released back to the jail, the treating free-world physician ordered that the prisoner receive a minimum of four weeks of physical and occupational therapy. When the prisoner asked the jail nurses about the lack of treatment, they responded that "they would do what they wanted," if the prisoner "didn't like it, too bad," and "no one could tell them how to run their hospital."

As in other areas of correctional health care, the monitor's jail inspections and the prisoners' letters to the court monitor provide evidence that some jail health provides withhold medical therapy and treatment as a means to inflict pain. Moreover, prisoners' letters show complicity between some medical and custodial staff members to deny medical care.

Exposing Prisoners to Temperature Extremes and Sleep Deprivation

Storr (1990:305) asserted that "sensory deprivation techniques could be used to produce what was equivalent to a temporary episode of insanity." In fact, isolating prisoners in segregated cells decreases their ability to cope and increases their psychological distress (Cooke, Baldwin, and Howison 1990; Holtz 1998:30; Members of the Special International Tribunal 1991:395–96; Miller and Young 1997). Segregated isolation, combined with temperature extremes and sleep deprivation, produces extreme suffering among prisoners (Lippman 1979; Power, McElroy, and Swanson 1997; Weinstein and Cummins 1996).

Prolonged exposure to cold temperatures is a form of segregated detention developed by Nazi (Lippman 1993; Taylor 1992) and Japanese (Tanaka 1996; Williams and Wallace 1989) doctors, implemented in Soviet gulags (Solzhenitsyn 1974), and perfected by Israeli security police (Human Rights Watch/Middle East 1994), in which prisoners are required to "strip down and sleep in cold cells with very little bedding" (King 1994:76). Solzhenitsyn (1974) reported that the purpose of cold therapy was to impair prisoners' health and break their spirit. In very cold cells, prisoners' normal sleep patterns are disrupted; this disruption undermines their concentration and self-control (Human Rights Watch/Middle East 1994) and compounds their inability to adjust and cope ("Psychological Torture" 1997).

In our study, letters to the jail monitor revealed that prisoners were exposed to temperature extremes and sleep deprivation as part of the medical regimen. One problem that prisoners continually faced was lack of immediate medical care for acute health problems. Some prisoners with acute conditions, who were targeted for punishment, were refused medical treatment, but staff members offered them a Hobson's choice: To receive prompt medical care, they must be suicidal.

In January 1993, for example, a prisoner suffered a broken jaw as a result of a prisoner-to-prisoner assault (Letter 025). Despite severe pain and a jaw the size of a "softball," he was denied prompt medical treatment. A correctional officer, however, informed the prisoner that emergency medical care was available only for prisoners who claimed they were "going to hurt themselves." The prisoner said he would "hurt himself if . . . that's what it would take . . . to be seen by a doctor and be treated." Moments later he was escorted to "Bravo Wing," where suicidal prisoners were placed under a 24-hour suicide watch. Once in Bravo Wing, these prisoners were stripped, given a sleeveless paper gown, and placed in a cell in which cold air conditioning blew constantly. The cell contained only a metal bed that was "filled with germs and bacteria," and it reeked of "old dried-up food and human waste." Under suicide watch, prisoners were checked every few minutes with a flashlight, which prevented meaningful sleep or rest. Under appropriate medical care, a flashlight is shined on truly suicidal prisoners every 20 minutes to ensure that they do not harm themselves (Danto 1997; Hayes 1997). This standard medical procedure, however, becomes a means of ill-treatment and torture when nonsuicidal prisoners are placed on suicide watch and are prevented from sleeping for extended periods.

In October 1994, a prisoner who had been diagnosed in the free world with posttraumatic stress disorder (PTSD) was awakened abruptly at 2 a.m. by a correctional officer (Letter 159). Upset and surprised by the sudden awakening, the prisoner "assumed a combative stance," which infuriated the officer. When the jail psychiatrist was summoned, the prisoner explained his combative reaction as symptomatic of PTSD: When awakened quickly from a deep sleep, PTSD sufferers may exhibit a "hyper-alertness and exaggerated startle response." As a result of this exchange and after input from custodial officers, the psychiatrist believed that the prisoner "was going to hurt" himself. Although he vehemently denied that he was suicidal, he was medically committed to Bravo Wing under suicide watch. There he suffered "nakedness, sleeplessness, no mattress, no pillow, no cover, and the cold temperatures for three days."

The practices reported at the jail under study here are reminiscent of Soviet gulag methods of intimidation, "accompanied by enticement and by promises which were, of course, false" (Solzhenitsyn 1974:105). Prisoners' letters illustrate the merging of the pain-inflicting and the medical functions in Bravo Wing, where prisoners ostensibly were placed to receive acute medical treatment, but in fact were subjected to humiliating false promises and punishment.

In January 1993, a prisoner who requested acute medical care was locked into the suicide watch cold room, stripped of his clothing, and denied sleep for several days (Letter 025). In September 1993, a prisoner was transferred to the medical Bravo Wing for a strip search and was placed in a suicide cell after an officer reported that "he heard the prisoner say I was going to harm myself" (Letter 086). Although the prisoner denied making the statement, he was stripped and locked into the cell with strong air conditioning for several days. In October 1994, when a prisoner sought medical care for PTSD, he was stripped and placed on suicide watch in the "cold room" for three days (Letter 159). These letters show a pattern of ill-treatment and torture stretched over a 20-month period in which prisoners seeking acute medical care were subjected to temperature extremes and sleep deprivation.

Using Dental Care as a Means of Ill-Treatment and Torture

Two types of dental ill-treatment and torture were identified in the letters to the jail monitor and in the monitor's jail inspections (Federal Court Monitor 1994–1996). In the first type, prisoners were forced to wait weeks or months for dental care for abscessed teeth; when care finally was available, the correctional dentist pulled the wrong teeth (Walens 1997:86). This practice was implemented at the jail, when a dentist pulled a good tooth, from a prisoner's mouth while leaving the abscessed tooth to be pulled weeks or months later (Letter 104). Several hours after the procedure, when the prisoner complained that the wrong tooth had been pulled, a dental assistant altered his dental chart to make it appear that the prisoner had asked the dentist to pull the good tooth (Letter 106).

In the second practice, the medical staff provided only extractions but no routine preextraction dental maintenance (Letter 236). "Most dentists will agree that it is the object of dentistry to retain as many teeth as possible for as long as possible. One interested in good oral hygiene does not extract teeth indiscriminately" (Schafler 1996:86). According to Murton (1971:27), however, correctional practitioners historically were paid on the basis of the number of teeth they pulled, not on routine dental maintenance (Murton and Hyams 1969:99). Apparently little has changed since that practice was reported: Rasmussen (1990:37) and Belknap (1996:36) observed more recently that preventive dental care was rare and that correctional dental "services are limited to pulling teeth."

Similar practices were reported in the letters to the jail monitor and in the monitor's jail inspections (Federal Court Monitor 1992, 1994, 1995). In Letter 047, for example, a prisoner stated that he suffered from "unbearable pain" due to two abscessed teeth. Jail officials informed him that they did not fill cavities, and scheduled him for an extraction. The prisoner waited over six weeks for the tooth to be pulled.

In Letters 124 and 149, a prisoner with a severe toothache was examined by the jail dentist seven days after submitting a request for treatment. The dentist X-rayed the tooth and informed the prisoner that it was infected. After "prescribing Advil for pain and antibiotics for an infection," the dentist "advised [him] that [the] tooth would need to be extracted or have root canal performed." The jail dentist said "that root canal therapy was the best option" for the prisoner; yet, because the "jail would not pay for root canal work," extraction was the prisoner's only option (Letter 149).

Themes in the letters to the jail monitor and in the monitor's subsequent investigations, which question whether the jail's dental care fell below acceptable levels, are corroborated by research reporting that the practice of correctional medicine frequently falls below professional standards of care commonly available in the free world (Vaughn and Carroll 1998). Although the consent decree provided that "extraction should be utilized only as a last resort" ("Final Proposal" 1979:9), prisoners in Letters 047, 124, 138 and 149 were told that extraction was the only dental service offered at the jail. The tactics used by the jail also forced prisoners to wait for dental services; typically the appointment for extraction was made early in the consulting process, but the actual extraction required a wait of weeks or months (Federal Court Monitor 1994, 1995).

Falsifying Prisoners' Medical Records

Medical personnel are uniquely qualified to document abuse of prisoners because they are "often the first to interview [prisoners] who have been ill-treated or tortured" (Audet 1995:609; Berat 1989:501–02; Shenson 1996). Although ethical medical practice requires the keeping of accurate and comprehensive health records (BMAWP 1992; Thomsen and Voigt 1988), Nazi pediatricians and psychiatrists during World War II, falsified death certificates of mentally ill and retarded children and adults to mask their own involvement in medical experimentation, euthanasia, and extermination (Grodin, Annas, and Glantz 1993; Lifton 1986; Taylor 1992). Japanese doctors used prisoners of war as "human guinea pigs" and disposed of their remains by burning the bodies in an "electric furnace to leave no trace" (Williams and Wallace 1989:32). Health professionals practicing apartheid medicine in South Africa falsified prisoners' medical records and autopsy reports to hide ill-treatment and torture (Nightingale et al. 1990:2100). At the infamous Cummins and Tucker Prison Farms in Arkansas, medical files reported that prisoners with glass eyes possessed "normal" vision (Murton and Hyams 1969:111).

More recently, criminal justice personnel have been implicated in destroying and/or altering incriminating documents to thwart investigation of official lawlessness (*Harris v. Roderick* 1997; Kappeler, Sluder, and Alpert 1998). Perjury commonly is recognized as the most widespread form of official wrongdoing in criminal justice agencies (Barker and Carter 1994; Commission to Investigate 1994). In the 1960s, at one correctional facility in the United States, prisoners returning from the prison hospital were accompanied by thick medical files, but most of these consisted of blank sheets of paper (Murton and Hyams 1969:111). At this facility, the state pathologist concluded that deceased prisoners showed no "evidence of trauma or a violent death . . . [despite] the fact that two of the bodies had been decapitated prior to burial and the skull of the third had been crushed to the size of a grapefruit" (Murton 1971:29).

Although conspiracies involving forged health records are difficult to sustain, prisoners' letters to the jail monitor and the monitor's subsequent investigations showed that some medical personnel at the jail falsified medical documents to hinder detection of ill-treatment and torture of prisoners (Federal Court Monitor 1992–1996). The prisoner author of Letter 052 stated "I have personally seen medical employees watch prisoners on Bravo-Wing get brutally beat [by custodial officers] and then consistently go along with a false report. . . . Usually, officers are walking around looking for an opportunity to roll a cell door and beat the hell out of someone, while a nurse is waiting . . . to come in and shoot the prisoner with a sedative." Letter 052 repeats a theme prevalent in the ill-treatment and torture literature: Health care workers observe and monitor physical abuse, and provide treatment only to cover up atrocities committed by the custodial staff (Nightingale 1990).

In Letter 027, a prisoner reported hearing two correctional officers say they were going to "take care" of him. Minutes later, when one of the officers was escorting the prisoner to a holding area within the jail, the officer struck his head, knocking a gold tooth from his mouth. Then the officer slammed his head to the floor; as a result, the prisoner suffered severe headaches, swelling of the brain, and nerve damage to the right hand. When he sought medical treatment for his injuries, the health care staff refused him an examination by a physician.

The nurse called the prisoner a "punk," saying "I hope you rot to death" (Letter 027). More important, no notes or entries were made in the medical records to document the injuries. Because the outward physical manifestations of the assault healed while the prisoner was jailed, the medical files held no record of these injuries. Thus it was "exceptionally difficult subsequently to prove that torture occurred and [to] prosecute the torturers" (Iacopino et al. 1996:397).

Maintenance of prisoners' medical records in some U.S. correctional facilities is so inadequate as to border on criminal negligence (Vaughn and Carroll 1998). Inadequate health records result in "chaotic medical files that impede the work of even the most conscientious physicians" (King 1979:277). In such situations, prisoners' medical conditions, symptoms, and care are neither recorded nor documented; therefore subsequent caregivers are uninformed about prisoners' medical histories and the success or failure of previous treatments (Hudson 1987; Sparks, Bottoms, and Hay 1996).

One way in which the jail falsified medical records was to systematically omit prisoners' health complaints from bookkeeping processes; this omission resulted in failure to document and record prisoners' illnesses and injuries (Iacopino et al. 1996). In 1994 the Federal Court Monitor wrote "[T]here isn't any system (such as a numbering system) which would allow a tracking of [prisoners' requests for medical care]. There isn't any doubt that there are [prisoners' requests for medical care] missing out of the [prisoners'] medical records, casting suspicion that not all of [these requests] . . . actually are processed." Then, in 1996, the Federal Court Monitor wrote "[The] method [of medical record keeping at the jail] is not working. The [prisoners' medical] requests are being ignored by medical staff, medical staff are not signing the [medical] forms, correctional officers are picking up the . . . forms, and the [forms] are not being answered in a timely manner or they are not being answered at all . . . At this point, I don't think that [the medical provider] has any plans to correct this problem."

Similar failures in medical documentation were reported in letters to the jail monitor. In Letter 170 a female prisoner, who was nine months pregnant and had been in labor for 16 hours, had not eaten or drunk anything for six days because of pregnancy-induced vomiting. Because of her condition, she was transferred to a high-risk clinic maintained by the jail medical provider. At the clinic, however, she was not treated because the medical staff at the jail had "not document[ed] any [of her health problems,] so the clinic didn't even know there was a problem." The prisoner was returned to the jail, where jail medical authorities administered the prisoner "liquids and ice" but refused other medication or health services.

Some letters to the jail monitor indicated that jail health providers deliberately forged medical charts to document medical procedures where none had been performed, to record health examinations where none had been conducted, and to report administration of medications where none had been distributed (Letter 092; Letter 152; Letter 219). In Letter 092, a prisoner with hypertension and advanced heart disease was under a free-world physician's orders to receive a morning transdermal patch of nitroglycerin and an oral dose of cardiovascular medication. One morning, the prisoner went to court and missed the pill line. After he experienced chest pains and requested his medication and nitroglycerin patch throughout the day, the evening "nurse showed [the prisoner his medical file] where the chart was marked that [he] received the nitro patch that morning." At the exact time recorded on the chart when the prisoner presumably received the nitro patch, he was in "court on the other side of the jail complex." Failure to administer the physician-prescribed nitroglycerin patch increased his risk of a serious cardiac event.

Letters to the jail monitor and the monitor's investigations showed misplaced loyalties in the jail's medical unit: The custodial subculture had coopted some medical personnel to conspire to violate the consent decree, medical ethics, and prisoners' constitutional rights. Although much has been written about ideological conflicts between custodial and medical staff members, these letters revealed a workplace culture in which some medical providers adopted a custodial worldview predicated on prisoners' suffering, denial of medical care, disregard for the Hippocratic Oath, and forged medical records.

Conclusion

Correctional medical personnel operate in an occupational subculture where issues of treatment and issues of custody compete for their loyalties. The Hippocratic Oath mandates that health care professionals must not harm patients; penal harm advocates contend that prisoners should be punished, and reject therapeutic measures as pro-offender or antivictim. Just as Nazi doctors participated in "psychic numbing," a reasoning process that made their Jewish victims "less than human and therefore not capable of evoking empathy or moral restraint" (Lifton 1986:442; Markusen 1992:153), correctional medical personnel find "themselves in morally ambiguous circumstances, without sharp limits or clear moral boundaries to restrain them" (Brown 1987:158). In this environment, some of the medical workers identify with custodial mandates and pattern their behavior after "the perceived collective needs of society, not the rights of individual 'subhuman'" prisoners (Brown 1987:158). Nazi doctors were able to abandon the Hippocratic Oath because they believed that their actions served the "larger purpose of bettering human life" (Markusen 1992:152). Similarly, dehumanization of prisoners permits correctional medical personnel to engage in ethical relativism and to abandon allegiance to the Hippocratic Oath.

From an organizational perspective, collective demonization of prisoners allows individual medical workers to deviate from ethical canons. Obedience to the pain-inflicting mandates of the custodial subculture overwhelms the ethical standards and humanistic obligations that the medical professional is sworn to uphold. The practice of penal harm medicine also fits the new penal managerialism or the new penology, whereby individual prisoners' rights are deemphasized and the efficient control of aggregate prisoner populations predominates. In this environment, it is acceptable to harm "subhuman" prisoners. Correctional health care systems committed to implementing the penal harm movement and the rationality of the new penal managerialism do not appear to favor institutional treatment settings ideally based on morality, justice, and respect for human dignity.

Prisoners' letters to the jail monitor and the monitor's subsequent investigations showed that some of the health care staff members in the jail had a custodial-punishment orientation. Advocates of penal harm predict the merging of custodial and medical functions because imprisonment is intended to personify pain: "[The] penal sanction is to harm" (Clear 1994:4). Letters and the monitor's investigations supported our thesis that for some health care employees, practicing in an environment dominated by a philosophy of penal harm led to ill-treatment and torture of prisoners.

We found a persistent pattern of medical ill-treatment and torture at the jail, which extended over the entire five-year period. Given the explosion of correctional populations, the penal harm movement, and the disturbing (although tentative) nature of our findings, penologists, criminologists, and criminal justicians should more fully investigate medical ill-treatment and torture in correctional facilities throughout the United States. Although the secretive, insular world of corrections poses obstacles to access, ethnographic studies in correctional health care systems, uncovering the epidemiology of ill-treatment and torture of prisoners, are in great demand.

References

Acoca, L. 1998. "Defusing the Time Bomb: Understanding and Meeting the Growing Health Care Needs of Incarcerated Women in America." *Crime and Delinquency* 44:49–69.

Alderslade, R. 1995. "Human Rights and Medical Practice, Including Reference to the Joint Oslo Statements of September 1993 and March 1994." *Journal of Public Health Medicine* 17:335–42.

Allen, H. E. and J. C. Abril, 1997. "The New Chain Gang: Corrections in the Next Century." *American Journal of Criminal Justice* 22:1–12.

American Correctional Association. 1997. *Jail Directory.* Laurel, MD: American Correctional Association.

American Psychiatric Association. 1994. *Diagnostic and Statistical Manual of Mental Disorders.* 4th ed. Washington, DC: American Psychiatric Association.

Amnesty International. 1975. *Report on Torture.* New York: Farrar, Straus and Giroux.

———. 1984a. *Codes of Professional Ethics.* 2nd ed. London: Amnesty International.

———. 1984b. *Torture in the Eighties.* London: Amnesty International.

———. 1988. *Amnesty International Report.* London: Amnesty International.

———. 1990. *Amnesty International Report.* London: Amnesty International.

Angell, M. 1988. "Ethical Imperialism? Ethics in International Collaborative Clinical Research." *New England Journal of Medicine* 319:1081–83.

Anno, B. J. 1991. *Prison Health Care: Guidelines for the Management of an Adequate Delivery System*. Chicago: National Commission on Correctional Health Care.

———. 1997. "Correctional Health Care: What's Past Is Prologue." *Correct Care* 11(3):6–11.

Arrigo, B. A. 1996a. "Subjectivity in Law, Medicine, and Science: A Semiotic Perspective on Punishment." Pp. 69–92 in *Punishment: Social Control and Coercion*, edited by C. T. Sistare. New York: Peter Lang.

———. 1996b. *The Contours of Psychiatric Justice: A Postmodern Critique of Mental Illness, Criminal Insanity, and the Law*. New York: Garland.

Asad, T. 1996. "On Torture, or Cruel, Inhuman, and Degrading Treatment." *Social Research* 63:1081–1109.

Audet, A. M. 1995. "The Role of the Physician and the Medical Profession in the Prevention of International Torture in the Treatment of Its Survivors." *Annals of Internal Medicine* 122:607–13.

Ball, R. A. 1997. "Prison Conditions at the Extreme: Legal and Political Issues in the Closing of West Virginia's Prisons for Men and Women." *Journal of Contemporary Criminal Justice* 13:55–72.

Bankowski, Z. 1996. "Ethics and Human Values in Health Policy." *World Health Forum* 17:146–49.

Barak, G. 1990. "Crime, Criminology, and Human Rights: Towards an Understanding of State Criminality." *Journal of Human Justice* 2(1):11–28.

Barker, T. and D. L. Carter. 1990. "Fluffing Up the Evidence and Covering Your Ass: Some Conceptual Notes on Police Lying." *Deviant Behavior* 11:61–73.

———. 1994. "Police Lies and Perjury: A Motivation-Based Typology." Pp. 139–53 in *Police Deviance*, 3rd ed., edited by T. Barker and D. L. Carter. Cincinnati: Anderson.

Beaman-Hall, L. 1996. "Legal Ethnography: Exploring the Gendered Nature of Legal Method." *Critical Criminology* 7(1):53–74.

Belknap, J. 1996. "Access to Programs and Health Care for Incarcerated Women." *Federal Probation* 60(4):34–39.

Bendfeldt-Zachrisson, F. 1985. "Special Report on Torture as a Medical Problem—State (Political) Torture: Some General, Psychological, and Particular Aspects." *International Journal of Health Services* 15:339–49.

Bennett, K. and R. V. del Carmen. 1997. "A Review and Analysis of Prison Litigation Reform Act Court Decisions: Solution or Aggravation?" *Prison Journal* 77:405–55.

Berat, L. 1989. "Doctors, Detainees, and Torture: Medical Ethics v. the Law in South Africa." *Stanford Journal of International Law* 25:499–542.

Bernheim, J. 1993. "Medical Ethics in Prison." *Criminal Behavior and Mental Health* 3:85–96.

Bierma, P. 1994. "Torture behind Bars: Right Here in the United States of America." *Progressive* 58(7):21–27.

Blanco, E. 1989. "Torture in Emergency Situations." *Leiden Journal of International Law* 2:209–28.

Bloche, M. G. 1987. *Uruguay's Military Physicians: Cogs in a System of State Terror*. Washington, DC: American Association for the Advancement of Science.

Blumberg, M. 1990. *AIDS: The Impact on the Criminal Justice System*. Columbus, OH: Merrill.

Blumberg, M. and C. Mahaffey-Sapp. 1997. "Health Care Issues in Correctional Institutions." Pp. 333–44 in *Corrections: An Issues Approach*, 4th ed., edited by M. D. Schwartz and L. F. Travis. Cincinnati: Anderson.

Bonta, J. and P. Gendreau. 1990. "Reexamining the Cruel and Unusual Punishment of Prison Life." *Law and Human Behavior* 14:347–72.

Breed, A. F. 1998. "Corrections: A Victim of Situational Ethics." *Crime and Delinquency* 44:9–18.

Brewer, T. F. and J. Derrickson. 1992. "AIDS in Prison: A Review of Epidemiology and Preventive Policy." *AIDS* 6:623–28.

Bright, S. B. 1996. "The Electric Chair and the Chain Gang: Choices and Challenges for America's Future." *Notre Dame Law Review* 71:845–60.

———. 1997. "Casualties of the War on Crime: Fairness, Reliability, and the Credibility of Criminal Justice Systems." *University of Miami Law Review* 51:413–24.

British Medical Association Working Party. 1986. *The Torture Report*. London: British Medical Association.

———. 1992. *Medicine Betrayed: The Participation of Doctors in Human Rights Abuses*. London: British Medical Association.

Browde, S. 1989. "Doctors, Ethics and Torture." *Social Science and Medicine* 28:766.

Brown, T. M. 1987. "Doctors in Extremity." *Law, Medicine, and Health Care* 15(3):156–59.

Buchanan, A. 1996. "Judging the Past: The Case of the Human Radiation Experiments." *Hastings Center Report* 26(3):25–30.

Bunce, C. 1997. "Doctors Involved in Human Rights Abuses in Kenya." *British Medical Journal* 314:166.

Burger, T. 1987. *Max Weber's Theory of Concept Formation: History, Laws, and Ideal Types*. Expanded ed. Durham: Duke University Press.

Burkhalter, H. J. 1995. "Barbarism behind Bars: Torture in U.S. Prisons." *Nation* 261(1):17–18.

Butler, A. M. 1997. *Gendered Justice in the American West: Women Prisoners in Men's Penitentiaries*. Urbana: University of Illinois Press.

Carroll, L. 1992. "AIDS and Human Rights in the Prison: A Comment on the Ethics of Screening and Segregation." Pp. 162–77 in *Correctional Theory and Practice*. edited by C. A. Hartjen and E. E. Rhine. Chicago: Nelson-Hall.

———. 1998. *Lawful Order: A Case Study in Correctional Crisis and Reform*. New York: Garland.

Cassese, A. 1996. *Inhuman States: Imprisonment, Detention, and Torture in Europe Today*. Cambridge, UK: Polity.

Centere for Human Rights. 1988. *Human Rights: A Compilation of International Instruments*. New York: United Nations.

———. 1994. *Human Rights and Pre-Trial Detention: A Handbook of International Standards Relating to Pre-Trial Detention*. New York: United Nations.

Chilton, B. S. 1991. *Prisons under the Gavel: The Federal Court Takeover of Georgia Prisons*. Columbus: Ohio State University Press.

Christie, N. 1981. *Limits to Pain*. Oxford: Martin Robertson.

———. 1993. *Crime Control as Industry*. London: Routledge.

Chung, C. C., C. O. Mok., K. H. Kwong, E. K. Ng, W. Y. Lau, and A. K. Li. 1997. "Obturator Hernia Revisited: A Review of 12 Cases in 7 Years." *Journal of Royal College of Surgeons of Edinburgh* 42:82–84.

Clark, E. B. 1995. "The Sacred Rights of the Weak: Pain, Sympathy, and the Culture of Individual Rights in Antebellum America." *Journal of American History* 82:463–93.

Clear, T. R. 1994. *Harm in American Penology*. Albany: SUNY Press.

Cockburn, A. 1997. "The Torture of Susan McDougal." *Nation* 265(2):9.

Commission to Investigate Allegations of Police Corruption and the Anti-Corruption Procedures of the Police Department (Mollen Commission). 1994. *Commission Report*. New York: Commission to Investigate Allegations of Police Corruption and the Anti-Corruption Procedures of the Police Department.

Committee on the Judiciary, House of Representatives. 1991. *Medical Care for the Prison Population*. Washington, DC: U.S. Government Printing Office.

Cooke, D. J., P. J. Baldwin, and J. Howison. 1990. *Psychology in Prisons*. London: Routledge.

Council of Europe. 1987. *European Prison Rules*. Strasbourg: Council of Europe.

———. 1995. *Human Rights in Prison: The Professional Training of Prison Officials*. Strasbourg: Council of Europe.

Crouch, B. M. and J. M. Marquart. 1989. *An Appeal to Justice: Litigated Reform of Texas Prisons*. Austin: University of Texas Press.

Cullen, F. T. 1995. "Assessing the Penal Harm Movement." *Journal of Research in Crime and Delinquency* 32:338–58.

Danish Medical Association/International Rehabilitation and Research Center for Torture Victims 1987. "Doctors, Ethics, and Torture: Proceedings of an International Meeting, Copenhagen, August 1986." *Danish Medical Bulletin* 34(4):185–216.

Danto, B. L. 1997. "Suicide Litigation as an Agent of Change in Jail and Prison: An Initial Report." *Behavioral Sciences and the Law* 15:415–25.

Denzin, N. K. 1997. *Interpretive Ethnography: Ethnographic Practices for the 21st Century.* Thousand Oaks, CA: Sage.

Downie, R. S. 1993. "The Ethics of Medical Involvement in Torture." *Journal of Medical Ethics* 19:135–37.

Drob, S. L. 1992. "The Lessons from History: Physicians' Dual Loyalty in the Nazi Death Camps." Pp. 167–71 in *Review of Clinical Psychiatry and the Law*, Vol. 3. edited by R. I. Snow. Washington, DC: American Psychiatric Press.

DuBose, E. R. 1996. "Prison Infirmary Nurses: Professionalism and Principles." *Making the Rounds* 1(21):1–4.

Duncan, M. G. 1996. *Romantic Outlaws, Beloved Prisons: The Unconscious Meanings of Crime and Punishment*. New York: New York University Press.

Engdahl, B. E. and R. E. Eberly. 1990. "The Effects of Torture and Other Maltreatment: Implications for Psychology." Pp. 31–47 in *Psychology and Torture*, edited by P. Suedfeld. New York: Hemisphere.

"Ex-F. B. I. Man Sentenced in Ruby Ridge Case." 1997. *New York Times*, October 11, p. A-8.

Federal Court Monitor. 1992–1996. *Court Monitor's Reports: Davis v. Roberts* 75–411-Civ-TGC.

Feeley, M. and J. Simon. 1992. "The New Penology: Notes on the Emerging Strategy of Corrections and Its Implications." *Criminology* 30:449–74.

———. 1994. "Actuarial Justice: The Emerging New Criminal Law." Pp. 173–201 in *The Futures of Criminology*, edited by D. Nelken, London: Sage.

"Final Proposal for Entry of Consent Decree." 1979. *Davis v. Roberts* 75–411-Civ-TGC.

Fleisher, M. S. and R. H. Rison. 1997. "Health Care in the Federal Bureau of Prisons." Pp. 327–34 in *Correctional Contexts: Contemporary and Classical Readings*, edited by J. M. Marquart and J. R. Sorensen. Los Angeles: Roxbury.

Fogel, D. 1979. *We Are the Living Proof: The Justice Model for Corrections*, 2nd ed. Cincinnati: Anderson.

Foster, D. H., D. Sandler, and D. M. Davis. 1987. "Detention, Torture, and the Criminal Justice Process in South Africa." *International Journal of the Sociology of Law* 15:105–20.

Gallo, E. and V. Ruggiero. 1991. "The Immaterial Prison: Custody as a Factory for the Manufacture of Handicaps." *International Journal of the Sociology of Law* 19:273–91.

Gannon, C. C. 1997. *Health Records in Correctional Health Care: A Reference Manual*. Chicago: National Commission on Correctional Health Care.

Garland, D. 1997. "Governmentality and the Problem of Crime: Foucault, Criminology, Sociology." *Theoretical Criminology* 1:173–214.

Geiger, H. J. and R. M. Cook-Deegan. 1993. "The Role of Physicians in Conflicts and Humanitarian Crises: Case Studies from the Field Missions of Physicians for Human Rights, 1988 to 1993." *Journal of the American Medical Association* 279:616–20.

Genefke, I. 1993. "Torture, the Most Destructive Power against Democracy. *International Journal of the Humanities* 10(1):73.

Gibbons, D. C. and D. L. Garrity. 1959. "Some Suggestions for the Development of Etiological and Treatment Theory in Criminology." *Social Forces* 38:51–58.

———. 1962. "Definition and Analysis of Certain Criminal Types." *Journal of Criminal Law, Criminology, and Police Science* 53:27–35.

Gill, G. V. and I. A. MacFarlane. 1989. "Problems of Diabetics in Prison." *British Medical Journal* 298:221–23.

Glazier, A. K. 1997. "Genetic Predispositions, Prophylactic Treatments, and Private Health Insurance: Nothing Is Better Than a Good Pair of Genes." *American Journal of Law and Medicine* 23:45–68.

"Glossary of Terms in Health Care." 1995. *Business Journal Serving Southern Tier, CNY, Mohawk Valley, Finger Lakes, North*, December 11, p. 23B.

Goffman, E. [1957] 1997. "Characteristics of Total Institutions." Pp. 97–108 in *Correctional Contexts: Contemporary and Classical Readings*, edited by J. M. Marquart and J. R. Sorensen. Los Angeles: Roxbury.

———. 1962. *Asylums: Essays on the Social Situation of Mental Patients and Other Inmates*. Chicago: Aldine.

———. 1963. *Stigma: Notes on the Management of Spoiled Identity*. New York: Aronson.

Goldstein, R. H. and P. Breslin. 1986. "Technicians of Torture: How Physicians Become Agents of State Terror." *Sciences* 26(2):14–19.

Gostin, L. O. and Z. Lazzarini. 1997. *Human Rights and Public Health in the AIDS Pandemic*. New York: Oxford University Press.

Goulet, D. 1977. "Prolegomenon to a Policy: Thinking about Human Rights." *Christianity and Crisis* 37(8):100–104.

Greenspan, J. 1996. "Prisoners Respond to AIDS." Pp. 115–23 in *Criminal Injustice: Confronting the Prison Crisis*, edited by E. Rosenblatt. Boston: South End.

Griffin, M. M., J. G. Ryan, V. S. Briscoe, and K. M. Shadle. 1996. "Effects of Incarceration on HIV-Infected Individuals." *Journal of the National Medical Association* 88:639–44.

Grodin, M. A., G. J. Annas, and L. H. Glantz. 1993. "Medicine and Human Rights: A Proposal for International Action." *Hastings Center Report* 23(4):8–12.

Haritos-Fatouros, M. 1988. "The Official Torturer: A Learning Model for Obedience to the Authority of Violence." *Journal of Applied Social Psychology* 18:1107–20.

Harris, M. K. and D. P. Spiller. 1977. *After Decision: Implementation of Judicial Decrees in Correctional Settings*. Washington, DC: U.S. Government Printing Office.

Hayes, L. M. 1997. "From Chaos to Calm: One Jail System's Struggle with Suicide Prevention." *Behavioral Sciences and the Law* 15:399–413.

Henry, S. and D. Milovanovic. 1996. *Constitutive Criminology: Beyond Postmodernism*. London: Sage.

Holtz, T. H. 1998. "Refugee Trauma versus Torture Trauma: A Retrospective Controlled Cohort Study of Tibetan Refugees." *Journal of Nervous and Mental Disease* 186:24–34.

Hornblum, A. M. 1997. "They Were Cheap and Available: Prisoners as Research Subjects in Twentieth Century America." *British Medical Journal* 315:1437–41.

Howard League for Penal Reform. 1991. *Suicides and Strip Cells*. London: Howard League for Penal Reform.

Hudson, B. 1987. "Prison Medical Service: Serving Health from Behind Bars." *Health Service Journal* 97:958–59.

Human Rights Watch/Middle East. 1994. *Torture and Ill-Treatment: Israel's Interrogation of Palestinians from the Occupied Territories*. New York: Human Rights Watch.

Iacopino, V. 1996. "Turkish Physicians Coerced to Conceal Systematic Torture." *Luncet* 348:1500.

Iacopino, V., M. Heisler, S. Pishevar, and R. H. Kirschner. 1996. "Physician Complicity in Misrepresentation and Omission of Evidence of Torture in Postdetention Medical Examinations in Turkey." *Journal of the American Medical Association* 276:396–402.

International Military Tribunal for the Far East. 1946–1948. *Record of Proceedings*. Tokyo: International Military Tribunal for the Far East.

Irwin, J. 1985. *The Jail: Managing the Underclass in American Society*. Berkeley: University of California Press.

Jacobs, F. G. and R. C. A. White. 1996. *The European Convention on Human Rights* 2nd ed. New York: Oxford University Press.

Jaranson, J. M. 1995. "Government-Sanctioned Torture: Status of the Rehabilitation Movement." *Transcultural Psychiatric Research Review* 32:253–86.

Jayawardena, H. 1996. "AIDS and Professional Secrecy in the United States." *Medicine, Science, and Law* 36:37–42.

Jones, G. E. 1980. "On the Permissibility of Torture." *Journal of Medical Ethics* 6:11–15.

Jonsen, A. R. and L. A. Sagan. 1985. "Torture and the Ethics of Medicine." Pp. 30–44 in *The Breaking of Bodies and Minds: Torture, Psychiatric Abuse, and the Health Professions*, edited by E. Stover and E. O. Nightingale. New York: Freeman.

Jurgens, R. and N. Gilmore. 1994. "Divulging of Prison Medical Records: Juridical and Legal Analysis." *Criminologic* 27(2):127–63.

Kappeler, V. E., M. Blumberg, and G. W. Potter. 1996. *The Mythology of Crime and Criminal Justice*, 2nd ed. Prospect Heights, IL: Waveland.

Kappeler, V. E., R. D. Sluder, and G. P. Alpert. 1998. *Forces of Deviance: Understanding the Dark Side of Policing*. 2nd ed. Prospect Heights, IL: Waveland.

Kelman, H. C. 1995. "The Social Context of Torture: Policy Process and Authority Structure." Pp. 19–34 in *The Politics of Pain: Torturers and Their Masters*, edited by R. D. Crelinsten and A. P. Schmid. Boulder: Westview.

Kemp-Genefke, I. 1991. "Perspective on the Present and the Future." *Journal of Medical Ethics* 17(Supplement):11–12.

Keve, Paul W. 1996. *Measuring Excellence: The History of Correctional Standards and Accreditation*. Lanham, MD: American Correctional Association.

King, L. N. 1979. "Public Policy and Administrative Aspects of Prison and Jail Health Services." *Prison Law Monitor* 1(11):265, 277–79.

King, R. D. 1994. "Russian Prisons after Perestroika: End of the Gulag?" *British Journal of Criminology* 34(Special Issue):62–82.

Kooijmans, P. H. 1995. "Torturers and Their Masters." Pp. 13–18 in *The Politics of Pain: Torturers and Their Masters*, edited by R. D. Crelinsten and A. P. Schmid. Boulder: Westview.

Kratcoski, P. C. 1989. *Correctional Counseling and Treatment*, 2nd ed. Prospect Heights, IL: Waveland.

Laborde, J. M. 1989. "Torture: A Nursing Concern." *Image: Journal of Nursing Scholarship* 21(1):31–33.

La Forte, R. S., R. E. Marcello, and R. L. Himmel. 1994. *With Only the Will to Live: Accounts of Americans in Japanese Prison Camps 1941–1945*. Wilmington, DE: Scholarly Resources.

Laing, J. M. 1996. "The Police Surgeon and the Mentally Disordered Suspects: An Adequate Safeguard?" *Web Journal of Current Legal Issues*. I. [Online]. Available at http://www.nel.ac.uk/~nlawwww/1996/issue1/laing1.html.

Laurence, R. 1992. "Part I: Torture and Mental Health: A Review of the Literature." *Issues in Mental Health Nursing* 13:301–10.

Liebling, A. and P. Hall. 1993. "Seclusion in Prison Strip Cells." *British Medical Journal* 307:399–400.

Lifton, R. J. 1982. "Medicalized Killing in Auschwitz." *Psychiatry* 45:283–97.

———. 1986. *The Nazi Doctors: Medical Killing and the Psychology of Genocide*, New York: Basic Books.

Light, D. W. 1997. "The Real Ethics of Rationing." *British Medical Journal* 315:112–15.

Lindlof, T. R. 1995. *Qualitative Communication Research Methods*. Thousand Oaks, CA: Sage.

Lippman, M. 1979. "The Protection of Universal Human Rights: The Problem of Torture." *Universal Human Rights* 1(4):25–55.

———. 1993. "The Nazi Doctors Trial and the International Prohibition on Medical Involvement in Torture." *Loyola of Los Angeles International and Comparative Law Journal* 15:395–441.

———. 1997. "Crimes against Humanity." *Boston College Third World Law Journal* 17:171–278.

Loeb, G. H. 1993. "Protecting the Right to Informational Privacy for HIV-Positive Prisoners." *Columbia Journal of Law and Social Problems* 27:269–318.

Logan, C. H. and G. G. Gaes. 1993. "Meta-Analysis and the Rehabilitation of Punishment." *Justice Quarterly* 10:245–63.

Machan, T. R. 1990. "Exploring Extreme Violence (Torture)." *Journal of Social Philosophy* 21:92–97.

MacPherson, P. 1989. "In a Padlocked Society, Good Health Care Remains an Elusive Goal." *Governing* 2(April):50–54.

Maeve, M. K. 1997. "Nursing Practice with Incarcerated Women: Caring within Mandated [sic] Alienation." *Issues in Mental Health Nursing* 18:495–510.

Magill, F. N. 1996. *International Encyclopedia of Psychology*, Vol. 2. London: Fitzroy Dearborn.

Markusen, E. 1992. "Comprehending the Cambodian Genocide: An Application of Robert Jay Lifton's Model of Genocidal Killing." *Psychohistory Review* 20:145–69.

Marquart, J. W., D. E. Merianos, S. J. Cuvelier, and L. Carroll. 1996. "Thinking about the Relationship between Health Dynamics in the Free Community and the Prison." *Crime and Delinquency* 42:331–60.

Marquart, J. W., D. E. Merianos, J. L. Hebert, and L. Carroll. 1997. "Health Condition and Prisoners: A Review of Research and Emerging Areas of Inquiry." *Prison Journal* 77:184–208.

Mastrofski, S. D. 1998. "Police Agency Accreditation: A Skeptical View." *Policing: An International Journal of Police Strategies and Management* 21:202–205.

McCoy, C. 1997. "Review Essay: Sentencing and the Underclass." *Law and Society Review* 31:589–612.

Melamed, B. G., J. L. Melamed, and J. C. Bouhoutsos. 1990. "Psychological Consequences of Torture: A Need to Formulate New Strategies for Research." Pp. 13–30 in *Psychology and Torture*, edited by P. Suedfeld. New York: Hemisphere.

Members of the Special International Tribunal. 1991. "Verdict of the Special International Tribunal: On the Violation of Human Rights of Political Prisoners and Prisoners of War in United States Prisons and Jails." *Humanity and Society* 15:375–99.

Meyer-Lie, A. 1986. "Ethics in Prison Health Care." Pp. 63–69 in *Health and Human Rights*, edited by International Commission of Health Professionals. Geneva: International Commission of Health Professionals.

Miller, H. A. and G. R. Young. 1997. "Prison Segregation: Administrative Detention Remedy or Mental Health Problem?" *Criminal Behavior and Mental Health* 7:85–94.

Milovanovic, D. 1996. "Postmodern Criminology: Mapping the Terrain." *Justice Quarterly* 13:567–610.

Moore, J. M. 1986. "Prison Health Care: Problems and Alternatives in Delivery of Health Care to the Incarcerated—Part 1." *Journal of the Florida Medical Association* 73:531–35.

Morgan, R. and M. Evans. 1994. "Inspecting Prisons: The View from Strasbourg." *British Journal of Criminology* 34(Special Issue):141–59.

Moynihan, D. P. 1997. "The Culture of Secrecy." *The Public Interest* 128 (Summer): 55–72.

Murton, T. 1971. "Prison Doctors." *Humanist* 31(3):24–29.

Murton, T. and J. Hyams. 1969. *Accomplices to the Crime*. New York: Grove.

National Commission on Correctional Health Care. 1996. *Standards for Health Services in Jails*. Chicago: National Commission on Correctional Health Care.

Naude, G. and F. Bongard. 1997. "Obturator Hernia Is an Unsuspected Diagnosis." *American Journal of Surgery* 174:72–75.

Neale, K. 1991. "The European Prison Rules: Contextual, Philosophical, and Practical Aspects." Pp. 203–18 in *Imprisonment: European Perspectives*, edited by J. Muncie and R. Sparks, London: Harvester.

Nightingale, E. O. 1990. "The Role of Physicians in Human Rights." *Law, Medicine, and Health Care* 18(1–2):132–39.

Nightingale, E. O. and J. C. Chill. 1994. "The Health Professions and Human Rights." *Family and Community Health* 17(2):30–37.

Nightingale, E. O., K. Hannibal, H. J. Geiger, L. Hartmann, R. Lawrence, and J. Spurlock. 1990. "Apartheid Medicine: Health and Human Rights in South Africa." *Journal of the American Medical Association* 264:2097–2102.

Nursing97 Drug Handbook. 1997. Springhouse, PA: Springhouse.

"Order Granting Defendants' Motion to Dissolve Consent Decree." 1998. *Davis v. Roberts* 75–411-Civ-T-21(c).

Osofsky, H. M. 1997. "Domesticating International Criminal Law: Bringing Human Rights Violators to Justice." *Yale Law Journal* 107:191–226.

Paden, R. 1984. "Surveillance and Torture: Foucault and Orwell on the Methods of Discipline." *Social Theory and Practice* 10:261–71.

Parmentier, S. 1992. "Book Review: The International Fight against Torture." *Human Rights Quarterly* 14:568–72.

Pellegrino, E. D. 1993. "Societal Duty and Moral Complicity: The Physician's Dilemma of Divided Loyalty." *International Journal of Law and Psychiatry* 16:371–91.

Penal Reform International. 1990. *International Instruments on Imprisonment: Briefing No. 1*, London: Penal Reform International.

Peters, E. 1986. *Torture*. New York: Basil Blackwell.

Peters, T. 1992. *Liberation Management*, New York: Knopf.

Petersen, H. D. and O. V. Rasmussen. 1992. "Medical Appraisal of Allegations of Torture and the Involvement of Doctors in Torture." *Forensic Science International* 53:97–116.

Platt, A. 1971. "The Politics of Riot Commissions, 1917–1970: An Overview." Pp. 3–54 in *The Politics of Riot Commissions, 1917–1970: A Collection of Official Reports and Critical Essays*, edited by A. Platt. New York: Macmillan.

Power, K., J. McElroy, and V. Swanson. 1997. "Coping Abilities and Prisoners' Perception of Suicidal Risk Management." *Howard Journal of Criminal Justice* 36:378–92.

"Psychological Torture, CIA-Style." 1997. *Harper's* 294(1763):23–25.

Punamaki, R. L. 1988. "Experiences of Torture, Means of Coping, and Level of Symptoms among Palestinian Political Prisoners." *Journal of Palestine Studies* 17:81–96.

Ramsbotham, S. D. 1996. "Patient or Prisoner? A New Strategy for Health Care in Prisons." Discussion Paper, Home Office, London.

Rasmussen, O. V. 1990. "Medical Aspects of Torture: Torture Types and Their Relation to Symptoms and Lesions in 200 Victims, Followed by a Description of the Medical Profession in Relation to Torture: A Monograph." *Danish Medical Bulletin* 37(Supplement 1):1–88.

Rayner, M. 1987. *Turning a Blind Eye? Medical Accountability and the Prevention of Torture in South Africa*. Washington, DC: American Association for the Advancement of Science.

Reed, J. and M. Lyne. 1997. "The Quality of Health Care in Prison: Results of a Year's Program of Semistructured Inspections." *British Medical Journal* 315:1420–24.

Renzetti, C. M. 1997. "Confessions of a Reformed Positivist." Pp. 131–43 in *Researching Sexual Violence against Women: Methodological and Personal Perspectives*, edited by M. D. Schwartz. Thousand Oaks, CA: Sage.

Reyes, H. 1995. "The Conflicts between Medical Ethics and Security Measures." Pp. 41–47 in *Torture: Human Rights, Medical Ethics, and the Case of Israel*, edited by N. Gordon and R. Marton. London: Zed Books.

Reynaud, A. 1986. *Human Rights in Prisons*. Strasbourg: Council of Europe.

Rodley, N. S. 1987. *The Treatment of Prisoners under International Law*, Paris: United Nations Educational. Scientific, and Cultural Organization.

Roling, B. V. A. and C. F. Ruter. 1977. *The Tokyo Judgment: The International Military Tribunal for the Far East, 29 April 1946–12 November 1948*. Amsterdam: APA-University Press Amsterdam.

Rosalki, J. 1993. "The Hippocratic Contract." *Journal of Medical Ethics* 19:154–56.

Rosenberg, T. 1997. "To Hell and Back." *New York Times Magazine*, December 28, pp. 32–36.

Ross, J. I. 1995. "Controlling State Crime: Toward an Integrated Structural Model." Pp. 3–33 in *Controlling State Crime: An Introduction*, edited by J. I. Ross. New York: Garland.

Roth, E. F., I. Lunde, G. Boysen, and I. Kemp-Genefke. 1987. "Torture and Its Treatment." *American Journal of Public Health* 77:1404–1406.

Rynerson, B. C. 1989. "Cops and Counselors." *Journal of Psychosocial Nursing and Mental Health Services* 27(2):12–17.

Sagan, L. A. and A. Jonsen. 1976. "Medical Ethics and Torture." *New England Journal of Medicine* 294:1427–30.

Saunders, J. L. 1993. "When Your Patients Are Murderers and Thieves." *Medical Economics* 70(4):131–35.

Savage, S. P., G. Moon, K. Kelly, and Y. Bradshaw. 1997. "Divided Loyalties? The Police Surgeon and Criminal Justice." *Policing and Society* 7:79–98.

Schafler, N. L. 1996. *Dental Malpractice: Legal and Medical Handbook*, Vol. 1. 3rd ed. New York: Wiley.

Scroggy, G. A. 1993. "Managing Conflicts between Custody and Health Care Staff." Pp. 130–32 in *The State of Corrections: Proceedings ACA Annual Conference 1992*, Laurel Lakes, MD: American Correctional Association.

Sheleff, L. S. 1987. *Ultimate Penalties: Capital Punishment, Life Imprisonment, Physical Torture*, Columbus: Ohio State University Press.

Shenson, D. 1996. "A Primary Care Clinic for the Documentation and Treatment of Human Rights Abuses." *Journal of General Internal Medicine* 11:533–38.

Shichor, D. 1997. "Three Strikes as a Public Policy: The Convergence of the New Penology and the McDonaldization of Punishment." *Crime and Deliquency* 43:470–92.

Shields, K. E. and D. de Moya. 1997. "Correctional Health Care Nurses' Attitudes toward Inmates." *Journal of Correctional Health Care* 4:37–59.

Shue, H. 1978. "Torture." *Philosophy and Public Affairs* 7:124–43.

Silver, M., R. Conte, M. Miceli, and I. Poggi. 1986. "Humiliation: Feeling, Social Control, and the Construction of Identity." *Journal for the Theory of Social Behavior* 16:269–83.

Simon, J. and M. Feeley. 1995. "True Crime: The New Penology and Public Discourse on Crime." Pp. 147–80 in *Punishment and Social Control*, edited by T. G. Blomberg and S. Cohen. New York: Aldine.

Slee, V. N., D. A. Slee, and H. J. Schmidt. 1996. *Health Care Terms*, 3rd ed. St. Paul: Tringa.

Solzhenitsyn, A. I. 1974. *The Gulag Archipelago, 1918–1956: An Experiment in Literary Investigation, I-II*. New York: Harper and Row.

Sorensen, B. 1992. "Modern Ethics and International Law." Pp. 511–19 in *Torture and Its Consequences: Current Treatment Approaches*, edited by M. Basoglu. Cambridge, UK: Cambridge University Press.

Sparks, R. 1996a. "Prisons, Punishment, and Penalty." Pp. 197–247 in *Controlling Crime*, edited by E. McLaughlin and J. Muncie. London: Sage.

———. 1996b. "Penal Austerity: The Doctrine of Less Eligibility Reborn?" Pp. 74–93 in *Prisons 2000*, edited by R. Matthews and P. Francis. New York: St. Martin's.

Sparks, R., A. Bottoms, and W. Hay. 1996. *Prisons and the Problem of Order*. New York: Oxford University Press.

Steadman, H. J., D. W. McCarthy, and J. P. Morrissey, 1989. *The Mentally Ill in Jail: Planning for Essential Services*. New York: Guilford.

Steadman. T. L. 1995. *Steadman's Medical Dictionary*. 26th ed. Baltimore: Williams and Wilkins.

Stein, G. L. and L. D. Headley. 1996. "Forum on Prisoners' Access to Clinical Trials: Summary of Recommendations." *AIDS and Public Policy Journal* 11:3–20.

Storr, A. 1990. *Churchill's Blackbox, Kafka's Mice, and Other Phenomena of the Human Mind*. New York: Ballantine.

Stover, E. 1987. *The Open Secret: Torture and the Medical Profession in Chile*. Washington, DC: American Association for the Advancement of Science.

Stover, E. and E. O. Nightingale. 1985. "Introduction: The Breaking of Bodies and Minds." Pp. 1–26 in *The Breaking of Bodies and Minds: Torture, Psychiatric Abuse, and the Health Professions*, edited by E. Stover and E. O. Nightingale. New York: Freeman.

Summerfield, D. 1997. "Medical Ethics: The Israeli Medical Association." *Lancet* 350:63–64.

Tanaka, Y. 1996. *Hidden Horrors: Japanese War Crimes in World War II*. Boulder: Westview.

Taylor, T. 1992. "Opening Statement of the Prosecution December 9, 1946." Pp. 67–93 in *The Nazi Doctors and the Nuremberg Code: Human Rights in Human Experimentation*, edited by G. J. Annas and M. A. Grodin. New York: Oxford University Press.

Tesoriero, J. M. and M. L. McCullough. 1996. "Correctional Health Care Now and into the Twenty-First Century." Pp. 214–36 in *Visions for Change: Crime and Justice in the Twenty-First Century*, edited by R. Muraskin and A. R. Roberts. Upper Saddle River, NJ: Prentice Hall.

Thomas. J. 1988. *Prisoner Litigation: The Paradox of the Jailhouse Lawyer*. Totowa, NJ: Rowman and Littlefield.

Thomsen, J. L. and J. Voigt. 1988. "Forensic Medicine and Human Rights." *Forensic Science International* 36:147–51.

Tindale, C. W. 1996 "The Logic of Torture: A Critical Examination." *Social Theory and Practice* 22:349–74.

Toch, H. 1992a. *Living in Prison: The Ecology of Survival*, 2nd. ed. Washington, DC: American Psychological Association.

———. 1992b. *Mosaic of Despair: Human Breakdowns in Prisons*, 2nd. ed. Washington. DC: American Psychological Association.

Tomasevski, K. 1992. *Prison Health: International Standards and National Practices in Europe*. Helsinki: Helsinki Institute for Crime Prevention and Control.

Trager, J. 1979. *The People's Chronology: A Year-by-Year Record of Human Events from Prehistory to the Present*. New York: Holt, Rinehart, and Winston.

Trevelyan, J. 1988. "Agents of Repression." *Nursing Times* 84(42):45–47.

Turnbull, P. J., K. A. Dolan, and G. V. Stimson. 1993. "HIV Testing, and the Care and Treatment of HIV-Positive People in English Prisons." *AIDS Care* 5:199–206.

Turner, S. and C. Gorst-Unsworth. 1990. "Psychological Sequelae of Torture: A Descriptive Model." *British Journal of Psychiatry* 157:475–80.

Ugalde, A. and R. R. Vega. 1989. "Review Essay: State Terrorism, Torture, and Health in the Southern Cone." *Social Science and Medicine* 28:759–67.

van Heerden, J. 1995. "Issues Affecting the Reform of Prison Health Care in South Africa." *South African Medical Journal* 85:345–46.

Van Maanen, J. and B. T. Pentland. 1994. "Cops and Auditors: The Rhetoric of Records." Pp. 53–90 in *The Legalistic Organization*, edited by S. B. Sitkin and R. J. Bies. Thousand Oaks, CA: Sage.

Van Willigen, L. H. M. 1992. "Organization of Care and Rehabilitation Services for Victims of Torture and Other Forms of Organized Violence: A Review of Current Issues." Pp. 277–98 in *Torture and Its Consequences: Current Treatment Approaches*, edited by M. Basoglu. Cambridge, UK: Cambridge University Press.

Vaughn, M. S. 1995. "Section 1983 Civil Liability of Prison Officials for Denying and Delaying Medication and Drugs to Prison Inmates." *Issues in Law and Medicine* 11:47–76.

———. 1996. "Prison Civil Liability for Inmate-against-Inmate Assault and Breakdown/Disorganization Theory." *Journal of Criminal Justice* 24:139–52.

———. 1997. "Civil Liability against Prison Officials for Prescribing and Dispensing Medication and Drugs to Prison Inmates." *Journal of Legal Medicine* 18:315–44.

Vaughn, M. S. and L. Carroll. 1998. "Separate and Unequal: Prison versus Free-World Medical Care." *Justice Quarterly* 15:3–40.

Vaughn, M. S. and R. V. del Carmen. 1997. "The Fourth Amendment as a Tool of Actuarial Justice: The Special Needs Exception to the Warrant and Probable Cause Requirements." *Crime and Delinquency* 43:78–103.

Vause, R. C., A. Beeler, and M. Miller-Blanks. 1997. "Seeking a Practice Challenge? PAs in Federal Prisons." *JAAPA/Official Journal of the American Academy of Physician Assistants* 10(2):59–67.

Veatch, R. M. 1987. "Nazis and Hippocratists: Searching for the Moral Relation." *Psychohistory Review* 16:15–31.

Vesti, P. and N. J. Lavil. 1995. "Torture and the Medical Profession: A Review." *International Journal of the Humanities* 11(1):95–99.

Veysey, B. M., H. J. Steadman, J. P. Morrissey, and M. Johnsen. 1997. "In Search of the Missing Linkages: Continuity of Care in U.S. Jails." *Behavioral Sciences and the Law* 15:383–97.

Walens, S. 1997. *War Stories: An Oral History of Life behind Bars*. Westport, CT: Praeger.

Waring, T. 1996. "Prisoners with Diabetes: Do They Receive Appropriate Care?" *Nursing Times* 92(16):38–39.

Weber, R. P. 1990. *Basic Content Analysis*, 2nd ed. Newbury Park, CA: Sage.

Wei, C. S. 1997. *Courage to Stand Alone: Letters from Prison and Other Writings*. New York: Viking.

Weinert, F. 1996. "Weber's Ideal Types as Models in the Social Sciences." Pp. 73–93 in *Verstehen and Humane Understanding*, edited by A. O'Hear. Cambridge, UK: Cambridge University Press.

Weinstein, C. and E. Cummins. 1996. "The Crime of Punishment: Pelican Bay Maximum Security Prison." Pp. 308–21 in *Criminal Injustice: Confronting the Prison Crisis*, edited by E. Rosenblatt. Boston: South End.

Welsh, W. N. 1995. *Counties in Court: Jail Overcrowding and Court-Ordered Reform*. Philadelphia: Temple University Press.

Wessner, D. W. 1996. "From Judge to Participant: The United States as Champion of Human Rights." *Bulletin of Concerned Asian Scholars* 28(2):29–45.

White, L. W. 1996. "The Nazi Doctors and the Medical Community: Honor or Censure? The Case of Hans Sewering." *Journal of Medical Humanities* 17(2):119–35.

Williams, P. and D. Wallace. 1989. *Unit 731: Japan's Secret Biological Warfare in World War II*. New York: Free Press.

Wilson, C. R. M. 1993. "Going to Europe: Prisoners' Rights and the Effectiveness of European Standards." *International Journal of the Sociology of Law* 21:245–64.

Winn, R. G. 1996. "Ideology and the Calculation of Efficiency in Public and Private Correctional Enterprises." Pp. 21–30 in *Privatization and the Provision of Correctional Services: Context and Consequences*, edited by G. L. Mays and T. Gray. Cincinnati: Anderson.

Witherington, R. 1987. "The Acute Scrotum: Lesions That Require Immediate Attention." *Postgraduate Medicine* 82:207–16.

World Medical Assembly. 1975. "Declaration of Tokyo: Guidelines for Medical Doctors Concerning Torture and Other Cruel, Inhuman, or Degrading Treatment or Punishment in Relation to Detention and Imprisonment." *World Medical Journal* 22:87, 90.

Wu, H. H. 1994. *Bitter Winds: A Memoir of My Years in China's Gulag*. New York: Wiley.

Yackle, L. W. 1989. *Reform and Regret: The Story of Federal Judicial Involvement in the Alabama Prison System*. New York: Oxford University Press.

Zupan, L. L. 1991. *Jails: Reform and the New Generation Philosophy*. Cincinnati: Anderson.

Cases Cited

Bell v. Wolfish 441 U.S. 520 (1979).

Estelle v. Gamble 429 U.S. 97 (1976).

Harris v. Roderick 126 F.3d 1189 (9th Cir. 1997).

Harris v. Thigpen 727 F.Supp. 1564 (M.D. Ala. 1990). aff'd in part and vacated and remanded in part, 941 F.2d 1495 (11th Cir. 1991), on remand, *Onishea v. Hopper* No. 87-V1109-N, Slip Opinion (M.D. Ala. 1995), vacated and remanded, 126 F.3d 1323 (11th Cir. 1997).

Howard v. City of Columbus 466 S.E.2d 51 (Ga. App. 1995).

Madrid v. Gomez 889 F.Supp. 1146 (N.D. Cal. 1995).

Nelson v. Prison Health Services 991 F.Supp. 1452 (M.D. Fla. 1997).

Appendix: Provisions in Consent Decree Concerning Medical Facilities and Treatment

A. All inmates shall continue to have the services of a physician available on a regular basis during the business week for sick call while a physician shall also be on call on a 24 hour-a-day basis.

B. Immediate steps shall be taken to institute an efficient communication system for the purpose of insuring that inmates are able to notify a member of the medical staff of the need for medical assistance. Said information shall be contained in the information packet distributed to inmates upon entering the jail. This communication system shall require that a member of the medical staff immediately be notified of any inmate's health complaint and the nature of said complaint; that the member of the medical staff shall immediately evaluate the inmate's complaints and determine if further emergency agency is needed. A written report of all complaints of inmates seen by the medical staff shall be submitted to the physician on sick call the next day.

C. Arrangements shall be made with an outside, medically qualified and licensed facility to provide emergency services and major surgical services on a 24 hour-a-day basis.

D. Daily sick call shall be provided and a licensed nurse shall be present on the jail grounds on a 24 hour-a-day basis. All inmate complaints shall result in treatment within 24 hours of the complaint.

E. Inmates shall be furnished such special diets as are prescribed by a physician or any other member of the jail medical staff.

F. Upon recommendation of the medical staff any inmate, due to a potentially infectious or contagious disease, mental illness or any other ailment or injury shall be hospitalized and not housed in the County Jail.

G. No jail personnel shall administer or handle prescription medication prescribed by medical authority unless acting under the direct and immediate supervision of a member of the medical staff.

H. Immediate steps shall be taken to insure that inmates who suffer from toothaches or other tooth or gum ailments which are evaluated by the medical staff as causing serious pain which cannot be dealt with a medical doctor, are provided with dental treatment other than extraction, if the problem can be handled without extraction. This treatment should be available within 24 hours of the complaint. Extraction should be utilized only as a last resort. Dental problems not causing significant pain need not be treated at the old downtown jail. All future facilities shall provide for dental treatment upon the advise of the medical staff within the overall medical program. As a continuing policy inmates may elect to have their personal physicians or dentist provide treatment, at their own expense.

I. As a continuing policy, within 24 hours of being processed into the jail, every inmate shall be screened, including a medical history and visual inspection along with vital signs. In the event of an emergency this screening may be delayed up to 48 hours after processing, so long as a written explanation of the emergency delay is included in the inmate's records and copy provided to the inmate.

(Final Proposal 1979:8–9)

JUSTICE QUARTERLY, Vol. 16 No. 1, March 1999.

13. Meeting the Health Care Needs of the New Woman Inmate: A National Survey of Prison Practices

Vernetta D. Young
Rebecca Reviere

The number and characteristics of women in prison have changed dramatically in recent years. Prisoners are older, more likely minority, and more likely to be substance abusers than in the past. We surveyed 65 state and federal prisons for women to assess health care personnel and services available to meet the needs of the present inmate population. Institutions generally reported that basic health care staff, like physicians and registered nurses, was located on-site. However, specialists, such as gynecologists and dieticians, were often located off-site, whereas there was a reported need for various other specialties. Similarly, most respondents reported that basic health care services were available. On the other hand, the availability of services for chronic disease, disability, and mental health care, all conditions that disproportionately occur among the changing female inmate population, was less consistent.

Individuals enter the prison system with disproportionately high rates of chronic and acute physical and health problems, and health conditions vary by gender (Acoca, 1998; Baillargeon, Black, Pulvino, & Dunn, 2000; Lindquist & Lindquist, 1999). Because women have poorer health in general than men and because women's rates of incarceration are increasing so quickly, health care for women in prison is becoming a pressing issue.

This pilot survey of women's penal institutions in the United States was designed to describe the health services available to the female prison population. This detailed view will allow us to theorize the match between services and needs and to suggest needed changes in prison health care policy.

Review of the Literature

Today, the typical adult female prisoner is a member of a racial or ethnic minority (48% African-American, 15% Hispanic, 4% American Indian, Asian, and other races), between 25 and 34 years of age, single, with at least one child under age 18. She is a high school dropout who started using drugs and/or alcohol by age 13 or 14 and is a frequent drug abuser. She has a history of physical or sexual abuse. She has worked at a number of minimum wage jobs and received welfare assistance (American Correctional Association, 1990; GAO, 1999). This changing profile, and the increase in average sentence length, suggests that health care systems that have traditionally worked best in prisons may no longer be most efficient.

Health of Women in Prison

Women enter prison with a multitude of physical and mental health problems (Lindquist & Lindquist, 1999). These are a result of many factors such as poor health habits before incarceration (Brewer & Baldwin, 2000), poverty, exposure to traumatic events (Jordan, Schlenger, Fairbank, & Caddell, 1996) and lack of access to decent health care. A study of inmates in the Texas Department of Justice indicated that for a number of physical health conditions, prevalence rates among the prison population were significantly higher than for the general population and that rates varied substantially by gender (Baillargeon, Black, Pulvino, & Dunn, 2000). In addition, female inmates have higher rates of certain psychiatric disorders and mental distress than women in the community (Jordan, Schlenger, Fairbank, & Caddell, 1996; Lindquist & Lindquist, 1997). Further, according to the CDC, the prevalence of sexually transmitted diseases (STDs) among incarcerated women is high, with about 35% positive for syphilis, 27% for chlamydia, and 8% for gonorrhea (Morbidity and Mortality Weekly Report, 1998).

Ingram-Fogel's (1991) interviews and follow-up interviews with incarcerated women in North Carolina found that over 50% of her respondents reported menstrual difficulties and alcohol abuse. Other commonly reported problems were headaches, back problems, fatigue, drug abuse, and a history of sexually transmitted disease. Obesity was present in almost half of the respondents on entry and increased over time; abnormal pap smears were present in about 78% of cases. Ingram-Fogel (1991) also found that the majority of the sample reported depressive symptomology. On follow-up, 100% of the respondents indicated that they had experienced health problems since the first interview. Only about 28% sought health care for these problems, citing an unresponsive health care system as the primary reason.

Studies of Health Care for Women in Prison

Glick and Neto (1977), in an early study of women's correctional programs, surveyed the availability of health and medical care. They reported that although all institutions had some type of medical care, women's prisons, in general, failed to provide adequate health and medical care service. According to Glick and Neto (1977:62) medical services provided in women's institutions included:

> . . . intake examinations; sporadic "routine" examinations, primarily in response to a problem or a specific request; emergency care available with evening coverage by paramedical personnel; and limited dental care.

A few recent studies have surveyed health care programs and services for female inmates. Crawford (1988) reported that at least 70% of the facilities surveyed offered inmates' intake screening, yearly checkups, gynecological and obstetrical care and prenatal/postpartum services on-site. Lillis (1994) surveyed 49 correctional systems. Forty-seven of the 49 responding systems had on-site medical staff to provide screening at intake. Forty-four offered yearly health checkups; 42 offered obstetrical and gynecological care; 46 offered prenatal and postpartum care; 47 tested female inmates for AIDS with 25 providing tests at the inmate's request, 16 upon entry and 15 when inmates were at risk or with symptoms. However, limited information is available about the extent of STD diagnosis and treatment services in correctional facilities. During the summer of 1997, the CDC (Morbidity and Mortality Weekly Report, 1998) conducted a survey of STD testing and treatment policies and practices and found that most facilities treat STDs based on symptoms or by arrestee request and do not routinely screen asymptomatic persons.

Recently, the General Accounting Office (GAO, 1999) surveyed the Federal Bureau of Prisons, the California Department of Corrections, and the Texas Department of Criminal Justice. They reported that although all three jurisdictions had policies and procedures for providing health care for female specific issues, none routinely evaluated the quality of this care. While these studies give an overview of available health care, they do not allow us to ascertain the adequacy of these procedures for a changing female inmate population with specific health care needs. Here, we focus specifically on the health care needs of three major groups of female inmates: substance abusers, older women, and minority women.

Substance Abusers

According to Henderson's review (1998), drug abuse is the primary reason women enter prison and the primary health problem of women in prison. This coincides with the steady increase of women incarcerated for drug and alcohol and related crimes (Lillis, 1994). Snell (1994) reported that one change in the female inmate population was the number of women incarcerated for drug offenses. Nearly one in three women inmates in state prisons was serving a sentence for drug offenses in 1991 compared with one in eight in 1986 (Snell, 1994).

An increasing proportion of female inmates reported regular drug use before incarceration (Acoca, 1998; GAO, 1999), and a significant proportion has addictive disorders (Guyon, Brochu, Parent, & Desjardins, 1999). In a study of 805 women entering prison in North Carolina, inmates were found to have high rates of substance abuse relative to women in community studies (Jordan, Schlenger, Fairbank, & Caddell, 1996). According to one study of 651 women felons in North Carolina, 73% had used drugs prior to incarceration, with crack the most commonly used (Cotten-Oldenburg, Jordan, Martin, & Kupper, 1999).

In addition to the problems of drug and alcohol use, substance abuse may signal a broad set of other physical and mental health problems. According to a GAO survey (1999), substance abusers are likely to have a prior history of physical or sexual abuse and a history of mental illness. Particularly troubling is the fact that women who abuse drugs and/or alcohol also exhibit behaviors that put them at high risk for HIV/AIDS (Cotten-Oldenburg, Jordan, Martin, & Kupper, 1999; Guyon, Brochu, Parent, & Desjardins, 1999). High rates of substance abuse among female inmates indicate a need not only for treatment programs but also for other mental and physical health services. Despite high rates of substance abuse problems, inmate participation in drug treatment declined from 19% in 1991 to 10% in 1997, whereas about one-third of the inmates with mental illness did not receive mental health services while incarcerated (GAO, 1999). Morash and Harr (1994:220), in a recent study comparing prison programming for women and men, concluded that regardless of gender "the prison experience . . . leaves many who have a history of drug abuse . . . untouched by relevant programming."

Older Women

Although the population of women in prison is relatively young compared to the general population, the numbers of older women and the length of sentences are both on the rise (Kratcoski & Babb, 1990; Singletary, 1993; Rosenfeld, 1993). Kratcoski and Babb (1990) reported that inmates age 50 and above accounted for almost 12% of the prison population in 1989. This is expected to increase to more than 16% by 2005. Moreover, the median age of female inmates has steadily increased from 29 years in 1986 to 31 years in 1991 to 33 years in 1997 (GAO, 1999). Kratcoski and Babb (1990) noted that although prisons will remain predominately male and young, older women are becoming a larger segment of the inmate population. And older women have different sets of health care problems than younger women.

Aday (1994) reported that among older female inmates, there was a high incidence of chronic health problems such as hypertension, heart diseases, diabetes, alcoholism, cancer, emphysema, arthritis, asthma, ulcers, and stroke. Aday (1994) added that most of the new elderly offenders reported high levels of co-morbidity. In addition, he indicated the need for attention to psychological reactions to incarceration, declining health and death, and the impact of the failure to maintain family and peer relationships.

Morton (1992) noted that elderly inmates face unique problems: they are more susceptible to debilitating injury due to falls; they are more sensitive to heat and cold; their ability to see, distinguish colors, perceive changes in depth, and respond to light diminishes; cataracts, glaucoma, and retinal disorders are more common; they lose perception of high tones and hearing diminishes; there is frequent urination or incontinence; and older people are quite vulnerable to tuberculosis and other contagious diseases and may need additional immunization.

Minority Women

Approximately two-thirds of incarcerated women are women of color (Acoca, 1998). Harrison Ross and Lawrence (1998) reported that minority women in large correctional systems had the highest rates of HIV infection and associated tuberculosis. They also noted the high incidence of sexual and physical abuse. Harrison Ross and Lawrence (1998:122) concluded:

> The medical problems of women are associated with these conditions and behaviors; they most often include asthma, diabetes, HIV/AIDS, TB, hypertension, unintended, interrupted or lost pregnancy, dysmenorrhea, chlamydia infection, papillomavirus (HPV) infection, herpes simplex II infection, cystic and myomatic conditions, chronic pelvic inflammatory disease, anxiety neurosis and depression.

The risk of cervical cancer for black women is more than twice that for white women, with mortality rates three times higher for blacks than for whites (McGaha, 1987). The incidence of hypertension is also higher for black females (McGaha, 1987; Acoca, 1998), with one in four African-American women having high blood pressure. Diabetes mellitus is twice as prevalent in the female population as in the male and is highest among black females, and rates of infant and maternal mortality are higher in minority women. Sickle cell anemia is significantly more common in the African-American population. Finally, the leading cause of death for black women 25 to 44 is breast cancer with lung cancer deaths not far behind.

Summary

Women enter prison with poorer health than men who enter prison, and prisons have been slow to meet the specialized health care demands that female prisoners pose. Our review of the literature suggests that three groups of female inmates–substance abusers, older women, and minority women–have both unique and overlapping health care needs. All three populations have increased need for mental health services, particularly counseling for drug abuse and physical and sexual abuse. Older women and women of color share many chronic health problems, such as increased risk of diabetes, hypertension, and breast cancer. All three groups have relatively high rates of HIV. And importantly, these three groups share with other women in prison a pressing need for quality health care, given their poor health status entering prison and the stress of prison life itself.

Ignoring the gap between the potential needs and available services and resources for female inmates could be costly for corrections in the United States. If not treated effectively, many health conditions such as hypertension and diabetes may worsen and lead to complications requiring more intensive treatment and possibly hospitalization. In some instances, the failure to provide adequate care results in incapacitation or death. Furthermore, in the past, the issue of adequate medical care has resulted in a number of legal challenges (Ruiz v. Estelle, 1980; Estelle v. Gamble, 1976; United States v. DeColegro, 1987). Geballe and Stone (1988), in a study of women's prison litigation, reported increased emphasis on reproductive health care due to the increased incidence of hepatitis, drug addiction and AIDS and on the inadequacy of prenatal and postpartum care that leads to miscarriages, birth defects and unnecessary hysterectomies. Geballe and Stone (1988) also discussed litigation resulting from inadequate substance abuse, dental, and general medical care. Although the courts seem to have adopted the doctrine of "due deference," there is still a willingness to hear cases involving substantive rights issues (Jones, 1992). The initiation of such challenges based on violations of equal protection would be disruptive to the peaceful management of these facilities.

Considering the rise in incarceration rates among women, the potential for deleterious health outcomes for the prisoners, and the need to avoid litigation for institutions, we assess the resources and procedures available to women in prison, with specific emphasis on the health care concerns of these specific inmate groups.

Method

Procedure

After receiving clearance from the Federal Bureau of Prisons and appropriate state Departments of Corrections, we pretested the survey instrument on 15 institutions. After refining the instrument, we mailed a cover letter, the assessment instrument, and a return envelope to 123 state and federal institutions that housed women; those that also housed men or were work release centers were not included. Two weeks after the initial mailing we sent reminder cards to institutions that had not responded.

Sample

Of the 123 packets mailed, we received completed questionnaires from 58 state and 7 federal institutions. Analysis revealed that there were no differences between responding and nonresponding institutions in terms of size of institution and part of the country.

Results

Medical Staff

Respondents were asked to describe their medical staff and to indicate their status on-site or off-site. A number of respondents reported that some members of their medical staff were contract workers. However, this identification was not consistent across institutions, thereby making comparisons of contract workers unreliable. The majority reported that they had physicians (92%), registered nurses (95%), psychiatrists (83%) and psychologists (89%) on-site (see Table 1). Most facilities also reported that their licensed social workers (55%) and other mental health specialists (62%) were on-site. One-third did not employ these two groups of specialists.

TABLE 1 Medical Staff

Location	*On-Site*	*Off-Site*	*Not Available*
Physician*	92% (60)	8% (5)	0%
Obstetrician	45% (29)	45% (29)	11% (7)
Gynecologist	43% (28)	48% (31)	9% (6)
Registered Nurse*	95% (62)	5% (3)	0%
Dietician	40% (26)	49% (32)	11% (7)
Psychiatrist	83% (54)	12% (8)	5% (3)
Psychologist	89% (58)	8% (5)	3% (2)
Licensed Social Worker	55% (36)	8% (5)	37% (24)
Other Mental Health Specialist	62% (40)	5% (3)	34% (22)

*All federal physicians and registered nurses were located on-site.

On the other hand, gynecologists (48%) and dieticians (49%) were more likely to be located off-site than on-site, 43% and 40% respectively. Obstetricians were about equally likely to be on-site (45%) as off-site. A small number of respondents did not have gynecologists, obstetricians, or dieticians on staff.

Respondents were also asked: *Do you have other health staff available?* The most frequently named were licensed practical nurses, dentists, physician assistants, and nurse practitioners. A few institutions also had contracts with orthopedists, optometrists, physical therapists, and midwives. There were only three psychiatric or mental health nurses, one psychiatric social worker, one mental health nurse practitioner, and three psychiatric assistants or mental health technicians. There was one mention of an HIV counselor, HIV training specialist, HIV/AIDS physician, and HIV nurse, surprising given the rising incidence of HIV among women, especially those likely to be incarcerated. Similarly, with the frequency of alcohol and drug abuse problems among incarcerated women, just one institution reported a substance abuse counselor.

In-Take and Physical Examinations

Almost all reported that they asked about past drug/alcohol use, menstrual cycles, menopause, medication history, mental health problems, asthma, arthritis, and pregnancy history during in-take and/or physical examinations (see part A of Table 2). Even though most institutions reported asking about past physical abuse (75%) and past sexual abuse (68%), a significant percentage did not ask about either. All of the federal respondents asked about both past and physical sexual abuse. A majority, 71%, reported that they asked about urinary incontinence, a chronic problem for older women, but a sizeable proportion failed to ask about this important condition for older women.

TABLE 2 Health Assessment

A. Do you ask about the following during in-take and/or physical examinations?

In-Take	*Yes*	*No*	*No Response*
past drug/alcohol abuse	98% (64)		2% (1)
past physical abuse	75% (49)	22% (14)	3% (2)
past sexual abuse	68% (44)	29% (19)	3% (2)
transfusions	69% (45)	29% (19)	2% (1)
sickle cell anemia	72% (47)	26% (17)	2% (1)
sensitivity to heat and cold	48% (31)	48% (31)	5% (3)
recent weight loss/gain	82% (53)	17% (11)	2% (1)
mental health problems	95% (62)	3% (2)	2% (1)
arthritis	88% (57)	12% (7)	2% (1)
asthma	92% (60)	5% (3)	2% (1)
menstrual cycles	98% (64)	2% (1)	
menopause	98% (64)	2% (1)	
pregnancy history	94% (61)	6% (4)	
medication history	98% (64)	2% (1)	
urinary incontinence	71% (46)	29% (19)	

B. Do you test/screen for the following on admission?

Test/Screen	*Yes*	*No*	*No Response*
cervical cancer (PAP)	92% (60)	6% (4)	2% (1)
HIV	71% (46)	25% (16)	5% (3)
other sexually transmitted diseases	94% (61)	3% (2)	2% (1)
hepatitis	63% (41)	31% (20)	6% (4)
diabetes	85% (55)	14% (9)	2% (1)
hypertension	86% (56)	11% (7)	3% (2)
breast cancer (mammogram)	71% (46)	25% (16)	5% (2)
manual breast exam	88% (57)	11% (7)	2% (1)
glaucoma	40% (26)	54% (35)	6% (4)
cataracts	46% (30)	49% (32)	5% (3)
hearing	54% (35)	40% (26)	6% (4)
heart disease	88% (57)	8% (5)	5% (3)
respiratory system	88% (57)	6% (4)	6% (4)
pneumonia	80% (52)	17% (11)	3% (2)
tuberculosis	94% (61)	5% (3)	2% (1)
general mental status	94% (61)	3% (2)	3% (2)

Finally, sickle cell anemia, a disease that disproportionately affects minorities, especially African-Americans, requires sufferers to get transfusions more frequently than the general population. Although most respondents asked about sickle cell anemia at in-take, 26% did not ask, and 29% failed to ask about transfusions.

Prior medical history is a valuable tool for assessing the medical condition of a client. Eighteen percent of the respondents, none of them federal, reported requesting prior medical history for all women, and 72% for some women. Most (30) reported requesting prior history to facilitate diagnostic work-ups or treatment plans, while others indicated that the request was dependent upon the current medical illness.

Test/Screen on Admission

Over 90% of the respondents tested or screened for cervical cancer, other sexually transmitted diseases, tuberculosis, general mental status, and thoughts about suicide. Between 83 and 90% tested or screened for diabetes, hypertension, breast lumps, general vision, heart disease, respiratory system, and reflexes.

On the other hand, most respondents (54%) did not test/screen for glaucoma. Even though the female prison population is aging, the median age of 33 is below the age that tests for glaucoma are encouraged among the general population. Still, glaucoma is more common in African-Americans and those over 60; consequently it may be necessary to increase both the number of tests given and the pool being tested as the population continues to age. Similarly, one-half of the respondents reported that they did not test/screen for cataracts. The caution is the same as that concerning glaucoma. Forty percent did not test/screen for hearing loss. Even though the elderly are more likely to suffer from hearing loss, the younger population is increasingly at risk, and as a result, this should be addressed.

Most of the respondents (71%) did test/screen for HIV. Some indicated that there were restrictions; ten tested/screened only if the inmate consented, two if the inmate consented or it was determined necessary by the practitioner, and two if the inmate was at risk. Conversely, almost one-quarter of the respondents reported that they did not test/screen for HIV. In addition, over 30% of the respondents did not test/screen for hepatitis which could be related to HIV-infection and to the poor living conditions many women experience before incarceration.

Although most institutions indicated that they did mammograms, seven respondents tested/screened for breast cancer only if inmates were over 35, if they met certain criteria, or if it was medically necessary. The remaining 25% did not test/screen for breast cancer. A number of institutions tested or screened for glaucoma, cataracts, diabetes, and hypertension if the inmate was a certain age, if her history indicated a problem, if tests were ordered by a practitioner, if it was requested by the inmate, or if a physical exam indicated the need for further attention.

Services Offered

Respondents were asked about the availability of various health care services. Over 90% of the institutions reported regularly scheduled physical examinations. Seventeen respondents gave annual physical examinations to all inmates; the remaining respondents scheduled examinations based upon age of the inmate, the need for special exams, and the nature of presenting illnesses. The largest number of respondents reported (13) that those 50 years of age and older were given annual exams. Annual physical examinations were also given in four facilities for those with chronic illnesses, such as hypertension and diabetes. Those with major problems (1) and those working in the kitchen (2) were also given annual physical examinations. In addition, pap smears (6) and breast exams (3) were provided annually. Inmates under 40 years of age were given physical examinations every five years in one facility and every three years in four facilities. Other institutions scheduled physical examinations for all inmates every two years (1), every two–three years (3), or every five years (1).

Almost all of the institutions offered dental care, fitting for dentures, drug counseling, bereavement counseling, other mental health services and special diets (see Table 3). A large proportion, 76%, also offered pre-natal care. But only 57% of the institutions reported that they offered birth control. Fewer institutions provided vision care (72%) and hearing screening (53%) than dental care. A majority of the institutions reported that X-ray equipment (64%) and lab tests (79%) were included in the services that they offered. In addition, pharmacies

TABLE 3 Available Services

Services Offered	*On-Site*	*Off-Site*	*Not Available*
pre-natal care	78% (51)	8% (5)	14% (9)
birth control	57% (37)	8% (5)	35% (23)
vision care	75% (49)	23% (15)	2% (1)
hearing screening	58% (38)	41% (24)	5% (3)
dental care (not dentures)	91% (59)	8% (5)	2% (1)
fitting for dentures	89% (58)	3% (2)	2% (1)
drug counseling	91% (59)		9% (6)
bereavement counseling	92% (60)		8% (5)
other mental health services	92% (60)	3% (2)	5% (3)
special diets	88% (57)	2% (1)	11% (7)
X-ray equipment	68% (44)	29% (19)	3% (2)
lab tests	82% (53)	15% (10)	3% (2)
hospice	28% (18)	23% (15)	49% (32)
pharmacy	69% (45)	29% (19)	2% (1)
other	9% (6)	3% (2)	88% (57)

were available in 66% of the institutions. Federal institutions differed somewhat in that they all offered pre-natal care, vision care, hearing screening, dental care, denture fitting, drug counseling, x-ray equipment, lab tests, and a pharmacy, on-site.

Although most of the respondents reported that they did screen for HIV/AIDS, only 2%, none of them federal institutions, offered separate HIV facilities. Nevertheless, 28% of the responding institutions offered hospice. It is assumed that the hospices would cater to HIV/AIDS cases as well as those needing terminal care for other diseases.

Disability Services

Respondents were asked: *Do you have any disabled inmates?* Over 7 out of every ten institutions reported that they did have disabled inmates. A wide range of services was reported. Four respondents provided all services necessary to meet the requirements of the Americans with Disabilities Act, and an additional nine reported that they provided accessible facilities, such as dorms (5) and handicap cells or rooms (5). Wheelchairs (12), walkers (5), canes (2) and handicapped showers (4) were also available.

A small number of institutions provided services for the deaf, the blind, and the mentally ill. Special communication devices (5) and interpreters (4) were provided for deaf inmates. One facility indicated that they had special light alarms and an escort program for the blind. Three facilities reported housing for inmates with acute psychiatric problems and staff for the mentally disabled.

Drug Treatment

There were a plethora of drug treatment programs reported. Alcoholics Anonymous (16) and Narcotics Anonymous (15) were the most frequently mentioned drug treatment programs, followed by counseling (7), group (3) and individual therapy (4). In addition, the Therapeutic Community program and Al-Anon were available in four facilities and 12-Step Programs, in three. Other programs included Waldon House, Hazeldon, Hearts, Tapestry, Gateway, Summit House, and First Step. One jurisdiction provided a drug and alcohol treatment program for Spanish speaking inmates, and another offered a smoking cessation program.

Other Health Services

Respondents were asked: *What other health services do you provide?* Health education (7) and the monitoring of chronic illness (7) were the services provided most often. Other services included residential treatment for the chronically mentally ill (4), dialysis (4) and an infirmary (4). HIV pre- and post-test counseling (2), HIV training (2), individual counseling for chronic illness patients (2), minor surgery (2), telemedicine (2), and access to specialty clinics or consultants (2). One institution provided a nursery for newborns for up to 18 months and special training for officers in transporting pregnant inmates in labor and emergency delivery.

Other Health Issues

Respondents included a laundry list of health problems. The most frequently mentioned problems were HIV and TB (18), the incarceration of the mentally ill (10), and hepatitis B and C (8). Other issues were the need for health education (3), substance abuse (3), chronic illness (3), diabetes (3), high-risk pregnancy (3), smoking (2), asthma (2), respiratory problems (2) and compliance with medications (2).

Discussion

As the population of women in prison continues to grow and to change, health care services for those women must also grow and change. Considering the three fastest growing groups of women are older women, women of color, and women with substance abuse problems, we ask the question here: Do reported health care services seem to meet the unique needs of these women?

First, the average age of women in prison is now over thirty years of age (GAO, 1999). Clearly this is not an "older" population by any definition, but because many women who go to prison have never had adequate health care at any point in their lives, it follows that they are likely to experience health problems more typical of "older women." Unique problems faced by women growing older in prison are chronic diseases and co-morbidity, disability, vision and hearing problems, and mental health problems.

Most, but not all, institutions did screen for arthritis, a major problem for older women, heart disease, hypertension, diabetes, and menopause. A smaller percentage tested for glaucoma, cataracts, and hearing problems. The need for frequent physical examinations as age increases was evident. Most offered services appropriate to the aging inmate, such as fitting for dentures. However, current reports did not indicate that institutions were prepared to address "debilitating" injuries due to falls that are likely to increase with an aging population, and there were relatively few services or facilities for inmates with disabilities.

Second, women who are incarcerated are increasingly likely to be women of color, particularly African-American women. In some ways the health profile of African-American women matches that of aging women in general. Specifically, both share high rates of chronic disease, mental health problems, and disabilities. However, there are a number of health problems that are more specific to minority women. These include HIV infection, cervical and breast cancers, hypertension, diabetes, and sickle cell anemia.

Most of the institutions reported that upon admission women were examined, tested, and screened for a number of health problems that are more prevalent among minority women. The data indicate that counselors, nurses and other staff trained to treat HIV patients were generally unavailable, however. In addition, close to 1 out of every 3 failed to ask about or screen for physical and sexual abuse, sickle cell anemia, or breast cancer.

Our third group of interest is women with substance abuse problems. This group has particular needs for mental health treatment, especially in the areas of physical and sexual abuse, and HIV and STD screening and treatment. They also enter the institution with a number of chronic disorders and illnesses related to poor dietary habits. As noted above, staff trained to treat HIV patients were generally unavailable and a sizeable number of institutions failed to screen for physical and sexual abuse. Although there were a number of drug treatment programs listed, there were few that provided readily available professional help. In fact, there was only one reported counselor devoted solely to substance abuse.

Most institutions report high rates of available services and access to treatments. We focus our discussion below on areas that are particularly salient to these three groups but where gaps in provision of care appear: mental health problems (including substance and alcohol abuse), chronic disease, and disability.

Mental Health

African-Americans (Gupta, 1993), older women, and substance abusers have relatively high rates of mental health problems. One study revealed that 64% of the women who were tested on a symptom inventory were in the clinical range for mental health problems (Singer, Bussey, Song, & Lunghofer, 1995). Mental health problems may be present at the time of incarceration or may be a response to incarceration itself. Prior physical or sexual abuse and stressors from poverty may predispose these women to poor mental health. They are separated from their children and their social support systems, and they may be afraid of victimization while detained (McCorkle, 1993). Importantly, rates of mental illness may be underdiagnosed and undertreated in prison populations, especially among women, because of misdiagnosis, reluctance to discuss problems and seek help, and a lack of understanding that services are available. In addition, traditional mental health treatment is generally less effective with poor patients for many reasons: there are wide status differences between patient and therapist, poorer individuals have less experience in "talking out" their problems, definitions of problems and expectations for cure may differ between therapist and patient.

For further refinement of the health care protocol and for future research in general, we suggest that particular attention be paid to the specific types of treatment available, the procedure for referrals, the type of therapists involved with actual patient care, and the evaluation of these mental health treatments. In contrast to Harrison Ross and Lawrence (1998), our research suggests that mental health professionals and services are available at most facilities. Roughly 88% of responding institutions reported having a psychiatrist on-site, and 93% reported doing a mental status exam on in-take and having mental health services available. The services of clergy or psychiatric nurses might be more salient for much of the prison population than the services of psychiatrists or psychologists.

Chronic Disease

Substance abusers, minority women, and older women are all at higher risk for chronic disease. Problems such as sickle cell anemia, arthritis, hepatitis C, hypertension, diabetes, and asthma pose long-term problems with needs for long-term solutions. Although most institutions reported assessing these types of disorders upon admission to the institution, only seven reported regularly monitoring chronic illnesses.

Other factors, which may contribute to the worsening of these disorders, include the lack of control that women in prison might have over their diets, the inability to avoid stress, and failure to take the necessary medications. One important aspect of dealing with chronic disease for most individuals is self-care. This could be enhanced for women in prison and for their subsequent release through health education. However, only seven institutions indicated that they provided health education, while three stressed the need for health education. An infusion of health education programs would benefit the inmates by reducing pain and suffering, the correctional administration through savings in health care costs, and the larger community through reduced need for health care upon their release.

Disability

As noted above, wide ranges of services for disabled inmates were provided by only a few institutions. The aging of the inmate population and the long-term effects of chronic diseases such as arthritis and HIV may require that in the future institutions provide more services for disabled inmates. The number of accessible facilities will have to be increased. Additional equipment and advanced technology will be needed to improve conditions. Specific services for the deaf, the blind, and the mentally ill must be expanded. This will also necessitate the hiring of staff trained to address the special needs of this population of inmates.

Summary

Women in prison are indeed a captive audience. Entering with poor health, poor health habits, and poor health education, these women receive a range of examinations and tests that provide a profile of health care needs. However, the available services are often not in line with specific health care needs of the changing inmate population. Our findings lead us to suggest an approach that is tailored more toward this changing population, particularly around the issues of mental health, chronic disease, and disability. Moreover, because a number of the predominant health conditions were chronic, it is suggested that these women can greatly benefit from opportunities to acquire health education. We know very little, however, about the health education programs provided by the institutions or the health care knowledge of inmates. Women in prison should be given every opportunity to improve their health and to increase their health knowledge; it is for the benefit of the women themselves, the communities of which they will become a part, and ultimately their children.

References

Acoca, L. (1998). Defusing the time bomb: Understanding and meeting the growing health care needs of incarcerated women in America. *Crime and Delinquency, 44*, 49–69.

Aday, R. (1994). Aging in Prison: A Case Study of New Elderly Offenders. *International Journal of Offender Therapy and Comparative Criminology, 38*, 79–91.

American Correctional Association. (1990). *The female offender: What does the future hold?* Washington, DC: American Correctional Association.

Baillargeon, J., Black, S. A., Pulvino, J., & Dunn, K. (2000). The disease profile of Texas prison inmates. *Annals of Epidemiology, 10*, 74–80.

Brewer, M. K. & Baldwin, D. (2000). The relationship between self-esteem, health habits, and knowledge of BSE practice in female inmates. *Public Health Nursing, 17*, 16–24.

Cotten-Oldenburg, N., Jordan, B., Martin, S., & Kupper, L. (1999). Women inmates' risky sex and drug behaviors: Are they related? *American Journal of Drug and Alcohol Abuse, 25*, 129–149.

Crawford, J. (1988). *Tabulation of a nationwide survey of state correctional facilities for adult and juvenile female offenders*. Prepared for the Task Force on the Female Offender of the American Correctional Association.

Geballe, S. & Stone, M. (1988). The new focus on medical care issues in women's prison cases. *The Journal of the National Prison Project, 15*, 1–7.

General Accounting Office. (1999). *Women in prison: Issues and challenges confronting U.S. correctional systems*. GAO/GGD-00-02, Washington, DC.

General Accounting Office. (2000). *State and federal prisoners: Profiles of inmate characteristics in 1991 and 1997*. GAO/GGD-00-117, Washington, DC.

Glick, R. & Neto, V. (1977). *National study of women's correctional programs*. Washington, DC: U.S. Government Printing Office.

Gupta, G. (1993). *The sociology of mental health*. Boston: Allyn-Bacon.

Guyon, L., Brochu, S., Parent, I., & Desjardins, L. (1999). At-risk behaviors with regard to HIV and addiction among women in prison. *Women and Health, 29*, 49–66.

Harrison Ross, P. & Lawerence, J. (1998). Health care for women offenders. *Corrections Today, 60*, 122–128.

Henderson, D. J. (1998). Drug abuse and incarcerated women. A research review. *Journal of Substance Abuse Treatment, 15*, 579–587.

Ingram-Fogel, C. (1991). Health problems and needs of incarcerated women. *Journal of Prison & Jail Health, 10*, 43–57.

Jones, C. (1992). Recent trends in corrections and prisoners' rights law. In C. Hartjen and E. Rhine (Eds.), *Correctional theory and practice*. Chicago: Nelson Hall.

Jordan, B. K., Schlenger, W. E., Fairbank, J. A., & Caddell, J. M. (1996). Prevalence of psychiatric disorders among incarcerated women. II. Convicted felons entering prison. *Archives of General Psychiatry, 53*, 513–519.

Kratcoski, P. & Babb, S. (1990). Adjustment of older inmates: An analysis of institutional structure and gender. *Journal of Contemporary Criminal Justice, 6*, 264–281.

Lillis, J. (1994). Survey summary: Programs and services for female inmates. *Corrections Compendium, 19*, 6–7.

Lindquist, C. H. & Lindquist, C. A. (1997). Gender differences in distress: Mental health consequences of environmental stress among jail inmates. *Behavioral Science and Law, 15*, 503–523.

Lindquist, C. H. & Lindquist, C. A. (1999). Health behind bars: Utilization and evaluation of medical care among jail inmates. *Journal of Community Health, 24*, 285–303.

McCorkle, R. (1993). Fear of victimization and symptoms of psychopathology among prison inmates. *Journal of Offender Rehabilitation, 19*, 27–41.

McGaha, G. (1987). Health care issues of incarcerated women. *Journal of Offender Counseling, Services & Rehabilitation, 12*, 53–59.

Morash, M. & Haar, R. (1994). A comparison of programming for women and men in U.S. prisons in the 1980s. *Crime and Delinquency, 40*, 197–221.

Morbidity and Mortality Weekly Report. (1998). *Assessment of sexually transmitted disease services in city and county jails–United States, 1997, 47*, 429–431.

Morton, J. (1992). *An administrative overview of the older inmate*. U.S. Department of Justice, National Institute of Corrections.

Rosenfield, H. A. (1993). The older inmate—Where do we go from here? *Journal of Prison & Jail Health, 12*, 51–58.

Singer, M., Bussey, J., Song, L., & Lunghofer, L. (1995). The psychosocial issues of women serving time in jail. *Social Work, 40*, 103–113.

Singletary, H. (1993). *Status report on elderly inmates*. Florida Department of Corrections.

Snell, T. (1994). *Women in prison: Survey of state prison inmates, 1992. Special report*. Washington, DC: Department of Justice: Bureau of Justice Statistics.

Cases

Estelle v. Gamble, 97 S. Ct. 285 (1976).

Ruiz v. Estelle, F. 2d 115 (1980).

United States v. DeColegro, 821 F. 2d. Ist Circ., (1987).

JOURNAL OF OFFENDER REHABILITATION, Vol. 34, No. 2, 2001.

14. Implications for Corrections of an Aging Prison Population

Joana Brown Morton

America is undergoing a quiet revolution. You can see it almost everywhere you go. There are more and more older people in society and they are living longer. According to the U.S. Bureau of Census, in 1900 the number of Americans 65 years of age or older was 3.1 million or 4.1 percent of the population. In 1995, that number had grown to 33.4 million or 12.3 percent of the population. By 2030, it is estimated that those 65 years of age and older will number almost 70 million and make up over 20 percent of the population. Life expectancy in 1900 was 47 years of age; in 2000, people lived to an average of 76 years of age (American Association of Retired Persons, 1998). This dramatic change in the demographic makeup of the country is affecting every facet of society, including the prison system. Management issues related to older inmates in state and federal prisons are reviewed in this article. The issues include defining the older inmate, providing needed program services, planning for release, and staffing older offender programs. Also included is a discussion of the need to take a systems approach to addressing the challenges older inmates pose in the prison system.

Older inmates, both as a percentage of the total prison population and in actual numbers, are increasing in state and federal prisons. In 1990, inmates 50 years of age and older made up 4.9 percent of the total prison population. By 1998 this same group made up 7.2 percent of state and federal prison populations (Camp & Camp, 1998). Of the more than 92,000 inmates 50 years of age and older in 1999, the Federal Bureau of Prisons had the largest number with 15,216; among the states, Texas with 12,162 and California with 9,820 had the largest numbers (Camp & Camp, 1999). In the 16 states covered by the Southern Legislative Council, between 1991 and 1997, the total inmate population increased by 83.39 percent while the inmate population 50 years of age and older grew by 115.12 percent (Edwards, 1998).

The prediction for the future is more of the same. Demographic forecasts indicate that the nation's population will continue to age as 75 million baby boomers reach their 50s (Sultz & Young, 1999). Also, the average life expectancy, although not anticipated to increase as much as it has in the past, will continue to rise.

The number of older people in prison will also continue to rise. The Federal Bureau of Prisons predicted in 1988 that its 5,014 inmates 50 years of age and older would number 7,930 by 2005 ("Looking Ahead," 1989). Instead, by 1999 the Bureau of Prisons had more than 15,216 inmates in that age group. Studies of state systems including South Carolina (Morton & Anderson, 1982), New Jersey (Walsh, 1989), Florida (Duggen, 1988), and Louisiana (Turley, 1990) predicted similar growth in numbers of inmates over 50 years of age. The growth in the older prison population is not limited to the United States. In 1996, Uzoaba (1998) reported there were 1,379 inmates in the Correctional Services of Canada's facilities who were 50 years of age or older. By 2000, that number had increased to 3,752 and represented 17 percent of the overall federal offender population (M.A. Drouin, personal communication, May 19, 2000).

The change in demographics is only one factor that is increasing the number of older inmates in prison. Also important is the effect of longer sentences, truth-in-sentencing statutes that limit judicial and parole board discretion, "two-strikes" and "three-strikes" legislation, the war on drugs, and the politicization of the crime problem that has led to calls for getting tough on offenders. All these changes in sentencing patterns and social concerns have resulted in more people going to prison and staying there longer.

Older offenders, while still making up a small percentage of the total inmate population, began to merit serious study in the 1980s because of incompatibilities between the prison system and the needs of these offenders. Areas of concern included the failure to provide legally mandated, safe, and fully accessible living environments and age-appropriate programs and services for this population. Based on individual agency and nationwide studies, researchers concluded that prisons were ill-equipped to handle older inmates (Bernat, 1989; Chaiklin & Fultz, 1983; Dickenson & Wheeler, 1980; Dugger, 1988; Morton & Anderson, 1982; Newman, Newman, & Gewirtz, 1984; Walsh, 1989). One nationwide study conducted in 1985 by the National Institute of Justice found that little had been done to address the needs of older inmates. Only 11 states had specialized units for older inmates, and most had limited programming systemwide that would facilitate maximum use of limited resources or minimize legal challenges to agency policies and institutional operations for this group (*Elderly inmates*, 1985). A similar study in 1992 found that only 13 states and the Federal Bureau of Prisons had some type of program for older inmates (Morton, 1992).

It was also noted that older inmates are a heterogeneous group whose medical and other problems change with increasing age. For example, King and Bass (2000), in a survey of medical problems among older inmates in five southern state prisons, found hypertension and diabetes were the most prevalent medical problems of inmates 45–55 years of age. Among those 55–64 years of age, heart disease became a problem and there was an increase in arthritis, chronic obstructive pulmonary disease, and prostate maladies. Among the 65–74 age group, there was another increase in arthritis and heart disease with psychological and respiratory problems also increasing. The smallest percentage of the population, the 75–84 age group, had the most serious medical problems with heart disease, arthritis, hypertension, and mental conditions such as dementia and disorientation being among the most prevalent.

Defining the Older Inmate

Some of the problems in obtaining a full picture of older inmate issues are the difficulties encountered in defining those who should be included in this category. The lack of consistency in a definition creates problems in assessing demographic trends among age groups within and across agency lines. It also makes it difficult to determine the potential effect of differential treatment strategies on older inmates. Without this information, policymakers and administrators cannot ensure agencies are complying with legal mandates for older inmates or maximizing limited resources by implementing preventive health care programs and other activities that have the potential to reduce catastrophic medical and other costs.

There are two dimensions to defining what constitutes older inmates. The first is the need to have a common chronological age as a starting point for categorizing someone as an older inmate. The second area that must be addressed is the issue of an individual's level of functioning that encompasses how well inmates can care for themselves and participate fully in everyday life activities.

There is no uniform definition of what constitutes an older person in the community. Federal employment law defines older workers as being from 40 to 70 years of age. For Social Security purposes, 62 and 65 years of age have traditionally been the beginning of eligibility for retirement benefits, but these are being extended as persons live longer. The Older Americans Act of 1965 as amended, which provides federal funding for a variety of programs in the community, cites 55 years of age as the beginning of eligibility.

Among criminal justice agencies, there is also no definitive definition as to what constitutes an older inmate, but more agencies are moving toward defining an older inmate as one who has reached the chronological age of 50 (Camp & Camp, 1998; Morton 1992; Ohio Department of Rehabilitation and Correction, 1997). This relatively young age is based on the at-risk lifestyle of many inmates that results in their physiological age being as much as 10 years older than others of the same social-economic group. Also relevant is the fact that health care and other costs rise after 50, with experience showing that as many as 30 percent of inmates 50 years of age and over have medical and other problems that require specialized attention (Criminal Justice and Corrections Council, 1999). Beginning to look at this population at the relatively young age of 50 can enable correctional agencies to implement preventive programs that may reduce or delay expensive medical and other costs later on (Morton, 1992).

Defining individual levels of functioning is much more complex than identifying chronological age. The Americans with Disabilities Act (ADA) defines those with disabilities as people who have a physical or mental condition that substantially impairs one or more of the basic activities of life. These activities include such things as walking, talking, thinking, breathing, hearing, attending to personal hygiene and working. Individuals are also considered as having a disability if they have a record of such impairment or have ever been regarded as being impaired.

This definition does not take into account that in some cases, functioning in the prison setting can be more difficult than coping with limitations in one's own home. Different levels of functioning can be needed to live effectively even among different correctional facilities. There is less stress and hassle, for example, in a small minimum-security facility than there is in a large maximum-security institution. A facility that is designed to provide universal access for those with disabilities will enable older people to function independently longer than will a facility designed for younger more physically active inmates.

Although age does not necessarily mean one is disabled, the potential for impairment increases as one ages (King & Bass, 2000). Although not all states maintain adequate records for the number and kinds of disabilities encountered in the prison system, there are indications that problems exist in meeting the needs of this population (Long & Sapp, 1992). Researchers also know that the level of functioning can change rapidly among elderly people or can creep up so slowly that it is hardly noticed until it has reached a crisis stage. This fact means that correctional personnel, particularly correctional officers who have the most contact with older inmates, have to monitor and assess the levels of functioning of older inmates carefully.

Basics of Aging

To address the special needs of older inmates, it is important to understand the basic factors related to aging and the effect they have on people's ability to function. The term "special needs" is used because older inmates as a group have problems that are not addressed in normal supervision and management of general population inmates. For example, although medical care is made available to all inmates, age-specific medical problems will require administrators to take actions for older inmates beyond what is normally provided.

To further complicate the matter, each person ages differently based on a series of factors, including his or her heredity and environment. "While heredity may set the cellular stopwatch, environmental factors can influence how fast it runs" ("What is normal aging?," 1997, p. 3). So life expectancy is based on how long a person's parents, grandparents, and other family members lived and how a person lives his or her life. Smoking, lack of exercise, a high-fat diet, drug and alcohol abuse, exposure to environmental hazards including toxic chemicals and even too much sun, stress, excessive weight, and poor health can accelerate aging and deteriorate the quality of life. Because of these variables, some people might be physically or mentally old at 50 years of age whereas others may be active and "young" at age 70. Thus, older people are more heterogeneous than any other age group (Feldman, 1989; Foner, 1986).

The lifestyles many inmates have before coming to prison can damage their systems and cause premature aging. Once they are incarcerated, however, the availability of good medical care, a proper diet, limited access to drugs and alcohol, and other facets of a controlled environment can slow the decline.

Profile of Older Inmates

Older inmates can fall into one of at least three categories, each with problems that must be addressed by the prison system. There are those inmates sentenced to prison after age 50, those who have spent a number of years in prison with short periods of freedom, and those who were sentenced to prison at an early age and grew up there. States differ in the numbers of inmates they have in these three groups, and there is no clear explanation for this variation.

The first group of older inmates consists of those who committed their crimes after the age of 50. Those in this group are often sentenced to prison for the first time for serious or heinous crimes (Ohio Department of Rehabilitation and Correction, 1997). The offenders in this group are likely to have led law-abiding lives in the past and will have difficulty adjusting to prison life. Because they are new to the system, they may be the most vulnerable to being victimized by younger inmates. Given the nature of their crimes, their age, and the lengths of their sentences, their chances for parole are limited and many will die in prison.

The second group are those who have been in and out of prison most of their lives. This group includes habitual offenders who may have considerable skill in coping with prison but lack the ability to function adequately in the community. Given that inmates in this group often have serious substance abuse problems—usually alcohol addiction—they may suffer more degenerative medical problems than do those in the other groups.

The third group consists of inmates who committed their crimes and received long sentences before the age of 50. Their crimes are often heinous. More recently, some offenders in this group may be caught up in the war on drugs or "three-strikes" legislation that mandate long terms or life without parole for specific types of crimes. This latter group may or may not have committed crimes that are violent in nature. These individuals will likely circulate in and out of disciplinary segregation and prison mental health units the majority of their prison stay. If they are released, older inmates in this group will probably be the most difficult to place in the community because they will have grown up in prison and will lack community ties or the skills to live in society.

Special Needs

There are a number of policy and procedural issues that arise when one works with wardens and superintendents to help them design services for this group and when one looks at the research on aging and the way prisons are planned and operated. Of major concern is the cost involved in providing needed services. Two studies found similar differences in costs for services for older inmates compared with younger ones. The Center on Juvenile and Criminal Justice found the average cost of imprisoning a young inmate was $21,000 per year, whereas the costs for those over 60 years of age was $60,000 annually (Edwards, 1998). Similarly, the National Criminal Justice Commission reported the average incarceration cost for a younger inmate was $22,000 per year. For those over 35 years of age, the costs soared to $69,000 per year or more than three times the costs for a younger inmate (Holman, 1997).

Medical Care

One of the major costs of incarcerating older inmates is that of providing comprehensive medical care. In at least two cases. *Estelle vs. Gamble* in 1976, and *Capps vs. Ariyeh* in 1983, court rulings require correctional agencies to provide medical services to inmates. In Capps, the court mandated that inmates have the right to make their medical problems known, have professionally competent medical staff examine and diagnose their medical problems, and be referred to outside medical care if needed (Edwards, 1998).

Beyond legal mandates and ethical considerations, it is eminently practical for a correctional agency to take a wellness approach to managing older inmates. Providing prevention programs as well as chronic and acute medical services for older inmates will keep them healthy and functioning independently as long as they can. This, in turn, will save money and resources over time. If testing and treatment of high cholesterol, for example, delay a debilitating stroke or heart attack, it is much cheaper than providing 24-hour per day care for a bedridden inmate.

The majority of state correctional agencies appear to be providing specialized medical care for older inmates. A 1991 national survey reported that 21 correctional agencies provided specialized medical care for older inmates (Morton, 1991). By 1997, that number had increased to 38 with chronic care clinics, preventive care, and increased physical examinations being the most common services provided (National Institute of Corrections, 1997).

Of concern, however, is the tendency to consolidate specialized medical programs at one or two sites to save money and other resources. Although this may reduce the medical costs of providing services to older inmates in the short term, it may result in additional costs in the long term. Generally, when correctional agencies consolidate medical services, they place these services in maximum- or medium-security settings so they can serve inmates from all security levels. Although many older inmates have committed serious crimes, they generally pose less of a security threat than do younger violent offenders, and a large number can be safely housed in a minimum-security setting if medical care is available. This frees up more expensive secure bed space for those younger offenders who present a serious threat to themselves or others.

Another issue in consolidation of medical services is the need to mainstream or place the heterogeneous older inmate population throughout the system. This practice will help ensure that older inmates are not denied access to programs and services available to other inmates. It will aid correctional administrators in complying with the Rehabilitation Act of 1973 and the ADA. Such compliance is necessary because the Rehabilitation Act requires that any agency receiving federal funds must ensure that those with disabilities have access to programs and services provided to other inmates. Also, in the case of *Pennsylvania v. Yeskey* in June 1998, the U.S. Supreme Court clarified that inmates are covered under ADA and that those with disabilities have the same rights to programs and services as do those inmates who are not disabled (Edwards, 1998).

Mainstreaming older inmates can enable them to be closer to home and have a better chance to develop or maintain family and community ties. Family members of older inmates are often elderly and may not be able to travel long distances but could visit facilities closer to their homes. Again, this is an expedient policy because it may make older inmates easier to place on release.

A final issue in the medical area is the practice of requiring inmates to pay for medical services. Inmates for a variety of reasons use medical services at higher rates than their counterparts in free society, with incarcerated men averaging about 20 visits per year and women averaging about 24 (National Institute of Corrections, 1997). In too many situations, inmates abuse the medical system because it is free, it provides a way to alter their routine, and, in some cases, it enables them to avoid work assignments. To remedy this problem, a number of correctional agencies require inmates to pay part of the cost for visits to sick call and other medical services. According to administrators, these copayment arrangements have cut medical costs and reduced malingering.

In spite of its benefits, this policy has three problems when applied to older inmates. First, the practice can discriminate against older inmates unless work programs provide for accommodations so they have an opportunity to earn money or credits for their copayment. Twenty-four departments of corrections charge a fee or copayment for medical care, and only seven provide exceptions for older inmates and then only to those with special medical needs (Edwards, 1998).

Second, copayment programs have a differential effect on older inmates because they normally have more ailments than their younger counterparts. Care should be taken when applying copayment policies to older women because female offenders already use medical services more than do males, particularly because of gynecological-related needs. Requiring copayments could discriminate based on gender as well as age.

The third and perhaps the most important reason for examining copayment programs as they relate to older inmates is that they can discourage inmates from seeking medical care. For older inmates, discouraging the seeking of care is really the opposite of what ideally should happen. To implement a wellness model and practice preventive medicine, older inmates should be made to feel comfortable in seeking guidance and help from medical personnel. Their failure to seek medical attention in a timely manner for some ailments such as high blood pressure, for example, can result in the development of expensive and debilitating illnesses or even death.

Housing

Another issue related to older inmates involves housing. The vast majority of older people function quite adequately in the community with often only simple modifications of their environment to allow them to live independently or with minimum care. Similarly, modifications of the prison physical plant and operating practices may make it possible for correctional agencies to avoid or delay costly hospitalization and nursing home care for some older inmates.

As noted, most inmates should be placed in the general population. For some, few if any, modifications in their environment will be necessary to enable them to function fully in everyday activities of a standard facility. As inmates grow older or develop chronic medical problems, accommodations will need to be made to help them maintain their independence. These accommodations can range from making certain older inmates are placed on the bottom bunk to housing older inmates on a separate wing. Even allowing older inmates more time to eat can mean that they may get the proper nutrition necessary to stay healthy and active.

Older people are a lot more resilient than they get credit for being, and helping them maintain an active lifestyle while minimizing some of the noise, stress, and lack of privacy of a general population dormitory can go a long way in helping them successfully cope with prison. It is also important to ensure that new facilities are built and existing ones renovated using universal design criteria. This means the institution will be fully accessible so that older and infirm inmates as well as staff and visitors can participate fully in all the facility's programs.

It is inevitable that some older inmates will become so infirm that they cannot continue to function in the general population. For this group, a small separate facility or a section of a larger facility should be developed as a protected environment for older inmates. Studies indicate as few as 14 or as many as 18 states have specialized housing units or facilities for older, frail inmates, and those who have physical disabilities (English, 1999; Morton & Anderson, 1982). Of concern in comparing the lists of states having programs is some agencies appear to have stopped delivering specialized services as others were beginning. Canceling specialized units for older inmates sometimes occurs when administrators who may not be knowledgeable about the issues take over a correctional system. Special units may also be the victims of the desires of governors and legislators to get tough on inmates and eliminate programs or to pressures to use the space and resources to try to cope with overcrowding.

Release Services

Release services for older inmates can be broken into three types: release from the institution under community supervision or at the expiration of a sentence, compassionate release, and, increasingly, hospice services for inmates who are terminally ill and who cannot be released. The first type of release into the community is the most typical for older inmates and is the one correctional agencies are most accustomed to providing. Even here, however, older inmates are often more difficult to place than are younger ones. Social Security and Medicare and Medicaid eligibility takes time to process and frequently requires special arrangements with other governmental agencies to ensure the benefits are available when the person is released. Arrangements may have to be made to ensure continuity of medical care. In some cases, nursing homes may have to agree to take those being released who are in need of such care. Coordination with other agencies, including parole boards and community aging service providers, is often complicated by differences in mission, philosophy, client groups, and politics. Unfortunately, given that older inmates are usually not a high priority with other agencies, it falls on correctional program managers to be proactive to ensure that those who are eligible for release do not stay in prison because they have no place to go.

In some cases, outside organizations can assist in release planning and monitoring of older inmates. Professor Jonathan Turley began one such program in

Louisiana while at the Tulane Law School. Using law students as volunteers and strict eligibility criteria, the program provided screening of low-risk older inmates and planning for community placement. Because the program depends on student volunteers and excludes sex offenders and murderers, it can only work with a small number of older inmates. It does illustrate, however, the need to have a specialized assessment of older inmates to see whether they can be released.

The need for timely release of older inmates is occurring as parole is being abolished in some systems and the number of inmates granted parole is being curtailed in those jurisdictions that still have it. To fill the gap, correctional agencies, in conjunction with other social services agencies and community groups, must establish review and placement procedures to obtain release of those older offenders who pose a limited risk to society regardless of their initial crime. Eventually, states may have to develop multidisciplinary boards that include both correctional personnel and specialists on aging to review, place, and supervise older inmates in the community.

Once released to the community, many older inmates will need specialized supervision. One study of those on probation found that older offenders often rationalize their behavior and are therefore labeled as unwilling to accept responsibility for their crime. Because they are seen as problems but not as security risks, they tend to be ignored in favor of working with younger offenders.

Compassionate release is the second area that requires consideration when dealing with releasing older inmates from the corrections system. States that do have compassionate release programs usually establish requirements that inmates must be totally incapacitated or terminally ill and not a threat to themselves or others to be released. The process for release is usually complex and involves other agencies and a parole board or the judiciary. Even though the number of people who will be eligible is limited, more states will probably need to consider compassionate release legislation as the number of incapacitated older inmates rise. Data are not available on the effectiveness of these programs or even how those who are released are functioning in the community.

Although not normally considered a release program, in a way hospice care provides a compassionate way for inmates who are in the final stages of life and who cannot be released to the community to die.

All correctional agencies will have to face the issue of providing hospice care to dying inmates in the future. No one wants to die in prison, and the kinds of care necessary to ease the trauma of inmates who are terminally ill and their families lie outside the normal role of correctional personnel. Even inmates who have lived with the dying inmate and correctional personnel, particularly the correctional officers who have worked closely with the inmate for a long time, will need help in adjusting to the loss. Whether the program is inhouse or contracted with the community, prison staff must work with outside specialists in the design and implementation of hospice care.

For those inmates who have no family or others to be responsible for their burial, the correctional system should have procedures in place to handle transportation and burial. Having a graveside or memorial service can help staff and inmates who knew the inmate to have closure. It also provides some peace of mind to the older inmates who are left behind to know that they will be treated with respect on their death.

Personnel Issues

Only a limited number of states have considered the problems of selecting and preparing staff to work with older inmates. Not everyone is capable or suited to work with older inmates. As in the community, elder abuse can occur in correctional facilities when those who work with older people take out their frustration and anger on the job. Correctional managers and other personnel can be held legally liable for such behavior. The keys to preventing abuse are careful screening, selection, training, and monitoring of staff and implementation of multidisciplinary teams that include correctional officers and other staff who can combine their knowledge and expertise to ensure the most efficient and effective programs are provided.

Specialized training for all staff members who come in contact with older inmates whether in the general population or in specialized units is needed to help them work more effectively with this group. Training should not be limited to security personnel and managers. Those in the helping professions including medical personnel and social workers may not have had specialized training in geriatrics. All staff must come to grips with how they feel about aging themselves and resolve any conflicts they have about working with older people. Some staff will fear aging themselves and others will have had difficult relationships with aging relatives or others close to them. Others may resent providing programs and services for inmates that their own family members have difficulty obtaining in the community. It is unfortunate when all the care older people in the community need is not provided. This does not, however, absolve the correctional community from the legal and ethical responsibility to meet the needs of those under its care, and staff members will need to understand their obligations in this area (Morton, 1992).

Gender-Related Issues

It would be remiss not to mention the small but growing number of older women inmates in correctional facilities. Although they have many of the same general needs as do older male inmates, older women have a number of issues that must be addressed because they differ physically from men and are acculturated differently (Morton, 1993a). For example, older women need different medical procedures such as gynecological examinations and mammograms, and the requirements for these examinations increase as they age. They have greater propensity than men for certain chronic diseases such as strokes, macular degeneration, arthritis, other autoimmune diseases, and osteoporosis, and they are more likely to die from their first heart attack than are men.

On the environmental side, older women are more likely to be poor, have suffered from abusive relationships, lack the ability to earn a living wage, and have fewer family ties than do older males. Any planning and programming for older inmates must be gender responsive to older women and take their particular needs into account.

A Systems Approach

The bottom line for correctional administrators in dealing with older inmates is the need to take a systems approach to planning and implementing programs and services for them (Morton, 1999). This approach can best be accomplished by using a multidisciplinary, multiagency task force to examine current programs and future needs. The team should involve staff from throughout the agency and from all security levels to ensure that the needs of mainstreamed elderly are met and the issues of those in special units are addressed. It should also incorporate specialists from outside the system to provide a different perspective on the issues and relevant expertise in programming for older people. These specialists can be found in state and local agencies on the aging, universities, and the private sector. Additionally, representatives from the aging network advocacy system such as the American Association of Retired Persons can provide input and at the same time become familiar with problems faced by the corrections system. Using outside people is important because correctional agencies are not going to be able to go it alone. They are going to need ideas, assistance, advocacy, and resources from a variety of sources.

References

Aday, R. H. (1994). Golden years behind bars: Special programs and facilities for elderly inmates. *Federal Probation, 58*(2), 47–54.

American Association of Retired Persons. (1998). *A profile of older Americans,* Washington, DC: Author.

Americans with Disabilities Act of 1990, 42 U.S.C. Sec. 12101 (1991).

Bernat, B. (1989). Dramatic rise in number of elderly prisoners means special care, increased costs. *National Prison Project: Journal, 20,* 9–11.

Camp, C. G., & Camp, G. M. (1998). *The corrections yearbook 1998.* Middletown, CT: Criminal Justice Institute.

Camp, C. G., & Camp, G. M. (1999). *The corrections yearbook 1999.* Middletown, CT: Criminal Justice Institute.

Capps v. Ariyeh 559. A Supp. 394 Supp. on D. Or (1983).

Chaiklin, H., & Fuitz, L. (1983). *Service needs of older offenders.* Rockville, MD: National Institute of Justice.

Criminal Justice and Corrections Council. (1999, December) *An examination of elder inmate services: An aging crisis.* Tallahassee, FL: Florida House of Representatives.

Dickenson, G., & Wheeler G. (1980). The elderly in prison. *Corrections Today, 42*(10), 3–5.

Duggen, R. L., (1988). The graying of American prisons. *Corrections Today, 50(3)*, 26–30.

Edwards, T. (1998). *The aging inmate population*, Atlanta, GA: Southern Legislative Council. The Council of State Governments.

Elderly inmates, (1985). Boulder, CO: National Institute of Corrections.

Elsworth, T., & Helle, K. (1994). Older offenders on probation. *Federal Probation, 58*(4), 43–50.

English, D. (1999, July). *Project for older prisoners: Programs for geriatric inmates.* Unpublished manuscript.

Esteile vs. Gamble 429 U.S. 97 (1976).

Federal Medical Center (1994, September 1). *Inmate hospice program procedures*. Fort Worth, TX: Federal Bureau of Prisons, Federal Medical Center.

Feldman, S. L. (1989). Gerontological health education research: Issues and recommendations. In Feldman, R. H. L., & Humphrey, J. H. (Eds.), *Advances in health education* (pp. 161–193). New York: AMS.

Foner, A. (1986). *Aging and old age: New perspectives.* Englewood Cliffs, NJ: Prentice Hall.

Holman, J. R., (1997, March–April). The costliest convicts. *Modern Maturity*, 30–36.

King, K., & Bass, P. (2000). Southern prisons and elderly inmates: Taking a look inside. In Stevens, J. D. (Ed.). *Corrections Perspectives* (pp. 66–69). Madison, WI: Coursewise.

Long, L. M., & Sapp. A. D. (1992). Programs and facilities for physically disabled inmates in state prisons. *Journal of Offender Rehabilitation, 13*(1–2), 191–204.

Looking ahead—The future BOP population and their costly health care needs. (1989, January). In *Research Bulletin* (pp. 1–5). Washington, DC: U.S. Department of Justice. Federal Bureau of Prisons.

Lyons, J., & Bonebrake, L. (1995). *Elderly inmate profile: 1985 and 1995*. Albany, NY: New York Department of Correctional Services.

Morton, J. B. *An analysis of prison systems' response to older inmates*. Unpublished manuscript.

Morton, J. B. (1992). *An administrative overview of the older inmate.* Washington, DC: National Institute of Corrections.

Morton, J. B. (1993a). The older female offender. In *Female offenders meeting the needs of a neglected population* (pp. 30–35). Laurel, MD: American Correctional Association.

Morton, J. B. (1993b, February). Training staff to work with elderly and disabled inmates. *Corrections Today, 55*(1). 42, 44–47.

Morton, J. B. (1999). A systems approach to programming for older offenders. In *The state of corrections* (pp. 23–35), Lanham, MD: American Correctional Association.

Morton, J. B., & Anderson, J. C. (1982). Elderly offenders: The forgotten minority. *Corrections Today, 44,* 14–16.

National Institute of Corrections, (1997). Prison medical care: Special needs populations and cost control. In *Special issues in corrections* (pp. 1–7). Longmont, CO: NIC Information Center.

Newman, E. S., Newman, D. J., & Gewirtz, M. L. (1984). *Elderly criminals,* Boston, MA: Oelgeschlager, Gunn, & Hain.

Ohio Department of Rehabilitation and Correction, (1997). *Older offenders: The Ohio initiative.* Columbus, OH: Author.

Older Americans Act of 1965 (P.L. 89–73).

Pennsylvania v. Yeskey 542 U.S. 206 (1998).

Rehabilitation Act of 1973, 29 U.S.C. Sec. 504 (1982).

Rubin, P. N., & McCampbell, S. (1994, July). The Americans with Disabilities Act and criminal justice: Providing inmate services. In *National Institute of Justice Research in Action* (pp. 1–7) Washington, DC: U.S. Department of Justice.

Sultz, H. A., & Young, K. M. (1999). *Health Care USA: Understanding its organization and delivery.* Gaithersburg, MD: Aspen Publishers.

The elderly inmate in Michigan (1996). Lansing, MI: Michigan Department of Corrections.

Turley, J. (1990). Tulane project for older prisoners. In *Long term confinement and the aging inmate population: A record and proceedings.* Washington, DC: Federal Bureau of Prisons.

Uzoaba, J. H. E. (1998, May). *Managing older offenders: Where do we stand?* (research report) Ottawa, Ontario: Correctional Services of Canada.

Walsh, C. E., (1989). Older and long-term inmates growing old in New Jersey prison system. *Journal of Offender Counseling Services and Rehabilitation, 13*(2), 245–248.

What is normal aging? (1997, June). *Women's Health Watch,* 1–4.

CORRECTIONS MANAGEMENT QUARTERLY, 2001, 578–88.

15. High-Risk HIV Transmission Behavior in Prison and the Prison Subculture

Christopher P. Krebs

Nearly two million people are currently housed in state and federal prisons. The rate of AIDS infection is 5 times higher in prisons than in the general population. High-risk HIV transmission behaviors take place inside prisons, and there is little doubt that intraprison HIV transmission occurs. What is not well understood is what determines whether high-risk HIV transmission behaviors occur and how they can be prevented inside prison. In this article, an integrated theoretical framework, which merges the importation and deprivation models of inmate behavior, is proposed to explain intraprison high-risk HIV transmission behavior. Data from an inmate survey suggest that sex and tattooing are the two most prevalent intraprison high-risk HIV transmission behaviors and that the majority of high-risk behavior in prison can be attributed to the deprivation model. These data, coupled with insightful inmate comments, carry important policy implications and should inform future HIV education and prevention efforts.

Although HIV is transmitted in an instant during a "risky" behavior or event, many factors affect the likelihood that such a risky behavior or event will occur. In other words, although contracting HIV may occur in a matter of seconds, the behaviors and experiences that ultimately put one in a situation of risk occur over time (an exception to this might involve the risk associated with certain instances of rape). It is not as simple as exchanging tainted blood or semen. HIV transmission involves a behavioral process, and the behaviors that facilitate transmission are not uniformly practiced by all members of society. This explains why certain individuals and groups are at greater risk than others. It is important to understand what leads certain individuals or groups to indulge in risk behaviors at a higher rate than others if one hopes to prevent those behaviors and/or make them safer.

Although rates of infection vary from institution to institution and from state to state, it is estimated that the proportion of inmates in state and federal prisons who are infected with AIDS is about 5 times higher than for persons in the general population (Maruschak, 2001). (Similar figures are not available for HIV because it is difficult to estimate the number of people in the general population who are HIV infected). These high estimates are not surprising because prison inmates represent a population that is at high-risk of contracting HIV and therefore developing AIDS, and this level of risk is by no means diminished on entering prison. Many inmates continue to indulge in high-risk HIV transmission activities after entering prison. In fact, inmates sometimes engage in a greater number of high-risk HIV transmission behaviors and engage in these behaviors more frequently than members of the general population (Pagliaro & Pagliaro, 1992).

Although estimates vary, research indicates that a substantial proportion of inmates engage in sexual contact while in prison. Wooden and Parker (1982) estimated that more than 65% of 200 inmates in California engaged in consensual homosexual sex while in prison. Nacci and Kane (1983) concluded that 30% of 330 inmates in 17 federal prisons engaged in consensual sex while in prison. Tewksbury (1989) found that 19% of 150 inmates and Saum, Surratt, Inciardi, and Bennet (1995) estimated that only 2% of 101 inmates engaged in homosexual activity while in prison. The majority of this sexual contact is likely of the unsafe variety because few correctional facilities address the issue of intraprison sex or distribute condoms, the most effective mechanism for preventing the sexual transmission of HIV. Most state prison systems (96%) and all but four jails consider condoms to be contraband and do not allow them inside facilities (Hammett, Harmon, & Maruschak, 1999). The fact that much of the sexual contact occurring in male prisons is of the same-sex anal variety does nothing but further increase the risk of HIV transmission behind bars. Anal intercourse is considered to be significantly more risky than either vaginal intercourse or oral sex because the mucosal lining of the rectum is significantly more delicate than both the vaginal and oral linings and therefore more susceptible to rupture, thus making HIV transmission more likely (Schoub, 1995). Although specific estimates of the prevalence of intraprison anal intercourse in particular are hard to come by, research indicates that it does occur (Davis, 1982; Lockwood, 1994; Saum et al., 1995).

Whereas the research discussed above covers voluntary participation, rape, another fact of prison life, occurs involuntarily. The taboo nature of rape in society and prison makes estimating its prevalence problematic; however, it does occur and is germane to any discussion regarding HIV transmission inside prison. In an early study by Davis (1982), it was found that 2,000 of 60,000 (3%) Philadelphia jail inmates had been sexually assaulted, two thirds of whom endured "completed" rapes. Wooden and Parker (1982) estimated that 14% of 200 inmates had been sexually assaulted inside prison. A more current study by Lockwood (1994) found that 25 of 89 (28%) New York State prison inmates had been the target of sexual aggression, but only 1 had endured a completed rape. Struckman-Johnson, Struckman-Johnson, Rucker, Bumby, and Donaldson (1996) determined that 12% of almost 500 male inmates were sexually assaulted. Hensley (2000) reported that 14% of 174 inmates had been sexually threatened and 1% had endured rape. Struckman-Johnson and Struckman-Johnson (2000) found that 21% of 1,788 inmates had experienced at least one incident of pressured or forced sex and 7% of them endured a completed oral, anal, or vaginal rape while in prison.

Estimates of the prevalence of intravenous drug use (IDU) inside prison also indicate that HIV transmission risk may accelerate upon entry into prison. Forty percent of inmates report knowledge of needle sharing inside prison, and of those who inject drugs inside prison, 40% report sharing injection equipment with others (Monroe, Colley-Niemeyer, & Conway, 1988). Eleven percent of Canadian federal prison inmates report injecting drugs inside prison, only 57% of whom thought the equipment they used was clean (Correctional Service Canada, 1996). Although the proportion of inmates who continue to inject drugs once inside prison seems to decrease, those inmates who continue to inject are more likely to share equipment and less likely to clean the shared equipment between uses. Injection equipment and bleach, which is used to clean the equipment, are difficult to acquire in the correctional setting because they are considered contraband (Mahon, 1996). Furthermore, they are sharing injection equipment with a population (fellow inmates) that has a very high rate of HIV/AIDS infection (Gore, 1995; Thomas, 1990; Turnbull, Dolan, & Stimson, 1992).

An additional high-risk HIV transmission activity that continues to occur inside prison is tattooing. Because needles, which are used to make tattoos, are considered contraband, they are difficult to obtain in the correctional setting. The shortage of needles causes many inmates to share tattooing equipment, thereby accelerating their risk of contracting HIV (Doll, 1988; Mahon, 1996).

Much of the research on intraprison HIV transmission has been epidemiologic in nature. Researchers have sought to determine if HIV is transmitted inside prison, how HIV is transmitted inside prison, and how often HIV is transmitted inside prison. Researchers have dedicated little time to explaining why HIV is transmitted inside prison or what leads inmates to indulge in high-risk behaviors that are known to facilitate HIV transmission. A tested theoretical framework that helps explain the factors that lead certain groups, specifically the incarcerated population, to practice risky behaviors could prove to be valuable in the effort to reduce those factors and ultimately the specific behaviors and events that facilitate intraprison HIV transmission.

For a variety of reasons, some choose to involve themselves in risky behaviors whereas others do not. With the exception of rape, the risky events that lead to transmission in the prison setting, namely, unprotected sex, IDU, and tattooing, are essentially behaviors chosen by the participants, and many things affect the decision to indulge in such risky events. It is the preprison characteristics, behaviors, and experiences of an inmate and the current, or in-prison, characteristics, behaviors, and experiences of an inmate that work together to determine whether these risky events will be practiced by a given inmate. Contracting HIV is more of a process than an event, and understanding this process both substantively and theoretically will assist in the effort to make risky events less common and/or less dangerous. Reducing the risk, and ultimately the incidence of infection, will improve not only inmate health but also public health, as most inmates serve relatively short prison sentences of fewer than 3 years (Ditton & Wilson, 1999).

What percentage of prison inmates indulges in high-risk HIV transmission activities? Of those who indulge in high-risk activities, what percentage of them indulged in that same activity prior to incarceration? Are high-risk HIV transmission behaviors imported into prison with inmates as part of the criminal subculture or are these behaviors in response to the characteristics of confinement or the deprivations imposed by imprisonment?

Theoretical Framework

Sociology and criminology share rich theoretical traditions that have sought to explain inmate behavior and the prison subculture. However, to date, few researchers have drawn on this theoretical tradition to explain HIV transmission in prison. In this article, an integrated theoretical framework is proposed that outlines intraprison HIV transmission as a process, rather than how it is conventionally viewed, as an event. The framework is integrated because it incorporates two existing, though often competing, theoretical perspectives, namely, the deprivation and importation models of inmate behavior. The framework is process oriented because it involves the accumulation of preprison characteristics, experiences, and behaviors and in-prison characteristics, experiences, and behaviors of inmates. In other words, preprison and in-prison factors are theorized to coalesce to affect the behavioral tendencies of inmates and establish the level of intraprison HIV transmission risk.

A major tenet of the study of the prison and the inmate subculture is the process of prisonization. The concept of prisonization was popularized by Donald Clemmer in 1940. Underlying Clemmer's notion of prisonization is a stimulus of deprivation that results in a patterned response. The response of many inmates is to develop and perpetuate the inmate subculture to cope with the deprivations imposed by incarceration.

Evolving from the early work on the prison community and prisonization, two competing theoretical models were developed to explain the prison subculture and the patterns of inmate behavior. These models are the deprivation and importation models.

The deprivation model, which is an extension of the prisonization hypothesis, assumes that particular characteristics of prison life affect an inmate's attitude, self-image, values, and behavior, which once changed produce a unique culture that embodies certain behaviors and viewpoints. The prison environment deprives inmates of certain needs, and it is believed that the absence of these needs leads to behavioral changes in the inmate, known as modes of response. Gresham Sykes (1958), in his classic study *The Society of Captives,* referred to the loss of these basic needs as the "pains of imprisonment." The pains are produced by the loss of liberty, goods and services, heterosexual relationships, autonomy, and security. The loss of these basic needs results in an array of behavioral responses, most of which involve the adherence to an "inmate code," which opposes the institutional authority of the prison staff. As a result, the inmates' modes of response often entail the internalization of deviant normative prescriptions, a feature of the inmate social system that carries special importance in a study of this kind.

Although deprivationists believe prison changes people and view prison as radically different from society, importationists view prison as simply an extension thereof. The importation model was first proposed by Clarence Schrag (1961), who held that the values of the prison subculture are imported into prison from the outside world. Importationists argue that criminals foster certain attitudes in society and these tendencies remain intact when the criminal is incarcerated and guide his or her behavioral responses to imprisonment. John Irwin's (1970) classic work, *The Felon*, further claims that inmate behavior is not merely a reflection of the unique deprivations of imprisonment but an extension of the behavioral patterns of the inmates prior to incarceration. In other words, the preprison characteristics, behaviors, and experiences of inmates are imported into the prison with the inmate.

Historically, the deprivation and importation models have been employed in a mutually exclusive manner. Early researchers either endorsed the importation model and sought to measure to what extent inmates bring their subcultures to prison with them, or they endorsed the deprivation model and tried to determine to what extent inmates adapt to incarceration by adhering to an inmate code that is institutionally born. Several researchers, however, eventually acknowledged the viability and value of theoretical integration in prison subculture research (Akers, Hayner, & Gruninger, 1977; Grapendaal, 1990; Tittle, 1972). Despite their insight, prison subculture research did not experience widespread integration until the late 1980s and early 1990s. Today, integration is commonplace and a number of recent studies have simultaneously tested the models.

Reisig and Ho Lee (2000) conducted a prison subculture study in several Korean prisons. Their results suggest that deprivation plays a more significant role in constructing the prison subculture than the importation model. This finding manifested itself at both the individual and aggregate levels. Paterline and Petersen (1999) examined the structural and social psychological determinants of prisonization by integrating measures of importation, deprivation, and inmate self-conceptions. They found that deprivation model variables were a better predictor of inmate responses than importation model variables, but they also found that the integration of the two models produced the most explanatory power. Stevens (1994) found that the prison environment affects inmate violence levels regardless of the personal attitudes of inmates toward violence prior to their confinement. This finding suggests that deprivation plays a substantive role in affecting inmates' attitudes toward violence. Stevens concluded that some inmate values and attitudes seem to be shaped before their entry into prison, which supports the importation model, but not to the extent that some research would like us to believe. Lawson, Segrin, and Ward (1996) found support for both models and endorsed future theoretical integration in prison subculture research. Grapendaal (1990) also found support for both models; however, he concluded that deprivation is of greater importance. Cao, Zhao, and Van Dine (1997) employed both models, and their data indicate the importation model is a stronger predictor of prison rule violations, a measure of prisonization.

With the exception of this last study, the above studies largely seem to support the predictive ability of the deprivation model over the importation model. However, a number of the authors found that integration of the two models provides more explanatory value than either of the two models employed independently.

The mere individual application of these models would be of limited utility, especially in an attempt to explain the events and behaviors that facilitate HIV transmission in prison. The deprivation and importation models actually complement each other nicely, in an end-to-end format, to explain how the preprison characteristics, experiences, and behaviors of inmates coalesce with the in-prison characteristics, experiences, and behaviors of inmates to create a subculture and a situation that embody high-risk HIV transmission behavior and events.

The linear nature of the deprivation and importation models becomes readily apparent when the various high-risk events and behaviors that likely facilitate HIV transmission are considered. It is important to learn about who and what inmates are prior to incarceration to better understand what characteristics, experiences, and behaviors, as well as the level of risk, they import into prison. Following is a review of what the importation and deprivation models suggest about the activities that likely facilitate HIV transmission in prison.

First, inmates are demographically similar, in terms of age, socioeconomic status, and race, to people who are at relatively high risk of contracting HIV in the general population. Second, some inmates adhered to preprison lifestyles that put them at significant risk of contracting HIV. Similarly, some inmates import their injection drug–using lifestyle into prison. Some inmates enjoy obtaining tattoos as part of their preprison lifestyle. Inmates who import certain high-risk traits, or histories, are likely to adapt to prison by maintaining their identity and continuing to adhere to their high-risk lifestyles. Whether inmates import their sexual, IDU, or tattooing proclivities, these activities may continue inside prison and place inmates at risk of contracting HIV (Irwin, 1970).

In addition to the high-risk HIV transmission characteristics that inmates import into prison, the deprivations associated with imprisonment and the conditions of confinement cause some inmates to indulge in high-risk HIV transmission activities. Obviously, not all inmates import high-risk HIV transmission characteristics into prison. Many inmates, some of whom display no high-risk behavioral characteristics upon entering prison, become prisonized and respond to the deprivations of imprisonment by having sex, injecting drugs, and obtaining tattoos. Some inmates respond to the deprivation of heterosexual relationships by experimenting sexually with fellow inmates of the same sex. Some inmates, due to the deprivation of security, cannot defend themselves and become partners in coercive homosexual liaisons. Some inmates respond to the deprivations of imprisonment by seeking psychological escape in the form of intravenous drugs. Others respond to the deprivation of security by trying to appear tough to avoid becoming the target of victimization, and tattooing is one way to obtain a label of toughness. Intraprison sex, intravenous drug use, and tattooing are high-risk HIV transmission behaviors, but the deprivation of goods and services renders these events and behaviors even more risky. Most inmates do not have access to condoms, clean needles, or bleach, which are preventive mechanisms that are readily available and used in the general population to make high-risk HIV transmission activities less risky. Inmates are not able to diminish their risk by using such products due to the deprivations imposed by imprisonment.

Methodological Approach

This study uses a mailed inmate survey to capture the inmate perspective on some of the matters discussed above. Questions delve into the preprison and in-prison experiences and behaviors of inmates.

A minimum, medium, and maximum security prison were randomly selected from each of four state regions. However, there was not a minimum security institution located in one of the regions, so only a medium and maximum security prison were selected from this region. Eleven prisons were selected in all. From these 11 prisons, the department of corrections randomly selected 500 male inmates and provided their names, unique identification numbers, and where they were housed. Each inmate was then mailed a survey and a postage-paid return envelope. Women were excluded from the sample because the transmission dynamics of HIV/AIDS are likely substantially different for women in the correctional setting.

For the questions that were used in the survey analysis, inmates were asked to estimate the percentage of inmates they know who indulge in a particular activity, a methodological tactic typically used when surveying inmates. The mean percentage for each question is presented so as to convey the average opinion of the inmates who responded to the survey.

Findings

Of the 500 surveys that were mailed to randomly selected male inmates from 11 state prisons representing various security levels and geographic locations, 222 never reached the inmates. Of these 222, 8 were returned because the inmate was released between the time his name was obtained from the state department of corrections and the time the survey was sent (5 days), and another 214 surveys were returned because staff at four of the prisons did not distribute the surveys. Prisons screen all inmate mail, and for unknown reasons, the survey was deemed to be inappropriate by staff at these 4 institutions. These prisons were contacted, and each indicated that they were unwilling to distribute the surveys unless the central department of corrections office instructed them to do so. Prison staff members have the discretion to reject inmate mail, and little could be done to avoid losing this portion of the sample. Therefore, 278 surveys seemingly reached inmates at the 7 correctional facilities remaining in the sample.

It is difficult to know if these four prisons refusing to distribute the survey affected the representativeness of the sample. Three of the four institutions are not at all unique in terms of security level or the custody grades of inmates they house. All three accept minimum-, medium-, and close-custody-risk inmates and have a 4 or 5 security designation, on a scale ranging from 3 to 7, with 7 being the most secure. The fourth, on the other hand, is a youthful offender institution housing males between the ages of 19 and 24. It accepts minimum- and medium-risk inmates and has a security designation of 3. Given that the institutions that excluded themselves from the study are not dramatically different than those that did distribute the survey, it seems unlikely that excluding the four prisons had a major impact on the sample, but this possibility cannot be ruled out.

Of the 278 surveys mailed, 134 were returned. Several of the respondents (13) returned the survey but did not answer any of the questions. These surveys are obviously not included in the analysis; therefore, 121 surveys (44% of those that seemingly reached inmates) were returned and deemed usable.

Of the 121 respondents whose surveys were deemed usable, the average age was 36. The youngest respondent was 20, and the oldest respondent was 69. Fifty-eight of the respondents were White (43%), 44 were Black (33%), 16 were Latino (12%), 3 were Native American (2%), and 4 were of another race (3%). Eleven of the respondents had been in prison for less than 1 year (8%), 32 for 1 to 3 years (24%), 33 for 4 to 8 years (25%), and 48 for 8 or more years (36%).

Compared to the state prison population, this sample seems to be fairly comparable in terms of age. The average age of state prison inmates was 36. The youngest inmate was 14 and the oldest 88. The sample has the same proportion of White inmates as the state prison population but a lower proportion of Black inmates and a higher proportion of inmates of other races. 54% of state inmates were Black, 43% were White, and 2% were of other races. In terms of time served, the sample consists of inmates who have served more time than the state prison population. 34% of state prison inmates had been in prison for less than 1 year, 31% for 1 to 3 years, 23% for 4 to 8 years, and 12% for 8 or more years (Department of Corrections, 2001).

Inmate Responses to Survey Questions

It is simplest to report the mean response to each question, so as to convey the general opinion of the respondents. In response to the question, "Of the inmates you know, what percentage of them have gotten tattoos inside prison?" the 121 respondents reported a mean of 53%. In other words, the respondents reported that about half of the inmates in prison get tattoos inside prison. When asked, "Of the inmates you know who have gotten tattoos inside prison, what percentage of them do you think had tattoos before coming to prison?" the 121 respondents reported a mean of 44%.

When asked, "Of the inmates you know, what percentage of them have injected drugs inside prison?" the 121 respondents reported a mean of 19%. When asked, "Of the inmates you know who have injected drugs inside prison, what percentage of them do you think injected drugs before coming to prison?" the 121 respondents reported that of the 19% of inmates who inject drugs inside prison, a mean of 52% of them injected drugs before coming to prison. When asked, "Of the inmates you know who have injected drugs inside prison, what percentage of them share injection equipment with other inmates inside prison?" the 121 respondents reported a mean response of 41%. This suggests that despite the illegality of drug injection equipment in prison, only about 41% of inmates who inject share equipment.

When asked, "Of the inmates you know, what percentage of them have had sexual contact with other inmates inside prison?" the 121 respondents reported a mean response of 44%. When asked, "Of the inmates you know who have had sexual contact with other inmates inside prison, what percentage of them do you think had sexual contact with someone of the same sex before coming to prison?" the 121 respondents reported that of the 44% of inmates who have sex inside prison, only 30% of them had sexual contact with someone of the same sex before coming to prison. This suggests that the majority (70%) of inmates who have sex in prison did not have homosexual relations prior to imprisonment, which supports the deprivation hypothesis. When asked, "Of the inmates you know who have had sexual contact with other inmates inside prison, what percentage of them have had oral sex?" the 121 respondents reported a mean of 58%. When asked, "Of the inmates you know who have had sexual contact with other inmates inside prison, what percentage of them have had anal sex?" the 121 respondents reported a mean of 51%. When asked, "Of the inmates you know, what percentage of them have been raped inside prison?" the 121 respondents reported a mean of 16%.

Interpretation of the Inmate Responses. The responses to the survey questions are interesting and show some support for both the deprivation and importation models. In general, the respondents indicated that tattooing behavior is fairly common in prison, with about 53% of inmates getting tattoos. They also suggested that, although some inmates who get tattoos come in with tattoos, many do not, which seems to support both theoretical models.

The respondents indicated that injection drug use is somewhat rare, with only about 19% of inmates injecting drugs inside prison. Of the inmates who inject drugs inside prison, it seems that about 52% of them were injection drug users before coming to prison. This suggests that injection drug behavior can be imported into prison but can also occur in response to the prison environment (deprivation). Surprisingly, the respondents reported that only about 41% of the inmates who inject drugs inside prison share injection equipment. This contradicts some of the literature (Jurgens, 2000; Mahon, 1996), which suggests rates of needle sharing are quite high because injection equipment is difficult to acquire in correctional institutions. It may be that inmates in this state are fairly adept at acquiring injection equipment or that correctional officers in this state are less effective at keeping injection equipment out of prisons.

The respondents indicated that about 44% of inmates have had sexual contact inside prison. Of the 44%, only about 30% of them had homosexual contact with someone before coming to prison, which largely supports the deprivation hypothesis. Inmates who are willing to have sex with men undoubtedly come to prison (importation), but it seems that the majority (70%) of inmates who have sex in prison are responding to the deprivation of heterosexual relationships or are victims due to various other prison deprivations. The respondents seemed to believe that oral and anal sex are equally as common among those who have sex inside prison (58% and 51%, respectively). Finally, respondents suggested about 16% of inmates are raped inside prison. These data indicate that both deprivation and importation account for some portion of each of the high-risk HIV transmission activities that occur in prison.

Inmate Comments Related to the Survey Content

What is perhaps more interesting than the responses to the survey questions are the inmate comments, in which many inmates urged further contact, several asked for legal advice, and a few requested assistance with various matters, such as getting a job, starting a band, distributing artwork, and receiving a picture of their favorite college football team. Several of the inmates, however, made very insightful comments. It is these comments that help paint a picture of what living in prison is all about and why the events and behaviors that likely facilitate HIV transmission in prison occur and how they can be prevented.

The comments are as diverse as the inmates who provided them, but the comments have been categorized so as to connote their general perspective. Inmate comments are placed into three categories: (a) statements supporting importation, (b) statements supporting deprivation, and (c) comments on behavior and policy matters. Inmate comments are presented and discussed within these categories and in this order. All inmate comments are reproduced verbatim. Any explanatory statements that have been added appear inside brackets.

Inmate Comments in Support of the Importation Model. Several of the inmate comments seem to support the importation model by indicating that certain events and behaviors are a part of the inmates' lifestyles before they come to prison.

> I don't know of anyone who has injected drugs but I know of quite a few who smoke pot or crack and the ones who have done it here also did it before coming to prison.
>
> As for I.V. drug use; it's rare and the people who do it, did it on the street when it does occur, they almost have to share the needle because they are so difficult to obtain.

The following respondents indicate that tattooing behaviors are often imported into prison, but the second respondent indicates that the age of the inmate seems to play some part in determining tattooing behavior.

> A lot of guys have them [tattoos], about 86% of them have tattoos all over there bodys. 70% had tattoos before they came to prison.
>
> Questions 5 and 6 mainly depends on age brackets; 18–30 90% will either get tattoos and will get their old tattoos redone; 30–45 90% of the ones with tattoos will get them redone and the ones without tattoos at least 95% don't care for any; 45 or older don't worry about it no more.
>
> Most already had them but the ones who didn't can't get a better deal than in prison from the outside and some of the best "ink slingers" come from prison.

This second comment suggests that younger inmates will get tattoos if they do not already have them, which actually supports the deprivation model, or get their tattoos redone if they already have some. According to this comment, older inmates are less likely to get tattoos at all, which seems to support the importation hypothesis in that the older inmates adhere to their preprison behavioral tendencies. Older inmates with tattoos get them redone, and older inmates without tattoos do not bother getting any inside prison.

Inmate Comments in Support of the Deprivation Model. Although several comments seem to support the importation model, many more seem to support the deprivation model. These comments suggest that the deprivations imposed by prison—the loss of liberty, goods and services, heterosexual relationships, autonomy, and security—elicit modes of response by inmates. These modes of response can take the form of events and behaviors that likely facilitate HIV transmission in prison.

The following comment simply indicates that very few of the inmates who have sex in prison had sexual contact with someone of the same sex before coming to prison.

> About 23% of men in here are homosexuals, 15% of them were gay before they came to prison.

The following comment suggests several deprivations lead to high-risk behavior:

> The tattoos are a macho part of being in prison—trying to appear strong so as not to be preyed upon by homos "mostly blacks intimidating whites." The sex thing is limited, books—used to allow sexually explicit books in here now they don't. Also—when you get a visit from wife or girl friend you are allowed one hug and one kiss only—which makes it all that much harder on the woman—divorce rates are high in prison. Homos run rampant in prison—they actually allow people with AIDS to work in the kitchen.

The respondent indicates that inmates get tattoos to gain status and appear tough so as to not be preyed upon (deprivation of security), he alludes to the idea that prison officials have taken away pornography and that this affects the amount of sexual activity that occurs inside prison (deprivation of goods and services), and he implies that due to limited contact with loved ones, inmates seek other contact (deprivation of heterosexual relationships).

The following comment suggests that the decision to remove pornography from prisons has had a direct effect on prison sex. In fact, this inmate believes that removing pornography has not only resulted in an increase in homosexual sex but an increase in the transmission of HIV.

> The reason homosexuality ratings are so high is because they have taken and stopped all adult magazines from coming into the prison system. There has also

been and out spread of the H.I.V. virus cause of this. Some people get released and spread it to others. The Department of Corrections is promoting homosexuality by taking this type of action.

The following comments suggest that the deprivation of autonomy and security result in inmates' being able to coerce and force more vulnerable and lonely inmates into sexual relationships.

> The anser to my No. 14 [question regarding rape] may seem kind of high to you. But you must understand there are more ways to rape someone than just by force. Most guys are young and scared just by being in here the first place, so it not hard to talk someone young into doing thing that they wouldn't ever think of doing other wise. Plus threat will work also, if you are bigger than them. And then alot of these guy are lonely. So just shown them a little tender loving care T.L.C. and you can get about the same thing.
>
> Question # 14 [question regarding rape] Most of the people (85–90%) what are referred to in here as (punk or girls) were raped in one way or another. There are two kinds of rape in prison, in my opinion. Forsed to physically and forsed to out of fear before in get physical. Fear is by far the most widely used tactic to get people to do things they wouldn't do on the out side.
>
> Now a days it [rape] doesn't happen as much, but the people I know, 1 was raped and he became a homosexual.

The following comments are similar in that they indicate why inmates indulge in or are pressured into having sexual relations in prison or using drugs.

> Most of what happens inside is due to peer pressure or due to debts owed from gambling or borrowing from another.
>
> They get raped not by force, but by pressure or influence that they cannot avoid. The reason it's higher in prison is because of pressure others put on those who are "weak", "raped", or want protection and also those who don't have money coming in and want things to eat, gamble, drugs.

Due to the deprivation of security and autonomy, it seems that inmates are pressured into sex. Inmates who are pressured either owe something, which they probably borrowed because of the deprivation of goods and services, or are unable to fend off more powerful predators (deprivation of security).

The following comment indicates that inmates use drugs to escape the stresses of prison. The inmate goes on to suggest that because he is in a "soft camp" with a lot of "new cox" (first-timers) who are serving relatively short sentences, few of the inmates are willing to do anything wrong. In other words, the deprivations have not yet taken their toll. This portrayal supports the deprivation hypothesis in that it indicates persons serving shorter sentences do not respond to the deprivations in the same way as inmates serving longer sentences.

> You got to understand drug is a excape from here that's why we go on trips here . . . it make times go by . . . this is a soft camp they picking the inmate to send here, not being old timers all new cox with a little time so they not going to shake noting . . . they scared to do anything so it slow here. But other places are real sweet, wine and the rest, just as long you got Money you in shape.

The following comment indicates that needles are hard to come by in prison, which suggests that inmates who inject drugs inside prison likely share injection equipment. The inmate also indicates that the amount of sexual activity that an inmate is involved in is directly related to the amount of time he has spent in prison. This strongly supports the original prisonization hypothesis proposed by Sykes (1958). The longer an inmate is deprived of heterosexual relationships and the comforts of home, the more the inmate becomes "prisonized" and indulges in behaviors associated with the inmate subculture.

> Regarding the tattoo issue: it's regarded as status. Drugs: the needles are almost nil here. Sex: due to the length of sentence determines more accurately if there is sexual activity and the extent of that activity with no regard to spouse or girl friend.

The following comments indicate that most of the inmates who have sex in prison have long sentences, thus supporting the deprivation model.

> There are quite a few homosexuals, most have a great deal of time [are serving long sentences].

> It's amazing to me what these men will do for their pleasure to me it's very sick. When I see a new young inmate come in here you can watch the wolves stare and that inmate over! It's sick. This is what happens in here especially those with long time, and the officers look the other way!

The following comment suggests that young inmates are more likely to have sex in prison and the inmates who have been convicted of sexual crimes are more likely to become gay inside prison.

> Most of all sexual convicted inmates tend to become gay or bi-sexual. Most young guys ages 15 to 23 tend to start the gay acts.

The following comment illustrates why many inmates indulge in sex in prison. The comment indicates that very few inmates who have sex in prison had sex with someone of the same sex before coming to prison. The inmate goes on to explain that relationships in prison are primarily in response to loneliness, thus strongly supporting the deprivation hypothesis.

> [in response to the question concerning what percentage of inmates who have sex in prison had sex with someone of the same sex before coming to prison] Probably very few has ever liked the same sex. Prison is one of the lonliest place's in the

> world And in you will fine yourself loving someone or something That you never thought could be. For example, A inmate use to walk around with a beetle bug in his pocket. He loved that bug. He die with the bug in his pocket. One of the greatest Power in the world is love.

The following comment supports both the importation and deprivation models. The respondent indicates that inmates are "trapped by their lifestyle of crime," which seems to support importation, but he goes on do discuss how inmates must become prisonized to survive, thus supporting the deprivation model.

> Prisoners are mostly a society of persons who are trapped by their lifestyle of crime and consequently forced to live and act according to the ways of the majority of the prison population out of ignorance and in some cases for survival. Those who will not or do not conform to their ways in my opinion will eventually become martyrs.

The following comments indicate that guards encourage homosexual behavior and why.

> The sexual activity is rampant and encouraged by guards. Guards believe that the sex will provide release for sexual tension; this is faulty logic though, as more tension is produced from the dislike of homosexuals, the bartering of homosexuals, and the protection of gays by other prisoners.

> I sincerely believe that the promiscuous sexual activity here is encouraged to alleviate the tension here. The authorities it is my belief don't give a damn if we kill each other so whats they say he is a fag or they are just inmates. Who cares.

The following comments support deprivation by indicating that needles are difficult to obtain and how this likely contributes to needle sharing, a behavior known to facilitate HIV transmission (deprivation of goods and services).

> . . . the needles aren't really used because of the fact there close to impossible to get. If one was to surface I'm sure every dope head on the compound would use the same needle. As far as homosexual activity goes, the ones I know that are involved in that which isn't many have not had sex with another male on the street. As for injecting drugs, there are no needles on the compound. The only place you're going to get a needle, is in medical. And that's like asking the devil for a glass of ice water.

The following statements indicate that tattooing is often not a result of importation.

> A lot of blacks are getting tattoos, just passed a cell and a friends getting one finish and got 3 friend that never had a tattoos in there life tell they come to prison.

> I can see more here with tattoos in their stay So I assume they have it done while here.

One inmate wrote back and said he wanted to know what the survey was for before he answered it. He was told about the general mission of the survey, which is to determine if high-risk HIV transmission behaviors are imported into prison or in response to deprivation. He responded, and one of his comments directly addressed this issue.

> "Imported"? How can you say what on a man mind you lock his ass up for life, sure he going to get high, fight, pick on weak prick maybe even get him ashot of ass or head, you say imported [author's name] when a man been in the chaingang for 15–20 year he changes with time his mind work different.

This comment does not refute the importation hypothesis, but it certainly suggests that living in prison takes its toll. This toll of prisonization/deprivation results in inmates' changing and behaving in ways they likely never would have had they not been incarcerated.

Discussion

Theoretically, this study supports integration of the deprivation and importation models when explaining the universe of high-risk HIV transmission behaviors that occur inside prison. However, although both deprivation and importation account for some portion of each high-risk behavior, it is clear that certain behaviors can be largely explained by a single model. Sex in prison, for example, can be largely explained by the deprivation model. These findings are informative and provide support for further theoretical integration; although behavior specific, and sometimes independent, application of these models can still be effective when explaining certain behaviors.

Beyond the theoretical contribution, these findings are substantively informative and carry important policy implications. Although it is difficult to have great confidence in the validity of the inmate responses to the survey questions, the coupling of the responses and the inmate comments bolsters the validity of the data. The data indicate what proportion of inmates indulge in various high-risk HIV transmission behaviors, and this information is needed so correctional and public health officials understand the potential risk of contracting HIV inside prison.

In addition, this study carries some important policy implications that correctional and public health officials ought to consider. Deprivation and the conditions of confinement seem to explain much of the sex occurring in prison, which suggests that intraprison sex could be prevented by changing the prison environment. The inmates commented on various conditions of confinement that lead to sex in prison. Several inmates indicated that because pornography was removed from prisons, sexual activity has been on the rise. Pornography may have provided a sexual outlet, which once removed resulted in inmates looking for alternative, sometimes more dangerous, outlets. Allowing pornography inside prisons might result in less sex and therefore fewer instances of HIV transmission risk, at least according to some of the inmates who responded to the survey. Several inmates cited limited supervision by correctional staff members as a reason sexual activity is common. If correctional officers provided additional supervision, there might be fewer opportunities to indulge in sex and therefore transmit HIV. A few inmates discussed limited contact with loved ones as a reason sexual contact is prevalent among prison inmates. It might be that if inmates had more intimate contact, such as conjugal visits, with their loved ones, then sex between inmates would occur less frequently. Currently, the state under study does not allow conjugal visits.

IDU, although not as common as tattooing and sex inside prison, is a high-risk behavior, and knowing that it does occur suggests that certain policies might be in order to prevent IDU and/or make it safer. Several comments suggest that inmates might inject drugs to escape the reality in which they find themselves. Being locked up takes its toll, and some inmates respond by getting high on whatever drugs may be available. Making prison environments not so psychologically taxing could reduce reliance on mind-altering substances and therefore the risk of contracting HIV inside prison. A couple inmates indicated that inmates use drugs less often since the prisons started testing inmates for drugs. It might be that testing inmates for drugs more regularly would reduce IDU and therefore the risk of contracting HIV; however, testing is often believed to be more expensive and less effective than public health responses, such as drug education and rehabilitation approaches (A. G. Bird, S. Gore, & cosignatories, letter to M. Forsyth, Secretary of State for Scotland, September 14, 1995). In addition, there is evidence that drug testing causes inmates to switch from low-risk drugs like marijuana, which can remain in urine for up to 30 days, to higher-risk drugs like cocaine and heroin, which can only remain in urine for a few days (Jurgens, 1996; Riley, 1995). Although no prison systems in the United States officially make bleach available to inmates for the purposes of cleaning drug injection equipment, a number of international systems make bleach available and have not experienced any negative consequences as a result (Jurgens, 2000). Similarly, no prisons in the United States furnish sterile injection equipment, yet several international prisons, many of which are in Switzerland, provide clean injection equipment, and needle sharing and HIV transmission is down as a result (Jurgens, 2000).

Another policy option would be to provide methadone maintenance to inmates who are addicted to opiates. Methadone maintenance has proven to be a successful approach to reducing drug injection and therefore HIV transmission risk, and several groups have called for the introduction of methadone programs in prison (Advisory Committee on the Misuse of Drugs, 1993; World Health Organization, 1993). McLeod (1991) indicated that methadone maintenance is likely the most effective way to prevent needle sharing in prisons.

Tattooing, a behavior often thought to be relatively safe in the community, is believed to be a high-risk HIV transmission behavior in prison. This is because tattooing and needles, which are used to make tattoos, are not allowed in prison. Inmates, therefore, often share the needles that do exist, thus increasing the risk of transmitting HIV (Heilpern & Eggers, 1989). The present study indicates that tattooing is rather common inside prison. Increasing security and supervision, something inmates who responded to the survey call for, could reduce tattooing. In addition, providing clean tattooing equipment and bleach to sterilize equipment could reduce the HIV risk associated with tattooing inside prison.

There is clearly risk of contracting HIV inside prison as these findings, as well as those from other studies, indicate that high-risk HIV transmission activities occur inside prison and that a decent proportion of inmates indulge in these behaviors. Although a number of policy options already discussed may not be realistic in the United States, a number of international systems have successfully implemented them and are enjoying the benefits. In addition to policy reforms, discussed above, what might be necessary is a new approach to managing HIV risk in prisons and jails. Actively preventing HIV transmission inside prison will require the introduction of programs that contradict current correctional policies and acknowledgment by correctional officials that some behaviors are not preventable, but the benefits of making the behaviors safer would be borne by society, not just those who reside in correctional facilities. As stated by the United Nations Commission on Human Rights (1996),

> There is no doubt that governments have a moral and legal responsibility to prevent the spread of HIV among prisoners and prison staff and to care for those infected. They also have a responsibility to prevent the spread of HIV among communities. Prisoners are the community. They come from the community, they return to it. Protection of prisoners is protection of our communities.

References

Advisory Committee on the Misuse of Drugs. (1993). *AIDS and drug misuse update.* London: HMSO.

Akers, R. L., Hayner, N., & Gruninger, W. (1977). Homosexual and drug behavior in prison: A test of the functional and importation models of the inmate system. *Social Problems, 21,* 410–422.

Beck, A. J., & Karberg, J. C. (2001). *Prison and jail inmates at midyear 2000* (NCJ 185989). Washington, DC: Bureau of Justice Statistic.

Cao, L., Zhao, J., & Van Dine, S. (1997). Prison disciplinary tickets: A test of the deprivation and importation models. *Journal of Criminal Justice, 25,* 103–113.

Clemmer, D. (1940). *The prison community.* Boston: Christopher.

Correctional Service Canada. (1996). *1995 National Inmate Survey: Final report.* Ottawa, Canada: The Service, Correctional Research and Development.

Davis, A. J. (1982). Sexual assault in the Philadelphia prison system and sheriff's vans. In A. M. Scacco, Jr. (Ed.), *Male rape: A casebook of sexual aggressions* (pp. 107–120). New York: AMS.

Ditton, P. M., & Wilson, D. J. (1999). *Truth in sentencing in state prisons* (NCJ Publication No. 170032). Washington, DC: National Institute of Justice.

Doll, D. (1988). Tattooing in prison and HIV infection. *Lancet, 2*(9), 66–67.

Department of Corrections. (2001). *FY 1999–2000 annual report.* [Location anonymous]: Bureau of Research and Data Analysis.

Gore, S. M. (1995). Drug injection and HIV prevalence in inmates of Glenochil Prison. *British Medical Journal, 310,* 293–296.

Grapendaal, M. (1990). The inmate subculture in Dutch prisons. *British Journal of Criminology, 30,* 341–355.

Hammett, T. M., Harmon, P., & Maruschak, L. M. (1999). *1996–1997 update: HIV/AIDS, STDs, and TB in correctional facilities.* Washington, DC: U.S. Department of Justice, National Institute of Justice.

Heilpern, H., & Eggers, S. (1989). *AIDS in Australian prisons: Issues and policy options.* Canberra, Australia: Department of Community Services and Health.

Hensley, C. (2000, March). *Consensual and forced sex in male Oklahoma prisons.* Paper presented at the annual meeting of the Academy of Criminal Justice Sciences, New Orleans, LA.

Irwin, J. (1970). *The felon.* Englewood Cliffs, NJ: Prentice Hall.

Irwin, J., & Cressey, D. (1962). Thieves, convicts, and the inmate culture. *Social Problems, 10,* 142–155.

Jurgens, R. (1996). *HIV/AIDS in prisons: Final report.* Montreal: HIV/AIDS Legal Network and Canadian AIDS Society.

Jurgens, R. (2000). HIV/AIDS and drug use in prisons: Moral and legal responsibilities of prisons. In D. Shewan & J. B. Davies (Eds.), *Drug use and prisons: An international perspective.* Amsterdam: Harwood Academic.

Lachat, M. (1994). *Account of a pilot project for HIV prevention in the Hindelbank Penitentiaries for Women—Press conference, May 16, 1994.* Berne, Switzerland: Information and Public Relations Bureau of the Canton.

Lawson, D. P., Segrin, C., & Ward, T. D. (1996). The relationship between prisonization and social skills among prison inmates. *The Prison Journal, 76,* 293–309.

Lockwood, D. (1994). Issues in prison sexual violence. In M. C. Braswell, R. H. Montgomery, Jr., & L. X. Lombardo (Eds.), *Prison violence in America* (2nd ed., pp. 97–102). Cincinnati, OH: Henderson.

Mahon, N. (1996). New York inmates' HIV risk behaviors: The implication for prevention policy and programs. *American Journal of Public Health, 86,* 1211–1215.

Maruschak, L. M. (2001). *HIV in prisons and jails, 1999* (NCJ No. 187456). Washington, DC: Bureau of Justice Statistics.

McLeod, F. (1991). Methadone, prisons and AIDS. In J. Norberry, M. Gaughwin, & S. Gerull (Eds.), *HIV/AIDS and prisons.* Canberra: Australian Institute of Criminology.

Monroe, M. C., Colley-Niemeyer, B. J., & Conway, G. A. (1988). *Report of studies of HIV seroprevalence and AIDS knowledge, attitudes, and risk behaviors in inmates in South Carolina Department of Corrections.* Columbia: South Carolina Department of Corrections.

Nacci, P., & Kane, T. R. (1983). The incidence of sex and sexual aggression in federal prisons. *Federal Probation, 47*(4), 31–36.

Pagliaro, L. A., & Pagliaro, A. M. (1992). Sentenced to death? HIV infection and AIDS in prisons—Current and future concerns. *Canadian Journal of Criminology, 34*, 201–214.

Paterline, B. A., & Petersen, D. M. (1999). Structural and social psychological determinants of prisonization. *Journal of Criminal Justice, 27*, 427–441.

Reisig, M. D., & Ho Lee, Y. (2000). Prisonization in the Republic of Korea. *Journal of Criminal Justice, 28*, 23–31.

Riley, D. (1995). Drug testing in prisons. *The International Journal of Drug Policy, 6*, 106–111.

Saum, C., Surratt, H., Inciardi, J., & Bennett, R. (1995). Sex in prison: Exploring the myths and realities. *The Prison Journal, 75*, 413–430.

Schoub, B. D. (1995). *AIDS & HIV in perspective: A guide to understanding the virus and its consequences.* New York: Cambridge University Press.

Schrag, C. (1961). Leadership among prison inmates. *American Sociological Review, 19*, 37–42.

Stevens, D. J. (1994). The depth of imprisonment and prisonization: Levels of security and prisoners' anticipation of future violence. *The Howard Journal, 33*, 137–157.

Struckman-Johnson, C., Struckman-Johnson, D. (2000). Sexual coercion rates in seven Mid-western prison facilities for men. *The Prison Journal, 80*, 379–390.

Struckman-Johnson, C., Struckman-Johnson, D., Rucker, L., Bumby, K., & Donaldson, S. (1996). Sexual coercion reported by men and women in prison. *The Journal of Sex Research, 33*(1), 67–76.

Sykes, G. (1958). *The society of captives.* Princeton, NJ: Princeton University Press.

Tewksbury, R. (1989). Measures of sexual behavior in an Ohio prison. *Sociology and Social Research, 74*(1), 34–39.

Thomas, P. A. (1990). HIV/AIDS in prisons. *The Howard Journal of Criminal Justice, 29*, 1–13.

Tittle, C. (1972). *Society of subordinates.* Bloomington: Indiana University Press.

Turnbull, P. J., Dolan, K. A., & Stimson, G. V. (1992). *Prison decreases the prevalence of behaviors but increases the risks.* Poster abstract no. PoC4321, VIIIth International Conference on AIDS, Amsterdam.

United Nations Commission on Human Rights. (1996). Fifty-second session, item 8 of the agenda. HIV/AIDS in prisons—Statement by the Joint United Nations Programme on HIV/AIDS (UNAIDS). Geneva, Switzerland.

World Health Organization. (1993). *Guidelines on HIV infection and AIDS in prisons.* Geneva, Switzerland: World Health Organization Global Programme on AIDS.

Wooden, W., & Parker, J. (1982). *Men behind bars: Sexual exploitation in prison.* New York: Plenum.

THE PRISON JOURNAL, Vol. 82 No. 1, March 2002, 19–49.

16. Surviving in the Time Machine

Suicidal Prisoners and the Pains of Prison Time

Diana Medlicott

Because of the nature of prison, with its forcible suspension of everyday life and its emphasis on time-discipline, prisoners are forced to confront the issue of passing time and personal identity. Suicidal prisoners experience time as an acute source of suffering and connected to the deterioration of their sense of self. The accounts of prisoners demonstrate patterned differences between suicidal and coping prisoners in their relationship with prison time.

Introduction

Time is integrally and internally bound up with our sense of identity. Psychological definitions of personal identity, such as "I am all that I inherited as well as all I have acquired" (Mann 1991) are always propositions about the essential temporality of identity formation and development. The self-organization of events takes place against the backdrop of two primordial experiential principles, (1) that certain phenomena repeat and (2) that life change is irreversible (Leach, 1961).

The force of these principles in prison is monolithic: prison life consists of endless repetitions, and prisoners are aware that although their free life in society has been suspended, their bodies and identities continue to age and change. To cope with prison life is to cope with this painful awareness without letting it destroy self-identity.

In prison, the time of inmates is appropriated in the name of punishment, and individuals must learn to live by prison time, which necessarily involves the destruction of temporal autonomy. Time-discipline is enacted through the routines of each day which are compulsively thrust upon inmates. The timetable itself is a structural practice (Foucault 1979) with historical roots in rational and Enlightenment views on the achievement of order and discipline. The rigidity of timetables, the preoccupation with counting and observing prisoners, the compilation of personal files, are all disciplinary measures seemingly designed to produce psychological effects in inmates (Scraton et al., 1991). Accompanying these measures is, however, the phenomenon of dead time, those stretches of time which are emptied of events and human interaction, and generally passed in a cell, so that the features of spatial deprivation and hardship accompany the temporal deprivations.

In a literary evocation of his own imprisonment Serge (1970: 30) describes the resulting relationship of unreality with the landscape of time:

> Here I am back in a cell. Alone. Minutes, hours, days slip away with terrifying insubstantiality. Months will pass away like this, and years. Life! The problem of

> time is everything. Nothing distinguishes one hour from the next: the minutes and hours fall slowly, torturously. Once past, they vanish into near nothingness. The present minute is infinite. But time does not exist.

It was Serge's depiction of time that struck the prisoners in Cohen and Taylor's (1972) study of a maximum security wing as the most accurate in relation to time and their fears of deterioration over the passage of their life sentence. The painful problem of time for lifers has been long recognized (Sapsford, 1983). But this recognition is implicitly predicated on the assumption that it is only the length of sentence which produces a painful relationship with the passage of time.

My research, however, focuses on the interaction of *suicidal* prisoners with the nature of prison time itself, regardless of the length of sentence. I chose a large local male prison for the study. Suicides in prison are most prevalent in male local prisons, where overcrowding, operational pressures and high numbers of receptions of remand prisoners are daily stresses. In 1878, the medical inspector for local prisons observed that rates at local prisons were four times greater than at convict prisons, and surmised that remand prisoners underwent specific torture through suspense and anxiety about future outcomes (Second Report of the Commissioners of Prisons, 1878–9). In the 1990s, local prisons and remand prisoners still figure persistently and disproportionately in the suicide statistics: 39 percent of those who took their own lives in prison in 1997 were on remand. Remand prisoners have not been convicted and many will be acquitted or receive a non-custodial sentence: their time is still appropriated in the same manner as for convicted prisoners.

During the 1980s, suicides in the general population among men between the ages of 15 and 44 rose steadily, with a 16 percent rise in 1988. It is this age group which dominates the male prison population, and the social trends which underpin the rise in suicide in the community also contribute to the heightened levels of vulnerability within the prison system (H. M. Prison Service, 1992). In 1984, the rate in the general population for males between the ages of 15 and 59 was 14 per 100,000; the rate for male prisoners in this group in the same year was 52 per 100,000. In 1997, the total rate of self-inflicted deaths in prisons in England and Wales was 115 per 100,000 population (Samaritans, 1998).

Adopting what Corradi di Fiumara (1990) defined as a "philosophy of listening," I conducted semi-structured interviews in a large local male prison, using the strategy of disciplined empathy.

The interview focused on the time and place aspects of prison which are experienced in entirely individual and personal ways by each prisoner. Half of my sample were defined by the prison as "at risk of suicide."

The other half of my sample were defined as "good copers." There are no formal procedures for identifying prisoners in this way, and I was obliged to rely on the considerable experience and expertise of senior officers on the four wing locations where these prisoners were being managed. As far as possible, the number of remanded and convicted prisoners were matched in each group, as were the range of offences.

"Poor copers" have previously been identified in research typologies (Dooley, 1990; Liebling and Krarup, 1993) and the distinction between poor and good copers has been a fruitful and useful one in previous prison research. But my pilot work disclosed that distinctions between "poor" and "good" copers, and between "suicidal" and "coping" prisoners, *cannot be sustained across time and changing circumstances*. Additionally, "coping" itself is defined by prison staff with reference to their own interests and responsibilities. Nevertheless, despite these reservations, the official definitions were a useful primary organizing principle.

Denying the Enemy

On the level of regret for the crime or event which has brought inmates into prison, reflection on time proves a great source of suffering for all prisoners. Many speak obsessively about turning the clock back to a time prior to their offence. This is particularly true of those who have committed crimes on impulse. "If only . . ." is a stream of thought which produces its own form of torture, especially for lifers. But even those with a few weeks to face speak of the implacable enemy of time. This enemy is central to individual fate, for each has been sentenced to either a known or unknown slice of time, and yet it is an enemy too elusive for inmates to grasp in thought.

The response of the not now "coping" prisoners is to deny the centrality of this enemy. The pain of this enemy is so great for them that they cannot bear to acknowledge it. Bud's emphatic denial is typical:

> With the issue of time, the only thing you can do is shut your mind off from it, and just get on with it.

After a pause for reflection, the same speaker continues:

> Everyone deals with the thing differently: my way is to shut myself off from the time. If I looked at my sentence, I'd probably be in awe of it, and totally daunted. But I'm not expecting to be here too long, I'm hoping to die, so it's easier. (Bud, not now "coping," medical centre)

There are several circuitous ironies here. Bud is avoiding looking at the issue of the "time" he has to serve, in case he is "totally daunted." But he is on his twelfth day of hunger strike, and as he goes on to demonstrate in our interview, it is precisely the issue of time which is so distressing to him and which he thinks and talks about obsessively. Here he speaks of the pains of "empty" time:

> My time here is so very empty. I've used my mind all my life, but all I can do in here is write. You can only write so much, and read, and you can only read so much before you get bored. I listen to music, I play Gameboy, and that's it. When I first came in, I wrote about six letters a day, but there's only so much you can say in a

> letter, and only so many people you can write to. I tend to spend a lot more of my time thinking now.

In complete contrast to the claim that he has shut himself off from time, he goes on to say:

> Time passes extremely slowly. I've been in 12 days, and it seems like four weeks. Time just doesn't go. It was the same situation on the wings, when I was on remand.

Bud's sentence is only 19 months, and it is a light sentence for his offence. Friends cannot understand his inability to accept the time that must pass before his release:

> They say "Are you a bit touched or something?"—but to me, it seems that 19 months is a hell of a long time to be separated from the life you're used to. To be separated from your family, your partner, your friends . . . that length of time . . . well . . . (Extremely articulate, Bud cannot find words to express his response to the sentence time, and stares down at his hands)

Later, he returns to the struggle to express the unhappiness he associates with the length of time he has to serve:

> I can't do 19 months. I could probably just touch on nine months or a year, with it doing me in completely. But 19 months . . . No. No hope. I'm strong enough mentally to know what I'm capable of withstanding, and I just can't address 19 months. I can't keep myself going. It'd just break me down. I know they will . . . I've experienced unhappiness before [when a relationship broke up] . . . but that unhappiness didn't even begin to touch this, because this is like . . . although it sounds like a year and a half isn't that long, when you are in here it is, it's a tremendously long time. It's too frightening.

Although by his own admission Bud is "petrified by fear" and utterly degraded by the routines of prison, his daily life is marked by some things worth anticipating. But the time he has to serve appears to him, a young man, as *long-term*, and while he could bear short-term suffering, he cannot face what appears to him to be long-term suffering:

> On a day-to-day basis, there's different things, speaking to my partner or my family on the 'phone. But on a long-term basis, all I look forward to is dying. That's it, it ends there.

Bud's failure to accept his sentence, the length of which strikes others as bearable, is typical of prisoners whose relationship with prison time is filled with fear and pain. They cannot see the sentence length as manageable: the length is immaterial in a way, because the present-timeness of it is so filled with terror. The only escape route seems to be through death.

Retreating from the Enemy

Sean (not now "coping," medical centre) echoes Bud in finding the emptiness of time a source of acute suffering. Despite their best attempts to fill the time, they both fall victim to the grip of empty time in which destructive thoughts can get a hold:

> Most of the time when I try to read, you just can't focus on the books, you know what I mean? So you spend most of the day daydreaming, thinking things, things you shouldn't think . . . I spend most of the time sitting by myself, looking into the distance, you know. There's nothing. Empty. Nothing.

This retreat into oneself is partly forced upon inmates who do not necessarily feel themselves to have much in common with the surrounding talk:

> You try to talk to people, but when you talk to people in here, all they want to do is talk about crimes, you know. I can't really talk about them sort of things . . . they are always effing, swearing and blinding you know. Talking about what they are going to do when they do get out. Them's the things I don't want to know about, you know.

Like Bud, Sean tries not to think about the years ahead, but inevitably finds that the subject he most tries to avoid, is in fact the one he thinks about constantly:

> You don't lose track of time, no matter how you try. You just keep thinking of the years ahead . . . You just take each day as it comes, but the date's always in your mind, the years ahead you know. Each day that goes by, you're one day closer to getting out, that's the way you do think about it, all the time, you know.

Sean looks forward to sleep, "but not to waking up." The nights are painful for him, because he expects the time to pass in a flash, and yet, because he cannot sleep properly, it drags as slowly as the day. He marks the passing of the time in the night by a series of regular noises:

> When you go to sleep at night, you hate waking up in the morning, you know. Every morning I hear one noise first, and that's the noise of a plane going up, so I know it's half-four in the morning. Then the noise I wait for after that is the noise of keys. So that's what I wait for every morning. The noise of the plane and then the noise of the keys. You keep thinking, Oh let me go to sleep again. I want to go to sleep again, but you can't, you know. So you only get four hours' sleep a night . . . Makes the days even longer, you look at your watch and it's 6 o'clock and you try your best to go down and sleep again, but you still keep thinking of how you're waiting for the keys, you know, so you end up staying awake.

He does not find anything else to look forward to on a daily basis, except the television being put on in the ward:

> I wait for the TV, at 12 or 1.30. Then again, at 4 o'clock, it's on again. Then, once it goes out, you're lost for things to do. You might play a game of dominoes or draughts, but people aren't into that, you know, you just can't focus on things you know.

But one of the problems with looking forward to supposedly regular occurrences, such as the TV, is that they cannot be relied on, as Marty (not now "coping," medical centre) explains:

> I look forward to the television going on in the evening from 4 till 8, because it makes the time go a little bit quicker . . . But if someone doesn't get out of bed in the morning at half seven, then they turn it off an hour earlier. And if it happens twice in a row, it'll be two hours, and so on.

So even these time-markers are precarious and cannot be relied upon. But Marty, like the others who are not coping, gets over-involved in present time and the slowness with which it moves. Like many, he is trying hard not to think of the time ahead:

> I try not to think about the future . . . if I do think about it, it gets me thinking about all the things I could be doing, and it knocks me back, and I end up feeling very depressed and contemplating suicide. Time just drags . . . one day seems like three days. Like I say, I can't deal with time, even a day seems too long.

Jimmy (not now "coping," medical centre) is a person who has never thought of the future. With intense highs and lows of mood, he says ruefully: "The present has always been abundant enough for me." But he experiences the passing of time acutely painfully:

> It's just like a matter of waiting for the end of waiting, you know. Killing time before time kills you. Like I say, I am able to retreat into an inner world. And I do write a bit . . . sometimes I'll just sit there, still, for three or four hours . . . I'm self-contained in a way.

Speaking of his feelings in his last, almost-successful suicide attempt, Jimmy tries to express the torture he suffered, and the part played by his internal time-sense:

> I was tormented, I was so stretched. There are no words to describe how I felt . . . in those dark days . . . you feel tortured, your spirit feels like it's stuck in sticky pitch blackness. But imagery . . . like inky crows and blind men's dreams . . . none of it comes even close to a description. Literally, the seconds ticking away, that's the Chinese water torture of what it's like.

Distorting the Enemy

The long periods of empty time, which Jimmy refers to as "enforced idleness," are harmful for inmates whose mental state is very precarious. It can sometimes lead to "lost time," where the thinker retreats entirely into another world. Time can even seem to speed up, as Pradeep's remarks show:

> It's so terrible here . . . there's nothing to do. I can be sitting on my chair thinking about a lot of things in life, and before you know it, time has just gone. Time just flies past, I don't really know it and it's dark again.

That this kind of "speeding up" is not healthy is illustrated when Pradeep (not now "coping," medical centre) goes on to say:

> One thing I do when I'm sitting, I've got a few pictures of my wife, and sometimes when I'm looking at them for a little while, she actually starts talking to me. Sometimes I snap out of this place, and I see people walking around, sitting next to me, and I actually talk back to them.

The phenomenon of time seeming to be utterly empty and yet moving too fast seems to be something that many inmates experience from time to time, when they are in extreme distress:

> Sometimes when I've been on the wing, it's just too fast, you can't think to yourself, you just can't think. You lie there, you want to think, people go past your door, keys clanging. You want to concentrate on one thing, but you can't, with keys jangling, steps going past, everything too fast. It makes me angry. (Jock, not now "coping," medical centre)

Pradeep, like the other non-copers, cannot bear to contemplate the length of his sentence, but that is just what his mind returns to again and again. The thought of what will happen to loved ones, and being powerless to help, is an agony that many cannot help reflecting on:

> If I was to walk out of here tomorrow, I'd have a chance of pulling my life back–but when I think of the time ahead, the 12 years, I just slip into depression. I start thinking of all the possibilities of things that could happen in that time, what will happen to my parents. And what could have happened if I'd been outside . . . I just can't seem to get out of that.

An additional pain suffered by the non-coping prisoners is the knowledge that, along with the placelessness they suffer, the space they occupy and the time they spend is in no sense their own. It is distorted by the purposes of the prison, because they are observed all the time:

> I just feel suicidal, but I'm being observed all the time. I am being watched and watched and watched. It's been over a month they've watched me, sitting in that chair. (Pradeep)

The lack of a private space and a private time means that inmates on the wards are deterred from requesting a visit from a Samaritan. Their perception is that this encounter would take place in full view of all.

> Who wants a Samaritan walking across the ward and sitting down beside you, with everyone watching? If you talk to them, you're going to cry—it's like being in a goldfish bowl. (Marty)

Lifers must cope with the pains of the present, and accept that the future means more of the same pains. Brendan (not now "coping," medical centre), a lifer who has served time previously, finds an added pain in that there is no point in looking forward, and this contrasts bitterly with past times in prison:

> In my first sentence, I used to look forward to going home and being with my girlfriend. And music—I'm a musician and I'd look forward to hanging round with my friends, and being loved in a physical aspect. It kept me going. But in a life sentence, there's absolutely nothing to look forward to. There's visits, letters, phone calls, canteen—that's about it. No future.

He describes his time as empty, and slow-moving, but tries to cheer himself up by mentioning markers which, ironically, could only be relevant in a cheering sense if he were free:

> Time's slow, yes it is. Since I got sentenced. You know . . . maybe it's just because it's the tail end of the year that passes slowly for me. Because once Christmas is gone, I'm sure Christmas will be round again before I know it. Then my birthday, my wife's birthday, Christmas, New Year—those are all points in time.

Brendan has not yet received his tariff, but already he is learning to block out thoughts about the length of sentence:

> I don't think about it. I'm numb. If I think about it, it gets me down, so I stop. I black it out. Most of the time I try numbing myself. I'm quite . . . "Oh, well! It might be 18, it might be 20 years!" . . . It's just a number, you know. I don't know whether I'm ever going to be released, so it's not exactly something I can look forward to.

Positive Struggle with the Enemy

Of the non-copers, Brad (not now "coping," medical centre) is the only one who is managing to confront the future. He has attempted suicide many times, in overdoses on the outside, and two attempted hangings in this six-week remand period. He is in visibly bad shape: his eyes droop involuntarily, his speech is slurred and he cannot control the movements of his mouth. He is aware that he cannot control his suicidal impulses, and needs an enormous amount of help. But an extraordinary spirit blazes from him, although he speaks slowly and with difficulty. Although aware of his own extreme vulnerability, he is beginning to believe that he is on the way to putting suicidal behaviour behind him. There are long pauses between every sentence, and he concentrates hard to say exactly what he means:

> I still take things one day at a time, but I do look ahead now. Yeah. I've got time on my hands so,—how can I put it—instead of putting my energies into destructive ways, I will put 'em into constructive ways, I hope. I'm expecting to go to hospital and get psychological help for my past, because I'm a manic, I'm . . . I get depressed a lot, and that's why I take drugs . . . I think about the future a lot. I think about what I want to do with myself.

But it is only the thought of constructive help in future time which is giving him something to hold onto:

> My time here is just wasted, and wasting. I'm wasting time being here, I'm wasting time. I just sit around, or sleep. It's a waste of my time . . . I talk to the others, sometimes we have a laugh. But we're just wasting away.

Brad has done time before, and never achieved this impulse toward a positive relationship with time that he seems to be experiencing:

> I've realized a lot. I've done a lot of thinking, like I always do when I come into prison. I do a lot of thinking. But I kept on coming out with the attitude that I've done my bird, and it was nothing, and I can do it again. But now, I look at it now as wasted time.

So Brad, like others on the cusp of change, is changing his internal time-awareness: he is becoming aware of a future with possibilities, and he is trying to map his awareness of future possibilities onto a horrific past filled with abuse and pain:

> "Time is a great healer." [Sighs] Maybe I'll always keep certain barriers up, so I can't get hurt like that again. But, maybe I will trust someone again, I don't know.

Living with the Enemy

The relationship that the now-copers have with their internal time-sense is qualitatively different. They have far less to say than the non-copers about the phenomenon of time, and are not helplessly immured in the agonies of present time. Somehow, they have learned to put time into the general perspective of their prison experience, and their time-sense sits in their consciousness in a less obsessive way. Hal (ambivalently "coping," through repeated self-cutting, in the medical centre) is subject to the life of the ward which the other non-copers find so difficult to adjust to. But, in contrast to them, he describes himself as "always busy," making greeting cards which he then sells to other prisoners.

> Time goes slowly, yes. But I've only got four to five weeks left to do, and next Thursday, I'll have exactly 28 days to do. And believe me, the further it goes down, the more happier I feel! I feel happier getting out, but of course when I do get out . . . I just don't want the problems I had last year when I got out.

Some, like Ken (now "coping"), have improvised their own personal time-sense:

> I telephone the wife every day, and twice at weekends. We get up at 5 a.m. and write to each other. Then we have a cup of tea together at about 8 o'clock. She's changed her meal times, so that we eat together at lunch and tea.

This "time together" occurs between two people who are 300 miles apart, and demonstrates the innovative ways in which "copers" deal with the issue of time. Ken's wife has reorganized the domestic clock of her life, and is living to the timetable of prison with her husband. This is a source of emotional comfort and strength for them both. Ken feels that it has been significant in pulling him through from a suicidal to a coping stage.

Alistair (coping, "C" Wing) lives according to prison time. His life, spent in one institution after another since the age of 9, has trained him perfectly for the prison experience. He grumbles tolerantly if he is banged up early, but does not feel any unusual discomfort if his time is disrupted in this way:

> I don't like to say it, but I'm an institutions person. You just go along with the flow. I just take each day as it comes, really. There's not a lot you can do about it. If they decide to bang us up early, you've just got to accept it.

He sits passively enough in present time, but admits that toward the end of all of his many sentences, he begins to orientate himself in rather an automatic way toward future time, and looks forward in time to his release, but it is difficult even for him to understand why he does so:

> What keeps me going is looking forward to the day I get out, and what I'm going to do when I get out. I look forward to getting out, and my problems start the day I get out. Once you walk out that door, you've gotta think where you're gonna get money from again, and that's the tragedy about prison. You can be in prison 10, 12, 14 years, easy. The trouble starts the day you walk out, because you've got to try and get somewhere again. How do I cope in prison? Well, it's more a case of having to, really. I mean, there's no alternative. You go out there, you do what you do, you know full well at the end of the day that you're gonna get caught, and you're gonna end up back in prison. What can I say . . . my life has been H.M.P. from day one to the end, you might near enough say, because that's how much time I've spent in prison custody.

So Alistair's life-*time* has been appropriated by Her Majesty's Prison Service. From somewhere far back in his past, he still has a personal time-sense which embodies looking forward and making plans. But this time-sense is dissonant with what he has learned—that he can cope easily with prison time but not with time outside.

Mike (now "coping," "C" Wing), with a life sentence behind him, gives a succinct summary of prison:

> Everything in prison works through time. It's like a time machine. At a quarter past eight, you do this. At half past eight, you do that. Time controls your life.

But this adjustment has been a long process for him, and a painful road to self-knowledge. In the first four years of his life sentence, he was simultaneously "in a trance," and belligerent and violent. Eventually he was stabbed by a fellow inmate and nearly lost his life. He took a long look at himself and began the process of adjustment to prison time. He followed every course that was on offer, and he began to read voraciously, taking a special interest in the history of slavery. He says that it was *looking at the past* of his people that began to give him the tools to look at his own future. Over the years, he learnt to exercise autonomy over his time:

> I didn't choose to come to prison, but I can choose how to spend that time. I choose to watch a film—that's a positive choice for me, and so I'm passing those couple of hours positively.

Bill (now "coping," "C" Wing) is only five months into a life sentence, and is perhaps still in the "trance period" referred to by Mike. In his case, it has not made him belligerent.

> I just keep my head down, and try to do what is asked of me. I don't look forward to anything, I just keep busy, with my cleaning job. I don't ever sit there thinking how I'm going to pass the next couple of days or couple of hours. As soon as I've done one thing, I do another, without thinking about it.

An overriding desire to seek the positive structures George's (now "coping," "B" Wing) approach:

> There's enough negativity about, so you try and fill your time with a focus on good things. You might get out at exercise, and see someone from another wing, so you focus on talking to him. Sometimes I'll be able to go to the gym and meet some lifers who have done a lot of time already, so I like to talk to them, and they try to point out how things are, and how things were, and how things will go . . . I find that useful . . . you think to yourself if you can get onto the right plane . . . even when you do talk to the ones that have made the mistakes and caused uproar, they will admit it, and be straight with you, and say, well that's not the way you want to go . . . So it's helping you through it as well: if you can get into it, and keep in a predominantly positive frame of mind, then the time will take care of itself.

Unlike the non-copers, George does not over-invest the dimension of time with painful meaning, even though he is a lifer. For him, prison time naturally interrelates with the efforts he makes to turn the prison into a place where he interacts with others and lives in a positive way. Other lifers have valuable and special time-knowledge: they can say *how things are, how things were*, and *how things will go*. This is the significance of learning to cope in prison—acceptance of the time-frame, and knowledge of what it permits the imprisoned self in terms of self-development. George is eager to learn from prisoners who have adjusted to this time-frame, and enlarge his own time-place perspective.

Conclusion

Within the prison, the subjective experience of time produces discomfort. Whether an inmate is in prison for a month or for life, the horrible mismatch of one's internal time-consciousness and the reality of prison time produces dissonance. As Serge (1970: 35) pointed out, "there are swift hours and very long seconds. Past time is void. There is *no chronology of events* to mark it; *external duration no longer exists*" (my italics).

It is the comparative eventlessness of prison life which produces discomfort, stress and enforced passivity (Toch, 1992: 28). Time in prison seems cyclical rather than linear, in its endless repetition: events either repeat endlessly, or, just when inmates have come to rely upon them, fail to repeat because staff are too hard-pressed. So acquiring a manageable personal and internal time-sense is a major challenge. The external duration of each life has been brought to an end: henceforward the prisoners must live to prison time, unable to choose freely how to spend any time inside, and unable to participate in the chronology of events that made up their life on the outside and helped to construct and maintain their identity. Family birthdays, football matches, religious feast days, leaving parties for work colleagues—all the chronology of birth, life and death flows on outside the prison, and the prisoner remains bitterly aware of it while forcibly restrained from participation in it. Liberal theorists may assert that people are sent to prison as punishment, and not for punishment. But the fracture of their time-sense is an ongoing and punitive experience for the entire duration of their stay in prison. It is the nature of prison to produce repetitive experience and enforce normalization practices (Foucault, 1979).

This capacity of the prison causes cruel and unusual pain to prisoners who are suicidal for a wide variety of reasons, some of which will undoubtedly reside in the nature of prison itself. For non-coping prisoners, time itself is a source of pain, and the linear view that has been implicit in their socialization pattern cannot help them adjust to prison time.

The non-copers exemplify the way in which time can be the most potent instrument of punishment. It is empty, slow, relentless, and it has been appropriated by a powerful agency. This agency has the power to fill the time, but, for those defined as needing the special "care" of the medical centre, it chooses not to do so. During the period of my research, staff shortages meant that no one in the medical centre was able to visit the library on a regular basis. No one I interviewed in the medical centre during the year of my research had had the benefit of anything approaching the six hours of daily purposeful activity, which is the standard of the Health Care Directorate.

Stretches of empty time can produce the breakthrough into consciousness of much material which the prisoner would rather not revisit, or a retreat into fantasy (such as Marty described), or an obsession with activities to kill time (Toch, 1992: 28). So the time-markers are trivial matters, such as the television going on. Even these markers are tenuous and unreliable, since they lie within the control of the staff, a power which they exercise as a weapon in the maintenance of conformity.

The non-coping inmates feel both in the grip of an obsession with time and yet a peculiar *timelessness*, in that they have failed to evolve a workable relationship with their internal sense of time. Some feel watched, but are not aware of any source of help or comfort which might slacken the grip of the obsession, or enable them to develop a *personal timeness*. For others, time either speeds up or stretches out in unpredictable and disorientating ways. Their responses to prison time tend to fall toward *denial, retreatism and distortion*, as the necessarily limited quotations in this paper have shown.

Coping prisoners employ a variety of strategies, some passive and some more innovative, in order to maintain a reasonable coexistence with the enemy of time. Alistair (now "coping," "C" Wing) illustrates the passive acceptance of prison time, so common among many prisoners who have been shuffled from one institution to another all their lives. His years of training have taught him how to wait, and so he waits for time to pass. For those who have adapted to prison time, such as George (now "coping" "B" Wing) and Mike (now "coping," "C" Wing), this lesson in "learning to wait" has been acquired in prison, and is combined with their innovative capacity to make best use of personal time, while acknowledging the inevitable constraints. George and Mike exemplify a time-place integration. Acceptance of the prison *time-place* was acquired painfully, and with it came acceptance and adjustment to the dominant characteristic of the place, its subtle management of repetitive *time*. It is not possible to generalize about the manner and order of acceptance: it is an individual journey of integration, the originating threads of which are elusive for prisoners to grasp unless they are the recipients of care in the form of prolonged talk.

Non-copers keep returning to the issue of time; they are saturated in now-time awareness; they cannot move through time but must endure the feeling of its slow passing as a kind of personal torture. This saturation renders them unable to engage with the most complex representations of time-consciousness, which attempt to grasp at the unity of future, past and present. It is this deep temporal awareness which they must acquire if they are to accept the fact of the penal appropriation of their time, adapt to it and learn to talk to themselves about how best to move through the present and into the future.

The past of each prisoner casts a long shadow: the prison adds its own special capacity to crush identity, and prisoners speak sorrowfully of experiencing the extremes of anger, loneliness, boredom, guilt, apathy and self-loathing. Through reflective talk—sometimes with self, often with others—prisoners can enter into a dialogue with self which is grounded in time-consciousness and which provides the nutrition for overcoming suicidal behaviour and feelings. Talk with chaplains, Samaritans, senior officers and Listeners was identified by prisoners as a crucial but scarce commodity.

This study has outlined the painful and problematic relationship with time suffered by suicidal prisoners: the anguish of this relationship, which is produced by their interaction with the prison, is a significant dimension of a larger pain which immures them in suicidal behaviour and thought. The difficulties of time consciousness have no necessary relationship with the length of sentence, and the length of time spent in prison does not have a direct relationship with the pain suffered, because the ability of inmates to handle time varies so markedly from person to person (Porporino, in Toch, 1992). Suicidal prisoners need help in order to learn to live with prison time and develop a dialogic inner relationship with their internal time-sense. Such a relationship can act as a protective factor in the struggle against suicidal feelings. Unless this qualitative aspect of suffering in prison is properly appreciated and addressed in regimes and prisoner care, policies to prevent suicide will always suffer from a major awareness deficit.

References

Cohen, S. and Taylor, L. (1972) *Psychological Survival: The Experience of Long-term Imprisonment*. Harmondsworth: Penguin.

Corradi di Fiumara, Gemma (1990) *The Other Side of Language: A Philosophy of Listening*. London: Routledge.

Dilthey, W. (1976) *Selected Writings*, ed. and trans. H. P. Rickman. Cambridge: Cambridge University Press.

Dooley, E. (1990) 'Prison Suicide in England & Wales, 1972–1987,' *British Journal of Psychiatry* 156: 40–5.

Douglas, Jack (1985) *Creative Interviewing*. Beverley Hills, CA: Sage.

Foucault, M. (1979) *Discipline and Punish*. Harmondsworth: Penguin.

Giddens, A. (1984) *The Constitution of Society*. Cambridge: Polity.

Her Majesty's Chief Inspector of Prisons (1991) *The Woolf Report: Prison Disturbances*. London: HMSO.

Her Majesty's Prison Service (1992) *Caring for Prisoners at Risk of Suicide and Self-Injury: The Way Forward*. London: HMSO.

Leach, E. R. (1961) *Rethinking Anthropology*. London: Athlone.

Liebling, A. and Krarup, H. (1993) *Suicide Attempts & Self Injury in Male Prisons*. London: Home Office.

Lynch, K. (1972) *What Time is this Place?* Cambridge, MA: MIT Press.

Mann, David W. (1991) 'Ownership: A Pathography of the Self,' *British Journal of Medical Psychology* 64: 211–23.

Medlicott, Diana (1994) *History of the Modern Soul: Foucault's Genealogy and the Problem of the Subject*, Occasional Paper, School of Sociology & Social Policy, Middlesex University.

Ricoeur, P. (1984) *Time and Narrative*, Vol. I, trans. K. McLaughlin and D. Pellaner. Chicago: University of Chicago Press.

Samaritans (1998) *Prison Suicides*, Fact Sheet 27. Slough: Samaritans.

Sapsford, R. (1983) *Life Sentence Prisoners*. Milton Keynes: Open University Press.

Scraton, Phil, Sim, Joe and Skidmore, Paula (1991) *Prisons under Protest*. Milton Keynes: Open University Press.

Second Report of the Commissioners of Prisons, PP, 1878–9 (C.2442), xxxiv

Serge, Victor (1970) *Men in Prison*. London: Gollancz.

Thompson, E. P. (1967) 'Time, Work-Discipline and Industrial Capitalism,' *Past & Present* 38 (December): 56–97.

Toch, Hans (1992) *Living in Prison: The Ecology of Survival*. Washington: American Psychological Association.

Towl, Graham and Hudson, Danielle (1997) 'Risk Assessment and Management of the Suicidal' in *Suicide and Self-Injury in Prisons*, ICLP 28. Leicester: British Psychological Society.

17. Drug Use in Prison The Experience of Young Offenders

Nina Cope

This article explores young offenders' drug use in prison. Qualitative research with inmates highlighted the importance of understanding drug use in prison as a continuum of behaviour, where inmates' drug use inside was related to their drug use before custody. The inmates made choices and decisions around their drug use inside, considering the compatibility of drugs with the prison environment and their need to seek the "right high." Availability of drugs was crucial and the article discusses the routes of drug supply into prison via visits and the informal prison economy, where the distribution of drugs was facilitated by close inmate friendship networks.

Setting the "Scene": Young People's Drug Use in Context

Young people's drug use is increasing (cf. Parker et al., 1998; Shiner & Newburn, 1999; Denham-Wright & Pearl, 1995) and is no longer the preoccupation of subcultural groups as it was in the 1960s and 1970s (cf. Becker, 1963; Young, 1971). The current trend towards recreational drug use is described as a process of normalization (cf. Parker et al., 1998) where illicit drug use has become part of everyday life (South, 1999) and is integrated into generally conforming lifestyles. Although some criticise the normalization thesis noting that many young people continue to express negative views towards illegal drugs and drug users (Shiner & Newburn, 1999), the relationship between negative views about drugs and their use is unclear.

Studies of drug use in prison amongst predominantly adult male prisoners reveal that drugs are widely used before and during custody (Keene, 1997a; Maden et al., 1991; Turnbull et al., 1994). Evidence from research that includes young offenders confirms high levels of drug and alcohol use outside prison (Collison, 1996; Keene, 1997a) and indicates that young offenders are at risk of developing problematic patterns of drug use (Newburn, 1998). However, young offenders report less drug use in prison compared to adults (Edgar & O'Donnell 1998), although studies have not explored the dynamics of young offenders' drug use in detail to explain how it might differ to that of adult offenders. Furthermore, the relative lack of research, particularly qualitative research, means less is generally known about how inmates make drug choices and maintain drug supply.

This article explores young offenders' decisions to use drugs in prison, the drug choices they make and how they maintain drug supplies in custody. The inmates' decisions to use drugs in prison were influenced by the level and type of drug use before custody and the compatibility of the drug with the prison environment.

Availability of drugs was crucial and the article goes on to discuss the routes of drug supply into prison via visits and the internal prison economy.

Methodology

The research on which this article is based forms part of a PhD thesis, which explores young offenders' experiences of drug use in prison. Unstructured interviews were conducted in a young offenders institution with 30 inmates aged between 16 and 21 years of age. Thirteen inmates in the study were African-Caribbean, 12 white, three Asian and two described themselves as "mixed race." All of the inmates had recently been transferred into the prison and, in order to trace their experiences of drugs as they settled into the regime, each inmate was interviewed on three occasions. The inmates had committed serious crimes including robbery (18 inmates), rape (four inmates) and murder (two inmates). Although long sentences (of 3 years and above) reduced the transient nature of the prison population, of the original 30 first interviewed, 26 and 18 were interviewed on second and third occasions. To verify information from the interviews, the inmates' prison records were consulted and while they offered further insight into their offences, they lacked comprehensive information about their drug history. Ten interviews were also conducted with prison staff.

An Outside Connection: The Drug Continuum

The drug careers of the young offenders in my research varied and, compared to the extent and levels of poly drug use before incarceration, prison was a relatively "dry time" for inmates. Understanding the context and pattern of inmates' drug use before custody is important because it influenced the nature of drug use in prison. In line with the theory of normalization (Parker et al., 1998), the inmates were highly tolerant of cannabis and 28 of the 30 used the drug before custody. The inmates did not define it as a "real drug" and use was not considered deviant or illegal, as Martin, a regular user explained: "[cannabis], well that's just an every day thing for me, it'd be like smoking cigarettes." While the prison environment forced changes in the pattern and intensity of use, consistent with other studies of drug use in prison (Edgar & O'Donnell, 1998; Inciardi et al., 1993; King & McDermott, 1995), cannabis remained popular with the inmates after conviction (19 used the drug regularly and seven used it occasionally). Only three of the 30 inmates interviewed refrained from using cannabis inside prison. One inmate had never used any drugs, including cannabis, and two had already served long periods in custody (of 6 and 4 years) and were nearing parole or seeking a lower security category status. This probably influenced their decision to stop using drugs as the inmates often controlled and modified their drug use to achieve particular goals, such as a transfer to another wing within the prison or a transfer to another institution.

Similar to outside prison, staff and inmate attitudes towards cannabis inside created an environment where use of the drug was largely tolerated. Research has shown that staff and inmates express negative attitudes towards mandatory drug tests because they disproportionately punish cannabis use and prison officers rarely perceive the private use of cannabis as harmful to the general order of the prison (Edgar & O'Donnell, 1998; Keene, 1997b). This suggests rules against cannabis use might be sacrificed to maintain order and preserve positive staff/inmate relationships. Discretion when enforcing all rules is a fundamental characteristic of prison life (Sparks et al., 1996), as officers have to balance rule enforcement with maintaining the harmony of an institution. However, in my research, officers who expressed tolerant attitudes towards cannabis did not believe this affected how they enforced prison rules. As a senior officer explained:

> I have a very tolerant attitude towards cannabis, from what I've read they have no positive proof it has an effect on your health, well compared to things like nicotine, so I'm very tolerant towards it but at the same time we're in prison . . . To be honest my tolerant attitude is different to a lot of peoples. Their tolerant attitude is that [cannabis] keeps [the inmates] quiet and keeps them happy, if they're happy, then it's not a problem for me. My attitude is the fact, well it's an illegal drug but I'm very cynical about the fact we allow tobacco and alcohol [outside prison] but we don't allow cannabis . . . [But] at the end of the day I work within the rules of prison and society.

The inmates commented that cannabis use would be punished or ignored depending on the officer, as Kevin, serving 5 years for robbery, explained:

> I don't think officers do really care about you smoking drugs . . . cos at the weekends we'll be smoking weed in front of the T.V. and they can smell it, they just can't be bothered and they just say "you'll get a piss test" and then [they] don't worry about it. That's what they're like on my wing, on another wing they're like DRUGS, DRUGS and start goin' mad.

As individual cannabis use was considered unproblematic, the staff justified their intervention based on the bullying and debt associated with drug dealing and supply in the prison. Although the members of staff I interviewed did question intervention and the legitimacy of drug testing without treatment (at the time of the research the prison had no comprehensive drug treatment strategy) that meant testing simply amounted to identifying and punishing users. As one officer explained: "We don't do anything with them. You get added days and whatever, we don't even give them a bloody drug leaflet, just you failed your test, you're nicked."

The logic of the drug continuum, where the context and pattern of drug use before custody influenced drug use in prison, meant the high levels of cannabis use and tolerance towards the drug resulted in it being very popular amongst the inmates in the young offenders' institution. Conversely, low reported use of heroin outside (three inmates admitted to using heroin daily and five used the drug occasionally) meant generally inmates were less likely to use the drug inside. The inmates who were addicted to heroin before custody were at greater risk of using the drug throughout their sentence. For example, Dan (21) was serving 7 years for robbery. He explained his introduction to drugs and his problem with heroin and crack:

> I started smoking pot when I was about 15, somethin' like that. I started taking acid and from acid, ecstasy to drugs like that. Then, all of a sudden someone introduced me to heroin and I was takin' that now and again and then crack came along and that was it. It all went haywire . . . it's addictive . . . you get a rush, you blow the smoke out, but it's only for a couple of seconds, then it's gone . . . then you feel stressed out and paranoid . . . It was crack and heroin 24–7 (24 hours a day, 7 days a week). I'd wake up in the mornings and when I was smokin' crack and needing heroin, takin' heroin to sort of take the bad one away, level your head a bit.

Dan described his fear and anxiety about being released before he was able to come to terms with his crack and heroin problem. He had not addressed his drug problem in prison, partly because there was no drug treatment programme available at the time of the research and he did not trust the prison staff or feel comfortable talking to them about his addiction. As a consequence he coped alone with the transition from intense heroin use outside and regular use on remand, to withdrawal when convicted. During the research he made contact with a drug dealer on one of the wings and started using heroin again. After getting into debt he was eventually transferred to another prison as he later wrote to me to explain: "I was stupid enough to dabble in some [heroin] in [the young offenders institution] and ended up owing some guy money so, I thought it'd be best to go on my travels. I haven't looked back since then."

The drug continuum meant inmates were at greater risk of using drugs in prison if they had used outside, although drug use was not inevitable. Other factors needed to be taken into consideration, for example, irregular and limited supplies of heroin made habitual drug use logistically and physically less viable after conviction. Research outside prison suggests more specialized drug supply networks may be needed to access harder drugs (Forsyth et al., 1992). Prison officers in my research suggested younger inmates were too impetuous, unsophisticated and "out for themselves" to operate as an organized inmate group that would be able to establish a regular supply of hard drugs into the prison. The nature of the prison drug economy, based on cannabis, offered some support for this, although the young inmates did organize themselves to ensure effective drug distribution. However, hard drugs were less available in the prison than cannabis and inmates who had used heroin regularly outside and on remand explained that the principal motivator for stopping when convicted was the lack of supply. One inmate, Ian, stopped using heroin when he started to serve his 6-year sentence for robbery. Fewer visits and the move to a national prison severed his local networks and dramatically reduced supply. The alternative was to access heroin internally through a dealer but a regular supply could not be guaranteed and the expense increased the risk of debt. Low supply meant he was unable to alleviate the withdrawal symptoms or balance them with the pleasure of using the drug (Lindesmith, 1938, p. 593):

> My mates were still there in the jail but cos the visits weren't so regular, you were gettin' every two weeks instead of every day. Like if I'm gonna go from one weekend to the next weekend without having none [heroin] and then through the next week you're not so dependent on it . . . after that it wasn't such a big thing, it was a treat once in a while, on remand I was takin' [heroin] for granted.

Generally heroin is less prevalent in young offenders institutions compared to adult prisons (Edgar & O'Donnell, 1998) and the comparatively low levels of use in my research influenced demand for the drug in prison. There is no way to know if more inmates would have been inclined to use heroin for the first time in prison if the drug were more available. Confinement and inflated prices made the relationship between supply and demand in prison difficult to assess, mainly because fluctuating street prices and the length of time it takes users to find a drug supply are used to gauge the impact that supply reduction has on user demand outside (Murji, 1998). However, it can be assumed that demand does influence supply (see Sutton, 1995, 1998 as an example). In my research, the regular users of heroin found it more difficult to resist their latent addiction and appeared to seek out a supply of the drug more readily. However, the occasional users (five inmates outside) did not seek the drug inside and substituted their heroin use with the cheaper, less risky and more available cannabis.

The perception of heroin amongst the inmates probably had some influence on their levels of use or their willingness to report use of the drug. The stereotype of a physically dependent heroin addict was not compatible with the inmates' view of themselves as being able to exert control over their drug use (Glassner & Loughlin, 1987). Appearances especially in the very masculine environment of the prison were vital. Signs of strength, size, stature and good looks were important to the inmates and were all qualities not associated with the image of the unattractive, retreatist heroin user. Other drugs were not labelled in the same way, for example, while heroin was seen as a "physical drug," crack was perceived to be a "mind drug." Kevin, a regular user of crack, explained this paradox:

> Crack just relaxes your brain. But it's not like brown [heroin], I'd never touch brown . . . Brown's like a physical thing and crack's like a mental thing . . . Crack is bad enough but crack for me seemed like a better drug than skag [heroin] . . . it's everything, just the name of it, skag, and when you see those skagheads now and they've got those white things by their mouths, oh no, I couldn't touch heroin.

Heavy crack users do experience some physical deterioration, such as weight loss (Jacobs, 1999), however the inmates neutralized the harm (Sykes & Matza, 1959) of crack and only stigmatized heroin. John was a heavy drug user who, like Dan, synchronized his use of heroin to control the "high" of crack. John suggested the distinction between the drugs was based on the relationship between crack and the recreational drug scene that made it appear more glamorous and acceptable. John's comments also reveal how the stigma of heroin did not deter use indefinitely:

> Crack is seen as quite a glamorous drug, you're standing around drinking champagne and smoking crack, you're thinking you're a superstar and others are thinking, wow, and you're smoking crack, but everyone's thinking, that guy's off his head. Heroin, I can't explain it, I think 'cos it's seen as a dirty drug, I took it anyway. When you come down off the crack and you were just stoned it was a really nice feeling of just comfort and well-being. You had sort of a warm glow, like the Ready Brek man.

The drug continuum highlights the relationship between drug use outside and inside prison. However, the inmates in my research continued to make decisions and choices about the drugs they used during their sentence.

Drug Choices and Compatibility: Being High Makes Time Fly

A second influential factor on inmates' drug choices was the compatibility of the drug with the prison environment. Similar to recreational use outside, inmates prioritized their drug use according to their current life situation and the practical considerations of space, predictability and seeking the right "high." The inmates explained that smoking cannabis helped them to cope with their sentence. The prospect of months or years in prison profoundly affected the inmates. While time is usually "a deeply taken for granted aspect of social life" (Adam, 1990, p. 9), for the prisoner "concern for time seems to be an almost constant and painful state of mind" (Galtung, 1961, p. 113). The inmates would often subtract the years in custody from their age. As one life sentence prisoner described: "I'm 17 now, I'll be 30 odd when I get out but I'll still be doin' things that a 17-year-old would be doin'. You don't grow up mate, time stops dead [in jail]." Essentially prison time was futureless and the inmates' lives were characterized by waiting and sameness (cf. Brown, 1998; Meisenhelder, 1985).

Drugs played a role in the management of time and was one of a number of strategies inmates developed to cope with their sentences. They turned to the regime, marking time with the purchase of their weekly "canteen" [supplies such as magazines, food and music] or abandoned visits because to look forward to an event slowed the passage of time. Smoking cannabis made time fly because it meant rather than "doing their time" it would pass effortlessly and unconsciously as the inmates were sleeping. As Craig (21), serving a 7-year sentence for rape, described: "With cannabis you can smoke it at night and it makes you get your head down, it makes me relaxed and makes me fall asleep. The way I look at it is it makes time go faster." Research amongst young people who live highly unstructured lives outside prison suggests drugs can fulfil a similar function, helping them to "fill the void" (McAuley, forthcoming).

The attractiveness of cannabis, the predictability of the "high" and good availability meant it was perceived to be a relatively low risk drug to use in prison.

However, this had to be reconciled with the high risk of detection through mandatory drug tests because of the length of time cannabis remained detectable in the body after use, although punishment for cannabis use (14 added days on a sentence usually with some loss of pay or association) was more lenient than for opiates. Rather than stop or switch their use to other drugs, the inmates developed techniques they thought would evade positive drug test results. Tom used cannabis throughout his sentence stopping for a brief period when he wanted to be transferred to another establishment. After using the drug in his cell, he described how he would drink lots of water in the belief it would "flush out his system":

> Well water, you can do it with water, but you've got to drink it straight away and then go to the toilet twice and then you're ready to go to the toilet for them, but sometimes you ain't got time because they surprise you.

Tom had a positive test for cannabis during the research. Further methods of evasion included promoting excessive sweating, eating orange or lemon peel and drinking vinegar. Adulteration of the MDT also hid traces of drug use, although the prison undermined this practice by introducing adjudication procedures when samples were contaminated.

The importance of seeking the "right high" and the compatibility of the drug to the prison environment meant the inmates, who were mainly "poly-drug users" outside prison, often combining cannabis with ecstasy or LSD, avoided stimulant cocktails inside. The popularity of crack outside prison (10 inmates used it regularly and seven binged on the drug more occasionally) would suggest inmates were at greater risk of using the drug inside, however, none used crack in prison. The general perception amongst the inmates was that crack, with its short high and potent craving, was a dangerous drug to use inside. Tom, a regular crack user outside prison, explained:

> I'd have [crack] if I wanted it but I don't want it when I'm in here. If I was gonna get some, say I was gonna get like 50 quid, then I'd smoke it but after I'd be wanting more, but I wouldn't be able to send out to get any more or get anyone to bring any up, just stuck in my cell and can't do nothing.

The inmates wanted a "low drug" that helped them to sleep, as Martin, serving a 4-year sentence for robbery, explained:

> I don't know why they bring E's in here. A couple of boys come to me yesterday and said about having an E, I said to them, "if I take an E, what am I gonna do?" They said, "turn up your radio and listen to some jungle." But I told them to keep that . . . see if you're gonna be takin' a drug yeah, you can't be takin' none of that, I 'ave to be takin' a low drug yeah, otherwise it's not helping me [to sleep] . . . [On remand] I took an E and was goin' loops, I said to the guy, "this drug is rubbish man, I had to stay up all night" . . . That's the reason why you smoke [cannabis],

> you just conk out, go to sleep quick and wake up the next morning. But if you don't have anything to smoke, you just lay up and get bored the day goes long . . . if you smoke cannabis the day whizzes through.

Occasionally the inmates did use ecstasy in prison to offer them an escape from their mundane sentence by bringing a little of their life outside into their cells. For example Josh, a heavy user of amphetamines before prison, looked forward to taking ecstasy: "I should've a E comin' up at the weekend . . . I have got my system [stereo] comin' this week as well, a big system, just turn it up."

Essentially the inmates approach to drug use in prison was similar to outside or became even more strategic. Parker et al.'s (1998) description of "*drugwise*" young people, making "cost benefit assessments" where they weigh the risk of bad drug experiences and getting caught "against the pleasure and enjoyment of particular drugs and their ability either to blank out stress and distress or most often help deliver cost effective, deserved 'time out' through relaxation and enjoyment from the grind of ordinary, everyday life" (1998, pp. 19–20), can be closely aligned to the inmates' approach to drug choices in prison.

Supplying Inside

The inmates experiences of using cannabis or heroin demonstrated the importance of maintaining a good drug supply in prison. The principal routes of access were divided between external (drugs brought in from outside the prison) and internal, where drugs were exchanged inside with other inmates (Turnbull et al., 1994).

The main external source of drugs was through visits with family and friends. In the young offenders' institution an inmate was entitled to a visit every 2 weeks, or once a week if they were on the enhanced regime wing. Visits took place midweek and over the weekend. The latter was the favoured time for passing over drugs as inmates knew staffing levels were lower and as a consequence it was rare for mandatory drug tests to be carried out on a Saturday or Sunday. The inmates appeared to find it relatively easy to get their visitors to bring cannabis into the prison and rarely regarded the request for drugs as coercive. As one inmate described: "I don't even have to ask [my visitors], they know to bring it, like when my girl or my friends come they'll just give it to me and I don't have to ask." Nevertheless, inmates sometimes became stressed and threatened to withdraw their visits altogether if a visitor refused to bring drugs for them or let them down on a visit. While the inmates did not interpret this as coercive, family members struggling to maintain contact with them during a long sentence may have done.

To prevent drug trafficking into the prison the staff adopted profiling techniques similar to those used in policing to target high-risk individuals and groups (cf. Ericson & Haggerty, 1997). Limited staff numbers meant it was not feasible to search all visitors, although the officers did not deny that anyone could be a potential trafficker. Profiling was often reduced to stereotyping and the inmates were aware that elderly visitors, groups of girls and young children attracted less staff attention than black, male groups and the inmate's mother. Kevin used a range of drugs outside prison and attempted to maintain a supply, particularly of cannabis, while inside. Aware of the officers' tendency to select "high-risk" visitors to search, he used this knowledge to his advantage:

> When he [father] was in jail, my mum used to bring it up for him. Now I'm in jail and they bring it up for me . . . but I try to get them to bring it up with the baby [his own child], so when you 'ave it with a baby you can just put it away . . . It's disrespect really, with the baby.

Despite the presence of officers and cameras in the visiting room, the inmates found ways to obscure the transfer of drugs by kissing, handshakes or putting the drugs into drinks, confectionery or crisps to disguise the pass by eating or drinking. Even during closed visits, the ultimate drug-trafficking prevention strategy where the inmates were separated from their visitor by a screen, drugs were passed over. Inmates described the cubical as "make-shift," with a large gap above the screen that meant drugs could be thrown over and collected by the inmates.

Once in their possession, the inmates had to hide their drugs inconspicuously. An increase in the number of strip searches meant the only safe place to hide their drugs was to insert them intra-anally (Turnbull et al., 1994), a practice known as "plugging." Any revulsion at retrieving plugged or swallowed drugs was overcome by its necessity to avoid detection. Once retrieved, drugs were either hidden in the cell or more preferably about the person, as one inmate, Tom explained:

> I put a spliff under [the door] for someone and they got caught with it at dinner and they [the prison staff] come straight to my cell so I just stuck it in my sugar but usually I just keep it up my bum, and then you squat and I mean it might drop out but it doesn't always drop out. If I know I'm gonna have a cell search, then I'll just keep it up my bum, after that I'll just keep it in my pocket.

The Internal Route: Drugs and the Prison Economy

Exchanging drugs for money or goods and the more altruistic sharing of drugs between friendship groups (Turnbull et al., 1994) were the main ways inmates accessed drugs inside the prison. An unintended consequence of the routine deprivation of goods was that almost all material objects were potential forms of currency. Inmates were allowed to spend a maximum of £10 a week from their wages or private cash. It was common for a range of other goods to be dealt and exchanged for tobacco and cannabis. The majority of inmates engaged in some sort of dealing that was usually opportunistic to satisfy their immediate needs. Elory (21) used cannabis but knew no one else from his area outside. When I asked if he ever shared his drugs, he said: "Oh no, no. This is jail man, you don't get nothing for free man. As soon as you come to jail y'know it's double back [get owed double what you lent out] and as simple as that."

The exchange value varied according to the goods and who the deal was with. Kevin traded his supply of cannabis with other inmates around the prison and he explained his pricing index:

> A spliff is £3 in here, some people charge more but I charge three . . . Say I give you the spliff and I want cocoa white shampoo, just buy me that. Or give someone £6, I want 3 months of FHM magazines or GQs. That's the currency of jail, drugs. Hash, like the resin but you get skunk weed and that, people don't want to part with their weed 'cos it tastes better than the resin.

Cannabis formed the foundation of the prison economy and was often referred to as the currency inside. However, there were no cannabis dealers as such and the drug was broadly distributed across the prison population. Heroin was treated differently to cannabis by the internal prison economy. Similar to outside, more specialized networks were required to access harder drugs (Forsyth et al., 1992) and because it was "cut" more with other substances in prison than on the street, the profit margin was high. As Dan said: "They cut [heroin] down three sizes to sell it in prison, so they're making three, four times as much, for a gram, which cost about £70. They're making £200 [in prison], a lot of money."

The Cost Without Culture: Sharing Cannabis and the RSPs

As cannabis was linked to the inmate culture, being part of the subculture was crucial for favourable treatment when making deals and was vital for sharing drugs. In this respect, the rules of the prison inmate culture were simple: if you were in, you had access to drug-sharing networks and cheap deals; if you were out, you had little access to drugs aside from your own supply, and any deals available were expensive. For this reason, understanding the nature of the inmate culture and how friendship networks were organized offered a vital insight into the drug distribution in the prison.

A gang whose structure and organization was imported from outside dominated the inmate culture in the prison. The RSPs were drawn from a particular area in a large city. Five of the inmates interviewed for the research were related to the gang. All were African-Caribbean, and four of the five had been arrested for robbery. Martin (16), a member, explained the organization of the gang:

> We all hang together [and] everyone knows us as the RSPs, like bad and that. Like you've got the younger youngens, that's under me yeah but they're the same age and the same year but I move with a bigger lot. Then there is the youngers and that's the older lot, like 17, 18, 19 and that's my lot yeah, that's who I move with. Then there is a higher lot, that's like 21 all up to 30, like big man and that. Like they call themselves the RSPs men and that's different to us.

Drug use was synonymous with the RSPs. They were predominantly cannabis users who shared drugs across their broad friendship networks, as Gary, a member of the gang explained: "I have my own [cannabis] but say I've been on a visit and I have mine but my friend doesn't have any, then I'll give him a few spliffs, I'll settle him a few spliffs, like we'll look after each other." Sharing was limited to cannabis and inmates usually only exchanged drugs with those they knew from outside, or had met during previous sentences or whilst on remand. The assumption was that friends would automatically share their drugs and it was unacceptable to need to ask.

Sharing reintroduced an element of social exchange into drug use and reinforced the sense of camaraderie amongst the RSPs. It also facilitated drug supply. As individuals, the inmates could only get smaller amounts into the prison often because of the practicalities of hiding drugs. However, when a number of friends had a supply of cannabis to share, supply could be guaranteed between visits.

Those inmates not integrated into the subculture had limited access to drugs inside as deals to "outsiders" were expensive and attracted the risk of debt. The price of drugs was not fixed and fluctuated according to the perception of the inmate wishing to acquire drugs. The desperation associated with addiction meant even higher prices could be charged, especially to weaker inmates or "fraggles" as they were called. Phil was one such outsider who was not in a position to do deals. At 21 he was serving a 4-year sentence for robbery. He was white, came from out of town and had few friends in the prison. He had stopped using cannabis deterred by high prices and difficulties of access, as he said: ". . . 5 quid for a bit of draw and all the hassle you get for it . . . I'm not interested in doin' deals with people."

Conclusion

This article has explored some of the drug choices young inmates made in prison. The paper highlights the importance of understanding drug use in prison as a continuum of behaviour, where inmates' drug use inside was related to their drug use before custody. Therefore, gathering information on inmates' drug use outside (when they first arrive at an institution) can help to identify those who are at risk of drug use inside, ensuring the prison is better placed to meet their needs and respond proactively to drug problems. In my research, inmates made choices and decisions around their drug use in prison, considering the compatibility of drugs with the prison environment and using cannabis in particular to help them to pass their time. A good local understanding of how an institution potentially influences the patterns of drug use and drug supply, through the regime, searches and the frequency of mandatory drug tests, is important. Furthermore, understanding the informal prison economy and how inmate friendship networks operate offers an insight into the distribution of drugs across the prison.

References

Adam, B. (1990). *Time and Social Theory*. Cambridge: Polity Press.

Becker, H. (1963). *Outsiders Studies in Sociology of Deviance*. New York: Free Press.

Bennett, T. (1986). A decision making approach to opioid addiction. In D. B. Cornish & R. V. Clarke (Eds), *The Reasoning Criminal: rational choice perspectives on offending* (pp. 83–102). New York: Springer-Verlag.

Brown, A. (1998). Doing time: the extended present of the long-term prisoner. *Time and Society*, 7, pp. 93–103.

Collison, M. (1996). In search of the high life: drugs, crime, masculinities and consumption. *British Journal of Criminology*, 36, pp. 428–43.

Cromwell, P., Olson, J., & Wester Avary, D. (1991). *Breaking and Entering: an ethnographic analysis of burglary*. California: Sage.

Denham-Wright, J. & Pearl, L. (1995). Knowledge and experience of young people regarding drug misuse 1969–1994. *British Medical Journal*, 310, pp. 20–24.

Edgar, K. & O'Donnell, I. (1998). *Mandatory Drug Testing in Prisons: the relationship between MDT and the level and nature of drug misuse*. Research Study No. 189. London: Home Office.

Ericson, R. V. & Haggerty, K. (1997). *Policing the Risk Society*. Oxford: Oxford Clarendon Press.

Felson, M. & Clarke, R. V. (1998). *Opportunity Makes the Thief: practical theory for crime prevention*. Police Research Series Paper 98. London: Home Office.

Forsyth, A., Hammersley, R., Lavelle, T. & Murray, K. (1992). Geographical aspects of scoring illegal drugs. *British Journal of Criminology*, 32, pp. 292–309.

Galtung, J. (1961). Prison: the organisation of dilemma. In D. Cressey (Ed.), *The Prison* (pp. 107–45). New York: Holt, Rinehart and Winston.

Glassner, B. & Loughlin, J. (1987). *Drugs in Adolescent Worlds: burnouts and straights*. Basingstoke: Macmillan Press.

Inciardi, J., Lockwood, D. & Quinlan, J. (1993). Drug use in prison: patterns, processes and implications for treatment. *The Journal of Drug Issues*, 23, pp. 119–29.

Jacobs, B. A. (1999). *Dealing Crack: the social world of streetcorner selling*. Boston: North Eastern University Press.

Keene, J. (1997a). Drug use among prisoners before, during and after custody. *Addiction Research*, 4, pp. 343–55.

Keene, J. (1997b). Drug misuse in prison, views from inside: a qualitative study of prison staff and inmates. *Howard Journal*, 36, pp. 28–41.

King, R. & McDermott, K. (1995). *The State of Our Prisons*. Oxford: Oxford Clarendon Press.

Lindesmith, A. (1938). A sociological theory of drug addiction. *American Journal of Sociology*, 43, pp. 593–613.

Maden, A., Swinton, M. & Gunn, J. (1991). Drug dependence in prisoners. *British Medical Journal*, 302, p. 880.

McAuley, R. (forthcoming). The enemy within: economic marginalisation and the impact on crime amongst young adults. PhD thesis, University of Cambridge.

Meisenhelder, T. (1985). An essay on time and the phenomenology of imprisonment. *Deviant Behaviour*, 6, pp. 39–56.

Murji, K. (1998). *Policing Drugs*. Aldershot: Ashgate.

Newburn, T. (1998). Young offenders, drugs and prevention. *Drugs: education, prevention and policy*, 5, pp. 233–43.

Parker, H., Aldridge, J. & Measham, F. (1998). *Illegal Leisure: the normalisation of adolescent recreational drug use*. London: Routledge.

Preele, E. & Casey, J. (1969). Taking care of business: the heroin user's life on the street. *International Journal of the Addictions*, 4, pp. 1–24.

Shiner, M. & Newburn, T. (1999). Taking tea with Noel: the place and meaning of drug use in everyday life. In N. South (Ed.), *Drugs: cultures, controls and everyday life* (pp. 138–59). London: Sage.

South, N. (Ed.) (1999). *Drugs: cultures, controls and everyday life*. London: Sage.

Sparks, R., Bottoms, A. E. & Hay, W. (1996). *Prisons and the Problem of Order*, Oxford: Clarendon Press.

Sutton, M. (1995). Supply by theft. *British Journal of Criminology*, 35, pp. 400–14.

Sutton, M. (1996). *Handling Stolen Goods and Theft: a market reduction approach*, Research Study No. 178. London: HMSO.

Sykes, G. & Matza, D. (1959). Techniques of neutralisation: a theory of delinquency. *American Sociological Review*, 22, pp. 664–670.

Turnbull, P., Stimson, G. & Stillwell, G. (1994). *Drugs in Prison*. West Sussex: Avert.

Young, J. (1971). *The Drugtakers*. London: Paladin.

DRUGS: EDUCATION, PREVENTION AND POLICY, 7(4), 335–336.

18. Smoke 'Em If You Got 'Em: Cigarette Black Markets in U.S. Prisons and Jails

Stephen E. Lankenau

Since the mid-1980s, cigarette-smoking policies have become increasingly restrictive in jails and prisons across the United States. Cigarette black markets of various form and scale often emerge in jails and prisons where tobacco is prohibited or banned. Case studies of 16 jails and prisons were undertaken to understand the effects of cigarette bans versus restrictions on inmate culture and prison economies. This study describes how bans can transform largely benign cigarette "gray markets," where cigarettes are used as a currency, into more problematic black markets, where cigarettes are a highly priced commodity. Analysis points to several structural factors that affected the development of cigarette black markets in the visited facilities: the architectural design, inmate movement inside and outside, officer involvement in smuggling cigarettes to inmates, and officer vigilance in enforcing the smoking policy. Although these factors affect the influx of other types of contraband into correctional facilities, such as illegal drugs, this study argues that the demand and availability of cigarettes creates a unique kind of black market.

Since the mid-1980s, cigarette-smoking policies have become increasingly restrictive in jails and prisons across the United States. Currently, two thirds of U.S. jails and one quarter of U.S. prisons ban inmates from smoking cigarettes or possessing tobacco (Falkin, Strauss, & Lankenau, 1998, 1999). In institutions where bans are enforced, inmates are prohibited from smoking any form of tobacco inside the facility or outside on the facility grounds. Despite this trend toward banning tobacco in correctional facilities, virtually no studies have examined the effect of this policy change on inmate culture and prison economies. In particular, no research has focused specifically on cigarette black markets that invariably emerge in jails and prisons where tobacco is prohibited.

We conducted ethnographic case studies of smoking policies in 16 jails and prisons to understand the effects of cigarette bans (the prohibition of tobacco) and restrictions (the sanctioning of tobacco smoking) on the exchange and use of cigarettes among inmates. In the following analysis, we contrast relatively benign cigarette "gray markets," where cigarettes are traded and used as currency in facilities that restrict tobacco, with more problematic black markets, where cigarettes are a highly priced contraband item in facilities that ban tobacco. In particular, our analysis points to several structural factors that affect the development of cigarette black markets in the facilities that we visited: the architectural design of the institution, including the configuration of inmate-housing units;

the degree to which inmates move around and outside of an institution; and the vigilance of correctional officers and staff in enforcing the smoking policy and their involvement in smuggling cigarettes to inmates. Although these factors affect the influx of other types of contraband in to correctional facilities, such as illegal drugs, we argue that the demand and availability of cigarettes creates a unique kind of black market.

The Function of Cigarettes in a Prison Economy

The legitimate and illicit exchanges of goods and services occurring inside jails and prisons comprise both a formal and informal economic system (Williams & Fish, 1974). The formal economy constitutes a prison's legitimate economic system that includes prison industries, work release programs, and other licit activities that generate income for inmates (and the correctional facility). This official system includes inmate monetary accounts, which are supplemented through prison employment and deposits made by associates, as well as the commissary, which dispenses goods, such as soap, snack foods, and sometimes cigarettes. For many inmates, however, the formal prison economy does not provide enough opportunities to earn income and offers too few desirable goods and services from the commissary. Consequently, an informal economy develops that is premised on consuming prohibited or contraband items and "hustles" (Gleason, 1978) to earn extra resources to pay for contraband and legitimate commissary goods.

Traditionally, cigarettes have been used by inmates as a standard form of currency in informal prison economies. Radford's (1945) description of a Nazi Germany prisoner of war (POW) camp was the first to discuss the economic and social importance of cigarettes in an inmate economy. Radford, a former POW, indicated that although active trading of other goods and services existed, only cigarettes were transformed from a commodity to a form of currency due to their durability, portability, supply, and demand. Likewise, Williams and Fish (1974) reported that cigarettes functioned as an ideal currency in prison because they were often smoked and replaced by new packs before the old packs became mangled and worn out.

The packaging of cigarettes into cartons, packs, and individual cigarettes creates natural denominations that foster convenient transactions among inmates. Kalinich's (1986) study of one prison economy found that stable prices evolved for contraband items that were expressed in terms of packs and cartons of cigarettes, such as five packs for a joint of marijuana or two cartons for a tattoo. Likewise, Radford (1945) reported that prices evolved for certain commodities and were expressed in number of cigarettes, such as 40 cigarettes for a loaf of bread or 15 cigarettes for a chocolate bar.

Another defining feature of the camp described by Radford (1945) was the development of an embryonic labor market, such as laundrymen earning two cigarettes per washed garment, and the emergence of entrepreneurial services, such as coffee stall proprietors selling coffee for two cigarettes per cup. Labor marketers and entrepreneurs using cigarettes as currency is also commonly found in jails and prisons. One practice, "mushfaking," involves manufacturing contraband items out of available materials in exchange for cigarettes or other goods and services (Foster, 1982). Examples include inmates creating dice from cubes of sugar marked with a black felt pen or making shivs or knives from silverware. Likewise, tattooing (Demelco, 1993), drug dealing (Gleason, 1978), and gambling (Kalinich, 1986) are common hustles that generate illicit income tied to the exchange of cigarettes.

A primary feature of the prison environment is the policing of hustles and the management of contraband problems through occasional or frequent shakedowns. Shakedowns are accomplished by correctional officers searching through an inmate's cell and possessions and ferreting out and seizing unauthorized items (Guenther, 1978). Shakedowns typically focus on more serious contraband, such as weapons, illegal drugs, and escape equipment, rather than on less serious "nuisance contraband," such as pornography, gambling equipment, and personal effects. In prisons that allow smoking, cigarettes constitute contraband only when amassed in large quantities (Kalinich, 1986).

Despite the integral role that cigarettes have traditionally played in the prison economy, both as a commodity and as a currency, no formal research has investigated the effects of cigarette bans on inmate culture. Rather, research examining cigarettes in prisons or jails has focused on housing-unit smoking policies (Falkin et al., 1998; Romero & Connell, 1988; Vaughn & del Carmen, 1992), rates of smoking among inmates (Vaughn & del Carmen, 1992), and legal issues surrounding cigarette bans (Vaughn & del Carmen, 1992). Prison and jail research has focused on topics that relate to informal prison economics, such as changes in prison culture (Hunt, Riegel, Morales, & Waldorf, 1993), new generation jails (Jackson & Stearns, 1995), and sex in prison (Saum, Surratt, Inciardi, & Bennett, 1995), without mentioning the recent trend to ban cigarettes.

This article addresses an important gap in the existing literature on the role of cigarettes in informal prison economies. In particular, this research examines how changes in institutional policy, namely, restricting or banning cigarettes in jails and prisons, affects the informal prison economy and inmate culture.

Method and Sample

We began by contacting jails and prisons that were changing their smoking policy (or had recently changed), were viewed as authorities on the subject of banning cigarettes in correctional facilities, or were located in regions of the country where tobacco was an important part of the local or regional economy. Based on these criteria, we selected jails and prisons for qualitative exploration after individually examining hundreds of previously collected surveys (Falkin et al., 1998) or learning about cases while attending jail and correctional association annual meetings.

Following the screening process, 10 jails and 6 prisons in eight states (California, Connecticut, Indiana, Kentucky, Michigan, New Jersey, North Carolina, and Washington) were identified as possessing smoking policies of interest and later visited. All of the site visits were conducted between May 1998 and April 1999.

Ten of the case study sites (6 jails and 4 prisons) banned cigarettes for staff and inmates, whereas 6 of the sites (4 jails and 2 prisons) restricted smoking, that is, staff and inmates were permitted to smoke in certain parts of the institution at specific times. Visits lasted 2 days and included touring the facility, interviewing key administrators, conversing with correctional officers and staff at their posts (e.g., medical clinic, control center, jail cell), and talking to inmates.

Interactions with line staff and inmates consisted of informal conversations and formal interviews to obtain information on inmate access to cigarettes and cigarette prices in facilities that permitted smoking and to describe three main aspects of the cigarette black market in facilities that banned smoking: smuggling, dealing, and smoking practices. In total, 50 staff and 140 inmates were interviewed.

In addition to directly asking administrators, staff, and inmates about cigarette practices and policies, inmates were observed interacting with other inmates and with officers in the jails and prisons. Finally, department of corrections officials in three states were interviewed to understand smoking policy formulation at the state level and to learn how these officials viewed problems surrounding the enforcement of cigarette restrictions in prisons.

To provide a context for understanding how and why cigarette black markets emerged and functioned in the facilities that banned tobacco, we first describe the gray market cigarette economy in facilities that permitted smoking.

The Gray-Market Cigarette Economy

Access to Cigarettes

In the six facilities that permitted smoking, inmates purchased cigarettes as well as other commodities, such as snack foods, beverages, personal hygiene products, medication, and clothing, from a commissary or in-house store. Whereas new inmates received basic hygiene items, such as toothpaste and soap, from the commissary on admission, all inmates were responsible for paying for luxury items as well as necessities after admission. In lower security facilities, inmates went to the commissary to buy cigarettes and tobacco, whereas in higher security facilities, purchased items were delivered directly to their cells.

Because U.S. currency was regarded as contraband inside all of the facilities visited, inmates were given personal debit accounts, and the costs of commissary items were deducted from their accounts. Money could be added to inmate accounts via deposits made by inmates themselves, families, or associates. Inmates also accrued income through institutional jobs, and these earnings were added directly to their accounts. Depending on their level of skill and job responsibility, inmates earned between $15 and $35 per month. For instance, an inmate working as a welder earned more than a janitor. In some cases, inmates earned a wage for attending general equivalency diploma classes or drug abuse treatment programs. In addition, inmates who were prohibited from working, chose not to work, or attended classes received "idle pay," a minimal monthly allowance that provided for basic hygiene purchases.

Depending on the facility, inmates ordered commissary items between one and three times per week. Commissary purchases, including cigarettes, were limited to a maximum weekly amount, such as $50 or $60. The commissary was the only source for these products because inmates were prohibited from receiving such items from friends or family. Outside gifts were prohibited because they could serve as conduits for tobacco and other contraband, such as illegal drugs and weapons.

In the six institutions that sold tobacco, the price, quality, and diversity of tobacco products varied from facility to facility. For example, inmates in a small jail could purchase only a generic brand of cigarettes costing $1.25 for a pack of 20 cigarettes, whereas inmates in a large prison could buy cigars, loose tobacco, and name brand cigarettes, such as Marlboro, for $2.25 per pack. Cartons with 10 packs of cigarettes were also sold but typically without any discounted pricing. Loose tobacco, which was sold in 6-oz cans or 1-oz boxes along with cigarette rolling papers, was the cheapest form of tobacco. For instance, in one prison, a 6-oz can of Bugler cost $4, which could then be rolled into 300 cigarettes, the equivalent of 15 packs of cigarettes costing about $0.40 per pack.

Cigarettes as Currency

All of the facilities that allowed inmates to smoke prohibited them from trading cigarettes for other goods and from giving cigarettes to each other as gifts. However, cigarette exchanges among inmates were difficult to police, and sanctions for trading were rarely imposed, according to both inmates and officers at these six facilities. Furthermore, because U.S. currency was prohibited, cigarettes functioned as a local form of currency in these prisons and jails. In particular, a pack of cigarettes stood as the basic unit of exchange and favored form of currency for several reasons. First, compared with other common commissary items, such as candy bars, soups, and soap, a pack of cigarettes cost enough to be a meaningful object of exchange. Second, a pack of cigarettes is a portable, semidurable object that could be conveniently exchanged; however, because trading or giving away cigarettes constituted a rule violation in these facilities, the unit of currency had to be inconspicuous. Third, because the great majority of inmates smoked, a pack of cigarettes served the dual function of acting as currency and as a consumable good. Rather than trading other items for a pack of cigarettes, an inmate could simply smoke up his winnings or earnings.

A pack of cigarettes was used as payment for a variety of services and exchanges. For instance, a visit to the prison barber sometimes required a pack of cigarettes as a tip to ensure the desired haircut. In several facilities, inmates who wanted their laundry properly folded had to tip the laundryman a pack of cigarettes for each load of clothes washed. In some cases, inmates who failed to tip not only received poorly folded clothes but had their belongings subjected to a "state wash," that is, a laundryman washed and dried an inmate's clothes without ever removing them from the laundry bag, which often left clothes still dirty and wrinkled.

Apart from inmates who used their institutional jobs to gain income, such as laundrymen or barbers, other inmates devised various hustles to earn extra income. For instance, one inmate created cards and envelopes that he exchanged for cigarettes. He also ran a "store" where he bought items from inmates at one price, such as a shirt for two packs of cigarettes, and then sold the items later for a higher price, such as three packs of cigarettes for the same shirt. Gambling debts were also frequently paid in packs of cigarettes.

One particular inmate's hustle, to roll loose tobacco into cigarettes, clearly illustrates the value of cigarettes and how cigarettes can circulate within a jail or prison economy. In one prison, a 6-oz can of loose tobacco sold for $4, and the buyer would pass it to an inmate who was highly skilled at rolling cigarettes. Using 4 oz of tobacco, he rolled 200 cigarettes, the equivalent of 10 packs of cigarettes, and he kept the remaining 2 oz as payment for his labor. He then rolled the extra tobacco into 100 additional cigarettes. Because his cigarettes were so skillfully rolled, other inmates were often willing to trade a pack of 20 cigarettes, valued at $2, for his 100 cigarettes. He then traded packs of cigarettes for commissary items. This inmate, who also worked a night job as a janitor, rolled between two and seven cans of tobacco per day. Whereas his janitor job paid only $16.50 per month, he earned the equivalent of $4 to $14 per day rolling cigarettes. Although rolling and exchanging tobacco was forbidden under the institution's rules, this inmate was able to succeed because the dorm officers often looked the other way.

The Black Market in Cigarettes

Contraband Cigarettes in Facilities That Permit Smoking

As mentioned earlier, the six facilities that sold cigarettes all restricted inmate smoking in certain ways. Depending on the facility, these restrictions included the following: barring inmates from smoking anywhere inside the facility but allowing them to smoke on the prison grounds, prohibiting inmates from smoking in their individual cells but permitting smoking in the attached dayrooms, and prohibiting inmates from smoking in their cells if their cellmate objected. Violating the smoking policy led to further smoking restrictions, such as the loss of smoking privileges for certain periods of time.

In all the facilities that allowed inmates to smoke, smoking was prohibited in the isolation cells, known as the administrative segregation unit, which are reserved for egregious rule violators. However, when placed in the administrative segregation unit, inmates procured cigarettes in a secretive and costly manner, a practice that foreshadowed the emergence of black markets in facilities that banned tobacco.

For instance, a well-developed black market existed in the administrative segregation unit at one maximum security prison where smoking was permitted among the general population. According to several officers assigned to the unit, cigarettes entered the unit in a variety of ways. Inmates involved in the black market hid cigarettes in food trays or in bundles of laundry that were sent into the units. Cigarettes were also placed inside tennis balls, tossed into the outdoor recreational area, and then retrieved by inmates. Other inmates purposefully became involved in incidents requiring disciplinary action or requested protective custody in order to be temporarily placed in administrative segregation. Once in the unit, the new inmate provided smuggled cigarettes to other inmates at a substantial markup.

Because cells in the unit were frequently searched and monitored, inmates had to carefully smoke and hide their tobacco. One clever technique involved an inmate's placing tobacco and matches in a tightly sealed plastic toothbrush holder and then putting the holder in a toilet located in the inmate's cell. The inmate then flushed the holder, but the buoyant plastic became trapped in an air pocket located inside the toilet plumbing. When the inmate wished to smoke, he drained the toilet water into the sink. Removing the water caused the toothbrush holder to drop into the base of the toilet bowl. The tobacco and matches, still dry, were then removed from the holder. On lighting the cigarette, smoke was blown into the air-filled toilet plumbing. In this case, the toilet served the dual function of hiding the tobacco and concealing cigarette smoke.

Black Markets in Facilities That Banned Smoking

Among the 10 facilities that banned smoking, all prohibited administrative staff, correctional officers, and inmates from smoking tobacco anywhere inside of the facility, that is, both the administrative offices and the secured areas. However, certain policy variations existed that had implications for the development of a black market. For instance, one facility allowed inmates to smoke while they were off-site performing community service or while they were on work release. Most facilities allowed staff and officers to smoke on facility grounds in designated areas that were outside of the view of inmates. The most restrictive policy prohibited staff and officers from possessing or using tobacco while on facility property. In this case, staff and officers were pat-searched specifically to ferret out tobacco before entering the facility's secured area.

Ultimately, at all 10 facilities, the smoking bans produced subterranean, sometimes elaborate, practices for acquiring, exchanging, and smoking tobacco. In certain ways, these practices and exchanges are variations on other types of black market activity, such as illegal drugs, that emerge inside of correctional facilities. However, we describe how cigarette bans produce a unique black market because of the high demand by inmates for tobacco and the more pervasive involvement of correctional staff in the black market. In this section, we discuss three aspects of the cigarette black market: methods of acquiring and smuggling tobacco into a facility, dealing tobacco inside a facility, and smoking, lighting, and hiding practices.

Acquiring and Smuggling Tobacco. The defining feature of a black market and its ability to thrive is the relationship between black marketers and individuals with access to cigarettes in the nonsecured sections of the facility as well as areas outside of the facility. The greater access inmates had to other inmates, visitors, staff, and officers, the more likely it was that a more organized black market arose. Interaction among inmates and others was typically influenced by the security level of the facility, facility architecture, and policing pragmatics, such as single-person cells versus two-person cells, cells versus dorm-housing units, indoor recreational areas versus outdoor recreational spaces, and security fences versus no fences. Essentially, greater interaction among inmates created more opportunities to exchange tobacco, resources, and information. Facilities with a higher security level, which meant greater restrictions among inmates, did have less black market activity.

An important dimension of security and interaction among inmates is whether a facility allowed certain inmates clearance, that is, permitted inmates to move into and out of the secure areas of the facility, including leaving the facility. Inmate trustees, who often work in the secured and nonsecured areas of a facility, represented one end of the clearance continuum and were referred to as having a low level of clearance. Typical trustee jobs included kitchen and janitorial work. Community service and work release inmates, who left the facility and returned to the community during scheduled times each day, denoted the other end of the continuum and were described as having a high level of clearance. Common jobs in the community included mowing fields along highways or painting city buildings and other properties. In facilities that had less black market collusion from staff and officers, inmates with a higher clearance status were the primary tobacco runners and suppliers. Overall, the great majority of jail and prison inmates had no clearance or low clearance and had to rely on the few inmates with higher levels of clearance or on officers to smuggle tobacco into the facility.

Inmates with a relatively low level of clearance at one jail, trustees who worked in the kitchen, had a successful smuggling operation for a period of time, until the scheme was uncovered by staff. The kitchen was staffed by inmate workers who lived together in one pod or section within the jail. These trustees were housed together due to their atypical schedule—they rose earlier than other inmates to prepare meals—and to minimize the possible flow of contraband between them and other inmates. Kitchen workers also wore white uniforms to distinguish them from other trustees and nontrustees. The kitchen was located behind the jail in an area that was infrequently patrolled and was fenced off from pedestrians. The kitchen's exterior wall consisted of vinyl siding that met directly with an outside, unsecured space. At some point, a hole about 1 inch in diameter was drilled or banged through the base of the exterior wall and into the kitchen. This small hole, which connected the interior of the kitchen directly to the outside world, became an artery for cigarettes and other contraband until it was discovered. Kitchen workers retrieved the cigarettes placed in the hole and either smoked them later or distributed them within the jail. Despite being housed together in one area, the kitchen staff had contact with other trustees during the day, which afforded them opportunities to route contraband around the jail. The civilian staff who managed the inmate kitchen workers represented an additional point of contact with the outside world and may have facilitated the smuggling operation. Hence, despite a jail's attempt to minimize the flow of contraband by segregating trustees from other inmates and civilians, this example highlighted a security breach that allowed a supply of cigarettes to enter the jail.

Community service workers and work release inmates represented a more reliable, steady supply of cigarettes. Such workers devised their own smuggling efforts, such as procuring cigarettes from civilian workers or having them drop off cigarettes in designated outdoor areas. Alternatively, inmates with no clearance reported arranging for civilian associates to leave bundles of cigarettes to be retrieved and later smuggled in by a "mule," such as an inmate working on a road crew.

These smuggling efforts were typically financed by a "send-in." Broadly, a send-in involved an inmate sending money out of the facility in exchange for a certain quantity of tobacco to be brought in, typically a carton or more. Send-ins were accomplished by one inmate sending money to an outside source who then bought the cigarettes and left them in a designated area for pick-up. Send-ins were risky investments because cigarettes could be lost, stolen, or confiscated before reaching their purchaser. However, send-ins were generally viewed as worthwhile risks because the street cost of a carton was relatively low compared with its black market price inside a jail or prison, which ranged from $200 to $500.

Work release inmates who smuggled in cigarettes faced certain risks. Depending on the attitudes projected by workers themselves and the number of officers staffing a post on particular times and days, returning workers might be strip-searched, pat-searched, or waved in without being explicitly searched. To evade detection during searches, inmates hid contraband in a variety of ways. For instance, the soles of shoes or sneakers were hollowed out, filled with loose tobacco or cigarettes, and then meticulously restored with glue to avoid suspicion. Likewise, linings of jackets and coats were sometimes cut open, filled with tobacco, and then resewn. Inmates who were permitted to take gear to a work site reported hiding tobacco inside tool belts or plastic mugs. A more invasive smuggling method involved wrapping cigarettes in plastic and then carrying them inside one's rectum.

Inmates who successfully smuggled in tobacco for other inmates generally received a portion of the tobacco as a form of payment. For instance, one inmate who bought tobacco via a send-in paid a mule 5 packs out of a 30-pack delivery, a 17% cost. Another inmate who bought five cans of tobacco paid his mule 9 oz of the 30 oz smuggled in, a 30% cost.

That such large amounts of tobacco, multiple cartons or cans, were often smuggled into certain facilities indicated a force beyond sheer cleverness or luck on the part of smugglers. Rather, correctional staff were complicit in some of these larger smuggling efforts. In fact, some mules developed relationships with the officers in charge of pat searches. For instance, certain mules paid officers a $20 "gate fee," which allowed reentry to the facility without any search.

Compared to other black market enterprises, such as illegal drugs, cigarettes represented a unique commodity because officers typically viewed them differently from other forms of contraband. Most officers interviewed did not view cigarettes as immoral or dangerous, as they might regard heroin, cocaine, or marijuana, because many were current or former smokers themselves. Rather, a cigarette's legal status in the civilian world placed it in a qualitatively different category than a sleeve of heroin or a vial of crack. Consequently, some correctional officers directly fueled the cigarette black market by smuggling or aiding the smuggling of tobacco into a facility.

An officer's participation in the black market consisted of developing explicit relationships with inmates focused on delivering certain quantities of tobacco. Some officers passed on a few cigarettes or a pack of cigarettes to an inmate in exchange for money or a job well done. More serious transactions involved officers working as suppliers of cigarettes into a facility or as couriers of inmate cigarette profits out of a facility. Inmates financed tobacco purchases indirectly through send-ins and more directly through accumulated cigarette profits. Regarding send-ins, inmates reported contacting civilian associates to deliver the appropriate money to an officer. On receipt of the money, the officer delivered the agreed on amount of tobacco. Inmates who generated large profits inside a facility, several hundred dollars at a time, reported paying officers directly inside the facility.

Significantly, officers collected large amounts of money supplying cigarettes. Inmates reported that officers charged between $20 and $50 for one pack of cigarettes, whereas cartons and cans of tobacco sold for between $50 and $100. That cigarettes are legal in the civilian world made procurement both easy and stigma-free. Ultimately, officers who earned between $7 and $10 as an hourly wage could earn an entire week's salary in one cigarette transaction. Consequently, officers who participated in the cigarette black market were motivated by multiple factors, some of which were easily rationalized.

Dealing Tobacco. The tremendous markups enjoyed by officers who fueled the cigarette black market point to the great earning potential of dealing cigarettes. Apart from officers, two primary layers of inmate dealers existed in well-developed cigarette black markets. Inmates who had the resources to coordinate send-ins to officers or other civilian suppliers represented the primary dealers. These inmates purchased bulk amounts of tobacco, cartons and cans, and then sold packs and ounces to secondary dealers. Secondary dealers bought tobacco by trading commissary items or other possessions for tobacco. Alternatively, secondary dealers also did send-ins to primary dealers, which was accomplished by a secondary dealer sending money to a primary dealer's inmate account or to an outside location, such as a post office box or a civilian address. Tobacco was dispensed once the money "hit" the primary dealer's account or outside location.

Primary dealers reported amassing substantial amounts of money through black market participation. For instance, one dealer claimed that he sent $400 to $500 to his girlfriend each week, whereas another dealer reported saving $900 after dealing cigarettes for 3 months. Smuggling out such large amounts of cash often required the assistance of officers. One inmate said that he paid an officer $100 to deliver $400 to a civilian associate.

Compared to primary dealers, secondary dealers typically sold enough tobacco to pay for their own smoking habit, while earning a small profit on the side. For instance, a secondary dealer at one facility periodically spent $50 on a 6-oz can of tobacco and then recouped his investment by selling three 1-oz bags of tobacco for $20 per bag. Typically, $20 worth of commissary items, such as soap, snacks, and soups, were exchanged for the ounce or the ounce was purchased with "green money," U.S. currency. The remaining 3 oz were then smoked or periodically sold off for additional commissary items or other prison commodities. This example demonstrates that buying a $50 can of tobacco on the black market yields far greater returns, in terms of commissary purchasing power, than does adding $50 to an inmate account. Consequently, some inmates requested that family members undertake send-ins for tobacco rather than adding money directly to their accounts.

In facilities with less developed black markets and where tobacco was less plentiful, packs of cigarettes (as compared to cartons) were the main quantities smuggled into facilities. For instance, primary dealers at one facility bought packs from officers for $20 in U.S. currency and then sold individual cigarettes for $5 a piece. Secondary dealers then broke the cigarettes down into "rollies," smaller cigarettes constructed out of tobacco and rolling papers, that sold for $2 or $3 a piece.

Like smuggling, dealing cigarettes carried certain risks. The penalties for possessing or selling tobacco varied from facility to facility, but the offense typically fell under the broader category of possessing or distributing contraband. In some institutions, dealing tobacco was regarded as seriously as dealing a controlled substance, such as marijuana or cocaine. In other facilities, tobacco was viewed more benignly, similar to possessing unauthorized clothing or books. Across facilities, sanctions ran the gamut from loss of certain privileges, such as commissary or visitors, to being moved to a higher security facility or increasing the length of one's sentence. Hence, established dealers were careful about handling tobacco.

In fact, some more experienced dealers, both primary and secondary, did not handle tobacco at all. Rather, the risks of possessing tobacco were absorbed by lower profile inmates who were not likely to have been "ticketed" for tobacco possession. In some cases, dealers chose nonsmokers to hold and deal tobacco for them. Other dealers hired two inmates: one to deal their tobacco and another to hold their tobacco for personal use. In turn, these subdealers and handlers were often paid in commissary items and/or tobacco for their work. For instance, one dealer paid an inmate $5 in commissary and 10 rollies to hold 6 oz of tobacco, which had a yard value between $50 and $60.

Hiding tobacco in personal space, such as lockers, cells, and beds, was difficult because these were the places that correctional officers searched during inmate shakedowns. Consequently, tobacco was hidden throughout some facilities in library books, behind lighting fixtures, underground, inside walls, and outside in recreation areas. In addition to hiring subdealers to hide tobacco, established dealers distributed free cigarettes, essentially hush money, to those inmates who threatened the secrecy of their operation.

Smoking, Lighting, and Hiding Practices. Jail and prison inmates spent most of their waking and nonwaking hours in their housing units, that is, cells, day rooms, and dormitories, which were also the primary places where inmates exchanged and smoked cigarettes. Depending on the facility's architecture, inmates were either directly supervised by officers while in their housing units or indirectly monitored from remote locations. Under either approach, burning tobacco was readily discernible in spaces that were supposed to be smoke-free. Before charging an inmate with violating the smoking policy, an officer typically needed concrete evidence that an inmate had been smoking, such as a cigarette butt. To avoid detection, inmates craftily hid cigarettes, masked the smell of smoke with electric fans or cologne, and flushed cigarette butts down toilets. These evasion techniques frustrated many officers from actively pursuing cigarette smokers, whereas other officers simply looked the other way when detecting smoke. Some officers only pursued flagrant rule violators, such as inmates who openly smoked without any respect for the officer's authority.

Officers generally caught inmates with tobacco in one of three ways: while smoking a cigarette in a cell, dayroom, or bathroom; during a cell or bed area shakedown; or while attempting to smuggle tobacco into the facility. Among these three scenarios, smoking a cigarette was a frequent way of getting caught because a burning cigarette emitted both visual and olfactory evidence, despite an inmate's best efforts to hide it. Also, the act of smoking caused some smokers to cough, which would attract an officer's attention. In addition, lighting a cigarette required a flame or spark that also transmitted visual, olfactory, and auditory clues of a smoking violation. Because matches and lighters were frequently more scarce than cigarettes, inmates devised a host of techniques to create fire, some of which occasionally led to their being caught.

A common lighting method was to place two pencil leads in an electrical outlet and set a third lead wrapped in toilet paper across the first two. Generally, the toilet paper caught fire, the cigarette was lit, and the lighting kit was discarded. Occasionally, the lighting process went awry and caused an outlet to short out, which then drew an officer's attention to the particular cell or section of the day room.

Overall, inmates reported adeptness at masking the smell of smoke, lighting cigarettes without detection, and discarding cigarette butts before they could be confiscated by officers as evidence. Rather, both inmates and officers reported that most tobacco violators were caught during shakedowns. Shakedowns were typically conducted for one of three reasons: periodic facility-wide shakedowns, random housing-unit shakedowns, and cell shakedowns following suspicious inmate activities or tips from other inmates. During periodic shakedowns, the entire facility—offices, classrooms, work sites, housing units, and recreational areas—were inspected to ferret out contraband and uncover hiding places. During cell shakedowns, inmate cells were examined for extraneous possessions, such as clothing, plus contraband items, such as lighters, cigarettes, and illicit drugs.

Despite the policing mechanisms aimed at enforcing a smoking ban, inmates regularly violated the smoking policy. In the four prisons that banned smoking, at least half of the inmates interviewed in each facility smoked on a weekly basis. The amount and frequency of smoking varied from a few cigarettes per week at one facility to nearly half a pack of cigarettes every day at another. Typically, inmates smoked less in higher security facilities. Inmates were more likely to be caught smoking or possessing tobacco in facilities where inmates detailed a more pervasive black market. Regardless of the facility, however, the number of violators who reported ever being caught and the rate of smoking violations per month was very low compared to the amount of smoking that occurred on a regular basis.

The amount of regular smoking occurring in certain facilities was influenced by officer ambivalence toward vigorously pursuing policy violators, as demonstrated by officers who looked the other way when smelling smoke or spotting tobacco. One particularly reluctant officer went so far as to proclaim, "Smoke 'em if you got 'em," on entering a dormitory at the beginning of his shift, thereby signaling to inmates that smoking would be tolerated. In general, part of this ambivalence may have stemmed from the fact that many officers smoked cigarettes themselves and empathized with an inmate's desire to smoke. In addition, some officers who smoked cigarettes were embittered by the facility's smoking ban because it curbed their own smoking habit. Also, prior to smoking bans, cigarettes were a primary way for officers to motivate inmates, particularly poorer inmates, to accomplish certain tasks. Consequently, some officers reported that enforcing the smoking ban was counterproductive to carrying out their job, particularly more senior officers who had worked at a facility prior to the enactment of a smoking ban.

Discussion

The preceding description of the structural components of the cigarette black market points to several factors that appear to influence the development of cigarette black markets. First, the design and age of a facility affected cigarette smuggling and smoking prospects among inmates. Black market activity seemed greater in older facilities that were less secure and that had less direct supervision of inmates by officers. Second, the security level of the institution, that is, the movement within and outside of the institution, affected smuggling activity. Higher level security facilities, which restricted movement within the institution and which prohibited inmates from leaving the institution, appeared to have less organized black markets. Third, officer attitudes toward the smoking policy affected the development of cigarette black markets in two ways. Officers who did not enforce the policy, that is, those who overlooked smoking violations, indirectly stimulated inmate demand for cigarettes by allowing inmates to develop or maintain a smoking habit. More serious, officers who smuggled cigarettes or aided smugglers fueled both a supply and a demand for cigarettes among inmates.

Other factors leading to a more developed black market were greater organization, communication, and black market skills among inmates. The structure of the cigarette black market as outlined here, with its kingpins, smugglers, middlemen, and dealers, is not too different from illegal street-level drug markets. In fact, inmates involved in the cigarette black markets were frequently individuals who had been incarcerated for drug crimes. These inmates were already skilled at financing and obtaining illegal substances; managing lieutenants, adversaries, and turf; and eluding social control agents. Consequently, banning an addictive substance in a setting filled with sophisticated inmates created an environment ripe for the development of a black market. As one inmate, who was serving a 90-year sentence in a maximum security prison for drug trafficking, lamented, "I would've never messed with coke on the street if I knew how much money I could've made selling cigarettes here in the joint."

Interestingly, prison wardens and jail administrators often reported a decline in illegal drugs entering their facilities since banning cigarettes and attributed the decline to a greater demand for cigarettes among inmates. Inmates suggested that demand is, in fact, greater for tobacco than other drugs. For instance, several inmates claimed that kicking nicotine had been more difficult than quitting heroin, and others said that they would much prefer a cigarette to a line of cocaine. However, in addition to demand for tobacco, an equally significant factor dampening the drug economy was that tobacco was a more profitable substance to sell than other drugs. Whereas illicit drugs, such as marijuana, heroin, or cocaine, may yield greater profits per sale, the volume of tobacco sold and its high profit margin made it a more lucrative commodity to sell.

Conclusion

Jails and prisons ban cigarettes for a variety of reasons, including tobacco control laws and ordinances that legislate bans throughout state and county buildings, inmate lawsuits and grievances that sue for smoke-free environments, jail and prison overcrowding that increases the amount of cigarette smoke within facilities, and new institutional architecture and technology that are harmed by tobacco smoke (Lankenau, Falkin, & Strauss, 1999). The elimination or reduction of the amount of potentially harmful cigarette smoke contacting staff, inmates, or facility infrastructure has been a primary objective of bans. Despite this seemingly positive intention, the cigarette black markets that emerged in response to cigarette bans typically had a negative impact on inmates in the facilities we visited. We conclude by describing several of the effects of the cigarette black market on inmates.

First, since smoking cessation aids, such as smoking cessation classes or nicotine replacement therapies, were virtually nonexistent in the facilities where bans were enforced, the inmates interviewed were compelled to quit cold turkey or contend with the vagaries of the black market. Most inmates interviewed chose to participate in the black market because their tobacco use rarely abated on entering a facility that banned cigarettes.

Second, the majority of inmates were compelled to pay considerably higher prices to continue their cigarette habits. For instance, prior to a ban at a maximum security prison, one inmate said he spent about $5 per week on a can or about $15 per week on a carton. Following the ban, he smoked about three cigarettes per day at a cost of $60 to $70 per week. Consequently, the high cost of cigarettes prompted many inmates to undertake various hustles or to become low-level dealers because paying for only a few cigarettes could cost a third of an inmate's monthly institutional pay. For instance, one 60-year-old inmate used his pension money to pay for black market cigarettes. He said he had been robbed six times and manhandled twice over cigarettes. Prior to the ban, he said he was never robbed or assaulted. Other inmates increasingly relied on family members to add money to commissary accounts or to finance send-ins, whereas the poorest inmates reported trading hygiene items, such as soap and toothpaste, or sexual favors for cigarettes.

Third, just as the criminalization of cocaine and heroin gives rise to impure drugs and a scarcity of sterile drug paraphernalia, cigarettes sold on the black market are often more harmful than those sold legally and are combined with less healthy smoking practices. For instance, because rolling papers were scarce, some inmates resorted to rolling tobacco with toilet paper wrappers or with pages from a Bible. Both contain ink or dyes that are harmful when burned. Also, inmates reported removing the filters on manufactured cigarettes to increase the potency of each drag of tobacco. Furthermore, inmates who might otherwise have smoked a lower tar cigarette had little choice but to smoke higher tar cigarettes.

Fourth, the great majority of inmates who smoked or dealt cigarettes eluded detection, but the consequences for cigarette violations caused certain hardships. Whereas violations in some facilities were handled informally by correctional officers, such as merely confiscating the cigarettes, more formal punishments included losing privileges, such as commissary and visitations; being confined to administrative segregation; being transferred to a higher security facility; and having the length of a sentence extended. Also, many inmates complained of tensions between themselves and officers over the policing of cigarette contraband and tensions among inmates, stemming from a fear of being ratted out by snitches.

Finally, despite the fact that an appreciable amount of cigarette smoking occurred in facilities where tobacco was banned, most inmates smoked considerably less than they did prior to entering the criminal justice system. For instance, inmates at one prison smoked approximately 30 fewer cigarettes per day under the cigarette ban compared to their daily smoking habits outside of prison. However, despite this large reduction, most of these inmates did not report many noticeable health improvements, such as improved breathing, lessened fatigue, or a heightened sense of taste or smell. Perhaps, this was the case because these inmates continued a habit of 5 to 10 cigarettes per day.

References

Demelco, M. (1993). The convict body: Tattooing among male American prisoners. *Anthropology Today, 9*(6), 10–13.

Falkin, G., Strauss, S., & Lankenau, S. (1998). Cigarette smoking policies in American jails. *American Jails, 8*(3), 9–14.

Falkin, G., Strauss, S., & Lankenau, S. (1999). *Cigarette smoking policies in state prisons.* Unpublished manuscript, National Development and Research Institutes, Inc., New York.

Foster, T. (1982). "Mushfaking": A compensatory behavior of prisoners. *Journal of Social Psychology, 117*, 115–124.

Gleason, S. (1978). Hustling: The "inside" economy of prison. *Federal Probation, 42*, 32–40.

Guenther, A. (1978). Compensation in a total institution: The forms and functions of contraband. *Crime and Delinquency, 21*, 243–254.

Hunt, G., Riegel, S., Morales, T., & Waldorf, D. (1993). Changes in prison culture: Prison gangs and the case of the "Pepsi Generation." *Social Problems, 40*(3), 398–409.

Jackson, P., & Stearns, C. (1995). Gender issues in the new generation jail. *The Prison Journal, 75*(2), 203–221.

Kalinich, D. (1986). *Power, stability, and contraband: The inmate economy*. Prospect Heights, IL: Waveland.

Lankenau, S., Falkin, G., & Strauss, S. (1999). *Social forces shaping and resisting the trend toward banning cigarettes in U.S. jails and prisons*. Unpublished manuscript, National Development and Research Institutes, Inc., New York.

Radford, R. (1945). The economic organization of a P.O.W. camp. *Economica, 35*, 189–201.

Romero, C., & Connell, F. (1988). A survey of prison policies regarding smoking and tobacco. *Journal of Prison & Jail Health, 7*(1), 27–36.

Saum, C., Surratt, H., Inciardi, J., & Bennett, R. (1995). Sex in prison: Exploring the myths and realities. *The Prison Journal, 75*(4), 413–430.

Vaughn, M., & del Carmen, R. (1992). Research note: Smoking in prisons—A national survey of correctional administrators in the United States. *Crime and Delinquency, 39*(2), 225–239.

Williams, V., & Fish, M. (1974). *Convicts, codes, and contraband: The prison life of men and women*. Cambridge, MA: Ballinger.

THE PRISON JOURNAL, Vol. 81 No. 2, June 2001, 142–161.

Part 5: Programming

If we believe that the main purpose—or one of the main purposes—of sending offenders to prison is to change their behavior from criminal to law-abiding, we would believe that prisons should emphasize programs for inmates. Working with inmates to identify, understand, and overcome the problems that are associated with committing crime is a centerpiece of the rehabilitation ideal, and the core of any efforts to change behavior. However, programs for inmates have been scaled back and even eliminated since the early 1990s. This has occurred as the number of prison inmates has skyrocketed. In large part, curtailing programs and working with inmates to address their crime-related problems has been done in an attempt to control the ever-increasing costs of operating prisons. As more inmates come in, costs go up. To help absorb these increasing costs, "extras" (such as programs) have been cut, and funds have been redirected to basics (such as housing, food, and security personnel). However, this does not mean that programs are a bad idea or that administrators and inmates do not want programs to be available. Some programs are considered very valuable in prisons, and administrators work hard to see that these programs and services are not eliminated. The articles in this section look specifically at three basic needs of inmates and how prison programs can address these needs.

The first article discusses one of the most basic, yet more controversial, forms of programming in prisons: education, especially higher education. As Welsh points out, due to federal legislation in the early 1990s, prison inmates lost their eligibility for federal higher education tuition assistance. Up until this time, higher education had been shown to be the most successful form of rehabilitation programming in prison. However, due to political influences, this programming option was significantly reduced in American prisons. The issues involved, politically and in terms of recidivism, are outlined in this article.

The second article in this section discusses a program variety that most people would not think of as a "program" per se: religion. However, as the authors of this article point out, religion has been a part of American correctional efforts from the very beginning and has many benefits to offer. The importance of programs for maintaining internal order and a smooth-running prison are highlighted in this discussion. As a "program," religion offers benefits both to individual inmates who choose to participate and to institutions and administrators. Correctional officials are legally required to provide access to religious observances and activities, and for the most part, this has never been opposed or debated. This discussion outlines the reasons for this and shows the benefits that such a "program" offers.

The third article in this section looks at the prevalence of a type of program that is more in the public eye: psychotherapy. Morgan, Winterowd, and Ferrell report that one in five male prison inmates participates in group therapy sessions. The most common goals for such groups are assisting inmates to adjust to prison life, preparing inmates for life after prison, and teaching social skills. Obviously, with a majority of prison inmates having at least one type of diagnosable mental health problem, there is a great need for mental health services. In addition to simply reviewing what types of services are provided and how frequently, the authors discuss some of the reasons for this disparity and the ways psychologists could better address these needs.

Finally, Latessa, Cullen, and Gendreau discuss the problem of programs and "new ideas" that are advanced and implemented with little evidence of their likely success. Focusing on what they call "correctional quackery," these authors criticize the field of corrections for failing to consider research about what is or is not likely to work when developing new programming options for offenders. Their argument is that corrections, in order to be truly a profession, needs to become an "evidence-based profession" and look to both theories about criminal behavior and evaluations of current and past programs in order to identify what is a promising approach to working with criminal offenders. Their discussion also presents arguments supporting the importance of building evaluations into all new programs, and principles (based on research) for what constitutes effective an correctional program.

As was the case with some of the previous sections in this book, the articles in this section challenge the reader to consider what the purpose of prison is and if and how various approaches to programming help to further that goal. When we think about programs in prison, we see that we need to think broadly and consider all forms of activities that are (or could be) organized and goal oriented. Programming can mean many different things in prison, and the articles in this section push us to examine what can and should be included in this idea.

Discussion Questions

Programming

1. What are the major goals of prison programs?
2. What distinguishes a good, or "successful," inmate program from an unsuccessful program? How can correctional officials design and implement programs to enhance the likelihood that they will be successful?
3. What are the positive and negative impacts of programs for the operations of a prison?

19. Opportunities Lost: The Consequences of Eliminating Pell Grant Eligibility for Correctional Education Students

Richard Tewksbury
David John Erickson
Jon Marc Taylor

Post-secondary educational opportunities for incarcerated offenders have declined in recent years. The passage of the Violent Crime Control Act of 1994 marked the elimination of all state and federal inmates' eligibility for Pell entitlement grants, effective in the 1995–96 academic year. The present study serves as a re-evaluation of the state of PSCE programming within U.S. correctional systems. Two academic years have passed since the original evaluation conducted in 1995–96 (see Tewksbury & Taylor, 1996), allowing the opportunity to assess the intermediate consequences of the loss of Pell Grant funding for inmates. The present study assesses the degree to which the loss of Pell funding has affected PSCE opportunities for inmate-students and how correctional systems have adapted and changed as a result of the elimination of Pell Grant funding.

Post-secondary educational opportunities for incarcerated offenders have declined in recent years. Initiated declines were attributed to state-level reductions in funding (Lillis, 1993); additionally, the passage of the Violent Crime Control Act of 1994/95 marked the elimination of all state and federal inmates' eligibility for Pell entitlement grants, effective in the 1995–96 academic year (Tewksbury & Taylor, 1996). (Five states (California, Michigan, Missouri, Nebraska and New Jersey) had their inmates declared ineligible for Pell Grant funding in the 1994–95 academic year as the result of violations of the 1994 Higher Education Reauthorization Act's supplant/supplement clause.)

In addition to the elimination of inmates' access to post-secondary education through Pell Grant funding, fully one-half of all state correctional systems reduced technical and vocational training programs following the passage of the Violent Crime Control Act (Worth, 1995). The purpose of the present study is to assess the current state of post-secondary correctional education (PSCE) programming within U.S. correctional systems three years after the elimination of Pell Grant eligibility.

Prior to the exclusion of inmates from Pell entitlements, 92 percent of correctional systems offered some form of post-secondary educational programming (Ryan & Woodward, 1987) in 772 prisons (Stephan, 1992), enrolling more than 38,000 inmate-students (Lillis, 1994). In the first academic year after inmates were excluded from Pell funding, inmate enrollment in PSCE programs decreased 44 percent to just over 21,000 inmate-students (according to data from 43 reporting jurisdictions) (Tewksbury & Taylor, 1996). Furthermore, the number of correctional systems offering PSCE opportunities decreased from 82.6 percent in 1994–95 to 63 percent in 1995–96. The elimination of Pell Grant funding also brought about significant decreases in curriculum diversity as well. Systems offering certificate programs decreased from 52 to 39 percent; associate degrees from 71 to 50 percent; baccalaureate degrees from 48 to 33 percent; and graduate programs from 13 to 6 percent. (Although Pell Grant funding is not available for graduate studies, the grants do fund undergraduate programs that qualify students for subsequent graduate study. Without the undergraduate "feeder programs" PSCE graduate opportunities cease to exist.) Moreover, nine correctional systems reported the complete elimination of all PSCE opportunities for inmates in the first year of inmates' exclusion from Pell Grant funding. Surviving PSCE programs reported reductions in overall program stability and the number of educational institutions operating on-site PSCE programs. Only 20 percent of jurisdictions reported minimal or no changes in PSCE programming in the first year following the elimination of Pell Grant funding for inmates (Tewksbury & Taylor, 1996). The consequences of large-scale reductions in PSCE programming can be measured by examining the benefits that both inmates and correctional administrators derive from such programming.

Benefits of PSCE Programming

In spite of political rhetoric to the contrary, the American public has held fast to the notion that rehabilitation should be one of the major goals of correctional processes (Cullen, Skovron, Scott & Burton, 1990; Doble, 1987; Quinney, 1979; Rotman, 1986). The central question is whether or not PSCE programming serves as an effective agent of rehabilitation; that is, does PSCE reduce recidivism? Unfortunately, there has historically been little consensus in addressing the efficacy of PSCE programming (Maltz, 1984). Furthermore, much of the research that is available is plagued by inconsistent methodology (Janic, 1998; Wreford, 1990), giving both opponents and proponents the opportunity to hold their ground in the PSCE debate.

Opponents of PSCE programming are quick to dismiss the validity of research in support of higher education for inmates on methodological grounds. Opponents argue further that the type of offenders that seek, or are selected for, educational opportunities bias the reported success of PSCE in that these individuals are likely to be the type of offenders with the highest likelihood of successful reintegration into society, regardless of educational attainment (Ross & McKay, 1978). In this case, although they have the advantage of a higher education, the argument is that these individuals would have succeeded anyway; although, there is no data to support this contention.

Rudin (1998:105) however, "provides indirect evidence which counters the self-selection argument as an explanation of the benefits of higher education programs for prisoners." Moreover, research literature suggests several statistical methods for negating selection bias. Berk (1987), and Harer (1995) utilized two of these (multivariate models and the propensity score approach) to mediate the bias in his recidivism research. Other researchers have employed the same and similar techniques as well.

Proponents of PSCE programming contend that, despite the acknowledged methodological inconsistencies, extant research suggests that prison education programs yield significant reductions in recidivism rates (Adams, Bennett, Flanagan, Marquart, Cuvelier, Fritsch, Gerber, Longmire & Burton, 1994; Batiuk, Moke & Rountree, 1997; Center on Crime, Community & Culture, 1997; Duguid, Hawkey & Knights, 1998; Gerber & Fritsch, 1995; Holloway & Moke, 1986; Janic, 1998; Jenkins, Steurer, & Pendry, 1995, Palmer, 1984; Ross & McKay, 1978; Stevens & Ward, 1997; Taylor & Tewksbury, 1998; Windham School System, 1994; Wreford, 1990). PSCE programming reduces recidivism through a fundamental change in the cognitive processes of the inmate-student. Higher education serves as a catalyst to the maturation process for the maladaptive offender by providing organized exposure to, and development of, a more mature sense of values, improved self-esteem, and a more pro-social worldview (Benson, 1991; Haber, 1983; Homant, 1984; O'Neil, 1990; Parker, 1990; Pittman & Whipple, 1982; Rountree, Edwards & Dawson, 1982; Taylor, 1994; Taylor & Tewksbury, 1998; Toch, 1987). Or, as adult educator Mezirow (1990) explains it, higher education induces "critical reflection" that leads to "transformative learning." Positive changes in the offender's cognitive processes also lead to a more positive attitude, improved coping skills, and improved behavior (Adams, 1968; Anklesaria & Lary 1992; Harer, 1995; Johnson, 1987; Taylor & Tewksbury, 1998). With that, proponents of PSCE programming suggest that the question of the validity of PSCE recidivism studies can be suspended, and PSCE programming may be supported from a purely pragmatic perspective—the improved management of inmates.

"Educational programming has long been recognized as an important management tool" (Luttrell, 1991:55; see also Dilulio, 1991) for correctional administrators. Dilulio (1991) suggested that correctional education programming serves as an important management tool that reduces disciplinary problems, increases inmate-staff interactions and provides incentives for good behavior. While a direct cause-effect relationship has not been established, inmates that participate in educational programming are better behaved than the general inmate population (Dilulio, 1991; Taylor, 1993). Davis (1988) found that participation in PSCE was a significantly greater influence for positive institutional behavior than even the opportunity to participate in conjugal visitation programs. Buser (1996) found that inmates who participated in PSCE in the year prior to the elimination of such programming in Maryland spent approximately four times as many days in disciplinary segregation during the following year when no college program was available. It has also been suggested that inmate-students foster a more peaceful atmosphere within the prison (Duguid, 1987; Taylor, 1992). Moreover, higher education often serves as a catalyst to improved inmate-inmate, staff-staff, and inmate-staff relations by enhancing social interactions and decreasing social distance between these groups (Carroll, 1974, 1982; Dilulio, 1991; Pass, 1988; Reasons, 1974; Taylor, 1992).

The present study serves as a re-evaluation of the state of PSCE programming within U.S. correctional systems. Two academic years have passed since the original evaluation conducted in 1995–96 (see Tewksbury & Taylor, 1996), allowing the opportunity to assess the intermediate consequences of the loss of Pell Grant funding for inmates. The present study will not only assess the degree to which the loss of Pell funding has affected PSCE opportunities for inmate-students, but also how correctional systems have adapted and changed as a result of the elimination of Pell Grant funding.

Methods

Data for the present analysis were obtained via surveys mailed to directors of adult education programming in all 50 states and the District of Columbia. Initial surveys were mailed during fall 1998 with follow-up requests mailed to all non-responding systems approximately six weeks after the initial mailing. The final research sample consisted of 48 systems. In the present study only three systems did not report: District of Columbia, West Virginia, and Wyoming. Of those in the current study, only West Virginia did not report to the 1996 survey, when a total of six systems failed to report. Thus, the results of this survey are more comprehensive.

Requested data focused on the size of PSCE programming in the particular system (number of educational institutions, number of PSCE students, types of degrees available to inmates), perceptions regarding the impact of elimination of Pell Grant eligibility, perceptions regarding PSCE program stability, and sources of funding for PSCE programming. Directors were asked to report all data for the 1997–1998 academic year. In this way we could devote attention to identifying intermediate changes in program scope and operations three academic years following Pell Grant elimination.

Findings

As predicted in the original evaluation conducted in 1995–96 (Tewksbury & Taylor, 1996), the present analysis finds further erosion of PSCE programming across the nation. Three years after the elimination of Pell Grant funding for incarcerated students, the number of correctional systems offering PSCE programming has dropped from 82.6 percent in 1994–95 to 63 percent in 1995–96, and 54.9 percent in 1997–98. Not only do fewer systems offer opportunities, but the range of program options has further decreased as well. The number of systems offering certificate programs decreased from 52 percent in 1994–95 to 39 percent in 1995–96, but rose to 49 percent in 1997–98. The number of systems offering associate degrees has decreased from 71 percent in 1994–95, to 50 percent in 1995–96, and 37.3 percent in 1997–98. Likewise, the number of systems offering baccalaureate degrees has decreased from 48 percent in 1994–95, to 33 percent in 1995–96, and 19.6 percent in 1997–98. Holding position, the number of systems offering graduate degrees decreased from 13 percent in 1994–95, to 6 percent in 1995–96, and remained at 6 percent in 1997–98.

TABLE 1 Primary Forms of Funding Still Available

Type of Funding	*1995–96*	*1997–98*
State Version of Pell	15.9	2.1
Other State Grants	18.2	27.1
Student's Own Money	43.2	27.1
Student's Family	20.5	4.2
Perkins Grants/Federal Funds	27.3	14.6
Private Foundation Grants/Social Organizations	34.1	31.3
General State Funds	34.1	31.3
No Funds/Program	25.0	54.2

Note. The values represent the percentage of systems reporting that a particular form of funding was available to inmates for PSCE programming.

The present analysis finds that the total number of enrolled PSCE students has increased since the original evaluation conducted in 1995–96. However, this finding is misleading. To accurately interpret these findings, the total number of students enrolled must be adjusted for the increase in inmate populations during the same period. When the total number of PSCE students is adjusted for increases in inmate populations, we find that the percentage of inmates enrolled in PSCE programming has decreased from 7.3 percent in 1994–95, to 4 percent in 1995–96, and 3.8 percent in 1997–98.

More telling than the modest decrease in the percentage of PSCE inmates since the original evaluation is the percentage of inmates eligible for participation in PSCE programming that actually enroll. Correctional education directors indicated that while approximately 41 percent of the inmate population is eligible to participate in PSCE programming, only 10 percent of the eligible inmates were enrolled in PSCE programming. We are not able to distinguish between eligible inmates who do not participate for lack of interest and/or motivation, and those who simply cannot access funding needed to participate in PSCE programming. As the following discussion will make clear, however, it is likely that a significant portion of eligible inmates who do not participate are prevented from doing so by the lack of funding options available to them.

The sources of funding available to inmates for PSCE are limited. When correctional education directors were questioned regarding sources of funding available in their systems, the source most commonly reported as the "primary" source of funding was general state funds (31.3 percent, N = 15). Table 1 shows the range of funding sources available to inmates, as reported by correctional education directors. While it appears that there are several funding options possible for inmates, it is important to note the actual availability of the funding. For example, the two most prominent sources of funding reported (private foundation/social organization grants and general state funds) are only available in 15 of the reporting systems, leaving inmates in at least 33 systems without access to one or

TABLE 2 Reported Impact of Pell Grant Elimination on PSCE Programs

Response	*% of Systems*
All PSCE Programming Eliminated	18.6
Completely Changed Program	16.3
Very Significant Impact	20.9
Somewhat Significant Impact	7.0
Some Impact, but Not Much	11.6
Very Little Impact	14.0
No Changes at All	11.6[a]

[a]Of the systems reporting "no changes," 40 percent never made Pell Grant funding available to inmate students and a further 40 percent had no PSCE programming and, thus, reported "no changes."

both of these funding sources. The number of funding options reported by each system further exacerbates the availability of funding. For example, the Texas Department of Corrections reported that five of the eight sources listed in Table 1 were available to PSCE students, while 26 other systems (54.2 percent) reported that none of the sources listed in Table 1 were available. Furthermore, some of the funding options that were previously available to inmates have declined substantially. While 15.9 percent of systems reported that a state version of the Pell Grant was available in 1995–96, only 2.1 percent reported that such funding was available to inmate students in 1997–98. Likewise, 27.3 percent of systems reported that Perkins loans and/or other federal funding was available to inmate students in 1995–96, while only 14.6 percent reported that such funding was still available in 1997–98. It is clear, then, that funding limitations prevent significant portions of eligible inmates from participating in PSCE programming.

Obviously, there continue to be significant changes in the scope and delivery of PSCE programming. So as to better understand the magnitude of these changes, we again asked correctional education directors to report how the elimination of Pell Grants impacted their programs. Nearly 35 percent of correctional education directors reported that curtailing Pell Grant eligibility had "completely changed" or "eliminated" all PSCE programming. A further 20.9 percent indicated that the elimination had a "very significant impact" on their programs. Although 11.6 percent indicated that there had been "no changes" to their programs, it is important to note that of the systems reporting no changes, 40 percent never made Pell Grant funding available to inmate students and a further 40 percent had no PSCE programming and, thus, reported no changes.

More specifically, we also looked at how the elimination of Pell Grant funding has affected PSCE programs in the following areas: number of enrolled students, curriculum diversity, number of degrees offered, number of degrees conferred, and number of educational institutions operating within each system. Fully 69 percent of systems reported that the number of students enrolled had decreased since the elimination of Pell Grant funding, while only 4.8 percent reported increases in the

Table 3 Number of Educational Institutions Operating PSCE Programs in the States

	1994–95[a]	*1995–96*[b]	*1997–98*[c]
Total Number of Educational Institutions	232	138	245
Average Number of Participating Educational Institutions per State	5.27	3.14	7.9
Total Number of Prisons in Reporting States	690 ($\bar{x}$ = 15.68)	688 ($\bar{x}$ = 15.64)	1077 ($\bar{x}$ = 22.5)
Ratio of Average Number of Prisons to Average Number of Educational Institutions	2.97/1	4.98/1	2.8/1

[a]46 systems reporting. [b]46 systems reporting. [c]48 systems reporting.

number of students enrolled. Similarly, 59 percent of systems reported that curriculum diversity had decreased, while only 2.6 percent reported increases in curriculum diversity. The majority of systems reported significant decreases in the number of degrees offered (62.5 percent), as well as the number of degrees conferred (65 percent). When asked how the elimination of Pell Grant funding had impacted the number of educational institutions operating within their systems, 95 percent of correctional education directors indicated that the number of institutions had decreased (40 percent) or remained the same (55 percent). The impact of Pell Grant elimination on the number of educational institutions operating, as reported by the correctional education directors surveyed, points to an inconsistency in our findings on this point.

Correctional education directors were asked to indicate the total number of educational institutions operating PSCE programs in their systems. As Table 3 illustrates, the aggregate number of educational institutions reported for 1997–98 was 245, a 76 percent increase above the 138 reported in 1995–96. Even more surprising, the 245 educational institutions reported in 1997–98 is higher than the 232 reported for the 1994–95 academic year—prior to the elimination of Pell Grant funding for PSCE programming. With that, the average number of educational institutions participating in PSCE programming per state went from 5.3 in 1994–95 to 3.1 in 1995–96, and 7.9 in 1997–98. These findings, obviously, stand in sharp contrast to the 95 percent of correctional education directors who reported that the number of educational institutions had decreased or remained the same.

While unlikely, it is possible that some share of the inconsistencies regarding changes in the number of educational institutions operating PSCE reported here is due to correctional education directors' misperceptions of the actual number of such institutions prior to the elimination of Pell Grant funding. It is also possible that the inconsistencies reported here could be, in part, a result of reporting errors in the original—or present—analyses. It is most likely, however, that the inconsistency in the number of participating educational institutions is a direct result of the proliferation of prisons across the nation. Directors of correctional education see some schools bowing out of PSCE programming, and this surely leaves a lasting impression on their perceptions. At the same time, however, the average number of prisons is steadily increasing (see Table 3). As new prisons initiate PSCE programs, they must recruit new schools to provide programming. Another possible explanation is that correctional systems are increasingly contracting with local community colleges (and universities) to provide literacy/ ABE/GED programming, and thus the directors have included any college or university service provider in their response (although these educational institutions do not offer PSCE programming). As Table 3 illustrates, the ratio of the average number of prisons to the average number of educational institutions was at a low point (2.8/1) in 1997–98; which provides a viable explanation for the inconsistency regarding the number of educational institutions reported by correctional education directors.

Discussion

The elimination of Pell Grant eligibility for incarcerated students has had a substantial negative impact on PSCE programs and the men and women who enroll in PSCE. In the last year of Pell Grant eligibility for inmates, four-fifths of state correctional systems offered PSCE opportunities. Three academic years later just over one-half provide the same option. Programming scope dropped from 67 percent offering associate degree programs to only 37 percent offering the same option. Baccalaureate programs have been similarly reduced. Whereas one-half of the states offered baccalaureate degrees previously, in 1997–98 only 20 percent did so. Most important, the percentage of inmates participating in PSCE programming continues to drop, as does the percentage of inmates eligible to participate that actually enroll in PSCE programs.

There is no question that the elimination of Pell Grant funding for inmate students has severely impacted PSCE programming throughout the nation. Despite significant losses in programs, program diversity, programming dollars, and student participation, however, hope remains as PSCE survives in many places. The continued degradation of PSCE measured in the present analysis pales in comparison to the initial losses in the first year following the exclusion of inmates from Pell Grant eligibility. It appears, then, that surviving PSCE programs may be stabilizing somewhat as they recover from the initial blow dealt by the Pell Grant elimination. Whether surviving PSCE programs stabilize, or further erode, remains to be seen. What is clear, however, is that the catastrophe foreshadowed in our previous analysis—thankfully—did not fully come to pass. As a consequence, those systems that found the courage and wherewithal to ensure PSCE survived will continue to reap the benefits that PSCE programming provides.

While the present analysis offers no empirical support for the rehabilitative efficacy of PSCE programming, the authors-and many others-believe that extant research supports the position that PSCE programs seem as effective in (re)integrating participants more successfully than virtually any other option (Adams et al., 1994; Center on Crime, Community & Culture, 1997; Gerber & Fritsch, 1995; Holloway & Moke, 1986; Janic, 1998; Linden & Perry, 1982; Martinson, 1974; Palmer, 1984; Ross & McKay, 1978; Stevens & Ward, 1997; Windham School System, 1994; Wreford, 1990). It is imperative that further research be conducted to resolve the rehabilitative efficacy issue so that surviving programs can be (re)improved, further (re)developed, and so that PSCE can be (re)expanded to those systems that currently do not offer such programming.

In the interim, proponents of PSCE should "sell" and call for the (re)expansion and (re)development of PSCE as an effective and essential management tool for the administration of the nation's prisons. The reinstitution of inmates' Pell Grant eligibility would be the best alternative for successfully achieving this goal (Rudin, 1998).

Inmate populations are not getting any smaller, nor are correctional facilities getting any less crowded. In this respect, the civilizing influence and thus, the institutional value of PSCE programming cannot be overlooked.

References

Adams, S. (1968). *The San Quentin Prison College Project*. Berkeley, CA: University of California Press.

Adams, K., Bennett, K. J., Flanagan, T. J., Marquart, J. W., Cuvelier, S. J., Fritsch, E., Gerber, J., Longmire, D. R., & Burton, V. S. (1994). A large-scale multidimensional test of the effect of prison education programs on offender behavior. *Prison Journal, 74*, 433–499.

Anklesaria, F. & Lary, S. (1992). A new approach to offender rehabilitation: Maharishi's integrated system of rehabilitation. *Journal of Correctional Education, 43*, (1), 6–13.

Batiuk, M. E., Moke, P. and Rountree, P. W. (1997). Crime and rehabilitation: Correctional education as an agent of change—a research note. *Justice Quarterly, 14*, (1), 107–178.

Benson, I. (1991). Prison education, and prison education in the UK. *Yearbook of Correctional Education*, Burnaby, BC: Institute for the Humanities, Simon Fraser University: 3–10.

Berk, R. (1987). Causal inference as a prediction problem. In D. M. Gottfredson and M. Tonry (Eds.) *Prediction and Classification: Criminal Justice Decision Making*, Chicago: University of Chicago Press.

Buser, C. E. (1996). *The Relationship Between College Participation and Institutional Adjustment Problems for Incarcerated Women*. (Unpublished doctoral dissertation, University of Maryland College Park).

Carroll, L. (1974). *Hacks, Blacks, and Cons: Race Relations in a Maximum Security Prison* (reissued 1988). Prospect Heights, IL: Waveland.

Carroll, L. (1982). *Race, ethnicity, and the social order of the prison*. In Johnson and Toch (Eds.). The Pain of Imprisonment. Beverly Hills, CA: Sage.

Center on Crime, Community & Culture (1997). *Education as Crime Prevention* (Research Brief No. 2).

Cullen, F., Skovron. S., Scott, J. & Burton, V. (1990). Public support for correctional treatment: The tenacity of rehabilitative ideology. *Criminal Justice and Behavior, 17*, (1), 6–18.

Davis, R. (1988). Education and the impact of the family reunion program in a maximum security prison. *Journal of Offender Counseling, Services and Rehabilitation, 12*, (2). 153–159.

DiIulio, J. (1991). *No Escape: The Failure of American Corrections*. New York: Basic Books.

Doble, J. (1987). *Crime and Punishment: The Public's View*. New York: Public Agenda Foundation.

Duguid, S. (1987). *University Education in British Columbia*. Burnaby, BC: Prison Education Program, Simon Fraser University.

Duguid, S., Hawkey, C. and Knights, W. (1998). Measuring the impact of post-secondary education in prison: A report from British Columbia. *Journal of Offender Rehabilitation, 27*, (1/2), 87–106.

Gerber, J. & Fritsch, E. J. (1995). Adult academic and vocational correctional education programs: A review of recent research. *Journal of Offender Rehabilitation, 24*, (1/2), 119–142.

Haber, G. (1983). The realization of potential by Lorton, D. C. Inmates with UDC education compared to those without UDC education. *Journal of Offender Services, Counseling, and Rehabilitation, 7*: 37–55.

Harer, M. D. (1995). *Prison Education Program Participation and Recidivism: A Test of the Normalization Hypothesis*. Washington, D.C.: Federal Bureau of Prisons Office of Research and Evaluation.

Holloway, J. & Moke, P. (1986). *Post-Secondary Correctional Education: An Evaluation of Parolee Performance*. Wilmington College, OH (ERIC Document ED 269–578).

Homant, R. (1984). On the role of values in correctional education. *Journal of Correctional Education, 35*, (1), 8–12.

Janic, M. (1998). Does correctional education have an effect on recidivism? *Journal of Correctional Education, 49*, (4), 152–161.

Jenkins, H. D., Steurer, S. J. and Pendry, J. (1995). A post-release follow-up of correctional education program completers released in 1990–1991. *Journal of Correctional Education, 46*, (1), 20–24.

Johnson, R. (1987). *Hard Time: Understanding and Reforming the Prison.* Pacific Grove, CA: Brooks Cole.

Lillis, J. (1993). Cutbacks may endanger inmate education. *Corrections Compendium, 18,* (9), 1–4.

Lillis, J. (1994). Prison education programs reduced. *Corrections Compendium, 19,* (3), 1–4.

Linden, R. & Perry, L. (1982). The effectiveness of prison education programs. *Journal of Offender Counseling, Services and Rehabilitation, 6,* (4), 43–57.

Luttrell, M. (1991). The impact of sentencing reform on prison management. *Federal Probation, 55,* (4), 54–57.

Maltz, M. (1984). *Recidivism.* Orlando, FL: Academic Press.

Martinson, R. (1974). What works?–Questions and answers about prison reform. *The Public Interest, 35,* 22–54.

Mezirow, J. (1990). How critical reflection triggers transformative learning and emancipating education. In J. Mezirow and Associates (Eds.) *Fostering Critical Reflection in Adulthood.* San Francisco: Jossey-Bass.

O'Neil, M. (1990). Correctional higher education. Reduced recidivism. *Journal of Correctional Education, 41,* (1), 28–31.

Palmer, T. (1984). Treatment and the role of classification: A review of basics. *Crime and Delinquency, 30,* 245–267.

Parker, E. (1990). The social-psychological impact of a college education on the prison inmate. *Journal of Correctional Education, 41,* (3), 140–146.

Pass, M. (1988). Race relations and the implications of education within prison. *Journal of Offender Counseling, Services and Rehabilitation, 13,* 145–151.

Pittman, V. & Whipple, E. M. (1982). The inmate as college student. *Lifelong Learning, the Adult Years, 5,* (4/5), 30.

Quinney, D. (1979). *Criminology* (2nd ed.). Boston: Little Brown and Company.

Reasons, C. (1974). Racism, prison, and prisoners' rights. *Issues in Criminology, 9,* 3–20.

Ross, R. & McKay, H. (1978). Behavioral approaches to treatment in corrections: Requiem for a panacea. *Canadian Journal of Criminology, 20,* (2), 279–295.

Rotman, E. (1986). Do criminal offenders have a Constitutional right to rehabilitation? *International Journal of Offender Therapy and Comparative Criminology, 32,* 29–35.

Rountree, G., Edwards, D. & Dawson, S. (1982). The effects of education on self-esteem of male prison inmates. *Journal of Correctional Education, 32,* (4), 12–17.

Rudin, J. P. (1998). Teaching undergraduate business management courses on campus and in prisons. *Journal of Correctional Education, 49,* (3), 100–106.

Ryan, T. A. & Woodward, J. (1987). *Correctional Education: A State of the Art Analysis,* Washington, DC.: National Institute of Corrections.

Stephan, J. (1992). *Census of State and Federal Correctional Facilities, 1990,* Washington, D.C.: Bureau of Justice Statistics.

Stevens, D. J. & Ward, C. (1997). College education and recidivism: Educating criminals is meritorious. *The Journal of Correctional Education, 48,* (3), 106–110.

Taylor, J. (1992). Post-secondary correctional education: An evaluation of effectiveness and efficacy. *Journal of Correctional Education, 43,* 132–141.

Taylor, J. (1993). Pell Grants for Prisoners. *The Nation* (Jan. 25), 88–91.

Taylor, J. M. (1994). Deny Pell Grants to prisoners? That would be a crime. *Criminal Justice, 9,* (2), 18–19, 23–25, 54–56.

Taylor, J. & Tewksbury, R. (1998). Post-secondary correctional education: The imprisoned university. In R. Gido & T. Alleman (Eds.). *Contemporary Correctional Issues: The Practice of Institutional Punishment.* New York: Prentice-Hall.

Tewksbury, R. A. & Taylor, J. M. (1996). The consequences of eliminating Pell Grant eligibility for students in post-secondary education programs. *Federal Probation, 60,* (3), 60–63.

Toch, H. (1987). Regenerating prisons through education. *Federal Probation, 51,* (3), 61–66.

Windham School System (1994). *Prison Education Research Project Final Report.* Texan State Department of Criminal Justice, Windham School, Sam Houston State University.

Worth, R. (1995). A model prison. *The Atlantic Monthly* (November), 12.

Wreford, P. (1990). *Community College Prison Program Graduation and Recidivism.* (Unpublished doctoral dissertation. University of Michigan).

JOURNAL OF OFFENDER REHABILITATION, Vol. 31, No. 1, 2000.

20. The Value of Religion in Prison

An Inmate Perspective

Todd R. Clear
Patricia L. Hardyman
Bruce Stout
Karol Lucken
Harry R. Dammer

In recent years, religious programming for inmates is being applauded by some as the latest answer to recidivism. Policy makers and correctional officials alike are among the supporters of these programs that go well beyond conventional prison ministry. The emphasis in promoting the expansion of religion-based programs indeed lies in the claim that faith in a higher power prevents relapse into criminal activity better than secular strategies. Whether this claim can be consistently validated remains unclear. Moreover, the sustained focus on religion's utility in preventing future criminal conduct diminishes religion's immediate value to the inmate during the term of incarceration. With this latter function in mind, this article reports findings from qualitative inquiries conducted in several prisons nationwide. Designed to reveal the meaning of religion to inmates, the study calls attention to the role of religion in preventing devaluation and fostering survival.

Religion has always been a part of penal history, although its role and importance in the punishment process have shifted over time. In colonial America, biblical precepts provided the justification for punishment and, at times, a guideline for its severity. Hence, in Massachusetts, the maximum number of whippings was set at 40, as indicated by Old Testament scripture. Religion's influence in punishment remained apparent in the 19th century with the development of the penitentiary (Ignatieff, 1978; McKelvey, 1977). Time spent in labor and reflection was to equip the offender with a spiritual coat or armor, capable of deflecting the most virulent of moral diseases. By the turn of the 20th century, scientific knowledge had displaced religion as a paradigm for explaining and controlling crime. Governed by the rule of empiricism, the new penal science made no accommodation for the mystical musings of religion. Consequently, throughout the 20th century, religion was seen foremost as a constitutionally protected right rather than as a formal strategy of correction or control.

Entering the 21st century, conservative politics and a declining faith in science-made cures have fostered religion's comeback. Religious organizations have become the new providers of a variety of offender programs that go beyond conventional prison ministry; it even includes Christian-contracted prison units. Whether religion-based interventions are effective or better than secular interventions at reducing recidivism is unclear (Ames, Gartner, & O'Connor, 1990; Clear et al., 1992; Young, Gartner, O'Connor, Larson, & Wright, 1995), but the idea is taking hold nevertheless.

If history is any indicator, religious programs will likely undergo the same scrutiny as their rehabilitation predecessors. In addition, should this latest panacea fall short of its highly touted potential, as decided by scientific measures of success and failure, will it not meet with the same fate as other reform strategies? Put differently, if it is cast into the heap of "nothing works" strategies, what will become of the humanizing presence that expanded religious programming brings to dehumanizing places?

It is recognized that the personal change that presupposes reduced recidivism necessarily conveys benefits for the offender in the long term. Yet, when program expectations are bound up in social defense objectives—crime prevention and reduced recidivism—the immediate value of religion to the inmate is generally not communicated. Rather than measure religion's effectiveness via expected odds on rearrest, projected outcomes, and the like, this article focuses on the effectiveness of religious programming from the perspective of inmates.

Methodological Framework

There is a way in which social science fits poorly to religion as a tool of investigation. Science deals with things that are observed, measured, and inferred by logic. Religion so often deals with mystery not to be captured by observation, namely, the experiences of the spirit that happen within individuals. In our analysis, we seek to treat with respect the reports of these experiences and to treat them as important to the speaker regardless of their truth or reality. This is not hard when we are trying to understand the meanings that our respondents attach to their experiences. It is less easy when we try to evaluate the importance within the prison setting of those experiences.

A series of interviews and an ethnography were the most appropriate methods of studying the meaning of religion in prison. Individual and group interviews with inmates were conducted in prisons in Delaware, Texas, Indiana, Missouri, and Mississippi. The ethnography was based on 10 months of intense participant observation in Western Prison (pseudonym). At least 3 days per week, the ethnographer visited the prison from 9 in the morning until 9 in the evening. During that time, religious activity was observed in the context of general prison activity. Standard ethnographic procedures were followed for the maintenance, coding, and interpretation of field notes. During the final 2 months, 50 interviews were conducted with a variety of religious and nonreligious inmates. During a 3-month period, a validation study was conducted in a different, but similar, maximum-security prison (with a pseudonym of Eastern Prison). Here, 20 interviews were carried out, each of which was recorded and transcribed.

Realistically, we must recognize that our research is but an entry into the general area of prison and religion. Still, it provides a way of indicating certain patterns of practice that apply to the intersection of these two social institutions. We believe that our work illuminates aspects of both, although we feel that we have provided grist for further hypotheses more so than we have answered, with finality, any particular questions of immediate concern.

Conceptual Framework

What religion means in prison can be described at two levels. There is the individual level, in which the meaning is highly subjective. Each inmate experiences religion in prison in a highly personal way, and its meaning for him is precisely the same as his experience of it. In a prison of 1,000 inmates, there are 1,000 meanings. Any attempt to make sense of this personal aspect of meaning must follow the rules of classification and focus on similarities of experience to build something of a typology of religious experience. Adopting such a strategy, we must recognize that some of the richness of individual experiences will be lost in the process of grouping these experiences into larger, broader categories. Nevertheless, by taking this approach, we will be able to construct something of a typology of religious meanings in prison, at least insofar as these relate to individual experiences.

Religion also has meaning as a group phenomenon. This meaning is inextricably tied up with individual experiences and their interpretations, but it is broader than these as well. The prison is an interconnected network of social groups, and the religious constitute some of those groups. The interconnections are determined by shared members, by shifts in the prison environment as members come and go, and by the continuing interactions of the groups on a day-to-day basis. Thus, seen from the perspective of a group phenomenon, religion in prison will have whatever meaning the inmates who comprise those groups give it by their actions with other groups.

Neither of these meanings is static. We have rich anecdotal data that individuals' religious experiences undergo change, sometimes profoundly so, during a single incarceration and from one prison term to another. Some of these stories play significantly in our own explanation of the religion phenomenon in prison.

A comprehensive view of religion in prison must recognize the rich variety of faiths within the walls. The two dominant faiths are Christianity and Islam, but within these is a multitude of variations. Yet, when we refer to religious participation, we are referring to adherents to these two worldviews. We take this approach, not because we feel that they are the only legitimate vehicles of faith in the prison but because they are so dominant in the prison setting. To try to discuss fully all the variations in faiths would not be feasible. Therefore, the picture of the meaning of religion that we portray must be understood as a strategic simplification. First, we are focusing our discussion on Christianity and Islam. Second, we are describing religion as though it were static, knowing that in any prison and for any prisoner, the experiential aspect we seek to portray might shift or be in the process of shifting.

To clarify the role that religion plays in incarceration, we use Gordon Allport's (1960) well-known concepts of intrinsic and extrinsic religious orientations. People are thought to be involved in religion for intrinsic reasons when their lives' master motives are defined by their religious beliefs. Their orientation is extrinsic when religious activity is chosen for its instrumental or utilitarian benefits. These orientations toward religious devotion are quite prominent outside the walls, and we believe that they are also important dimensions of religious practice within the prison setting.

The understanding of religion in prison is equally informed by the concept of prison society. We believe that religion in prison is deeply influenced by prison society, not in the general sense but in terms of the particular characteristics of the prison under consideration. There is, of course, some controversy about precisely what is meant by the term *prison society*. We have taken an interactionist perspective, so to speak, by relying on both the deprivation and importation perspectives on prison society. We assume that religion in the prison is shaped by the prison culture, which is itself a product of the deprivations of the prison and the imported social values. Religious programming will fit into and coincide with whatever mechanisms have evolved within a prison to provide inmates with supports of which they have been deprived. For instance, the degree of threat in the prison environment will influence the degree to which religion is sustained as a technique of safety. The degrees of race and ethnic pride mold the social configuration of religious groups. Likewise, the appeal of dogmatic and doctrinaire versions of faith is consistent with the younger, less experienced faithful. From this observation, it follows that there is no universal prison religion. Rather, there are variants that derive from the combined influences of the particularities of the prison housing the religious activity and the idiosyncrasies of the people in those programs. Each of these differences helps to shape the role of religion in the prison. However, within this vast and differentiated array of prison religious life lies common themes. These themes, which communicate the value of prison religion to the inmate, are presented in terms of the intrinsic and extrinsic orientations to religiosity.

The Meaning of Religion in Prison

Intrinsic Orientations

One of the most common answers to our questions about the motivations for religion in prison had to do with the dissonance the inmate feels about being in prison. Being in prison serves as a disconfirmation of the worth of one's life. The prisoner has to confront the fact of his imprisonment, one way or another. "Being incarcerated makes you bitter toward the world. They think it is going to make you better, but it does not." Many do so by fighting the circumstances of their sentence. They invest their time in appeals, blame lawyers and criminal compatriots for their fates, or arrange for better possibilities for when they are released. In addition, to sustain their image of self-importance, they may seek to achieve status within the prison society. "I have adjusted quite well without me being religious. I've done what I needed to do to adjust. Not going to church helped me get along better here." Of course, all these subterfuges can be taken by inmates who are religious. It is a way of adapting to the fact of imprisonment by denying the symbolic message of the sentence.

But for some inmates, there can be no denying. For these, the attack against the self, represented by the prison term, is too real to be denied. A certain truth about their lives must be confronted: the final failure of their choices. Religion, in its substance, holds possible routes out of the dilemma, for it not only explains the cause of the failure, it also prescribes the solution. In the logic of fundamentalist religious thought, both Muslim and Christian, the cause of all unhappy life consequences, such as imprisonment, is the failure of the individual to live within the doctrines of faith. The cure is fidelity to the teachings of the faith. "The true religious, they become stronger. They can deal with the ills that affect them, and they can ease the ills that affect you, and [they can] cause you to be able to avoid more crimes."

In this regard, it is worth noting that when inmates discuss their religious views, they often take a literal interpretation of the teachings of their faith. This is particularly true for Christians, but it is also true for Muslims. Direct quotation of the Bible or the Qur'an is very common, as are zealous urgings about the nearly magical quality of simple faith. Thus, inmates seem to experience religion as a basic truth that is presented without complexity or nuance in the holy teaching and is experienced without subtlety or ambiguity in holy rituals. As a consequence, the rhetoric of religious fervor can take on the quality of intolerance, as prisoners seek to convince each other of the merits of their own interpretations.

Although proselytizing was fairly common among the inmates we interviewed, the natural tension we might expect between Muslims and Christians was often downplayed. Although the inmate religious practitioners clearly recognized their own faiths as correct, they seemed sensitive to the strains faced by the devoted follower of any spiritual orientation. In fact, religious inmates often expressed more disappointment in the failings of those who profess similar religious views than in those of another faith group. Certainly, there were plenty of examples of inmates downplaying the accuracy of other religious views, but these instances were far less common than the expression of mutual respect that pertained to their relations in most prisons in our sample. "All religions promote love. If we are to promote love, we have to prove it in the way we get along with each other." What bonded the religious to each other was their mutual understanding of the needs that motivated them toward faith—in particular, the need to find meaning while spending a portion of their lives in prison. In fact, the way that religion translated into meaning was quite similar for all religious faiths that we encountered. Religious inmates described three separable but related varieties of intrinsic meanings.

Dealing with Guilt

With the exception of the loss of freedom, the most powerful message of imprisonment is guilt. The period of incarceration stands as a public shaming of the offender and a confirmed accusation of moral fault. Few accusations against self-esteem carry more potent damage than the reproach contained within the punishment act. Of course, not every offender feels the shame implied in the imposition of the prison term, as there is the common claim among prisoners that they are innocent or that they feel no contrition. But for those who do, confronting the damaging, ringing shame of imprisonment is central to survival in prison.

Most of the prison programs are evangelical. They meet the needs of guilt. They say, "Jesus can save me." Evangelical faiths offer unconditional acceptance. There are two ways that prisoners can turn to religion to relieve guilt. The first is a kind of exculpatory acceptance of the workings of evil in the world. The second is atonement and forgiveness.

Exculpatory uses of religion to relieve guilt employ the idea of evil to explain how the prisoner ended up in prison. This might be a simple belief that the person's previous rejection of religious obligations put him into circumstances in which crime was possible. Inmates of various faith persuasions would describe how their criminality resulted from undisciplined feeding of urges, the resistance of which is a core role of faith. Thus, because the person avoided religious fidelity, desires for drugs, thrills, sex, and other excitements were allowed free reign, and these desires eventually led to crimes. This is a view of evil as an inactive part of all of us against which we must build internal disciplines if we are to resist them. Religion, it was offered, was an important internal discipline for combating the baser urges. Christians and Muslims alike could resist these urges by prayer, fidelity in practice, and faith. "Being a Christian, I can go and ask Jesus Christ to forgive me for my sins and to give me the strength to deal with my problems." Some inmates viewed the evil as active—a real devil who would work within the bodies of those who would let them. Almost exclusively, this view was adopted by fundamental, charismatic Christians who would say that their criminality was a result of letting the devil into their lives and that Christ helped them drive Satan out.

Although both views of the personal cause of crime attribute blame to external forces, we should note that the latter version is particularly exculpatory. If evil is the undisciplined life, than it is up to the individual to maintain the disciplines necessary to combat it. If, on the other hand, evil is an active devil, then who can blame the sinner for his crimes once the devil has been cast out?

> Beware of the tricks of the devil. He has a lot of tricks. He uses the things of the world. He will use people to get in your face. . . . He uses different ways, but you have to be wise. You have to avoid it.

We heard references to this devil metaphor about men convicted of sex offenses, particularly crimes against children. These offenses are so stigmatized in Western society and so detested within prison that it must be exceedingly difficult to face oneself after having been labeled a child rapist. To cite an example, one of the ways in which the inmate can accept his crime, but reject the most damning aspects of the label, is to literally attribute the crime to a power that no one could defeat without special assistance—in this case, the devil. Understandably, laying responsibility for the crime as the work of an external agent can free the inmate of terrible burdens of guilt, while providing a worldview that enables him to align with positive adjustment models.

Many religious inmates refused to adopt an exculpatory view of their guilt. Instead, they seemed to accept a profound personal responsibility for their crimes and for the wrongfulness of their conduct. As one inmate said,

> If you talk to everyone here, they'll tell you they're in prison because of a mistake. Most of them, it was a bad attorney, a judge, a stupid mistake in the way they did the crime. The religious inmate, he realizes the mistake was doing the crime in the first place.

Rather than being exculpatory for these inmates, religion was a way to atone for the wrong that they had done and to receive the forgiveness that they needed to reestablish their personal self-worth. The teachings of Islam and of Christianity provide ways for the believer to admit guilt without experiencing guilt as a dead end. Instead, guilt can be experienced as a doorway to a better life. By adopting a religious identity, the inmate aligns with a logic that allows guilt but also surpasses it with a stronger self-image intact.

Finding a New Way of Life

One of the main themes that religious inmates provide in discussing the importance of their faith is that it has changed them. One inmate puts it eloquently with "My faith has made me excited about when I go home." This person has never been on the streets before. When searching for meaning, there is no more comprehensive place to find it than in the textbook of a religious order. The bible, the Qur'an, and other religious writings constitute complete explanations of the rights and duties of a human life. The inmate who desires an alternative to the prison lifestyle does not need to look further than these teachings. "Religion is a guide not to get out of hand; it gives you a straight path."

It is easy to discount the importance of these books. The idea that the inmate in prison might be looking for a packaged alternative to previous ways of living may seem far-fetched, but even a moments reflection will convince otherwise. Treatment systems such as Narcotics Anonymous and Guided Group Interaction are nearly total systems for living, and they do very well in the prison environment. The major religions are even more of a total system than these treatments, so it should not be surprising that they also do well in prison.

Inmates who adopt religion seem for the most part, as we have said, deeply committed to doctrinaire models of religious living. This is an indication of how attractive the certainty of religious doctrines can be for inmates. It facilitates a type of total replacement, whereby the ways of the past are subordinated to a new, fully developed way of living, one that can be thought of as proven. "Before I became a Muslim, I would not even think of the consequences. But religion teaches you these things, it makes you more conscious to every act you do."

A second way that inmates draw meaning from their religious orientation is the way in which they feel an active role of God in their lives. They report a change in their sense of personal power, and they say it enables them to cope with the pressures of being in prison. "We ain't did nothing. Anything that's happened in our lives. He [God] has done. . . . The Father wants you to be completely empty so he can fill you." Of course, there is no way to measure God as active in someone's life. However, it is possible to understand how this feeling can alter a person's life. An inmate who feels this change is constantly poised to listen for the voice of God in day-to-day decisions and dealings. Such an attitude may have a profound impact on an inmate's behavior, making him more reflective, less cynical, and more introspective.

This language is more common among Christians than among those of other faiths, but it is not unheard of among Muslims, who speak of Allah as making choices for them and exerting His will within their lives. The point for both faiths is to take a more accepting stance toward life, understanding the event as an act of God's will that is not to be resisted.

Obviously, this kind of thinking can have a penetrating significance within the prison, where unpleasant events can be so common. Inmates seeking to accept God's will can reinterpret these events, not as hostile environment but as almost friendly challenges from the hand of a benefactor.

Dealing with the Loss, Especially of Freedom

Finally, there is what might be thought of as the central intrinsic motivation for religiousness: a personal sense of peace. This was perhaps the most common way that inmates explained the value of adopting religion as a life guide. It enabled them to find peace. We also heard this from nonreligious inmates, although less frequently. The impression is that some religious inmates value faith because it provides a type of freedom within the walls of the prison.

> It is not the prison that incarcerates us, it is a man's mind. I am able to live a normal life and uphold my character with dignity. The first objective of prisons is to strip you of your dignity. It takes your self-esteem, your dignity, and everything about you. Religion has helped me to regain this.

Certainly, this freedom is an important doctrine of certain branches of Islam and Christianity. In both, a sharp distinction is made between things of the world and that which is spiritual or belongs to God. Followers are taught to value the latter, giving it primacy of attention and interest, while being careful to avoid inordinate concern about the former. In prison, where there is such a dominance of threat and deprivation, this is very sage teaching, because the person who focuses on losses incurred by being incarcerated is likely to become embittered. "My faith was not as strong until after being incarcerated. Suddenly, I found myself alone and with no one. That is when religion and belief in God became stronger. It kept me sane." A fruitful way to understand this idea of peace is to relate it to the primary deprivation of the prison: freedom. There is no deprivation more fundamental to the prison than the loss of freedom. Whatever else the prison does, it makes the inmate stay in a place he would not choose. Unlike other deprivations, such as safety or affiliation, there appears no obvious way to meet this need in prison.

Yet, inmates who are deeply committed to their religiousness often report that the main benefit of their faith is a sense of inner peace. When we would probe about the source of the peace, the inmates would tell us of their new life, of the way God (or Allah) was working in their lives, and of the fact that whatever happened to them, it was the will of God, and therefore was something they could handle.

> The only thing that is lacking in here is freedom of movement and women, but that is only a state of mind. I've seen some guys who don't really realize that they are in prison because it is not the prison that they see, it is the walk with God. Prison doesn't bother them anymore.

There is, frankly, no way that social science can test these statements. When people say that they feel peace or that they have found freedom within their imprisonment, any listener cannot help but be swayed by the obvious emotion with which they speak. When nonbelievers affirm their respect for the few whom they see as devout, the comments by people who claim they have found peace ring true.

A final comment on the role of religion in ameliorating this loss of freedom is deserved. Our research indicates that religion plays a role in softening the pains of this loss, but perhaps not in the way that is thought of commonly. The imagery of jailhouse religion is a cynical one. It connotes a manipulation of prison authorities and parole authorities to achieve special consideration—fewer restrictions inside the facility and, eventually, early release entirely. The image is so common that we were surprised to hear so little confirmation of it in our interviews. Religiously active inmates flatly denied that they received special treatment by parole or prison authorities. Even the non-religious, who described prison religion as a game, were skeptical that it led to special favors in prison or (and perhaps especially) in parole. The most optimistic type of answer we got was a kind of halfhearted affirmation that it cannot hurt.

Nevertheless, our observation (in other settings) of parole hearings confirms that claims of prison conversion are exceedingly common. In addition, there was much talk about getting chaplains to write favorable letters to outside authorities, including parole boards, on behalf of the actively religious and to contact community members for promises of support upon release. Within the prison lore, there are references to former inmates returning as pastors.

Therefore, it is the case that some inmates believe their religious affiliation stands to help them achieve freedom, if for no other reason than for it helping them avoid troublemaking associations in the prison setting. Nobody seems to think that the religious route is an automatic doorway to the outside, and even the hopeful seem to entertain a feeble confidence in their chances. As an extrinsic drive, the desire for freedom is poorly served by religious practice. The more profound impact of religion on freedom appeared to exist for the intrinsically oriented religious prisoner. They internalize the loss of freedom, redefining it as not a place where a person lives but the point of view that a person takes while living there. This profound redefinition of freedom is consistent with the master message of religious doctrine, and its adoption allows the religious experience to be related to the most penetrating deprivation imposed by the prison sentence.

Extrinsic Orientations Although these intrinsic reasons for religious involvement are a predominant aspect of the talk about prison religion, especially among the actively religious, they are not the only motivations for religion in prison. The combination of the deprivations imposed by prison life and the negative culture imported into it make the environment of the prison a difficult setting in which to live. It is understandable that religious programs would be designed to ameliorate the environment. These extrinsic functions of prison religion are many and varied, depending on the inmate and the prison setting.

Safety

The most immediately observable difficulties presented by the prison environment are the most basic, including safety, material comforts, and heterosexual contact. These leap first to the mind of the observer because they are apparent from the moment that one enters a prison. Of these, safety is perhaps the least complex. It stands to reason that prisons would be places where concerns for safety are raised. The image of the prison as a kind of concentrated community of threatening men is widely shared.

There are ways in which this image is misleading. First, most prison officials give first-order importance to maintaining a safe prison, and the disciplines of the prison regime are largely designed with safety in mind. But more to the point is the prisoners themselves, for they have a substantial interest in creating environments where daily living is possible without constant fear. Often, inmate leaders will give importance to safe living in the prison. Moreover, even prisoners who are inclined toward violence are not always violent. As a result, although the prison is in fact a place where safety is a concern, popular images may overplay the constancy of the threat to the ordinary prisoner.

There are unusual prisoners for whom safety concerns may be heightened, especially the physically weak, effeminate, openly homosexual, or convicted sex offenders. Even in prisons with minimal problems of safety, inmates of these kinds can normally expect to be challenged and to have their security disturbed.

> The sex offenders show up in the Christian group so they won't get hurt. They need to get protected. A person with a nasty crime is accepted into the group. Whether you did the crime or not, they are going to protect you.

Below, we have more to say about the special inmates. Our point here is to underscore the complexity of prison safety threats, which exist for some inmates but do not necessarily exist for all. Thus, a mix of factors come together to determine the degree to which safety is a pressing concern for a given inmate in a particular institution. These factors include the mix of inmates incarcerated therein, the capability of authorities in promoting institutional safety, the physical plant of the prison, and the particular characteristics of the inmate in question.

Inmates report that religion can play a role in improving a prisoner's personal safety in a prison. The most direct way that this is accomplished is physical. The chapel is a safe haven, a place where an inmate can go where the safety threats of prison life are excluded. We found this to be the case in several prisons in our sample. The chapel was off-limits to the normal strains of prison life, and inmates could go there to get away from these strains. The inmate could also expect to encounter inmates in the chapel who were equally interested in avoiding such problems. "When I am talking about 'protection,' I am talking about it as protection against myself. I can protect myself from the things that I would do that would cause me to violate and get more time."

However, this was by no means always true. Indeed, in one prison, the chapel toilet had an inside bolt (for the privacy of occasional female visitors to services), and it had the reputation as frequently serving as a place for homosexual liaisons between inmates. Concerns about safety are mainly dealt with through group support provided by religious inmates for their compatriots. For example, if a religious participant is being threatened by another inmate, an inmate leader of his religious affiliate group might speak to the threatener to convince him to cease his aggression. We are told that such support can carry considerable authority so long as (a) the threatened inmate's religious involvement is generally perceived as sincere (a point we discuss in greater detail below), (b) the authority of the inmate intervening on his behalf is respected, and (c) the aggression was not a result of a failure to pay debts or some other legitimate prison economic transaction.

> Being a Muslim will benefit you spiritually, your soul, and then there are other aspects, like protection. Muslims are obligated to protect another Muslim if they aren't doing anything wrong. We don't support anything that is wrong. If the guy is weak, and we know that he is weak, we are obligated to protect him and help him grow spiritually, because we don't know what is in his heart.

When an inmate religious leader intervenes on behalf of a religious peer who is under threat, there does not need to be any physical threat in his manner. Because all mainstream religions in prison profess nonaggression as a part of their doctrine, it is important that the inmate leader be able to handle such threats without resorting to actual force. The mere fact that a respected inmate is standing up for a colleague can be enough support to defuse an aggressive threat. Of course, the religious leader who, by virtue of a personal intervention such as this, can guarantee others' safety from aggression stands to gain considerable respect in the general population.

> If you are not tough or a fag, you need a group. Everyone has to be a part of something. They get protection. The Islamics are good for protection. Islamic people will help one another. He will jump in and help you. It's their job.

It may also be that a formal intervention on behalf of a specific target is unneeded. Some religious groups might carry enough social credibility within the prison that mere association with them can serve to guarantee a suppression of aggression by nonparticipants. We heard prisoners and officials tell us that some sects of Islamic inmates held this degree of authority in the prison. In some prisons, mere association with an Islamic sect might be sufficient to promise a certain level of safety. In others, Islamic leaders could, by selecting their associates, allocate enhanced safety almost as if it were a good that is subject to the rules of barter. Certainly, we have heard accounts of the origins of the Muslim movement in prisons that centered on the participants' desire to increase their power and influence within the prison and in relation to the prison administrators.

Our interviews with inmates left us with the distinct impression that the Muslim movement in some American prisons was undergoing a shift in focus, away from internal institutional politics and toward devotional practice. Our sample is inadequate to allow us to say more than this speculation: The justification of Islamic faith lies less in safety/power concerns and more in the intrinsic value that inmates find in its doctrines and in its practice.

Finally, although the Muslim faith is best known for its relationship to safety concerns within the prison (perhaps because of its recent and unique history with American prisons), it is by no means the only example of this phenomenon. Every inmate religious group that we interviewed described as important the support that they got from their religious colleagues in dealing with the often hostile, nonreligious inmate population at large. In one Southwestern prison, the nondenominational, evangelical Christian group was widely perceived as a safe haven for sex offenders, and it was said that "all the guys in the church are snitches."

With a couple of exceptions, however, the prisons in our sample were reported by inmates to be comparatively safe environments. This meant that the description of the role of religion in promoting safety was often discussed in secondhand references to experiences in other facilities. The modal religious inmate in our sample feels limited personal threat, and although he is able to relate instances when being religious helped to increase someone's safety, these tend to not be personal stories.

Material Comforts

The role of religion in increasing access to material comforts is described consistently by the inmates in our sample, although there are particularities that vary across institutions. The need for material sustenance flows from the starkness of material comforts in the prison. Inmates are paid minuscule wages and provided with only the basics of daily living. To make life in prison approach tolerability, a prisoner must find a way to soften the impact of material deprivations. Often, what constitutes material comfort in the context of the prison can seem pathetic by free-world standards. However, when a prisoner has to pay 50 cents for potato chips and this constitutes 2 hours of pay, a free helping of cookies or a couple of soft drinks can be an important benefit of a program. "The big thing is that everyone knew that the father was bringing in cookies and cakes and doughnuts and so forth. So naturally, everyone wanted to come." In every prison in our sample, there were advantages in material sustenance for those who would participate in religious activities. In a couple of prisons, the chaplain would allow extra phone calls for the faithful. In others, he would provide extra postage for letters. Church services were often followed by informal gatherings, in which punch and various cookies and cakes would be served. Leftovers could be taken back to cells for later or to be sold or traded for other goods. Always, the willingness to attend a service enabled the inmate to leave the monotony of his cell or dorm.

Access to Outsiders

Participation in religious programs provided access to outsiders, particularly women. When we asked inmates to talk to us about the deprivations that they experienced in prison, contacts with "free worlders" were mentioned, and special emphasis was given to the opportunities to meet women provided by religious services. "Because a lot of women come from the outside. There are a couple of cuties coming in, the word gets around. They have been in jail, so they want to see the women." Because this issue was discussed so frequently by those whom we interviewed, it is worth elaborating on the point. All prisons allow volunteers to enter as a part of religious programming. In some prisons, volunteers are a key component of religious programming. Because volunteers are outsiders, free-world people, many inmates seek them out. Having an outsider to talk to can play an enormous role in reducing the excruciating sense of being forgotten by society. The interest of an outsider in his fate helps the inmate to take his own life more seriously. It is self-confirming to have a significant other, who is free to walk the streets, take a sincere interest in the prisoner's life behind bars.

When the outsider is a woman, the self-confirming nature of these contacts takes on a different meaning, for the inmate is able to experience a prison rarity—to meet a woman who is a stranger.

> Sometimes there will be some good-looking ladies [volunteers] in the chapel on a Sunday. Then you're likely to see this place filled, with all the guys coming here to stare and laugh and say rude stuff to each other.

The inmate who can meet women is thus able to defeat the walls in a way, for he can reclaim one of the amenities of life that he lost when he entered the prison, albeit the achievement is only partial and is distorted. Inmates often discussed this aspect by recalling unusual events that took on the importance of prison legends.

> I know one guy that went to a seminar, and there was a woman there and he ran this line . . . [and] convinced her that Jesus wanted them to get married, and they got married. All he really wanted was jelly beans [sex]. He told me so.

Access to outsiders can also lead to much more diabolical strategies to relieve the deprivations of prison life, for it avails the inmate with opportunities to exploit the outsider for personal gain. Stories of inmate exploitation of volunteers are infrequent, but it only takes a few such stories to create a legend within a facility. We heard accounts of inmates arranging for money to be deposited into their accounts by outsiders, bank credit scams orchestrated by inmates and unwittingly carried out by religion volunteers, and solicitations of legal aid. If an inmate can think of a way to take advantage of naive volunteers through confidence games, there will be an incentive for them to try it.

The most cynical con games involve romance. A woman volunteer who is single meets a fast-talking, convincing, remorseful inmate and falls in love. The resulting marriage makes her personal and financial resources available to the inmate and creates an automatic parole plan. Prison weddings are common. Although the jailhouse courtship is something of a penological cliché, one chaplain commented wryly, "There are more people out there trying to get in than there are people in here trying to get out."

None of this should be taken to suggest that the religious inmate's desire to interact with outsiders is wholly manipulative. The sincerely religious inmate seeks outside supports to help reinforce the changes that he is trying to solidify in his own life inside and to improve his chances of staying out after he is released. It would take a narrow view of the inmate's lot to think of these actions as purely orchestrated. In addition, it would be inexcusably cynical of us to think of prison romance as simply a maneuver on the inmate's part.

Our point is that, when the inmate enters the prison, his access to the outside world is strictly limited. The arrangements of religious programming represent an opening in the wall of isolation, and inmates who participate in religious activities can overcome, however slightly, the isolation of incarceration.

Inmate Relations

Religion can provide important social support within the prison society. Prisoners feel desires for social interaction that is not much different in substance from those that we all feel, such as companionship, friendship, and the intimacy of family. For example, the simple desire for suitable companionship can be very important. In prison, a person is often assigned to housing partners without much regard to their ability to get along well or to become friendly. Many inmates will look for opportunities to see homeboys—people from their neighborhood. The chapel can be that opportunity.

> I wanted to see a friend of mine that was in another unit. . . . It was the only place we could meet. A lot of people attend services just to get out of their . . . 6-by-9 cell. It's just an opportunity to get out of your cell and socialize with somebody else.

Patterns of social interaction are very important in the prison. An inmate is often known by his friends. However, in prison, friendships are not always simple relationships. Calling someone a friend implies that you will stand with someone in the face of trouble. It may entail being involved in their businesses within the prison, businesses that are more than likely illegal. In prison, friendship is not merely an emotional relationship, it is a reciprocal one involving trade-offs and obligations.

There are reasons why some prisoners may not want the traditional prison friendship, because it may carry with it commitments to share aspects of the prison environment that the inmate wishes to avoid. This may be particularly true for an inmate who is alarmed by the power machinations within the prison and wants to avoid them or for one who feels alienated from, or weary of, the street culture that defines much of prison life. "What these people need now is a friend, a confidant, someone to talk to . . . someone you can share your last candy bar with." Affiliations between religious inmates can provide an alternative to traditional inmate relationships, especially when the religious groups subscribe to a different standard of conduct. They see adherence to traditional prison cultural rules as contrary to their own interests or well beyond their own capacity. Associating with others who subscribe to religious values can help the inmate avoid the difficulties of traditional inmate life.

> It has helped me to change and to hang with people who don't get into nothing. . . . They don't fight, they don't steal. . . . If you are somewhere else [than the chapel], you are apt to be stealing, then you get into trouble, then you get more time. . . . There's all kinds of things going on in prison.

For other inmates, the religious groups are the only ones who will accept them due to their heinous—by prison standards—crimes or other personal background factors.

> Anybody with a sex beef [conviction] or child beef will find himself in Christian programs. Anybody who is looking for something in prison is one step away from protective custody. It's sad because that is what happens. Most cases, they are not sincere. They got to have some friend who is going to hang out with them, and only other Christians will do that.

The adaptation is somewhat different for different faith groups. Muslims can demonstrate the seriousness of their affiliation to the religious lifestyle by adherence to the laws, particularly through individual and group prayer. The discipline of daily devotions is not only a public symbol of obedience to Allah, it is also a personal reminder of the commitment to the requirements of the Qur'an. In one of our prisons, the sight of a half-dozen Black inmates walking down main street with their prayer blankets under one arm, strolling off to the morning's work, was an eloquent testimony to all who wished to see that these prisoners were, by self-determination, different from their peers.

For Christians, it is not so easy to be obviously different. Therefore they report that, in addition to talking the talk, they are under continual scrutiny by other inmates who would see if they also walk the walk, to see if they live by the different standards of the Christian religion. In particular, this means they feel that they are being watched by the nonbelievers to see if they eschew the normal conduct of the inmate lifestyle. Of course, regular chapel attendance is an option, but there are so many other reasons for attending the chapel that mere attendance is not enough of a walk. Faced with the routine challenges and temptations of the cell or dormitory, the Christian inmate is watched to see how serious he is about the faith that he professes. "Sincere people are judged harder. If you are with them, you are judged harder. . . . It's what has helped me to change [because] I got to do things right."

The social needs of religious inmates stem in part from this desire to be different from the remaining population. It is not easy to avoid getting caught up in the inmate code; it is more difficult to reject it outright. Inmates who embrace religion stand as a kind of a challenge to their peers, representing a symbolic argument that their way is better and more righteous. It is understandable that some inmates will resent the religious prisoner and that most will be suspicious. Their reaction commonly takes the form of a testing—baiting, provoking, taunting—which often has the quality of hostility. For support, religious inmates turn to each other.

Social support can have the flavor of a community within a community. In some of the prisons in our sample, gatherings of religious inmates were occasions in which discussions of the travails of their walk were openly encouraged, but whether this was a formal agenda or not, most discussion with religious inmates included a description of the ways in which they try to help each other keep their vows of faith and avoid the temptations of prison life within the code.

> In Islam, we don't separate the secular from the religious. In Islam, anything could be addressed. We open with a prayer; we close with a prayer. But we could talk about just about anything in between. That's how we help each other to see things, to understand about doing our time here.

In a way then, the religious inmate has social needs that are not materially different than anyone else's, but he seeks to meet them without the normal asset of traditional inmate collegiality. The other religious inmates make this possible by being available and supportive. This is one of the reasons that many religious inmates emphasize the importance of hanging together.

> The [religious] group makes me feel like a hypocrite when I don't keep staying with my religion. I know I hurt my family; I see so much of myself in everyone's testimonies. I do this [come to fellowship] in order to be around positive people and to strengthen my faith.

An affiliation with the religious has other benefits that accrue to inmates who are themselves not inclined to the devout lifestyle. These benefits stem from the fact that many religious groups will try to avoid conflicts with inmates and prison officials. Religious affiliation may attract inmates who want to avoid trouble and find ways to occupy prison time without the distractions of the game. By going to chapel at night, the inmate is avoiding the free time in the living area, where the inmate culture of the prison is likely to be the most intense and lead toward violations of prison rules of conduct. The exception to this pattern is the fringe religious group that is formed precisely to confront and challenge prison administration on the basis of the First Amendment right to religious practice. In our study, these groups were uncommon.

Inmates also described religious involvement as helpful in the maintenance of family ties. Quite understandably, the process of being convicted of a crime and sent to prison can easily make an offender's family lose faith in him. They can come to see him as an embarrassment or a failure. The conviction and imprisonment are a humiliation for the inmate, and the family may feel it as well.

When the inmate embraces religion while in prison, it is a public way of claiming to be a different person from the one who was sentenced to prison. This can give the family hope and can help them justify continuing their contact with the prisoner. In one of our prisons, family supports were openly integrated with the religious activity because family members were allowed to attend services together with the inmate on Sundays. They would be together for over an hour, holding hands, touching, singing, and crying. The chapel as a vehicle for reuniting with family has potential symbolic substance everywhere. Here the symbolism was transformed into instrumental practice.

Finally, we must point out that not all religious inmates appreciate the social utility of religious practice in prison. We heard consistent references to the existence of a small number of quietly devout prisoners who stay away from the prison religious programs. This was particularly true in one prison where the religious program was seen as taken over by snitches and sex offenders, turning the chapel into a safe haven. Their dominance of the religious functions in that facility repulsed other inmates and led them to avoid open involvement in religious programming. In other prisons, the reason for this phenomenon is less clear. Perhaps some are annoyed by the tendency of these programs to orient toward extrinsic religious concerns. Perhaps their religious views are inconsistent with the predominately fundamentalist twist of Christian sentiments in the prison or with the comparative orthodoxy of Muslim activity. Perhaps they view the religious practice in prison as being too deeply infected with the game, and they want to avoid hypocrisy. The fundamentalist quality of much prison religiousness may explain why there are some inmates who are widely thought to be devout but who stay away from institutional practice. Perhaps these inmates' religious tastes are not satisfied by the ritualistic fervor of most prison religious practice; perhaps it is difficult for them to rationalize their participation in light of their less dogmatic views of religion.

Summary and Discussion

A prisoner is a social outcast. It is hard to imagine a more direct interpretation of the fact of imprisonment—the offender has been banned from society. Legal philosophers tell us that shame is an express function of incarceration. The law violator has, by virtue of his misconduct, taken advantage of others, ignored their rights, and treated them as objects. This is conduct deserving of shame and humiliation, and the expressive function of the law is precisely to promote such moral regret on the part of the offender. The symbolic message of the prison term is that he is unworthy of normal life, and the principle of least eligibility is a tangible realization of the symbol of punishment. Even if they are not aware of it, most offenders who arrive in prison get it; they are being told that their lives lack social worth.

Prison is also experienced as a survival challenge. The first time a person enters, he encounters an alien society over which he has almost no say. The message is "Do what you can to survive this experience." There may be a feeling of shock or dread—or basic fear—that the newly admitted inmate feels upon finding himself facing a sentence of imprisonment. The new arrival will feel hard-pressed to make a livable place for himself in this seemingly hostile environment. Many will search for a niche in which the prison sentence can be best survived. It would be unfair to overstate the difficulties of the prison, for nearly all offenders who are sentenced there survive and leave. That does not mean that they leave unharmed or unaffected. Even the prisoners who skate through their time are likely to say that they do not want to return. Almost anyone who was ever locked up will be willing to tell about how the prison experience was oppressive. So every prisoner must face incarceration as a survival struggle, and for those not entering prison for the first time, it is a longer term struggle. They also face an additional fact; they know that merely coping with their sentence may not keep them from returning.

In light of the enduring equivocal nature of program effectiveness (of any kind), defense of expanded religious programming should not lose sight of these overarching points of preventing devaluation and promoting survival. It is in these respects that religious programs serve a more certain purpose. Our closing argument, then, is not unlike Rotman's (1990) reconceptualization of rehabilitation. Rotman claims that we should move beyond effectiveness justifications for rehabilitation and locate the need for rehabilitation in the inmate's right to not deteriorate. We are not blind to the fact that a philosophy that elevates offender welfare, but cannot guarantee society's welfare, is a hard sell in these punitive times. Nor are we blind to the fact that religious program advocates must emphasize reduced recidivism (or increased institutional order) (Johnson, 1984; O'Connor, Ryan, & Parikh, 1997a, 1997b) to justify and expand their presence. We only issue the reminder that, although the two are not unrelated, what qualifies as working in the spiritual realm is not precisely the same as what qualifies as working in the criminal justice realm.

References

Allport, G. W., (1960). *The individual and his religion: A psychological interpretation*. New York: Macmillan.

Ames, D. B., Gartner, J., & O'Connor, T. (1990, August). *Participation in a volunteer prison ministry program and recidivism*. Paper presented at the Meeting of the American Psychological Association, Boston.

Clear, T. R., Stout, B. D., Dammer, H. R., Kelly, L., Hardyman, P. L., & Shapiro, C. (1992). *Religion in prison: Final report*. Newark, NJ: School of Criminal Justice, Rutgers University.

Goffman, E. (1961). On the characteristics of total institutions: The inmate world. In D. R. Cressey (Ed.), *The prison: Studies in institutional organization change* (pp. 15–67). New York: Holt, Rinehart & Winston.

Ignatieff, M. (1978). *A just measure of pain: The penitentiary in the industrial revolution, 1750–1850*. London: Macmillan.

Irwin, J. (1970). *The felon*. Englewood Cliffs, NJ: Prentice Hall.

Irwin, J., & Cressey, D. R. (1962). Thieves, convicts, and the inmate culture. *Social Problems, 10*, 142–155.

Johnson, B. R. (1984). Religiosity and institutional deviance: The impact of religious variables upon inmate adjustment. *Criminal Justice Review, 3*, 21–30.

McKelvey, B. (1977). *American prisons: A history of good intentions*. Montclair, NJ: Patterson Smith.

O'Connor, T., Ryan, P., & Parikh, C. (1997a). *The impact of prison fellowship on inmate infractions at Lieber prison in South Carolina (evaluation)*. Silver Spring, MD: Center for Social Research.

O'Connor, T., Ryan, P., & Parikh, C. (1997b). *The impact of religious programs on inmate infractions at Lieber prison in South Carolina (evaluation)*. Silver Spring, MD: Center for Social Research.

Rotman, E. (1990). *Beyond punishment: A new view of the rehabilitation of offenders*. New York: Greenwood Press.

Sykes, G. (1958). *The society of captives*. Princeton, NJ: Princeton University Press.

Young, M., Gartner, J., O'Connor, T., Larson, D., & Wright, K. (1995). The impact of a volunteer prison ministry program on the long-term recidivism of federal inmates. *Journal of Offender Rehabilitation, 22*, 97–118.

JOURNAL OF CONTEMPORARY CRIMINAL JUSTICE, Vol. 16 No. 1, February 2000, 53–74.

21. A National Survey of Group Psychotherapy Services in Correctional Facilities

Robert D. Morgan
Carrie L. Winterowd
Sean W. Ferrell

Facilitating group psychotherapy in correctional settings presents dilemmas and concerns that are unmatched in other environments, often leaving clinicians grasping for therapeutic advantages. This article provides information regarding national practices of group psychotherapy services for male inmates in state correctional facilities (n = *79) as reported by correctional mental health providers* (n = *162).*

Group psychotherapy services are frequently recommended in managed care organizations and institutional settings (with the latter including jails and prisons). However, only three survey studies have been conducted on group work in penitentiaries in the last 40 years (Arnold & Stiles, 1972; McCorkle, 1953; McCorkle & Elias, 1960). The results of these early studies indicated that group methods were widely used in correctional treatment programs, including group psychotherapy services.

The goal of psychotherapy in penitentiaries is to modify inmates' attitudes and behaviors "so that their internal and external conflicts are resolved in constructive rather than antisocial ways" (Mathias & Sindberg, 1985, p. 265). Because of limited clinical personnel and the high inmate population, individual therapy has traditionally been less common in penitentiary settings, and group psychotherapy became the treatment of choice in the early 1960s (e.g., Corsini, 1964; Yong, 1971). Another important benefit is that group psychotherapy provides clients with an opportunity to experience therapeutic factors (e.g., group cohesiveness, universality, altruism, the development of socializing techniques) that are difficult to create in individual psychotherapy (Yalom, 1995). These therapeutic factors appear especially relevant for inmates who may have never experienced any of these factors before their incarceration. Group therapy also offers clients the opportunity to actively focus on interpersonal relationships in the here and now (Yalom, 1995) and helps inmates learn to develop functional peer relationships (Yong, 1971). In addition, the group support may aid inmates in coping with problems encountered in a penitentiary setting (Mathias & Sindberg, 1986).

Correctional Group Psychotherapy Services Survey

In the present study, we examined the use of group psychotherapy services offered by professionals in psychological (i.e., mental health) departments in correctional settings and described the types of group psychotherapy services offered in penitentiaries and correctional facilities. A five-page survey was developed to assess a wide range of areas related to group therapy programs in correctional facilities, including group facilitator demographies, group therapies offered, group therapy structure and procedures, group therapy goals, areas of discussion and progress in group work, perceived overall effectiveness of specific psychotherapy groups, professional identity issues, and level of administrative support for group programming. A cover letter explaining the purpose of this study and postage-paid, self-addressed envelopes were provided with each survey.

For this study, 113 state penitentiaries (correctional facilities) were randomly selected from the American Correctional Association's *Directory* (1995), which includes a listing of current institutions.

Of the 113 facilities randomly selected, personnel at 79 state correctional facilities verbally agreed to participate in this study. We sent 386 surveys to these 79 facilities. Respondents completed and returned 162 surveys (return rate of 42%).

On average, group therapists in correctional facilities spent about equal amounts of time in the provision of individual psychotherapy services (32% of their total work time) and group psychotherapy services (29% of their total work time), with an average of 6.5 years ($SD = 6.1$) of group psychotherapy experience. These participants reported that there were various types of professionals who facilitated psychotherapy groups at their institutions over the past year, including psychologists (71%), professional therapists/counselors (52%), addiction counselors (47%), social workers (44%), master's students in training (29%), psychiatrists (19%), other professionals (13%), nonprofessionals (12%), and doctoral students in training (11%). It is interesting to note that some therapists (20%) reported that no supervision of group work was offered. Of those group facilitators receiving supervision, the following modes of supervision were reported: (a) individual/one-on-one (62%), (b) group/team (55%), and/or discussions with cofacilitators (48%).

In general, professionals who provided group therapy services to male inmates in state correctional settings facilitated a variety of psychotherapy groups that were evaluated as fairly effective in achieving positive outcomes with male inmates. See Table 1 for the list of therapy groups reported in this study and questions related to the type of facilitation for each psychotherapy group (e.g., perceived effectiveness, use of pregroup screening interviews, type of facilitation).

Group therapists reported that on average 20% ($M = 19.73$, $SD = 22.36$) of their male inmate populations received group therapy. With regard to inmate selection for group psychotherapy services, participants reported that on average 46% of male inmates were selected on a volunteer basis, and the other 54% were selected by staff referral or were required (mandated) to participate. Of further interest, 24% of the participants reported that they did not conduct pregroup screening interviews. Those who conducted pregroup screening interviews indicated that they focused

TABLE 1 Types of Psychotherapy Groups Offered in State Correctional Settings With Male Inmates

Type of group	*Group therapists facilitating groups*		*Type of facilitation*				*Use of pregroup screening interviews*				*Level of structure*		*Composition of group membership*		*Perceived effectiveness of group*	
			Individual		*Cotherapy*		*Yes*		*No*							
	n	%	*n*	%	*n*	%	*n*	%	*n*	%	*M*	*SD*	*M*	*SD*	*M*	*SD*
Anger management group	95	59	67	71	25	26	56	59	36	38	5.15	1.55	6.08	1.60	5.10	1.17
Stress management group	74	46	48	65	21	28	38	51	33	45	4.97	1.62	6.07	1.73	5.31	1.07
Problem-solving group	68	42	43	63	22	32	36	53	30	44	4.91	1.76	6.22	1.77	4.99	1.28
Recidivism group	31	19	22	71	8	26	20	65	9	29	4.93	1.82	6.07	1.53	4.94	1.48
Institutional adjustment group	40	25	31	78	10	25	20	50	16	40	4.38	1.93	5.63	2.22	5.14	1.40
Men's issues group	37	23	24	65	12	32	17	46	19	51	4.34	1.89	5.44	2.20	5.50	1.19
General psychotherapy group	74	46	50	68	19	26	47	64	25	34	3.79	1.93	5.75	1.97	4.99	1.08
Sex offender group	41	25	16	39	25	61	36	88	4	10	5.44	1.24	3.49	2.40	5.43	1.24
Substance abuse group	20	12	12	60	8	40	12	60	6	30	5.58	1.22	5.50	2.37	5.70	0.98
Cognitive restructuring group	10	6	4	40	6	60	5	50	4	40	6.30	0.95	6.90	0.32	5.60	1.71
Other psychotherapy groups	57	35	39	68	17	30	34	60	22	39	4.93	1.70	5.72	2.23	5.72	2.23

Note. Likert-type scale ranges were as follows: level of structure ranged from 1 (*unstructured*) to 7 (*highly structured*); composition of group membership ranged from 1 (*homogeneous*) to 7 (*heterogeneous*); perceived effectiveness of group ranged from 1 (*not effective*) to 7 (*very effective*).

on establishing a therapeutic alliance with clients (38%), preparing inmates for group therapy (e.g., explanation of goals, process, expected behavior: 76%), assessing inmates' readiness (e.g., motivation, interest) for group participation (76%) and compatibility (e.g., personality style) with the group (46%), as well as gathering information from the potential group member (66%).

Participants were asked to identify (a) the important group goals with their male inmate group members, (b) the amount of time devoted to discussing or processing topics in group work, and (c) the level of progress made by male inmates in the psychotherapy groups they facilitated. Table 2 provides a complete listing of the mean and standard deviation scores for each of the 33 items on the three questions of interest.

With regard to group psychotherapy research, approximately 16% of the participants reported that their departments were conducting group therapy research, whereas 80% of participants reported no such research, activities in their departments. Finally, using a 7-point Likert-type scale ranging from 1 (*strongly disagree*) to 7 (*strongly agree*), group therapists reported that they felt fairly safe when facilitating group therapy (M = 5.73, SD = 1.48); however, they appeared neutral with regard to their perceptions of support from prison administration (M = 4.19, SD = 1.89), and on average, mildly disagreed with a statement that rehabilitation is an important goal of their institution (M = 3.64, SD = 1.87).

Implications and Applications

Psychologists who are employed in state correctional facilities will likely be working with a wide range of professionals in providing group psychotherapy services with male inmates. Given psychologists' advanced training, it would appear that psychologists in correctional settings, as in other mental health settings, are likely to become extensively involved in the administration and development of group psychotherapy services as well as the provision of supervision for other group psychotherapy providers. Nevertheless, given the plethora of mental health professions available to provide group psychotherapy services, (e.g., psychologists, counselors, social workers), it is important for psychologists to collaborate with other mental health professionals to ensure high-quality group psychotherapy services for male inmates.

One ethical dilemma that psychologists and other mental health professionals face when providing services to inmates is confidentiality (e.g., Brodsky, 1980; Clingempeel, Mulvey, & Reppucci, 1980). It is critical that psychologists discuss issues of confidentiality during the pregroup screening interview as well as in their group meetings. Inmate group members need to understand that confidentiality in groups is an important group norm; however, confidentiality cannot be guaranteed. No matter how hard group facilitators prepare inmates for group therapy, there is always the possibility that one or more group members may break confidence by disclosing details of group discussions or by identifying group members to other inmates or personnel who are not participating in these groups. In addition, there are issues unique to the prison environment that may

TABLE 2 Means and Standard Deviations for 33 Potential Areas of Progress, Topics for Group Discussion, and Group Goals in Psychotherapy Groups With Male Inmates in State Correctional Facilities

	Level of progress		*Focus of group discussion*		*Importance as a group goal*	
Item assessed	*M*	*SD*	*M*	*SD*	*M*	*SD*
Institutional adjustment	4.90	1.07	4.43	1.56	4.95	1.64
Preparing inmates for life outside of prison	4.60	1.36	4.95	1.54	5.82	1.38
Teaching social skills	4.59	1.38	4.62	1.57	5.22	1.54
Existential issues (e.g., coping with loss of freedom)	4.27	1.47	3.96	1.65	4.30	1.77
Teaching career planning	2.87	1.34	2.70	1.46	3.30	1.80
Improving relationships with inmates	4.92	1.27	4.59	1.41	4.96	1.48
Improving relationships with prison staff	4.83	1.23	4.54	1.41	5.01	1.52
Imitating new behaviors	4.82	1.24	4.89	1.56	5.53	1.42
Stress management	5.03	1.36	4.96	1.56	5.47	1.52
Insight/personal growth	4.96	1.35	5.23	1.42	5.71	1.44
Diet/nutrition and exercise	2.91	1.52	2.69	1.56	3.11	1.68
Mood adjustment	4.44	1.36	4.50	1.56	5.09	1.51
Developing more realistic thoughts/beliefs	5.22	1.28	5.62	1.24	6.18	1.00
Group cohesion	4.81	1.49	4.45	1.59	4.97	1.55
Conflict resolution	5.01	1.18	5.22	1.33	5.65	1.25
Working through substance abuse and/or dependency problems	4.09	1.78	4.16	2.03	4.97	2.04
Reducing addictive behaviors/relapse prevention	4.02	1.63	4.70	1.84	5.64	1.81
Impulse/anger control	4.91	1.27	5.45	1.42	6.10	1.05
Exploration of early childhood events/traumas and working through them	3.66	1.80	3.67	1.84	4.01	1.97
Assertiveness training	4.03	1.57	4.03	1.73	4.60	1.73
Self-esteem enhancement	4.63	1.58	4.63	1.75	5.24	1.67
Improving relationships with partners and family members	4.18	1.54	4.37	1.71	4.91	1.69
Catharsis (venting feelings)	4.55	1.71	4.45	1.70	4.67	1.84
Group members learn to help each other	4.76	1.47	4.73	1.53	5.30	1.41
Strategies to avoid reoffense cycle	4.69	1.55	5.35	1.47	5.98	1.23
Group members offering advice and suggestions to one another	5.16	1.48	4.86	1.61	5.30	1.44
Group members recognize similarities in each others' problems	5.29	1.36	5.02	1.40	5.39	1.32
Normalizing group members' problems	4.62	1.43	4.39	1.47	4.76	1.56
Complying with institution rules and regulations	4.67	1.56	4.63	1.64	5.14	1.61
Crisis intervention	4.37	1.54	4.19	1.66	4.50	1.81
The importance of relationships within the group	4.57	1.60	4.37	1.66	4.72	1.73
Developing leisure activities	3.30	1.54	3.31	1.70	3.66	1.78
Having hope/faith in group treatment	4.46	1.47	4.41	1.67	4.95	1.68

Note. Following are the questions that were asked regarding each item and the range of possible responses on a Likert-type scale. Level of progress: How much progress do you believe your group clients make in the following areas? (1 = *no progress or improvement*, 7 = *much progress or improvement*). Focus of group discussion: In general, how much time do you and/or your cofacilitators spend discussing or processing the following topics in group? (1 = *no time spent on topic*, 7 = *much time spent on topic*). Importance as a group goal: In considering the overall goals of your groups, how important are the following as group goals? (1 = *not at all important*, 7 = *very important*).

compromise the safety of individuals as well as the integrity of the institution. Group psychotherapists should be required to discuss these limits to confidentiality with their inmate clients before the initiation of group services. Examples of these limits to confidentiality include knowledge of escape plans, intentions to commit a crime in prison, introduction of illegal items (e.g., contraband) into prison, in addition to suicidal or homicidal ideation and intention, court subpoenas, and reports of child or elder abuse or neglect.

Furthermore, given the frequency with which nondoctoral-level practitioners facilitate group psychotherapy services and the less frequent use of cotherapy, it does not seem unreasonable to suggest that group therapists could benefit tremendously from receiving ongoing supervision or consultation regarding their group work. Interestingly, 20% of the group therapy participants reported that no supervision of group work was offered at their facilities. Although many seasoned clinicians and therapists at some point may not require individual or team supervision, group facilitators could benefit from discussing group content and process issues with their cotherapist as a peer supervisory option or from consulting with another professional in their facility as needed for feedback. Because there are more clients to attend to in group therapy as well as more dynamics to address, it seems that continued supervision of group work would be important in ensuring that group facilitators are providing the best services possible to their male inmate clients. Thus, doctoral-level psychologists may fulfill an important role by providing supervision to mental health professionals with less training or experience in group psychotherapy. Furthermore, the need for supervision offers a potential area of consultation for experienced psychologists not directly involved in the correctional system.

The emerging trend of hiring nondoctoral-level practitioners to provide direct client services is a particularly salient issue for psychologists. Several questions need addressing if this is becoming a de facto model. As mentioned earlier, psychologists typically have more extensive training and the skills to provide group psychotherapy services as well as supervision of group services offered by other mental health professionals. This leads to the following question: Is adequate quality assurance being provided? Second, what are the implications of such a model for doctoral-level psychologists? It is possible for psychologists to get squeezed out in favor of the lowest "bidder." If nondoctoral-level mental health professionals are willing to run groups at a lower cost to the institution, then many administrators may adopt such a model. This possibility again points to the need for psychologists to become proactive regarding their role in the correctional setting. In addition to providing group psychotherapy services, psychologists, with their specialized training, should assume a leading role as program developers and evaluators of services. Such a role would certainly add to the viability of psychologists in correctional settings.

As prison populations continue to rise, the correctional philosophy of punitive models versus a rehabilitative models remains an important political debate (e.g., Irwin, 1996). Therefore, given the current trend toward punitive systems (e.g., Haney & Zimbardo 1998), it is possible that psychologists and administrators in correctional settings have different ideologies or philosophies with regard to the purpose and utility of group psychotherapy services with inmates. Other studies have found that conflict frequently exists between administrative staff and correctional workers (e.g., Check & Miller, 1983; Pogrebin, 1980). Thus, it does not seem unreasonable to suggest that similar conflicts may exist between mental health professionals who are in the business of providing a service to help people and correctional administrative staff who are in the business of confining people (i.e., carrying out sentenced punishment) for the protection of society. Psychologists could address this issue in two ways. First, given psychologists' expertise in psychotherapy, they should use their communication skills to improve the relationship between correctional staff and mental health staff. All too often, psychologists (and other mental health professionals) find themselves feeling isolated and segregated from other correctional administrators and staff. Second, educating correctional staff about the benefits of group psychotherapy treatment with inmates might have a significant impact on administrators' understanding of the utility of such services in creating meaningful changes in inmates' behavior: psychologists could demonstrate that group psychotherapy is not simply an activity to keep inmates busy while they serve their time.

When facilitating group psychotherapy with male inmate populations, what are group therapists' overarching group goals and foci? Unfortunately, very little has been written regarding important group goals or topics for discussion or group process. The following items were commonly identified by group therapists as important group goals, topics for discussion, and areas of noted progress: they may provide direction for group therapists struggling with where to begin: learning to recognize the similarity of inmates' problems (universality), developing more realistic thoughts and beliefs, learning to offer advice and suggestions to others (altruism), learning stress management skills, developing insight and personal growth, learning impulse and anger control, and learning conflict resolution skills. Furthermore, preparing inmates for life outside of prison, learning strategies to avoid the reoffense cycle, and teaching inmates to imitate (practice) new behaviors in group were commonly identified as important group goals and important topics for discussion in group therapy. Finally, reducing addictive behaviors and relapse prevention was identified by group therapists as an important group goal. Thus, this survey provides new insight and increased practice direction for what correctional group psychotherapists perceive as important and effective group psychotherapy processes and outcome goals with male inmates.

With regard to type of treatment, Scott (1976) indicated that no one theoretical approach is most effective with inmate populations: however, group therapists viewed cognitive–behavioral strategies (e.g., helping inmates in developing realistic thoughts or beliefs) as highly important and effective with regard to group psychotherapy topical issues. That cognitive–behavioral theory was incorporated into the rehabilitation process was reassuring as, according to Gendreau (1996), it is imperative for effective correctional rehabilitation to occur. Although cognitive–behavioral theory is critical to the rehabilitation process for offenders (Gendreau, 1996) and is in fact being implemented in correctional psychology, there remains a lack of structured cognitive–behavioral treatment programs available for practitioners.

Although only 20% of male inmates in correctional settings participated in group psychotherapy programs, ideally such programs should be available to most inmates who seek them, because inmates may benefit from services that focus on helping them alter dysfunctional patterns. As Boudouris (1984) indicated, rehabilitation is a process that includes a variety of treatments: therefore, although not all psychotherapy groups are geared toward reducing recidivism rates, inmates' participation in a variety of group psychotherapy programs might increase the likelihood that they will cope better in society. Furthermore, group psychotherapy may be superior to individual psychotherapy in helping inmate clients prepare to relate to others in society. By learning to relate to their inmate peers as well as group facilitators, they have more opportunities to learn about their interpersonal world.

Contrary to previous theoretical conclusions that group psychotherapy is the treatment of choice in correctional settings given the number of inmates needing services and the economic constraints (e.g., Corsini, 1964; Wilson, 1990; Yong, 1971), mental health professionals tend to spend equal amounts of time in the provision of individual and group psychotherapy services. Given the obvious economic benefits and the lack of data to suggest that individual psychotherapy is superior to group psychotherapy services with male inmates, it appears that increased attention should be placed on group methods. Individual psychotherapy certainly holds its place in correctional psychology; but given the current growth in the prison population and resources of psychology departments, increasing the use of group psychotherapy may offer rehabilitation to more inmates than can be reached through individual psychotherapy. Therefore, increasing the use of group psychotherapy and evaluating the efficacy of such programs appears to be a necessity rather than an opportunity.

References

American Correctional Association. (1995). *Directory: Juvenile & adult correctional departments, institutions, agencies & paroling authorities.* Laurel, MD: Author.

Arnold, W. R., & Stiles, B. (1972). A summary of increasing use of "group methods" in correctional institutions. *International Journal of Group Psychotherapy, 22,* 77–92.

Belar, C. D. (1998). Graduate education in clinical psychology: "We're not in Kansas anymore." *American Psychologist, 53,* 456–464.

Boudouris, J. (1984). Recidivism as a process. *Journal of Offender Counseling, Services & Rehabilitation, 8,* 41–51.

Brock, T. C., Green, M. C., Reich, D. A., & Evans, L. M. (1996). The *Consumer Reports* study of psychotherapy: Invalid is invalid. *American Psychologist, 51,* 1083.

Brodsky, S. L. (1980). Ethical issues for psychologists in corrections. In J. Monahan (Ed.), *Who is the client?* (pp. 63–92). Washington, DC: American Psychological Association.

Cheek, F. E., & Miller, M. D. S. (1983). The experience of stress for correction officers: A double-blind theory of correctional stress. *Journal of Criminal Justice, 11*, 105–120.

Clingempeel, W. G., Mulvey, E., & Reppucci, N. D. (1980). A national study of ethical dilemmas of psychologists in the criminal justice system. In J. Monahan (Ed.). *Who is the client?* (pp. 126–153). Washington, DC: American Psychological Association.

Corsini, R. J. (1964). Group psychotherapy in correctional rehabilitation. *British Journal of Criminology, 4*, 272–274.

Gendreau, P. (1996). Offender rehabilitation: What we know and what needs to be done. *Criminal Justice and Behavior, 23*, 144–161.

Haney, C., & Zimbardo, P. (1998). The past and future of U.S. prison policy: Twenty-five years after the Stanford Prison Experiment. *American Psychologist, 53*, 709–727.

Hare, R. D. (1991). *The Hare Psychopathy Checklist—Revised*. Toronto: Multi-Health Systems.

Hollin, C. R. (1990). *Cognitive–behavioral interventions with young offenders*. Elmsford, NY: Pergamon.

Irwin, J. (1996). The march of folly. *The Prison Journal, 76*, 489–494.

Kotkin, M., Daviet, C., & Gurin, J. (1996). The Consumer Reports mental health survey. *American Psychologist, 51*, 1080–1081.

Mathias, R. E., & Sindberg, R. (1985). Psychotherapy in correctional settings. *International Journal of Offender Therapy and Comparative Criminology, 29*, 265–275.

Mathias, R. E., & Sindberg, R. M. (1986). Time limited group therapy in minimum security. *Journal of Offender Counseling, Services & Rehabilitation, 11*, 7–17.

McCorkle, L. W. (1953). The present status of group therapy in United States correctional institutions. *International Journal of Group Psychotherapy, 3*, 79–87.

McCorkle, L. W., & Elias, A. (1960). Group therapy in correctional institutions. *Federal Probation, 24*, 57–63.

Meloy, J. R. (1988). *The psychopathic mind: Origins, dynamics, and treatment.* Northvale, NJ: Jason Aronson.

Murray, B. (1998, January). PhDs apply talents to emerging careers. *APA Monitor*, pp. 1–28.

Pogrebin, M. (1980). Challenge to authority for correctional officers. *Journal of Offender Counseling, Services & Rehabilitation, 4*, 337–342.

Rappaport, R. G. (1982). Group therapy in prison. In M. Seligman (Ed.). *Group psychotherapy and counseling with special populations* (pp. 215–227). Baltimore: University Park Press.

Scott, E. M. (1976). Group therapy with convicts on work release in Oregon. *International Journal of Offender Therapy and Comparative Criminology, 20,* 225–235.

Wilson, G. I. (1990). Psychotherapy with depressed incarcerated felons: A comparative evaluation of treatments. *Psychological Reports, 67,* 1027–1041.

Yalom, I. D. (1995). *The theory and practice of group psychotherapy* (4th ed.). New York: Basic Books.

Yochelson, S., & Samenow, S. E. (1976). *The criminal personality: Vol. 1. A profile for change.* Northvale, NJ: Jason Aronson.

Yong, J. N. (1971). Advantages of group therapy in relation to individual therapy for juvenile delinquents. *Corrective Psychiatry and Journal of Social Therapy, 19,* 34–39.

22. Beyond Correctional Quackery—Professionalism and the Possibility of Effective Treatment

Edward J. Latessa
Francis T. Cullen
Paul Gendreau

Long-time viewers of *Saturday Night Live* will vividly recall Steve Martin's hilarious portrayal of a medieval medical practitioner—the English barber, Theodoric of York. When ill patients are brought before him, he prescribes ludicrous "cures," such as repeated bloodletting, the application of leeches and boar's vomit, gory amputations, and burying people up to their necks in a marsh. At a point in the skit when a patient dies and Theodoric is accused of "not knowing what he is doing," Martin stops, apparently struck by the transforming insight that medicine might abandon harmful interventions rooted in ignorant customs and follow a more enlightened path. "Perhaps," he says, "I've been wrong to blindly follow the medical traditions and superstitions of past centuries." He then proceeds to wonder whether he should "test these assumptions analytically through experimentation and the scientific method." And perhaps, he says, the scientific method might be applied to other fields of learning. He might even be able to "lead the way to a new age—an age of rebirth, a renaissance." He then pauses and gives the much-awaited and amusing punchline, "Nawwwwwww!"

The humor, of course, lies in the juxtaposition and final embrace of blatant quackery with the possibility and rejection of a more modern, scientific, and ultimately effective approach to medicine. For those of us who make a living commenting on or doing corrections, however, we must consider whether, in a sense, the joke is on us. We can readily see the humor in Steve Martin's skit and wonder how those in medieval societies "could have been so stupid." But even a cursory survey of *current* correctional practices yields the disquieting conclusion that we are a field in which quackery is tolerated, if not implicitly celebrated. It is not clear whether most of us have ever had that reflective moment in which we question whether, "just maybe," there might be a more enlightened path to pursue. If we have paused to envision a different way of doing things, it is apparent that our reaction, after a moment's contemplation, too often has been, "Nawwwwwwww!"

This appraisal might seem overly harsh, but we are persuaded that it is truthful. When intervening in the lives of offenders—that is, intervening with the expressed intention of reducing recidivism—corrections has resisted becoming a true "profession." Too often, being a "professional" has been debased to mean dressing in a presentable way, having experience in the field, and showing up every day for work. But a profession is defined not by its surface appearance but by its intellectual core. An occupation may lay claim to being a "profession" only to the extent that its practices are based on research knowledge, training, and expertise—a triumvirate that promotes the possibility that what it does can be effective (Cullen, 1978; Starr, 1982). Thus, medicine's professionalization cannot be separated from its embrace of scientific knowledge as the ideal arbiter of how patients should be treated (Starr, 1982). The very concept of "malpractice" connotes that standards of service delivery have been established, are universally transmitted, and are capable of distinguishing acceptable from unacceptable interventions. The concept of liability for "correctional malpractice" would bring snickers from the crowd—a case where humor unintentionally offers a damning indictment of the field's standards of care.

In contrast to professionalism, *quackery* is dismissive of scientific knowledge, training, and expertise. Its posture is strikingly overconfident, if not arrogant. It embraces the notion that interventions are best rooted in "common sense," in personal experiences for clinical knowledge, in tradition, and in superstition (Gendreau, Goggin, Cullen, and Paparozzi, forthcoming). "What works" is thus held to be "obvious," derived only from years of an individual's experience, and legitimized by an appeal to custom ("the way we have always done things around here has worked just fine"). It celebrates being anti-intellectual. There is never a need to visit a library or consult a study.

Correctional quackery, therefore, is the use of treatment interventions that are based on neither 1) existing knowledge of the causes of crime nor 2) existing knowledge of what programs have been shown to change offender behavior (Cullen and Gendreau, 2000; Gendreau, 2000). The hallmark of correctional quackery is thus ignorance. Such ignorance about crime and its cures at times is "understandable"—that is, linked not to the willful rejection of research but to being in a field in which professionalism is not expected or supported. At other times, however, quackery is proudly displayed, as its advocates boldly proclaim that they have nothing to learn from research conducted by academics "who have never worked with a criminal" (a claim that is partially true but ultimately beside the point and a rationalization for continued ignorance).

Need we now point out the numerous programs that have been implemented with much fanfare and with amazing promises of success, only later to turn out to have "no effect" on reoffending? "Boot camps," of course, are just one recent and salient example. Based on a vague, if not unstated, theory of crime and an absurd theory of behavioral change ("offenders need to be broken down"—through a good deal of humiliation and threats—and then "built back up"), boot camps could not possibly have "worked." In fact, we know of no major psychological theory that would logically suggest that such humiliation or threats are components of effective therapeutic interventions (Gendreau et al., forthcoming). Even so, boot camps were put into place across the nation without a shred of empirical evidence as to their effectiveness, and only now has their appeal been tarnished after years of negative evaluation studies (Cullen, Pratt, Miceli, and

Moon, 2002; Cullen, Wright, and Applegate, 1996; Gendreau, Goggin, Cullen, and Andrews, 2000; MacKenzie, Wilson, and Kider, 2001). How many millions of dollars have been squandered? How many opportunities to rehabilitate offenders have been forfeited? How many citizens have been needlessly victimized by boot camp graduates? What has been the cost to society of this quackery?

We are not alone in suggesting that advances in our field will be contingent on the conscious rejection of quackery in favor of an *evidence-based corrections* (Cullen and Gendreau, 2000; MacKenzie, 2000; Welsh and Farrington, 2001). Moving beyond correctional quackery when intervening with offenders, however, will be a daunting challenge. It will involve overcoming four central failures now commonplace in correctional treatment. We review these four sources of correctional quackery not simply to show what is lacking in the field but also in hopes of illuminating what a truly professional approach to corrections must strive to entail.

Four Sources of Correctional Quackery

Failure to Use Research in Designing Programs

Every correctional agency must decide "what to do" with the offenders under its supervision, including selecting which "programs" or "interventions" their charges will be subjected to. But how is this choice made (a choice that is consequential to the offender, the agency, and the community)? Often, no real choice is made, because agencies simply continue with the practices that have been inherited from previous administrations. Other times, programs are added incrementally, such as when concern rises about drug use or drunk driving. And still other times—such as when punishment-oriented intermediate sanctions were the fad from the mid-1980s to the mid-1990s—jurisdictions copy the much-publicized interventions being implemented elsewhere in the state and in the nation.

Notice, however, what is missing in this account: The failure to consider the existing research on program effectiveness. The risk of quackery rises to the level of virtual certainty when nobody in the agency asks, "Is there any evidence supporting what we are intending to do?" The irrationality of not consulting the existing research is seen when we consider again, medicine. Imagine if local physicians and hospitals made no effort to consult "what works" and simply prescribed pharmaceuticals and conducted surgeries based on custom or the latest fad. Such malpractice would be greeted with public condemnation, lawsuits, and a loss of legitimacy by the field of medicine.

It is fair to ask whether research can, in fact, direct us to more effective correctional interventions. Two decades ago, our knowledge was much less developed. But the science of crime and treatment has made important strides in the intervening years. In particular, research has illuminated three bodies of knowledge that are integral to designing effective interventions.

First, we have made increasing strides in determining the *empirically established* or *known predictors* of offender recidivism (Andrews and Bonta, 1998; Gendreau, Little, and Goggin, 1996; Henggeler, Mihalic, Rone, Thomas, and Timmons-Mitchell,

1998). These include, most importantly: 1) antisocial values, 2) antisocial peers, 3) poor self-control, self-management, and prosocial problem-solving skills, 4) family dysfunction, and 5) past criminality. This information is critical, because interventions that ignore these factors are doomed to fail. Phrased alternatively, successful programs start by recognizing what causes crime and then *specifically design the intervention to target these factors for change* (Alexander, Pugh, and Parsons, 1998; Andrews and Bonta, 1998; Cullen and Gendreau, 2000; Henggeler et al., 1998).

Consider, however, the kinds of "theories" about the causes of crime that underlie many correctional interventions. In many cases, simple ignorance prevails; those working in correctional agencies cannot explain what crime-producing factors the program is allegedly targeting for change. Still worse, many programs have literally invented seemingly ludicrous theories of crime that are put forward with a straight face. From our collective experiences, we have listed in Table 1 crime theories that either 1) were implicit in programs we observed or 2) were voiced by agency personnel when asked what crime-causing factors their programs were targeting. These "theories" would be amusing except that they are commonplace and, again, potentially lead to correctional quackery. For example, the theory of "offenders (males) need to get in touch with their feminine side" prompted one agency to have offenders dress in female clothes. We cannot resist the temptation to note that you will now know whom to blame if you are

TABLE 1 Questionable Theories of Crime We Have Encountered in Agency Programs

- ✓ "Been there, done that" theory.
- ✓ "Offenders lack creativity" theory.
- ✓ "Offenders need to get back to nature" theory.
- ✓ "It worked for me" theory.
- ✓ "Offenders lack discipline" theory.
- ✓ "Offenders lack organizational skills" theory.
- ✓ "Offenders have low self-esteem" theory.
- ✓ "We just want them to be happy" theory.
- ✓ The "treat offenders as babies and dress them in diapers" theory.
- ✓ "Offenders need to have a pet in prison" theory.
- ✓ "Offenders need acupuncture" theory.
- ✓ "Offenders need to have healing lodges" theory.
- ✓ "Offenders need drama therapy" theory.
- ✓ "Offenders need a better diet and haircut" theory.
- ✓ "Offenders (females) need to learn how to put on makeup and dress better" theory.
- ✓ "Offenders (males) need to get in touch with their feminine side" theory.

mugged by a cross-dresser! But, in the end, this is no laughing matter. This intervention has no chance to be effective, and thus an important chance was forfeited to improve offenders' lives and to protect public safety.

Second, there is now a growing literature that outlines what does *not* work in offender treatment (see, e.g., Cullen, 2002; Cullen and Gendreau, 2000; Cullen et al., 2002; Cullen et al., 1996; Gendreau, 1996; Gendreau et al., 2000; Lipsey and Wilson, 1998; MacKenzie, 2000). These include boot camps, punishment-oriented programs (e.g., "scared straight" programs), control-oriented programs (e.g., intensive supervision programs), wilderness programs, psychological interventions that are non-directive or insight-oriented (e.g., psychoanalytic), and non-intervention (as suggested by labeling theory). Ineffective programs also target for treatment low-risk offenders and target for change weak predictors of criminal behavior (e.g., self-esteem). Given this knowledge, it would be a form of quackery to continue to use or to freshly implement these types of interventions.

Third, conversely, there is now a growing literature that outlines what *does* work in offender treatment (Cullen, 2002; Cullen and Gendreau, 2000). Most importantly, efforts are being made to develop principles of effective intervention (Andrews, 1995; Andrews and Bonta, 1998; Gendreau, 1996). These principles are listed in Table 2. Programs that adhere to these principles have been found to achieve meaningful reductions in recidivism (Andrews, Dowden, and Gendreau, 1999; Andrews, Zinger, Hoge, Bonta, Gendreau, and Cullen, 1990; Cullen, 2002). However, programs that are designed without consulting these principles are almost certain to have little or no impact on offender recidivism and may even risk increasing reoffending. That is, if these principles are ignored, quackery is likely to result. We will return to this issue below.

TABLE 2 Eight Principles of Effective Correctional Intervention

1. Organizational Culture

Effective organizations have well-defined goals, ethical principles, and a history of efficiently responding to issues that have an impact on the treatment facilities. Staff cohesion, support for service training, self-evaluation, and use of outside resources also characterize the organization.

2. Program Implementation/Maintenance

Programs are based on empirically-defined needs and are consistent with the organization's values. The program is fiscally responsible and congruent with stakeholders' values. Effective programs also are based on thorough reviews of the literature (i.e., meta-analyses), undergo pilot trials, and maintain the staff's professional credentials.

3. Management/Staff Characteristics

The program director and treatment staff are professionally trained and have previous experience working in offender treatment programs. Staff selection is based on their holding beliefs supportive of rehabilitation and relationship styles and therapeutic skill factors typical of effective therapies.

4. Client Risk/Need Practices

Offender risk is assessed by psychometric instruments of proven predictive validity. The risk instrument consists of a wide range of dynamic risk factors or criminogenic needs (e.g., anti-social attitudes and values). The assessment also takes into account the responsivity of offenders to different styles and modes of service. Changes in risk level over time (e.g., 3 to 6 months) are routinely assessed in order to measure intermediate changes in risk/need levels that may occur as a result of planned interventions.

5. Program Characteristics

The program targets for change a wide variety of criminogenic needs (factors that predict recidivism), using empirically valid behavioral/social learning/cognitive behavioral therapies that are directed to higher-risk offenders. The ratio of rewards to punishers is at least 4:1. Relapse prevention strategies are available once offenders complete the formal treatment phase.

6. Core Correctional Practice

Program therapists engage in the following therapeutic practices: anti-criminal modeling, effective reinforcement and disapproval, problem-solving techniques, structured learning procedures for skill-building, effective use of authority, cognitive self-change, relationship practices, and motivational interviewing.

7. Inter-Agency Communication

The agency aggressively makes referrals and advocates for its offenders in order that they receive high quality services in the community.

8. Evaluation

The agency routinely conducts program audits, consumer satisfaction surveys, process evaluations of changes in criminogenic need, and follow-ups of recidivism rates. The effectiveness of the program is evaluated by comparing the respective recidivism rates of risk-control comparison groups of other treatments or those of a minimal treatment group.

Note: Items adapted from the *Correctional Program Assessment Inventory—2000*, a 131-item Questionnaire that is widely used in assessing the quality of correctional treatment programs (Gendreau and Andrews, 2001).

Failure to Follow Appropriate Assessment and Classification Practices

The steady flow of offenders into correctional agencies not only strains resources but also creates a continuing need to allocate treatment resources efficaciously. This problem is not dissimilar to a hospital that must process a steady flow of patients. In a hospital (or doctor's office), however, it is immediately recognized that the crucial first step to delivering effective treatment is diagnosing or *assessing* the patient's condition and its severity. In the absence of such a diagnosis—which might involve the careful study of symptoms or a battery of tests—the treatment prescribed would have no clear foundation. Medicine would be a lottery in which the ill would hope the doctor assigned the right treatment. In a similar way, effective treatment intervention requires the appropriate assessment of both the risks posed by, and the needs underlying the criminality of, offenders. When such diagnosis is absent and no classification of offenders is possible, offenders in effect enter a treatment lottery in which their access to effective intervention is a chancy proposition.

Strides have been made to develop more effective classification instruments—such as the Level of Supervision Inventory (LSI) (Bonta, 1996), which, among its competitors, has achieved the highest predictive validity with recidivism (Gendreau et al., 1996). The LSI and similar instruments classify offenders by using a combination of "static" factors (such as criminal history) and "dynamic factors" (such as antisocial values, peer associations) shown by previous research to predict recidivism. In this way, it is possible to classify offenders by their level of risk and to discern the types and amount of "criminogenic needs" they possess that should be targeted for change in their correctional treatment.

At present, however, there are three problems with offender assessment and classification by correctional agencies (Gendreau and Goggin, 1997). First, many agencies simply do not assess offenders, with many claiming they do not have the time. Second, when agencies do assess, they assess poorly. Thus, they often use outdated, poorly designed, and/or empirically unvalidated classification instruments. In particular, they tend to rely on instruments that measure exclusively static predictors of recidivism (which cannot, by definition, be changed) and that provide no information on the criminogenic needs that offenders have. If these "needs" are not identified and addressed—such as possessing antisocial values—the prospects for recidivism will be high. For example, a study of 240 (161 adult and 79 juvenile) programs assessed across 30 states found that 64 percent of the programs did not utilize a standardized and objective assessment tool that could distinguish risk/needs levels for offenders (Matthews, Hubbard, and Latessa, 2001; Latessa, 2002).

Third, even when offenders are assessed using appropriate classification instruments, agencies frequently ignore the information. It is not uncommon, for example, for offenders to be assessed and then for everyone to be given the same treatment. In this instance, assessment becomes an organizational routine in which paperwork is compiled but the information is ignored.

Again, these practices increase the likelihood that offenders will experience correctional quackery. In a way, treatment is delivered blindly, with agency personnel equipped with little knowledge about the risks and needs of the offenders under their supervision. In these circumstances, it is impossible to know which offenders should receive which interventions. Any hopes of individualizing interventions effectively also are forfeited, because the appropriate diagnosis either is unavailable or hidden in the agency's unused files.

Failure to Use Effective Treatment Models

Once offenders are assessed, the next step is to select an appropriate treatment model. As we have suggested, the challenge is to consult the empirical literature on "what works," and to do so with an eye toward programs that conform to the principles of effective intervention. At this stage, it is inexcusable either to ignore this research or to implement programs that have been shown to be ineffective. Yet, as we have argued, the neglect of the existing research on effective treatment models is widespread. In the study of 240 programs noted above, it was reported that two-thirds of adult programs and over half of juvenile programs did not use a treatment model that research had shown to be effective (Matthews et al., 2001; Latessa, 2002). Another study—a meta-analysis of 230 program evaluations (which yielded 374 tests or effect sizes)—categorized the extent to which interventions conformed to the principles of effective intervention. In only 13 percent of the tests were the interventions judged to fall into the "most appropriate" category (Andrews et al., 1999). But this failure to employ an appropriate treatment approach does not have to be the case. Why would an agency—in this information age—risk quackery when the possibility of using an evidence-based program exists? Why not select effective treatment models?

Moving in this direction is perhaps mostly a matter of a change of consciousness—that is, an awareness by agency personnel that quackery must be rejected and programs with a track record of demonstrated success embraced. Fortunately, depending on the offender population, there is a growing number of treatment models that might be learned and implemented (Cullen and Applegate, 1997). Some of the more prominent models in this regard are the "Functional Family Therapy" model that promotes family cohesion and affection (Alexander et al., 1998; Gordon, Graves, and Arbuthnot, 1995), the teaching youths to think and react responsibly peer-helping ("Equip") program (Gibbs, Potter, and Goldstein, 1995), the "Prepare Curriculum" program (Goldstein, 1999), "Multisystemic Therapy" (Henggeler et al., 1998), and the prison-based "Rideau Integrated Service Delivery Model" that targets criminal thinking, anger, and substance abuse (see Gendreau, Smith, and Goggin, 2001).

Failure to Evaluate What We Do

Quackery has long prevailed in corrections because agencies have traditionally required no systematic evaluation of the effectiveness of their programs (Gendreau, Goggin, and Smith, 2001). Let us admit that many agencies may not have the human or financial capital to conduct ongoing evaluations. Nonetheless, it is not clear that the failure to evaluate has been due to a lack of capacity as much as to a lack of desire. The risk inherent in evaluation, of course, is that practices that are now unquestioned and convenient may be revealed as ineffective. Evaluation, that is, creates accountability and the commitment threat of having to change what is now being done. The cost of change is not to be discounted, but so too is the "high cost of ignoring success" (Van Voorhis, 1987). In the end, a professional must be committed to doing not simply what is in one's self-interest but what is ethical and effective. To scuttle attempts at program evaluation and to persist in using failed interventions is wrong and a key ingredient to continued correctional quackery (more broadly, see Van Voorhis, Cullen, and Applegate, 1995).

Evaluation, moreover, is not an all-or-nothing procedure. Ideally, agencies would conduct experimental studies in which offenders were randomly assigned to a treatment or control group and outcomes, such as recidivism, were measured over a lengthy period of time. But let us assume that, in many settings, conducting this kind of sophisticated evaluation is not feasible. It is possible, however, for virtually all agencies to monitor, to a greater or lesser extent, the *quality* of the programs that they or outside vendors are supplying. Such evaluative monitoring would involve, for example, assessing whether treatment services are being delivered as designed, supervising and giving constructive feedback to treatment staff, and studying whether offenders in the program are making progress on targeted criminogenic factors (e.g., changing antisocial attitudes, manifesting more prosocial behavior). In too many cases, offenders are "dropped off" in intervention programs and then, eight or twelve weeks later, are deemed—without any basis for this conclusion—to have "received treatment." Imagine if medical patients entered and exited hospitals with no one monitoring their treatment or physical recovery. Again, we know what we could call such practices.

Conclusion—Becoming an Evidence-Based Profession

In assigning the label "quackery" to much of what is now being done in corrections, we run the risk of seeming, if not being, preachy and pretentious. This is not our intent. If anything, we mean to be provocative—not for the sake of causing a stir, but for the purpose of prompting correctional leaders and professionals to stop using treatments that cannot possibly be effective. If we make readers think seriously about how to avoid selecting, designing, and using failed correctional interventions, our efforts will have been worthwhile.

We would be remiss, however, if we did not confess that academic criminologists share the blame for the continued use of ineffective programs. For much of the past quarter century, most academic criminologists have abandoned correctional practitioners. Although some notable exceptions exist, we have spent much of our time claiming that "nothing works" in offender rehabilitation and have not created partnerships with those in corrections so as to build knowledge on "what works" to change offenders (Cullen and Gendreau, 2001). Frequently, what guidance criminologists have offered correctional agencies has constituted *bad* advice—ideologically inspired, not rooted in the research, and likely to foster quackery. Fortunately, there is a growing movement among criminologists to do our part both in discerning the principles of effective intervention and in deciphering what interventions have empirical support (Cullen and Gendreau, 2001; MacKenzie, 2000; Welsh and Farrington, 2001). Accordingly, the field of corrections has more information available to find out what our "best bets" are when intervening with offenders (Rhine, 1998).

We must also admit that our use of medicine as a comparison to corrections has been overly simplistic. We stand firmly behind the central message conveyed—that what is done in corrections would be grounds for malpractice in medicine—but we have glossed over the challenges that the field of medicine faces in its attempt to provide scientifically-based interventions. First, scientific knowledge is not static but evolving. Medical treatments that appear to work now may, after years of study, prove ineffective or less effective than alternative interventions. Second, even when information is available, it is not clear that it is effectively transmitted or that doctors, who may believe in their personal "clinical experience," will be open to revising their treatment strategies (Hunt, 1997). "The gap between research and knowledge," notes Millenson (1997, p. 4), "has real consequences . . . when family practitioners in Washington State were queried about treating a simple urinary tract infection in women, eighty-two physicians came up with an extraordinary 137 different strategies." In response to situations like these, there is a renewed evidence-based movement in medicine to improve the quality of medical treatments (Millenson, 1997; Timmermans and Angell, 2001).

Were corrections to reject quackery in favor of an evidence-based approach, it is likely that agencies would face the same difficulties that medicine encounters in trying base treatments on the best scientific knowledge available. Designing and implementing an effective program is more complicated, we realize, than simply visiting a library in search of research on program effectiveness (although this is often an important first step). Information must be available in a form that can be used by agencies. As in medicine, there must be opportunities for training and the provision of manuals that can be consulted in how *specifically* to carry out an intervention. Much attention has to be paid to implementing programs as they are designed. And, in the long run, an effort must be made to support widespread program evaluation and to use the resulting data both to improve individual programs and to expand our knowledge base on effective programs generally.

To move beyond quackery and accomplish these goals, the field of corrections will have to take seriously what it means to be a *profession*. In this context, individual agencies and individuals within agencies would do well to strive to achieve what Gendreau et al. (forthcoming) refer to as the "3 C's" of effective correctional policies: First, employ *credentialed people*, second, ensure that the *agency is credentialed* in that it is founded on the principles of fairness and the improvement of lives through ethically defensive means; and third, base treatment decisions on *credentialed knowledge* (e.g., research from meta-analyses).

By themselves, however, given individuals and agencies can do only so much to implement effective interventions—although each small step away from quackery and toward an evidence-based practice potentially makes a meaningful difference. The broader issue is whether the *field* of corrections will embrace the principles that all interventions should be based on the best research evidence, that all practitioners must be sufficiently trained so as to develop expertise in how to achieve offender change, and that an ethical corrections cannot tolerate treatments known to be foolish, if not harmful. In the end, correctional quackery is not an inevitable state of affairs—something we are saddled with for the foreseeable future. Rather, although a formidable foe, it is ultimately rooted in our collective decision to tolerate ignorance and failure. Choosing a different future for corrections—making the field a true profession—will be a daunting challenge, but it is a future that lies within our power to achieve.

References

Alexander, James, Christie Pugh, and Bruce Parsons, 1998. *Functional Family Therapy: Book Three in the Blueprints and Violence Prevention Series*. Boulder, CO: Center for the Study and Prevention of Violence, University of Colorado.

Andrews, D. A. 1995. "The Psychology of Criminal Conduct and Effective Treatment." Pp. 35–62 in James McGuire (ed.), *What Works: Reducing Reoffending*. West Sussex, UK: John Wiley.

Andrews, D. A., and James Bonta, 1998. *Psychology of Criminal Conduct*, 2nd ed. Cincinnati: Anderson.

Andrews, D. A., Craig Dowden, and Paul Gendreau, 1999. "Clinically Relevant and Psychologically Informed Approaches to Reduced Re-Offending: A Meta-Analytic Study of Human Service, Risk, Need, Responsivity, and Other Concerns in Justice Contexts." Unpublished manuscript, Carleton University.

Andrews, D. A., Ivan Zinger, R. D. Hoge, James Bonta, Paul Gendreau, and Francis T. Cullen, 1990. "Does Correctional Treatment Work? A Clinically Relevant and Psychologically Informed Meta-Analysis." *Criminology* 28:369–404.

Bonta, James, 1996. "Risk-Needs Assessment and Treatment." Pp. 18–32 in Alan T. Harland (ed.), *Choosing Correctional Options That Work: Defining the Demand and Evaluating the Supply*. Thousand Oaks, CA: Sage.

Cullen, Francis T. 2002. "Rehabilitation and Treatment Programs." pp. 253–289 in James Q. Wilson and Joan Petersilia (eds.), *Crime: Public Policies for Crime Control*. Oakland, CA: ICS Press.

Cullen, Francis T. and Brandon K. Applegate, eds. 1997. *Offender Rehabilitation: Effective Correctional Intervention*. Aldershot, UK: Ashgate/Dartmouth.

Cullen, Francis T. and Paul Gendreau, 2000. "Assessing Correctional Rehabilitation: Policy, Practice, and Prospects." Pp. 109–175 in Julie Horney (ed.), *Criminal Justice 2000: Volume 3—Policies, Processes, and Decisions of the Criminal Justice System*. Washington, DC: U.S. Department of Justice, National Institute of Justice.

Cullen, Francis T. and Paul Gendreau, 2001. "From Nothing Works to What Works: Changing Professional Ideology in the 21st Century." *The Prison Journal* 81:313–338.

Cullen, Francis T., Travis C. Pratt, Sharon Levrant Miceli, and Melissa M. Moon, 2002. "Dangerous Liaison? Rational Choice Theory as the Basis for Correctional Intervention." P. 279–296 in Alex R. Piquero and Stephen G. Tibbetts (eds.), *Rational Choice and Criminal Behavior: Recent Research and Future Challenges*. New York: Routledge.

Cullen, Francis T., John Paul Wright, and Brandon K. Applegate. 1996. "Control in the Community: The Limits of Reform?" Pp. 69–116 in Alan T. Harland (ed.),

Choosing Correctional Interventions That Work: Defining the Demand and Evaluating the Supply. Thousand Oaks, CA: Sage.

Cullen, John B. 1978. *The Structure of Professionalism*. Princeton, NI: Petrocelli Books.

Gendreau, Paul, 1996. "The Principles of Effective Intervention with Offenders." Pp. 117–130 in Alan T. Harland (ed.), *Choosing Correctional Options That Work: Defining the Demand and Evaluating the Supply*. Newbury Park, CA: Sage.

Gendreau, Paul. 2000. "1998 Margaret Mead Award Address: Rational Policies for Reforming Offenders." Pp. 329–338 in Maeve McMahon (ed.), *Assessment to Assistance: Programs for Women in Community Corrections*. Lanham, MD: American Correctional Association.

Gendreau, Paul and D. A. Andrews, 2001. *Correctional Program Assessment Inventory—2000*. Saint John, Canada: Authors.

Gendreau, Paul and Claire Goggin, 1997. "Correctional Treatment: Accomplishments and Realities." Pp. 271–279 in Patricia Van Voorhis, Michael Braswell, and David Lester (eds.), *Correctional Counseling and Rehabilitation*, 3rd edition. Cincinnati: Anderson.

Gendreau, Paul, Claire Goggin, Francis T. Cullen, and D. A. Andrews. 2000. "The Effects of Community Sanctions and Incarceration on Recidivism." *Forum on Corrections Research* 12 (May): 10–13.

Gendreau, Paul, Claire Goggin, Francis T. Cullen, and Mario Paparozzi. Forthcoming. "The Common Sense Revolution in Correctional Policy." In James McGuire (ed.), *Offender Rehabilitation and Treatment: Effective Programs and Policies to Reduce Re-Offending*. Chichester, UK: John Wiley and Sons.

Gendreau, Paul, Claire Goggin, and Paula Smith. 2001. "Implementing Correctional Interventions in the 'Real' World." Pp. 247–268 in Gary A. Bernfeld. David P. Farrington, and Alan W. Leschied (eds.), *Inside the "Black Box" in Corrections*. Chichester, UK: John Wiley and Sons.

Gendreau, Paul, Tracy Little, and Claire Goggin. 1996. "A Meta-Analysis of the Predictors of Adult Offender Recidivism: What Works?" *Criminology* 34:575–607.

Gendreau, Paul, Paula Smith, and Claire Goggin (2001). "Treatment Programs in Corrections." Pp. 238–263 in John Winterdyk (ed.), *Corrections in Canada: Social Reaction to Crime*. Toronto, Canada: Prentice-Hall.

Gibbs, John C., Granville Bud Potter, and Arnold P. Goldstein. 1995. *The EQUIP Program: Teaching Youths to Think and Act Responsibly Through a Peer-Helping Approach*. Champaign, IL: Research Press.

Goldstein, Arnold P. 1999. *The Prepare Curriculum: Teaching Prosocial Competencies*. Rev. ed. Champaign, IL: Research Press.

Gordon, Donald A., Karen Graves, and Jack Arbuthnot. 1995. "The Effect of Functional Family Therapy for Delinquents on Adult Criminal Behavior." *Criminal Justice and Behavior* 22:60–73.

Henggeler, Scott W., with the assistance of Sharon R. Mihalic, Lee Rone, Christopher Thomas, and Jane Timmons-Mitchell. 1998. *Multisystemic Therapy: Book Six in the Blueprints in Violence Prevention Series*. Boulder, CO: Center for the Study and Prevention of Violence, University of Colorado.

Hunt, Morton. 1997. *How Science Takes Stock: The Story of Meta-Analysis*. New York: Russell Sage Foundation.

Latessa, Edward J. 2002. "Using Assessment to Improve Correctional Programming: An Update." Unpublished paper, University of Cincinnati.

Lipsey, Mark W. and David B. Wilson. 1998. "Effective Intervention for Serious Juvenile Offenders." Pp. 313–345 in Rolf Loeber and David P. Farrington (eds.), *Serious and Violent Juvenile Offenders: Risk Factors and Successful Intervention*. Thousand Oaks, CA: Sage.

MacKenzie, Doris Layton. 2000. "Evidence-Based Corrections: Identifying What Works." *Crime and Delinquency* 46:457–471.

MacKenzie, Doris Layton, David B. Wilson, and Suzanne B. Kider. 2001. "The Effects of Correctional Boot Camps on Offending." *Annals of the American Academy of Political and Social Science* 578 (November):126–143.

Matthews, Betsy, Dana Jones Hubbard, and Edward J. Latessa. 2001. "Making the Next Step: Using Assessment to Improve Correctional Programming." *Prison Journal* 81:454–472.

Millenson, Michael L. 1997. *Demanding Medical Excellence: Doctors and Accountability in the Information Age*. Chicago: University of Chicago Press.

Rhine, Edward E. (ed.). 1998. *Best Practices: Excellence in Corrections*. Lanham, MD: American Correctional Association.

Starr, Paul. 1982. *The Social Transformation of American Medicine: The Rise of a Sovereign Profession and the Making of a Vast Industry*. New York: Basic Books.

Timmermans, Stefan and Alison Angell. 2001. "Evidence-Based Medicine, Clinical Uncertainty, and Learning to Doctor." *Journal of Health and Social Behavior* 42:342–359.

Van Voorhis, Patricia. 1987. "Correctional Effectiveness: The High Cost of Ignoring Success." *Federal Probation* 51 (March):59–62.

Van Voorhis, Patricia, Francis T. Cullen, and Brandon K. Applegate. 1995. "Evaluating Interventions with Violent Offenders: A Guide for Practitioners and Policymakers." *Federal Probation* 59 (June):17–28.

Welsh, Brandon C. and David P. Farrington. 2001. "Toward and Evidence-Based Approach to Preventing Crime." *Annals of the American Academy of Political and Social Science* 578 (November):158–173.

Part 6: Institutional Violence

One of the first images to come to many people's minds when they think of a prison is of a group of large, muscular, mean, aggressive men who fill their days with violence and exploitation of both other inmates and institutional staff. Our popular cultural views of prisons in this country emphasize the idea of violence. Common assumptions hold that prisons are violent places and inmates are either violent predators or victims.

While it is true that violence does happen in prison—and some inmates are violent predators and some inmates are victims—these are not universal and constant. In fact, as the articles in this section will show, while different types of violence do occur in prisons, among a range of inmates, it is the recognition of the possibility of violence that is more profound and has more of an effect on day-to-day life for inmates than actual occurrences of violence.

In the first article in this section, Hemmens and Marquart look at fear of crime among prison inmates. This question is one that would not come to mind for most people, based on the assumptions that inmates are dangerous and bad people themselves. However, as this research shows, inmates do express a fair amount of concern about the possibility of being victimized in prison. It is important, just as when looking at patterns of misconduct (as above), to look at inmates' personal characteristics and criminal histories. Both of these factors are important influences on fear of victimization, just as they are influential on rates of misconduct.

In the second article in this section, Jiang and Fisher-Giorlando specifically look at the ability of three major theoretical perspectives (importation, deprivation, and situational) to explain misconduct by inmates. They report that all three models are useful for explaining inmate misconduct, although they have different degrees of importance for different types of misconduct. However, they also conclude that in order to fully understand how, when, where, against whom, and—most important—why inmates violate institutional rules, it is necessary to draw on multiple theoretical explanations. No single theory is able to explain fully inmate misconduct.

The third article presents a look at a special and particularly worrisome group of inmates: gang members. In this article Fleisher and Decker outline a brief history of prison gangs, identify some of the major gangs found in American prisons, discuss ways in which prison gangs are involved in and associated with violence, and suggest some ways that may prove—or already have been proven—to be effective means of response for prison administrators.

The fourth and fifth articles in this section turn attention away from violence in general and focus on sexual violence, specifically. Growing attention has been focused in recent years on the issue of sexual assaults, and as these two articles point out, sexual violence (including rape, assault, coercion, and intimidation) occur in both men's and women's prisons. The article "The Evolving Nature of Prison Argot and Sexual Hierarchies" highlights the ways that different labels are used to denote male inmates who either aggress against others or are targeted for sexual victimization. As the data from interviews reported in this article makes clear, the ways that sexual aggressors, sexual victims, and men who engage in consensual sex with other male inmates are viewed has changed in some important ways in recent years.

Struckman-Johnson and Struckman-Johnson, in the next article, focus attention on an issue that many observers believe to be a "small" or infrequent form of violence in prison: sexual coercion among female inmates. Their research documents that, in fact, sexual coercion and abuse of female inmates does occur, and both staff members and other female inmates are perpetrators. As many of the other articles in this book suggest, the frequency and severity of this form of behavior is largely dependent on the characteristics of the prison and the prison staff. Women who are sexually coerced, abused, or assaulted, however, are not likely to report being victimized—similar to the situation in free society. What this article shows us very clearly is that sexual victimization does happen in prisons, even among women. However, the issue gets relatively little attention from scholars and policy makers.

In the last article in this section, the issue of prison riots, one of the biggest concerns expressed by many new staff and outside observers, is addressed. Boin and Van Duin present a somewhat different approach to thinking about how and why prison riots develop and end as they do. As they discuss, traditionally we have looked at prison riots with a focus on what caused them, and then assume that riots with a particular type of cause are likely to end in particular types of ways. However, these authors argue that one extremely important factor has been overlooked in these traditional approaches: how administrators respond to the situation. This article makes the argument, using evidence from the two most violent prison riots in American history, that how prison administrators prepare for and respond once a riot situation begins are critically important to the resolution and consequences of a riot. In other words, in order to understand how things happen in prison, we cannot look just at prison inmates; we need to look also at the actions of prison staff and administrators.

Violence is fairly common in American prisons, and inmates encounter violence, or more likely the consequences of potential violence, on a daily basis. However, the types of violence; the frequency of violence; and the dynamics of violent events, inmates, and situations are not as numerous as the media has led us to believe. Rather, violence is often done for multiple purposes, and violence is not rampant and constant in prison. However, the questions that are not addressed by these articles and that the reader should keep in mind, are (1) Why does violence happen in prison? and (2) What could corrections officials do to better control—or even eliminate—violence in their institutions? To answer these questions, however, you need to keep in mind what you believe the main goal of prison is, or what it should be. That will guide your thinking about where violence comes from and how it should be controlled.

Discussion Questions

Institutional Violence

1. What are the common forms of violence found in prisons?
2. What types of inmates are most likely to be involved in violence, both as perpetrators and as victims?
3. What could prison officials do to decrease the likelihood of violence happening in a prison? What factors would be more or less important for one-on-one and collective forms of violence?

23. Straight Time: Inmates' Perceptions of Violence and Victimization in the Prison Environment

Craig Hemmens
James W. Marquart

Although fear of crime among the public is well-documented, little attention has been paid to fear of crime within inmate populations. This gap in the literature is all the more surprising given the documented high level of violence in prisons. This paper presents results from a survey of 775 adult male inmates regarding their perceptions of violence in prison. Relationships between perception of the level of prison violence and individual background characteristics such as race, ethnicity, and prior criminal history are examined.

The stereotype of prison is that of a dangerous place, where strong inmates prey upon the weak. According to one unusually literate inmate, fear of assault is so pervasive, "everyone is afraid" (Abbott, 1981:144). Not surprisingly, research has shown that a feeling of personal safety is crucial in establishing a high quality of prison life (Toch, 1977). While there has been much study of the relationship between sociodemographic and criminal history characteristics and inmate adjustment to prison (Goodstein & MacKenzie, 1984; MacKenzie, 1987; Wright, 1989; 1991; 1993), relatively little attention has been paid to the relationship between these characteristics and perceptions of violence and victimization in prison.

This paper presents results from a survey of 775 recently released adult male inmates regarding their perceptions of violence in prison. Relationships between perceptions of the level of prison violence and individual sociodemographic and criminal history characteristics such as race/ethnicity, age, education level, age at first arrests, number of prior incarcerations, and number of years in prison are examined.

Life in Prison

What is the effect of incarceration on those subjected to it? There are a number of accounts of prison life, written by prisoners, current (Shakur, 1993) and former (Abbott, 1981), wardens (Ragen, 1954), and outside observers (Earley, 1992). These can best be described as case studies, anecdotal accounts of life in one institution at one point in time, as experienced by one man. While these provide an enormous amount of information, and a very real human touch, they are lacking in generalizability.

The sociological literature is rife with studies of prison life and inmate adjustment patterns. Modern sociological research on prison life dates from Clemmer's (1940) pioneering work *The Prison Community*. He observed that the written rules and regulations of the institution explained only a part of how a prisoner adjusted to life in the "Big House." Equally, if not more important, was the informal social system created by the inmates. He developed the concept of "prisonization" (Clemmer, 1940:299) to explain how a prisoner is assimilated into the informal social structure of the prison.

Sykes, in *The Society of Captives* (1958) and elsewhere (Sykes & Messinger, 1960), developed further Clemmer's concept of prisonization, explaining the cause of inmate alienation as a reaction to the "pains of imprisonment" (1958:63–83). Sykes identified five pains: loss of one's liberty, loss of material possessions, loss of heterosexual contact, loss of personal autonomy, and loss of personal security. Suffering these pains, Sykes believed, caused inmates to become insecure, bitter, and led them to "reject their rejecters" (McCorkle & Korn, 1954:98). The result was the pains of imprisonment forged an inmate population degree unified by its shared pains. Prisoners developed their own informal social structure based on their responses to the pains of imprisonment. This subculture reinforced a set of norms and values in opposition to those espoused by the prison staff. This was known as the "inmate code" (Sykes & Messinger, 1960).

The model of prison life developed by Clemmer and extended by Sykes became known as the "deprivation" model (Allen & Simonsen, 1992) or the "indigenous" or "functional" model (Irwin & Cressey, 1962). It focuses on the humiliations and degradations inherent in forced confinement. The model has received mixed empirical support.

The deprivation model was challenged by researchers who decried its disregard for the effect of the outside world and individual characteristics on how inmates adjust to prison (Irwin & Cressey, 1962; Irwin, 1970; Carroll, 1974; Jacobs, 1977). These writers noted that an inmate did not come into prison a blank slate, but rather brought with him the code of the streets, which he used in modified form within the prison walls. This was referred to as the "importation model." Irwin and Cressey (1962) argued that pre-institutional experiences and backgrounds have a major impact on how an inmate adapts to incarceration.

Later writers suggested that both the deprivation and importation models presented an incomplete picture of inmate life. The "integrated model" (Thomas, 1970; 1977; Zingraff, 1975) incorporated elements of both the deprivation and importation models in an attempt to provide a more complete picture of inmate adjustment patterns, and points out that Clemmer acknowledged that pre-prison experiences play some role in adjustment and that Irwin and Cressey admit there are some inmates who are more affected by the prison environment than other inmates.

More recent research has focused on the relationship of selected sociodemographic and criminal history characteristics and inmate adjustment patterns (Goodstein & MacKenzie, 1984; MacKenzie, 1987; Wright, 1989; 1993). The current research extends this trend and includes an understudied group, Hispanic inmates.

Prison Violence

There are a number of studies which have documented the relatively high level of aggression and victimization in prisons. Bowker (1980) provides a comprehensive review of the literature on victimization in prison, including physical, psychological, economic, and social victimization of inmates by other inmates, as well as victimization of inmates by correctional staff. He found that self-report data indicated a much higher level of inmate victimization than official data. This finding is in line with research on victimization studies in the general population (Bureau of Justice Statistics, 1992).

Research indicates that the vast majority of inmates experience feelings of vulnerability to victimization and attack, creating a mental state in which they are "constantly on guard against danger one cannot hope to locate, to anticipate, or to guard against" (Toch, 1977:42). Toch found that certain inmate characteristics are related to the degree of fear experienced. These characteristics include physical size and age (Toch, 1977). There is also evidence that White inmates have a higher fear of victimization, in part because they are more likely to be victims of interracial assault (Fuller & Orsagh, 1977; Irwin, 1980).

An early study of victimization in North Carolina state prisons by Fuller and Orsagh (1977) found that while victimization was not uncommon, the rate of unprovoked victimization was quite low. They examined official records and interviewed approximately 400 inmates. Their comparison of official records and self-report data indicated that official reports seriously underreported victimization in prison, similar to what occurs in the free world. They also found that victimization in prison was a much more likely occurrence than in the free world—by their estimate, an inmate had a fifty percent greater chance of being assaulted than did a person in the free world (Fuller & Orsagh, 1977).

Another study by Mabli et al. (1979) found that violence within an institution was largely a function of age. They studied assault rates in two federal prisons, one for young offenders and one for older offenders, and found that assault rates were higher in the institution which housed the younger offenders. When some of the younger offenders were transferred to the prison for older offenders, and some of the older inmates were moved to the prison for younger offenders, assault rates increased in the facility for older offenders and decreased in the facility for younger offenders.

McCorkle (1992, 1993a, 1993b) surveyed inmates of a Southern maximum security facility to determine the impact of living in a violence-prone institution. Where prior studies concentrated on victimization rates, he focused on the effect of victimization on inmate attitudes and actions. He found that inmate fear of victimization was higher than fear of victimization in the general population (McCorkle, 1993b), a not surprising finding given the well-documented levels of violence in prisons. McCorkle also discovered that the inmates with the highest fear of victimization were the young, socially isolated inmates, who also tended to be the most frequent targets of victimization (McCorkle, 1993b). This finding validates the anecdotal and participant observation literature of the 1970s and 1980s which suggested that gang affiliation served to protect inmates (Jacobs, 1977; Fong, 1990; Ralph, 1992), and empirical research which suggests those most likely to be victims are those without prior institutional experience (Wright, 1991).

McCorkle found that over half of the respondents in his study had been the target of a serious threat during their imprisonment, and over a third had been struck by fists, while a quarter of the respondents had been attacked with something more serious, such as a weapon (McCorkle, 1993a). When asked how safe they considered the prison, over half considered it at least reasonably safe, while only fourteen percent considered it very unsafe (McCorkle, 1993b). When asked what was the chance of being attacked while incarcerated, 44% said low, while 41% said medium and only 14% said high (McCorkle, 1993b). McCorkle found a strong association between prior victimization and fear of future victimization, and also found that young inmates and White inmates had higher levels of fear (McCorkle, 1993a).

McCorkle points out that it is unclear whether these levels of fear are higher than in the past, since no studies of fear of victimization exist. He suggests, however, that the fear level is probably higher, because the inmate population has changed, and the control policies of prisons have changed. A study by Crouch and Marquart (1990) of victimization and levels of fear in Texas before, during, and after court intervention provides an excellent explication of this hypothesis.

Texas prisons prior to the 1970s were run under what DiIulio (1987) has called the "control model." Inmate activity was highly regimented and controlled. Correctional staff, severely undermanned as a result of poor funding, utilized the some of the more aggressive, dominant inmates to control the other inmates, a control mechanism referred to as the "building tender" or "BT" system (Marquart, 1986). In this manner correctional officers "coopted" (Marquart, 1986) many potential discipline problems and were able to oversee a large number of inmates with a small number of staff. Texas prisons were acclaimed as some of the best run and safest institutions in the country (DiIulio, 1987). During the 1970s and 1980s Texas prisons became increasingly overcrowded, and the subject of a massive class action lawsuit alleging unconstitutional practices, *Ruiz v. Estelle* (503 F. Supp 1265 (S.D. Texas 1980)). The building tender system was ordered dismantled by the court, and TDC eventually complied, but failed to provide additional control measures to replace the building tender system. At the same time prison gangs increased in power and stepped into the power vacuum (Fong, 1990; Ralph, 1992). The result was several years of virtually unchecked violence, culminating in 52 inmate-on-inmate homicides in 1985 (Fong, 1990). During the later part of the 1980s, TDC began to regain control of its prisons, hiring additional staff and building units to relieve the overcrowding. Violence apparently decreased, at least according to the official statistics.

Crouch and Marquart (1990) studied inmate perceptions of violence in TDC during this turbulent period. Contrary to popular perception, they found that inmates did not feel safer during the building tender era than during the height of inmate violence during the mid-1980s. Crouch and Marquart surveyed a sample of 416 inmates who had been incarcerated in TDC from between 1978 and 1981 until 1987. Of these, almost 40 percent had begun serving time prior to 1978. They asked the respondents to describe how safe they felt in TDC during several different periods between 1978 and 1987. Their findings were striking. Inmate perceptions of safety did not, on the whole, vary significantly from the control period through the late 1980s, despite the fact that official reports of inmate violence increased dramatically. One would expect inmate fear to increase as prison became more violent, but this did not occur in the aggregate. What Crouch and Marquart did note, however, was that perceptions of safety over time varied based on race and age of the individual inmate. During the control period, Black inmates were much less likely to feel safe than White inmates. During the early reform period the number of White inmates who reported feeling safe declined dramatically, relative to Black and Hispanic inmates. During the period of highest institutional violence, the inmates did not indicate any greater fear for their safety.

Crouch and Marquart provide several explanations for these findings. First, while the control period was marked by low numbers of officially reported violent acts, during this period White inmates comprised the vast majority of the building tender population. As the number of Black inmates increased and the building tender system began to be dismantled, the group in power, the White inmates, began to experience a concomitant increase in their fear level. And during the period of high institutional violence, most of it occurred in isolated areas, the segregation units where gang members were housed. The average inmate was not involved in the gang violence, and hence had no reason to fear inter-gang violence (Crouch & Marquart, 1990).

Assuming prison is a dangerous place, what is the impact on the mental and emotional well-being of the inmates? Toch's research (1977) indicates that fear of victimization is high in prison. Others have demonstrated that fear of victimization is associated with higher levels of psychological and physical problems (Zamble & Porporino, 1988). McCorkle (1993) found that older inmates and those incarcerated for a longer period of time had higher levels of mental health (or what he termed "general well-being"), as do those inmates who have several friends in prison and who receive visitors regularly. Significantly, he noted that an inmate's level of fear was the strongest predictor of an inmate's mental health.

Given that prison is a dangerous place, and some inmates are more susceptible to attack than others, what can an inmate do to reduce his likelihood of victimization? McCorkle (1992) found that inmates pursue one of two strategies. The older, more fearful, and more socially isolated inmates often use avoidance behavior to reduce the possibility of victimization. These avoidance behaviors include "keeping to themselves" (McCorkle, 1992:164), avoiding certain areas of the prison, and spending more time in one's cell. The second strategy, employed by younger inmates, is to employ more proactive, aggressive tactics such as using violence, lifting weights, and "getting tough" (McCorkle, 1992:165).

Methods

The data for this paper were obtained from a survey administered, over a six-week period, to 775 men just released from incarceration in the Texas Department of Corrections-Institutional Division (TDCJ-ID). These former inmates, or "exmates," were interviewed at the bus station in downtown Huntsville. While there are over 100 prisons in TDCJ-ID, virtually all inmates are processed and released through one institution.

A total of 775 surveys were completed. None of the 775 completed surveys were unusable, although exmates did occasionally choose not to answer a particular question. Some exmates did, of course, elect not to participate. Still others were not contacted by the interviewers, due to a lack of time and/or interviewers. According to TDCJ-ID data, some 1,900 inmates were released during this six-week time period, and 775 inmates were in fact interviewed. This represents a response rate of forty-one percent.

Findings

Sample Characteristics

Descriptive statistics for the sociodemographic and criminal history characteristics of the 775 male exmates who comprise the sample are summarized below. Sample characteristics are similar to Texas and national level data regarding sociodemographic characteristics of male inmates in 1994. Blacks are the largest racial/ethnic group in the exmate sample, comprising almost half (48%) of all respondents. Whites account for approximately one-third (33.7%) of all respondents, while Hispanics make up just over seventeen percent (17.2%) of the sample. The average age of the exmate sample is 32.98 years. White exmates are slightly older, with a mean age of 33.84, compared with a mean age of 32.67 for Black exmates and 32.16 for Hispanic exmates. The difference in mean ages among the three racial/ethnic groups is not statistically significant.

The mean years of education completed for the exmate sample is just under eleven (10.96) years, or less than a high school degree (12 years). Over half (55.4%) of all the exmates have not completed high school. Slightly over one quarter (28.8%) of the exmates have a high school degree or GED, while fifteen percent have at least some college experience. The three groups do demonstrate some difference in education level. Black exmates have the highest mean for years of education, 11.27. Whites have a mean education level of 11.00 years. Hispanic exmates have a mean education level of 10.06 years, over a full year less than Black exmates.

Almost half (48.9%) of all exmates report having been arrested before they turned eighteen. Slightly over eleven percent (11.4%) report being arrested for the first time at age 18. Just over fourteen percent (14.3%) report being arrested for the first time between the ages of 19 and 21, while slightly more (16.5%) report being first arrested between the ages of 22 and 29. Less than eight (7.2%) report their age at first arrest at 30 or older. Hispanic exmates report their first arrest occurring at a younger age than the White or Black exmate groups. Hispanic exmates had a mean age at first arrest of 17.72 years, while White exmates had a mean age at first arrest of 19.11 years and Black exmates had a mean age at first arrest of 20.26 years.

Almost half (45.3%) of the exmates were serving their first prison term. Just less than eight (7.9%) percent of the sample had served time once before, while over a quarter (27.7%) of the exmates had served time in prison on two prior occasions. Twelve percent report having been incarcerated on three prior occasions, and approximately seven (7.1%) percent report having served time on four or more prior occasions. White exmates had the highest mean for number of prior incarcerations, at 2.58. Black exmates had a mean of 2.40, while Hispanic exmates had a mean of 2.33 prior incarcerations.

Over a third (35%) of the exmates indicate they served between one and two years in prison on their current sentence before their release. Approximately one-quarter (21.7%) of the exmates served between two and three years, and fifteen percent (15.6%) served between three and four years. Less than twenty percent (19.9%) served more than five years of their current sentence. Black exmates report serving the longest sentences, with a mean of 38.69 months served on their current offense. White exmates served 35.75 months on average, and Hispanic exmates served 35.33 months on their current offense.

Violence/Victimization

To measure exmates' perceptions of violence and fear of victimization in prison today, they were asked their level of agreement with five statements regarding violence and victimization. The possible range of scores for each of these items is from 1 ("strongly agree") to 4 ("strongly disagree"). A lower mean score indicates that an exmate tends to agree with the statement; a higher mean score indicates that an exmate tends to disagree with the statement. Table 1 presents the scores for each of the three racial/ethnic groups. The group mean, standard deviation, F ratio, and associated probability level are displayed.

Racial/ethnic identity does not appear to be a major factor in perceptions of violence and danger in prison. Comparison of the mean scores on the five items on violence and victimization reveal a statistically significant difference on only one item, "I worried a lot about getting beaten up or attacked while I was in TDC" (item 15). This item was reverse coded, so a higher mean score indicates agreement with the statement. Black exmates had a mean score of 2.031, while White exmates had a mean score of 2.204 and Hispanic exmates had a mean score of 2.200. The difference in the mean score of Black exmates relative to both White and Hispanic exmate mean scores is statistically different at the .05 level. Thus, Black exmates as a whole are less concerned with being attacked in prison than either White or Hispanic exmates. This lower level of concern may be a function of the numerical superiority that Blacks currently enjoy in prison.

The other variables are presented in Table 2. These include the sociodemographic variables age and education level, and the criminal history variables age at first arrest, number of prior incarcerations, and number of years incarcerated. For

Table 1 Means, Standard Deviations, and F Ratios in Analysis of Variance (One-Way Classification) of Subjects' Responses to Survey Instrument

Item 15: "I worried a lot about getting beaten up or attacked while I was in TDC"					
Race/Ethnicity	*N*	*Mean*	*Std. Deviation*	*F*	*p*
White	260	2.204	0.634		
Black	360	2.031	0.733		
Hispanic	132	2.200	0.691	6.261	.002
Item 19: "I almost never had any problems with other inmates while in TDC"					
Race/Ethnicity	*N*	*Mean*	*Std. Deviation*	*F*	*p*
White	260	2.400	0.752		
Black	363	2.284	0.768		
Hispanic	133	2.316	0.722	1.823	.1622
Item 20: "There are enough guards to provide safety and security for the inmates"					
Race/Ethnicity	*N*	*Mean*	*Std. Deviation*	*F*	*p*
White	259	2.568	0.776		
Black	362	2.547	0.773		
Hispanic	130	2.592	0.723	0.178	.8366
Item 39: "Inmates attack other inmates very often"					
Race/Ethnicity	*N*	*Mean*	*Std. Deviation*	*F*	*p*
White	258	2.508	0.690		
Black	356	2.477	0.737		
Hispanic	130	2.646	0.703	2.683	.069
Item 42: "Overall it is pretty safe in TDC"					
Race/Ethnicity	*N*	*Mean*	*Std. Deviation*	*F*	*p*
White	254	2.504	0.664		
Black	355	2.559	0.736		
Hispanic	133	2.639	0.644	1.926	.146

these continuously measured variables, the coefficient of correlation (Pearson's r) and the associated probability level are displayed.

Age appears to be a major determinant of perceptions of violence and victimization in prison. The age of the exmate, both at first arrest and at the time he completed the survey, shows up repeatedly on the five violence items. Exmates arrested at an earlier age experience more problems with other inmates (item 19), do not believe there are enough guards to provide safety and security (item 20), are more likely to agree with the statement "inmates attack other inmates very often" (item 39), and perceive prison as less safe overall (item 42) than do exmates arrested who were older at first arrest.

TABLE 2 Coefficients of Correlation Between Continuous Variables and Subjects' Responses to Survey Instrument

Item 15: "I worried a lot about getting beaten up or attacked while I was in TDC"		
Variable	*r*	*p*
Age	□ .0328	.364
Education level	□ .1110	.002
Age 1st arrest	□ .0657	.071
Time served (years)	.0414	.400
Number of prior sentences	□ .0472	.334
Item 19: "I almost never had any problems with other inmates while in TDC"		
Variable	*r*	*p*
Age	□ .2528	.000
Education level	□ .0173	.632
Age 1st arrest	□ .1405	.000
Time served (years)	.0379	.440
Number of prior sentences	□ .0406	.405
Item 20: "There are enough guards to provide safety and security for the inmates"		
Variable	*r*	*p*
Age	□ .1635	.000
Education level	□ .0020	.956
Age 1st arrest	□ .1259	.001
Time served (years)	.0394	.425
Number of prior sentences	□ .0620	.205
Item 39: "Inmates attack other inmates very often"		
Variable	*r*	*p*
Age	□ .2476	.000
Education level	□ .0774	.034
Age 1st arrest	□ .1432	.000
Time served (years)	.0555	.262
Number of prior sentences	□ .0637	.195
Item 42: "Overall it is pretty safe in TDC"		
Variable	*r*	*p*
Age	□ .2447	.000
Education level	□ .0510	.162
Age 1st arrest	□ .1824	.000
Time served (years)	.1399	.005
Number of prior sentences	.0504	.305

Younger exmates are generally more likely than older exmates to perceive prison as a dangerous place. While exmate age is not a statistically significant factor in fear of being attacked (item 15), it is statistically significant on all of the other items. Younger exmates indicate they have more problems with other prisoners, are less likely to believe there are enough guards to ensure inmate safety, are more likely to agree with the statement "inmates attack other inmates very often," and perceive prison as more dangerous overall than older exmates. Clearly, then, age matters, at least in regard to an exmate's perception of the level of violence and danger in prison. Younger exmates are consistently more likely than older exmates not to believe violence is common, but to have actually experienced problems while incarcerated. These findings are in accord with anecdotal accounts and news reports which suggest that it is the younger inmates who are more often involved in disputes and altercations resulting in disciplinary action.

Interestingly, while younger exmates as a whole describe prison as more dangerous than do older exmates, younger exmates do not admit to being worried about being attacked at a greater rate than older exmates. There are several possible explanations for this phenomena. Younger exmates may have a false sense of personal security, despite being cognizant of violence in prison. This may be because they are members of inmate gangs which provide their membership with protection from assault, or it may be because they still possess that youthful belief in their own invulnerability.

The other criminal history variables seem to have little relationship with perceptions. These include number of prior incarcerations and number of years spent in prison.

Conclusion

This research suggests that inmate perceptions of the level of violence and victimization do vary, and that a substantial portion of this variance can be explained by selected sociodemographic and criminal history characteristics. Age is a particularly important variable. Analysis of variance reveals that exmate age, both at the time interviewed and at time of first arrest, is significantly related to perceptions.

As a group, over half of all exmates agree with the statement "overall, it is pretty safe in TDC." Slightly over ten percent strongly disagree with the statement. Yet it appears that there is some degree of fear, and an awareness that prison is a dangerous place. This is in accord with prior research by McCorkle (1993b). Over half the inmates he surveyed considered prison at least reasonably safe, while only fourteen percent considered it very unsafe, despite the fact that a significant percentage of the inmates reported having been victimized while in prison.

Inmates react to incarceration differently, based on a number of factors. Sociodemographic characteristics appear highly correlated with perceptions of the institutional experience generally, and this research confirms the importance of factors such as race and age. Further research is needed to determine how the differential response to incarceration may be utilized by correctional administrators to improve institutional security.

References

Abbott, J. (1981). *In the Belly of the Beast*. New York: Bantam.

Allen, H. E., & Simonsen, C. E. (1995). *Corrections in America*. Upper Saddle River, New Jersey: Prentice Hall.

Babbie, E. (1995). *The Practice of Social Research (6th ed.)*. Belmont, California: Wadsworth.

Berk, B. B. (1968). Organizational goals and inmate organization. *American Journal of Sociology* 71, 522–534.

Bowker, L. H. (1980). *Prison Victimization*. New York: Elsevier.

Bureau of Justice Statistics. (1992). *Drugs, Crime, and the Criminal Justice System*. Washington, D.C.: Department of Justice.

Camp, G. M., & Camp, C. G. (1993). *Corrections Yearbook*. South Salem, New York: Criminal Justice Institute.

Carroll, L. (1974). *Hacks, Blacks, and Cons*. Lexington, Massachusetts: Lexington.

Clemmer, D. (1940). *The Prison Community*. New York: Holt, Rinehart and Winston.

Crouch, B. M., & Marquart, J. W. (1990). Resolving the paradox of reform: litigation, prisoner violence, and perceptions of risk. *Justice Quarterly* 7, 103–123.

DiIulio, J. J. (1987). *Governing Prisons: A Comparative Study of Correctional Management*. New York: The Free Press.

Earley, P. (1992). *The Hot House: Life Inside Leavenworth Prison*. New York: Bantam.

Faine, J. R. (1973). A self-consistency approach to prisonization. *The Sociological Quarterly* 14, 576–588.

Fong, R. S. (1990). The organizational structure of prison gangs: A Texas case study. *Federal Probation*, 36–43.

Fuller, D. A., & Orsagh, T. (1977). Violence and victimization within a state prison system. *Criminal Justice Review*, 35–55.

Garabedian, P. G. (1963). Social roles and processes of socialization in the prison community. *Social Problems*, 139–152.

Goodstein, L., & MacKenzie, D. L. (1984). Racial differences in adjustment patterns of prison inmates-prisonization, conflict, stress, and control. In D. Georges-Abeyie (Ed.): *The Criminal Justice System and Blacks*. New York: Clark Boardman Company.

Grusky, O. (1959). Organizational goals and the behavior of informal leaders. *American Journal of Sociology*, 59–67.

Irwin, J. (1970). *The Felon*. Englewood Cliffs, New Jersey: Prentice-Hall.

Irwin, J. (1980). *Prisons in Turmoil*. Boston: Little Brown.

Irwin, J., & Cressey, D. R. (1964). Thieves, convicts and the inmate culture. *Social Problems* 10, 142–155.

Jacobs, J. B. (1977). *Stateville*. Chicago: The University of Chicago Press.

Lawson, D. P., Segrin, C., & Ward, T. D. (1996). The relationship between prisonization and social skills among prison inmates. *The Prison Journal* 76, 293–309.

Mabli, J., Holley, C., Patrick, J., & Walls, J. (1979). Age and prison violence: Increasing age heterogeneity as a violence-reducing strategy in prisons. *Criminal Justice and Behavior* 6, 175–186.

Mabli, J., Glick, S. M., M. Hilborn, Kastler, J., Pillow, D., Karlson, K., & Barber, S. (1985). Prerelease stress in prison inmates. *Journal of Offender Counseling, Services, and Rehabilitation* 9, 43–56.

MacKenzie, D. L. (1987). Age and adjustment to prison: Interactions with attitudes and anxiety. *Criminal Justice and Behavior* 14, 427–447.

Marquart, J. W. (1986). Prison guards and the use of physical coercion as a mechanism of prisoner control. *Criminology* 24, 347–366.

Maxfield, M. G., & Babbie, E. (1995). *Research Methods for Criminal Justice and Criminology*. Belmont, California: Wadsworth.

McCorkle, L., & Korn, R. (1954). Resocialization within the walls. *The Annals of the American Academy of Political and Social Sciences* 293, 88–98.

McCorkle, R. C. (1992). Personal precautions to violence in prison. *Criminal Justice and Behavior* 19, 160–173.

McCorkle, R. C. (1993a). Fear of victimization and symptoms of psychopathology among prison inmates. *Journal of Offender Rehabilitation* 19, 27–41.

McCorkle, R. C. (1993b). Living on the edge: Fear in a maximum-security prison. *Journal of Offender Rehabilitation* 20, 73–91.

Ralph, P. H. (1997). From self-preservation to organized crime: The evolution of inmate gangs. In J. W. Marquart & J. R. Sorensen (Eds.): *Correctional Contexts: Contemporary and Classical Readings*. Los Angeles: Roxbury.

Ruiz v. Estelle, 503 F. Supp 1265 (S.D. Texas 1980).

Schrag, C. (1961). Some foundations for a theory of correction in the prison. In D. Cressey (Ed.): *The Prison*. New York: Holt, Rinehart, and Winston.

Shakur, S. (1993). *Monster: The Autobiography of An L. A. Gang Member*. New York: The Atlantic Monthly Press.

Street, D. (1970). The inmate group in custodial and treatment settings. *American Sociological Review* 33, 40–55.

Sykes, G. M. (1958). *The Society of Captives: A Study of A Maximum Security Prison.* Princeton, New Jersey: Princeton University Press.

Sykes, G. M., & Messinger, S. L. (1960). The inmate social system. In R. Cloward (Ed.): *Theoretical Studies in Social Organization of the Prison.* New York: Social Science Research Council.

Thomas, C. W. (1970). Toward a more inclusive model of the inmate contraculture. *Criminology* 8, 251–262.

Thomas, C. W. (1977). Theoretical perspectives on prisonization: A comparison of the importation and deprivation models. *The Journal of Criminal Law and Criminology* 68, 135–145.

Tittle, C. R. (1968). Inmate organization: Sex differentiation and the influence of criminal subcultures. *American Sociological Review* 30, 492–504.

Toch, H. (1977). Social climate and prison violence. *Federal Probation* 4, 21–25.

Wellford, C. (1967). Factors associated with adoption of the inmate code: A study of normative socialization. *The Journal of Criminal Law, Criminology and Police Science* 58, 197–203.

Wheeler, S. (1961). Socialization in correctional communities. *American Sociological Review* 26, 697–712.

Wilson, T. P. (1968). Patterns of management and adaptations to organizational roles: A study of prison inmates. *American Journal of Sociology* 71, 146–157.

Wood, B. S., Wilson, G. G., Jessor, R., & Bogan, J. B. (1968). Troublemaking behavior in a correctional institution: Relationship to inmates' definition of their situation. *American Journal of Orthopsychiatry* 36, 795–802.

Wright, K. N. (1989). Race and economic marginality in explaining prison adjustment. *Journal of Research in Crime and Delinquency* 26, 67–89.

Wright, K. N. (1991). The violent and the victimized in the male prison. *Journal of Offender Rehabilitation* 16, 1–25.

Wright, K. N. (1993). Prison environment and behavioral outcomes. *Journal of Offender Rehabilitation* 20, 93–113.

Zamble, E., & Porporino, F. J. (1988). *Coping, Behavior, and Adaptation in Prison Inmates.* New York: Springer-Verlag.

Zingraff, M. T. (1975). Prisonization as an inhibitor of effective resocialization. *Criminology* 13, 366–388.

JOURNAL OF OFFENDER REHABILITATION, Vol. 28 (3/4), 1999, 1–21.

24. Inmate Misconduct: A Test of the Deprivation, Importation, and Situational Models

Shanhe Jiang
Marianne Fisher-Giorlando

This article examines the effectiveness of three theoretical models (deprivation, importation, and situational) in explaining violent incidents, incidents against correctional staff, and incidents against other inmates in prison. Based on a sample of 431 disciplinary reports from a men's state prison in the deep South, the authors have found all three models help explain violent incidents. The deprivation and situational models help explain incidents against correctional staff. The situational and importation models contribute to explanations of incidents against other inmates. With regard to the relative power of each theoretical model in explaining inmate misconduct in prison, the situational model is the most powerful based on the total chi-square change of the model. According to the average of chi-square change per variable in each model, however, the deprivation model is the most powerful and the situational is the least in explaining violent incidents and incidents against correctional staff.

Prisoners' adjustment to confinement has been a major topic of prison research for 60 years, beginning with Donald Clemmer's (1940) classic *Prison Community* and theory of prisonization. As incarceration rates rise to unprecedented levels in the history of the U.S.'s imprisonment, not only are more people incarcerated but also more families are touched by corrections as increasing numbers of family members either live or work in correctional institutions. Accordingly, concern about social control of the incarcerated, that is, prisoners' behavior, has also increased.

This article examines inmate disciplinary reports that are an indicator of prisons' effective social control. There are several reasons for the examination. First, inmate misconduct reflects inmates' adjustment to prison. Many prison studies use disciplinary infractions as a measure of prison adjustment. Second, inmate disciplinary infractions affect the prison order (DuIulio, 1987; Flanagan, 1980; Wooldredge, 1991). High inmate disciplinary infractions, especially violent infractions, could be a threat to the safety of prisons, of correctional staff, and of other inmates (Goetting & Howsen, 1986; O'Donnell & Edgar, 1999; Patrick, 1998). Third, inmate disciplinary infractions are closely related to prison classification. They are not only one of the measures of classification effectiveness but also a necessary element for reclassification in prison. Fourth, the issue of discipline in prison is also important from an economic perspective (Goetting & Howsen,

1986; Lovell & Jemelka, 1996). An estimated average cost per infraction at a medium-security prison is $970 (Lovell & Jemelka, 1996). Finally, from a humanitarian perspective, a high number of disciplinary infractions can have devastating physical and emotional repercussions for correctional staff, inmates (Wooldredge, 1991), and the families of both (Goetting & Howsen, 1986).

In this article, we focus on three explanations of prison adjustment: the deprivation, importation, and situational models. The deprivation model emphasizes the effect of deprivation on prison adjustment. The importation model focuses on the effect of preprison factors on prison adjustment. The situational model emphasizes the effect of situational factors on prison adjustment. The major purposes of the study are, first, to examine the effectiveness of the three theoretical models in explaining inmate misconduct in prison. That is, does each of these models help explain inmate misbehavior? If yes, which one is the most powerful or which is the least powerful? Are they additive in explaining inmate misconduct? The final purpose is to examine and briefly discuss the effect of individual variables on inmate infractions.

Although there are thousands of studies on prison life and the adjustment of prisoners to their confinement (Goodstein & Wright, 1989), this study has several characteristics that make this work significant. First, this research applies all three models to assess their effectiveness in explaining inmate behavior. Previous studies either compare the deprivation with the importation models (i.e., Cao, Zhao, & Van Dine, 1997; Harer & Steffensmeier, 1996; Sorensen, Wrinkle, & Gutierrez, 1998; also see Paterline & Petersen, 1999, for the summary of the limits of the previous literature) or test only one (i.e., Steinke, 1991). Because none of these models alone can completely explain inmate misconduct (MacDonald, 1999; Paterline & Petersen, 1999; Thomas, Petersen, & Zingraff, 1978), this study contributes to a better understanding and explanation of inmate infractions.

Second, this work includes some variables that have rarely or never been examined that might be significant in explaining inmate misconduct. The variables are differences in age, education, and race between correctional officers and inmates. Because of the ambiguity of institutional rules and other factors, no officer enforces all the rules all the time or enforces all rules equally (Cressey, 1959; Johnson, 1987; Kauffman, 1988). Which rules are applied and to whom they are applied is dependent on officers' judgment. Differences in age, education, and race between correctional officers and inmates can exert a great impact on correctional officers' judgment. For example, correctional officers have been charged with being racially discriminatory in issuing disciplinary reports (Carroll, 1974; Jurik, 1985; Van Voorhis, Cullen, Link, & Wolfe, 1991). However, only one study analyzed the correlation between correctional officers' race and their behaviors, such as the numbers and types of disciplinary reports they issue (Fisher-Giorlando & Jiang, 2000). Moreover, only Fisher-Giorlando and Jiang examined and compared both interracial disciplinary responses (the race of the officers is different from that of the inmates they sanction) and intraracial disciplinary response (the race of the officers is the same as the race of the inmates they sanction). Finally, we found no research that examines the effect of differences in age and education between correctional officer and inmate on inmate misconduct.

Third, this research divides rule infractions into three groups and examines the application of the importation, deprivation, and situational models to each group. The three groups consist of the following three pairs of dichotomous variables: violent misconduct (yes or no), misconduct against staff (yes or no), and misconduct against inmates (yes or no). Most studies treat inmate infractions as one dependent variable (i.e., Flanagan, 1980; Goetting & Howsen, 1986; McShane & Williams, 1990; Sorensen, et al., 1998). Two recent quantitative studies on the correlates of inmate misconduct include four or more categories of rule violations (Craddock, 1996; Steinke, 1991). They, however, have few independent variables.

Finally, the study site is one facility but two levels of security—medium and maximum. The findings based on different levels of security have implications for those facilities that have similar situations.

Previous Research

Three Theoretical Perspectives

Three major theoretical models have been used to explain inmate adjustment to prison. They are the deprivation, importation, and situational models. According to the deprivation model, prison is a total institution completely cut off from the free world (Goffman, 1961). This kind of environment encourages the process of prisonization through adaptation to the losses or "pains of imprisonment" (Sykes, 1958; Sykes & Messinger, 1960). According to Sykes, pains of imprisonment include deprivation of liberty, goods and services, heterosexual relationships, autonomy, and security. Inmates' adjustment to these pains leads to the development of an inmate subculture that is in opposition to the administration. Accordingly, inmates exhibit negative attitudes, values, and self-concepts that are in opposition to the prison administration and staff (Paterline & Petersen, 1999; Sykes & Messinger, 1960; Thomas, 1977). Such oppositional culture and negative attitudes then lead prisoners to be aggressive (Cao et al., 1997; Harer & Steffensmeier, 1996; see Wright, 1991), resist authority (see Goodstein & Wright, 1989; Wright, 1991), attack other inmates, or violate other prison rules (see Wright, 1991, for more references).

In contrast to the deprivation model, the importation model focuses on the influence of preprison socialization and experience. It argues as follows: First, inmates' own distinctive traits and social backgrounds largely determine their behavior in prison (Irwin, 1981; Irwin & Cressey, 1962). Moreover, inmate subcultures reflect preprison belief systems and norms rather than a simple result of prisonization in a total institution (Irwin, 1970; Irwin & Cressey, 1962). Second, not all inmates universally experience pains and deprivation of imprisonment (Bonta & Gendreau, 1990; Bukstel & Kilmann, 1980). Their adaptation to prison depends on individual prisoners' ability to find a "niche" that meets their needs

(Seymour, 1977; Toch, 1977). Third, prison should be viewed as a "somewhat-less-than-total" institution (Farrington, 1992; Jacobs, 1976). Prison control today is shared between inmates, correctional officers and staff, the courts, and a number of other external groups (Stastny & Tyrnauer, 1982). Also, inmates are not a solitary group: they are comprised of different subgroups with different belief systems and norms (Carroll, 1974; Irwin & Cressey, 1962; Jacobs, 1974, 1976, 1977; Paterline & Petersen, 1999; Toch & Adams, 1986; Wooldredge, 1991).

Both the deprivation and the importation models have come under attack by correctional researchers (Goodstein & Wright, 1989). Methodologically, the two models have used varying and ambiguous measures (Porporino & Zamble, 1984) and have implemented only a small number of variables (Paterline & Petersen, 1999). Conceptually, the two models have been criticized as too general (Porporino & Zamble, 1984) and have failed to incorporate other theories of prisonization (Paterline & Petersen, 1999).

Finally, the situational model criticizes the importation model for ignoring the situational factors in explaining inmate adjustment to prison (Steinke, 1991). This model assumes that the sources for initiation and direction of behavior come primarily from situational factors (Endler & Magnusson, 1976), such as season of the year and location, or from a complex interplay between inmates, officers, and the settings in which the interactions occur (Flanagan, 1983). For example, because of the heat, inmates may commit more rule infractions in the summer than in the winter regardless of their personal background or their relative level of deprivation. Within the situational approach, three general questions are usually considered: Where, when, and with whom does the behavior occur (Steinke, 1991; also see Goldstein, 1994, for more information).

Empirical Evidence

In testing the deprivation model, researchers have used measures such as crowding, visiting patterns, involvement in prison programs, stringency of rule enforcement, security level in prison and sentence length (Cao et al., 1997; also see Goodstein & Wright, 1989; McCorkle, Miethe, & Drass, 1995, for extensive reviews).

Many variables have been used to test the importation model, most commonly, race, sex, and age (Goodstein & Wright, 1989; Wooldredge, 1991; Wright, 1991). Other frequently used variables include social class, marital status, education, number of convictions, employment, type of crime, area of origin, gang membership, drug use, and some personality variables (see Goodstein & Wright, 1989; Wooldredge, 1991; Wright, 1991, for extensive reviews).

The situational model focuses on the effect of situational variables on inmate adjustment. Situational variables are grouped into categories of where, when, and with whom. The category "where" includes both the place where the incident occurred and the type of residence in which the inmate was housed (Kratcoski, 1988; Steinke, 1991; see Goldstein, 1994, for more reviews). The category "when" includes the season (or temperature), the time of day, and/or the work shift during which the incident occurred (Haertzen, Buxton, Covi, & Richards, 1993; Kratcoski, 1988; Steinke, 1991). The category "with whom" includes who writes up the incident report and whether any other inmates were involved in the incident (Kratcoski, 1988; Steinke, 1991).

Studies Before 1991

In their extensive reviews of the literature prior to 1991. Goodstein and Wright (1989), Wright and Goodstein (1989), and Wright (1991) pointed out that deprivation variables at both the institutional and individual levels did have effects on inmates' behaviors, although the effects were not always the same in strength or even in the same direction. Identified variables include sentence length, length of time served, type of facility, physical characteristics of the prison, the social ecology of prison and prison-related policy changes (see Wright, 1991; Wright & Goodstein, 1989, for details).

In empirical tests of the importation model prior to 1991, it was found that individual (background and personality) variables had effects on inmates' behaviors, although findings varied from one study to another. Some research found no relationships or mixed results among inmate adjustment and age, race, and sex, yet the majority of findings generally provided support for a relationship among them (see Bukstel & Kilmann, 1980; Goodstein & Wright, 1989; Paterline & Petersen, 1999; Wooldredge, 1991; Wright, 1991, for extensive reviews). Researchers also found a relationship between inmate adjustment and other individual variables such as social class, marital status, number of convictions, employment, history of alcohol and drug use, and education (Goetting & Howsen, 1986; Toch & Adams, 1989; Zamble & Porporino, 1988).

There have been few studies conducted on the relationship between situational factors and inmate incidents in prison before 1991 (Steinke, 1991). Kratcoski (1988) suggested that the location of the assault and time of day in addition to work experience of the correctional officer assaulted varied with assaultive behavior by prisoners.

1991 and After

Researchers have continued to test the deprivation, importation, and situational models since 1991. Steinke (1991) tested the effects of situational variables on violent behavior in a male prison. She found situational variables such as site and type of residence in the prison, temperature, work shift, and type of staff served as predictors of aggressive behavior against staff, other inmates, self, or property. To test the temperature-aggression hypothesis. Haertzen et al. (1993) found that rule infractions occurred more frequently during the hot summer months (June, July, and August) than during the three other seasons.

In a test of the deprivation, management, and "not-so-total" institutional models. McCorkle et al. (1995) found that poor prison management practices were predictors of rates of assault on inmates and staff and that the deprivation model was least useful. Finn (1995) examined the effects of race, economic deprivation, urban background, and criminal justice history on officially recorded violent and nonviolent disciplinary reports for inmates (sample size = 2.496) released from a northern state prison system. Her findings indicated that after controlling for predictor variables such as employment, marital status, education, crime type, and prior violent crime, race and prior prison incarceration had no significant main effects on incident rates. Urban background was significantly related only to nonviolent misconduct. Economic deprivation (as measured by education and employment status at arrest) was significantly related to nonviolent and violent misconduct. Based on a sample of 239 male inmates in a maximum-security prison. Paterline and Petersen (1999) found that deprivation variables were better predictors of prisonization than were importation variables. The significant deprivation variables included oppositional attitudes toward the institution and attitudes supportive of the use of violence.

Harer and Steffensmeier (1996) used data from 58 male institutions in the federal correctional system to test for racial differences in both violent and alcohol and/or drug misconduct, controlling for a large number of individual, prison environment, and community background variables. Their findings indicated that net of controls, Black inmates had significantly higher rates of violent behavior but lower rates of alcohol and/or drug misconduct than did White inmates. They interpreted these findings as support for the importation model of prison adjustment over the deprivation model. Cao et al. (1997) tested the efficacy of the importation and deprivation models of inmate adjustment to prison in Ohio. The results from the study provided support for the importation model.

In examining rule violations among long-term inmates from 1978 to 1987 at the Missouri Department of Corrections, Sorensen et al. (1998) found that age and race were predictors of prison rule violations. They claimed their findings provided strong support for the importation model. Patrick (1998) examined differences in inmate-inmate and inmate-staff altercations. His findings suggested that inmate-inmate altercations were related to structural and interpersonal variables. Inmate-staff altercations were related to the extent to which inmates were involved in social relationships with other inmates and saw the correctional staff as a physical threat to them.

In examining the determinants of prisonization. Paterline and Petersen (1999) found that months of employment before imprisonment was a significant predictor. However, as noted, the total effect of the importation variables in their study was weaker than that of the deprivation model.

To summarize, the three models—the deprivation, importation, and situational—have proposed different ways to explain inmate behavior. All three models have supportive evidence. However, researchers have not examined the three models simultaneously. Also, most research includes a limited number of variables in each study. Finally, we rarely find research that examined one facility with different levels of security. This study intends to fill these gaps.

Methods

Research Site

Data were collected from a men's state prison in the deep South. The institution has an operational capacity of approximately 1,200 beds and houses, both medium- and maximum-security prisoners. This prison is one of many built in response to a mid-1970s federal court order. Constructed in 1980. Moreover, approximately one third of the prisoners are maintained in disciplinary cell blocks and have no interaction with the rest of the prison population (Foster, 1995).

Data Collection Procedures and Sampling

Data for this analysis were drawn from the official records of inmates' rule violations.

Data were collected for a 6-month period covering May 2, 1994, through November 2, 1994. A period of 6 months was chosen to ensure that enough disciplinary reports and a good representative sample were drawn.

Variables and Measurement

Dependent Variables. Three dependent variables were used in this study. They are dichotomous variables. Therefore, this study uses logistic regression analysis. The following are the three dependent variables:

Violent versus nonviolent. Violent misconduct includes five rule violations listed in the state prison handbook "Disciplinary Rules and Procedures for Adult Inmates" (1993 ed.). They are defiance, fighting, aggravated fighting, property destruction, and self-mutilation.

Misconduct against staff. This variable is based on the following six rule violations, which include both violent and nonviolent misconduct. The six items are defiance, disobedience, aggravated disobedience, disrespect, favoritism, and aggravated work offenses.

Misconduct against inmates. This variable includes three rule violations, including violent and nonviolent misconduct, as follows: fighting, aggravated fighting, and theft.

Independent Variables. This study examines the effects of 36 independent variables on the dependent variables. They are classified into three groups of measurement according to the three theoretical models—deprivation, importation, and situational.

Four variables that are indicators of the deprivation mode include sentence length (SLENGTH), length of time served (PRISONT), and two dummy variables, working cell blocks (WORKCELL) and dormitories (DORMS). The base category for the dummy variables is cell blocks. At the facility under study, cell blocks are lock-down units that are more restricted than working cell blocks, although both of these units are classified as maximum security. Dormitories are medium security and the least restrictive of all housing units.

There are 13 variables considered as measures of the importation model. All of these variables refer to characteristics and behaviors of prisoners. They include age at admission (AGEI) in years, education at admission (EDI) in years, race (RACEI; White = 1, Black = 0), gang membership at admission (GANG; yes = 1, no = 0), number of children (CHILDREN), drug-related crime at admission (DRUGCRIM; yes = 1, no = 0), conviction history (CONVICTH; total number previous), and self-reported substance abuse (including alcohol use and drug use) at admission (SUBSTANC). Two dummy variables relate to marital status of prisoners at admission, divorced and separated (DIVORCED) and single (SINGLE). The base category is married. The other two dummy variables relate to admission offenses and include conviction for a property offense (OFENSEPR) and conviction for a drug offense (OFFENSED). The base category is conviction for a violent offense.

This study uses 19 variables as indicators of the situational model. Correctional officer variables include race (RACEO; White = 1, Black = 0), seniority (WORKO) in years, education (EDO) in years, and age (AGEO) in years. Comparison variables include differences between writing officers' age and inmates' age (AGECOMP) in years, difference between writing officers' education and inmates' education (EDCOMP) in years, and racial differences between writing officers and inmates (RACECOMP). The remaining variables are month of incident (INCIDENM; May through September = 1, October and November = 0) and 11 dummy variables. The first 2 dummy variables refer to correctional officers' marital status, divorced or separated (DIVORCEO) and single (SINGLEO); the base category is married. Three dummy variables refer to inmates' daily schedule. They are free time (FREETIME), work time (WORKTIME), and sleeping time (SLEPTIME). The base category is movement time. The next 6 dummy variables relate to the place of the incident. They are working cells (INWCELL), corridors (INCORRID), recreation areas (INRECREA), working areas (INWORK), dorms (INDORMS), and dining rooms and kitchens (INDINING).

Findings

In this section, we first describe disciplinary reports based on the dependent variables. Then, we examine the predictors of each dependent variable using logistic regression.

Table 1 shows frequency and percentage distributions of violent versus nonviolent incidents and offenses against staff, inmates, and others. As noted, others includes property, self, and public order offenses. First, there are more nonviolent than violent incidents. Second, more than 50% of incidents are against staff.

Table 2 presents the odds ratio and coefficients from logistic regression of violence on three types of independent variables—the deprivation, the importation, and the situational variables. For the deprivation model, two dummy variables are statistically significant. Inmates living in working cell blocks (less restricted) are less likely than those living in cell blocks (most restricted) to commit violent incidents.

TABLE 1 Frequency Distribution of Disciplinary Reports

Variable	n	*Percentage*
Violent incident	121	28.3
Nonviolent incident	307	71.7
Incident against staff	216	50.5
Incident against inmate	47	11.0
Incident against other[a]	165	38.6

NOTE: There are 3 missing cases in this table.
a. It includes incidents against property, self, and prison security and/or order.

For the importation model, five variables are statistically significant. The first, CHILDREN, indicates that the more children an inmate has, the higher number of violent infractions he commits. The second variable, SUBSTANC, indicates that inmates who reported greater use of drugs and alcohol prior to incarceration had higher numbers of violent incidents in prison than did those who reported using less drugs and alcohol. The third variable, DRUGCRIM, illustrates that inmates who were convicted of drug-related crimes are more likely than those who were not convicted of drug-related crimes to commit violent behaviors in prison. The fourth variable, DIVORCED, indicates that divorced inmates (as reported at admission) are less likely than married inmates (as reported at admission) to commit violent infractions in prison. Finally, Table 2 shows that inmates convicted for drug offenses are less likely than those convicted for violent offenses to commit violent behaviors in prison.

For the situational model, one dummy variable, INWORK, is statistically significant. The result, as is shown in Table 2 indicates that a violent incident is less likely to occur in the working areas than in the cell blocks.

Combining the three models yields the following results. First, according to the chi-square changes and Nagelkerke R^2, as is shown in the combined model and the three separate models, each of the three models explains inmates' violent behavior in prison. They are also additive. Second, comparing the relative effect of each, the deprivation model explains less violent behavior than do the other two models.

Table 3 presents the odds ratios and coefficients from the logistic regression of incidents against correctional staff on the three types of independent variables that are the same, as shown in Table 2. The deprivation model shows that WORKCELL is statistically significant in a negative direction. That is, inmates living in the working cell blocks are less likely than are those living in the most restricted cell blocks to commit acts against correctional staff.

The situational model of Table 3 shows that two dummy variables are statistically significant. The first is SINGLEO. Its logistic coefficient indicates that an incident against correctional staff is more likely to occur when an officer who writes up the incident is single than when he or she is married. The second variable is INCORRID. The value of the coefficient for this variable indicates that an

TABLE 2 Odds Ratio and Coefficients from Logistic Regression of Violence on Three Types of Independent Variables

	Deprivation Model		*Importation Model*		*Situational Model*		*Combined*	
Variable	B	*Odds Ratio*	B	*Odds Ratio*	B	*Odds Ratio*	B	*Odds Ratio*
WORKCELL (yes = 1)	−.997** (.331)	.369					−1.164* (.567)	.312
DORMS (yes = 1)	−.861** (.307)	.430					−1.051* (.475)	.350
INWORK (yes = 1)					−1.347** (.466)	.260	−1.448* (.582)	.226
CHILDREN			.286* (.145)	1.286			.444* (.197)	1.559
SUBSTANC			−.183** (.062)	.832			−.197* (.085)	.821
DRUGCRIM (yes = 1)			1.102** (.389)	2.811				
DIVORCED (yes = 1)			−1.601** (.508)	.368			−2.179* (1.075)	.113
OFFENSED (yes = 1)			−1.531** (.520)	.216				
−2 log likelihood	495.50		444.72		378.90		317.49	
Chi-square change	16.23**		28.17**		29.49		63.71**	
Degrees of freedom	4		13		19		36	
Nagelkerke R^2	.05		.10		.12		.26	
Proportion of correct predictions	.72		.71		.71		.75	

NOTE: WORKCELL = working cell blocks; DORMS = dormitories; INWORK = working areas (the place of incident); CHILDREN = number of children; SUBSTANC = substance abuse; DRUGCRIM = drug-related crime; DIVORCED = divorced and separated; OFFENSED = drug offenses. Only those significant variables are shown in this table. The base category for WORKCELL and DORMS is cell blocks. The base category for INWORK is cells. The base category for DIVORCED is married. The base category for OFFENSED is violent offenses. CHILDREN is an interval-ratio variable. Values for SUBSTANC are from 0 to 8. DRUGCRIM is a dichotomous (yes or no) variable. Numbers in parentheses are standard errors.

$^*p < .05$. $^{**}p < .01$.

TABLE 3 Odds Ratio and Coefficients From Logistic Regression of Incident Against Correctional Staff on Three Types of Independent Variables

	Deprivation Model		*Importation Model*		*Situational Model*		*Combined*	
Variable	B	*Odds Ratio*	B	*Odds Ratio*	B	*Odds Ratio*	B	*Odds Ratio*
SLENGTH							−.028* (.014)	.972
WORKCELL (yes = 1)	−.700** (.267)	.497						
DIVORCEO (yes = 1)							1.600* (.669)	4.952
SINGLEO (yes = 1)					.078* (.036)	1.081		
WORKTIME (yes = 1)							−.733* (.351)	.481
FREETIME (yes = 1)							−.678* (.325)	.508
INCORRID (yes = 1)					−1.369* (.482)	.254		
−2 log likelihood	581.70		525.15		438.42		377.08	
Chi-square change	15.79**		22.01*		32.34		54.75*	
Degrees of freedom	4		13		19		36	
Nagelkerke R^2	.05		.07		.12		.21	
Proportion of correct predictions	.59		.61		.62		.66	

NOTE: SLENGTH = sentence length; WORKCELL = working cell blocks: DIVORCEO = divorced and separated; SINGLEO = single; WORKTIME = work time (the time of the incident); FREETIME = free time (the time of the incident); INCORRID = corridors (the place of the incident). Only those significant variables are shown in this table. SLENGTH is an interval-ratio variable. The base category for WORKCELL is cell blocks. The base category for INCORRID is cells. The base category for DIVORCEO and SINGLEO is married. The base category for WORKTIME and FREETIME is movement time. Numbers in parentheses are standard errors. None of the importation variables in the importation model is significant.
$*p < .05$. $**p < .01$.

incident is less likely to occur in the corridor area than in the cell blocks. There is no other variable that is statistically significant in the importation model.

Again, putting all three models together and comparing one with another, the following results are apparent in Table 3. First, according to the chi-square changes and Nagelkerke R^2, as shown in the combined model and the three separate models, each of the three models explains inmates' incident against correctional staff in the prison. Also, the three models are additive. Second, the situational model explains inmate misconduct against staff the most, with the importation model next and the deprivation model last.

Table 4 presents the odds ratios and coefficients from the logistic regression of an incident against other inmates on the three types of independent variables. The deprivation model does not show any variable that is statistically significant. The importation model shows that OFENSEPR is statistically significant. This finding reveals that inmates convicted for property offenses are more likely to be involved in incidents against other inmates than are those convicted for violent offenses.

The situational model shows that four variables are statistically significant. First, correctional officers' working experience affects writing inmate-on-inmate reports. The odds ratio tells us that the odds of inmate-on-inmate reports are higher for more experienced officers. It is possible that the "old timers" have less education and in fact are tougher in their general attitude toward inmates.

Second, the values of the coefficients for the three significant dummy variables indicate that incidents against other inmates are more likely to occur in the working cell blocks, corridors, and recreation areas than in the cell blocks. These results make sense because inmates in lock-down cell blocks do not have much chance to interact with other inmates.

Putting all three models together and comparing one with another, the following findings regarding incidents against other inmates stand out in Table 4. First, according to the chi-square changes and Nagelkerke R^2, as is shown in the combined model and the three separate models, the importation variable and the situational model help explain disciplinary reports against other inmates in the prison. Second, the situational model explains inmate-against-inmate incidents the most, with the importation model next and the deprivation model last.

Summary and Discussion

Before we summarize and discuss our findings, we want to point out the limitations of this study. Although the data set used in this study comes from a random sample, the study population consists of inmates and their behavior in one prison. Thus, the generalizability of the findings found in this study is statistically limited to the prison from which the data were collected. Furthermore, the analysis unit in this study is disciplinary reports. Therefore, the findings in this study can be generated to only those who did have disciplinary records from May to November in 1994, the period of time from which the data were collected. Finally, although this research used 36 independent variables in the models, they are not an exhaustive list of variables in explaining the three theoretical models.

TABLE 4 Odds Ratio and Coefficients From Logistic Regression of Incident Against Other Inmates on Three Types of Independent Variables

Variable	Deprivation Model		Importation Model		Situational Model		Combined	
	B	Odds Ratio	B	Odds Ratio	B	Odds Ratio	B	Odds Ratio
WORKO					.148** (.053)	1.160		
INWCELL (yes = 1)					1.3246* (.5392)	3.7608		
INCORRID (yes = 1)					1.630** (.616)	5.104	2.518** (.746)	12.401
INRECREA (yes = 1)					2.357*** (.651)	10.557	2.164** (.762)	8.704
FREETIME (yes = 1)							1.055* (.512)	2.871
DIVORCED (yes = 1)							−3.419** (1.326)	.033
OFENSEPR (yes = 1)			.840* (.395)	2.317			1.236* (.563)	3.440
−2 log likelihood	315.99		285.41		222.52		186.32	
Chi-square change	1.41		10.77		31.73*		45.90	
Degrees of freedom	4		13		19		36	
Nagelkerke R^2	.01		.05		.17		.26	
Proportion of correct predictions	.87		.88		.88		.90	

NOTE: WORKO = correctional officers' seniority; INCELL = working cells; INCORRID = corridors (the place of the incident); INRECREA = recreation areas; FREETIME = free time (the time of the incident); DIVORCED = divorced and separated; OFENSEPR = property offenses. Only those significant variables are shown in this table. WORKO is an interval-ratio variable. Cells are the base category for the three incident place variables. INCELL, INCORRID, and INRECREA. The base category for FREETIME is movement time. The base category for DIVORCED is married. The base category for OFENSEPR is violent offenses. Numbers in parentheses are standard errors. None of the deprivation variables in the deprivation model is significant.
$*p < .05$. $**p < .01$. $***p < .001$.

This article has examined the effectiveness of the deprivation, importation, and situational models in explaining inmate misconduct in prison. We have found that all three models and the model variables help explain violent incidents. The deprivation and situational models help explain incidents against correctional staff. The situational and importation models contribute to explanations of incidents against other inmates. These findings suggest that disciplinary reports may result from a combination of different factors related to different theoretical models, as suggested in Paterline and Petersen's (1999) recent study. All three models are complementary in explaining inmate infractions. Therefore, we need to use multiple theoretical models to explain inmate behavior in prison.

Regarding the relative power of each theoretical model in explaining violent incidents, incidents against correctional staff, and incidents against other inmates, this study has found that the situational model is the most powerful and that the deprivation model is the weakest.

At the individual variable level, this research has not found any effect of race and age on the three types of incidents, although it was given considerable attention. This finding is consistent with Fisher-Giorlando and Jiang's (2000) study. This research also finds that security level is a predictor of rule violations. To be more specific, inmates residing in working cell blocks and dormitories are less likely than are those in lock-down cell blocks to commit violence, whereas inmates residing in working cell blocks are less likely than are those in lock-down cell blocks to commit incidents against correctional staff. This finding is consistent with Steinke's (1991) research and makes logical sense. Inmates residing in lock-down cell blocks have less freedom than do those residing in working cell blocks and dormitories and may feel more deprived than do their counterparts in working cell blocks. Accordingly, they experience higher levels of deprivation that in turn lead to higher frustration and violence. Because they are limited to contact with correctional officers only, they are involved in misconduct against correctional staff but not other inmates. With regard to incidents against other inmates, those who live in working cell blocks and dormitories are more likely to be involved in these incidents than are those who live in lock-down cell blocks because of the presence of other residents, lack of privacy, and more contact with other inmates.

All these findings contribute to the understanding of inmate adjustment to prison. As noted, many of these findings are consistent with previous research and/or make logical sense. However, this work also has some surprising findings that require some explanation. In fact, our findings about the connection between marital status and violent misconduct and number of children and violent misconduct fly in the face of commonly accepted knowledge about men's behavior in prison.

As for marital status, data were collected at the time of admission in this study. Enough of these "married" men could have been divorced after being admitted into prison. Divorce law in this particular state allows uncontested divorce when a spouse is convicted of a felony. By definition, it is not only possible but also highly probable that some of these men "married at admission" were divorced when they committed the violent rule infraction.

The finding that the more children inmates have, the higher the number of violent infractions they commit also does not appear to make logical sense. It is commonly believed that prisoners' connections with their families through letters, phone calls, and visits indicate some level of stability for inmates, who are then less likely to engage in misconduct. Furthermore, prisoners know that punishment for misconduct can severely limit future visits with their families. However, as Martin (2002) observed. "We know relatively little about incarcerated fathers as a group" (p. 90). In the case of our study, we do not know the quality of the relationship these fathers had or have been able to maintain with their children. Although Martin studied men in jails, not prison, her work has some implications for understanding our findings. Martin pointed out that fathers differ in terms of the quality of relationships they had with their children before they were incarcerated. Not all prison fathers were "deadbeat dads" or biological fathers. Some fathers took major child care and economic responsibilities before incarceration and suffer pains of separation from their children. Although our data set does not provide the information, these fathers with more children could be fathers who were more involved with their children before incarceration and are thus more frustrated with having that role eliminated from their lives. Their frustration can in turn lead to more violent offenses. We do know that fathers have less contact with their children than do mothers either through phone calls, letters, or visits (Mumola, 2000). We have always assumed this is so because fathers do not care. However, we really do not know about fathers, and more research about relationships between fathers and prison misconduct needs to be conducted.

Other findings related to drug use before conviction and drug offenders also have implications for policy recommendations. Our study found that those inmates who reported a greater use of drugs and alcohol prior to incarceration had higher numbers of violent incidents in prison than did those who reported using less drugs and alcohol. We also found that inmates who were convicted of drug-related crimes had a higher number of violent incidents than did those who were not convicted of drug offenses. Clearly, this finding indicates the necessity of implementing serious substance abuse programming in prison.

Finally, findings from this research indicate that research about prisoner misconduct must be conducted. Furthermore, programs based on the issues raised in this research must be implemented to make correctional institutions safe and secure places for those who live and work there.

References

Bonta, J., & Gendreau, P. (1990). Re-examining the cruel and unusual punishment of prison life. *Law and Human Behavior, 14*, 347–372.

Bukstel, L. H., & Kilmann, P. R. (1980). Psychological effects of imprisonment on confined individuals. *Psychological Bulletin, 88*, 469–493.

Bureau of Justice Statistics (1989). *Special report: Prison rule violators*. Washington, DC: U.S. Department of Justice.

Cao, L., Zhao, J., & Van Dine, S. (1997). Prison disciplinary tickets; A test of the deprivation and importation models. *Journal of Criminal Justice, 25,* 103–113.

Carroll, L. (1974). *Hacks, Blacks, and cons: Race relations in a maximum security prison.* Lexington, MA: Lexington Books.

Clemmer, D. (1940). *The prison community.* Boston: Christopher.

Craddock, A. (1996). A comparative study of male and female prison misconduct careers. *The Prison Journal, 76,* 60–80.

Cressey, D. (1959). Contradictory directives in complex organizations: The case of the prison. *Administrative Science Quarterly, 4,* 1–19.

DiIulio, J. J., Jr. (1987). *Governing prisons: A comparative study of correctional management.* New York: Free Press.

Endler, N. S., & Magnusson, D. (1976). Toward an interactional psychology of personality. *Psychological Bulletin, 83,* 956–974.

Farabee, D., Prendergast, M., Carter, J., Wexler, H., Knight, K., & Anglin, M. D. (1999). Barriers to implementing effective correctional drug treatment programs. *The Prison Journal, 79,* 150–162.

Farrington, K. (1992). The modern prison as total institution? Public perception versus objective reality. *Crime & Delinquency, 38,* 6–26.

Finn, M. A. (1995). Disciplinary incidents in prison: Effects of race, economic status, urban residence, prior imprisonment. *Journal of Offender Rehabilitation, 22,* 143–156.

Fisher-Giorlando, M., & Jiang, S. (2000). Race and disciplinary reports: An empirical study of correctional officers. *Sociological Spectrum, 20,* 169–194.

Flanagan, T. J. (1980). Time served and institutional misconduct: Patterns of involvement in disciplinary infractions among long-term and short-term inmates. *Journal of Criminal Justice, 8,* 357–367.

Flanagan, T. J. (1983). Correlates of institutional misconduct among state prisoners. *Criminology, 21,* 29–39.

Foster, B. (1995). Angola in the seventies. In B. Foster, W. Rideau, & D. Dennis (Eds.), *The wall is strong: Corrections in Louisiana* (pp. 54-69). Lafayette, LA: University of Southwestern Louisiana, the Center for Louisiana Studies.

Goetting, A., & Howsen, R. M. (1986). Correlates of prisoner misconduct. *Journal of Quantitative Criminology, 2,* 49–67.

Goffman, E. (1961). *Asylums: Essays on the social situation of mental patients and other inmates.* Garden City, NY: Anchor Books.

Goldstein, A. P. (1994). *The ecology of aggression.* New York: Plenum.

Goodstein, L., & Wright, K. N. (1989). Inmate adjustment to prison. In L. Goodstein & D. L. MacKenzie (Eds.), *The American prison: Issues in research and policy* (pp. 229–251). New York: Plenum.

Haertzen, C., Buxton, K., Covi, L., & Richards, H. (1993). Seasonal changes in rule infractions among prisoners: A preliminary test of the temperature-aggression hypothesis. *Psychological Reports, 72*, 195–200.

Harer, M. D., & Steffensmeier, D. J. (1996). Race and prison violence. *Criminology, 34*, 323–355.

Irwin, J. K. (1970). *The felon*. Englewood Cliffs. NJ: Prentice-Hall.

Irwin, J. K. (1981). Sociological studies of the impact of long-term confinement. In D. A. Ward & K. F. Schoen (Eds.). *Confinement in maximum custody*. Lexington, MA: D. C. Heath.

Irwin, J. K., & Cressey, D. (1962). Thieves, convicts, and the inmate culture. *Social Problems, 10*, 142–155.

Jacobs, J. B. (1974). Street gangs behind bars. *Social Problems, 21*, 395–409.

Jacobs, J. B. (1976). Stratification and conflict among prison inmates. *Journal of Criminal Law and Criminology, 66*, 476–482.

Jacobs, J. B. (1977). *Stateville: The penitentiary in mass society*. Chicago: University of Chicago Press.

Johnson, R. (1987). *Hard time: Understanding and reforming the prison*. Pacific Grove, CA: Brooks/Cole.

Jurik, N. C. (1985). Individual and organizational determinants of correctional officer attitudes toward inmates. *Criminology, 23*, 523–539.

Kauffman, K. (1988). *Prison officers and their world*. Cambridge, MA: Harvard University Press.

Kratcoski, P. C. (1988). The implications of research explaining prison violence and disruption. *Federal Probation, 52*, 27–32.

Lovell, D., & Jemelka, R. (1996). When inmates misbehave: The costs of discipline. *The Prison Journal, 76*, 165–179.

MacDonald, J. M. (1999). Violence and drug use in juvenile institutions. *Journal of Criminal Justice, 27*, 33–44.

MacKenzie, D. L. (1987). Age and adjustment to prison. *Criminal Justice and Behavior, 14*, 427–447.

Martin, J. S. (2002). Jailed fathers. Paternal reactions to separation from children. In R. L. Gido & T. Alleman (Eds.). *Turnstile justice* (pp. 89–114). Englewood Cliffs, NJ: Prentice Hall.

McCorkle, R. C., Miethe, T. D., & Drass, K. A. (1995). The roots of prison violence: A test of the deprivation, management, and "not-so-total" institution models. *Crime & Delinquency, 41*, 317–331.

McShane, M. D., & Williams, F. P. (1990). Old and ornery: The disciplinary experiences of elderly prisoners. *International Journal of Offender Therapy and Comparative Criminology, 34*, 197–211.

Mumola, C. J. (2000). *Incarcerated parents and their children* (Bureau of Justice Statistics special report). Washington, DC: Department of Justice. Office of Justice Programs.

Norusis, M. J., & SPSS Inc. (1990). *SPSS advanced statistics user's guide*. Chicago: SPSS Inc.

O'Donnell, I., & Edgar, K. (1999). Fear in prison. *The Prison Journal, 79*, 90–99.

Paterline, B. A., & Petersen, D. M. (1999). Structural and social psychological determinants of prisonization. *Journal of Criminal Justice, 27*, 427–441.

Patrick, S. (1998). Differences in inmate-inmate and inmate-staff altercations: Examples from a medium security prison. *The Social Science Journal, 35*, 253–263.

Pearson, F. S., & Lipton, D. S. (1999). A meta-analytic review of the effectiveness of corrections-based treatments for drug abuse. *The Prison Journal, 79*, 384–410.

Porporino, F. J., & Zamble, E. (1984). Coping with environment. *Canadian Journal of Criminology, 26*, 403–422.

Seymour, J. (1977). Niches in prison. In H. Toch (Ed.), *Living in prison: The ecology of survival*. New York: Free Press.

Sorensen, J., Wrinkle, R., & Gutierrez, A. (1998). Patterns of rule-violating behaviors and adjustment to incarceration among murderers. *The Prison Journal, 78*, 222–231.

Stastny, C., & Tyrnauer, G. (1982). *Who rules the joint: The changing political culture of maximum security prisons in America*. Lexington, MA: Lexington Books.

Steinke, P. (1991). Using situational factors to predict types of prison violence. *Journal of Offender Rehabilitation, 17*, 119–132.

Sykes, G. M. (1958). *The society of captives*. Princeton, NJ: Princeton University Press.

Sykes, G. M., & Messinger, S. L. (1960). The inmate social system. In R. Cloward (Ed.), *Theoretical studies in social organization of the prison*. New York: Social Science Research Council.

Thomas, C. W. (1977). Theoretical perspectives on prisonization: A comparison of the importation and deprivation models. *The Journal of Criminal Law and Criminology, 68*, 135–145.

Thomas, C. W., Petersen, D. M., & Zingraff, R. M. (1978). Structural and social psychological correlates of prisonization. *Criminology, 16,* 383–393.

Toch, H. (1977). *Living in prison: The ecology and survival.* New York: Macmillan.

Toch, H., & Adams, K. (1986). Pathology and disruptiveness among prison inmates. *Journal of Research in Crime and Delinquency, 23,* 7–21.

Toch, H., & Adams, K. (1989). *Coping: Maladaptation in prisons.* New Brunswick. NJ: Transaction.

Van Voorhis, P., Cullen, F. T., Link, B. G., & Wolfe, N. T. (1991). The impact of race and gender on correctional officers' orientation to the integrated environment. *Journal of Research in Crime an Delinquency, 28,* 472–500.

Wooldredge, J. D. (1991). Correlates of deviant behavior among inmates of U. S. correctional facilities. *Journal of Crime and Justice, 14,* 1–25.

Wooldridge, J. M. (2000). *Introductory econometrics: A modern approach.* South-Western College Publishing.

Wright, K. N. (1991). A study of individual, environmental, and interactive effects in explaining adjustment to prison. *Justice Quarterly, 8,* 217–242.

Wright, K. N., & Goodstein, L. (1989). Correctional environments. In L. Goodstein & D. L. MacKenzie (Eds.). *The American prison: Issues in research and policy* (pp. 253–270). New York: Plenum.

Zamble, E., & Porporino, F. J. (1988). *Coping behavior and adaptation in prison inmates.* New York/Berlin: Springer-Verlag.

THE PRISON JOURNAL, Vol. 82 No. 3, September 2002, 335–358.

25. An Overview of the Challenge of Prison Gangs

Mark S. Fleisher
Scott H. Decker

A persistently disruptive force in correctional facilities is prison gangs. Prison gangs disrupt correctional programming, threaten the safety of inmates and staff, and erode institutional quality of life. The authors review the history of, and correctional mechanisms to cope with prison gangs. A suppression strategy (segregation, lockdowns, transfers) has been the most common response to prison gangs. The authors argue, however, that given the complexity of prison gangs, effective prison gang intervention must include improved strategies for community re-entry and more collaboration between correctional agencies and university gang researchers on prison gang management policies and practices.

America now imprisons men and women with ease and in very large numbers. At the end of the year 2000, an estimated two million men and women were serving prison terms. The mission of improving the quality of life inside our prisons should be a responsibility shared by correctional administrators and community citizens. Prisons are, after all, public institutions supported by tens of millions of tax dollars and what happens inside of these costly institutions will determine to some degree the success inmates will have after their release. Oddly though, citizens often believe that anyone can offer an intelligent opinion about prison management and inmate programming. In recent years, elected officials have called for tougher punishment in prisons, stripping color televisions, removing weightlifting equipment, and weakening education programs as if doing these rather trivial things will punish inmates further and force them to straighten out their lives and will scare others away from crime. If criminals choose to commit crime, "let them suffer" seems to be the prevailing battle cry of elected officials and citizens alike, who have little formal knowledge of crimogenesis, punishment, and imprisonment.

A parallel argument would let smokers suffer the ravages of cancer because their behavior, above all others, caused their health problem. Similarly, we should allow students who do not choose to study to remain ignorant because their behavior led them to marginal illiteracy. As we sanction cigarette companies for selling a carcinogenic product, as we strive to improve public education, we also should continuously improve prison management and the quality of life inside these costly, tax-supported institutions. We do not advocate coddling inmates but we surely do not advocate allowing millions of imprisoned inmates to live with drug addictions, emotional difficulties, and educational and employment skills so poor that only minimum-wage employment awaits them. These are the disabilities that, to some degree, define the American inmate population, and these same disabilities will damage the quality of life in our communities when these untreated, uneducated, and marginal inmates return home.

Criminologists have argued for decades that persistent criminals often do not have the power to control the destructive forces in their environment, which created their disabilities. Many criminals are, in a real sense, victims of family abuse and neglect, school disciplinary practices that expelled them before they had sufficient education to get a good job, and impoverished neighborhoods well outside the opportunity networks in the dominant community.

Western civilization has used prisons as an experimental site where socially destructive human behavior supposedly is transformed into socially productive behavior. This experiment has yielded consistently poor results. As we begin the next century, we might want to rethink the mission of the prison, shifting the prevailing approach from punishing convicted offenders to using these public institutions as society's last chance to reform men and women who, for whatever reason, have not been able to conform to mainstream community norms.

American history shows prison inmates have, for the most part, been marginal to the dominant economy of the time and were the society's most poorly educated and least well-prepared citizens to hold gainful employment. But now the gap between the social and economic margin and mainstream grows wider and faster than it ever has grown. In the 1950s, a general equivalency diploma (GED) was sufficient to enable employment in America's expanding factory economy, but now the GED affords only minimum-wage employment in the fast-food industry and/or service work in hotels, malls, and restaurants. America's high-tech twenty-first century has decreasing career opportunities for the nearly two million poorly educated American prisoners whose economic future grows more distant from the mainstream economy as the nanoseconds pass. Prisons are our last best chance to help lawbreakers find a lawful, economically stable place in mainstream communities.

That is a lofty mission, indeed, especially with tens of thousands of inmates entering prison annually. To accomplish the difficult job of retraining, educating, and treating inmates, prisons must be well-managed public institutions. Every prison cell house that burns in a disturbance burns millions of tax dollars. Managing prisons is difficult and that task should be delegated exclusively to the correctional experts rather than to elected officials pandering to voters. The highest security prisons hold the most violent and disruptive inmates who are most likely to be as disruptive inside as they were outside. In such places and others of lower security, a social force is operating today that will thwart even our best efforts to create and sustain high-quality prison management. That disruptive social force is prison gangs.

A Brief History of Prison Gangs

Lyman (1989) defines a prison gang as

> an organization which operates within the prison system as a self-perpetuating criminally oriented entity, consisting of a select group of inmates who have established an organized chain of command and are governed by an established code of conduct. The prison gang will usually operate in secrecy and has as its goal to conduct gang activities by controlling their prison environment through intimidation and violence directed toward non-members (p. 48).

We have only a rudimentary knowledge of prison gangs as social groups operating inside prisons and of the interplay between street gangs and prison gangs. Thus the scope, understanding, and study of prison gangs are broader and somewhat different from street gangs. One thing we do know: prison gangs are gang researchers' final frontier and prison managers' biggest nightmare.

While we debate prison gang demographics and their distribution in American prisons, we know such groups have been in prisons a long time. The first known American prison gang was the Gypsy Jokers formed in the 1950s in Washington state prisons (Orlando-Morningstar, 1997; Stastny & Tyrnauer, 1983). The first prison gang with nationwide ties was the Mexican Mafia, which emerged in 1957 in the California Department of Corrections.

Camp and Camp (1985) identified approximately 114 gangs with a membership of approximately 13,000 inmates. Of the 49 agencies surveyed, 33 indicated that they had gangs in their system: Pennsylvania reported 15 gangs, Illinois reported 14. Illinois had 5,300 gang members, Pennsylvania had 2,400, and California had 2,050. In Texas, there were nine prison gangs with more than 50 members each, totaling 2,407 (Ralph & Marquart, 1991). Fong (1990) reported eight Texas gangs with 1,174 members. Illinois reported that 34.3 percent of inmates belonged to a prison gang, which was then the highest percent of prison gang-affiliated inmates in the nation (Camp & Camp, 1985).

Lane (1989) reported that the Illinois Department of Corrections (IDOC) estimated the inmate gang population to be nearly 90 percent of the entire population, attributing that number to the importation of gangs from Chicago's streets, which is supported by research (Jacobs, 1974). Rees (1996) shows that Chicago police estimated more than 19,000 gang members in that city and a high percent of IDOC inmates were arrested in Cook County. Other correctional agencies, however, report their gang troubles started inside rather than outside prison walls. Camp and Camp (1985) cite that of the 33 agencies surveyed, 26 reported street counterparts to prison gangs.

Knox and Tromanhauser (1991) suggest there are approximately 100,000 or more prison gang members across the nation. Subsequent to Camp and Camp (1985), the American Correctional Association found that prison gang membership doubled between 1985 and 1992 from 12,624 to 46,190 (Baugh, 1993), with relatively few gang members in minimum security units. Later, Montgomery and Crews (1998) argued that Knox and Tromanhauser overestimated the prison gang population and cited the American Correctional Association's 1993 study that reported some 50,000 prison gang members.

Obtaining data on the number of prison gangs and gang membership has been difficult. Most estimates are now 10 to 20 years old. Fong and Buentello (1991) suggest three major reasons for the lack of prison gang research. First, official documentation on prison gangs is weak. What documentation exists is generally only for departmental use. Second, prison managers are reluctant to allow outside researchers into facilities to conduct prison gang research. Fears over security and concern that research might hamper the welfare of the prison are the oft-cited reasons for excluding prison researchers. Third, prison gang members themselves are secretive and likely would not disclose sensitive information about their prison gang group to outside researchers.

Prison Gangs: Structure and Organization

Prison gangs share organizational similarities. Prison gangs have a structure usually with one person designated as the leader who oversees a council of members who make the group's final decisions. The rank and file form a hierarchy, making these groups look more similar to organized crime than their counterparts on the outside (Decker, Bynum, & Weisel, 1998). The United States Department of Justice (1992) suggests that leaders and hard-core members are some 15–20 percent of a gang's membership and that the majority of members do not have a vested interest in the organization leadership.

Prison gangs, like some street counterparts, have a creed or motto, unique symbols of membership, and a constitution prescribing group behavior. Absolute loyalty to one's gang is required (Marquart & Sorensen, 1997), as is secrecy (Fong & Buentello, 1991). Violent behavior is customary and can be used to move a member upward in the prison hierarchy. Prison gangs focus on the business of crime generally through drug trafficking. Such crime groups have an interest in protecting their membership (Montgomery & Crews, 1998).

Gang members are the essential capital in crime-oriented social groups; likewise, when members want to leave the group, such out-group movement jeopardizes group security, thus the so-called blood in, blood out credo, according to Fong, Vogel, and Buentello (1995). These researchers surveyed 48 former prison gang members who defected and found that the number of gang defectors was proportional to their prison gang's size. A number of reasons were cited for defecting. Most commonly, former members lost interest in gang activities; the next most common reason was a refusal to carry out a hit on a non-gang member; and the least common reason for leaving was a disagreement with the direction of the gang's leadership. A small number of former members violated a gang rule and were fearful of a gang violation against them, outgrew a sense of belonging to the gang, turned informant, or refused to commit gang crimes. We do not know, however, how many defectors were killed inside and outside prisons as a percentage of the total number of defectors.

Research suggests there are at least five major prison gangs, each with its own structure and purpose. The Mexican Mafia (La Eme) started at the Deuel Vocational

Center in Tracy, California, in the 1950s and was California's first prison gang (Hunt, Riegel, Morales, & Waldorf, 1993) composed primarily of Chicanos, or Mexican Americans. Entrance into La Eme requires a sponsoring member. Each recruit has to undergo a blood oath to prove his loyalty. The Mexican Mafia does not proscribe killing its members who do not follow instructions. Criminal activities include drug trafficking and conflict with other prison gangs, which is common with the Texas Syndicate, Mexikanemi, and the Aryan Brotherhood (AB) (Orlando-Morningstar, 1997).

The Aryan Brotherhood, a white supremacist group, was started in 1967 in California's San Quentin prison by white inmates who wanted to oppose the racial threat of black and Hispanic inmates and/or counter the organization and activities of black and Hispanic gangs (Orlando-Morningstar, 1997). Pelz, Marquart, and Pelz (1991) suggest that the AB held distorted perceptions of blacks and that many Aryans felt that black inmates were taking advantage of white inmates, especially sexually, thus promoting the need to form and/or join the Brotherhood. Joining the AB requires a 6-month probationary period (Marquart & Sorensen, 1997). Initiation, or "making one's bones," requires killing someone. The AB trafficks in drugs and has a blood in, blood out rule; natural death is the only nonviolent way out. The Aryan Brotherhood committed eight homicides in 1984, or 32 percent of inmate homicides in the Texas correctional system, and later became known as the "mad dog" of Texas corrections (Pelz, Marquart, & Pelz, 1991).

The Aryan Brotherhood structure within the federal prison system used a three-member council of high-ranking members. Until recently, the federal branch of the Aryan Brotherhood was aligned with the California Aryan Brotherhood, but differences in opinion caused them to split into separate branches. The federal branch no longer cooperates with the Mexican Mafia in such areas as drugs and contract killing within prisons, but as of October 1997, the California branch still continued to associate with the Mexican Mafia. Rees (1996) suggested that the Aryan Brotherhood aligned with other supremacist organizations to strengthen its hold in prisons. The Aryan Brotherhood also has strong chapters on the streets (Valentine, 1995), which allows criminal conduct inside and outside prisons to support each other.

Black Panther George Jackson united black groups such as the Black Liberation Army, Symbionese Liberation Army, and the Weatherman Underground Organization to form one large organization, the Black Guerilla Family, which emerged in San Quentin in 1966. Leaning on a Marxist-Leninist philosophy, the Black Guerilla Family was considered to be one of the more politically charged revolutionary gangs, which scared prison management and the public (Hunt et al., 1993). Recently, offshoots within the Black Guerilla Family have appeared. California reported the appearance of a related group known as the Black Mafia (Orlando-Morningstar, 1997).

La Nuestra Familia ("our family") was established in the 1960s in California's Soledad prison, although some argue it began in the Deuel Vocational Center (Landre, Miller, & Porter, 1997). The original members were Hispanic inmates from Northern California's agricultural Central Valley who aligned to protect themselves from the Los Angeles-based Mexican Mafia. *La Nuestra Familia* has a formal structure and rules as well as a governing body known as *La Mesa*, or a board of directors. Today, *La Nuestra Familia* still wars against the Mexican Mafia over drug trafficking but the war seems to be easing in California (Orlando-Morningstar, 1997).

The Texas Syndicate emerged in 1958 at Deuel Vocational Institute in California. It appeared at California's Folsom Prison in the early 1970s and at San Quentin in 1976 because other gangs were harassing native Texans. Inmate members are generally Texas Mexican Americans, but now the Texas Syndicate offers membership to Latin Americans and perhaps Guamese as well. The Texas Syndicate opposes other Mexican American gangs, especially those from Los Angeles (Hunt et al., 1993). Dominating the crime agenda is drug trafficking inside and outside prison and selling protection to inmates (Landre et al., 1997).

Like other prison gangs, the Texas Syndicate has a hierarchical structure with a president and vice president and an appointed chairman in each local area, either in a prison or in the community (Orlando-Morningstar, 1997). The chairman watches over that area's vice chairman, captain, lieutenant, sergeant at arms, and soldiers. Lower-ranking members perform the gang's criminal activity. The gang's officials, except for the president and vice president, become soldiers again if they are moved to a different prison, thus avoiding local-level group conflict. Proposals within the gang are voted on, with each member having one vote; the majority decision determines group behavior.

The *Mexikanemi* (known also as the Texas Mexican Mafia) was established in 1984. Its name and symbols cause confusion with the Mexican Mafia. As the largest gang in the Texas prison system, it is emerging in the federal system as well and has been known to kill outside as well as inside prison. The *Mexikanemi* spars with the Mexican Mafia and the Texas Syndicate, although it has been said that the *Mexikanemi* and the Texas Syndicate are aligning themselves against the Mexican Mafia (Orlando-Morningstar, 1997). The *Mexikanemi* has a president, vice president, regional generals, lieutenants, sergeants, and soldiers. The ranking positions are elected by the group based on leadership skills. Members keep their positions unless they are reassigned to a new prison. The *Mexikanemi* has a 12-part constitution. For example, part five says that the sponsoring member is responsible for the person he sponsors; if necessary, a new person may be eliminated by his sponsor (Orlando-Morningstar, 1997).

Hunt et al. (1993) suggest that the *Nortenos* and the *Surenos* are new Chicano gangs in California, along with the New Structure and the Border Brothers. The origins and alliances of these groups are unclear; however, the Border Brothers are comprised of Spanish-speaking Mexican American inmates and tend to remain solitary. Prison officials report that the Border Brothers seem to be gaining membership and control as more Mexican American inmates are convicted and imprisoned.

The Crips and Bloods, traditional Los Angeles street gangs, are gaining strength in the prisons as well as are the 415s, a group from the San Francisco area (415 is a San Francisco area code). The Federal Bureau of Prisons cites 14 other disruptive groups within the federal system, which have been documented as of

1995, including the Texas Mafia, the Bull Dogs, and the Dirty White Boys (Landre et al., 1997).

Prison Gangs and Violence

Prison gangs dominate the drug business and many researchers argue that prison gangs also are responsible for most prison violence (Ingraham & Wellford, 1987). Motivated by a desire to make money and be at the top of an institution's inmate power structure, prison gangs exploit the inherent weaknesses resulting from overcrowded, understaffed mega-prisons such as correctional staffers' inability to watch the activities of say, 3,000–5,000 inmates every moment of each day, month after month.

Where profits are at stake, research on street gangs shows that violence is often the outcome. Inside prisons, the same pattern appears. Camp and Camp (1985) noted that prison gang members were on aggregate 3 percent of the prison population but caused 50 percent or more of the prison violence. In a small confined area with a finite number of drug customers as well as customers of other gang-related services, such as gambling and prostitution (Fleisher, 1989), the stage is set for inter-gang competition (Fong, Vogel, & Buentello, 1992), especially in overcrowded prisons. "Turf wars" occur on the street as well as in prison, where gang members and non-gang members are packed together, leaving few options for retreat to a safe and neutral spot (Gaston, 1996).

Correctional Responses to Prison Gangs

Prison gangs have had adverse effects on prison quality of life. Those adverse effects have motivated correctional responses to crime, disorder, and rule violations. Many correctional agencies have developed policies to control prison gang-affiliated inmates. Carlson outlines the approaches used by major correctional agencies to handle prison gangs (see article in this issue).

Since the publication of Clemmer's (1958) classic *The Prison Community*, prison scholars have debated the effect that prison has on the formation of inmate groups and individual behavior. Do inmates form disruptive groups as a result of the actions of prison administrators? Will inmates form disruptive groups as a prison extension of their street behavior (Jacobs, 1977) in spite of the best efforts of prison managers to create a positive environment (Hunt et al., 1993)?

Fong and Buentello (1991) argue that inmates' need for social identity and belonging contribute to the formation of inmate prison groups; however, a need for identity and belonging does not explain the importation of outside gang structures, names, and symbols into a prison where security and continuous oversight are among the institution's principal organizational traits. That inmates form groups based on the need for identity, belonging, personal interests, and race/ethnicity conforms to well-known processes in all human groups, and such behavior inside a prison should not be a surprise. To try to suppress human tendencies to form social groups, as was tried in the early days of the Pennsylvania system, would be pointless as a general management strategy (Knox, 2000). In many respects, however, today's super-maximum security institutions attempt to do just that.

In institutions where prison management controls on inmate crime and violence are weak and where prisons routinely violate inmates' civil rights (Fong et al., 1995; DiIulio, 1987; Ralph and Marquart, 1991), it may be understandable that inmates form tips and cliques to ensure their own physical safety. Given this line of argument, if prisons want fewer inmate tips and cliques and by extension prison gangs, management must step forward proactively and offer inmates a meaningful alternative to prison gangs and gang crime and offer inmates treatment for personal issues such as addiction. Scott's article focuses on altering the prison environment. He argues that prisons, like mainstream communities, must broaden their approach to dealing with prison gangs. Hardening the environment, Scott argues, may fail as a long-term prison control strategy as law enforcement suppression, to the exclusion of social intervention, has failed to quell the street gang problem.

Adjusting prison environments most often happens in court. Jacobs (1977) argues that the courts weakened the authority of correctional officers to control gangs taking control since the earliest cases on inmates' rights; prison administrators are confined within the limits of case law. Federal Bureau of Prisons' lawyer Daniel Eckhart reviews recent federal legal cases on prison gangs. Eckhart's useful article informs correctional administrators who must develop gang control strategies that meet the limits of federal court precedents; such precedents are also useful information to correctional researchers who may evaluate prison control strategies.

Mainline prisons for the most part are expected to house inmates, independent of gang affiliation. Prison suppression and intervention strategies likely will affect gang-affiliated inmates differently from non-gang-affiliated inmates. Why? Shelden (1991) compared 60 gang members (45 black, 15 Hispanic) to 60 non-gang members. There were a number of similarities between the gang and non-gang groups: they shared similar socioeconomic backgrounds, education levels, and marital status; both groups had substance abuse problems. Gang members, however, were more likely to have never been employed, more likely to have a juvenile crime record (30 percent of them had juvenile court records compared with 8 percent of non-gang inmates); 32 percent of the gang members had 15 or more arrests compared with 7 percent of non-members; and gang members also were more likely to have used a weapon than non-members. Krienert and Fleisher show in their article in this issue that new admissions into the Nebraska Department of Corrections who report a prior gang affiliation are significantly different from those who do not report a gang affiliation on many of the same factors Shelden used. Their research documents the growing nature of this problem.

Shelden's contribution also shows that while imprisoned, gang members were twice as likely to have more than five rule violations, were more likely to violate drug use sanctions, were more likely to fight, and were less likely to be involved in treatment programs. Without in-prison treatment, education, and vocational training, the likelihood that gang-affiliated inmates would be prepared for a lawful lifestyle outside prison is low. The article by Davis and Flannery in this issue deals with special challenges that gang-affiliated inmates pose to therapists.

How have prison officials responded to prison gangs? Prisons have tried a variety of overt and covert strategies, including the use of inmate informants, the use of segregation units for prison gang members, the isolation of prison gang leaders, the lockdown of entire institutions, the vigorous prosecution of criminal acts committed by prison gang members, the interruption of prison gang members' internal and external communications, and the case-by-case examination of prison gang offenses. There are, however, no published research evaluations testing the efficacy of these suppression strategies on curbing prison gang violence and/or other criminal conduct inside correctional institutions. Below is a brief summary of some of these anti-prison-gang initiatives.

The Texas state legislature passed a bill in September 1985 that made it a "felony for any inmate to possess a weapon" (Ralph & Marquart, 1991, p. 45). The bill also limited the discretionary authority of sentencing judges: inmates convicted of weapons possession must serve that sentence subsequent to other sentences. Officials believe that laws like this might help to keep inmates, especially those in prison gangs, under control (Ralph & Marquart, 1991).

A popular control procedure is segregation. Inmates are isolated in a cell 23 hours a day, with one hour assigned to recreation and/or other activities. Texas used administrative segregation and put all known prison gang members into segregation in 1985 in the hope of limiting their influence on mainline inmate populations. Violence in the general population decreased, with nine prison gang-motivated homicides from 1985 to 1990; fewer armed assaults were reported as well. By 1991, segregation housed more than 1,500 gang members (Ralph & Marquart, 1991).

By contrast, Knox (2000) reports that more than half of the 133 prison officials interviewed in a national survey on prison gangs believe a segregation policy is not effective because gang activity still occurs. When an order is issued by a prison gang to commit a violent act, it is carried out, even in a segregation unit. Then, too, segregation is expensive and does not solve the problem of developing better prison management to control prison gangs.

Isolating gang leaders has become a popular control strategy. With a prison gang leader locked down, vertical communication within the gang ideally would weaken and the prison gang group's solidarity eventually would deteriorate. One version of isolating prison gang leaders is to transfer them among institutions or keep them circulating between prisons (United States Department of Justice, 1992). There are no published evaluations of isolation and/or "bus therapy."

Another attempt to reduce gang membership is "jacketing." This involves putting an official note in an inmate's file if he is suspected of being involved with a gang. This note follows him in prison and allows authorities to transfer him to a high-security facility. Many find this process inappropriate because it may involve suspected but unconfirmed gang activity, often reported by a snitch, which leads to incorrectly labeling an inmate as a prison gang member or associate.

When so labeled, an inmate can be controlled with threats of segregation and transfer. There are no published evaluations of this approach either.

Correctional agencies now use databases to track prison gang members and gang activities. This allows for effective communication between a correctional agency and a state police agency and improves data accuracy because data can be entered as soon as they are gathered (Gaston, 1996). The New York City Department of Correction uses a system that allows for digitized photos that document gang members' marks and/or tattoos. Database searches can be done by a tattoo, scar, or other identifying marks. The speed and capacity to update intelligence information make the use of a shared database an effective tool in prison gang management.

Providing alternative programming could become part of prison gang management strategy; however, prison gang members have not embraced such programming. The Hampden County Correctional Center in Ludlow, Massachusetts, developed a graduated program for prison gang members wanting to leave segregation. The program uses movies, discussion sessions, and homework. At the program's end, participants must write a statement certifying they will no longer participate in gang activities. Two years into the program, 190 inmates were enrolled and 17 were returned to segregation for gang activities (Toller & Tsagaris, 1996). Details of the program's evaluation are not available.

Another control strategy is the use of out-of-state transfers, which send key prison gang members out of state in the hope of stopping or slowing a prison gang's activities. If a gang already has been established, it is hoped that such a transfer would disrupt a gang to the point of its demise; however, there are no data showing the effectiveness of this type of control strategy. In fact, transferring a high-ranking prison gang member could be the impetus to transfer his prison gang to yet another institution (United States Department of Justice, 1992).

Correctional agencies have tried to weaken prison gangs by assigning members of different prison gangs to the same work assignment and living quarters in anticipation of limiting the power of one prison gang over another at a specific place. The Texas Department of Corrections, for instance, assigned prison gang members to two or three high-security lockdown institutions. Illinois tried this approach to no avail because the inmate prison gang population was too large to control effectively within a few locations (United States Department of Justice, 1992). Illinois developed a "gang-free" institution near Springfield, but as yet there are no published evaluations of its effectiveness on reducing gang-related/motivated crime within the Illinois Department of Corrections.

Camp and Camp (1985) surveyed facilities and asked officials which strategies they were most likely to employ against prison gangs. Transfer was cited by 27 of the 33 agencies (such an approach is analogous to schools expelling disruptive students to alternative schools); the use of informers was cited 21 times; prison gang member segregation was cited 20 times; prison gang leader segregation was cited 20 times; facility lockdown was cited 18 times; and vigorous prosecution and interception of prison gang members' communications were cited 16 times.

Knox and Tromanhauser (1991) surveyed prison wardens asking about prison gang control: 70.9 percent advocated bus therapy. Some prison officials tried to quell prison gang disruptions by discussing those disruptions with gang leaders. And another 5.5 percent of the wardens said they ignored prison gangs. These researchers show that fewer than half of the prisons surveyed provided any type of prison gang training; but recently, Knox (2000) shows that correctional officers training has improved, with a finding that more than two-thirds of the 133 facilities surveyed provided some gang training in 1999.

A Need for More Collaboration

We have little hard data on the demographics of today's prison gangs and the nature and levels of prison gang-related disorder in American prisons. This lack of data is a serious impediment to making progress against a serious and growing problem. The Camp and Camp (1985) inventory of prison gangs describes an earlier era in American corrections. Collaborative research between correctional officials and experienced gang and prison researchers can yield the data needed to develop effective prison gang intervention and suppression strategies as well as the data needed to test the efficacy of current strategies. Collaboration between correctional agencies and university researchers is a key to creating strong solutions to the difficult, persistent problem posed by prison gangs. Such collaboration should create the programs that will increase the likelihood that prison gang members, leaving institutions after decades of doing time, will remain crime free. Imagine how strange today's job market looks to the inmates who were imprisoned in 1980 or even 1990. To be sure, the challenge of beginning a career, even for a college graduate, is daunting. For a former inmate and a prison gang member, searching to find a lawful path will be difficult and alien.

Efforts to control prison gangs must be matched by thoughtful community initiatives. Such initiatives may include carefully designed community reintegration programs offering specialized education and training to meet the expectations of entry-level high-tech employment. Research shows that prison gangs' criminal influence extends into the community (Fong & Buentello, 1991). The important implication of this observation is that prison gangs will gain a stronger hold in communities if communities do not structure intervention to include more than law enforcement suppression. If that happens, street gangs may become better structured and drug gangs may become more powerful forces in the community. The article by Fleisher, Decker, and Curry in this issue urges correctional agencies to unite with communities to provide careful, post-imprisonment programming for gang-affiliated inmates. In this way, the response to gangs both on the street and in prison can be comprehensive and integrated.

References

Baugh, D. G. (1993). *Gangs in correctional facilities: A national assessment.* Laurel, MD: American Correctional Association.

Camp, G. M., & Camp, C. G. (1985). *Prison gangs: Their extent, nature, and impact on prisons.* Washington, DC: U. S. Government Printing Office.

Clemmer, D. (1958). *The prison community*. New York: Holt, Rinehart, and Winston.

Decker, S. H., Bynum, T. S., & Weisel, D. L. (1998). Gangs as organized crime groups: A tale of two cities. *Justice Quarterly, 15*, 395–423.

DiIulio, J. J. (1987). *Governing prisons: A comparative study of correctional management*. New York: Free Press.

Fleisher, M. S. (1989). *Warehousing violence*. Newbury Park, CA: Sage Publications.

Fong, R. S. (1990). The organizational structure of prison gangs: A Texas Case Study. *Federal Probation, 59*, 36–43.

Fong, R. S., & Buentello, S. (1991). The detection of prison gang development: An empirical assessment. *Federal Probation, 55*, 66–69.

Fong, R. S., Vogel, R. E., & Buentello, S. (1992). Prison gang dynamics: A look inside the Texas Department of Corrections. In P. J. Benekos & A. V. Merlo (Eds.), *Corrections: Dilemmas and directions*. Cincinprison culture: Prison gangs and the case of the "Pepsi generation." *Social Problems, 40*, 398–409.

Ingraham, B. L., & Wellford, C. F. (1987). The totality of conditions test in eighth-amendment litigation. In S. D. Gottfredson & S. McConville (Eds.), *America's correctional crisis: Prison populations and public policy*. New York: Greenwood Press.

Jacobs, J. B. (1974). Street gangs behind bars. *Social Problems, 21*, 395–409.

Jacobs, J. B. (1977). *Stateville: The penitentiary in mass society*. Chicago: University of Chicago Press.

Knox, G. W. (2000). A national assessment of gangs and security threat groups (STGs) in adult correctional institutions: Results of the 1999 Adult Corrections Survey. *Journal of Gang Research, 7*, 1–45.

Knox, G. W., & Tromanhauser, E. D. (1991). Gangs and their control in adult correctional institutions. *The Prison Journal, 71*, 15–22.

Landre, R., Miller, M., & Porter, D. (1997). *Gangs: A handbook for community awareness*. New York: Facts On File, Inc.

Lane, M. P. (1989, July). Inmate gangs. *Corrections Today, 51*, 98–99.

Lyman, M. D. (1989). *Gangland*. Springfield, IL: Charles C Thomas.

Marquart, J. W. & Sorensen, J. R. eds., (1997). *Correctional contexts: Contemporary and classical readings*. Los Angeles, CA: Roxbury Pub.

Montgomery R. H., Jr., & Crews, G. A. (1998). *A history of correctional violence: An examination of reported causes of riots and disturbances*. Lanham, MD: American Correctional Association.

Orlando-Morningstar, D. (1997, October). Prison gangs. *Special Needs Offender Bulletin, 2*, 1–13.

Pelz, M. E., Marquart, J. W., & Pelz, C. T. (1991). Right-wing extremism in the Texas prisons: The rise and fall of the Aryan Brotherhood of Texas. *The Prison Journal, 71*, 23–37.

Ralph, P. H., & Marquart, J. W. (1991). Gang violence in Texas prisons. *The Prison Journal, 71*, 38–49.

Rees, T. A., Jr. (1996, Fall). Joining the gang: A look at youth gang recruitment. *Journal of Gang Research, 4*, 19–25.

Shelden, R. G. (1991). A comparison of gang members and non-gang members in a prison setting. *The Prison Journal, 71*, 50–60.

Stastny, C., & Tyrnauer, G. (1983). *Who rules the joint? The changing political culture of maximum-security prisons in America*. New York: Lexington Books.

Toller, W., & Tsagaris, B. (1996, October). Managing institutional gangs: A practical approach combining security and human services. *Corrections Today, 58*, 100–111.

United States Department of Justice. (1992). *Management strategies in disturbances and with gangs/disruptive groups*. Washington, DC: U. S. Government Printing Office.

Valentine, B. (1995). *Gang intelligence manual*. Boulder, CO: Paladin Press.

Whitehead, J. (1986b). Job burnout and job satisfaction among probation managers. *Journal of Criminal Justice, 14*, 25–35.

Whitehead, J. (1987). Probation officer burnout: A test of two theories. *Journal of Criminal Justice, 15*(1), 1–16.

Whitehead, J., & Lindquist, C. (1986). Correctional officer job burnout: A path model. *Journal of Crime & Delinquency, 23*(1), 23–42.

Wright, K., & Saylor, W. (1991, December). Male and female employees' perception of prison work: Is there a difference? *Justice Quarterly, 8*, 505–524.

Zimmer, L. (1986). *Women guarding men*. Chicago: University of Chicago Press.

Zupan, L. (1986). Gender-related differences in correctional officer's perceptions and attitudes. *Journal of Criminal Justice, 14*, 349–361.

Zupan, L. (1992). The progress of women correctional officers in all-male prisons. In I. L. Moyer (Ed.), *The changing roles of women in the criminal justice system* (2nd ed., pp. 323–343). Prospect Heights, IL: Waveland Press.

CORRECTIONS MANAGEMENT QUARTERLY, 2001, 5(1), 1–9.

26. The Evolving Nature of Prison Argot and Sexual Hierarchies

Christopher Hensley
Jeremy Wright
Richard Tewksbury
Tammy Castle

Prison argot and sexual hierarchies have consistently been found to be present in U.S. correctional facilities. However, recent years have seen very few studies that focus specifically on argot labels and sexual hierarchies that exist in prisons. Using data collected from 174 face-to-face structured interviews with male inmates in multisecurity-level correctional facilities in Oklahoma, we found many similarities and differences with previous research on the issues of argot labels and the sexual hierarchy.

The rapid and continued growth of U.S. prison populations in the last 2 decades has brought with it increasing attention and concern about whether and how U.S. society can afford (financially, politically, and culturally) to maintain the correctional industry. However, although a great deal of attention has been directed toward these macrolevel issues, attention to microlevel issues, such as programmatic operations and inmate culture, have been largely neglected. This is clearly a shortcoming of the penological literature. Without a thorough understanding of how institutions operate on a day-to-day basis, it may not be possible to fully and adequately address larger scale issues, such as finances and the place of prisons in the political and social structure of society.

Understandings of the microlevel operations of correctional institutions are the world of the prison inmate. Inmates, obviously, live lives very different from their counterparts in free society; prison inmates live in a "total institution" (Goffman, 1961). Total institutions are closed, single-sex societies separated from society socially and physically. Inhabitants of total institutions have essentially all decisions about the structure and content of their daily lives made for them, and they share all aspects of their daily lives within these types of institutions. However, one area in which occupants of total institutions do retain some degree of control is in their individual and collective abilities to develop unique values, norms, and means for exercising social control over such. Central to this cultural construction is the delineation of specific social roles, which are accompanied by rigidly proscribed behavioral expectations. These distinct values and behavioral roles are referred to as the prison subculture.

Newly arriving inmates in a correctional facility who seek to ease their social transition must learn the values, attitudes, and behavioral expectations that structure the operations of the institution. According to Einat and Einat (2000). "The norms and values of the inmate code form the core of an inmate subculture, providing its members with informal means to gain power and status and, thereby, a way to mitigate their sense of social rejection and compensate for their loss of autonomy and security" (p. 309). When the new inmates have accepted the prison lifestyle and criminal values, they have been "prisonized." Any inmate whose behavior violates the values, behavioral codes, and traditions faces the likelihood of sanctions from other inmates, staff, or both. The inmate code is one of the most important aspects of their new culture that inmates are expected to adopt, and which can indicate acceptance of institutional values as well as the ability to avoid accidental affronts to others (via incorrect use of language).

Prison researchers who have studied male prison life have found that inmates use a special type of language or slang within the prison subculture that reflects the "distorted norms, values, and mores of the offenders" (Dumond, 1992, p. 138). As such, the vocabulary and speech patterns of prison inmates—what is known as prison argot—are largely distinct from those of noninmates. Language, as is well known, provides the parameters of understandings—and possibilities—for constructing a social and cultural milieu. Perhaps nowhere is this clearer than in correctional institutions, where inmates live, think, and function within the framework defined by the argot (Bondesson, 1989). Thus, the argot is centered on the functions that it serves for inmates. Einat and Einat (2000) document six functions of argot roles:

- the need to be different and unique
- alleviation of feelings or rejection and refusal
- facilitation of social interactions and relationships
- declaration of belonging to a subculture or social status
- a tool of social identification leading to a sense of belonging to a group
- secrecy (pp. 310–311)

One critical component of correctional institution culture, building on argot roles, is the prison sexual hierarchy. Sexual behavior among inmates does occur, although the sexual activities of individual inmates and with whom one engages in sex is governed by a hierarchical system of roles and relationships. Within this structure the roles, activities, and actors involved in sexual activities are assigned unique, institutionally specific labels. According to Dumond (1992). "While the terms may have changed somewhat over the decades, prison slang defines sexual habits and inmates' status simultaneously, using homosexuality as a means of placing individuals within the inmate caste system" (p. 138). These sexual scripts define an inmate's position within the prison society. Dumond (1992) also found that argot roles "help to define the treatment which an inmate is likely to receive from other inmates and corrections officers" (p. 138). Labels, then, are central elements in the structuring of social interactions.

Previous research has attempted to describe the inmate subculture, including sexual argot roles and the prison sex hierarchy. However, inmates in prison today face a myriad of new challenges, many of which are at least indirectly related to sexuality issues. Overcrowding, fears of contracting HIV, and widespread influence of gangs are just some of the issues inmates confront as they enter and become integrated into the prison subculture. Understanding the prison subculture is not only important but also necessary to inmates' survival while incarcerated. Recent years, however, have seen very few studies focusing specifically on argot labels and the sexual hierarchy that exists in prisons. The purpose of this study is to describe the sexual roles and hierarchy that exist in prison, with special emphasis on sexual argot, at the start of the 21st century and to assess how these factors have transformed prison subcultures (see also Hensley, 2002).

Literature Review

In 1934, Joseph Fishman, a former inspector for federal prisons, conducted one of the first ethnographies on sex in male prisons. Fishman found that homosexuality was an offense in many communities, and men were arrested and sent to prison for this offense. The Penitentiary at Welfare Island in New York was a prison where men were commonly sent for offenses such as attempting to corrupt a minor, indecent exposure, and soliciting members of the same sex for money. Men convicted of these offenses who came into prison were often passive and known by other inmates as "punks," "girls," "fags," "pansies," or "fairies." These inmates had feminine characteristics and often wore makeup. Other inmates, known as "top men" or "wolves," took advantage of these homosexuals. These sexual argot roles marked the passive prisoners as appropriate targets for sexual assault.

Research in the last 40 years, built on the foundation laid by Fishman, has expanded, yet largely reiterated the basic finding of victimized and victimizing inmates in prisons. Donaldson (1993), Sagarin (1976), Kirkham (1971), and Sykes (1958) studied social roles in male prisons and found that inmates engaging in homosexual activity were divided into three categories. The first category consisted of those inmates who played an active, aggressive (i.e., masculine) role in same-sex sexual relations. Inmates referred to these men as wolves, "voluntary aggressors," or "daddies." Inmates in the second and third categories played a more passive and/or submissive (i.e., feminine) role and were referred to as punks and fags.

In large part, adoption of a wolf role may be attributed to the strong emphasis in correctional institution culture on the maintenance of masculinity. To prove their masculinity to themselves and others—and therefore avoid being sexually victimized—some men may opt to be (sexually) aggressive. In essence, to avoid being a sexual victim it may be necessary to sexually victimize others. Wolves assumed an aggressive role and often preyed on other inmates, relying on either violence or coercion as their methods of sexually displaying their masculinity. Even though wolves engaged in same-sex sexual behavior with fags (often via force), the goal for wolves in these encounters was nothing more than physical release and enhancement of a social reputation. Raping punks reinforced the wolves' masculine identity, thereby solidifying the wolves' high position in the institutional status hierarchy. Through this aggressive behavior, wolves managed to escape the stigma of being labeled a homosexual, although they were engaged in sexual activities with other men (Donaldson, 1993; Kirkham, 1971; Sagarin, 1976; Sykes 1958).

Fags adopted the same role in prison as they are assumed to have adopted in the free community. The fag fulfilled the stereotype of the homosexual and was viewed by other inmates as playing a natural role. Fags engaged in sex with men because they were born that way. The fag was known by his exaggerated feminine mannerisms, often wearing makeup and dressing in women's clothing. They were considered gender nonconformists and posed little threat to the masculinity of other inmates. In fact, fags provided the feminine counterpart against which wolves could construct their masculinity. Fags were defined as having "pussies," not "assholes," and wore "blouses," not "shirts" (Donaldson, 1993). Although fags, "effeminates," or "queens" were accorded significantly less respect than wolves (because of their femininity), the fact that these inmates were fulfilling their "natural role" did accord them some degree of respect. Fags occupied a status below wolves but above that of the most despised, the punks (Donaldson, 1993; Kirkham, 1971; Sagarin, 1976; Sykes, 1958).

The label of punk or "jailhouse turnout" was assigned to those inmates who engaged in sexual activities with another inmate (almost always a wolf because of coercion, force, or rape. Punks were viewed as cowards who were morally weak and unable to defend themselves in prison. In short, a punk was a male who did not fulfill his role as a man. Unlike the fags, punks did not display feminine characteristics. However, because of their displays of weakness (physical) punks were often targets of sexual attacks. Donaldson (1993 found that punks had some common characteristics. These included being younger in age, inexperienced first-time offenders, middle class, White, and physically smaller in size. Punks were viewed as having forfeited their masculinity as a result of submitting to a more aggressive inmate. Punks were considered slaves, and wolves used them as commodities for protection of goods and services. Kirkham (1971) expanded on this idea, identifying inmates who declined to adopt a feminine role yet traded sexual activities for goods and services (i.e., prostitutes) "canteen punks." Universally, researchers have reported that punks occupied the lowest rungs on the institutional cultural hierarchy.

The idea that there is an important distinction between true homosexuals and those who engaged in sexual activity due to situational forces (situational homosexuality) has been a common theme throughout 20th-century prison sex research. Buffman (1972) focused on this distinction, further identifying two categories of inmates who engaged in situational homosexuality: victims and rapists. Victims were referred to as made homosexuals and were stigmatized as effeminate men. Rapists were referred to as "jockers." Jockers remained consistent with their masculine role: thus they were seen as maintaining their masculinity and therefore escaped stigmatization in prison.

Another variation on the approach to argot sexual roles emerged with Wooden and Parker's (1982) suggestion that argot roles were adopted based on simple distinction between sexually engaged inmates based on one's role as an insertor and insertee. The group that took the role of insertee was the homosexuals and vulnerable heterosexual "kids." These inmates were perceived and defined as feminine and encouraged (or forced) to present themselves with (often exaggerated) feminine characteristics. These inmates were commonly referred to as "broads," "bitches," "queens," and "sissies." The homosexuals usually conformed to this role and adopted feminine names. However, when the role was imposed on those who were not true homosexuals, these inmates were labeled as having been "turned out."

The dominant partner (the insertor) who maintained his masculine identity was known as the jocker, "stud," or "straight who uses." The jocker's sexual behavior with another male was viewed as situational, and therefore acceptable. The jocker exploited the vulnerable homosexual or heterosexual inmate in prison and treated his sexual partner as a surrogate female. In this way, jockers were attempting to replicate normal sexual roles outside of prison.

Wooden and Parker (1982) also added to the literature arguing that inmates tolerated sissies because they maintained their natural role. Heterosexual kids were tolerated as long as they did not attempt to change the role specification and accepted the scripts of the inmate subculture. However, submissive men were not respected or seen as real men. They were strictly commodities that jockers often used to satisfy a need, whether sexual or economic.

Most recently, Hersher (1989) reported that a wide range of terms were used to designate effeminate homosexuals at the U.S. Penitentiary at Lompoc, California, including, "skull buster," "punk," "queen," "fag," "homo," bitch, "faggot," "fruiter," broad, kid, and "old lady." However, four dominant categories and associated argot roles were found at the prison. These included fags, "fuck boys," "straights," and turn-outs.

Fags and fuck boys were the female sex role players in the institution. Both groups claimed homosexuality and were described as homosexual by other inmates, however, some differences were evident between the two. Fags were effeminate homosexuals who were often distinguishable by their gait, dress, hair, and speech. Fuck boys, on the other hand, were not distinguishable by these traits.

Straights and turn-outs were the male sex role players in the institution. They did not consider themselves homosexual, nor did the other inmates define them as homosexual. Straights used fags for sexual gratification although some straights developed long-term sexual relationships with other straights. When these relationships did develop they were very carefully guarded and remained very private. On the other hand, turn-outs took a passive strategy by seducing inmates with commissary privileges or other items.

What stands as a major gap in the research on prison culture is that during the last decade there have been essentially no studies on the role of argot and the prison sex hierarchy in male correctional facilities. Therefore, the purpose of this study is to shed new light on an integral part of the prison subculture, argot roles and the prison sex hierarchy.

Methodology

A total of 300 inmates (100 inmates from a minimum, medium, and maximum security facility in Oklahoma) were randomly selected and invited to participate in the study. However, only 58% (n = 174) of invited inmates elected to participate. Data were gathered during face-to-face, structured interviews with inmates from all three security-level institutions (minimum = 52, medium = 61, and maximum = 61).

Results

Interviews revealed that the three traditional sexual roles outlined by previous research (i.e., wolves, fags, and punks) were still present in the prison subculture in all three security-level institutions. However, results also show some important differences from previous research, especially in the structure of the institutional sexual hierarchy and in additional refinement of the traditional roles.

One of the primary differences uncovered in this study is the identification of two subcategories within the wolf and fag roles. Whereas previous research has presented these roles as rather unified, inmates in the present study detailed two distinct subcategories of the wolf category: the "aggressive wolf" and the "nonaggressive wolf." Aggressive wolves were depicted as inmates of African American descent who were considered physically and verbally tough. These inmates entered prison with a heterosexual orientation and maintained their masculinity by sexually assaulting younger, weaker inmates (punks). Masculine identification is also reinforced by restricting sexual involvement to only active roles (i.e., receiving oral sex from punks and inserting during anal sex). However, inmates also make clear that aggressive sexual interactions—such as raping punks—although providing a sexual release, had more to do with status and power than sex. When asked about their current sexual orientation, all of the self-described aggressive wolves maintained their heterosexual identity.

Nonaggressive wolves (or "teddy bears"), on the other hand, typically did not report sexually assaulting their sex partners. Rather, these inmates sought other inmates ("fish" or "closeted gays") who were predisposed and willing to voluntarily participate in sexual activities with another male while in prison. Nonaggressive wolves more often than not were Caucasian men who entered prison with a heterosexual identity. These inmates, similar to their aggressive counterparts, were also able to maintain their masculine role by participating in active roles during sex. However, when asked about their current sexual orientation, more than one half of the nonaggressive wolves indicated that they now identified as bisexual. Thus, many of these inmates—because of the lack of heterosexual sexual opportunities in prison—had modified their self-concepts regarding their sexual orientation.

Just as the traditional category of the wolf has been refined into two more specific categories, so too has the category of the prison fag been more closely distinguished. Fags, in the present study, have been distinguished as either fish or closet gays. Fish (a term previously reserved to refer to newly arriving inmates) is now a label for referring to (typically African American) inmates who present themselves with a feminine appearance and enacting stereotypically feminine role. Although violating institutional rules and regulations, these inmates wore makeup, displayed female mannerisms, and took on female nicknames. Fish entered into prison life with a homosexual identity and maintained this identity by assuming a passive role during sexual activity (i.e., performing oral sex and playing the insertee role during anal sex). Some fish also sold themselves for canteen goods and cigarettes, while others sought out relationships with nonaggressive wolves.

A closet gay is an inmate, typically Caucasian, who is believed to enter prison with a hidden homosexuality identity. Closet gays are perceived as having the ability to take on either an active or passive role during sexual activity. Such inmates, however, strive to maintain masculine appearance and mannerisms. They typically sought other closet gays in hopes of forming a "true love" relationship.

As evidenced in previous studies, there is a clearly defined prison sexual hierarchy with wolves on top, fags in the middle, and punks on the bottom. However, this study suggests that this ranking system may be being replaced with a newly defined hierarchy. Inmates in the present study reported that the status of fags had progressed upward to now be relatively equal to that of the wolves. Fish and aggressive wolves were the most respected and feared groups within the prison sexual hierarchy. Many inmates feared fish because they were known for their aggressive, albeit in nonsexual ways, behavior. For example, two incidents of fish killing other inmates because the other inmates had referred to them as punks were reported by the inmates in the maximum security facility. In addition, fish were also known for their jealousy; consequently, a number of inmates reported that they were scared to engage in sexual activities with the fishes' sex partners.

Closet gays and nonaggressive wolves typically occupied positions of relatively equal status. However, both of these groups of inmates were slightly lower in the institutional ranking system than the fish and aggressive wolves. Punks, however, remain at the bottom of the prison sexual hierarchy. All other inmates continued to view punks as cowards who were physically and morally weak. Punks often sold themselves for protection. Therefore, inmates saw them as inferior to other inmates within the correctional facility.

Discussion

Inmates in correctional institutions develop an institutional subculture, with a code of conduct, roles, behavioral expectations, and an institution-specific language at the core. The code of conduct consists of norms and values that, in turn, structure the informal patterns of life among inmates. According to Einat and

Einat (2000). "[This] code is directly linked to the process of socialization and adaptation to prison life" (p. 309). In other words, the inmate code has universal elements that cut across all correctional facilities because the normative society, its attributes, and its delegates are inherent opponents of prisoners. The language (argot) that characterizes institutional subcultures is one of the principal elements of prisonization, as well as the development and perpetuation of the inmate code.

Similarities between the early research regarding sexual argot roles and the present study are clear. Inmates who engage in same-sex sexual activity are labeled based on the sexual role they portray in the interaction. The findings of the present study on sexual argot roles and the prison sexual hierarchy in male facilities suggest that the nature of these sexual relationships is changing. In male facilities, wolves originally held the highest status in the prison sexual hierarchy. However, this study indicates that the status of fish is now gaining equality with the status of aggressive wolves. Nonaggressive wolves and closet gays maintain statuses of relative equality with each other, falling in the middle of the sexual hierarchy. The punks continue to remain on the bottom of the sexual hierarchy. Although the prison subculture is changing, punks continue to be the most despised inmates in the prison.

In conclusion, sexual argot roles in prison reflect and reinforce the organization, language, and status hierarchy of the prison subculture. To survive in prison, inmates must learn to reject the norms of free society and adopt the new normative order. It is also important for correctional administrators and staff to understand the organization of the prison subculture. Learning the language and normative codes help staff maximize the efficiency of the prison, as well as the safety of staff and inmates. According to Dumond (1992), "Such information may be particularly helpful in assisting prison administration . . . in defining and managing the prison ecosystem/environment" (p. 138).

References

Bondesson, U. (1989). *Prisoners in prison societies*. New Brunswick, NJ: Transaction Publishers.

Buffman, P. (1972). *Homosexuality in prisons*. Washington, DC: U.S. Department of Justice. Law Enforcement Assistance Administration.

Donaldson, S. (1993). *A million jockers, punks, and queens: Sex among male prisoners and its implications for concepts of sexual orientation*. Available from www.igc.apc.org/spr/docs/prison-sex-lecture.html.

Dumond, R. W. (1992). The sexual assault of male inmates in incarcerated settings. *International Journal of the Sociology of Law, 20*(2), 135–157.

Einat, T., & Einat, H. (2000). Inmate argot as an expression of prison subculture: The Israeli case. *The Prison Journal, 80*(3), 309–325.

Fishman, J. (1934). *Sex in prison: Revealing sex conditions in American prisons*. New York: National Library Press.

Fleisher, M. (1989). *Warehousing violence*. Newbury Park, CA: Sage.

Goffman, E. (1961). *Asylums: Essays on the social situation of mental patients and other inmates*. Garden City, NY: Anchor.

Hensley, C. (Ed.). (2002). *Prison sex: Practice and policy*. Boulder, CO: Lynne Rienner Publishers.

Kirkham, G. L. (1971). Homosexuality in prison. In J. M. Henslin (Ed.). *Studies in the sociology of sex* (pp. 325–349). New York: Appleton-Century-Crofts.

Sagarin, E. (1976). Prison homosexuality and it's effect on post-prison behavior. *Psychiatry, 39*, 245–257.

Sykes, G. (1958). *The society of captives*. Princeton, NJ: Princeton University Press.

Wooden, W., & Parker, J. (1982). *Men behind bars: Sexual exploitation in prison*. New York: Plenum.

THE PRISON JOURNAL, Vol. 83 No. 3, September 2003, 289–300.

27. Sexual Coercion Reported by Women in Three Midwestern Prisons

Cindy Struckman-Johnson
David Struckman-Johnson

The study was an anonymous self-report survey of coercive sexual experiences of women incarcerated in three Midwestern prisons.

The sexual coercion of women in prison, defined here as the experience of being pressured or coerced into unwanted sexual contact while incarcerated, has been described as one of America's "most open secrets" (Bell et al., 1999). According to several legal scholars, women who are incarcerated in American prisons face extensive problems with sexual harassment, molestation during strip searches, coercive sexual fondling, and pressured and forced sexual intercourse, most likely perpetrated by prison staff. This information has been revealed in an increasing number of court cases in which inmates have sued prisons for sexual exploitation (Bell et al., 1999; Springfield, 2000). Human rights groups have recently launched investigations of this problem. Human Rights Watch (1996) documented numerous cases of sexual abuse of imprisoned women by male correctional officers (custodial sexual abuse) in 11 state prison systems. A report by Amnesty International (1999) listed documented cases of custodial sexual misconduct for every state.

Although sexual coercion of women in prison is increasingly recognized as a serious social issue, the topic has received scant attention from social and sex scientists (Kunselman, Tewksbury, Dumond, & Dumond, 2002). A modest number of studies have been conducted on coercive sex in prison, but most have focused on male victims (Hensley, Struckman-Johnson, & Eigenberg, 2000). Between 1960 and 1990, there were about a dozen studies conducted in men's prisons (see Dumond, 1992), but we could find only two that included female inmates. In one early work, Kassebaum (1972) commented that many women in prison were vulnerable to sexual exploitation by prison staff and other female inmates. He described an incident in which a 16-year-old girl was beaten by five other inmates for refusing sexual advances. Bartollas and Sieverdes (1983) found that 9.1% of 561 adolescent offenders in six coeducational corrections facilities for juveniles had been sexually victimized, a measure based upon inmate attitudes and staff observation of "sex games." Victimization rates for males and females were said to be equal, although the number of participants was not provided. The authors noted that one female juvenile was raped.

It was not until the mid-1990s that this topic was investigated in depth by social scientists. Baro (1997) wrote about the chronic problems of custodial sexual abuse in a small women's prison facility (population of 45–50) in Hawaii. As a participant observer working at the prison, Baro interviewed female inmates and collected court and prison records of abusive practices. She found that between 1982 and 1994, Hawaii had 38 officially acknowledged cases of custodial sexual abuse. Thirty of the cases involved men and eight presumably involved female perpetrators. Alleged abuses included forced intercourse, unwanted pregnancies, and even service as prostitutes in a hotel near the prison. Baro concluded that many female inmates, vulnerable due to past histories of sexual abuse and drug addiction, were easy targets for male prison staff.

Struckman-Johnson, Struckman-Johnson, Rucker, Bumby, and Donaldson (1996) surveyed a small women's facility (population of 90) and found that 3 of 42 (7%) respondents had been sexually coerced. Two victims had been sexually fondled (one by a group of staff and one by a female inmate) and one had been groped by a group of inmates. The authors found much higher coercion rates in three men's facilities that were surveyed (16% to 22%). The lower rate for women, they speculated, reflected the smaller size of the women's facility, the less violent criminal history of female inmates, or perhaps women's general disinclination to initiate sexual coercion. One other study that assessed prevalence of sexual assault in adult female prisons was conducted by correctional and health agencies in New South Wales (Butler, 1997). The survey involved an intensive interview of 132 female inmates, or 40% of the total female population. Only 2 females (2%) reported engaging in non-consensual sex while in prison. However, 23 women (17%) reported awareness of sexual assaults occurring in prison in the previous 12 months.

More recently, Alarid (2000) published a qualitative analysis of one female inmate's observations and experiences of sexual assault over a 5-year period of incarceration. Although the study did not provide rates of sexual coercion, it suggested that female inmates regularly encountered sexual pressure in their daily interactions with other female inmates. The inmate observer gave an account of her own violent rape by other female inmates. Alarid wrote that rapes were the least common form of sexual behavior. When they occurred, they generally involved multiple female perpetrators who were seemingly expressing anger or resentment toward another inmate. Greer (2000) interviewed 35 female inmates in a Midwestern prison about their interpersonal and sexual relationships. Although sexual assault was not the topic of the interviews, inmates reported that most of the sexual interactions among inmates were brought about by game playing and economic manipulation.

This sparse literature stands in contrast to the hundreds of studies conducted on sexual coercion of women in campus and community settings (see Muehlenhard, Harney, & Jones, 1992). Why have social and sex scientists neglected this provocative and important issue for women in prison? One explanation is that there is a long-held belief that female inmates do not coerce each other into sexual contact. Several early studies of women's prisons (e.g., Selling, 1931) suggested that women in prison met their needs for intimacy and sexuality by forming make-believe families with other inmates. Thus, it has been argued, there was no need for force or subjugation to occur (Hensley, 1999). Tewksbury and West (2000) posited that the sexuality of female offenders has been studied less than male offenders because women are generally considered less sexual than men are.

Baro (1997) wrote that social science scholars have abandoned the study of sexual abuse of women in prison, perhaps because they believe that it is an isolated phenomenon and not suitable as a topic. She also charged that prejudice is part of the problem. According to Baro, women in prison are viewed as "bad girls" because of their crime backgrounds and probable connections to prostitution. Because they have presumably granted sexual access to men in the past, they are perceived as willing to consent to sex in general. Therefore, female inmates who complain of sexual abuse lack credibility and are denied legitimate victim status.

A major hindrance to research has been the difficulty in gaining access to inmate participants, male or female (Struckman-Johnson et al., 1996). Traditionally, prison administrations have been reluctant to allow research on coercive sexuality (Alarid, 2000; Ibrahim, 1974). Baro (1997) adds that incidents of custodial sexual abuse are typically buried deep in the personnel files. Prison administrations may discourage research because discovery of sexual assault cases may damage their reputations or may cause legislative bodies to demand expensive and impractical reforms. Obstacles may also be raised by community and prison Internal Review Boards who are wary of sex research.

Research Objectives

Our primary purpose was to estimate the incidence of sexual coercion of women in prison. In our review of the legal, journalistic, and social scientific literature, we could find few estimates of the prevalence of sexual coercion among adult female inmate populations. While the level of sexual abuse in prison has been described as "rampant" (Bell et al., 1999), and "extensive" (Springfield, 2000), there are almost no data on how many women are affected. The 7% sexual coercion rate found by Struckman-Johnson et al. (1996) is occasionally cited, but this rate was based on only one small women's facility.

Prison records of sexual coercion rates are also rare. Many corrections agencies do not keep records or are reluctant to publish them (Baro, 1997). For example, in a recent survey by the National Institute of Corrections (2000), only 36 of 54 state and federal departments of corrections (DOCs) were willing or able to provide data on substantiated incidents of sexual misconduct involving prison staff and female inmates for 1998. Of the 36 DOCs, 14 reported no incidents, 17 had between one and five incidents, and 5 reported more than five cases. These numbers suggest that sexual coercion rates are low. However, experts caution that statistics released by prison authorities may be serious underestimates because of the difficulties female inmates have in reporting and substantiating incidents (Baro, 1997; Springfield, 2000).

Another objective was to obtain inmates' and prison staff's perceptions of the sexual assault climate in a facility.

Another goal was to describe the characteristics of women who were the targets of sexual coercion and what happened in their worst-case incident. We were especially interested in finding out who perpetrated incidents of sexual coercion. Finally, we wanted to know how many women reported the incident to authorities.

Method

Selection of Facilities and Samples

The present study was part of a survey of multiple prison facilities for men and women. Due to past difficulties in obtaining permission to study prison populations, we sent out research requests to the DOCs in 14 states. We guaranteed that the identity of the facilities would be kept confidential. Five DOCs agreed to participate. We were given access to three women's facilities and seven men's facilities, all located in Midwestern states. Only the procedures and results of the women's facilities are presented in this study.

Surveys were administered to the total inmate population and security-related staff of the three facilities. Facility 1 was a maximum-medium-minimum security facility with 295 female inmates and 100 prison staff. Facility 2 was a maximum-medium-minimum security facility with 113 inmates and 26 staff. Facility 3 was a maximum-medium-minimum security facility with 60 female inmates and 154 staff who were responsible for male and female inmates.

Instruments

Inmate Survey. The inmate questionnaire was a modified version of an instrument used in a prior study (Struckman-Johnson et al., 1996). The inmate survey had sections for demographic data and crime background, perceptions of the prison environment, and opinions about sexual coercion. These led into more sensitive questions about experiences with sexual coercion.

Staff Survey. The staff survey had sections for demographic data and work history in corrections, perceptions of the prison environment, and opinions about sexual coercion. As in the inmate survey, staff answered questions about the perceived sexual coercion rate and facility protection level.

Results

Return Rates

In Facility 1, 148 inmates (50% of the sample) and 30 staff (30% of the sample) returned usable surveys. In Facility 2, 79 of the inmates (70% of the sample) and 13 staff (50% of the sample) sent back usable surveys. Thirty-six inmates (60% of the sample) and 57 staff (37% of the sample) in Facility 3 returned usable surveys.

TABLE 1 Sexual Coercion Rates and Estimates for Women's Prison Facilities

	Facility		
	1	*2*	*3*
Sample size—inmates	148	79	36
Sample size—staff	30	13	57
Inmates reporting a sexual coercion incident in any prison/jail in the state	40 (27%)	7 (9%)	3 (8%)
Inmates reporting a sexual coercion incident in this facility	28 (19%)	5 (6%)	3 (8%)
Inmates reporting a worst-case incident in this facility	27 (18%)	5 (6%)	2 (5%)
Inmates reporting a worst-case incident in this facility in the last 30 months	18 (12%)	3 (4%)	2 (5%)
Inmates reporting a worst-case incident of rape in this facility	8 (5%)	0 (0%)	0 (0%)
Inmates reporting a worst-case incident of rape in this facility in the last 30 months	5 (3%)	0 (0%)	0 (0%)
Inmate estimate of how many inmates are pressured/forced into sex in this facility (0–100%)	21%	11%	13%
Staff estimate of how many inmates are pressured/forced into sex in this facility (0–100%)	10%	2%	4%
Inmate rating of sexual assault protection level in this facility (1–7)	3.0 Low-Med	5.5 High	5.2 High
Staff rating of sexual assault protection level in this facility (1–7)	5.1 High	6.7 Very High	6.0 High

Note. All three facilities were of maximum, medium, minimum security levels. Staff from Facility 3 served both female and male inmates.

Sexual Coercion Rates and Climate

Facility 1. As shown in Table 1, a substantial percentage of inmates from Facility 1 (27%) had been sexually coerced while incarcerated in their state prison system. Nineteen percent had experienced an incident while residing in Facility 1. Eighteen percent of the respondents gave information about a worst-case incident that took place in Facility 1. Five percent of the respondents' worst-case incidents were classified as rape in that they involved a force tactic and an outcome of oral, vaginal, or anal intercourse. In the 30 months before the survey, 12% of the respondents had experienced their worst-case incident, while 3% had been raped.

Inmates guessed that 21% of the women in the facility had been pressured or forced into sex, an estimate that was lower than the statewide rate, but very close to the facility rate. Staff, however, guessed that only 10% of the inmates had been sexually coerced. Inmates generally disagreed and staff generally agreed that their prison system protected them from sexual coercion.

Facility 2. Sexual coercion rates in Facility 2 were substantially lower than in Facility 1. Only 9% of responding inmates said that they had been sexually coerced while incarcerated anywhere in their state, and 6% said that an incident had happened in Facility 2. None of the worst-case incidents that took place in the facility were classifiable as rape. Most of the worst-case incidents had happened during the 30-month period preceding the survey.

The inmate guess of an 11% sexual coercion rate was several points higher than the reported statewide and facility rates. The staff guess of 2% was much lower than the reported rates. Inmates generally agreed and staff strongly agreed that the prison system protected them from sexual coercion.

Facility 3. Sexual coercion rates were very similar to those in Facility 2. The statewide and facility sexual coercion rates were 8%. None of the worst-case incidents that happened in the facility qualified as rape. All of the worst-case incidents reported by inmates happened in the 30 months preceding the survey.

The inmate guess of a 13% sexual coercion rate was several points higher than the 8% report rate, while the staff guess was lower (4%). Inmates generally agreed and staff strongly agreed that the facility protected inmates from sexual coercion.

Worst-Case Incidents

Facility 1. Twenty-seven of the 28 women who had been coerced in Facility 1 gave information about a worst-case incident. As shown in Table 2, half of the targets were Caucasian, while the rest were Black, Hispanic, and Native American. Targets were predominantly heterosexual and about one fourth were bisexual or homosexual. Nearly 70% of the targets had committed a crime against persons, compared to 45% of all respondents in this facility.

Over one third of the targets said that they had been assaulted by one person, while over 40% had been accosted by a group of two to three persons. One half of the perpetrators were women and one half were men. Most perpetrators were Caucasian, although many were Black and Hispanic. About half of the incidents were perpetrated by inmates, while 45% of the incidents involved one or more staff persons.

As shown in Table 3, the perpetrator(s) used only a pressure tactic in 37% of the cases, usually persuasion and bribery. The most commonly reported force tactics (used in 63% of the incidents) were threats of harm and intimidation by size. One third of the targets were physically restrained and 11% were harmed. Most of the incidents resulted in sexual touching as opposed to completed intercourse. About a fourth of the targets were raped in that they were forced into oral, vaginal, or anal intercourse.

TABLE 2 Target and Perpetrator Characteristics for Worst-Case Incidents

	Facility		
	1	*2*	*3*
Number of targets	27	5	2
Age of target			
17–25	3 (11%)	1 (20%)	1 (50%)
26–36	8 (30%)	1 (20%)	0 (0%)
37–47	12 (44%)	3 (60%)	1 (50%)
48+	3 (11%)	0 (0%)	0 (0%)
Missing	1 (4%)	0 (0%)	0 (0%)
Average	37 years	36 years	34 years
Race of target			
White	14 (52%)	3 (60%)	1 (50%)
Black	3 (11%)	0 (0%)	0 (0%)
Hispanic	5 (18%)	1 (20%)	1 (50%)
Native American	4 (15%)	0 (0%)	0 (0%)
Asian/Other	1 (4%)	0 (0%)	0 (0%)
Missing	0 (0%)	1 (20%)	0 (0%)
Sexual orientation of target inmates			
Heterosexual	19 (70%)	4 (80%)	2(100%)
Bisexual	4 (15%)	1 (20%)	0 (0%)
Homosexual	3 (11%)	0 (0%)	0 (0%)
Missing	1 (4%)	0 (0%)	0 (0%)
Crime background of target inmates[a]			
Drug related	5 (18%)	2 (40%)	0 (0%)
Against property	9 (33%)	4 (80%)	2(100%)
Against persons	18 (67%)	1 (20%)	0 (0%)
Against public order	1 (4%)	1 (20%)	0 (0%)
Average maximum sentence	21.0 years	8.0 years	2.5 years
Year incident happened			
1970–1985	0 (0%)	0 (0%)	0 (0%)
1986–1990	3 (11%)	0 (0%)	0 (0%)
1991–1995	5 (18%)	2 (40%)	0 (0%)
1996–1998	18 (67%)	3 (60%)	2(100%)
Missing	1 (4%)	0 (0%)	0 (0%)
Number of perpetrators involved			
1	10 (37%)	2 (40%)	1 (50%)
2–3	12 (44%)	3 (60%)	0 (0%)
4–5	1 (4%)	0 (0%)	1 (50%)
6–10	1 (4%)	0 (0%)	0 (0%)
10+	0 (0%)	0 (0%)	0 (0%)
Missing	3 (11%)	0 (0%)	0 (0%)
Average	2.0	1.6	–

—*Cont.*

TABLE 2 *(Continued)*

	Facility		
	1	*2*	*3*
Sex of perpetrator			
Male	13 (48%)	1 (20%)	0 (0%)
Female	13 (48%)	4 (80%)	2 (100%)
Both	0 (0%)	0 (0%)	0 (0%)
Missing	1 (4%)	0 (0%)	0 (0%)
Race of perpetrator			
White	11 (41%)	4 (80%)	1 (50%)
Black	5 (18%)	0 (0%)	0 (0%)
Hispanic	5 (18%)	0 (0%)	0 (0%)
Native American	0 (0%)	0 (0%)	0 (0%)
Black with others	2 (7%)	1 (20%)	0 (0%)
White, Native, Hispanic mix	1 (4%)	0 (0%)	1 (50%)
Missing	3 (11%)	0 (0%)	0 (0%)
Relationship of perpetrator			
Inmate-stranger only	1 (4%)	0 (0%)	0 (0%)
Inmate-acquaintance only	11 (41%)	2 (40%)	0 (0%)
Inmate-stranger and acquaintance	1 (4%)	1 (20%)	1 (50%)
Staff only	11 (41%)	1 (20%)	1 (50%)
Inmate and staff only	0 (0%)	0 (0%)	0 (0%)
Other staff-involved combination	1 (4%)	0 (0%)	0 (0%)
Other visitor-involved combination	2 (7%)	1 (20%)	0 (0%)

[a]Percentages total more than 100 because respondents could check multiple categories.

Targets' written descriptions clarified the dynamics of sexual coercion in Facility 1. Most of the inmate-perpetrated incidents involved forceful sexual touching. For example, a perpetrator would block the door to a woman's cell and try to fondle her as the woman tried to escape. Or, a perpetrator would push a woman up against the wall and attempt to rub her body. There were more serious incidents when one or more inmates would isolate and trap a target and force her to submit to a variety of sexual acts. Some verbatim descriptions of incidents perpetrated by inmates follow.

> She would come up behind me & grab my breasts & run her body next to mine & I'd start pushing her away—She would say "come on baby let me turn you out," I'd say I'd die first. And I mean that too.

> She told me I wasn't her friend if I didn't agree then started kissing me locked the door pushed me on the bed and ripped my panties off she then pulled up her nightgown. She didn't have underwear on and started fucking me putting her pussy on mine moving up & down all over. I actually had an orgasium. But I was horrified, ashamed and bruised and battered. I wanted to kill her.

TABLE 3 Tactics and Sexual Outcomes for Worst-Case Incidents

	Facility		
	1	2	3
Number of targets	27	5	2
Perpetrator tactic[a]			
Persuasion	11 (41%)	4 (80%)	2 (0%)
Bribe	6 (22%)	1 (20%)	0 (0%)
Blackmail	3 (11%)	1 (20%)	0 (0%)
Love withdrawal	3 (11%)	0 (0%)	0 (0%)
Got victim drunk	0 (0%)	0 (0%)	0 (0%)
Threatened harm	11 (41%)	1 (20%)	2(100%)
Scared with size	12 (44%)	1 (20%)	1 (50%)
Physically held down	9 (33%)	1 (20%)	1 (50%)
Physically harmed	3 (11%)	0 (0%)	1 (50%)
Used a weapon	0 (0%)	0 (0%)	1 (50%)
Other	8 (30%)	4 (80%)	0 (0%)
Missing	1 (4%)	0 (0%)	0 (0%)
Pressure tactic only used	10 (37%)	3 (60%)	0 (0%)
At least 1 force tactic used	17 (63%)	2 (40%)	2(100%)
Sexual outcome			
Touching only	19 (70%)	5(100%)	2(100%)
Intercourse (oral, anal, vaginal)	8 (30%)	0 (0%)	0 (0%)
Rape (forced intercourse outcome)	7 (26%)	0 (0%)	0 (0%)

[a]Percentages total more than 100 because respondents could check multiple categories.

> 2 girls came in my room just playing at first. I thought it was funny. Then when I said no—because it was going to far—they threatened me. One played with my breast while the other one fingered me & made me finger the one playing with my breast.
>
> We were friends and were horse playing then got pinned down while they touched me then one of them removed her pants & underwear and the other one keep my head between her legs while the one without clothes moved back & forth and then made me lick her all over.
>
> Was tied down and everytime they would burn me if I didn't submit. They used different things.

The staff-perpetrated incidents at Facility 1 typically involved a male staff person who would sneak up on female inmates at work or in their cells and attempt to fondle and kiss them. Most of the targets were able to escape the situation, but they feared that the officer would repeat the attempt. One officer bribed and pressured two female inmates to have sex while he watched and masturbated. Some verbatim descriptions of staff incidents follow.

> I went to the shed several times to get clothes for new arrivals and he creeped into the shed with me. He rubbed himself across my rear end and got him off of me by hitting him with all of my might with a trash can lid and I told him that I'd gladly kill him if he tried it again. He sent me home for the day.

> Was asleep in my cell when an officer opened my cell & rubbed his penis on my face. While I wouldn't perform oral sex on him, he threatened me—I'll never get out, & trump up charges. You'll go to "the hole" etc. He constantly made sexual remarks & asked for sexual favors, grabbed at my private part. The other officer tried to rip my clothes off while in the hole. He was only escorted out of my cell then yelled at.

> I was taking a shower and an officer came into the shower room and made sexual comments to me about my breast. She described to me how good she could make me feel. I told her I would report her for harassing me sexually. She got angry and grabbed my left breast and squeezed it until I screamed with pain and fear. I tried to get her off but she is a very __ and strong woman. Finally, I gave in and she began to suck my breast and rub my vagina. I started to cry loudly and another inmate came into the shower and she backed off. She told me that no one here would believe me if I ever report her. I reported this officer and I was ignored . . . I am still currently being harassed by this officer.

> Tried to talk me into cooperating. Said "no" then grabbed and constantly touched me & cornered me & took out his penis & wanted sex—forced oral sex on me held me down, etc. We need help, lot of this going on—4 officers walked off property over sexual misconduct in last 2 years. Help US!

All targets experienced at least one bad effect of the incident. The most reported effects were nervousness around people, distrust of people, and worry that it would happen again. Half of the targets experienced flash backs and depression. Three targets (11%) reported physical injuries including an inmate who had permanent burn scars from the episode described above. The female inmates reported very high ratings of upset at the time the incident happened. Ratings of the lasting effects were in the high range. About 60% of the targets told someone about the incident, but only 30% reported it to the prison administration.

Facility 2. Only five women at Facility 2 reported a worst-case incident that had happened at their facility.

No incidents were classifiable as rape. According to written descriptions, most of the targets encountered a single, sexually aggressive female inmate who attempted to fondle and seduce them. In the one reported staff incident, a male officer subtly propositioned the woman. The targets reported high levels of upset and numerous bad effects from the incidents. Only one target told a prison administrator.

Facility 3. Only two women at Facility 3 reported a worst-case incident that had happened at their facility. The targets were Caucasian and Hispanic heterosexuals. Neither target was raped. According to written descriptions, one woman was forcefully held down and touched by another female inmate. The other was forcefully restrained and sexually touched by a female staff member during a strip search. The targets were very upset by the incidents and reported numerous bad effects. They did not report the incidents to the prison administration.

Discussion

Our study revealed that sexual aggression does take place in women's prisons, but that the frequency of the behavior may depend upon the characteristics of the facility and its inmate population. When we started this project, we anticipated that the sexual coercion rates would be somewhere close to the 7% rate found by Struckman-Johnson et al. (1996). The facility rates of 9% for Facility 2 and 8% for Facility 3 were expected. However, the 27% statewide rate and 19% facility rate for women in Facility 1 were surprising. These rates were comparable to those reported for several men's prisons in the Midwest (Struckman-Johnson & Struckman-Johnson, 2000.)

Our data suggested that Facility 1 was a vastly different place than Facilities 2 and 3. Facility 1 could be described as a rough prison where nearly half of the inmates had committed serious crimes against persons. The inmate population was racially and ethnically diverse and relatively large (n = 300) for a Midwestern women's facility. In addition, the facility appeared to have security and management problems. The inmates gave an unusually low rating to the protection level offered by the prison system. Many respondents cited problems with inadequate surveillance, predatory staff, noncaring and unresponsive staff, and policies that protected rather than punished staff and inmate sexual predators. Research on men's prisons shows that these factors which existed in Facility 1—inmate crime severity, large inmate population size, racial diversity, and low security—appear to contribute to higher sexual coercion rates (Struckman-Johnson & Struckman-Johnson, 2000).

Facilities 2 and 3, by contrast, were not rough prisons. Both facilities held a relatively small number of female inmates ($n < 120$) who, for the most part, had not committed crimes against persons. The inmates of Facility 2 and 3 were predominantly Caucasian and not as racially diverse as Facility 1 inmates. Also in contrast to Facility 1, the inmates of Facilities 2 and 3 generally had a favorable view of their prison's security level and management policies. Inmates in both facilities frequently commented that their staff watched out for them. Facility 2 inmates, in particular, praised their prison administration's "zero tolerance" policy for sexual coercion. However, there were dissenters in both facilities who alleged that staff covered up sexual coercion incidents.

Our findings about worst-case incidents are tentative because of the small sample size of targets (n = 34). We found that most targets were in their thirties, an age similar to the other inmates in the facilities. Female targets were most likely to be heterosexual and Caucasian, but women from all racial groups reported victimization. Although we expected that targets would have nonviolent crime backgrounds, most of the targets in Facility 1 had committed a crime against persons. Perhaps these women associated with other women with aggressive tendencies in the prison system and were more likely to be victimized. Or possibly the women tended to attract perpetrators—inmates or staff—because of their toughness or crime reputation. One target inmate wrote that she was "singled out" by a staff perpetrator because he wanted to prove that he was tougher than she was.

One of our most important findings was that nearly one half of the incidents of sexual coercion were carried out by female inmates. Incidents ranged from casual sexual grabs to injurious gang rapes. This finding contrasts with the assertion that same-sex sexual abuse in women's prison is rare (e.g., Human Rights Watch, 1996). We conclude that prison conditions can potentially foster female sexual aggression. We speculate that many women who go to prison are more aggressive than the typical woman, as evidenced by their crime background. Their aggressive tendencies may translate into sexual aggression in the confinement of a prison setting. The harshness and demands of prison life most likely contribute to sexual coercion among female inmates. According to Greer (2000), some women's prisons are becoming more like men's prisons in that many inmates meet their needs through manipulation and exploitation of other inmates.

Our study does support the claims in the literature that custodial sexual abuse is a serious problem. Almost half of the incidents reported by female targets were perpetrated by staff. Typically, a male staff member would corner an inmate in an isolated area and forcefully fondle her. However, a number of incidents involved female staff who used similar strategies to victimize women. We note this finding because so much of the literature presumes that male staff are the sole perpetrators of custodial sexual abuse. According to our findings, both men and women working at the prison used their authority to bribe, blackmail, and force inmates into sexual contact.

Another important finding of our study is that most of the incidents involved forceful fondling of genitals and breasts, but not forced oral, anal or vaginal intercourse. About one out of five incidents qualified as rape. The women had strong negative reactions to all types of incidents, including nervousness around people, fear that it would happen again, and depression. Two women said that they attempted suicide as a result of a sexual coercion incident. Many women came to hate their assailant(s) and one in five said that they were moved to commit violence. Our impression is that much of this trauma occurred because victims could not avoid the perpetrators. Many women said that their assailants, whether they were staff or other inmates, found ways to track them and harass them almost daily in the confines of the prison. One woman wrote that she wanted to cut her own face in order to make people leave her alone.

Finally, we found that women were not likely to report. Only about a third of the women told a prison administrator about the incident. When asked why they did not report, inmates typically responded that they feared retaliation from the perpetrators, especially staff who could make prison life very difficult for them. Also, targeted women anticipated that no one would believe them. The bad girl syndrome discussed by Baro (1997) exists in that these victimized women maintained their silence because they felt they had no credibility.

Conclusion

In summary, our study revealed a serious problem with sexual coercion in one prison facility for women and minor to moderate problems in two other facilities. This finding does not support the sweeping conclusions appearing in much of the literature that sexual abuse is extensive in women's prisons.

We strongly encourage social and sex scientists to conduct further research on this topic. It would be interesting to find out why certain women are chosen as targets. To what extent does physical attractiveness, passivity, toughness, or sexual orientation contribute to their victimization? It would also be important to learn the characteristics and motives of inmate and staff sexual predators. Is their behavior motivated by sexual desire and fantasies, misdirected quests for intimacy and romance, or needs for power and dominance? To what extent does race influence these interactions?

We found that sexual coercion has strong negative effects on victims. It would be valuable to explore what happens to these women when they leave prison and reenter or form new social-sexual relationships. Further research on questions such as these will not only add to our theoretical understanding of sexual aggression, but may enhance society's ability to provide protection and treatment for women in prison.

References

Alarid, L. F. (2000). Sexual assault and coercion among incarcerated women prisoners: Excerpts from prison letters. *The Prison Journal, 80*, 391–406.

Amnesty International. (1999). *United States of America: Not part of my sentence—Violations of the human rights of women in custody* (AI Index AMR 51/19/98). Retrieved July 2001 from http://www.amnestyusa.org/rightsforall/women/report/women.html

Baro, A. L. (1997). Spheres of consent: An analysis of the sexual abuse and sexual exploitation of women incarcerated in the state of Hawaii. *Women & Criminal Justice, 8*, 61–84.

Bartollas, C., & Sieverdes, C. M. (1983). The sexual victim in a coeducational juvenile correctional institution. *The Prison Journal, 58*, 80–90.

Beck, A. J., & Harrison, P. M. (2001). Prisoners in 2000. *Bureau of Justice Statistics Bulletin* (NCI 188207. pp. 1–15). Washington, D.C: U.S. Department of Justice.

Bell, C., Coven, M., Cronan, J. P., Garza, C. A., Guggemos, J., Storto, L. (1999). Rape and sexual misconduct in the prison system: Analyzing America's most "open" secret. *Yale Law and Policy Review, 18*, 195–223.

Butler, T. (1997, November). Preliminary findings from the inmate health survey of the inmate population in the New South Wales Correctional System. *Corrections*

Health Service (NSW Department of Health Report No. 365/66 09944 Butler, pp. 83–86). Sydney: NSWCHS.

Dumond, R. W. (1992). The sexual assault of male inmates in incarcerated settings. *International Journal of the Sociology of Law*, 137–157.

Greer, K. R. (2000). The changing nature of interpersonal relationships in a women's prison. *The Prison Journal, 80*, 442–468.

Hensley, C. (1999, September). *Attitudes toward homosexuality from behind bars.* Paper presented at the meeting of the Southern Criminal Justice Association, Chattanooga, TN.

Hensley, C., Struckman-Johnson, C., & Eigenberg, H. (2000). The history of prison sex research. *The Prison Journal, 80*, 360–367.

Human Rights Watch. (1996). *All too familiar: Sexual abuse of women in U.S. state prisons*. New York: Yale University Press.

Ibrahim, A. I. (1974). Deviant sexual behavior in men's prisons. *Crime and Delinquency, 20*, 38–44.

Kassebaum, G. (1972). Sex in prison. *Sexual Behavior, 2*, 39–45.

Kunselman, J., Tewksbury, R., Dumond, R. W., & Dumond, D. A. (2002). Nonconsensual sexual behavior. In C. Hensely (Ed.), *Prison sex: Practice and policy* (pp. 27–47). Boulder, CO: Ricnner.

Laumann, E. O., Gagnon, J. H., Michael, R. T., & Michaels, S. (1994). *The social organization of sexuality: Sexual practices in the United States*. Chicago, IL: University of Chicago Press.

Muehlenhard, C. L., Harney, P. A., & Jones, J. M. (1992). From "victim precipitated rape" to "date rape": How far have we come? *Annual Review of Sex Research, 3*, 219–253.

National Institute of Corrections (2000, May). Sexual misconduct in prisons. Law, remedies, and incidence, *Special Issues in Corrections* (NIC Information Center, pp. 1–12). Longmont, CO: LIS, Inc.

Ong, A. D., & Weiss, D. J. (2000). The impact of anonymity on responses to sensitive questions. *Journal of Applied Social Psychology, 30*, 1691–1708.

Selling, L. S. (1931). The pseudo family. *American Journal of Sociology, 37*, 247–253.

Springfield, D. (2000). Sisters in misery: Utilizing international law to protect United States female prisoners from sexual abuse. *Indiana International & Comparative Law Review, 10*, 457–486.

Struckman-Johnson, C., & Anderson, P. (1998). Men do and women don't: Difficulties in researching sexually aggressive women. In P. B. Anderson &

C. Struckman-Johnson (Eds.), *Sexually aggressive women: Current perspectives and controversies* (pp. 9–18). New York: Guilford.

Struckman-Johnson, C., & Struckman-Johnson, D. (2000). Sexual coercion rates in seven Midwestern prison facilities for men. *The Prison Journal, 80*, 379–390.

Struckman-Johnson, C. J., Struckman-Johnson, D. L., Rucker, L., Bumby, K., & Donaldson, S. (1996). Sexual coercion reported by men and women in prison. *The Journal of Sex Research, 33*, 67–76.

Tewksbury, R., & West, A. (2000). Research on sex in prison during the late 1980s and early 1990s. *The Prison Journal, 80*, 368–378.

THE JOURNAL OF SEX RESEARCH, Vol. 39 No. 3, August 2002, 217–227.

28. Prison Riots as Organizational Failures: A Managerial Perspective

R. Arjen Boin
Menno J. Van Duin

Most explanations of prison riots implicitly regard the causes of rebellious inmate behavior as the determinants of a riot's outcome. But little attention has been paid to the course of a riot. Here it is argued that what happens during the riot itself will influence the scope and outcome of that riot. In this article, the focus is on crisis management. We contend that the way in which prison administrations prepare for and handle this type of crisis can make the difference between a small-scale disturbance and a full-fledged riot. Crisis management should therefore be considered a critical variable in explaining a riot's outcome.

Introduction: Causes, Courses, and Outcomes of Prison Riots

The Attica Correctional Facility was designed to be the "perfect prison" when it opened its doors in 1931: escape-proof, riot-proof, and a "paradise for convicts" (New York State Special Commission, 1972, pp. 13–15). Four decades after its opening, Attica became arguably one of the most notorious prisons in the world. In September 1971, prisoners took over a large part of the institution, holding a group of correctional officers hostage for a period of 4 days. When negotiations between the revolting inmates and prison authorities failed, the institution was retaken by force. The final death toll of the Attica riot was 43 (32 inmates, 11 guards); 39 of them were killed during the recapturing of the institution.

The New Mexico prison riot was the most violent uprising in the correctional history of the United States. In the early hours of February 2, 1980, inmates took control of the entire institution, holding 12 correctional officers hostage while engaging in what is best described as an orgy of violence. The riot lasted 36 hours, caused over $100 million in damage, and left 33 inmates dead. Many guards and inmates were psychologically injured from their experiences in what the *Washington Post* described as "hell on earth" (quoted in Saenz, 1986, p. vii).

Having caused great social damage in terms of human life, financial costs, and the legitimacy of the U.S. correctional system, Attica and New Mexico stand tall. Why did these particular riots take such a high toll? What factors made these riots different from others that have struck the U.S. correctional system since 1774 (Dillingham & Montgomery, 1983)? The official commission investigating the Attica riot solemnly warned that "Attica is every prison and every prison is Attica" (New York State Special Commission, 1972, p. xii). Why, then, did the Attica and New Mexico riots turn out to be the bloodiest in U.S. history?

Over the past decades, social scientists have studied a substantial number of different prison riots and have proposed almost as many explanations of them. In these explanations, prison riots are often approached as one-shot events caused by a wide variety of factors. In most case studies, the causes of rebellious inmate behavior have been implicitly regarded as determinants of the outcome of a particular riot. What happens during the riot itself is often not a part of the analysis.

We argue that this is, at best, incomplete. To explain the outcome of a prison riot, one has to broaden the conventional focus on inmate behavior and security failures to include the events that occur during the course of the riot itself. What motivates inmates to rise against their keepers and how they succeed in escaping from their cells are relevant and necessary questions. However, they do not fully explain how inmates, in the course of a riot, can take over an entire institution. Why and when do inmates get the opportunity to riot on such an extensive scale as Attica and New Mexico? A closer look at the riot process itself might help to explain.

In developing a comprehensive approach to prison riots, we will focus in particular on the role of prison management. Recent administrative-oriented research indicates that prison management is an important variable to consider in the causation of prison riots (DiIulio, 1987; Useem & Kimball, 1989). We take this finding one step further. It is our assumption that ways in which prison authorities prepare for and handle this type of crisis can make the difference between a small-scale disturbance and a full-fledged riot. Effectively applied, crisis management can be an important instrument for deescalation. On the other hand, remedial actions by prison authorities may have an adverse effect, fueling the crisis instead of dampening it. In short, crisis management matters for our understanding of a prison riot's outcome.

Once the importance of the riot process is acknowledged as a determinant of riot outcomes, attention turns toward such issues as riot preparedness and crisis planning. Preparation and planning are often considered to be essential for adequate crisis management, but in the context of a penal institution, some delicate choices have to be made. A tension exists between the managerial style and administrative measures required for the daily functioning of a prison and those that are employed in the preparation for low-chance events. An exaggerated emphasis on preparedness may increase feelings of insecurity among correctional personnel and may have negative repercussions for the atmosphere in the institution. An overreliance on crisis planning could lead to unintended consequences; it may be conducive to a situation in which inmate rebellion becomes more likely.

In this article, we shall first present a short overview of conventional approaches to prison riots. We will show that the field has come a long way in understanding why riots are initiated, but that it doesn't help us enough in explaining the course and outcomes of riots once they are initiated. Second, we argue that crisis management is the critical intermediary variable that needs to be factored into the analysis. To illustrate its role, the Attica and New Mexico riots are briefly revisited.

In the final section, we move from theory to practice by discussing the feasibility of crisis planning and preparation in the light of the nature and requirements of routine performance of penal institutions.

The Conventional Orientation in Prison Riot Research: Studying Causes

Why Inmates Rebel: Living Conditions and Vulnerable Social Structures

Most explanations of prison riots are applications of collective behavior theories. This predominantly sociological field tries to explain why people, acting as a collective, revolt against existing social structures (Perry & Pugh, 1978; Rule, 1988). Two collective behavior approaches, *deprivation* and *breakdown* theories, appear to have been particularly influential in the formulation of prison riot explanations.

The collective-behavior school of deprivation proposes that people riot because conditions are bad (Gurr, 1970; Oberschall, 1973; Turner & Killian, 1987). These conditions may be caused by tyranny, poverty, or oppression and supposedly cause people to feel deprived, which in turn induces them to rebel. Gurr (1970) refined this theory using the concept of relative deprivation (Davies, 1962). According to Gurr, people revolt when they perceive an unacceptably wide gap between their aspiration level on the one hand and their level of satisfaction on the other hand.

Various explanations of prison riots have been postulated in which deprivation is a key variable. According to the well-known powder keg theory, inhuman conditions change the prison into a time bomb waiting to explode (Fox, 1971, 1973). The relative deprivation theory applied to prison riots proposes that inmates will riot when they perceive their living conditions to be significantly worse than other comparable prison environments, both in time and place (Dinitz, 1981; Flynn, 1980). The grievance dramatization explanation holds that prisoners prepare and organize themselves for a riot in order to protest against "bad" conditions by attracting outside attention to their plight (Adams, 1992; Ryan, 1992; Scraton, Sim, & Skidmore, 1991).

The breakdown approach, once the classical sociological line represented by Durkheim (1966), Parsons (1960), and Smelser (1962), holds that riots are the general result of a breakdown or disorganization of solidarity structures. It is presumed that in normal times, social structures keep people from mobilizing for conflict (Useem, 1985). Collective behavior is incited by the disappearance or breakdown of social structures and the development of a state of *anomie* (Barak-Glantz, 1983; Desroches, 1983; Durkheim, 1966).

Applied to prisons, the breakdown approach focuses on the structural relationship between inmates and prison authorities. The basic premise is that, by definition, prison authorities are not capable of controlling inmates and maintaining order without the consent and cooperation of the inmates (Cloward, 1960; Hartung & Floch, 1956; Sykes, 1958). In this approach, authorities depend on inmate cooperation for nearly anything they aim to accomplish within the prison. Prison authorities have to "buy" order from powerful inmates who function as unofficial leaders in the inmate society. It is argued that a semiofficial "prisoner government" is in place, which in effect is backed up by prison authorities.

This approach holds that a peaceful coexistence between prison officials and inmates is possible only when authorities recognize and respect inmate leaders. In exchange for their elevated position, the gang leaders will "keep order" for the authorities. As prison authorities supposedly lack real power, riots are viewed as resulting from a disturbed relation between officials and inmates. When authorities try to reorganize this system and "take back" the institution, they will find themselves with a riot on their hands (Cloward, 1960; Sykes, 1958).

The Management Approach: Administrative Failure as Cause

Both collective-behavior approaches have advanced theoretical insights with regard to the causes of prison riots. It seems plausible to assume that bad living conditions (as perceived by inmates) can be a strong riot incentive. On the other hand, breakdown-inspired explanations of prison riots have focused attention on the structural relationship between "the keepers and the kept." The management approach, to which we turn now, shifts attention from the study of the kept to a more administrative-oriented study of the keepers.

Studying inmates, the management approach argues, is only part of the study of prisons or prison riots. The missing half in many prison studies and most explanations of prison riots deals with the forgotten people in the penal institution: prison officials (Cullen, Latessa, Burton, & Lombardo, 1993; DiIulio, 1987; a notable exception is Jacobs, 1977). Although breakdown theorists implicitly acknowledge the importance of prison administrators, structural attention to the behavior of "barbed-wire bureaucrats" is lacking. Those researchers who did study prison administrators (see, for example, Kauffman, 1989; Kommer, 1991) focused exclusively on lower-level officials. Recently, however, some prison researchers have explicitly recognized prison management as a key variable (Useem, 1990).

One of the first to argue the point, DiIulio (1987, 1991a) has proposed that the focus in prison research should be shifted to prison administrators and the way they govern their institution. In his research into three American correctional systems, DiIulio (1987) found a strong relation between the quality of prison life and the way a prison was managed. His findings were similar to those in a number of studies on the functioning of schools and armies. The conclusion of these studies can be summarized in two words: management matters (see DiIulio, 1989; Wilson, 1989). The argument that management is an important variable in the functioning of organizations is, in itself, not a new one, as students of the institutional school have defended it for decades (see Selznick, 1957/1984; for an overview see Perrow, 1986). The argument, however, seemed new to prison researchers (or very old and forgotten; see DiIulio, 1991b).

In a management-oriented view, differences between good and bad prisons are traced back to the way these organizations are managed: "Poor prison and jail conditions are produced by poor prison and jail management; cruel and unusual conditions are the product of failed management" (DiIulio, 1991a, p. 12). Prison management then becomes an important key to analyzing problems within a prison. It follows from this approach that prison management is an important variable to consider in the explanation of prison riots.

The assertion that management matters for our understanding of prison uprisings finds empirical support in the pathbreaking work of Useem and Kimball (1989). In their detailed analysis of five American prison riots, the authors set out to integrate earlier research findings. To their surprise, prison administration turned out to be an important variable in all five cases:

> Prior to all the riots under study, there was a breakdown in administrative control and operation of the prison. Prison riots are a product of that breakdown and should be thought of as such. . . . Riots only occur in prisons with a particular sort of pathology. (p. 218)

This pathology amounts to developments and factors that on the one hand are detrimental to the authority's order-keeping abilities, and on the other hand convince inmates that the prison conditions are bad and unjust, if not unlawful.

Research on the Causes of Prison Riots: The State of the Art

A half century of research has taught us much about the causes of prison riots. Drawing on empirical findings and collective-behavior theories, prison sociologists have trained our attention on the delegitimizing effect of certain living conditions. The relation between living conditions and the inclination to riot seems well established. The administrative-oriented research discussed above has shifted attention to an obvious but often overlooked variable. Sloppy security procedures, the result of badly functioning prison administrations, may actually allow inmates to riot. The factors that have been proposed as important variables in the explanation of why inmates are inclined to riot and why prison management does not prevent them from doing so are here termed *first-order causalities.*

We can use these first-order causalities to characterize a prison organization in terms of riot proneness. Picturing the defining variables, living conditions and security level, as a continuum, a prison can be placed somewhere between the extreme ends of the two axes. On the first axis, the riot-proof end is marked by relatively good living conditions (as perceived by inmates). A prison is placed on the opposing riot-prone axis when living conditions are perceived as inhuman. The second axis runs from a high degree of security to sloppy security procedures. Juxtaposing the two dimensions of first-order causalities, four types of riot proneness can be identified, as shown in Figure 1.

Based on the research findings, the following inferences can be made. In a prison characterized by good living conditions (as perceived by inmates) and a high level of security, chances that inmates will initiate a riot seem relatively low. When living conditions are perceived to be inhuman and high security is used as

		Living Conditions Good	Bad
Institutional Security	High	riot-safe	riot-vulnerable
	Low	riot-vulnerable	riot-prone

FIGURE 1 Four Types of Riot Proneness (based on existing approaches to prison riots)

the proverbial lid, inmates might be willing to rebel but they are prevented from doing so. Still, the prison is characterized as "vulnerable" because small administrative errors may have grave consequences in such a tense environment. When inmates have little inclination to riot but sloppy security leaves ample room for the prisoners to incite one, prison administrators have developed a blind spot for riots. In this type of situation, a prison is vulnerable to a sudden change in perception among inmates. A prison that can be placed on the riot-prone ends of both the axes of security and living conditions is extremely susceptible to triggers that can inflame the institution at any given moment.

From Riot Causation to Riot as Process: The Study of Crisis Management

First- And Second-Order Causalities

If prison management can influence living conditions and the state of security, thus becoming an important variable in explaining the initiation of a riot, it seems important also to look at administrative practices that take place during the riot itself. Conventional approaches to prison riots have not done so, however. Thus far, even administrative prison studies have not been concerned with the riot process. Although causes of prison riots are viewed as developing over time, the riot itself is often treated as an event isolated in time. However, after its initiation, mostly by some sort of trigger, a riot develops over a course of time. It may be short-lived, or it may last for days, but a certain time span evolves between the onset of a riot and its ending. It seems only logical that the interaction between management practices and inmate behavior—so apparent in the pre-riot stage—may have significant bearings on the course and outcome of a riot.

Official post-riot investigations generally focus on first-order causalities, couching their findings in terms of "an accident waiting to happen." The official inquiry into the Attica riot went to great lengths to document the dismal living conditions and poor security procedures that were judged to have made the riot an inevitable occurrence (New York State Special Commission, 1972). In a similar vein, the New Mexico State Penitentiary was chastised by the state attorney's investigation for its cruel environment and security problems, which apparently dwarfed those present in Attica (State of New Mexico, 1980).

But these official analyses, although rich in detail and with a sharp eye for causal factors, appear incomplete. By focusing on first-order causalities, a riot-torn prison may be correctly diagnosed as riot prone, meaning that living conditions were very poor and security procedures were not adhered to (see Figure 1), thereby explaining why a riot was initiated. However, there appears to be no direct relation between first-order causalities and a riot's eventual course and outcome, once it has started. For instance, the Joliet (1975) and Michigan (1981) prison riots were characterized as a result of bad living conditions and failing security (Useem & Kimball, 1989), but these riots caused relatively modest damage in terms of injuries and financial costs. The dire warning that "Attica is every prison and every prison is Attica" (New York State Special Commission, 1972, p. xii) does not seem to apply to every prison riot's outcome.

Our central thesis is that riots causing large social damage cannot be explained completely by the factors and elements leading to the beginning of the crisis—the so-called first-order causalities—but have to be explained also by the way guards and prison administrators behave when the first signals and problems come to the fore, as well as the crisis-management techniques used during the entire riot. Riot explanations must take into account, explicitly, the ways in which prison authorities handled the crisis. We need to face the possibility that sometimes reactions of officials in crisis situations may—intentionally or unintentionally—add to, rather than prevent the occurrence of factors that contribute to the continuation of the riot. Thus the handling of the precipitating factors that "activate" the incubation period, and the way the crisis is "managed" in a number of cases may be considered factors that explain the severity, the magnitude, and the duration of the prison riot under study. These additional explanatory factors are called *second-order causalities* (Van Duin, 1992).

The Intricate Nature of Crisis Management

During the course of a riot, between its onset by some sort of trigger and its final ending, the behavior of prison officials may become of special importance to the riot's outcome. As prison authorities find themselves confronted with a riot, it is perceived by them as a threat to the routine functioning of the organization. Prison riots are "learned vulnerabilities" for prison administrators: problems that an organization has learned to try to avoid on the penalty of severe damage (Wilson, 1989). Therefore, prison authorities will have to take some sort of action in order to cope with the threat and restore a state of normalcy. It is in this stage that the actions of prison authorities may make the difference between a food strike in an isolated cell block (a riot you will never hear about) and the overtaking of an entire institution (a riot you might never forget).

Such a situation, where authorities perceive a situation as a severe threat to the organization while experiencing time pressure and uncertainty, may be characterized as a crisis. A crisis "constitutes a serious threat to the basic structures or the fundamental values and norms of a social system, which, under time pressure and highly uncertain circumstances, necessitates making critical decisions" (Rosenthal, Charles, & 't Hart, 1989). Whatever the nature of the threat, in this case a riot, an urgent need is perceived by members of the organization for administrative action aimed at mitigating the potential impact of the threat. In short, during prison riots administrative action is wanted, immediately.

For a better understanding of the impact prison administrators may have on the course and outcome of a riot, the interdisciplinary field of crisis management studies provides valuable insights. Finding its origins in studies of disasters, international crises, and public disorders, the field of crisis management is rapidly developing, with a considerable amount of empirical data being generated (see, for example, Drabek, 1986; George, 1991; Waddington, 1992). Certain regularities appear to exist in the coping behavior of decision makers in crisis situations (see, for example, Brecher, 1980; 't Hart, Rosenthal, & Kouzmin, 1993; Rosenthal, 't Hart, & Kouzmin, 1991).

The behavior of decision makers in crisis situations often differs from their behavior in day-to-day circumstances. Acute adversities, such as a riot or a fire, disrupt the routine functioning of an organization and are bound to influence the administrative functioning of organizational authorities. During crisis situations, decision makers may be confronted with periods of information overload, suddenly followed by information lapses. Rumors increase the uncertainty for crisis managers. Normal authority structures may be rendered obsolete during crises, as informal leaders and advisers can ascend to decision-making positions. The unexpected involvement of other organizations might create (or renew) interagency conflict. Time pressure and uncertainty can induce stress in small decision-making groups, which in turn may influence the decision-making process.

Administrative reactions to the often unexpected and sometimes bizarre stream of events during a crisis situation can have profound implications. Ideally, crisis management has a deescalating and mitigating effect; but crisis management can also fail to have a positive impact, or worse, it can contribute to the disastrous outcome of such a process. The positive connotation of crisis management is not always justified. Some authorities will find a way to deal with time pressure and uncertainty; other (groups of) decision makers under similar circumstances may be paralyzed by the adversity that befalls them.

Although the importance of emergency preparedness and crisis management is often acknowledged in "after-action reports" (Nacci, 1988), a scan of the prison riot literature reveals that administrative responses by prison authorities to calamities such as riots have been virtually neglected. The available empirical data on two of the best-researched U.S. prison riots, Attica and New Mexico, shows how flawed crisis management can play a significant part in determining the course and outcome of a riot.

Riot Management in Attica and New Mexico

An attempt to analyze both the Attica prison riot of 1971 and the New Mexico riot of 1980 in terms of second-order causalities has revealed at least three possible types of interrelated factors that appear to have contributed to the scope of these well-known prison tragedies (Boin, 1992). These three categories are: (a) lack of preparedness, (b) crisis response, and (c) management of the riot's aftermath.

Preparedness. In both the Attica and the New Mexico riots, the prison administrations turned out to be unprepared for an inmate rebellion. In the case of Attica, no riot plan existed at all. Although the New Mexico penitentiary had a riot plan, it could not be found by the administrators (although, ironically, copies of the plan circulated freely among inmates). It was useless anyway, because the plan had not considered the possibility that inmates would take over the entire institution. As no plan was used and prison personnel were generally unprepared and untrained for such emergencies, the Attica and New Mexico prison administrations were unable to respond in a quick, coherent, and coordinated manner. The administrative problems that resulted from the lack of preparedness were exacerbated by failing and inadequate communication systems. In Attica, an outdated communication system prohibited centralized command from communicating with more than one part of the institution at a time.

Response. Failures of crisis management were commonplace in both riots. In the cases of Attica and New Mexico, the decisional processes resulting in these second-order causalities were characterized by the presence of what Turner (1978) calls "strangers." After the immediate response by prison management failed and the news of the riot reached outside the prison walls, outside forces made their appearance in and around the prison. In the case of Attica, New York State Corrections Commissioner Oswald took over command from the superintendent within hours, staying in close contact with Governor Rockefeller. In Santa Fe, New Mexico, Acting Corrections Secretary Rodriguez assumed command with full backing of his superior, Governor King. In both cases, police troops were rushed to the scenes, bringing their own command structure with them. The role of the regular prison administration was degraded to an advisory one and subsequently became of minor importance. This centralization of command in the hands of relative strangers to the site, together with the difficult cooperation between the various agencies involved in such unique events, may have contributed to a number of erroneous decisions by both Oswald and Rodriguez, decisions that contributed to the disastrous outcomes of these riots. These decisions include the admission of reporters into Attica; the failure to control the so-called Observers' Committee, which mediated between Oswald and the Attica inmates; the planning failures of all authorities involved regarding the recapture of both prisons; and the failure of the New Mexico authorities to develop any strategy to stop the killings within the prison.

Aftermath. A third category of second-order causalities pertains to the aftermath of a riot. The aftermath is often ignored by analysts, but second-order causalities can still influence the scope of the riot after it has ended. It is in this stage that authorities can lessen the impact of a riot by carefully bringing the system back to normalcy. This is not an easy task, as relations between administrators and inmates are severely strained after a riot (especially if hostages had been taken). The aftermath is a period in which prison administrations are extremely vulnerable to illegal revenge-taking actions against rioters. Returning to a state of normalcy is a delicate process. Authorities may try to reemphasize the legitimate nature of their actions, or they may signal their willingness to prevent future administrative errors by attempting to develop learning mechanisms. In the case of Attica, moral transgressions on the part of correctional officers and police forces in the direct aftermath of the violent takeover delegitimized administrative efforts to resume the routine functioning of the institution. Although the riot had already started and ended, leaving many inmates and guards dead, administrative failure continued through the aftermath (Bell, 1985; New York State Special Commission, 1972). The absence of medical help caused unnecessary suffering for the many wounded on the scene, both inmates and guards. The massive and systematic beatings of inmates, administered by guards and police forces after the prison had been retaken, increased the social damage in terms of democratic legitimacy and excessive use of force.

First- And Second-Order Causalities: A Typology

The distinction drawn between first-order and second-order causalities offers a valuable perspective in the analysis of prison riots. It allows us to construe a more comprehensive typology of riot proneness. From existing prison riot explanations, two key variables (living conditions and state of security) have been deduced in assessing the degree of riot proneness. These variables were juxtaposed in Figure 1. We have argued that a more comprehensive approach to prison riots would include the management of second-order causalities as an additional variable. In this more comprehensive typology of riot proneness, therefore, the organization's vulnerability to the occurrence of first-order and second-order causalities are juxtaposed.

On the first axis, a prison is analyzed in terms of the likelihood that first-order causalities will occur. Judged by its living environment and state of security, a prison can be placed somewhere between the riot-safe and riot-prone end of this axis (the extreme types in Figure 1). It is our assumption that prison management can influence the level of prevention (with regard to the occurrence of first-order causalities) to a considerable degree, varying from adequate (decent living conditions/tight security) to inadequate (poor living conditions/low security). On the second dimension, the prison is analyzed in terms of the likeliness that second-order causalities will occur. Our hypothesis is that administrators are more likely to avoid second-order causalities when they are adequately prepared for crisis management. When the two dimensions are juxtaposed, four more comprehensive types of riot proneness are identified (see Figure 2).

The prison in which riots seem to be virtually impossible events (the riot-proof type) has the organization that manages to provide a decent living environment (as perceived by inmates) and tight security and that is adequately prepared for unlikely eventualities. The prison organization that neglects to prepare for such contingencies, notwithstanding good living conditions and security procedures that

		Managing Second-Order Causalities: Adequate	Managing Second-Order Causalities: Inadequate
Managing First-Order Causalities	Adequate	riot-proof	riot-management negligence
	Inadequate	riot-management engineering	riot-inducing

FIGURE 2 Four Types of Riot Proneness in a Processual Approach to Prison Riots

make the initiation of a riot appear unlikely, may be developing a blind spot for riots. Prison organizations in which living conditions are perceived by inmates to be relatively poor, while security is wholly inadequate, run a real-life risk of a riot. Still, the prison in which riot management is adequately prepared for (engineered) is less likely to suffer Attica-like disasters than the prison in which riot management is ignored. This last prison type is the one of the riot-inducing prisons.

Implications for Theory and Practice: The Feasibility of a Riot-Safe Prison

Responsible prison administrators look for ways to prevent riots from occurring in the first place. Ideally, administrative practices and organizational procedures would create a humane living environment for inmates, while maintaining an adequate level of security. In such a prison, riots would be unlikely events (see Figure 1). However, prison administrators entertain different management philosophies with regard to the meaning and achievement of adequate security levels and a humane living environment (DiIulio, 1987). Some correctional managers adhere to the more traditional belief that a strict disciplinarian climate for both inmates and employees is the key to riot prevention. Other correctional managers believe that a relaxed environment, in which inmates have considerable freedom of movement (within the prison), is instrumental to organizational safety. We believe that both approaches have merits for the performance of a prison organization, but that neither of these approaches can guarantee a riot-free institution.

Prevention does not suffice for two reasons. First, an overreliance on prevention presupposes near-perfect knowledge about the causes of riots. Although decades of detailed case studies have taught us that living conditions can be an important motive for inmates to riot, researchers know very little about what exact conditions, events, or developments will cause a substantial number of inmates to protest. Also, no evidence is available indicating why inmates engage in violent behavior (instead of peaceful actions such as strikes). Moreover, the relation between sloppy security practices and inmate riot behavior is unclear. How sloppy can security measures be before inmates will take advantage?

The issue of prevention has evoked intriguing debates among theorists who study organizations that manage high-risk technologies. Some scholars argue that the prevention of major accidents is indeed possible. So-called "high reliability theorists" argue that organizations, when properly designed and managed, are capable of maintaining a near-perfect safety record (see Roberts, 1993). Others consider this a fairly optimistic approach (Perrow, 1994; Sagan, 1993). From a more pessimistic perspective, it is argued that accidents are an integral characteristic of a complex system (Perrow, 1984; see also Bovens and 't Hart, 1995, Chapter 5). In this sense, accidents can be considered normal.

With these insights, a riot can be viewed as the result of unforeseen and unexpected developments in, and interactions between, the inmates' perception of living conditions and the level of security. For instance, a key preventive element in the New Mexico penitentiary was the unbreakable glass protecting the centrally located control room. From this room, all inmate traffic through the institution, as well as all gates, could be controlled by a single guard. Put to the ultimate test of inmate ferocity, the unbreakable glass held for less than a minute. The New Mexico prison administrators had neglected to consider such an eventuality. This unexpected contingency provided the inmates with access to all wings and gave them virtual control over the entire institution.

A second argument is that an overreliance on security as a preventive tool may have unintended consequences for the prison's living environment. Reliable security in large part depends on leadership involvement, redundancy, and a safety culture. However, increased safety measures are likely to have a negative impact on the living environment as perceived by inmates. When the warden makes the prevention of a riot the overriding goal of the organization, more personnel are allocated to security-related positions (redundancy). When organization culture dictates an interpretation of rules solely in terms of security, inmates are likely to perceive these developments as unwanted and unnecessary additional constraints on their freedom. Thus increased reliance on preventive security measures can disturb the routine functioning of a prison and, consequently, may have an adverse impact on the inmates' perception of legitimacy.

This is not to say that administrative efforts aimed at riot prevention should be abandoned. Naturally, security consciousness and administrative actions that explicitly take into consideration the possible consequences for the institution's living environment are instrumental to a safe prison. But administrators should be aware that despite the low chance of occurrence, riots may arrive unexpectedly and in unpredictable ways. Prison administrations can make the occurrence of a riot in their institution unlikely, but they cannot guarantee that it will never happen. Therefore, crisis preparation should be considered a critical but complementary effort in riot management.

Broadening the Theoretical Basis for Prison Riot Research

We have argued that conventional theoretical approaches to prison riots offer little explanation of the outcome of such events. Insights derived from collective-behavior theories have been useful for our understanding of what factors cause inmates to initiate a riot. A more administrative-oriented approach has established the importance of organizational variables relating to security and the inmates' perception of the legitimate nature of their living environment. But the question of why some riots are nipped in the bud and others are able to develop into deadly dramas has remained unaddressed.

Crisis management appears to be an important variable in understanding the outcome of a prison riot. In the course of a riot, prison administrators may receive or create opportunities to intervene and restore order within the institution. The performance of administrators during a riot may be a significant factor in understanding why some riots are afterwards perceived as mere incidents whereas others enter history as administrative tragedies.

An appreciation of the possibilities and promises of effective crisis management techniques focuses attention on the preparatory and planning stages of riot management. Although the importance of adequate planning and preparation is not easily overestimated, it creates heavyweight dilemmas for prison administrators. A tension exists between the dilemma-ridden administration of the prison's routine functioning and the relatively resource-consuming efforts of preparing for low-chance events. Therefore, crisis planning and preparation efforts are best considered as an integral part of prison management.

A focus on crisis management should be viewed as complementary to conventional prison riot approaches. By studying administrative behavior during prison riots, traditional approaches are broadened to include the riot process as object of study. Moreover, such an enlarged scope trains our attention explicitly on the interactions that are likely to exist between inmate living conditions and administrative practices. That a relation exists between inmate behavior and the organizational environment of the total institution seems well established (Goffman, 1961; see also Liebling, 1992). However, precious little research effort has been devoted to a more interdisciplinary approach in which inmate group behavior, the perceived legitimacy of the organizational environment of total institutions, and administrative processes are related.

In Figure 3, four clusters of prison riot research are identified. We distinguish between studies that focus on inmate behavior on the one hand and administrative practices on the other. We also distinguish between research that concentrates on riot causes and research that studies prison riots as a process. The application of

		Prison Riot As a	
		One-shot event	Process
Emphasis On	Inmate behavior	collective-behavior theories	coll-behavior/ group dynamics theories
	Administrative processes	organizational and management theories	crisis theories

FIGURE 3 A Chart for Prison Riot Research

collective behavior theories to inmate behavior has clarified the possible motives behind prison riots. Prison riot research has traditionally focused on this first cluster. The recent shift in attention to administrative practices as potential riot causes has provided us with valuable insights as to the delicate interplay between governing forces and inmate reactions. As the relevance of this cluster seems established, more empirical research into prison government is called for. Very little research has focused on the remaining two clusters in which riots are viewed as a process. We do not know what forces shape the behavior of inmate groups during a riot. Insights from collective behavior theories as well as social psychology appear to be the most promising starting points for research in this cluster. As we hope to have shown in this article, studying administrative behavior during riots (the fourth cluster) is important; more research on both successful and escalating interventions is needed.

An interdisciplinary approach to prison riots is truly absent. Our efforts to understand why inmates initiate a riot, why prison administrators cannot prevent inmates from rioting, why inmates go wild during a riot, why authorities fail during and after a riot, are limited by the scattering of research results throughout various fields by lack of a conceptual framework in which these results could be interpreted. Insights from social psychology, sociology, organizational theory, public administration, and political science should be integrated to enhance our understanding of these potentially harmful and disgraceful events.

Preparing for Riots: Implications for Prison Administration

To ensure adequate administrative responses during a riot, crisis planning and preparation are often assumed to be the answer. In general, crisis planning focuses on potential risks and threats, prescribing how personnel and management should cope with a crisis. Crisis response would be, in an ideal situation, a smooth process of implementing the crisis plan. The recovery programs would bring the system back to normalcy (compare with Rosenthal & Kouzmin, 1993). Many prison administrators are inclined to think that "that won't happen to us," simply because their organization does have a riot plan. However, although crisis planning is necessary and useful, it is no panacea for all problems that may occur during a crisis. Crisis planning may improve administrative coping patterns during a crisis situation, but crisis planning should not be considered a synonym for crisis management. Some valuable insights may be derived from the field of crisis management research (Quarantelli, 1985).

First, planning and preparation should closely fit reality as well as patterns of human behavior. Realistic expectations with regard to the types of potential disturbances and typical intervening factors (e. g., media interference) and the possible actors that may be involved should serve as the starting point of any planning acitivity. Next to assigning key roles during a crisis (for example, the role of negotiator during a hostage situation), the arrival of strangers to the organization should be expected (Turner, 1978). The shifts in the prison's authority structure due to the involvement of police chiefs, fire chiefs, and army units should be anticipated in a realistic plan. In addition, planning starts with taking into account basic human behavior. It recognizes that people may react differently than usual when under pressure and in fear.

Second, planning is a continuing process. Often, crisis planning constitutes no more than putting into writing a so-called emergency plan. Booklength documents collecting dust on shelves (or worse, unavailable and unknown to most organizational members) do not necessarily testify to an adequate preparation. Planning is more. The planning activity in itself (getting to know each other, creating an awareness of potential contingencies, gaining insight with regard to the [im]possible cooperation with outside agencies) fulfill an important function in achieving the final results of the plan.

Third, general planning should be preferred over specific planning. Emergency plans are often geared toward a specific type of calamity. Such planning may lead to feelings of false security because of the fact that situations, as well as specific details, change continuously and many different types of riots are possible. Different types of calamity, however unlikely, may occur simultaneously; a riot and a fire may render specific plans meaningless. Detailed planning for specific adversities should therefore be embedded in a more general, integral planning effort.

Fourth, planning is not the same as crisis management. Adequate planning and preparation are no guarantee of successful riot management. Although preparation is useful, unexpected situations are certain to occur, causing a discrepancy between plans and real-life administrative responses during a riot. However well prepared a prison administration may be, "riot reality" may cause administrators to err, sometimes without knowing that they made the wrong decision. Where planning generally aims at the prevention of failure, the reality of crisis management partially amounts to dealing with the consequences of one's own failures.

Fifth, planning presupposes flexibility and resilience. When a prison administration spends a fair amount of energy and resources preparing for riots, a sense of invulnerability may penetrate the organization. This is due to the persistent misunderstanding that an adequate crisis plan dictates and details the actions to be taken in a riot situation. However, crisis planning and preparation are better thought of as an awareness-creating process. In addition, planning should create an environment in which administrators are able to respond to uncertain and threatening situations. From this perspective, planning should teach correctional administrators that prisons are vulnerable institutions. Certain events cannot be anticipated; flexibility and resiliency then become key instruments in crisis response (see Wildavsky, 1988).

Conclusion: Integrating Crisis Planning and the Routines of Prison Management

Crisis planning and preparation may interfere in two ways with the routine functioning of a prison. First, an adequate planning and preparation effort requires sufficient resources. The continuing process of training, practice, and plan adaptation will necessarily involve most if not all members of the organization at set intervals. Unfortunately, the maintenance of personnel at a sufficient level is problematic in many penal organizations. For instance, high absenteeism rates and steadily declining resources have left Dutch prisons with very little slack in their organization (see Kommer, 1991). Increased planning and preparation efforts would therefore be likely to exert additional pressures on resource-strapped institutions. If more resources are allocated to planning and preparation efforts, less money and manpower will be available for the prison's routine tasks.

The price tag for crisis preparation creates an obvious dilemma for prison authorities. This dilemma is exacerbated by the possibility that preparation and planning may have unintended consequences. Just as an emphasis and strict reliance on security procedures may cause a deterioration in perceived living conditions, continuing preparation and planning efforts could be interpreted by inmates as unwarranted provocations that belie organizational intentions to offer a humane living environment. In the words of N. A. Carlson (personal communication, May 12, 1994), longtime director of the U.S. Federal Bureau of Prisons:

> I believe that administrators need to recognize that placing undue emphasis on [crisis] planning can result in a "self-fulfilling prophecy." Staff and inmates may both react to overemphasis on disturbance planning as a sign that problems are anticipated. It may also be interpreted as a signal that the administration is weak and unable to properly manage the institution.

Thus prison administrators will have to find an equilibrium between prison routines on the one hand and preparation and planning efforts on the other. This is no easy task. Difficult as the attainment of "routine goals" appears to be (Cressey, 1959; Dilulio, 1990; Morgan, 1994), there might be little organizational capacity for solving additional dilemmas and performing additional resource-consuming tasks. Still, the potential benefits of effective crisis management are immense. An increased awareness among practitioners and theorists of the promises and possible unintended consequences of crisis planning and preparation might eventually make for the incorporation of crisis management as an integral feature of prison management. Crisis planning and preparation then will have become a routine task of prison management.

References

Adams, R. (1992). *Prison riots in Britain and the USA*. London: St. Martin's.

Barak-Glantz, I. L. (1983, spring-summer). The anatomy of another prison riot. *The Prison Journal, 63*, 3–24.

Bell, M. (1985). *The turkey shoot*. New York: Grove.

Bennett, J. V. (1970). *I chose prison*. New York: Knopf.

Boin, R. A. (1992). *Over the edge: A thesis on the causes of prison riots*. Unpublished master's thesis, Leiden University, Department of Public Administration, Leiden, the Netherlands.

Bovens, M., & 't Hart, P. (1995). *Understanding policy fiascoes*. New Brunswick, NJ: Transaction Publishers.

Brecher, M. (1980). *Decisions in crisis: Israel, 1967 and 1973*. Berkeley: University of California Press.

Clemmer, D. (1958). *The prison community*. New York: Rinehart.

Cloward, R. A. (1960). *Theoretical studies in the social organization of the prison*. New York: Social Science Research Council.

Cressey, D. R. (1959). Contradictory directives in complex organizations: The case of the prison. *Administrative Science Quarterly, 4*(1), 1–19.

Cullen, F. T., Latessa, E. J., Burton, V. S., Jr., & Lombardo, L. X. (1993). The correctional orientation of prison wardens: Is the rehabilitative ideal supported? *Criminology, 31*(1), 69–92.

Davies, J. C. (1962, February). Toward a theory of revolution. *American Sociological Review, 27*, 5–19.

Desroches, F. (1983, April). Anomie: Two theories of prison riots. *Canadian Journal of Criminology, 25*, 332–351.

DiIulio, J. J., Jr. (1987). *Governing prisons: A comparative study of correctional management*. New York: Free Press.

DiIulio, J. J., Jr. (1989, March/April). Recovering the public management variable: Lessons from schools, prisons and armies. *Public Administration Review, 49*, 127–133.

DiIulio, J. J., Jr. (1990). Managing a barbed-wire bureaucracy: The impossible job of corrections commissioner. In E. C. Hargrove & J. C. Glidewell (Eds.), *Impossible jobs in public management* (pp. 49–71). Lawrence: University Press of Kansas.

DiIulio, J. J., Jr. (1991a). *No escape: The future of American corrections*. New York: Basic Books.

DiIulio, J. J., Jr. (1991b). Understanding prisons: The new old penology. *Law and Social Inquiry, 16*, 65–99.

Dillingham, S. D., & Montgomery, R. H., Jr. (1983, spring/summer). Prison riots: A corrections, nightmare since 1774. *The Prison Journal, 63*, 32–47.

Dinitz, S. (1981, March). Are safe and humane prisons possible? *Australian & New Zealand Journal of Criminology, 14*, 3–19.

Drabek, T. E. (1986). *Human system responses to disaster: An inventory of sociological findings*. New York: Springer-Verlag.

Durkheim, E. (1966). *Suicide*. New York: Free Press.

Flynn, E. E. (1980, May/June). From conflict theory to conflict resolution. *American Behavioral Scientist, 23*, 745–775.

Fox, V. (1971). Why prisoners riot. *Federal Probation, 35*(1), 9–14.

Fox, V. (1973). *Violence behind bars: An explosive report on prison riots in the United States*. Westport, CT: Greenwood.

Franke, H. (1990). *Twee eeuwen gevangen: Misdaad en straf in Nederland* [Two centuries of imprisonment: Crime and punishment in the Netherlands]. Utrecht: Het Spectrum BV.

George, A. L. (Ed.)(1991). *Avoiding war: Problems of crisis management*. Boulder, CO: Westview.

Goffman, E. (1961). *Asylums*. Middlesex: Penguin.

Gurr, T. R. (1970). *Why men rebel*. Princeton, NJ: Princeton University Press.

Hartung, F. E., & Floch, M. (1956). A social-psychological analysis of prison riots: A hypothesis. *Journal of Criminal Law, Criminology, and Police Science, 47*(1), 51–57.

Jacobs, J. (1977). *Stateville: The penitentiary in mass society*. Chicago: University of Chicago Press.

Kauffman, K. (1989). *Prison officers and their world*. Cambridge, MA: Harvard University Press.

Kommer, M. (1991). *De gevangenis als werkplek* [The prison as working place]. Arnhem, the Netherlands: Gouda Quint.

Liebling, A. (1992). *Suicides in prison*. London: Routledge.

MacDougall, E., & Montgomery, R. H., Jr. (1987). *American prison riots, 1971–1983*. Boulder, CO: Clearing House of the National Institute of Corrections.

Morgan, R. (1994). Imprisonment. In M. Maguire, R. Morgan, & R. Reiner (Eds.), *The Oxford handbook of criminology* (pp. 889–948). Oxford: Clarendon.

Morris, R. (1988). *The devil's butcher shop: The New Mexico prison uprising* (2nd ed.). Albuquerque: University of New Mexico Press.

Nacci, P. L. (1988, December). The Oakdale-Atlanta prison disturbances: The events, the results. *Federal Probation, 52*, 3–12.

New York State Special Commission on Attica. (1972). *Attica: The official report of the New York State Special Commission on Attica*. New York: Bantam.

Oberschall, A. (1973). *Social conflict and social movements*. Englewood Cliffs, NJ: Prentice Hall.

Parsons, T. (1960). *Structure and process in modern society*. New York: Free Press.

Perrow, C. (1984). *Normal accidents: Living with high-risk technologies*. New York: Basic Books.

Perrow, C. (1986). *Complex organizations: A critical essay* (3rd ed.). New York: McGraw-Hill.

Perrow, C. (1994). The limits of safety: The enhancement of a theory of accidents. *The Journal of Contingencies and Crisis Management, 2*(4), 212–220.

Perry, J. B., & Pugh, M. D. (1978). *Collective behavior: Response to social stress.* St. Paul, MN: West.

Quarantelli, E. L. (1985). *The need for planning, training, and policy on emergency preparedness* (Preliminary paper no. 101). Delaware: Disaster Research Center.

Roberts, K. H. (Ed.). (1993). *New challenges to understanding organizations.* New York: Macmillan.

Rosenthal, U., Charles, M., & 't Hart, P. (Eds.) (1989). *Coping with crises: The management of disasters, riots, and terrorism.* Springfield, IL: Charles C Thomas.

Rosenthal, U., 't Hart, P., & Kouzmin, A. (1991, Summer). The bureau-politics of crisis management. *Public Administration, 69,* 211–233.

Rosenthal, U., & Kouzmin, A. (1993). Globalizing an agenda for contingencies and crisis management: An editorial statement. *The Journal of Contingencies and Crisis Management, 1*(1), 1–11.

Rule, J. B. (1988). *Theories of civil violence.* Berkeley: University of California Press.

Ryan, M. (1992). The Woolf Report: On the treadmill of prison reform. *The Political Quarterly, 63*(1), 50–56.

Saenz, A. (1986). *Politics of a prison riot. The New Mexico prison riot: Its causes and aftermath.* Corrales, NM: Rhombus.

Sagan, S. D. (1993). *The limits of safety: Organizations, accidents, and nuclear weapons.* Princeton, NJ: Princeton University Press.

Scraton, P., Sim, J., & Skidmore, P. (1991). *Prisons under protest.* Buckingham: Open University Press.

Selznick, P. (1984). *Leadership in administration: A sociological interpretation.* Berkeley: University of California Press. (Original work published 1957)

Smelser, N. (1962). *Theory of collective behavior.* New York: Free Press.

State of New Mexico, Office of the Attorney General. (1980). *Report of the Attorney General on the February 2 and 3 riot at the penitentiary of New Mexico (Part I and II).* Santa Fe: Author.

Sykes, G. M. (1958). *The society of captives: A study of a maximum-security prison.* Princeton, NJ: Princeton University Press.

't Hart, P., Rosenthal, U., & Kouzmin, A. (1993). Crisis decision making: The centralization thesis revisited. *Administration & Society, 25*(1), 12–45.

Tumim, S. (1992). The inspector as critic: The job of HM Chief Inspector of Prisons. *The Political Quarterly, 63*(1), 5–11.

Turner, B. A. (1978). *Man-made disasters.* London: Wykeham.

Turner, R., & Killian, L. (1987). *Collective behavior* (3rd ed.). Englewood Cliffs, NJ: Prentice Hall.

Useem, B. (1985, October). Disorganization and the New Mexico prison riot of 1980. *American Sociological Review, 50*, 677–688.

Useem, B. (1990, February). Correctional management: How do we govern our "cities"? *Corrections Today*, 88–94.

Useem, B., & Kimball, P. (1989). *States of siege: U.S. prison riots, 1971–1986*. Oxford, UK: Oxford University Press.

Van Duin, M. J. (1992). *Van rampen leren* [Learning from disasters]. The Hague, the Netherlands: HDU.

Waddington, D. (1992). *Contemporary issues in public disorder*. London: Routledge.

Wicker, T. (1975). *A time to die*. New York: Quadrangle/The New York Times Book Company.

Wildavsky, A. (1988). *Searching for safety*. New Brunswick, NJ: Transaction Publishers.

Wilsnack, R. W. (1976). Explaining collective violence in prisons: Problems and possibilities. In A. K. Cohen, G. F. Bale, & R. G. Bailey (Eds.), *Prison violence* (pp. 61–78). Lexington, MA: D.C. Heath.

Wilson, J. Q. (1989). *Bureaucracy: What government agencies do and why they do it*. New York: Basic Books.

THE PRISON JOURNAL, Vol. 75 No. 3, September 1995, 357–379.

Part 7: Media Portrayals

Most people in society form their perceptions and get their information about prisons (and most issues) from what they see and hear in the media. Some forms of media, such as those focused on providing news and information, generally report "facts"—although many critics would argue that the facts are frequently presented in biased or unbalanced ways. Entertainment media, which reach more people, also provide information that helps in shaping people's perceptions and knowledge of the world around them. Both of these types of media are important in constructing the views Americans have about prisons and prison inmates. Some of the ways these media forms filled this role is the focus of the two articles in this section.

The first article in this section, by Welch, Weber, and Edwards, examines the ways that one of the nation's leading newspapers, *The New York Times,* reports on correctional issues. Through a review of the content of articles about corrections and an examination of who are used as "expert" sources in these articles, these authors report that the most common issues reported are violence, rehabilitation programs, health care, "get tough" policies, and privatization. Additionally, the majority of sources cited are government officials, and most of the quotes in these articles are supportive of governmental decisions and actions. Opposing views are noted; however, they are in the minority. The authors of this article contend that the news media largely function as a way for official (i.e., governmental) views on crime and justice issues to be legitimated and presented to the population as the dominant—if not the "only"—way to approach such issues.

In the second article, O'Sullivan looks at the way Hollywood movies have portrayed prisons. We see in this article that definite inaccuracies are presented in the entertainment media and that challenging the myths portrayed in movies can be problematic. However, it is also important to keep in mind that this may be the most common way people "learn" about prisons and prison inmates. If the types of messages and images this article identifies are, in fact, the norm for entertainment media presentations, we have to ask what the effects of such messages may be. As one of the most common, and perhaps most powerful, means of "educating" the public, it is important that we at least acknowledge what these messages are. The conclusions of this research may suggest that these messages should be challenged, and perhaps (in some way) corrected.

The last article in this section looks at a different role in producing and disseminating information about prisons: the role of news media coverage and how it is socially constructed regarding prison riots. News media tends to cover prison issues only when "something newsworthy," such as a riot, happens. As Mahan and Lawrence point out, corrections officials help to shape information available to news media and how the media approach and report on things such as riots. Most important in this discussion is the point that corrections officials can, and often do, have influence on what the news media report and, in turn, what the public comes to see and know about prisons. Therefore, rather than simply blaming the news media for the messages they present, it is important to consider what corrections officials can and should do in their relationship with the media.

Again, we have to come back to the question of what the roles of prisons and prison officials should be. Do we want the public truly to know and understand what happens in prisons? If we do want more accurate information, how can corrections officials and the media work to change these messages? Or do we believe that what happens in prisons is better left unknown? Although these seem to be rather simple questions, they are important issues to consider.

Discussion Questions

Media Portrayals

1. How accurate are the portrayals of prisons and prison issues in the news and entertainment media?
2. What are the possible problems that may arise from inaccurate information and stereotypes about prisons and inmates being presented to the public?
3. Should the public have access to "full and accurate" information about what happens in a prison? Why or why not?

29. "All the News That's Fit to Print": A Content Analysis of the Correctional Debate in the *New York Times*

Michael Welch
Lisa Weber
Walter Edwards

Scholarship over the past three decades has generated considerable insight into the roles of the media, politicians, and law enforcement officials in constructing images of criminal justice; still, that body of research has rarely ventured into the realm of corrections. Filling this void, we drew a sample of 206 newspaper articles on corrections published in the New York Times *for the purpose of examining news sources and their quoted statements. Our findings reveal that the* New York Times *relies heavily on political and government sources who—not surprisingly—express support for the prevailing correctional policies and practices. Whereas the* New York Times *also quoted sources critical of the government's correctional strategies, the dominance of political sources in the press offers evidence of agenda setting in the debate over corrections.*

Since the 1970s, scholars have generated significant research documenting various ways in which the media projects official images of crime and criminal justice (Barak, 1988, 1994; Chermak, 1994, 1997; Ericson, Baranek, & Chan, 1987, 1989, 1991; Fishman, 1978; Hall, Critcher, Jefferson, Clarke, & Roberts, 1978; Humphries, 1981; Kidd-Hewitt & Osborne, 1995; Surette, 1992). In particular, those investigations show that mediated information about crime is commonly traced to government sources; namely, political leaders, law enforcement officials, and other state managers. By occupying elevated positions within the hierarchy of credibility, politicians and government officials enjoy the privilege of offering to the media primary—and self-serving—definitions of crime (Becker, 1967, 1973). As a result of this social arrangement, the media afford political and government leaders valuable opportunities for advancing a criminal justice agenda that serves the state's political, ideological, and economic interests by generating public support, legitimizing power, and garnering funds for resources and manpower (Fishman, 1978; Hall et al., 1978; Kasinsky, 1994). The reciprocal relations between the state and the media contribute to the projection of governmental (or official) versions of crime to the public, producing what is *socially thinkable* about the nature of crime and strategies to control it.

Given the pivotal role of politicians in manufacturing the news, critics accuse the media of carrying out propaganda functions for the government's ideological machinery (Herman & Chomsky, 1988; Kappeler, Blumberg, & Potter, 1996; Tunnell, 1992). Similarly, our previous research uncovered important elements of ideology (i.e., beliefs on crime causation and crime control) contained in crime news (Welch, Fenwick, & Roberts, 1997, 1998). Those studies, the first of their kind, were based on a content analysis of experts' quotes appearing in feature articles about crime in four major newspapers (i.e., the *New York Times*, the *Washington Post*, the *Los Angeles Times*, and the *Chicago Tribune*). In sum, we discovered further evidence of journalism's reliance on politicians and law enforcement officials as news sources who in effect serve as primary definers of crime. Compared to intellectuals (i.e., professors and nonacademic researchers) also sourced in those articles, politicians spoke more ideologically about crime causation and crime control insofar as they routinely disavowed the relationship between social conditions and crime.

Applying a similar method of content analysis, this investigation examines newspaper articles devoted to corrections—a widely neglected area in media studies (Marsh, 1989, 1991). While remaining attentive to which issues comprise the corrections agenda, the study tracks chief patterns of news sourcing, particularly among sources supporting the government's correctional strategies vis-à-vis sources opposing such policies. In doing so, we set out to weigh the relative balance of press coverage in the debate over corrections, thus shedding a critical light on agenda setting in criminal justice.

Sample

While being able to generate mass attention to social issues, the media possesses a unique power to shape the nature of debate by defining parameters and selecting key items for public discourse. The debate over corrections presented in the press adheres to that pattern of news production, especially considering the selection process by which certain correctional issues are deemed more newsworthy than others. To further our understanding of how the correctional debate is framed by journalists, we turned our attention to the most circulated and arguably most influential newspaper in the nation.

Ranking first among metropolitan newspapers, the *New York Times* reports a daily circulation figure of 1,074,741, which surpasses its chief competitors, the *Los Angeles Times* (1,050,176), the *Washington Post* (775,894), and the *New York Daily News* (721,256) (*Detroit Free Press*, 1998). Largely due to its vast circulation, the *New York Times* is considered a highly influential newspaper that commands the attention of political, government, and business leaders, as well as the public.

To learn the extent to which correctional issues appeared in the *New York Times*, we administered a computerized literature search using the terms *corrections* and *prisons* as key words in locating appropriate articles. The search was limited to medium (6 to 18 column inches) and long (exceeding 18 column inches) stories to ensure depth of coverage. Between 1992 and 1995, the *New York Times* published 206 articles on corrections, spanning a wide array of 19 issues. Institutional violence (n = 40) and correctional programs (n = 34) were the most frequently covered topics, constituting 19% and 17% of all articles, respectively. Other notable correctional issues included health care (n = 17, 8%), "get tough" policies (n = 16, 8%), and privatization/corrections as industry (n = 16, 8%). By comparison, less attention was directed at overcrowding (n = 10, 5%), drugs (including the war on drugs) (n = 9, 4%), famous (and celebrity) inmates (n = 9, 4%), community concerns (including fear) (n = 8, 4%), correctional budgets (n = 8, 4%), and institutional issues (n = 8, 4%). Furthermore, even less coverage was aimed at juveniles (n = 6, 3%), officers (n = 6, 3%), the death penalty (n = 4, 2%), detention in Immigration and Naturalization Service (INS) centers (n = 4, 2%), contraband (n = 3, 1%), early release (n = 3, 1%), women prisoners (n = 3, 1%), and prison history (n = 2, 1%).

Method

A principle objective of the study was to examine in-depth the manner in which the *New York Times* covers corrections; in particular, we set out to evaluate the relative balance of coverage by attending to news sourcing. To achieve this undertaking, we administered a content analysis on the sample of 206 articles by identifying and coding all sources along with their direct quotes and attributed statements. While acknowledging the identity of every source (e.g., politicians, corrections officials, reform advocates), we analyzed the content of their quotes to determine whether they supported or opposed the government's correctional strategies. It should be noted that the research design relied on mutually-exclusive categories dichotomizing support and opposition to the government's correctional strategies.

Interestingly, there were no quotes that could be construed as neutral; perhaps the lack of neutrality stems from the nature of interview questions presented by journalists who force news sources to take firm positions on issues in the correctional debate. Each correctional issue (e.g., institutional violence, correctional programs) was scrutinized according to the classification scheme, thereby permitting us to ascertain whether the debate over corrections in the *New York Times* appeared balanced or biased. Upon delineating the pattern of sourcing, we delved further into the qualitative content of the articles to extract nuances of news coverage aimed at corrections.

Findings

Comparing various news sources in the correctional debate presented in the *New York Times*, we found that 62% (n = 593) of the sources supported the government's correctional strategies whereas 38% (n = 363) opposed them. A similar pattern also was evident among the sample of quoted statements: 62% (n = 1486) endorsed the government's prison policies whereas 38% (n = 893) expressed criticism of them. By examining the relative proportion of sources and quotes within each category of issues, the number of sources (and their quotes) supporting the government's correctional strategies consistently exceeded the sources (and quotes) voicing opposition; this pattern emerged in 15 of the 19 topics studied. On only four correctional issues (i.e., overcrowding, famous inmates, INS, and history) did the sources (and quotes) expressing opposition outnumber those supporting the government's stance on corrections. And on only one issue (i.e., budgets) did the number of sources (and statements) representing both sides of the debate reach parity.

The largest margin of imbalance emerged in articles on programs and rehabilitation (34 articles), a bias favoring the government's position with 83% (n = 174) of the sources and 84% (n = 392) of the quotes. The second widest gap was found in the articles on privatization/corrections as industry (16 articles); on that issue, 72% (n = 49) of the sources and 74% (n = 121) of the quotes supported the government's position. In due course, we shall explain precisely what the government's position is on each of the issues examined, thus allowing us also to interpret more fully the scope of the correctional debate in the *New York Times*. Nevertheless, in the next section we delineate the emergent pattern of sourcing that illuminates the perspectives from which the correctional debate is framed.

Sources and Quotes Supporting the Government's Correctional Strategies

Overall, 23 types of news sources (N = 593) supporting the government's correctional strategies were identified, altogether generating 1,486 total quotes. The leading sources in this category are officials in political and government positions (elected and appointed officials, e.g., legislators, attorneys general), accounting for 24% (n = 144) of the sources and 22% (n = 325) of the quotes. The second and third leading sources supporting are corrections officials (e.g., correctional commissioners, deputy commissioners) (20%, n = 116) and correctional managers (e.g., wardens, deputy wardens) (13%, n = 76), accounting for 24% (n = 352) and 15% (n = 220) of the total quotes, respectively. It should be noted that this emerging constellation of sourcing conforms to the government's hierarchy of state managers; indeed, the highest ranking officials were the most often quoted, followed by those officials occupying the lower strata of government power. The dominance of these groups is especially significant because they comprise 57% of the sources and 60% of the quotes endorsing the government's position on corrections. Interestingly, the fourth largest group of sources supporting the state version of corrections consists of inmates, representing 13% (n = 76) of all sources and 12% (n = 174) of all quotes.

Sources and Quotes Opposing the Government's Correctional Strategies

Overall, 24 types of news sources (N = 363) opposing the government's correctional strategies were identified, altogether contributing to 893 total quotes. Perhaps expectedly, the leading critics were reform advocates (e.g., correctional watchdogs, civil liberties activists) who represented 18% (n = 67) of all critics, offering 20% (n = 175) of all quotes. The second largest group of critics consisted of officials in political and government positions (elected and appointed officials, e.g., legislators, attorneys general), accounting for 15% (n = 55) of all sources and 12% (n = 105) of all quotes. Inmates (n = 52, 14%) emerged as the third most prevalent source of criticism, attributed to 20% (n = 180) of all statements, and attorneys representing inmates were the fourth most cited critics (n = 44, 12%, offering 95 quotes or 10%).

The government's correctional policies and practices also were called into question by numerous other critics, including 27 professors (7%), 21 corrections union officials (5%), 16 correctional staff members (e.g., officers) (4%), 14 corrections officials (e.g., correctional commissioners, deputy commissioners) (4%), 12 judges (3%), 12 residents (3%), 11 health care professionals (3%), 9 correctional managers (e.g., wardens, deputy wardens) (2%), 5 religious personnel (e.g., chaplains and various religious leaders) (1%), 3 program directors (0.8%), 2 researchers, attorneys representing correctional officers, "tough on crime" advocates, teachers of inmates, and prosecutors (0.5% each), as well as a collector, an auctioneer, a juror, a newspaper editor, and a volunteer (0.2% each).

Interpreting the Nature of the Debate over Corrections

Reaching beyond a basic quantification of sources and quotes, this study also set out to explore in-depth the content of articles on corrections, drawing more fully on the qualitative aspects of the data. This approach enables us to offer additional interpretations about how the correctional debate is formulated by the *New York Times*, while remaining attentive to the pattern of sourcing. In this section, we concentrate primarily on the five most prevalent correctional issues: institutional violence (n = 40 articles), programs and rehabilitation (n = 34), health care in corrections (n = 17), get-tough campaigns (n = 16), and privatization/corrections as industry (n = 16).

Institutional Violence and Riots. As the most common correctional topic, institutional violence (and riots) (n = 40) comprises 19% of the articles in the sample.

Not surprisingly, incidents of institutional violence were covered primarily as *events* (e.g., a particular riot, disturbance, or incident); by comparison, most other articles in our sample were presented as discussions or debates over certain correctional issues. Also prevalent in most of the articles in this category were exposés and other forms of investigative journalism, a type of media coverage rarely found among the other topics, except for a few articles on drugs, contraband, and the INS.

There is considerable reliance on sources supporting the government's correctional policies in this category (accounting for 59% of the sources and 63% of the quotes). Interestingly, the nature of opposition in several of those articles unveils an otherwise uncommon coalition in the correctional debate. Correctional watchdogs, attorneys representing inmates, prisoners, and correctional officers unions linked institutional violence (or the threat of violence) at Rikers Island to a lack of adequate funding and allocation of resources. Together, those groups opposed New York City's correctional policy that reduced spending for municipal jails. In the words of William H. Booth, chairman of the Board of Correction (a watchdog group). "I'm not one to predict riot, but I know very well when you make cuts like this and take away people's services and rights, they're going to react and you never know how" (Clines, 1994, p. B1). In response, New York City Mayor Giuliani adamantly defended the government's budgetary cuts for the city's jails, accusing the union of issuing "unfounded warnings" for the purpose of "budget manipulation" (Clines, 1994, p. B8). Stan Israel, president of the Correction Officers Benevolent Association injected further the alarming claim that "gang organization is on the rise" at Rikers Island (Clines, 1994, p. B8). As if in riposte, the Commissioner of Correction, Anthony Schembri, announced after a visit to Rikers Island that "a correctional officer, not an inmate had been arrested in possession of contraband—four razor blades and a sharpened knife blade presumably intended for sale to inmates" (Clines, 1994, p. B8). In projecting the government's interpretation of crime expressed through the media, Surette (1992, pp. 42–44) reminds us that animal metaphors abound in criminal justice rhetoric insofar as the role of police and corrections officers ("sheep dogs") is to protect the public ("sheep") from the criminal element ("wolves") (also see Welch, 1996, 1999; Welch et al., 1997, 1998). The wolf pack metaphor is especially popular in reference to gang violence. Conforming to this pattern of hyperbole, union president Israel referred to Hispanic and Black gangs at Rikers Island as "out-of-control wolfpacks roaming the prison at will and attacking any rival before correction officers can intervene" (Sullivan, 1994, p. B3).

As the debate on this issue suggests, even in articles about institutional violence, a theme of correctional economics is unmistakable. Moreover, political rhetoric and hyperbole is not only issued by the government to justify increased spending on corrections, but also by corrections officers unions who deploy similar tactics to protest budget cuts that affect adversely their membership. Equivocally, corrections officers unions either support or oppose the government's correctional policies depending on how it best serves their interests.

Programs and Rehabilitation. Although adequate funding for correctional programs has been denied greatly for the past three decades, contrary to the claims of some correctional pundits, the issue of rehabilitation is far from dead (see Clear, 1994; Flanagan, 1996; Welch, 1995, 1996, 1999). As a rough indicator of the degree to which correctional rehabilitation resonates in the mind of the press, our sample features 34 articles (17%) on programs, the second most common topic. Even more to the point, this grouping of articles generated more sources (n = 209) and quotes (n = 466) than other correctional topics in our sample; undoubtedly, the correctional debate over programs and rehabilitation is very much alive.

Consistent with the economic motif already acknowledged, the most common types of programs specified in these articles (n = 6) were those related to the promotion of meaningful work and gainful employment as a means of rehabilitation. Similarly, the subtopic of employment also alluded to the correctional value of instilling a work ethic. Perhaps underscoring the unspoken spiritual importance of a work ethic, an equally common subtopic in this section was religion as a source for reform (n = 6 articles). The next largest subsets of articles were devoted to the debate over the treatment of sex offenders (n = 5 articles) and for substance abusers (n = 4 articles). Although the virtues of the vocational, moral, and medical models were fairly well represented in this subsample, the education model, however, remained conspicuously neglected (n = 3 articles).

News sources (83%) and their quotes (84%) favoring the government's policies and practices overwhelmingly outnumbered voices of opposition; still, the government's stance on rehabilitation requires clarification. Remarkably, in all 34 articles, the government supported rehabilitation and programs, including those designed for sex offenders. The nature of criticism, however, centered typically on the complaint that correctional programs should be more available and better funded; likewise, many government officials concurred. Interestingly, opposition in the form of advocating harsher punishment rather than rehabilitation was minimal. More significantly, in 24 articles there was not a single news source (or quote) rejecting the government's claim that rehabilitation is an important aspect of its correctional strategy.

Upon reflection, the near absence of opposition on this issue could very well mean that the debate over rehabilitation constitutes a *false polarity*, insofar as it is more universally supported by citizens than politicians realize. Indeed, public opinion polls demonstrate that citizens generally favor correctional rehabilitation, especially in the form of substance abuse treatment (Maguire & Pastore, 1995, pp. 165, 176, 198; also see Cullen, Cullen, & Wozniak, 1988; Flanagan, 1996; Welch 1997a, 1997b; Welsh, Leone, Kinkade, & Pontell, 1991). True, citizens may also demand punishment (Maguire & Pastore, 1995), but contrary to the mindset of politicians who exploit the crime issue for campaign purposes, rehabilitation and punishment really do not exist as mutually exclusive categories (see Clear, 1994).

Health Care in Prisons. Given the amount of concern and anxiety about health care in the general population, it is of little surprise that medical issues in corrections ranked third among the topics in our sample (n = 17.8%). The most common subtopic in this category was the issue of AIDS/HIV (n = 8), followed by tuberculosis (TB) (n = 4) and smoking in correctional facilities (n = 3). News sources (56%) and quotes (59%) supporting the government's strategy for prison health care outnumbered the voices of opposition.

Consistent with the coverage on many of the topics, the theme of correctional economics is clearly evident in articles on health care. Indeed, the government's policies on prison health care were predicated largely by economic initiatives that, in turn, polarized the correctional debate. The government's plan to privatize prison medical services was staunchly opposed by correctional staff unions. Similarly, the government's policy requiring inmates to pay for health care was criticized by reform advocates and attorneys for inmates as well as inmates themselves. Government sources commonly pointed to the rising costs of medical care, including staffing and medication (especially for AIDS/HIV and TB) as reasons to reduce health care expenses.

Issues of correctional debate also included controversial prison management practices, particularly in the realm of AIDS/HIV, TB, and smoking. In 1992, the Eric County, N.Y. jail was sued by Louise K. Nolley, an inmate (charged with passing a check with insufficient funds and forgery) who was subjected to humiliating and improper treatment by correctional staff. The county government approved an institutional policy confining inmates with AIDS to an isolation unit, requiring them to wear plastic gloves while using the typewriter in the prison library and having their belongings labeled with red stickers identifying them as being infected with AIDS. Defending the county's correctional policy on AIDS, jail superintendent John Dray argued that the red stickers were introduced in 1986 when "AIDS became the epidemic that was terrorizing everybody in the business" and they are still necessary "to protect the 13,000 inmates we have in our system every year" (Sullivan, 1992, p. B4). Prisoners and reform advocates challenged the county's correctional policy and practice on AIDS. Eventually the courts intervened on behalf of the prisoners. Judge John T. Curtin of the Federal District Court in Buffalo, N.Y., awarded Nolley $155,000, commenting that, "there is no question that the red-sticker policy was developed, not in response to contagious diseases in general, but specifically in response to the hysteria over H.I.V. and AIDS" (Sullivan, 1992, p. B4).

In its coverage of smoking in prisons, the *New York Times* clearly pointed out that the government's correctional policies and practices included defending itself against inmates suing prisons for illnesses caused by secondhand smoke. In *Helling v. McKinney* (1992), a Nevada prisoner sued the state department of corrections for being housed (in a six-by-eight foot cell) with a cellmate who smoked five packs of cigarettes a day. The U.S. Supreme Court ruled in the case that prisoners who can show that exposure to smoking is a threat to their health may have a constitutional right not to be confined with a chain-smoking cell mate.

Get-Tough Campaigns. The fourth largest grouping of articles (n = 16, 8%) was devoted to get-tough campaigns, a punitive social movement that significantly impacts the form and function of corrections. A principle theme of those articles centered on the retributionist claim that correctional facilities are not tough enough to fulfill their mission of imposing punishment, instilling discipline, and deterring lawbreakers from committing future offenses. Advocates of get-tough campaigns insinuate that corrections coddles inmates and, confounding the issue, imply that high rates of recidivism are the result of institutional conditions that are inadequately punitive. While being driven by a staunch sense of retribution, those campaigns also are inspired by nostalgic sentiments involving criminal justice (Garland, 1990; Jameson, 1991; Simon, 1995; Stauth & Turner, 1988). Get-tough proposals include "three strikes" legislation, the return to hard labor (e.g., breaking rocks), chain gangs, correctional boot camps, the reduction or elimination of institutional amenities (e.g., programs, televisions, weight lifting), and the construction of super-maximum security penitentiaries.

The nostalgic worldview in corrections has emerged as a reaction to the modern and so-called liberal American prison where convicts are afforded certain constitutional protections, allowed to participate in institutional programs, and permitted to keep personal belongings while incarcerated (e.g., civilian clothes, televisions, coffee, cigarettes, snack food). Critics argue that depictions of prisons as country-clubs (or "three hots and a cot") are wildly exaggerated, inaccurate, and politically manipulative (Welch, 1997b, 1999). Nostalgia marks a return to harsh images of prison life, similar to those projected in such classic movies as *Cool Hand Luke*. In describing support for the get-tough campaigns in Arizona, Governor Fife Symington waxed his personal nostalgia with movie imagery which includes a sheriff's 400 member "executive posse" patrolling Phoenix in search of lawbreakers: "I remember, going way back, watching Tom Mix and Gene Autry and Roy Rogers . . . and I always remember the sheriff swearing in business people on a horse as posse men and saying, 'Go after the horse thieves'" (Mydans, 1995, p. A6; see Koppes & Black, 1987). Sounding the alarm of perceived lawlessness, social disorder, and moral panic, the nostalgic view of corrections expresses a need to regain control of convicts and penal institutions, as well as a return to a simpler society. In doing so, notions of retribution and deterrence are politicized to the extent that the locus of power is personified in criminal justice officials. Sheriff Joseph M. Arpaio, who was elected in 1992 to administer the Maricopa county jail, Arizona, announced to the press, "I want everybody in this country to know that if you commit a crime, you are going into a very bad jail. . . . I want people to say: 'I hate that sheriff. I hate his jails' (Mydans, 1995, p. A6). Correspondingly, Sheriff Arpaio proudly boasted his beliefs about the virtues of expanding of the criminal justice system, saying, "My whole philosophy is, put more people in jail. We've got a vicious crime problem out there, and the answer is to take them off the streets and educate them through punishment" (Mydans, 1995, p. A6).

Illuminating the tendency for elected leaders to resort to political hyperbole in justifying the government's financial commitment to increasing the criminal justice apparatus, Georgia Congressman Newt Gingrich proclaimed, "We should build as many stockades as necessary, and as quickly as though this were wartime and people were dying, because they are" (Berk, 1994, p. A9). Likewise, California Governor Pete Wilson blended populism and correctional economics into his personal vernacular of political crime-speak: "There's really no dispute that these reforms will require considerable additional expense for building prisons and operating them. That is an expense, I submit, that the public is willing to pay. We cannot afford not to pay" ("California Governor," 1994, p. A16). Joining the prevailing political mantra to expand the correctional machinery, New York Governor George F. Pataki pleaded to his constituents, "We cannot fail to build new [correctional] facilities if public safety requires it" (Levy, 1995, p. B4).

Whereas the divide between news sources supporting the government's correctional strategy of getting tough (53%) and its opposition (47%) was narrower than others, the total number of statements favored the government (61%). Nevertheless, many dissenters offered insightful and reasonable criticisms of get-tough campaigns. In particular, a critic of Alabama's revived chain gangs and rock-breaking ritual pointed to the futility of those practices. Dalmus Davidson, a highway director in Alabama, reported that the Department of Corrections' rock-breaking program would "provide no financial benefit to the state, which already has contracts with quarries to crush rock in various sizes that can be used along highway shoulders and for some road construction" ("Alabama to Make Prisoners," 1995, p. A5). In essence, get-tough campaigns often resort to a form of prison labor that ironically is void of utility and profit, suggesting that such penal exercises take on a purely punitive significance (Foucault, 1979; Welch, 1999).

Privatization and Corrections as Industry. Correctional economics evident in the growing correctional-industrial complex remained a principle theme in articles on privatization ($n = 9$) and corrections as industry ($n = 6$) (1 additional article focused on the privatization of health care; together these articles comprise 8% of our sample). Overall, 72% of news sources ($n = 49$) and 70% quotes ($n = 121$) supported the government's correctional strategy advocating both privatization and the use of corrections as local industry.

A case in point: In 1992, the federal government announced the closing of Fort Dix, N. J., army base, sending shock waves through a community that had deep financial ties to the military. (In fact, nearly 4,000 civilians worked at Fort Dix, one of the nation's largest employers.) An agreement between the Pentagon and the Federal Bureau of Prisons, however, softened the blow by converting Fort Dix into the federal system's biggest prison (housing 3,200 inmates). An estimated 700 new jobs were created, albeit little compensation for the massive civilian layoffs caused by the closing of the army base. According to Daniel R. Dunne, a spokesman for the Federal Bureau of Prisons,

> It's a win-win-win situation for everyone involved. . . . It's an excellent opportunity for the tax-payers. We'd move into a facility that's already established. Both organizations see the importance and economic significance this has and are looking to make it work. (Hanley, 1992, p. 33)

Similarly, in other articles describing the support for corrections as local industry, a Weed, California, city councilwoman retorted, "prisons don't go out of business" ("Residents of Dying," 1994, p. 28) whereas a resident in Appleton, Minnesota, quipped, "It's not a smoke-stack industry. . . . It's a renewable resource" (Terry, 1993, pp. 1,14).

On the other side of the debate, relatively few sources were quoted opposing the government's correctional strategy of privatization and use of prisons to generate revenue (n = 19 articles, 28%; n = 53 quotes, 30%). Six of the 16 articles did not cite a single source (or statement) of criticism, and in 4 articles, only one critic was quoted. Still, some critics of the government's correctional policies did shed light on the ironic nature of correctional economics contributing to the proliferation of the correctional enterprise.

> Ideally, prisons should be trying to put themselves out of business by doing everything in their power to reduce the recidivism rate. . . . But the very function of a for-profit prison company is to keep people locked up, as long as possible because the companies are paid a certain amount per prisoner, per day. (Jenni Gainsborough, spokeswoman for the National Prison Project of the American Civil Liberties Union [ACLU], quoted in Van Natta, 1995, p. A24)

In a similar vein, Alvin Bronstein, executive director of the National Prison Project of the ACLU, cited criminal justice as one of the few growth industries in the United States, adding, "Corrections today is a gigantic cash machine" (Holmes, 1994, p. 3).

Conclusion

Proponents of dominant ideology theory argue that the media's manufacturing of news relies heavily on government sources who, in turn, exploit public access to reinforce state power (Abercrombie, Hill, & Turner, 1980; Hall et al., 1978; Herman & Chomsky, 1988). From a Marxian view of the media, the power of the ruling class extends beyond the ownership and control of the means of material production by exerting influence over the means of mental production. Public pronouncements ratifying the government's criminal justice apparatus, for instance, are mental products transmitted in line with the imperatives of the dominant ideology (see Gramsci, 1971; Larrain, 1983; Marx, 1978; Sahin, 1980).

This research discovered considerable evidence of the politicization of punishment and criminal justice agenda setting. Emulating the hierarchy of state managers, political and government leaders were quoted considerably more often on correctional issues than any other news source, even corrections officials and prison managers. Our findings suggest that media discourse on corrections provides additional opportunities for high-ranking government figures to institutionalize their authoritative position (Becker, 1967, 1973; Chermak, 1997; Hall et al., 1978). In our sample, government sources pronounced repeatedly their agenda to expand the correctional system and to harshen the nature of incarceration, both of which are prominent features of coercive social control. Whereas political posturing on corrections serves to cultivate public support for criminal justice policy, it also functions to legitimize state power through the distribution of punishment (Foucault, 1979; Welch, 1999). By serving as primary news sources, politicians and government officials benefit ideologically, insofar as they determine what is *socially thinkable* about crime and criminal justice; likewise, they also gain materially by promoting their institutional goals and needs (e.g., increased spending on prison construction, maintenance, resources, and personnel) (see Chermak, 1994, 1997; Fishman, 1978; Hall et al., 1978; Humphries, 1981; Kappeler et al., 1996; Kasinsky, 1994; Surette, 1992; Tunnell, 1992).

The politicization of punishment and criminal justice agenda setting in the media have significant implications to correctional policy and practice. The correctional debate presented in the *New York Times*, whose motto is "All the news that's fit to print," concentrates heavily on issues of institutional violence and correctional programs. To a lesser degree, the *New York Times* addresses prison health care, get-tough policies, and privatization/corrections as industry, while neglecting other important correctional issues (e.g., capital punishment, juveniles, and female prisoners). More to the point of agenda setting, which influences correctional policies, those selected issues are introduced more often from the viewpoint of politicians and government officials whose perspectives determine the fate of policy and the flow of funding.

The phenomenon of agenda setting in corrections is highly relevant to criminal justice research, especially considering that popular notions about crime and criminal justice are constructed by the media, often according to the political views of government leaders. Criminal justice scholars entering the public debate over corrections should assess critically what is being reported in the media, remaining attentive to which issues are subject to discussion and which issues are ignored. Equally important, scholars should ascertain which groups serve as the dominant news sources and decipher their recommendations for correctional policy and practice. In doing so, it is crucial that scholars be mindful of the biases among news sources and confront the numerous myths and misconceptions shaping the government's correctional strategies.

In sum, our analysis of newspaper articles on corrections yields findings consistent with previous research documenting the media's dependence on government sources in manufacturing images of crime and criminal justice (Barak, 1994; Chermak, 1994, 1997; Ericson et al., 1987, 1989, 1991; Fishman, 1978; Hall et al., 1978; Humphries, 1981; Kasinsky, 1994; Surette, 1992; Welch, Fenwick, & Roberts, 1997, 1998). However, we also revealed that the press tends to include voices challenging the government's correctional strategies, suggesting perhaps a sense of pluralism. In fact, 38% of the sources (and their quotes) in our sample opposed the government's correctional policies and practices. Still, the degree of diversity evident in this study must be interpreted cautiously. Our examination of news sourcing was confined to the *New York Times*; as a result, the extent of pluralism in our findings may be unique to that newspaper. Additional research is needed to determine whether these findings are representative of other newspapers and media outlets. Despite these limitations, our investigation contributes further to a critical understanding of the social construction of crime news by offering an analysis of corrections: a vital component of criminal justice, though widely neglected by media researchers.

References

Abercrombie, N., Hill, S., & Turner, B. S. (1980). *The dominant ideology thesis.* London: Allen and Unwin.

Alabama to make prisoners break rocks. (1995, July 29). *The New York Times*, p. A5.

Barak, G. (1988). Newsmaking criminology: Reflections on the media, intellectuals, and crime. *Justice Quarterly, 5*(4), 565–587.

Barak, G. (1994). *Media, process, and the social construction of crime.* New York: Garland.

Becker, H. S. (1967). Who's side are we on? *Social Problems, 14*, 239–247.

Becker, H. S. (1973). *Outsiders: Studies in the sociology of deviance.* New York: Free Press.

Berk, R. (1994, January). G.O.P. sees crime as a major issue. *The New York Times*, p. A9.

California governor expected to back life terms for repeated felons. (1994, March). *The New York Times*, p. A16.

Chermak, S. (1994). Crime in the news media: A refined understanding of how crimes become news. In G. Barak (Ed.), *Media, process, and the social construction of crime* (pp. 95–130). New York: Garland.

Chermak, S. (1997). The presentation of drugs in the news media: The news sources involved in the construction of social problems. *Justice Quarterly, 14*(4), 687–718.

Clear, T. R. (1994). *Harm in American penology: Offenders, victims, and their communities.* Albany: State University of New York Press.

Clines, F. X. (1994, November 17). Rikers is tense as cuts loom, and official warns of crisis. *New York Times*, p. B1, B8.

Cullen, F. T., Cullen, J. B., & Wozniak, J. F. (1988). Is rehabilitation dead? The myth of the punitive public. *Journal of Criminal Justice, 16*, 303–317.

Detroit Free Press. (1998). *100 largest U.S. newspapers* [Online]. Available: http://www.freep.com/jobspage/links/top100.htm

Ericson, R. V., Baranek, P. M., & Chan, J. B. L. (1987). *Visualizing deviance: A study of news organizations.* Toronto, Canada: University of Toronto Press.

Ericson, R. V., Baranek, P. M., & Chan, J. B. L. (1989). *Negotiating control: A study of news sources.* Toronto, Canada: University of Toronto Press.

Ericson, R. V., Baranek, P. M., & Chan, J. B. L. (1991). *Representing order: Crime, law, and justice in the news media.* Toronto, Canada: University of Toronto Press.

Fishman, M. (1978). Crime waves as ideology. *Social Problems, 25*, 531–543.

Flanagan, T. J. (1996). Reform or punish: Americans' views of the correctional system. In T. J. Flanagan & D. R. Longmire (Eds.), *Americans' view crime and justice: A national public opinion survey* (pp. 75–92). Thousand Oaks, CA: Sage.

Foucault, M. (1979). *Discipline and punish: The birth of the prison.* New York: Vintage.

Garland, D. (1990). *Punishment and modern society: A study in social theory.* Chicago: University of Chicago Press.

Gramsci, A. (1971). *Selections from the prison notebooks.* New York: International.

Greenhouse, L. (1993, June 19). Court offers inmates a way to escape prison smokers. *The New York Times*, p. A8.

Hall, S., Critcher, C., Jefferson, T., Clarke, J., & Roberts, B. (1978). *Policing the crisis: Mugging, the state and law and order.* New York: Holmes and Meiser.

Hanley, R. (1992, August 30). Fort Dix may become federal prison. *New York Times*, p. 33.

Helling v. McKinney, 61 U.S. LW 3445 (1992).

Herman, E. H., & Chomsky, N. (1988). *Manufacturing consent: The political economy of the mass media.* New York: Pantheon.

Holmes, S. A. (1994, November 6). The boom in jails is locking up lots of loot. *The New York Times*, p. 3.

Humphries, D. (1981). Serious crime, news coverage, and ideology. *Crime and Delinquency, 27*, 191–205.

Jameson, F. (1991). *Postmodernism or the cultural logic of late capitalism.* Durham, NC: Duke University Press.

Kappeler, V. E., Blumberg, M., & Potter, G. W. (1996). *The mythology of crime and criminal justice.* Prospect Heights, IL: Waveland.

Kasinsky, R. G. (1994). Patrolling the facts: Media, cops, and crime. In G. Barak (Ed.), *Media, process, and the social construction of crime* (pp. 203–236). New York: Garland.

Kidd-Hewitt, D., & Osborne, R. (1995). *Crime and the media: The postmodern spectacle.* East Haven, CT: Pluto.

Koppes, C., & Black, G. (1987). *Hollywood goes to war: How politics, profits, and propaganda shaped the World War II movies.* New York: Free Press.

Larrain, J. (1983). *Marxism and ideology.* London: The MacMillan Press.

Levy, C. (1995, December 12). Pataki proposes a ban on parole in violent crimes. *The New York Times*, pp. A1, B6.

Maguire, K., & Pastore, A. L. (1995). *Sourcebook of criminal justice statistics 1994.* Washington, DC: U.S. Department of Justice, Bureau of Justice Statistics, U.S. Government Printing Office.

Maguire, K., & Pastore, A. L. (1996). *Sourcebook of criminal justice statistics 1995.* Washington, DC: U.S. Department of Justice, Bureau of Justice Statistics. U.S. Government Printing Office.

Marsh, H. L. (1989, September). Newspaper crime coverage in the U.S.: 1893–1988. *Criminal Justice Abstracts*, pp. 506–514.

Marsh, H. L. (1991). A comparative analysis of crime coverage in newspapers in the United States and other countries from 1960–1989: A review of the literature. *Journal of Criminal Justice, 19*, 67–79.

Marx, K. (1978). The German ideology. In R. D. Tucker (Ed.), *The Marx Engels reader* (2nd ed., pp. 146–200). New York: Norton.

Mydans, S. (1995, March 4). Taking no prisoners, in a manner of speaking. *The New York Times*, p. A6.

Residents of dying California town see future in a prison. (1994, May 8). *The New York Times*, p. 28.

Sahin, H. (1980). The concept of ideology and mass communication. *Journal of Communication Inquiry, 61*, 3–12.

Simon, J. (1995). They died with their boots on: The boot camp and the limits of modern penalty. *Social Justice, 22*(2), 25–48.

Stauth, G., & Turner, B. S. (1988). Nostalgia, postmodernism, and the critique of mass culture. *Theory, Culture, and Society, 52–53*, 509–526.

Sullivan, R. (1992, August 26). Ex-inmate wins award in bias case: Woman with AIDS granted $155.000. *The New York Times*, p. B4.

Sullivan, R. (1994, December 20). 7 stabbings and 5 others hurt in Rikers clash. *New York Times*, p. B3.

Surette, R. (1992). *Media, crime & criminal justice: Images and realities.* Pacific Grove, CA: Brooks/Cole.

Terry, D. (1993, January 3). Town builds a prison and stores its hope there. *The New York Times*, p. 1.

Tunnell, K. (1992). Film at eleven: Recent developments in the commodification of crime. *Sociological Spectrum, 12*, 293–313.

Van Natta, D. (1995, August 12). Despite setbacks, a boom in private prison business. *The New York Times*, p. A24.

Welch, M. (1995). Rehabilitation: Holding its ground in corrections. *Federal Probation: A Journal of Correctional Philosophy and Practice, 59*(4), 3–8.

Welch, M. (1996). *Corrections: A critical approach.* New York: McGraw-Hill.

Welch, M. (1997a). A critical interpretation of correctional bootcamps as normalizing institutions: Discipline, punishment, and the military model. *Journal of Contemporary Criminal Justice, 13*(2), 184–205.

Welch, M. (1997b). The war on drugs and its impact on corrections: Exploring alternative strategies to America's drug crisis. *Journal of Offender and Rehabilitation, 25*(1–2), 43–60.

Welch, M. (1999). *Punishment in America: Social control and the ironies of imprisonment.* Thousand Oaks, CA: Sage.

Welch, M., Fenwick, M., & Roberts, M. (1997). Primary definitions of crime and moral panic: A content analysis of experts' quotes in feature newspaper articles on crime. *Journal of Research in Crime and Delinquency, 34*(4), 474–494.

Welch, M., Fenwick, M., & Roberts, M. (1998). State managers, intellectuals, and the media: A content analysis of ideology in experts' quotes in featured newspaper articles on crime. *Justice Quarterly, 15*(2), 219–241.

Welsh, W., Leone, M. C., Kinkade, P., & Pontell, H. (1991). The politics of jail overcrowding: Public attitudes and official policies. In J. Thompson & G. L. Mays (Eds.), *American jails: Public policy issues* (pp. 131–147). Chicago: Nelson-Hall.

Wilkins, L. T. (1991). *Punishment, crime and market forces.* Brookfield, VT: Dartmouth.

THE PRISON JOURNAL, Vol. 80 No. 3, September 2000, 245–264.

30. Representations of Prison in Nineties Hollywood Cinema: From *Con Air* to *The Shawshank Redemption*

Sean O'Sullivan

The 1990s saw a steady growth in the world prison population with the USA contributing significantly to the upward trend. But, whilst it has been suggested that media-led panics and the propagation of "prison myths" have legitimated prison growth there has been little work done on the significance of representations of prison in popular cinema for social and cultural understandings of imprisonment. The current article attempts to redress this neglect. After a brief review of some of the existing literature, an analysis of four significant "prison films" of the nineties is presented. It is concluded that, with respect to film, the notion of challenging media misrepresentations of prisons and prisoners is problematic.

Throughout the 1990s and into the new millennium the size of the world's reported prison population and the conditions of its incarceration have been sources of concern amongst prison reform groups, academic criminologists and groups of activist prisoners and their families. The reported numbers of persons incarcerated in the United States, Britain and in most other countries in Western Europe saw a sustained and significant growth throughout the 1990s. By February 2000 the reported US prison population had passed the two million mark, an event thought by some to see the US replace Russia at the top of the world incarceration league (Walmsley 2000; Campbell 2000).

Opponents of prison growth have begun to investigate the role of the mass media in fuelling the growth of the prison population. Mathiesen (1995) and Walmsley (2000) have suggested that in Britain and Europe the increased willingness to incarcerate in the 1990s can be traced back to media reporting of isolated, high-profile dramatic events. More generally Mathiesen (1995, 2000) argues that the increased willingness to incarcerate could not be justified under conditions of unrestricted rational debate. In the light of the overwhelming evidence that prison fails to meet any of its stated objectives, Mathiesen terms the increased use of incarceration a "prisons fiasco." The continued use of imprisonment relies, he suggests, on a series of processes of denial which operate to conceal or avoid the contradictions between the stated aims of penal policy and the evidence of the recurring failure of prison to achieve its aims. The mass media play a significant role in these processes.

In a similar vein Walmsley (2000) argues that the public have a poor understanding of the characteristics of the offending population and their offences, and are poorly informed on the relative effectiveness of custodial and non-custodial sentences. There is a need, therefore, to counter selective and simplistic media representations of offenders and their offences and to educate the public in the reality of offending, the functions of prison and the human and social costs of imprisonment (Walmsley 2000).

For the United States specifically, the growth of the capacity of the prison system has been fuelled in part by the building of new capacity in the form of supermaximum security facilities. The growth of this "supermax" capacity, it has been suggested, was legitimated through the media's promulgation of a notion of an uncontrollable "worst of the worst" section of the inmate population in need of draconian measures of control and restraint (King 1999). As King has argued, this construction is an unfair misrepresentation of the characteristic inmate population or even that section of it to which the term might be applied.

Those who wish to slow or reverse the growth of the prison population now list amongst their campaign objectives "challenging media misrepresentations of prisons and prisoners." We might note however that the same campaigners also list "attempting to influence key decision-makers" amongst their objectives (Walmsley 2000). Whilst the two are not incompatible, and there is no reason why both should not feature in a list of objectives, they could be seen to reflect distinctly different ideas about how social change is effected. If penal policy can be influenced by targeting key decision makers directly does one need to challenge media (mis)representations in order to bring about a change in the public's attitudes? More work needs to be done to think through the role challenging media (mis)representations might play in opposing prison growth.

Mathiesen (1995) and more recently Mathiesen (2000) have speculated on the influence of television news reporting on penal policy. Mathiesen (2000) suggests that:

> the entertainment industry of television has transformed crime and prison to entertainment objects, thus corroding our doubts and worries about the prison solution. (p. vii)

How the entertainment industries more generally corrode our doubts and worries over imprisonment is, however, a relatively under-examined topic. One issue in particular that has been given scant consideration is the influence of representations of prison in mainstream popular film on people's perception of the legitimacy of imprisonment as a form of punishment. The remainder of this article will consist of an exploration of some of the issues that might be involved in opening up this area. A brief and selective review of some of the existing literature available on this topic is undertaken in order to suggest a number of issues that might be considered in an analysis of representations of prison in 1990s Hollywood cinema. The second section then examines four significant prison-related films of the 1990s. These are: *The Shawshank Redemption, American History X, Con Air* and

Convict Cowboy. The aim will be to suggest an interpretative reading of these films identifying the meanings and understandings that they might put into circulation concerning the legitimacy of prison as a form of punishment. The final section will suggest that arriving at an interpretative understanding of the films in question is problematic. Despite this some conclusions will be drawn as to the possible role of film in influencing social and cultural understandings of the legitimacy of prison as an institution. Finally some suggestions will be made as to whether "challenging media misrepresentations of prisons and prisoners" can and should include challenging representations of prison in film.

Prison in Film

There would seem to have been relatively little academic attention paid to the significance of representations of prison in mainstream popular film. Academics in film and cultural studies appear to have almost entirely ignored the issue. There are a handful of contributions coming from commentators with an interest in imprisonment and desire to engage with its representations. The main references here are Nellis (1988), Nellis and Hale (1981), and Wilson (1993). More recently, as academic criminologists have become increasingly interested in representations of crime and criminals within popular culture, further contributions have come from Mason (nd) and Rafter (2000).

However, whilst the above contributions are all individually valuable they do not provide a clearly mapped out area of study or an agreed methodology for investigating the relevant issues. Defining such an area of study would appear to be problematic. It can be observed that representations of prison occur in a number of different kinds of films taking in a range of settings. These would include futuristic prisons appearing in sci-fi movies and prisons arising in historical dramas. Some films are not only set within prisons but could be said to take "imprisonment and its consequences" as their theme or topic. Taking this as defining our area of study could include dramas set in prison or films set outside prison but whose narratives deal with the consequences of imprisonment following escape or release. Alternatively there are some films which, whilst set either in whole or in part in prison, deal only incidentally with imprisonment and its consequences, and which play more as action-adventure movies. These could easily be located within the category of "male rampage" films (Pfeil 1998). But should these be included in our study alongside the more conventional prison dramas? These definitional issues reduce in effect to the question of whether we can and should identify a *prison film genre*. We need also to consider how far identifying such a genre and its conventions will take us towards understanding the cultural significance of representations of prison in film.

One recent attempt to delineate a prison film genre is Nichole Rafter's (2000) *Shots in the Mirror: Crime Film and Society* which devotes a chapter to an examination of prison and execution movies. Rafter's book starts from the premise that film, and in particular Hollywood movies, are an important source of our ideas on crime and criminals. But what do these films say about the nature of crime, criminals and their relationship to society? Rafter defines her area of study as concerning films which *"focus primarily on crime and its consequences"* (Rafter 2000, p. 5, italics in original). Interestingly Rafter explicitly excludes from her category and analysis of "crime films" both comedies and action films! Significantly, she also expresses a preference for studying the important and significant and seeks to avoid the worst, the trivial and endless ephemera of the crime film category. It will be suggested below that these methodological choices skew the analysis developed.

Rafter suggests that within the crime film category the dominant tradition is the production of escapist fantasies in which aspects of the criminal justice system can be questioned, but in which the injustices of the system are eventually righted—the bent cop or brutal prison warden eventually get their come-uppance. Rafter's general approach to her topic is carried over into her discussion of prison films. Here she identifies the prison film genre as consisting of a series of stock characters (a young innocent, a knowing old con, the stool pigeon, the sadistic warden/chief of guards, etc.), stock themes (the struggle of the prisoners against the tyranny of the authorities) and stock plots (the culmination of the struggle in a riot or escape).

Such films she suggests:

> . . . are essentially escapist fantasies, films which purport to reveal the brutal realities of incarceration while actually offering viewers escape from the miseries of daily life through adventure and heroism. Presenting tales in which justice is miraculously restored after long periods of oppression, prison movies enable us to believe, if only briefly, in a world where long suffering virtue is rewarded. (Rafter 2000, p. 117)

Rafter goes on to examine the emergence of an alternative tradition of prison film taking in a variety of critical independent films and new documentaries. But her overall conclusion would seem to be that the mainstream will continue to produce feel-good prison movies which will appear increasingly out of place in a mass incarceration society.

Rafter's discussion makes a valuable contribution to the literature on the prison film genre. It is difficult to argue with her identification of the conventions of the genre or her general suggestions about the ways in which many mainstream crime/prison movies operate. But having said this the approach taken could be subject to a number of criticisms. In relation to prison films the analysis tends to assume unproblematically that there is a prison film genre. There is no real discussion of the problem of its definition and limits. Rather the discussion concentrates in the main on prison dramas and addresses films that would unambiguously be referred to as "prison movies." Less consideration is provided of films that might be on the margins of the genre. Indeed there are some notable films which might have been considered but which don't appear in the discussion. *American History X* and *Con Air* are two possible examples which will be discussed in more detail below.

Rafter's study avoids consideration of action-adventure films set in prisons. So although she mentions Sly Stallone's *Lock-Up*, the analysis doesn't consider the prison imagery present in a host of other action-adventure prison films or the ephemera of the prison film genre. It will be suggested below that consideration of these films would record a changing *mise en scene* of the "prison movie." Rafter's approach emphasises identifying the (unchanging) conventions of the genre, concentrating in particular on the narrative, but doesn't address the imagery through which the prison and its inmate subculture are portrayed. It will be suggested below that this imagery and its connotations needs to be considered if we are to understand the cultural significance of representations of prison in film.

Some of the relevant issues here are suggested by Wilson in a brief comment piece which appeared in the film journal *Screen* in 1993. Influenced in particular by his reading of three then recent films, *An Innocent Man* (1989), *Lock-up* (1989) and *Death Warrant* (1990), Wilson bemoans the representations of both the prison authorities (corrupt and rotten) and the prisoners (racially stereotyped, prone to violence) present in these films. Wilson observes that in these films it is usually a lone individual who is either "innocent" or inappropriately imprisoned who carries out the just struggle of the imprisoned against the tyranny of the prison authorities. But, he suggests, whilst redemption/rehabilitation is reserved for the "exceptional individual," prisoners in general are seen as collectively incapable and undeserving of rehabilitation. In these films the mass of ordinary prisoners are "not normally viewed in anything other than disparaging terms" (Wilson 1993, p. 79). Wilson goes on to underscore the point that prison films rarely show the inmate population as a whole of being capable of collective redemption/rehabilitation through a consideration of the sci-fi horror hybrid *Alien 3*. The action of the film is set in a penal colony, Prison Planet Fury 161. Despite a range of familiar prison clichés (mutinous and violent inmates, a threatened rape of Sigourney Weaver by the inmates—all sex offenders) the film:

> also uses its prison vehicle in new and important ways, not least of which is the eventual heroism, and self-sacrifice of the prisoners themselves. Their redemption is in marked contrast to how film normally views prisoners, and this is certainly to *Alien 3*'s credit. (Wilson 1993, pp. 78–9)

Wilson's concern seems to be that as long as prisoners are viewed in a negative light, with redemption/rehabilitation reserved for the exceptional individual, the message of prison movies is implicitly that prisoners deserve what they get. So, rather than asking why prison film fails to contribute to a climate of prison reform, we need instead to consider the ways in which representations of prison in film actively contribute towards legitimating prison as a form of punishment and, possibly, encourage the trend towards a growth in the prison population. It is interesting to note that Wilson's discussion implicitly records a shift in emphasis from the traditional prison drama (*Birdman of Alcatraz*) towards the action-adventure film set in a prison (*Tango and Cash, Lock-Up*). The discussion also implicitly records a shift in the prison *mise en scene* to a meaner, harder prison environment than that traditionally displayed in prison drama. In *An Innocent Man* Tom Selleck (playing the prison innocent) is forced in to a position where he is required to plan and execute the murder of a fellow inmate in order to survive incarceration. The prison *mise en scene* and the film's assumptions about the nature of the inmate subculture is significantly different to that portrayed in earlier prison films. The significance of this will be developed below.

Although Wilson (1993) detected a shift to a meaner prison environment in the films of the late 1980s and early 1990s, the 1990s went on to produce some mellower representations of imprisonment in films such as *The Shawshank Redemption* and *The Green Mile*. Are these films to be understood (and dismissed?) in the terms suggested by Rafter as escapist fantasies in which wrongs are miraculously righted and long-suffering virtue eventually rewarded? Or are they worthy of further consideration?

The arguments reviewed so far could go some way towards providing a basis for understanding what was going on in representations of prison in 1990s Hollywood cinema. But the analysis advanced by both Wilson and Rafter tends to assume that prison films have a meaning or message which can be identified and pinned down. The analysis developed below pays more attention to the problems involved in determining the ranging of possible meanings circulated by the prison-related films of nineties Hollywood cinema.

Representations of Prison in Nineties Hollywood Cinema

It is neither possible nor desirable to provide a comprehensive account of all the films that might qualify for consideration under the above heading. Rather four significant "prison films" of the 1990s will be discussed. The chosen films are: *The Shawshank Redemption* (1994), d. Frank Darabont, *American History X* (1998), d. Tony Kaye, *Convict Cowboy* (1995), d. Rod Holcomb, *Con Air* (1997), d. Simon West.

The Shawshank Redemption (1994) starred Morgan Freeman and Tim Robbins. Although not hugely successful on its initial cinema release it went on to achieve enormous success through video rental and sales. This incredibly popular film is set almost entirely within a prison and yet is often referred to in review and comment as being "not really a prison film." It both "fits" and does not "fit" the suggested conventions of the prison film genre and the arguments of the authors reviewed above. *American History X* (1998) is in some ways almost a mirror image of, or answer-film to, *The Shawshank Redemption*. Set in contemporary Los Angeles the story of the film concerns the drift of its main character (Derek Vinyard/Ed Norton) into right wing extremist violence and his redemption/rehabilitation whilst in prison for the murder of two young black men. The film attempts to be a hard-edged look at one aspect of life in contemporary urban America. The film is widely used as a basis for discussion across a variety of courses in American universities and in other educational settings.

Con Air (1997) is an action-adventure blockbuster whose story concerns the transportation of and bid for escape by a group of prisoners who in current US parlance might be described as "the worst of the worst" (sic) of the prison population. The film is an instance of Wilson's complaint about prisoners being represented in disparaging terms. Finally, *Convict Cowboy* (1995) is technically a "made for television" movie, but the film has a highly cinematic feel and will be discussed here as if it were a standard Hollywood product. The film is interesting as it operates as a kind of hybrid between a traditional prison drama (imprisonment and its consequences) and an action-adventure movie set in a prison (male rampage within a *mise en scene* of institutionalised inmate violence).

It should be said that the films chosen all feature male leads and, by implication, the male experience of imprisonment. No attempt has been made to select a film dealing with a female experience of imprisonment to include in the discussion, as the choice of films is believed to be defensible, and because there is no intention to develop a gender blind analysis of them. Having said this the comments of the gendered nature of these representations will be fairly limited.

Con Air

Released in the summer of 1997 *Con Air* was a blockbuster movie which grossed over $200,000,000 on its initial cinema release. It is widely available in video stores and has been screened on UK terrestrial television. Its "all-star" cast include Nicolas Cage, John Cusack, John Malkovich, Ving Rhames (*Pulp Fiction*) and Steve Buscemi (*Reservoir Dogs*). Cage plays Cameron Poe a (good guy) ex-army ranger about to be released from prison after serving eight years for manslaughter. He has the misfortune that on the day of his release he is to be transported on a plane also carrying Malkovich, Rhames, Buscemi and others, a set of hard-core murderers, serial killers, and serial rapists, to a supermax prison facility. As Cage's character observes: "Somehow they managed to get every creep and freak in the universe on this one plane." The passengers of *Con Air* are literally described in the dialogue of the film as "the 'worst of the worst' that the system has ever produced"—"pure predators." The film explicitly articulates the "supermax" discourse, although here the nightmare scenario of centralisation arises and the "super-crims" succeed in taking over the plane.

It is not the intention of the following discussion to mount a defence of *Con Air*, but before we move straight to filing it under the heading "disparaging representations of prisoners" it is perhaps worth making the following points. Firstly, *Con Air* is an action-adventure movie and one that is played to excess (spectacular special effects, explosions, our hero out-running flaming fire-balls, etc.). Cage's performance and body imagery articulate other "male rampage" films such as the *Die Hard* franchise (Pfiel 1998). Secondly, the film is built around two oppositions—first the struggle of Cage—the good-guy, time-served convict—in his efforts to thwart the plans of Malkovich and his motley crew, but also the struggle between John Cusack (good-guy US Marshal) and Colm Meaney, playing Malloy the hawkish DEA agent. Malloy wants to blow the plane, criminals and prison-service hostages, out of the sky, whilst Cusack wants to rely on Cage to bring it down safely. Thirdly, the outcome is that good-guy time-served convict Cage, defeats the assembled army of "the worst of the worst *the system* has ever produced," and in so doing rewards Cusack's faith in him. In the process Cusack wins the hawkish

DEA agent Malloy over to his point of view. Fourthly, Steve Buscemi, who plays Garland Green, a sick, psychotic, "incurable" serial killer, transported in a Hannibal Lecture style restraint suit, is redeemed/rehabilitated when a child with whom he has a chance tea party asks if he might like to join with her in singing: "He's got the whole world in his hands."

The significance of this scene may be worth pausing on. Allowing Buscemi/ Green redemption means that the film breaks the convention of allowing redemption only for the exceptional/innocent individual. The manner of the redemption could be taken to suggest either that redemption/rehabilitation is a random/chance event beyond the control of the authorities or it requires the opportunity for valued social interaction. I am not suggesting that the film's makers are attempting to make any serious point about rehabilitation here and I recognise that some people might find the scene in question distasteful. Nevertheless it is interesting that the film's makers chose to include it as it makes little contribution to the action taking place and could easily have been dropped to make way for yet another "explosion of billowing orange." One possible reason for the scene's inclusion could have been a desire on the part of the film's makers to "play" with any film critics or academics attempting to determine a "meaning" in the text!

Finally, the film ends with a montage reprising the main characters of the film giving the name of the actor and the character played. All are seen in action, but smiling broadly. The reprise ends with Cage giving a knowing wink, in effect, to the camera. The point of this montage is, of course, to draw to the attention of the members of the audience watching, that the film is, in fact, only joking.

Of course, more seriously, we have to consider whether the film, joking or not, operates to circulate or to subvert the notion of the "worst of the worst." Here we might have to record an open verdict although it is perhaps worth making the point that the general character of the film is one of cinematic excess. In addition to this, the choice of very well known screen stars, who never really escape their already established screen personalities, to play the "main parts," and more particularly the "monsters," could operate to suggest that the notion of "the worst of the worst" is a fiction, and one which most properly belongs within the confines of the hyperbolic action-adventure movie. By way of contrast, in the film *Face/Off* (Nic Cage again) there is a brief middle section set within a futuristic maximum-security prison. This is possibly a more "dangerous" representation. In *Face/Off* the *mise en scene* of the (super) maximum security prison operates as an unnoticed and unquestioned backdrop to the unfolding action. In *Con Air* it is put on a plane and "played to the max."

The Shawshank Redemption

Set initially in the 1940s. *The Shawshank Redemption* is the story of a Maine banker, Andy Dufresne (Tim Robbins), who is (wrongly) convicted of the murder of his wife and her lover and sentenced to life imprisonment in Shawshank Penitentiary. For the first three years of his sentence Andy has a tough time surviving, particularly as he becomes the object of attention of a gang of prison "gays" known as the sisters. However, when the captain of the prison guards and then the prison warden come to discover and benefit from Andy's financial acumen his star in the prison begins to rise. Andy becomes responsible for laundering the money generated by the warden's corrupt scams and in return is allowed to expand the prison library and start a prisoner education scheme. However, when the warden denies Andy an opportunity to prove his innocence (by murdering another inmate) Andy is left with no option but to escape Shawshank and to blow the whistle on the warden's corrupt schemes.

The above brief plot summary would suggest that *Shawshank* is, as Rafter (2000) suggests, an escapist fantasy. It is relatively easy to identify the ways in which the film reproduces the conventions and clichés of the prison film genre. Firstly, the prison authorities are shown to be rotten/corrupt (exploitative use of prison labour) and to use illegitimate violence to support their regime (fatal and maiming beatings, illegitimate use of solitary confinement, murder). Secondly, the prison is represented as a machine (initiation rituals—the de-lousing of new arrivees, the baiting by existing inmates of "new fish"; the ritual of parole application; the effects of longterm institutionalisation). Thirdly, inmate violence is represented by Andy's experience of male rape at the hands of the prison gang "the sisters." Fourth, the challenge to the authority of the system comes from a lone individual who is both innocent and exceptional. Fifth, the film uses the well known ploy of appearing to be highly critical of a social institution only for the actions of one principled individual to "allow the system to redeem itself in the last reel" (see Ryan and Kellner 1990).

But *The Shawshank Redemption* has quite a different feel to the prison films complained about by Wilson (1993). Rather than being shown as being beyond redemption the prisoners organise their own rehabilitation. Andy expands the library and provides an opportunity for prison education, but his fellow inmates assist, participate in, and support these activities. The prisoners in *Shawshank* are shown as being supportative of one another, with the activities of "the sisters" being the only real significant example of institutionalised inmate violence. The prison population, particularly the friendship group associated with Andy and Red, are a long way from being a cinematic equivalent of the popular conception of "the worst of the worst." This is significant.

Stylistically *Shawshank* is an interesting film to analyse. The film is set in the past, although the action unfolds chronologically, approaching but not reaching the present day. The visual action takes place in the present tense, whilst the wistful voice-over, supplied by the narrator (Red/Morgan Freeman), is given in the past tense. The voice-over serves to establish beyond doubt that Andy was/is someone special. There is no "frame story" provided within which to locate the past events. Despite the past tense of the voice-over the story does not unfold as if told in flash back. In addition to the use of these devices, the lighting, choice of camera shots, use of music, and the emotional pull of the viewer to identify with the heroic nature of Andy's struggle, all serve to give the film its fabular quality which is invariably recognised in discussions of the film. *Shawshank* does not in any way pretend to be a "realist" examination of the US prison system. It is "just" a story.

It would seem then that, as Rafter (2000) suggests, *The Shawshank Redemption* is an ideal candidate for the category of feel-good escapist fantasy. It is relatively easy to generate an unfavourable reading of the film which could be accused of being hypocritical on two counts. Firstly, that it puts a formulaic and superficial critique of prison which is in no way seriously critical of any actually existing experience of incarceration. Secondly, that through the casting of Morgan Freeman as co-lead, the film is given an appearance of racial equality which it in fact does not live up to. On closer examination the film reproduces a predominantly white main cast and only a weakly multi-racial *mise en scene*. However, the research undertaken for this article might suggest that a revision of this assessment is appropriate. *Shawshank* was produced against the background of a growth of action-adventure movies set in prisons. These often feature a *mise en scene* of racially divided prisons controlled by warring factions of "hard-core gang members" and characterised by high levels of institutionalised inmate violence. This representation of prison, it could be argued, resonated with the popular conception promoted by some sections of the US prison system that some prisons were becoming unmanageable and required a new generation of supermax institutions to house the "worst of the worst" of the inmate population (King 1999). But, it could be argued, both the notion of "the worst of the worst," and its cinematic equivalent, are a misrepresentation of the actual composition of the US prison population and its characteristics, and could be regarded as one of the "prison myths" that underpinned the substantial increase in the rate of incarceration witnessed in the US in the 1990s. *The Shawshank Redemption* clearly sets itself against this trend and attempts to circulate an alternative representation of prisoners as being worthy and capable of rehabilitation. In this respect the film might be welcomed by anyone wishing to transform prisons away from their role as "holding pens" and towards them becoming a more therapeutic environment (Wilson and Reuss 2000). *The Shawshank Redemption* could be regarded as an attempt at "doing good by stealth."

In her discussion of the film Rafter (2000) recognises that *Shawshank* knowingly deploys the conventions of the prison film genre but dismisses this as being merely an exercise in cinematic nostalgia. But it is possible to credit the film's director Frank Darabont with a more subtle intent. In effect the film operates as a kind of double bluff. First it declares itself to be a prison film—the Shawshank Redemption set in the Shawshank penitentiary. Then, its highly apparent, fabular and mythical nature immediately lay it open to the charge—you're not really a prison film! The audience and critics leave the cinema convinced that they have watched a film that isn't really a prison film at all. But as the film is set for almost all of its entirety in a penal institution it could succeed, almost by default, in circulating its alternative understanding of its prisoners and their capacity for redemption. Through the hyperbolic use of cliché Frank Darabont may have succeeded in escaping the redundancy of the traditional prison film and in finding a way of "saying the already said" (Eco 1984). Alternatively it may be, as Rafter might suggest, that most people will just see the fairy-tale and miss the message. But if we are to dismiss *Shawshank* as an escapist fantasy we would need to ask if a more hard-edged or "realist" approach to the cinematic representation of prison is in any way more preferable.

American History X

American History X could be seen as a mirror image of, or an answer-film to, *The Shawshank Redemption*. The contrasts between the two are so striking that it is almost as if the makers of *American History X* had set out to make a film that was not *The Shawshank Redemption*. Some of the main contrasts could be stated as follows.

The Shawshank Redemption is set in the past and works towards the present day. *American History X* is set in the present day but works back to the past by use of flashbacks. *The Shawshank Redemption* imagines a fairy-tale world in which racism is virtually absent. *American History X* seeks to put white racism on display in full view (the prejudice of Derek's father, the activities of the white supremacist group). In *The Shawshank Redemption* white liberal Andy "redeems," and saves the life of, black "Red" (Morgan Freeman). In *American History X* the white Derek Vinyard/Ed Norton is "redeemed" and life-saved by his black prison workmate (unnamed in the film). In *The Shawshank Redemption* the prison authorities are corrupt and rotten, the inmates are, to an extent, mutually supportive. In *American History X* the prison authorities are conspicuous by their absence. The gangs rule the prison and are shown to be rotten and corrupt (white supremacists engaged in drug dealing with people of colour, willingness to use rape and violence to discipline dissent). *The Shawshank Redemption* takes place almost entirely within the prison. In *American History X* the prison sequence occupies less than 25 minutes of a two-hour film. It is still nonetheless a film, which deals with "imprisonment and its consequences." *The Shawshank Redemption* is in colour. *American History X* makes use of black and white during the flashback sequences which make up a substantial portion of the film. Both films contain a scene in which a supporting character describes how they were arrested by police whilst holding a television set that they had just stolen from a store. In *The Shawshank Redemption* the character is white whilst in *American History X* the character is black. *The Shawshank Redemption* is "fabular"/mythical. *American History X* recognises that a film is a construction (use of flashbacks in black and white) but still attempts to stake a "realist" claim to be, in some way, anchored in an actually existing social reality of contemporary Los Angeles (discussions of Rodney King, a *mise en scene* of the struggle for the city and its basketball courts).

American History X sets out to avoid the charges of hypocrisy that could be levelled against *The Shawshank Redemption*. In *History X* the black characters (Bob Sweeny the High School principal, Derek's prison workmate) are responsible for the redemption of both Derek and his brother Danny. *History X* implicitly claims to be both more realistic, and more progressive, than *Shawshank*. But to what extent does it succeed in achieving its aims?

American History X has been widely criticised in reviews, comment and discussions of the film. Most of the criticism revolves around the charge that in making white racism its centrepiece the film commits a number of errors. Racism is represented in the film as being a question of individual racial prejudice and/or the activities of far right groups. Institutional or societal racism is virtually absent from view. Further, because the film is about Derek and Danny and their family, these characters have history, motives and depth. The black characters, particularly the youths killed whilst attempting to 'jack Derek's car, have no history and the story is not told from their perspective. Finally, it has been suggested that the film not only centres on the activities of Derek but implicitly valorises his racist behaviour. Derek's body imagery undergoes a transformation as he undergoes his political transformation from wimpy liberal teenager to built Aryan warrior. The reformed Derek is mostly seen fully clothed, is growing his hair and will, it is implied, revert to his less hyper-masculine body image. In addition to this we could add that the prison rape scene is shot and played in a manner that could be suggestive of "glorifying the white man's body" (Dyer 1997).

In effect it is being suggested that, despite its intention to challenge racism, the film succeeds only in reproducing it. Perhaps more germane to our purpose here is to note that the film explicitly trades on a view of Los Angeles as a "racially"/"ethnically" divided city (and here it resonates with the other key "white identity" film, *Falling Down*, also set in Los Angeles). *History X* then brings this "city of division" inside the prison to create the *mise en scene* of a post-liberal, post-reformist prison, ruled by "ethnically" self-segregating gangs. Although *History X* does contain instances of inter-racial harmony and co-operation, most significantly Derek's relationship with his prison workmate, the backdrop assumption to the film is that prison is a dangerous place where the prison authorities are either unable or unwilling to protect the lives and wellbeing of their charges. *History X* both trades on and circulates a particular understanding of the American city significantly that exemplified by one particular view of post-Rodney King LA. But, it is also a view of the character of the prison associated with this city. The film makes explicit a move, from city to prison, which is implicit in countless episodes of American television dramas. (How many times do American cop shows (*Homicide: Life on the Street*, etc.) or action dramas (*Reno: renegade*) feature a single episode that is set undercover in a prison or involve a visit to a prison to interview a suspect? How often are suspects or informers threatened with the dire consequences that will arise should they be "sent down"? These representations invariably trade on a backdrop assumption of a racially divided city and prison.)

Finally, we can suggest that to the extent that the discourses and imagery which articulate the (alleged/imagined) problems of the Southern California prisons have been used to legitimate the building "new generation" prisons elsewhere in America (King 1999), then it is possible that *American History X* contributes more to the production and circulation of the "prison myths" associated with the growth of America's prison population than does *Con Air*.

Convict Cowboy

Convict Cowboy is a film that operates as a kind of hybrid between two "genres." It is part "prison drama" and part "action-adventure movie set in a prison." The film is set in a Montana prison that has a prison ranch attached to it. The ranch is the pet scheme of the prison warden (Ben Gazzara), justified to his superiors as a rehabilitation initiative, but in fact a cover for him to pursue his interest in maintaining a competitive prison rodeo team. Ry Westen (Jon Voight) is the ageing con who runs the ranch and its workforce of convict cowboys. Serving life for having murdered a man in a bar room brawl, Ry is a hard man—tough, principled, and moral although a little unbending. He runs the ranch with a firm hand and makes a stand against the drugs trade in the prison.

Clay Treyton (Kyle Chandler) is a rebellious young man convicted for assault after being involved in a scuffle with the police officers trying to arrest him for a minor offence. After some initial hostility Ry and Clay come to be friends. Ry saves Clay from becoming caught up in the prison drug trade and redirects him towards a career as a rodeo rider. In the process Ry himself becomes a better person.

There are two aspects of particular interest in *Convict Cowboy*. Firstly, the film clearly shows how the prison system runs counter to the idea of rehabilitation. Clay is rehabilitated by the mentorship of Ry despite, rather than because of, the efforts of the prison authorities. But when Clay is released having served his sentence, Ry is left behind. The audience is left with the question as to why Ry is apparently serving life without possibility of parole for a crime he committed as a young man. Why isn't a recognition of his rehabilitation and his release possible?

The second interesting aspect of *Convict Cowboy* is its use of *mise en scene*. The action of the film takes place in two distinct locations: the prison and the prison ranch. The difference between the two is clearly emphasised. The ranch is, of course, an outdoor location. The convict cowboys and their guards ride horses over gently rolling hills. We see men working with animals. There is hard physical work but it is dignified. It is not hard labour. This *mise en scene* contrasts sharply with the usual prison interior and is even distinctly different to that of the rural prison and chain gang featured in *Cool Hand Luke*. In contrast, the prison interior in *Convict Cowboy* exhibits the by now familiar *mise en scene*—"racial"/"ethnic" divisions, organised gangs, drugs trade, institutionalised inmate violence, etc., etc. The prison drama sections of *Convict Cowboy* (the mentoring of Clay by Ry, Ry's abortive relationship with the (female) ranch vet) take place almost entirely on the ranch. The attempts of the drug cartel to ensnare Clay in trafficking and the actions of Ry in stopping them, take place mainly within the prison and play more like an action movie. Jon Voight is clearly chosen for the lead role because of the ability of his screen persona to convincingly play both "parts."

The hybrid genre/split *mise en scene* is clearly an intentional device, but whether it is one which assists the film in achieving its aims is less clear. The film succeeds in raising the question of why Ry can't be considered as rehabilitated and eligible for release, and in establishing that the prison-as-machine is counter-productive to an ideal of rehabilitation. But it does this at a cost. Despite its pro-rehabilitation intentions, the *mise en scene* of the interior set scenes of the film circulate the imagery of the "control-problem prison" and also confirm the previously discussed proposition, that as long as redemption/rehabilitation is reserved for the exceptional (Clay/Ry), the mass of the inmate population is, by default, seen as being incapable of reform and unworthy of rehabilitation.

Synthesis and Conclusion

One of the most striking things about the four films discussed above is their treatment of gender. In these films women are either conspicuous by their absence and/or used in entirely conventional ways. "Women motivate men to action" is a standard convention in Hollywood cinema and is a convention that is maintained in these films. Defence of the family is a significant theme in *Con Air* and *History X* and *Convict Cowboy* features a female vet as the "romantic interest." The clichéd roles allocated to women in these films can and should be criticised. Why these films chose to represent prison in the masculine also requires further discussion but is beyond the scope of this article.

It seems safe to say that the role of the prison film in generating social and cultural understandings of the legitimacy or illegitimacy of prison as a form of punishment has not attracted a significant amount of discussion. Previous work has suggested that films within the mainstream prison film genre tend only to produce escapist fantasies that are in no way relevant to or critical of any actual experience of incarceration. The four films discussed above could all be said to be in some way "uncritical" and to operate within the limits of dominant social understandings of imprisonment. It can be suggested that in focusing on higher tariff offenders and facilities the films do provide a skewed representation of the nature of the inmate population and the characteristics of its offences (Walmsley 2000). Further, all of the films tacitly accept imprisonment as a necessary part of the criminal justice system. None puts a radical critique of imprisonment and none articulate Mathiesen's (2000) concerns about the growth of the prison population as constituting a "prisons fiasco." In Mathiesen's terms the films could be seen as part of the processes that deny the prisons fiasco. In not drawing our attention to the irrationality of imprisonment they could be seen as "corroding our doubts and worries about the prison solution" (p. vii).

Whether the above observations support a case for challenging misrepresentations of prisons and prisoners in film is less clear. In cultural/film studies it has often been suggested that in the 1980s and 1990s films became more polysemic (that is, containing many meanings). Increasingly films are deliberately constructed so as to be open to different readings. The discussion of the films above has only offered some suggestions as to the possible readings these films might be open to. But the discussion does suggest that they can be read in different ways. *The Shawshank Redemption* could be seen as a hypocritical text or an instance of "doing good by stealth." *Con Air* could be seen as propagating disparaging representations of prisoners or sending up the discourse of "the worst of the worst."

American History X and *Convict Cowboy* may illustrate that in film making, as in many other walks of life, the road to hell is paved with good intentions. It is quite possible that these two films circulate meanings distinctly different to those intended by their makers.

It would follow from the above then, that with respect to film, a notion of "challenging media misrepresentations" of prisons and prisoners is problematic. Which representations are to be challenged and how? Could prison activists picket/boycott films of which they disapprove? Or target the producers of these films as being irresponsible in a manner similar to the targeting of the tobacco or arms industries? The discussion above would suggest that to organise such actions would be highly problematic. Who is to decide, and on what basis, which films are to be championed and which derided? And how much support could be gathered for boycotting films designated as undesirable? It is interesting to note that in constructing a blockbuster movie the makers of *Con Air* have in a sense already anticipated possible objections to the film they have produced. The film contains both a "liberal" and a "conservative" reading on crime and punishment.

Having noted these problems, it should be said that the discussion above does suggest that film (and television) drama do circulate a repertoire of prison imagery which carries connotations and which is meaningful. How exactly these representations contribute to the climate in which penal policy is debated, and whether and how they might have contributed to the growth of the prison population is less clear. Did the cinematic imagery of the control-problem prison "accompany" or "underpin" the growth of the prison population? More work would need to be done to understand the ways in which prison imagery circulated by film and television may have contributed to the growth of the prison population.

References

Campbell, D. (2000) "Anger grows as US jails its two millionth inmate." *The Guardian*. 15 February.

Davis, M. (1991) *City of Quartz*, London: Verso.

Davis, M. (1992) *Beyond Blade Runner: The Ecology of Fear*, Westfield NJ: Open Media.

Davis, M. (2000) *Magical Urbanism: Latinos Reinvent the U.S. Big City*, London: Verso.

Dyer, R. (1997) *White*, London: Routledge.

Eco, U. (1984) *Postscript to "The Name of the Rose,"* New York: Harcourt Brace.

Fiske, J. (1987) *Television Culture*, London: Methuen.

King, R. (1999) "The rise and rise of supermax: an American solution in search of a problem," *Punishment and Society*, *1*(2), 163–84.

Mason, P. (nd) "Systems and process: the prison in cinema," *Images, 6*, [online] available at: www.imagesjournal.com/issue06/features/prison6.htm

Mathiesen, T. (1995) *The Driving Forces Behind Prison Growth: The Mass Media*, Washington DC: The Sentencing Project.

Mathiesen, T. (1990) *Prison on Trial*, London: Sage.

Mathiesen, T. (2000) *Prison on Trial*, 2nd ed., Winchester: Waterside Press.

Nellis, M. (1988) "British prison movies: the case of 'Now Barabbus,'" *Howard Journal, 27*, 2–31.

Nellis, M. and Hale, C. (1981) *The Prison Film*, London, Radical Alternatives to Prison.

Olson, S. R. (1999) *Hollywood Planet: Global Media and the Competitive Advantage of Transparency*, London: Laurence Earlbaum Associates.

Pfeil, F. (1998) "From pillar to postmodern: race, class and gender in the male rampage film," in: J. Lewis (Ed.), *The New American Cinema*, Durham NC: Duke University Press.

Rafter, N. (2000) *Shots in the Mirror: Crime Film and Society*, Oxford: Oxford University Press.

Ryan, M. and Kelner, D. (1990) *Camera Politica: The Politics and Ideology of Contemporary Hollywood Cinema*, Bloomington, Indiana: Indiana University Press.

Sparks, R. (1992) *Television and the Drama of Crime*, Buckingham: Open University Press.

Walmsley, R. (1999) "World prison population list," *Home Office Research, Development and Statistics Directorate: Research Findings No. 88*, London: Home Office.

Walmsley, R. (2000) "The world prison population situation: growth, trends, issues and challenges" (paper given to the Association of Paroling Officers International Conference, Ottawa 2000, [online] available at: www.apaintl.org/Pub-Conf2000-PlenaryWalmsley-En.html).

Wilson, D. (1993) "Inside observations," *Screen, 34*(1), 76–9.

Wilson, D. and Ashton, J. (1998) *What Everyone in Britain Should Know About Crime*, London: Blackstone Press.

Wilson, D. and Reuss, A. (Eds.) (2000) *Prison(er) Education: Stories of Change and Transformation*, Winchester: Waterside Press.

HOWARD JOURNAL OF CRIMINAL JUSTICE, Vol. 40 No. 4, pp. 317–334.

31. Media and Mayhem in Corrections: The Role of the Media in Prison Riots

Sue Mahan
Richard Lawrence

Three of the most infamous prison riots in the United States took place in Attica, New York; Santa Fe, New Mexico; and Lucasville, Ohio in 1971, 1980, and 1993, respectively. Although an examination of the three riots reveals differences in the uprisings, there are important similarities in the underlying conditions behind them. Analysis of the three riots shows the significant role played by representatives of the media both in negotiating with inmates and taking back the three institutions. In this article, the authors discuss the influence and effect of media coverage on prison riots based on what was learned from the participation of the media in the Attica, Santa Fe, and Lucasville uprisings.

Prison riots involve a seizure of control, violence, and inmate demands for changes in the prison. Since the first prison riot in the United States in 1774, some 300 prison riots have been reported in this country in the past two centuries (Fox, 1972). Prison riots are major media events that draw scores of radio and television reporters as well as newspaper journalists to cover the drama unfolding during the course of the disturbance. The public takes little interest in prisons until a tragic and violent crisis such as a riot takes place, and then considerable attention is riveted on the prison, the administrators, the corrections system—and on the inmates. Not surprisingly, prison inmates stage disturbances and riots and take hostages to air grievances. These disturbances and riots often erupt as acts of desperation among inmate leaders who have come to believe that it is a last resort to get a hearing from prison officials, policy makers, and the public about unfair policies or deplorable conditions in prisons. During riots, inmates attempt to use news media representatives to make their points and gain concessions from prison officials. The nature of news media coverage and the content of news stories may affect the ongoing developments during a riot, negotiations between inmates and officials, and retaking control of the institution.

The role of the news media in reporting ongoing events during a riot, and the influence of the media in negotiations between inmates and prison officials has not been carefully examined. Corrections administrators have two concerns with regard to media coverage of prison riots. They are concerned that reporters may present an overly sympathetic image of rioting inmates and that media representatives will intrude and interfere with the actions of the state to control the riot. On the other hand, the primary concern of media representatives is access to firsthand information (Miller, 1982), and they view their right to gather information as guaranteed by the First Amendment to the Constitution. But journalists also have expressed concerns about the difficulties of acting as neutral reporters when they become part of the negotiating process to bring order back to the prison.

There is a need to balance the freedom of the press and the public's right to know with the necessity of corrections officials to move carefully and deliberately in regaining control of the prison while minimizing the possibility of injury and loss of life to inmates and corrections personnel. Few corrections departments have uniform or clear policies regarding the role of reporters during a riot or for providing information to the media. The absence of clear policies and the variations in news media roles in previous prison riots indicate a serious need to closely examine this issue. The purpose of this article is to study three of the nation's worst prison riots to suggest a meaningful role for news media representatives during riots.

The prison riots at the Attica State Correctional Facility in New York in 1971 and at the New Mexico Penitentiary in Santa Fe in 1980 are considered two of the most deadly riots in U.S. prison history. The 1993 riot at the Southern Ohio Correctional Facility in Lucasville is considered the longest prison takeover in the United States. These three riots have been selected to illustrate the origins and circumstances of prison riots. Having occurred over three decades in U.S. history, they also demonstrate changes over time. Although the role of the media in the three riots is the focus of the study, it is also possible to examine similarities and differences in precipitating factors of the riots. The goal is to offer suggestions for further research and for the development of more clear policies for the coordination and cooperation of news media and corrections officials during the course of a prison riot.

Hostage Taking and the News Media

Prison riots have been investigated from a number of perspectives, but available information about riots basically falls into one of two explanations: One focuses on the research literature about the causes and nature of riots, and the other concerns the more graphic and personal media coverage surrounding riots. Studies have either examined the idiosyncratic characteristics of the people involved, or they have searched for structural and organizational causes for riots. The criminology literature about prison riots is largely devoted to the study of organizational factors, whereas the media and investigative reports are more often concerned with individuals and personalities.

Braswell, Dillingham, and Montgomery (1985) suggest that the origins and conditions for riots fall into one of four categories: (a) inmate solidarity in the face of authority; (b) racial, political, and ideological tensions; (c) unmet inmate expectations for changes; and (d) organizational conflicts over basic goals for prison. Leger (1988) notes that racial antagonism among inmates is often related to prison violence, and others have considered various characteristics of inmates such as age or criminal history (Kratcoski, 1988) or inmates' family experiences and personal goals (Sechrest, 1991) to explain violence-prone inmates. The experience of corrections officers is also believed to explain some prison violence, in that less-experienced officers are most likely to be assaulted by younger inmates who were first convicted at an early age (Kratcoski, 1988). Situational factors that have been examined in relation to prison riots include the location, time of day, and prior inmate involvement in prison violence (Kratcoski, 1988; Porporino, 1986; Steinke, 1991). The most common environments for inmate violence against officers and themselves are in high-security-level and disciplinary or segregation units. The most common environments for violence against other inmates are settings such as day rooms, prison yards, or similar areas where inmates are congregating but are not engaged in structured activities.

In general, studies have concluded that overcrowding is the most significant organizational precondition for riots. It may be seen as an "interactive variable"—sometimes causing, sometimes the result, and often exacerbating the impact of other conditions and practices. Researchers have shown the relationship of overcrowding to idleness and lack of programs (Goodgame, 1985; Mahan, 1985). Also related to overcrowding is a breakdown of the classification system, depletion of resources, lack of space for classrooms or recreation, and a general buildup of tension in prisons (American Correctional Association [ACA], 1990). Many prisons in the United States far exceed their capacities, and inmates are very often double or triple celled or living in open dormitories. Irrespective of other factors and despite the range of negative consequences from overcrowding, riots are not everyday occurrences in U.S. prisons. Researchers must look to other conditions for a better explanation of riot preconditions (Eckland-Olson, 1986).

From an organizational perspective, DiIulio (1987) found that prison riots were a response to control: usually not too much control but a dangerous lack of it. He described a conflict between the punitive ideology, which encourages tight controls with the viewpoint that prisons are deterrents and necessary for the protection of society, and the radical ideology, which encourages the least control possible with the viewpoint that prisons are unnecessarily oppressive, discriminatory, and vengeful. Surette (1992) points out that the punitive ideology is a likely result of sensationalistic and shocking news media coverage of personal violence, such as is the case in a riot. Media images may foster a punitive ideology of strict control. They may encourage conflict over controls in prisons. In some ways the media plays a role in the riot-generating process.

From the point of view of criminologists, news media reports are not simply "reflections of reality" (Barlow, Barlow, & Chiricos, 1995). When it comes to crime, media coverage is socially constructed reality (Barak, 1988). The image presented by the media is shaped by career and organizational self-interests that support the larger power structures of society (Wright, Cullen, & Blankenship, 1995). Coverage may imply that crime is beyond remedy (Gorelick, 1989), and when a remedy for crime is implied, it is likely to be individualistic and forceful. "Newsworthy" items are those that are dramatic, violent, visual, and timely. A prison riot in which hostages are taken is an event that serves the purposes of the news media because it garners high ratings. It serves the purpose of rioting inmates because the event gives them a large audience (Surette, 1992). Because publicity is the primary concern of inmates taking hostages, there is danger of media manipulation by the rebellious, demanding inmates. However, reporters must rely on corrections authorities and state officials for reliable information and details about the riots (Fishman, 1978). Official viewpoints providing a limited perspective about violence may be overrepresented in news media reports. The climate of fear and resulting polarization of public opinion that is created by media reports of hostage taking also can be manipulated by political authorities (Poland, 1988). During "newsworthy" events, it may be a question of "who is being manipulated by whom?"

Most law enforcement and corrections departments have public information offices to coordinate the flow of information between the agency and the news media, as well as to promote a positive image of the agency (Surette & Richard, 1994). Although the public information officer provides a connecting link between the department and the community, the responsibilities of that individual may not be clearly defined and may vary broadly among agencies and in different circumstances. Both media reports and official reports of past prison riots show that public information officers were in critical communication positions during disturbances, but they were poorly prepared and inadequately informed of ongoing events and decisions (Bingaman, 1980; Tillson, 1994). The role of spokesperson or media representative acting as a liaison between authorities and journalists has been developing over the past decades. This is the role of gatekeeper to information, and it is critical to the process of negotiations and settlement even though this person is not a negotiator. Reports made public by the media have a critical influence on inmates during major prison riots. The responsibility of the public information officer during a riot is extremely important. Planning and preparation for the person in this role is basic to adequate riot preparation.

Methodology of Study

Two of the deadliest prison riots in American history occurred at the New York correctional facility in Attica in 1971 and at the New Mexico state prison in Santa Fe in 1980. The 1993 riot at the Southern Ohio Correctional Facility in Lucasville was the longest prison takeover in this country. These three prison riots were selected for study because they represent not only the deadliest and longest prison riots in U.S. history but also span three decades and occurred in three different regions of the country, thus offering an opportunity for multiple comparisons. Each prison shared common conditions that played a part in triggering the riots, but there were also unique circumstances that differentiate the three. Data for this study were derived from different kinds of documents published following each riot and included information from the criminology literature as well as media and investigative reports. Some of the more important factual data and distinguishing characteristics of each of the three prison riots are summarized for comparison in Table 1.

TABLE 1 A Comparison of Three Prison Riots

	Attica, NY	*Santa Fe, NM*	*Lucasville, OH*
Date	Sept. 9, 1971	Feb. 2, 1980	April 11, 1993
Length	36 hours	5 days	11 days
Prison cap	1,200	900	1,609
Actual population	2,000	1,136	1,820
Percentage overpopulated	166	126	113
Trigger	Inmate dragged to the "hole"	Security breaches	Threat of a lockdown
Hostages	38	12	12
Deaths caused by inmates during riot			
Inmates	3	33	9
Officer	1	0	1
Deaths during takeback			
Inmates	29	0	0
Officers	10	0	0
Cost estimate	$3 million	$28.5 million	$15 million
Inmate leadership	Black Muslims	Cliques	Three gangs
Official leadership	Commissioner Oswald, Governor Rockefeller	Management cliques, Governor King	Experts, Warden Tate
Official report	New York state court appointment, McKay Commission	Attorney General Bingaman	Governor and Department of Rehabilitation and Corrections appointment, two-citizen commission
Media role			
Officials contacted	Newspaper	Radio	All types
Inmates demanded	Newspaper	TV	All types
Negative aspects	Confused issues	Glorified mayhem	Blamed for a death
Positive aspects	Exposed cover-up	Exposed corruption	Assisted with takeback
Official view	Interfering	Antagonistic	Used as players

Similarities Among the Three Prison Riots

Study of the Attica, Santa Fe, and Lucasville riots reveals striking similarities in origins and conditions leading up to the uprisings, conditions that have persisted with very little change over the past three decades in most U.S. prisons. The following is not an exhaustive list of originating and precipitating factors in prison riots, but it does summarize some of the notable parallels in the three riots studied. The factors have been organized into three categories: (a) prison structural-organizational factors, (b) prisoner-individual factors, and (c) media-related factors.

Prison Structural-Organizational Factors

- Urban offenders were being held in rural settings with little connections to homes or families.
- The prisons were considered the "toughest" in the state. They housed inmates with the highest security levels and were end-of-the-line, "maxi-maxi" facilities.
- The prisons were large, overcrowded institutions, holding more than 1,000 prisoners, often housing high-security-level inmates in less than highly secure conditions.
- Inadequate and ineffective classification schemes made it impossible for administrators to transfer problem or special-needs inmates to other facilities.
- Inmates were idle most of the time due to a lack of meaningful educational and recreational programs.
- Power struggles existed at each prison between upper-level management and line staff.
- Role conflicts were common among the prison staff, pitting those who emphasized control and custody goals against those who emphasized case management and treatment.
- Disciplinary procedures were a source of conflict in the prisons; no systematic procedures to resolve inmate grievances were being followed.
- There had been complaints of harassment and brutality toward inmates at all three prisons just prior to the riots.
- Mentally ill inmates were not handled appropriately and were disruptive to prison routine.
- The prisons had no adequate plans for riots and other emergencies.
- Many of the corrections officers were poorly trained and ill-prepared for their duties. Inept handling of security details was a factor that triggered each of the riots.
- Administrative changes had led to periods of extreme tension just before the riots broke out; most employees had recognized warning signs and indications of trouble that gave clear signals that crises were imminent.
- Officials responded to tensions with ill-designed efforts meant to tighten controls. Attempts to maximize control backfired when inmates erupted into violence and took control over the prison.

Prisoners: Individual Factors

- Incoming inmates to the prisons were said to be a "new breed" and "more violent."
- The riots were considered both planned and spontaneous. There were many elements that were well thought out in advance, but the actual uprisings depended on taking advantage of opportunities and circumstances as they came up.
- Racial and ethnic conflicts were well documented at the three prisons; the conflicts existed between inmates, between inmates and prison staff, and between inmates and those living in surrounding communities.
- Inmates at each prison expressed high levels of frustration and desperation. They were prepared to die to get the respect they were demanding: "We're not going to bow down. We are not going to give up. We will remain strong until we either negotiate this to our liking or they will kill us," declared a Lucasville inmate.

Media-Related Factors

- Rioters were desperate for media coverage. Access to a legitimate public forum had been denied.
- Inmates were more willing to exploit attention of the media than authorities, who were more hostile to media attention.
- Rioting inmates attempted to use the media to achieve their demands for reforms and gain concessions from prison administrators.
- False or misleading reports about conditions were issued to the media by officials.
- Rioters were following media coverage of the riot while they held the prisons and recognized misinformation.

Attica

The inmates at the Attica prison began rioting on September 9, 1971, and the siege lasted 5 days. There were at least 2,000 inmates being held in the facility that had a stated capacity of 1,200 (166% of capacity). Thirty-eight officers were taken hostage, and the facility suffered $3 million in damage. During the uprising, three inmates were slain by other inmates under circumstances that remain unclear, and one hostage was killed. Early reports that the hostage died when thrown from a second-floor window proved false, and later reports claiming he was "beaten to death" left the perpetrators unknown. The rest of the deaths, an additional 39, were from "overkill" when the prison was taken back with extreme force by the state (*American Prisons in Turmoil*, 1979). Ten of the dead were hostages, and 29 were inmates. The incident that immediately precipitated the riot was a lockdown following a poorly handled disciplinary action against inmates in a part of the prison considered to be under the most tension.

The Black Muslims emerged as leaders of the riot in the highly organized inmate society that developed in the yard. New York Governor Rockefeller refused to take part in the event but gave his support to a forceful takeback. Negotiations involved a group of observers who reflected a broad political spectrum and included participants from the media, politics, and other professions. The diversity of this committee of outside observers was reported to have made it dysfunctional. State Commissioner of Correctional Services, Russell Oswald, took the leadership role in negotiating for the state and ordering the attack. His deputy, Walter Dunbar, was responsible for false reports of atrocities committed by inmates that persisted long after the riot was over. Rioters at Attica asked for removal of the warden, Mancusi, as one of their demands. He was removed several months later.

The Media Role at Attica. Prior to the riot, inmates complained that whenever there was media attention at Attica, "the prison authorities made sure no inmates were around unless they were locked in their cells, so on one would be able to talk to reporters" (Clark, 1973, p. 12). Yet inmates also reported they were keeping abreast of what was happening outside by listening to the news through the earphones provided in every cell. Once the siege was under way, rioters demanded access to the media as a means of making public any promises made to them by the state. Attorney William Keunstler, member of the Observers' Committee, remarked that the prisoners trusted the press more than the authorities. Included among the media representatives requested by the inmates was a reporter from the *New York Times*, "because the person who reads the Times is not like a working person. . . . We wanted to reach influential people, not just the people on the subway . . . and we wanted a whole cross-section of coverage" (Clark, 1973, p. 65). Tom Wicker, the *New York Times* representative who later wrote a book about Attica, said, "I couldn't be both a reporter and a negotiator. . . . The only time I told the New York Times I could not file was when I became part of the story" (Tillson, 1994, p. 25). Wicker acknowledged the conflict he felt as a journalist being part of an event rather than simply informing the public.

During the riot, prisoners watched themselves on the news, and there was constant radio coverage from a loud speaker system set up in the yard by an inmate electrician. Media coverage contributed to inmates' misunderstanding about the negotiating process and hostilities toward prison officials. When inmates heard that an officer had died from reportedly being thrown from a window, and knowing that all the windows had bars, they believed that the state had killed their own man and were blaming inmates.

Prison officials were also aware of media coverage of their actions during the riot. Commissioner Oswald was confronted at the outset with a barrage of questions from reporters that he considered to be "from the prisoners' point of view" (Oswald, 1972, p. 80). When he told reporters the inmates were asking for "the world," he did not realize that inmates would hear. He later found that his answers had been badly received by rioters listening inside.

The report from the New York State Special Commission on Attica, which investigated the riot, described the role of the media and noted that the presence of reporters and television cameras inside the prison gave inmates a sense of importance, dignity, and power by providing them with an unparalleled opportunity to tell the public about prison conditions. Inmates realized that they could command national attention only as long as they kept the hostages, and once the uprising ended, they "would return to the status of forgotten men, subject to all the humiliations of prison life. That feeling, coupled with their fear of reprisals and mistrust of the State, made it almost impossible to persuade them to give up the limelight and return to anonymity" (McKay, 1972, p. 211). The authors of the Commission report also noted that the presence of television cameras and the press tends to encourage rhetoric rather than serious concessions. The Commission agreed that prisons must be subject to public scrutiny and that the news media have a vital role to play in exposing inhumane conditions, but the Commission also noted that settlement negotiations during an uprising are not the occasion to exercise that function. "To maximize chances of agreement, negotiations must be conducted privately without the presence of the press, but with appropriate briefings to the press" (McKay, 1972, p. 213).

Santa Fe

Prisoners took over the New Mexico State Prison in Santa Fe in the early hours of February 2, 1980, and the riot lasted 36 hours. Security lapses had been common throughout the prison, making a takeover likely. The riot erupted when officers left a security gate open as they were closing down for the night. It began in a dormitory that housed high-risk inmates. Twelve officers were taken as hostages, and 33 inmates were killed by their fellow inmates. The most horrible brutality was reserved for "snitches" who had been given special treatment by prison officials in return for informing on other inmates either in court, inside prison, or both. No hostages died, and no one was killed in the assault to take back the prison. At the time of the riot, 1,136 inmates were being held in a facility designed for 900 (126% of capacity). The approximate damage to the prison facility totaled $28.5 million.

No identifiable inmate leadership emerged, and negotiators had no clear mandate from the prisoners. Hostages were traded for personal considerations. Social organization was described as cliques divided along racial lines. Blacks, who were greatly outnumbered by Hispanics and Whites, pleaded for protection from the state.

All negotiations for the state were handled by Acting Secretary of Corrections Felix Rodriquez, who had held various positions of leadership in state corrections, including warden at Santa Fe. As a result of his leadership, it was said that "cumulative corruption blocked any chance of outside help" (Morris, 1981, p. 166). Governor King deferred all decisions to Rodriguez, but he was the first to speak to inmates by phone early in the morning after the riot began. They told him they started the riot "to get somebody's attention" (Bingaman, 1980, p. 37). King promised inmates a meeting with the press, but that meeting was not forthcoming for more than 30 hours.

The warden at the time of the riot, Griffin, was made press spokesman, but he was not involved in negotiations and was said to be the furthest removed from decision making. He was replaced shortly after the riot was over. Recently appointed Secretary of Corrections Adolph Saenz had not yet been formally confirmed in office when the riot erupted. He called for the assault that took back control of the prison. By most accounts the riot had already ended before the order was carried out by a SWAT team that met no resistance.

The Media Role at Santa Fe. Prior to the riot, a radio show had been scheduled for broadcast from the Santa Fe prison. Inmates had planned to take hostages and use the broadcasting facilities as a public forum to air their complaints. The show was canceled when prison administrators learned of their plans. Prisoners described a long-standing dislike of the media on the part of prison officials. At the same time, media people were described by inmates as "being the trouble shooters of the world" (Stone, 1982, p. 19). During the riot, inmates, prison officials, and the public were admonished to "remember Attica" by banners and slogans at the scene and by media coverage that drew instant parallels between the two bloody revolts. These reminders may have discouraged officials from staging a forced "takeback" at Santa Fe in spite of the documented killing and mayhem going on inside. Throughout the riot, prisoners communicated with each other and with prison officials using CB radios, but they were also monitoring and interfering with each other's transmissions.

The first journalist on the scene was Ernie Mills, a radio announcer from Santa Fe. According to the attorney general's report, Mills joined in the talks in response to inmates' constant demands for access to news media. Mills realized the tenuous nature of his position and insisted he was there to assist the officials, remarking, "As soon as I went in, I was no longer a reporter." With Mills present, a hostage was released in exchange for talks between inmates and officials. The second journalist, a cameraman from an ABC affiliate, was allowed inside at midnight approximately 24 hours after the uprising started. He filmed inmates voicing their demands, and another hostage was released in exchange for his coverage. After another 12 hours, inmates were allowed the news conference they had been demanding. At this time three Hispanic and two White inmates, who had been identified by prison officials as riot leaders, negotiated in their own interests and arranged for the release of the remaining two hostages.

Throughout the riot, journalists complained about lack of consistent information and irregular briefings. The riot was considered major network news, and representatives from news organizations all over the United States descended on Santa Fe to cover the story. But the prison officials made little or no concession to their role. Riot plans and procedures were carried out without consideration for the media, and so journalists carried on without official communication. Because of this lack of reliable information, reporters and families were left to scramble for facts, barraging prison officials with questions. The crowd of reporters and family members even hampered emergency evacuation of the wounded. Rumors persisted without any facts to dispute them. Reports grew sensationalistic and inflammatory. Prison officials were said to be infuriated by media representatives, and the relationship between journalists and authorities was antagonistic. According to the official investigation, "the lack of effective public relations appear[ed] to handicap the operation of the penitentiary" (Bingaman, 1980, p. IIB-5).

Lucasville

The uprising at the Southern Ohio Correctional Facility at Lucasville broke out on Easter Sunday, April 11, 1993, and the siege lasted 11 days. At the time of the riot, there were 1,820 inmates held in the prison that had a stated capacity of 1,609 (113% of capacity). Inmates rebelled one day before a lockdown to force Black Muslim inmates to submit to TB skin testing. The cost of damages to the facility was estimated to be $15 million. Twelve officers were held hostage, one of whom was killed by inmates. Nine inmate deaths resulted from attacks by other inmates, but no prisoners were injured by authorities in the takeover of the prison.

Inmate leadership included roughly three groups: Black Muslims, Aryan Supremacists, and Black Gangster Disciples. Prison operations were led by Reggie Wilkinson, head of the State Department of Rehabilitation and Corrections, and his leadership was never questioned. Governor Voinovich answered no press questions and left negotiations to law enforcement and corrections experts. Reports indicate that, although Lucasville Warden Tate provided energetic leadership of the facility, he lacked confidence in his supervisory and midlevel staff, and there was disruptive tension between custody and unit management of the institution.

During the negotiation process, the state's top negotiators and corrections representatives, who had written the policy manual for negotiations in a hostage situation, were surprised to find that one of the leaders of the riot had found a copy of the book inside the prison and was following the strategy outlined in it. Inmates demanded to have an attorney during the negotiation process, and the one they chose was credited with being the catalyst for bringing both sides together, eventually leading to a resolution.

The Media Role at Lucasville. The Lucasville riot occurred during the time the Branch Davidian Complex in Waco, Texas was under siege. On the ninth day of the 11-day riot, the media were bombarded with images of the horror of the climax to the siege in Waco. Pressure to negotiate in Ohio intensified after the scenes of flames in Texas. It was described as "fear of the news" (McCarty et al., 1993, p. 9).

Shortly after the riot broke out, hundreds of journalists descended on the Lucasville area, and the press became an integral part of the drama. Reporters were caught sneaking through the woods, filming through doors, posing as family members, and trespassing on hostages' property. But the first press briefing was not held until late on the second day. A news blackout was imposed that proved to be a breeding ground for rumor. The local newspaper reported 50 to 150 bodies lying inside the prison, and friends and families of hostages said, "Everybody knows it's worse than what they're saying." Inmates were leaking false information to reporters about sadistic atrocities (Tillson, 1994).

Prison officials had decided to negotiate a way out, but the inmates were so sharply divided in their demands that negotiating with them was said to be "like boxing with an octopus." A single telephone line to negotiators was the inmates' only link to the outside. Frustrated prisoners took their message outdoors, broadcasting garbled announcements over a makeshift PA system. From the broken windows, rioters draped bedsheets painted with slogans: "We want the media." "We want to talk to the FBI." "The state is not negotiating."

Later, another sheet was hung from a prison window with a crudely written message: "If we don't have something in 3+ hours, we're going to kill a hostage." The prison spokesperson, Tessa Unwin, dismissed the threat, saying, "They have been threatening something like this from the beginning. It's part of the language of the negotiations" (McCarty et al., 1993, p. 9). Later, two released hostages blamed the spokesperson for the death of one hostage. Rioters were angered by broadcast remarks that were interpreted as downplaying the seriousness of their threat to kill hostages.

During the news conference a rioter confirmed, "From the outset of this we have tried desperately, desperately, desperately, to get in contact with the news media. We have beat our brains out. We have been stopped by this administration. They think they can hide everything, like they've been doing down here for years and years" (McCarty et al., 1993, p. 6). He traded a hostage for his interview. Later, a Black Muslim inmate also traded a hostage for an interview. The press was surprised to see a Black corrections officer come out dressed in Muslim garb and announce that he had chosen a Muslim name and "adjusted to the Nation of Islam" while being held hostage.

Throughout the riot, journalists also complained about their treatment. News conferences were called and canceled without regard for deadlines, and no explanations were offered. Early on in the uprising, a local radio announcer agreed to let state police, who believed rioters were listening, review the news before it was aired on radio. In spite of his attempts to cooperate during the first days of the riot, the journalist found himself unable to reach the state police to find out what he could use, and thus he was unable to air the news he was gathering.

At the same time, officials viewed the news representatives as "players" and used them as tools to arrange a successful outcome. The rioters began talking about surrendering, but there were unanswered concerns for which the media were pressed into service. Rioters were concerned about predatory prisoners attacking other prisoners and officer retaliation during the takeback. The state wanted media representatives to videotape the surrender to protect rioters from violence and ensure the safe release of hostages. Negotiators expected the media to clamor for the privilege of doing a live broadcast of the takeback, but media representatives were less than enthused. They disliked being kept "on call" by prison officials and resisted the restrictions placed on them: The entire takeback had to be filmed uninterrupted, without commercials; they had to feed the broadcast uninterrupted to other stations; and the reporters could only report what they saw happening—no commentary, no background, and no identification of the reporters or their affiliation. Only a regional station with an extra satellite truck could handle the task.

The Disturbance Cause Committee, established by the secretary of the Department of Rehabilitation and Corrections to study the Lucasville riot, proposed a list of 26 preliminary recommendations. Only one of those recommendations (no. 11) refers to the role of the media: "The Department of Rehabilitation and Corrections should develop a communication policy whereby information provided to the media about a prison uprising is carefully evaluated as to its impact and ramifications before release" (Mohr, 1993). A media task force also was established by the governor of Ohio to find out how the state could do a better job of dealing with the media in future disasters. The task force found that there was a prevailing tendency on the part of state officials (including public information officers) during the riot to withhold information, even when there was no operational reason for doing so. The primary recommendation of the task force was that all state officials, from the governor on down, be made aware of the state policy requiring release of information in a complete and timely manner during an emergency. The task force also recommended the media not be used as a direct participant in resolving crises or in other ways required to compromise the independence or credibility of their coverage (Tillson, 1994).

Discussion

The media role in prison riots has developed and expanded as the influence of mass communication has evolved, but certain key issues remain basic to the relationship between officials and the media during prison riots. At Attica, the roles of newspaper journalists were critical. A key issue raised then, and still unresolved after decades, is the position of journalists who cross over to become negotiators. When journalists take part in the negotiation, on whose behalf are they acting? Does a journalist cease to be a reporter when acting in support of authorities? At Santa Fe, the television coverage inflamed the riot and was carried on in an air of antagonism between journalists and authorities. A second key issue is this apparent conflict of interests between journalists' First Amendment rights and authorities' need to control strategic information. Their common interests to inform the public and to discourage further prison violence may be overlooked. At Lucasville, reporters' roles as media representatives and public servants were in conflict. Authorities expected journalists to video the entire takeback of the institution, but networks had other commitments. By calling for continuous broadcasting, officials were not considering commercial or other news and entertainment demands. Cooperation is a third key issue that was in conflict in the three riots. The cooperation of the media is far more useful to officials than their authority to exercise control over the media to coerce their compliance. Controls over journalists' access to information in the United States is likely to be self-imposed in the form of voluntary guidelines (Vetter & Perlstein, 1991). Professional guidelines and self-imposed, responsible reporting are reasonable alternatives to censorship but can only be effective if guidelines are enforced.

This study of three prison riots offers an explanation of media involvement on a duality of levels—individual and organizational. Journalists and investigative reporters often show an individualistic bias, preferring to report on personal stories and individual explanations. Using the records provided by journalists made it possible to examine the roles of the rioting inmates, prison officials, and media personalities as critical factors in the riots. News and commission reports helped to reveal more about the conditions and the spontaneous elements that contributed to the riots.

Social scientists tend to have an organizational bias, preferring to look for patterns and systemic explanations. Studying the structures, policies, and systems in place at Attica, Santa Fe, and Lucasville helped to uncover the long-standing elements that contributed to the riots. However, a combined explanation explores media influence on prison riots as both predictable and idiosyncratic. Despite the incidents that made each riot unique, there were common elements among them that made them similar to countless others as well as to each other.

Since 1971, the uprising at Attica has served as a grim reminder that prisons—especially overcrowded, maximum security facilities with inmate and staff problems—are ripe for disturbances that may turn into full-blown riots. Despite the deadly reminder of Attica, problems persist in American prisons, posing daily risks and hazards to prison staff and inmates. Many of the problems exist because of the unrealistic demands placed on prisons to house more offenders for longer periods of time without adequate funds to recruit and train qualified prison staff. The growing trend toward more punitive rather than rehabilitative approaches also contributes to the tense conditions in prison. Institutional programs and services that help inmates adjust to jail and prison life have been cut (Lawrence, 1985). Programs and amenities, such as exercise facilities and television, which help to reduce tension levels and aid prison staff in controlling a potentially violent prison community, are no longer provided. The tax-paying public is best served with a balanced perspective on prison uprisings, but the media image is often distorted for maximum impact. An inflammatory version of a prison riot may provoke drastic reactions and greater conflict between inmates and authorities. Media representatives are seldom in a position to consider institutional conditions, the individual needs of inmates, and the programs and policies that enable prison staff to control a population that vastly outnumbers them.

Miller (1982) offers a list of recommendations about the extent and nature of media coverage in hostage situations. Because Miller's list addresses hostage situations involving political terrorists, the following list has been revised to refer directly to prison riots:

- By naming individuals, the media give credit and strengthen what they are doing. By making their methods public, the media may be encouraging imitation. By publicizing what rioters say, the media help them accomplish what they want.

- If media coverage is part of the demands, it should be done in as limited a manner as possible, involving as few people as possible.
- Rioters should not be portrayed as heroes.
- The point should be made that no hostage situation has been successful.
- Direct calls to the rioters should be avoided because they tend to draw out the process.
- Site coverage should be limited because it gives away intelligence information to the rioters.
- Keep air time in proportion to the objective news value of the acts.
- Give documentaries and analyses on the problems facing the system and even access to the media for the voices of reason among dissident groups, thereby reducing the likelihood of their resorting to violence to have their grievances heard.

Miller's recommendations for media coverage in political terrorist situations must be considered in light of the particular characteristics of prison riots. Hostages are taken in familiar surroundings after a long-standing relationship of conflict that has erupted in a prison riot. It is not clear how these unique characteristics affect the potential for harm done by the media.

Smith (1990), in his book *Combating Terrorism*, points out media practices that are likely to cause problems in any hostage-taking situation, prisons or elsewhere:

- saturation coverage that can limit or preempt the authorities' options
- political dialogue with inmates or hostages that can delay resolution of the uprising
- coverage of obviously staged events that encourages violence
- Payments to inmates for access or interviews that interfere with inmates' social organization and promote self-serving actions
- coverage of authorities' tactical plans in advance, which causes problems in restoring order

These are practices that media representatives can be asked to avoid.

Patrick Murphy (1982) noted five ways that news media reporting may create problems when police are dealing with terrorists: (a) entering into negotiations, (b) talking directly to rioters, (c) casting doubt on the reliability of officials, (d) disclosing tactical information, and (e) raising rioters' anxieties. The study reported here suggests that these problems also characterized media coverage of the riots at Attica, Santa Fe, and, to some extent, Lucasville.

The repetitive interference of the "Observers Committee" at Attica contributed to the breakdown of negotiations and unresolved conflicts between the two sides and did nothing to stop the massacre.

The long-standing antagonism between the media and New Mexico state officials was played out in misunderstandings and hostilities during that riot. Although hostages were traded in exchange for access to the media, the sensational coverage of the event may have provided encouragement for the mayhem that ensued during the uprising. The media provided continuous on-site coverage, sympathetic images of the prisoners, and disproportionate air time, considering the riot's objective news value.

At Lucasville, a spokesperson was blamed for the death of a hostage after the media reported that officials were not taking rioters' threats seriously. Media representatives felt they were poorly used and manipulated by state officials throughout the 11-day siege. Yet state negotiators expected reporters and camera technicians to act as "players" assisting them in regaining control of the prison.

From studies of hostage-taking situations, an alternative role for the media during these crises has emerged. During riot situations, the appropriate approach to news gathering is twofold: (a) minimize intrusiveness so that journalists avoid inciting more violence and (b) provide complete coverage so that confidence and cooperation between the media and the authorities can be maintained (Vetter & Perlstein, 1991).

Prison officials must provide a riot control policy that includes the media in all phases. At the level of development, guidelines for the media during prison riots must be established. Standards and professional policies can best be drawn up by a commission of media, government, and civic members. Clear and reasonable standards, well enforced, are more useful than censorship imposed by officials.

At the level of reaction, authorities must establish operations centers during the emergency. Official command centers have many functions that contribute to better relations between authorities and media representatives: (a) They provide information by and for all departments of government; (b) they establish communications between all levels of authority; (c) they collect, analyze, and disseminate information; (d) they provide regular situation briefings; (e) they coordinate the release of information to the media; and (f) they recommend courses of action to decision makers (Vetter & Perlstein, 1991). Command centers that effectively provide these services offer the most efficient way to avoid inflaming events and prolonging incidents.

At the level of organization, authorities need three fundamental resources for riot control: (a) Prison plans must provide for adequate technical and professional apparatus to expedite communication. During the riot, media equipment and vehicles must not dominate the thoroughfares or be blocked from admittance. (b) Prison officials must make prompt, substantial information—for all agencies and to the media—a high priority. Information is a most valuable resource, and plans for its use must be fair and open if media cooperation is to be expected. (c) Prison officials also need effective spokespersons who can inspire public confidence in the authorities. Spokespersons are valuable resources who must be included in advanced planning. Adequate use of these three resources—equipment, information, and trained personnel—make it possible to establish a balance between too much and too little access to information (Smith, 1990).

At the same time, because a primary objective of rioting inmates is to air their grievances, media coverage can be useful in saving lives. For example, inmates may trade hostages for interviews. Informed coverage also can prevent future destruction by discouraging potential rioters in other prisons from imitating an uprising. The media can bring a quicker end to a disturbance by convincing the rioters to give up because their situation is hopeless. Clearly, the role of the news media before, during, and after a prison riot is essential.

Although it is not valid to blame the media for causing prison riots, it is valid to note that the media are a critical factor. Yet, in developing strategies to deal with riots, the media have been overlooked. For example, an in-depth study sponsored by the National Institute of Justice and the Federal Bureau of Prisons in 1995 examined eight prison disturbances. The media are not included among the key issues considered in that study, and no mention of the media is made in the conclusions (Useem, Camp, Camp, & Dugan, 1995). A study of state and federal prison systems' policies toward the media and a comparison of conditions with violent incidents at facilities that are more or less open to the media could aid in developing effective guidelines for media involvement. Media standards are needed that pursue goals of prevention, education, provision of information, and diffusion of prison riots.

The three riots described in this study offer some preliminary findings and suggestions. They took place in institutions with conditions similar to those found in many large maximum security prisons throughout this country. Information from studies of hostage situations by terrorists may apply to prison uprisings if the unique conditions of confinement are taken into account. Prison riots are last responses to the lack of attention to long-standing grievances. They are action as propaganda. Rioting inmates rarely expect to be released or escape during a riot. Their intention is to draw attention to their conditions and their experiences. Prison officials have rarely understood that the media are an essential element in prison riots. Their hostility and attempts to exclude the media are counterproductive.

References

American Correctional Association (ACA). (1990). *Causes, preventive measures, and methods of controlling riots and disturbances in correctional institutions.* College Park, MD: Author.

American prisons in turmoil: Hearings by the Select Committee on Crime, 92nd Cong., ¼C 86/3: pt. 2, p. 93. (1979).

Badillo, H., & Haynes, M. (1972). *A bill of no rights.* New York: Outerbridge & Lazard.

Barak, G. (1988). Newsmaking criminology: Reflections on the media, intellectuals, and crime. *Justice Quarterly, 5*, 565–587.

Barlow, M. H., Barlow, D. E., & Chiricos, T. G. (1995). Economic conditions and ideologies of crime in the media. *Crime and Delinquency, 41*(1), 3–19.

Bingaman, J. (Attorney General). (1980). *Report of the attorney general on the February 2 and 3, 1980 riot at the penitentiary of New Mexico.* Santa Fe, NM: Author.

Braswell, M., Dillingham, S., & Montgomery, R. (Eds.). (1985). *Prison violence in America.* Cincinnati, OH: Anderson.

Burlew, K. (Chair). (1994, January). *Final report and recommendations of the governor's select committee on corrections.* Columbus, OH: Author.

Clark, R. (1973). *The brothers at Attica.* New York: Links.

DiIulio, J., Jr. (1987). *Governing prisons.* New York: Free Press.

Eckland-Olson, S. (1986). Crowding, social control, and prison violence. *Law and Society Review, 20,* 389–420.

Fishman, M. (1978). Crime wave as ideology. *Social Problems, 25,* 531–543.

Fox, V. (1972). Prison riots in a democratic society. *Police, 16,* 33–41.

Goodgame, D. (1985, August 12). Mayhem in the cellblocks. *Time,* p. 20.

Gorelick, S. (1989). The construction of ideology in a newspaper crimefighting campaign. *Crime and Delinquency, 35,* 421–436.

Gould, R. (1974). The officer inmate relationship: Its role in the Attica rebellion. *Bulletin of the American Academy of Psychiatry and the Law,* 2(1), 34–35.

The killing ground. (1980, February 18). *Newsweek,* p. 66.

Kratcoski, P. (1988). The implications of research explaining prison violence and disruption. *Federal Probation, 52,* 57–62.

Lawrence, R. (1985). Jail educational programs: Helping inmates cope with overcrowded conditions. *Journal of Correctional Education, 36,* 15–20.

Leger, R. (1988). Perceptions of crowding, racial antagonism, and aggression in a custodial prison. *Journal of Criminal Justice, 16,* 167–181.

Lupsha, P., & Miler, G. (1981, July 7). Impact: Correcting corrections. *Albuquerque Journal Magazine,* pp. 4–13.

Mahan, S. (1985). An "orgy of brutality" at Attica and the "killing ground" at Santa Fe: A comparison of prison riots. In M. Braswell, S. Dillingham, & R. Montgomery (Eds.). *Prison violence in America.* Cincinnati, OH: Anderson.

McCarty, M., Beyerlein, T., Flynn, A., Miller, T., Reed, C., Rollins, R., & Theis, S. (1993, June 6). Eleven days in Lucasville. *Dayton Daily News.*

McKay, R. (Chairman). (1972). *ATTICA: The official report of the NY state special commission.* Praeger, NY: Author.

Miller, A. (Ed.). (1982). *Terrorism, the media and the law.* Dobbs Ferry, NY: Transnational.

Mohr, G. C. (Chair). (1993, June 10). *Southern Ohio correctional facility disturbance cause committee findings.* Columbus, OH: Author.

Montgomery, B. (Chair). (1994, April). *Interim report by the Correctional Institution Inspection Committee.* Columbus, OH: Author.

Morris, R. (1981, March). Thirty-six hours at Santa Fe. *Playboy*, p. 111.

Murphy, P. (1982). The police, the news media, and the coverage of terrorism. In A. Miller (Ed.). *Terrorism, the media and the law.* Dobbs Ferry, NY: Transnational.

Oswald, R. (1972). *Attica, my story.* New York: Doubleday.

Poland, J. (1988). *Understanding terrorism.* Englewood Cliffs, NJ: Prentice Hall.

Porporino, F. (1986). Managing violent individuals in correctional settings. *Journal of Interpersonal Violence, 1*, 213–237.

Ragheb, A. (1990). Mass media and terrorism: Cause and effect. In R. H. Ward & A. G. Ezeldin (Eds.). *International responses to terrorism: New initiatives.* Chicago: University of Illinois. The Office of International Criminal Justice.

Saenz, A. (1986). *Politics of a prison riot.* New York: Rhombus.

Sechrest, D. (1991). The effects of density on jail assaults. *Journal of Criminal Justice, 19*, 211–223.

Serrill, M., & Katel, P. (1980, April). New Mexico: The anatomy of a riot. *Corrections Magazine, 6*(2), 6–16, 20–24.

Smith, G. D. (1990). *Combating terrorism.* London: Routledge & Kegan Paul.

Steinke, P. (1991). Using situational factors to predict types of prison violence. *Journal of Offender Rehabilitation, 17*, 119–132.

Stone, W. G. (1982). *The hate factory.* New York: Dell.

Surette, R. (1992). *Media, crime & criminal justice.* Pacific Grove, CA: Brooks/Cole.

Surette, R., & Richard, A. (1994). *Public information officers: A descriptive study of crime news gatekeepers.* Unpublished paper, Florida International University.

Tillson, J. B. (Chair). (1994, March). *Lucasville media task force report.* Dayton, OH: Author.

Useem, B., Camp, C. G., Camp, G. M., & Dugan, R. (1995). *Resolution of prison riots.* Washington, DC: U.S. Department of Justice.

Vetter, H. J., & Perlstein, G. R. (1991). *Perspectives on terrorism.* Belmont, CA: Wadsworth.

Wicker, T. (1975). *A time to die.* New York: New York Times Books.

Wright, J. P., Cullen, F. T., & Blankenship, M. B. (1995). The social construction of corporate violence: Media coverage of the Imperial Food Products fire. *Crime and Delinquency, 41*(1), 20–36.

THE PRISON JOURNAL, Vol. 76 No. 4, December 1996, 420–441.

Part 8: Getting out of Prison

Almost all prison inmates will eventually be released and return to the community. For some this happens after only a relatively short period of incarceration. For others this could well be twenty years, twenty-five years, or even longer. Regardless of how long they have been in prison, as the time of their release approaches, they are likely to encounter a number of emotional, psychological, and social issues that can bring on stress and fear as well as excitement. As Schmid and Jones showed in the first reading in this book, the adjustment to being in prison can be stressful and trigger shifts in one's identity. The movement from inside to outside of prison also can be stressful and taxing. The three readings in this section address some of the issues and challenges that inmates may face as the possible transition to free society approaches.

In the first reading, the emotional and social experiences of being considered for parole, and having parole denied, are explored from the perspective of the inmate. The experience is discussed as one that many inmates enter with misunderstanding and typically find frustrating, confusing, and discouraging. The structure of the parole board hearing process, arguments inmates believe would be convincing to parole board members, and the way institutional staff are perceived to conspire with the parole board are examined from the perspective of the inmates.

In the second article, Fleisher and Decker discuss the challenges inherent in integrating ex-inmate gang members to the free community as law-abiding citizens. The problems they identify stem from both individual-level and community issues, and they pose both barriers and attractions for ex-inmates that may be exceptionally difficult, if not impossible, to overcome. In response to these difficulties, Fleisher and Decker present reasons that some of the common approaches to working with gang members in prison are likely to fail, and they outline several ways that communities in general and criminal justice system actors and agencies can address these challenges and promote community safety. Community involvement is central to successful integration of prison gang members to communities. Simplistic approaches that try to get offenders to disavow themselves of their gang, gang affiliation, and support systems are not helpful in this regard.

The final selection explores the strategies and resources that female ex-inmates report as critical for their successful return to the community. It is common knowledge that individuals arriving at prison must negotiate ways to adapt successfully to the restrictions and stresses of confinement. However, in this article O'Brien argues that inmates leaving prison must also find means and resources for adapting to their return to freedom. Interestingly, most of the forms of support that are identified are individual traits and characteristics—not programs, materials, or systems provided by correctional officials.

As we have seen throughout the sections and articles of this book, these issues bring us back to what the purpose of incarceration is and should be. If we believe the system exists for the purpose of punishing offenders, we may not see a significant need to address offenders' reentry issues. If we believe that prison exists to facilitate offenders' reformation or return to society as law-abiding and productive individuals, we are more likely to think that system actors and processes should address these needs. These are not necessarily easy questions, however, and we should not expect everyone to agree on the answers.

Discussion Questions

Getting out of Prison

1. Why is getting out of prison stressful for many prison inmates?
2. What are the common problems that prison inmates face when returning to the community?
3. How could corrections officials, and other government authorities, reduce the rate of recidivism among recent prison releasees?

32. Denial of Parole: An Inmate Perspective

Mary West-Smith
Mark R. Pogrebin
Eric D. Poole

Like many other discretionary decisions made about inmates (e.g., classification, housing, treatment, discipline, etc.), those involving parole are rather complex. Parole board members typically review an extensive array of information sources in arriving at their decisions, and empirical research has shown a wide variation in the decision-making process. The present study seeks to advance the work on parole decision-making from the point of view of those inmates who have had their release on parole denied.

Inmates denied parole have often been dissatisfied with what they consider arbitrary and inequitable features of the parole hearing process. While those denied parole are naturally likely to disagree with that decision, much of the lack of acceptance for parole decisions may well relate to lack of understanding. Even inmates who have an opportunity to present their case through a personal interview are sent out of the room while discussions of the case take place (being recalled only to hear the ultimate decision and a summary of the reasons for it). This common practice protects the confidentiality of individual board members' actions; however, it precludes the inmate from hearing the discussions of the case, evaluations of strengths and weaknesses, or prognosis for success or failure. More importantly, this practice fails to provide guidance in terms of how to improve subsequent chances for successful parole consideration. A common criticism of parole hearings has been that they produce little information relevant to an inmate's parole readiness (Morris, 1974; Fogel, 1975; Cole & Logan, 1977); thus, it is unlikely that those denied parole understand the basis for the decision or attach a sense of justice to it.

Parole Boards

The 1973 Supreme Court decision in *Scarpa v. United States Board of Parole* established the foundation for parole as an "act of grace." Parole is legally considered a privilege rather than a right; therefore, the decision to grant or deny it is "almost unreviewable" (Hier, 1973, p. 435). In fact, when federal courts have been petitioned to intervene and challenge parole board actions, the decisions of parole boards have prevailed (see *Menechino v. Oswald*, 1970; *Tarlton v. Clark*, 1971). While subsequent Court rulings have established minimal due process rights in prison disciplinary proceedings (*Wolff v. McDonnell*, 1974) and in parole revocation hearings (*Morrissey v. Brewer*, 1972), the parole hearing itself is still exempt from due process rights. Yet in *Greenholtz v. Nebraska* (1979) and *Board of Pardons v. Allen* (1987), the Supreme Court held that, although there is no constitutional right to parole, state statutes may create a protected liberty interest where a state's parole system entitles inmates to parole if they meet certain conditions. Under such circumstances, the state has created a presumption that inmates who meet specific requirements will be granted parole. Although the existence of a parole system does not by itself give rise to an expectation of parole, states may create that expectation or presumption by the wording of their statutes. For example, in both *Greenholtz* and *Allen*, the Supreme Court emphasized that the statutory language—the use of the word "shall" rather than "may"—creates the presumption that parole will be granted if certain conditions are met. However, if the statute is general, giving broad discretion to the parole board, no liberty interest is created and due process is not required. In Colorado, as in most other states with parole systems, the decision to grant parole before the inmate's mandatory release date is vested entirely within the discretion of the parole board. The legislatively-set broad guidelines for parole decision-making allow maximum exercise of discretion with minimal oversight.

In Colorado, the structure of parole board hearings depends on the seriousness of the inmate's offense. A full board review is required for all cases involving a violent crime or for inmates with a history of violence. A quorum for a full board review is defined as four of the seven parole board members and a decision to grant parole requires four affirmative votes. However, two parole board members conduct the initial hearing and submit their recommendation to a full board review. Single board members hear nonviolent cases. The board member considers the inmate's parole application, interviews the inmate, makes the release decision, and decides the conditions of parole. The personal interview may be face-to-face or by telephone. If the decision is to grant parole, an additional board member's signature is required. Given the variety of backgrounds and experiences board members bring to the job, individual interpretation and application of the broad statutory guidelines can make parole decision-making appear idiosyncratic.

In their 1986 study of parole decision-making in Colorado, Pogrebin and his colleagues (1986) concluded from their observations that the "overriding factor in parole decisions was not the relative merits of the inmate's case, but the structure of the board itself" (p. 153). At the time of their study, at least two board members rather than the current single board member made the majority of decisions. One may speculate that with only one decision-maker the decision to grant or deny parole is now even more dependent on the individual board member's background and philosophy.

Normalization and Routinization

Sudnow's (1965) classic study of the processes of normalization and routinization in the public defender's office offers insights into the decision-making processes in parole board hearings. Like Sudnow's public defender, who works as an employee of the court system with the judge and prosecutor and whose interests include the smooth functioning of the court system, the parole board member in Colorado works with the prison administration, caseworkers, and other prison personnel. Public defenders must represent all defendants assigned to them and attempt to give the defendants the impression they are receiving individualized representation. However, public defenders often determine the plea bargain acceptable to the prosecutor and judge, based on the defendant's prior and current criminal activities, prior to the first meeting with the defendant (Sudnow, 1965).

The parole board theoretically offers individual consideration of the inmate's rehabilitation and the likelihood of future offending when deciding whether or not to release an inmate. However, the parole board, like the public defender, places a great deal of emphasis on the inmate's prior and current criminal record. The tremendous volume of cases handled by the public defender necessitates the establishment of "normal crime" categories, defined by type and location of crime and characteristics of the defendant and victim, which permit the public defender to quickly and easily determine an appropriate and acceptable sentence. Such normalization and routinization facilitate the rapid flow of cases and the smooth functioning of the court system. Similarly, a two-year study of 5,000 parole decisions in Colorado in the early 1980s demonstrated that the parole board heard far too many cases to allow for individualized judgments (Pogrebin et al., 1986, p. 149).

Observations of parole hearings illustrate the rapid flow of cases and collaboration with other prison personnel. Typically, the case manager, in a brief meeting with the parole board member, discusses the inmate, his prior criminal history, current offense, institutional behavior, compliance with treatment programs, progress and current attitude, and makes a release or deferral recommendation to the parole board member prior to the inmate interview. The inmate and family members, if present, are then brought into the hearing room. The parole board member asks the inmate to describe his prior and current crimes, his motivation for those crimes, and the circumstances that led to the current offense. Typical inmate responses are that he was "stupid," "drunk," or "not thinking right." Inquiries by the parole board about the programs the inmate has completed are not the norm; however, the inmate is often asked how he thinks the victim would view his release. The inmate typically tries to bring up the progress he has made by explaining how much he has learned while institutionalized and talks about the programs he completed and what he learned from them. A final statement by the inmate allows him to express remorse for the pain he has caused others and to vow he will not get into another situation where he will be tempted to commit crimes. Family members are then given time to make a statement, after which the inmate and family leave the hearing room. A brief discussion between the parole board member and the case manager is followed by the recommendation to grant or defer parole. A common reason given for a deferral is "not enough time served." If parole is granted, the parole board member sets the conditions for parole.

"Normal" cases are disposed of very quickly. The time from the case manager's initial presentation of the case to the start of the next case is typically ten to fifteen minutes. Atypical cases require a longer discussion with the case manager before and after the inmate interview. Atypical cases also can involve input from other prison personnel (e.g., a therapist), rather than just the case manager. Those inmates who do not fit the norm, either through their background or the nature of their crime, are given special attention. The parole board member does not need to question the inmate to discover if the case is atypical since the case manager will inform him if there is anything unusual about the inmate or his situation.

During the hearing, the board member asks first about the prior and current crimes and what the inmate thinks were the causal factors that led to the commission of the crimes. Based on his observations of public defenders, Sudnow (1965) concludes, "It is not the particular offenses for which he is charged that are crucial, but the constellation of prior offenses and the sequential pattern they take" (p. 264). Like the public defender who attempts to classify the case into a familiar type of crime by looking at the circumstances of prior and current offenses, the parole board member also considers the criminal offense history and concentrates on causal factors that led the inmate to commit the crimes. It is also important for the board member that the inmate recognize the patterns of his behavior, state the reasons why he committed his prior and current crimes, and accept responsibility for them. The inmate, in contrast, generally wants to describe what he has learned while incarcerated and talk about the classes and programs he has completed. The interview exchange thus reveals two divergent perceptions of what factors should be emphasized in the decision-making process. In Sudnow's (1965) description of a jury trial involving a public defender, "the onlooker comes away with the sense of having witnessed not a trial at all, but a set of motions, a perfunctorily carried off event" (p. 274). In a similar manner, the observer at a parole board hearing has the impression of having witnessed a scripted, staged performance.

As a result of their journey through the criminal justice system, individual inmates in a prison have been typed and classified by a series of criminal justice professionals. The compilation of prior decisions forms the parole board member's framework for his or her perception of the inmate. The parole board member, with the help of previous decision-makers and through normalization and routinization, "knows" what type of person the inmate is. As Heinz et al. (1976) point out, "a system premised on the individualization of justice unavoidably conflicts with a caseload that demands simple decision rules. . . . To process their caseloads, parole boards find it necessary to develop a routine, to look for one or two or a few factors that will decide their cases for them" (p. 18). With or without the aid of parole prediction tools to help in their decision, parole board members feel confident they understand the inmate and his situation; therefore, their decisions are more often based on personal intuition than structured guidelines.

Theoretical Framework

Based on a combination of both formal and informal sources of information they acquire while in prison, inmates believe that satisfactory institutional behavior and completion of required treatment and educational programs, when combined with adequate time served, will result in their release on parole. They also believe that passing their parole eligibility date denotes sufficient institutional time. Denial of parole, when the stated prerequisites for parole have been met, leads to inmate anger and frustration. As stories of parole denials spread throughout the DOC population, inmates are convinced that the parole board is abusing its discretion to continue confinement when it is no longer mandated.

Control of Institutional Behavior

The majority of inmates appearing before the parole board have a fairly good record of institutional behavior (Dawson, 1978). Inmates are led to believe that reduction in sentence length is possible through good behavior (Emshoff & Davidson, 1987). Adjustment to prison rules and regulations is not sufficient reason for release on parole; however, it comprises a minimum requirement for parole and poor adjustment is a reason to deny parole (Dawson, 1978). Preparation for a parole hearing would be a waste of both the prisoner's and the case manager's time and effort if the inmate's behavior were not adequate to justify release.

Research suggests that good behavior while incarcerated does not necessarily mean that an inmate will successfully adapt to the community and be law-abiding following a favorable early-release decision (Haesler, 1992; Metchik, 1992). In addition, Emshoff and Davidson (1987) note that good time credit is not an effective deterrent for disruptive behavior. Inmates who are most immature may be those most successful at adjusting to the abnormal environment of prison; inmates who resist conformity to rules may be those best suited for survival on the outside (Talarico, 1976). However, institutional control of inmate behavior is a crucial factor for the maintenance of order and security among large and diverse prison populations, and the use of good time credit has traditionally been viewed as an effective behavioral control mechanism (Dawson, 1978). Inmates are led to believe that good institutional behavior is an important criterion for release, but it is secondary to the background characteristics of the inmate. Rather than good behavior being a major consideration for release, as inmates are told, only misbehavior is taken into account and serves as a reason to deny parole.

Inmates are also told by their case manager and other prison personnel that they must complete certain programs to be paroled. Colorado's statutory parole guidelines list an inmate's progress in self-improvement and treatment programs as a component to be assessed in the release decision (Colorado Department of Public Safety, 1994). However, the completion of educational or treatment programs by the inmate is more often considered a factor in judging the inmate's institutional adjustment, i.e., his ability to conform to program rules and regimen. Requiring inmates to participate in prison programs may be more important for institutional control than for the rehabilitation of the inmate. Observations of federal parole hearings suggest that the inmate's institutional behavior and program participation are given little importance in release decisions (Heinz et al., 1976). Noncompliance with required treatment programs or poor institutional behavior may be reasons to deny parole, but completion of treatment programs and good institutional behavior are not sufficient reasons to grant parole.

Release Decision Variables

Parole board members and inmates use contrasting sets of variables each group considers fundamental to the release decision. Inmates believe that completion of treatment requirements and good institutional behavior are primary criteria the parole board considers when making a release decision. Inmates also feel strongly that an adequate parole plan and demonstration that their families need their financial and emotional support should contribute to a decision to release on parole.

In contrast, the parole board first considers the inmate's current and prior offenses and incarcerations. Parole board members also determine if the inmate's time served is commensurate with what they perceive as adequate punishment. If it is not, the inmate's institutional behavior, progress in treatment, family circumstances and parole plan will not outweigh the perceived need for punishment. Inmates, believing they understand how the system works, become angry and frustrated when parole is denied after they have met all the stated conditions for release.

Unwritten norms and individualized discretion govern parole board decision-making; thus, the resulting decisions become predictable only in retrospect as patterns in granting or denying parole emerge over time.

Method

In October of 1997, Colorado-CURE (Citizens United for Rehabilitation of Errants), a Colorado non-profit prisoner advocacy group, solicited information through its quarterly newsletter from inmates (who were members of the organization) regarding parole board hearings that resulted in a "setback," i.e., parole deferral. Inmates were asked to send copies of their appeals and the response they received from the parole board to Colorado-CURE. One hundred and eighty inmates responded to the request for information with letters ranging in length from very brief one- or two-paragraph descriptions of parole board hearings to multiple page diatribes listing not only parole board issues, but complaints about prison conditions, prison staff, and the criminal justice system in general. Fifty-two letters were eliminated from the study because they did not directly address the individual inmate's own parole hearing. One hundred and twenty-eight inmate letters were analyzed; one hundred and twenty-five from male and three from female inmates. Some letters contained one specific complaint about the parole board, but most inmates listed at least two complaints. Several appeals also contained letters written to the parole board by family members on the inmate's behalf. Two hundred and eighty-five complaints were identified and classified into thirteen categories.

The purpose of the present study is not to explore the method the parole board uses to reach its release decisions; rather, our interest is to examine the content of the written complaints of inmates in response to their being denied parole.

Findings

Table 1 presents the frequency of complaints regarding parole denial and the percentage of inmates having each complaint.

Inadequate Time Served

Forty-eight percent of the inmates reported "inadequate time served" as a reason given for parole deferment. Their attempt to understand the "time served" component in the board's decision is exemplified by the following accounts:

> . . . if you don't meet their [the parole board's] time criteria you are "not" eligible. Their time criteria is way more severe than statute. . . . [The risk assessment] also says, if you meet their time amounts and score 14 or less on the assessment you

TABLE 1 Frequency of Complaints and Percentage of Inmates Having Complaint

Nature of Complaint	*Frequency of Complaints*	*Percentage of Inmates with Complaint*
1. Inadequate time served, yet beyond P.E.D.	61	48%
2. Completed required programs	45	35%
3. Denied despite parole plan	35	27%
4. Board composition and behavior	27	21%
5. Longer setbacks after parole violation	26	20%
6. Family need for inmate support ignored	22	17%
7. Case manager not helpful	17	13%
8. New sex offender laws applied retroactively	16	12%
9. Required classes not available	11	9%
10. Few inmates paroled on same day	7	5%
11. Appeals not considered on individual basis	6	4%
12. Miscellaneous	12	9%
	N=285	N=128

> "shall" receive parole. This does not happen. The board is an entity with entirely too much power. . . .
>
> I don't understand how your P.E.D. [parole eligibility date] can come up and they can say you don't have enough time in.
>
> If the court wanted me to have more time, it could have aggravated my case with as much as eight years. Now the parole board is making itself a court!
>
> . . . I [was] set back again for six months with the reason being, not enough time spent in prison. I've done 5 calendar years, I'm two years past my PED, this is my first and only felony of my life, I've never been to prison, it's a non-violent offense, it's not a crime of recidivism, I do not earn a livelihood from this crime or any criminal activity. So what is their problem?
>
> [Enclosed] is a copy of my recent deferral for parole, citing the infamous "Not enough time served" excuse. This is the third time they've used this reason to set me back, lacking a viable one.

These responses of the inmates to the "inadequate time served" reason for parole deferral demonstrate that they believe the parole board uses a different set of criteria than the official ones for release decisions. Inmates do not understand that the "time served" justification for parole deferment relates directly to the perception by the parole board member of what is an acceptable punishment for their crime. They believe the parole board is looking for a reason to deny parole and uses "time served" when no other legitimate reason can be found.

Completed Required Programs

Thirty-five percent of the inmates complained that their parole was deferred despite completing all required treatment and educational programs. Related complaints, expressed by 9 percent of the inmates, were the lack of mandatory classes and the long waiting lists for required classes. The following excerpts from inmate letters reflect this complaint:

> When I first met with them [the parole board] I received a 10 month setback to complete the classes I was taking (at my own request). But was told once I completed it and again met the board I was assured of a release. . . . Upon finishing these classes I met the board again [a year later]. . . . I noticed that none of my 7 certificates to date were in the file and only a partial section of the court file was in view. I tried to speak up that I was only the 5th or 6th person to complete the 64 week class and tell about the fact that I carry a 4.0 in work plus have never had a COPD conviction or a write-up. He silenced me and said that meant nothing. . . . I later was told I had been given another one year setback!!!
>
> They gave me a six month setback because they want me to take another A.R.P. class. . . . [I]t was my first time down [first parole hearing], and I have taken A.R.P. already twice. . . . I have also taken. . . Independent Living Skills, Job Search,

> Alternatives to Violence, workshops and training in nonviolence, Advanced Training for Alternatives to Violence Project, mental health classes conducted by addiction recovery programs. I also chair the camp's A. A. meetings every week and just received my two year coin. I have also completed cognitive behavioral core curriculum. . . .

Inmates view completion of required programs as proof that they have made an effort to rehabilitate themselves and express frustration when the parole board does not recognize their efforts. The completion of classes was usually listed with other criteria the inmates viewed as important for their release on parole.

Parole Denied Despite Parole Plan

Deferral of parole even though a parole plan had been submitted was a complaint listed by 27 percent of inmates. It is interesting to note that this complaint never appeared as a solo concern, but was always linked to other issues. These inmates seem to believe that a strong parole plan alone will not be sufficient to gain release and that the parole plan must be combined with good institutional behavior and the completion of required classes. Even when all required criteria are met, parole was often deferred. The frustration of accomplishing all of the requirements yet still being deferred is expressed in the following excerpts:

> . . . I was denied for the third time by the D.O.C. parole board even though I have completed all recommended classes (Alcohol Ed. I and II, Relapse Prevention, Cognitive Skills and Basic Mental Health). I have a place to parole to [mother's house], a good job and a very strong support group consisting of family and friends. . . . To the present date I have served 75% of my 3-year sentence.

> [After having problems with a previous address for the parole plan] . . . my parents and family . . . were assured . . . that all I needed to do is put together an alternative address. I managed to qualify for and arrange to lease a new low-income apartment at a new complex. . . . My family was helping with this. I also saw to it that I was preapproved at [a shelter in Denver], a parole office approved address, so that I could go there for a night or two if needed while I rented and had my own apartment approved by the parole office. My family expected me home, and I had hoped to be home and assisting them, too. I arranged employment from here, and looked forward to again being a supportive father and son. . . . I received a one-year setback! I was devastated, and my family is too. We are still trying to understand all of this. . . . I am . . . angry at seeing so many sources of support, employment, and other opportunities that I worked so hard at putting together now be lost.

Preparing an adequate parole plan requires effort on the part of both the inmate and the case manager. When a parole plan is coupled with completion of all required treatment and educational programs and good institutional behavior, the inmate is at a loss to understand how the parole board can deny parole. Inmates often expressed frustration that the plans they made for parole might not be available the next time they are eligible for parole. "Inadequate time served" is often the stated reason for parole deferment in these cases and does not indicate to the inmate changes he needs to make in order to be paroled in the future.

Parole Board Composition and Behavior

Twenty-one percent of the inmates complained about the composition of the parole board or about the attitude parole board members displayed toward the inmate and his or her family. Several inmates expressed concern that at the majority of hearings, only one parole board member is present and the outcome of an inmate's case might depend on the background of the parole board member hearing the case:

> The man [parole board member] usually comes alone, and he talks to the women worse than any verbal abuser I have ever heard. He says horrible things to them about how bad they are and usually reduces them to tears. Then he says they are "too emotionally unstable to be paroled!" If they stand up for themselves, they have "an attitude that he can't parole." If they refuse to react to his cruel proddings, they are "too cold and unfeeling." No way to win!! Why in the *world* do we have ex-policemen on the parole board?? Cops always want to throw away the key on all criminals, no matter what. Surely that could be argued . . . as conflict of interest!
>
> As I was sitting in the parole hearing for me I was asked some pretty weird questions. Like while I was assaulting my victim was I having sex with my wife also. My answer was yes. Then this man [the parole board member] says, "Sounds like you had the best of both worlds, huh?" I was taken back by this comment and wonder why in the world this guy would think that this was the best of any world.
>
> My hearing was more of an inquisition than a hearing for parole. All of the questions asked of me were asked with the intent to set me back and not the intent of finding reasons to parole me. It was my belief that when a person became parole eligible the purpose was to put them out, if possible. My hearing officer did nothing but look for reasons to set me back.

Inmates often expressed the view that the parole board members conducting their hearings did not want to listen to their stories. However, if parole board members have generally reached a decision prior to interviewing the inmate, as indicated by the routinization of the hearing process, it is logical that the board member would attempt to limit the inmate's presentation. In addition, if board members have already determined that parole will be deferred, one would expect the questions to focus on reasons to deny parole. One inmate stated, "I believe that the parole board member that held my hearing abused his discretion. I had the distinct feeling that he had already decided to set me back before I even stepped into the room."

Family's Need for Inmate's Support

Many inmates criticized the parole board for failing to take into account their families' financial, physical, and emotional needs. Seventeen percent of the inmates expressed this concern, and several included copies of letters written by family members asking the board to grant parole. The primary concerns were support for elderly parents and dependent young children:

> My mom has Lou Gehrig's disease. . . . [S]he can't walk and it has spread to her arms and shoulders. . . . [No] one will be there during the day to care for her. The disease is fast moving. . . . My mom is trying to get me home to care for her. . . . I am a non-violent first time offender. I have served 8 years on a 15. I have been before the parole board 5 times and denied each time. . . . (I got 6, 6, 9, 6, 12 month setbacks in that order). Why I'm being denied I'm unsure. I've asked the board and wasn't told much. I've completed all my programs, college, have a job out there, therapy all set up, and a good parole plan.
>
> I have everything going for me in the community. I have a full-time job. I have a 2 year-old son that needs me. I have a mother that is elderly and needs my help. This is all over an ounce of marijuana from [1994] and a walk-away from my own house. I have over 18 months in on an 18 month sentence.
>
> [My 85-year-old mother] has no one. Her doctor also wrote [to the chair of the parole board] as well as other family members, including my son. All begging for my release. She *needs* me!! I wish you could [see] . . . how hard I have worked since I have been in prison. . . . Being good and trying hard does not count for much in here. . . . This is my 5th year on an 8 year sentence.

The parole board does not consider a dependant family as a primary reason to release an inmate on parole; however, inmates regard their families' needs as very important and are upset that such highly personal and emotionally charged circumstances are given short shrift during their parole hearing. And if they believe they have met the conditions established for release, inmates do not understand why the parole board would not allow them to return home to help support a family.

Case Manager Not Helpful

Thirteen percent of the inmates expressed frustration with their case manager, with a few accusing the case manager of actually hurting their chances to make parole. Although the inmate was not present during the case manager's presentation to the board member, many inmates declared satisfaction with their case manager and felt that the board did not listen to the case manager's recommendation. Since the present study focuses on inmate complaints, the following excerpts document the nature of the dissatisfaction inmates expressed concerning their case managers:

> [The case manager] has a habit of ordering inmates to waive their parole hearings. Many inmates are angry and do not know where to turn because they feel it is their right to attend their parole hearings. . . . [He] forces most all of his caseload to waive their parole hearing. That is not right! . . . How and why is this man allowed to do this? I would not like my name mentioned because I fear the consequences I will pay. . . . [T]his man is my case manager and I have not seen the parole board yet.

> I have not had any writeups whatsoever and I have been taking some drug and alcohol classes since I have been back [parole revoked for a dirty U.A.]. I had a real strong parole plan that I thought that my case manager submitted but he never bothered to. I was planning on going to live with my father who I never asked for anything in my life and he was willing to help me with a good job and a good place to live. My father had also wrote to [the chair of the parole board] and asked if I could be paroled to him so he can help me change my life around.
>
> [Some] case managers are not trained properly and do not know what they are doing. Paperwork is seldom done properly or on time. Others are downright mean and work *against* the very people they are to help. Our liberty depends on these people, and we have no one else to turn to when they turn against us.

Inmates realize they must at least have a favorable recommendation by the case manager if they are to have any chance for parole. Yet they generally view the case manager as a "marginal advocate," often going through the motions of representing their interests but not really supporting or believing in them. Case managers after all are employees of the Department of Corrections, and their primary loyalties are seen by inmates to attach to their employer and "the system."

Few Inmates Paroled the Same Day

Five percent of the inmates related in their letters that very few inmates were paroled on a given hearing day, leading them to suspect that the parole board typically denies release to the vast majority of inmates who come up for a hearing.

> I just received a letter . . . and she told me that 2 out of 24 made parole from [a Colorado women's facility]. . . . [Also] out of 27 guys on the ISP non-res program from [a community corrections facility] only 4 made parole!! . . . What is going on here?!! These guys [on ISP] are already on parole for all intents and purposes.
>
> Went [before parole board] in June '97, 89 went, 2 made it (mandatory).
>
> I realize they're not letting very many people go on parole or to community. It's not politically correct to parole anyone. Now that Walsenburg is opening. I'm sure they will parole even less people. I have talked to 14 people that seen the Board this week, 2 setbacks. . . .

Inmates circulate such stories and cite them as evidence that the parole board is only interested in keeping prisoners locked up. Many inmates express their belief that the parole board is trying to guarantee that all the prisons are filled to capacity.

Appeals Not Considered on an Individual Basis

Although Colorado-CURE asked inmates to send copies of their appeal and the response to the appeal, the majority of inmates mailed copies of their appeal before they received the response. Thus, it is not surprising that only four percent of the inmates discussed the apparent uniformity of appeal decisions. The standard form letter from the chair of the parole board, included by those who stated this complaint, reads as follows:

> I have reviewed your letter . . ., along with your file, and find the Board acted within its statutory discretion. Consequently, the decision of the Board stands.

Word of the appeals circulates among the general prison population and between prisons via letters to other inmates. Inmates suggest that the form letters are evidence that the parole board is not willing to review cases and reconsider decisions made by individual board members.

Conclusion

The nature of the written complaints reflects the belief among many inmates that the parole board in Colorado is using criteria for release decisions that are hidden from inmates and their families. A parole board decision, made without public scrutiny by members who have no personal knowledge of the inmate, depends on the evaluation of the likelihood of recidivism by others in the criminal justice system. While guidelines and assessment tools have been developed to help with the decision-making process in Colorado, it is unclear the extent to which they are used. Release decisions by the parole board appear to be largely subjective and to follow latent norms that emerge over time. The emphasis on past and current crimes indicates that inmates—regardless of their institutional adjustment or progress in treatment, vocational, or educational programs—will continue to be denied parole until they have been sufficiently punished for their crimes.

Findings of this study indicate that the factors inmates believe affect release decisions are different from the factors the parole board considers and thus suggest why inmates fail to understand why their parole is deferred despite compliance with the prerequisites imposed upon them. As evidenced by the above examples, inmates are not only confused and angry when they believe parole should be granted, they begin to question whether or not it is worth the effort if they are only going to "kill their numbers" (i.e., serve the full sentence). The prison grapevine and the flow of information among the entire Department of Corrections inmate population allow such stories and theories to spread. Prison officials should be concerned that if inmates feel compliance with prison rules and regulations is pointless, they will be less likely to conform to the administration's requirements for institutional control. Currently, inmates who are turned down for parole see themselves as victims, unfairly denied what they perceive they have earned and deserve. Each parole eligible case that is deferred or set back becomes another story, duly embellished, that makes its rounds throughout the prison population, fueling suspicion, resentment, and fear of an unbridled discretionary system of power, control, and punishment.

Inmates denied parole are entitled to a subsequent hearing usually within one calendar year. But the uncertainty of never knowing precisely when one will be released can create considerable tension and frustration in prison. While discretionary release leaves them in limbo, it is the unpredictability of release decisions that is demoralizing. As we have found, this process has resulted in bitter complaints from inmates. Perhaps the late Justice Hugo Black of the U.S. Supreme Court best summarized the view of many inmates toward the parole board:

> In the course of my reading—by no means confined to law—I have reviewed many of the world's religions. The tenets of many faiths hold the deity to be a trinity. Seemingly, the parole boards by whatever names designated in the various states have in too many instances sought to enlarge this to include themselves as members (Quoted in Mitford, 1973, p. 216).

References

Board of Pardons v. Allen, 482 U.S. 369 (1987).

Carroll, J. S., Wiener, R. L., Coates, D., Galegher, J., & Alirio, J. J. (1982). Evaluation, diagnosis, and prediction in parole decision making. *Law and Society Review, 17*, 199–228.

Carroll, L., & Mondrick, M. E. (1976). Racial bias in the decision to grant parole. *Law and Society Review, 11*, 93–107.

Cole, G. F., & Logan, C. H. (1977). Parole: The consumer's perspective. *Criminal Justice Review, 2*, 71–80.

Colorado Department of Public Safety (1994). *Parole guidelines handbook*. Denver, CO: Division of Criminal Justice.

Conley, J. A., & Zimmerman, S. E. (1982). Decision making by a part-time parole board: An observational and empirical study. *Criminal Justice and Behavior, 9*, 396–431.

Dawson, R. (1978). The decision to grant or deny parole. In B. Atkins and M. Pogrebin (Eds.), *The invisible justice system: Discretion and the law* (pp. 360–389). Cincinnati: Anderson.

Emshoff, J. G., & Davidson, W. S. (1987). The effect of "good time" credit on inmate behavior: A quasi-experiment. *Criminal Justice and Behavior, 14*, 335–351.

Fogel, D. (1975). . . . *We are the living proof: The justice model for corrections*. Cincinnati: Anderson.

Garber, R. M., & Maslach, C. (1977). The parole hearing: Decision or justification? *Law and Human Behavior, 1*, 261–281.

Gottfredson, D. M., & Ballard, K. B. (1966). Differences in parole decisions associated with decision-makers. *Journal of Research in Crime and Delinquency, 3*, 112–119.

Greenholtz v. Nebraska Penal Inmates, 442 U.S. 1 (1979).

Haesler, W. T. (1992). The released prisoner and his difficulties to be accepted again as a "normal" citizen. *Euro-Criminology, 4*, 61–68.

Heinz, A. M., Heinz, J. P., Senderowitz, S. J., & Vance, M. A. (1976). Sentencing by parole board: An evaluation. *Journal of Criminal Law and Criminology, 67*, 1–31.

Hier, A. P. (1973). Curbing abuse in the decision to grant or deny parole. *Harvard Civil Rights-Civil Rights Law Review, 8*, 419–468.

Hoffman, P. B. (1972). Parole policy. *Journal of Research in Crime and Delinquency, 9*, 112–133.

Holsti, O. R. (1969). *Content analysis for the social sciences and humanities*. Reading, MA: Addison-Wesley.

Lombardi, J. H. (1984). The impact of correctional education on length of incarceration: Non-support for new paroling policy motivation. *Journal of Correctional Education, 35*, 54–57.

Menechino v. Oswald, 430 F.2d 402 (2nd Cir. 1970).

Metchik, E. (1992). Judicial views of parole decision processes: A social science perspective. *Journal of Offender Rehabilitation, 18*, 135–157.

Mitford, J. (1973). *Kind and unusual punishment: The prison business*. New York: Knopf.

Morris, N. (1974). *The future of imprisonment*. Chicago: University of Chicago Press.

Morrissey v. Brewer, 408 U.S. 471 (1972).

Pogrebin, M. R., Poole, E. D., & Regoli, R. M. (1986). Parole decision making in Colorado. *Journal of Criminal Justice, 14*, 147–155.

Rogers, J., & Hayner, N. S. (1968). Optimism and accuracy in perceptions of selected parole prediction items. *Social Forces, 46*, 388–400.

Sacks, H. R. (1977). Promises, performance, and principles: An empirical study of parole decision making in Connecticut. *Connecticut Law Review, 9*, 347–423.

Scarpa v. U.S. Board of Parole, 414 U.S. 934 (1973).

Scott, J. E. (1974). The use of discretion in determining the severity of punishment for incarcerated offenders. *Journal of Criminal Law and Criminology, 65*, 214–224.

Starosta, W. J. (1984). Qualitative content analysis: A Burkean perspective. In W. Gudykunst & Y. Y. Kim (Eds.), *Methods for intercultural communication research* (pp. 185–194). Beverly Hills, CA: Sage.

Sudnow, D. (1965). Normal crimes: Sociological features of the penal code in a public defender's office. *Social Problems, 12*, 255–276.

Talarico, S. M. (1976). The dilemma of parole decision making. In G. F. Cole (Ed.), *Criminal Justice: Law and politics*, 2nd edition (pp. 447–456). North Scituate, MA: Duxbury.

Tarlton v. Clark, 441 F.2d 384 (5th Cir. 1971), *cert. denied*, 403 U.S. 934 (1971).

Wilkins, L. T., & Gottfredson, D. M. (1973). *Information selection and use in parole decision-making: Supplemental report V*. Davis, CA: National Council on Crime and Delinquency.

Wolff v. McDonnell, 418 U.S. 539 (1974).

FEDERAL PROBATION, Vol. 64, No. 2, 2000.

33. Going Home, Staying Home: Integrating Prison Gang Members into the Community

Mark S. Fleisher
Scott H. Decker

Recidivism rates in the United States and Canada have hovered at approximately 60 percent for decades. To explain why six out of 10 former inmates return to prison, it is reasonable to assume that imprisonment, even under the best conditions, cannot prepare inmates adequately for productive life in a mainstream community. Prison gang members encounter challenges to post-imprisonment community life that non-gang members may not encounter or encounter with similar intensity. This article argues that the burden of inmate readjustment should fall on communities rather than on individual former inmates, and that successful community integration requires communitywide planning and an understanding of the realities of a gang lifestyle.

Introduction

It is arguable that most prison gangs are either street gangs imported into prisons (Jacobs, 1974) or prison equivalents of street gangs rather than the highly structured, traditionally defined prison gangs such as the Mexican Mafia, Texas Syndicate, and others described in the prison gang overview. Prison gangs are chronic, serious, criminal organizations. Prison gang groups are qualitatively and quantitatively different from the street and/or youth gangs that have occupied the attention of gang researchers (Decker & Van Winkle, 1996; Fleisher, 1998).

We would argue that the study of gangs needs a strong bifurcation between the hard-core criminals in the Mexican Mafia and Aryan Brotherhood, among others, and the youthful adolescents and young adults whose gang membership is transitory (Esbensen & Huizinga, 1993, Thornberry, 1998), whose crime is opportunistic (Klein, 1995), and whose behavior is focused more on drinking and drug use (Fagan, 1989) than on organized drug distribution, prostitution, gambling, and contract murder. Prison gang members are those men whose criminal lifestyles have become entrenched and difficult to break. These chronic gang offenders are the focus of this article.

This article focuses on two major topics. First, there is a discussion of issues affecting community integration (as opposed to reintegration) of former inmates who are also gang members as they moved into their home communities after release. Second, there are realistic, proactive proposals offered to community leaders that will enable them to meet the challenge of integrating former prison gang members. Street gangs in prison and traditional prison gangs—known also as disruptive groups and security threat groups (STGs) (Fleisher & Rison, 1999, discusses the characteristics of disruptive and STGs)—will be lumped and referred to as prison gangs for the purpose of this article.

In dealing with the first topic, we chose the word integration rather than reintegration for a specific reason. Research among youthful and adult gang members suggests these men probably were not integrated well into lawful economic networks in the community before they entered prison; rather, these men spent their lives in impoverished communities where they as well as their parents and other relatives had low-paying jobs and other social and economic difficulties and personal problems such as addictions, which threatened and/or worsened these men's link to legitimate employment markets. Street research shows that post-imprisonment, these men easily can reestablish neighborhood-based ties to gang social networks. A newly released gang-affiliated former inmate, within hours or minutes of returning home, can be selling drugs on a street corner. The challenge for community interventionists is one of finding realistic mechanisms to integrate into the lawful community former prisoners who are gang members. This is a formidable challenge and one not being met with standard forms of parole.

The rich literature on community intervention strategies and gang crime suppression lacks a specific approach prescribing the best practices of integrating prison gang members into the legitimate community. Community gang crime is a difficult problem for law enforcement and social service agencies to handle but when we add to an already difficult intervention problem the issue of prison gang members returning home, the challenges escalate and urgency is added to the need to create effective means of facilitating adult gang members' integration into the legitimate community. Suggestions offered here are a step in outlining the arguments that lead toward creating realistic approaches to the community integration of prison gang members.

The arguments advanced and the insights offered in this article are based on our numerous years of community gang research among youthful and adult gang members in cities such as St. Louis, Kansas City, Seattle, and Champaign (Illinois). In addition to conducting years of street gang research (Fleisher, 1995, 1998), Fleisher was employed by the Federal Bureau of Prisons as a correctional worker in a high-security penitentiary (Fleisher, 1989) and then as a regional administrator. Decker and Curry have years of community gang research and have collaborated closely with communities and police departments on community gang-related issues (see Curry, Ball, & Decker, 1996; Curry & Spergel, 1992; Decker, Bynum, & Weisel, 1998; Decker, Pennell, & Caldwell, 1996; Decker & Van Winkle, 1995). The observations and recommendations offered in this article are extracted from our professional experiences and are issues that communities must face if they are to develop effective strategies in response to prison and street gang members returning home.

State and Federal Prison Demographics: The Context for Prison Gangs

The number of prison gangs and prison gang members currently in American prisons is unknown. Correctional agencies consider data and information on prison gangs and their members to be law enforcement intelligence because prison gangs often pose egregious threats to institution security. With the need for controlling information and keeping it out of the hands of prison gang members themselves and their allies on the street, correctional agencies carefully guard such data. Despite that, however, we can get a general overview of the nature of the risk that prison gangs may pose to institutions by looking at publicly available correctional data. Table 1 documents the escalating rate of confinement in state and federal corrections since 1990. If we assume that at least one third of inmates have some tie to a prison gang, either as a member or an associate, that suggests there are nearly 400,000 gang members or affiliates inside American prisons.

The principal factors that have influenced such growth in federal and state prison populations also lead to the suggestion that the influence of prison gangs will not diminish inside prisons (Beck & Mumola, 1998). Such factors include: a 39 percent rise in the number of parole violators returned to state and federal prisons; a 4 percent increase in new court commitments; a decrease in release rates from 37 percent (1990) to 31 percent (1997); and an increase in average time served from 22 months (1990) to 27 months (1997). Four percent of America's prisoners will not be released. As inmates serve longer terms and as prisons receive more recidivists, the dilemma of controlling prison gangs escalates along with the prisoner population.

The size of correctional agencies has expanded differentially with some experiencing massive growth with others experiencing relatively little. When inmate populations expand, the risk of prison gangs also expands. Likewise, when incarceration rates are high, it is realistic to assume that the wide net of arrest and

TABLE 1 State and Federal Prison Populations and Incarceration Rates in the 1990s

On December 31	*Number of Inmates*		*Sentenced Prisoners per 100,000 Resident Population*	
	Federal	*State*	*Federal*	*State*
1990	63,326	708,393	20	272
1993	106,250	1,023,624	32	379
1996	105,344	1,077,824	33	394
1997	112,973	1,129,480	35	440
1998	123,044	1,478,978	38	423

Source: Data from Beck, A. J. & Mumola, C. J. Prisoners in 1998. Bulletin NCF–175687. Washington, D.C. : U.S. Department of Justice.

conviction will be cast over violent and non-violent drug offenders, many of whom will enter prison with street gang affiliations.

Nearly half of state prison inmates serve convictions on violent offenses while slightly more than 60 percent of federal inmates serve sentences for drug offenses. Violent offenders serving sentences with violent and non-violent drug offenders set the stage for expansion of prison gangs.

Gang and correctional researchers as well as correctional administrators will agree that one of the most difficult current challenges for correctional administrators is managing the effect of prison gang activity.

We argue that the problem of prison gangs originates in the community and that community problems linked to gangs do not end when gang offenders are convicted and sentenced to prison. The link between prison gangs and the community is unexplored. Among other issues, we know little about how street gangs facilitate the criminal activity of prison gangs, how prison gangs select new members from among street gangs, and how prison gang members' family members, friends, and associates strengthen criminal conduct within correctional institutions by participating indirectly and directly in prison gang-related crime. It is also critical to note that no published reports suggest that prison-based gang suppression and intervention have the effect of reducing gang involvement and gang crime in communities after the release of prison gang-affiliated inmates. This last observation is critical: Data noted above show that 96 percent of prisoners will be released into the community. This suggests an out-of-sight, out-of-mind approach to street and prison gangs and opens the door for more community gang-related crime, which in turn stretches the resources of community-based social and law enforcement agencies. With prison inmate populations expanding and parole violations nearing 40 percent and with state prisons housing mostly recidivists, community integration is a vital social and economic challenge to communities.

Core Features of Gangs: Impediments to Community Integration

Why do prison gangs pose such a difficult intervention problem? What can communities do about those problems? Gang research literature is clear on a number of issues affecting the emergence and perpetuation of community gangs; as long as these issues exist in the community, gangs will exist as well. Many issues have become axioms about street gangs and these often apply as well to prison gangs. These issues are critical in planning former prison gang members' community integration. We outlined a number of these key issues below.

First, gangs facilitate crime. This happens in at least two ways. A gang has a structure; some structures are formal. Other gangs have informal structures. Nevertheless, a gang group is a network of members who align themselves with other members. In forming such alignments, members who share propensities for various types of crime, ranging in severity from shoplifting to homicide, may find each other and in that relationship, commit more serious crimes than they would have had they not been in a gang. Because a gang is a social group whose members commit a wide range of offenses, members likely may have opportunities to commit types of crime that they may have bypassed previously.

Because gang groups accelerate the frequency and severity of crime, such groups have a measurable effect on their members' criminal behavior. In short, individuals in gang groups commit more crime than they would outside such a group. Although there are no published analyses of such crime acceleration for prison gangs (street gangs in prison or traditional prison gangs), such acceleration is reported widely in the street gang literature (Esbensen & Huizinga, 1993; Thornberry, 1998) and arguably would be a reasonable assumption about the influence of a prison gang group on the behavior of individual members.

Second, gangs are social groups with longevity. Gangs often persist longer than individual members, especially the most criminal and problematic gang groups. A Vice Lord neighborhood of 30 years ago likely may still be a Vice Lord territory now. Even if gang members are convicted and imprisoned for long terms, new gang members replace them year after year. This suggests that structural and economic forces in the neighborhoods establish conditions necessary for gang emergence. When a gang-affiliated inmate returns home, even after a 10-year prison term, likely waiting there will be members of his or another gang who will offer criminal opportunities but not opportunities of lasting social and economic value within the mainstream community. Repeatedly arresting these gang members has little effect on reducing the propensity for the emergence and perpetuation of street gangs (Klein, 1995) if these are a community's only efforts to curb community gang crime.

Third, self-identification to a gang may persist for years and/or decades, especially among adult offenders with extensive criminal histories; the blood in/blood out rule shared among the major prison gangs, argues for the gang group's effort to retain long-term membership. By contrast, youth gang membership may be short term and transitory (Decker & Van Winkle, 1996; Esbensen & Huizinga, 1993; Thornberry, 1998).

Recent research in Champaign shows that men and women now in their 40s and 50s have retained since their youth a self-identification to a gang and with that affiliation have retained social ties with people whom they have know since their teens (Fleisher, 2000). A gang member may not choose to exploit his or her gang affiliation to further criminal activity; a gang affiliation may not be the only prerequisite necessary to engage in lucrative drug crime activities; and a gang affiliation may not isolate self-identified members of different gangs from one another in daily interactions.

This research shows that these gang-identified men's daily interactions are fluid and influenced more by friendship ties than gang affiliation. Members of different gangs freely interact on the street unless personal biases otherwise alter the friendship relationship. This finding has significant implications for post-imprisonment community integration of prison gang members and suggests that former inmates of different prison gang affiliations may be able to cooperate in the community even though penitentiary life precluded such cooperation. Such cooperation may align these men in employment sites, training programs, and treatment venues.

Fourth, adult gang members may be unwilling to relinquish a gang identity even if they are not active gang members. A gang identity and the social ties it brings are significant in a person's neighborhood identity and help to create a sense of belonging to a persistent social group. In this sense, a gang identity is a proxy for a person's social history, for better or worse, as we see it because in a gang neighborhood, a sense of belonging to a local-area gang network may be achieved only with gang affiliation, prison experience, and a cultivated knowledge of the street.

Fifth, gang members are poor and as such are outsiders in the mainstream community. Research literature is clear on the social and economic marginality of gang members, especially the hard-core gangsters who are most likely to be involved in criminal conduct serious enough to affect a prison term. In our many years of gang research, we have not known hard-core gangsters who were honor students, had offers to attend college, had supportive and loving parents, and had strong social bonds to community institutions such as schools, athletic teams, and civic organizations. The profile of the street gang member who eventually enters prison for violent and/or drug-related offenses is the opposite of the characterization just noted. To such a sad picture, we realistically add the emotional and psychological deficits affected by violent victimization and post-traumatic stress (see Davis & Flannery in this issue) and multiple addictions.

Sixth, gang identity is linked to self identity. Street gang research shows that being a gang member may be a vital element in the self-definition of a gang member. Given that a formerly imprisoned gang member likely has failed at school and has few if any support ties to a mainstream community, a gang affiliation offers companionship, identity, and sense of belonging to a marginal community. Former prison gang members may not wish to shed the gang mantle. A gang identity may offer these men an identity in their neighborhoods that has social and economic value.

Try as we might, we most likely won't be able to strip the gang self-identification of a prison and/or street gang member. Adult criminals who claim a prison gang affiliation are likely to be serious offenders, especially those in high-security institutions. Preaching at them about the dangers of gang affiliation and/or threatening them with longer prison terms may move some prison gang members away from their gang groups but realistically will have little effect on the thousands of men who see themselves to be hard-core gangsters. Gangs are social groups and a sense of belonging and identity come with gang membership.

Community Re-entry and Integration

Adult gang members who also are former inmates face especially difficult problems when they return to the community. These men entered prison with poor work skills, little education, and alienated from high-paying employment; imprisonment does little to improve that situation and has worsened it in a number of ways. Former inmates are stigmatized by their "ex-con" status, which reinforces the middle-class notion of them as outsiders, and by virtue of serving 5-, 10-, or 15-year sentences or longer, have left community job markets behind. Imagine the economic plight of men imprisoned in the middle 1980s who return home in 1995.

When these men were imprisoned, computers were not being used in most offices and the Internet was an abstraction. In 1995, the best, most highly paid employment was open to men and women with college diplomas and high-tech skills. A 30-year-old former inmate is faced with an employment market unfamiliar to him and competition for the best jobs from college graduates. Where does that leave, and lead, the former inmate who has gang ties to the local Vice Lords, Gangster Disciples, or Mexican Mafia? To be sure, even if former prison gang members want to straighten out their lives, they likely cannot get jobs paying enough money to keep them away from lucrative drug markets; and to complicate this picture even more, it will be highly unlikely that a former inmate and prison gang member will have the community social support necessary to assume a lawful lifestyle.

Prison anti-gang (or "deganging") programs have not been evaluated or at least such evaluations have not been distributed publicly. Even if such institution-based programs serve to improve prison social order, former inmates' home neighborhoods are not highly controlled environments and as such pose social and economic difficulties that a street gang affiliation can overcome easily. Neighborhood illegal drug markets are easy to exploit, especially for men who have spent their lives selling drugs. Prison-based education and vocational programs coupled with longer prison terms do not resolve problems related to either prison gang management or prison-to-community transition for former gang-affiliated inmates. Bossler's, Fleisher's, and Krienert's (2000) research among federal inmates shows that full-time, legal employment, even at middle to upper income levels, is often an insufficient buffer to engaging in lucrative illegal drug markets and other forms of high-profit economic crime.

Former prison inmates, especially those with low levels of education, face low wages, low levels of social support in communities, and few realistic opportunities to earn wages high enough to divert them from high-income street crime. A realistic assessment of the economic future of prison gang members who may have long histories of juvenile and adult arrests and convictions is poor. Add to this dim financial outlook the social instability typical among persistent criminals, which includes a shifting residential pattern and/or a reliance on local shelters for temporary residences, and a dim outlook worsens. For men facing this bleak future, resuming an active affiliation with a local gang is a productive and perhaps the only way to live a relatively stable social and economic lifestyle.

Community Intervention

Given the reality of the street gang life and its social and economic advantages for former prison gang members, community leaders have a daunting challenge. What can communities do to assist prison gang members looking for legitimate opportunities? Before we offer specific suggestions, it is necessary to remind readers of the realities of dealing with former inmates who are also gang members.

First, it is unlikely that such men will relinquish gang ties; they may tell parole officers they no longer hang out with gangsters and former gang crime partners but what they say and what they do in the neighborhood are different. Unless a gang affiliation requires a man to become actively involved in gang crime, it should not matter if a man claims to be a Gangster Disciple, Black Gangster, or some other gang. Gang affiliation is much more than a link to a social group whose members commit crimes. For men who have been gangsters for decades, it is a form of personal identity most will be unwilling to relinquish. Were a former inmate residing in a gang neighborhood to disassociate from all of his gang companions, he may have to sever ties with parents, aunts and uncles, cousins, siblings, grandparents, and his own children as well as life-long friends. Such a loss of social capital would isolate a former inmate and leave him without social support. Shedding such social ties is unrealistic and if it were required as a condition of parole, the stage would be set for a quick parole violation and return to prison. We must be sure to recognize that hanging out with gang members does not mean involvement in crime and/or gang crime necessarily. We also must keep in mind that gang neighborhoods offer low-income housing and also may offer low-skill jobs to former inmates and may be the most economically accessible and socially suitable place for former prison gang members.

Second, we must expect that some percentage of former inmates who may or may not be gang members will violate parole and/or commit new offenses. Parole violations and the commission of new crimes by repeat offenders may have less to do with the quality of community problems than with the social, economic, and emotional instability of former inmates. Sitting in the Champaign County Correctional Center on his way to yet another state prison term, the leader of the Mickey Cobras in Champaign said it this way: "When your life's a mess and you have nowhere to stay, jail's a good place to go" (Fleisher, 2000).

Keeping in mind the realities of street life for former prison gang members, community planning must be realistic, which means overcoming those realities. Asking too much of former inmates sets them and us up for failure. Each time a parolee violates his parole and is re-arrested, the cost to the community may be higher than the cost to the parolee. Former inmates/gang members often comment that when a fellow gang member returns to prison, he is "going home" (Fleisher, 2000). We have outlined below a number of steps communities may take to facilitate community integration. These steps occur at both an individual and a community level.

Individual-Level Intervention

Bossler, Fleisher, and Krienert (2000) and particularly Bossler (1999) show that the resilience given by jobs and stable interpersonal relations may be eroded quickly by the persistent abuse of alcohol and other drugs. This fact suggests that former inmates need long-term drug and alcohol treatment. This we already know; however, where that treatment occurs is critical to its success.

Long-term treatment in prison therapeutic communities does little to help inmates when they return home. Follow-up treatment conducted in community-based treatment centers located miles away from former inmates' neighborhoods sets the stage for failure. Such men who need treatment likely are unwilling to spend several dollars on bus fare if a bus can take them to the treatment center. At home, a former inmate may have a wife or girlfriend who drinks alcohol and smokes marijuana, or uses other drugs, and in the neighborhood, his companions do the same. The likelihood of him resisting drug use is reduced if he has to travel at his own expense to find support. Easily accessible community-based treatment centers, preferably in gang neighborhoods themselves, may be a first step in improving a recovering drug addict's chances of staying clean.

Returning home from prison sounds like a joyous event. It is not. In the reality of street life in a gang neighborhood, there are no yellow ribbons tied around trees and no placards welcoming home a former inmate. An inmate released after years of imprisonment may find "home" to be rather inhospitable: he may find that the house he left behind is occupied by strangers, boarded up, or torn down; if he finds his house, his bed now may be occupied by someone else; his friends, siblings, and cousins may be residing in other neighborhoods or may be in prison or dead; his former girlfriend may have a new suitor and more children; and his pre-imprisonment behavior, if it included violence and/or ripping off local residents, now may exclude him from local social networks or, worse yet, set him up for retaliatory violence even after years away from the neighborhood. These are the realities of returning home for many former inmates. A realistic approach to overcoming the "worst case" as noted here also would bolster the integration of former inmates whose return home is less risky; even in the best case, a former inmate must have a stable residence, find and keep a job, and surround himself with companions supportive of a straight lifestyle. These seemingly simple things are difficult to do in an impoverished gang neighborhood.

Given the realistic limitations already noted, communities may wish to develop, in cooperation with local social service, alcohol and drug treatment, employment training agencies, community homes or dormitories for former inmates that offer a variety of treatment services, job training and placement, and continuous, post-release social support of a year or longer. Such homes located in gang neighborhoods could operate as residential therapeutic communities (Yablonsky, 1997). A residential center that serves as the focal point for a variety of services for former inmates could streamline parole officers' requirement to visit parolees, enable service providers to meet clients' needs in an environment comfortable to the clients, and strengthen former inmates' social ties to the community.

Community-Level Intervention

Parole agents' case loads are high and parole offices often are located dozens of miles from parolees' homes. There is only so much that a parole agent can do for a parolee if the agent sees the parolee once or twice every 60 to 90 days. It would seem reasonable that if correctional agencies would establish community-based parole offices in local neighborhoods, parole officers would have immediate access to parolees. While it may be difficult to establish such offices in large urban centers, metropolitan communities with populations of approximately 100,000 may be well-chosen test sites. Champaign, for instance, is such a community and dozens of former prison gang members return to specific, well-defined neighborhoods annually; but these men and women have few contacts with parole officers and fewer contacts with community members who can offer them employment. It is helpful to keep in mind that poor gang neighborhoods are social and economic isolates located in the midst of urban and suburban prosperity. A primary objective of a state correctional agency should be to create and sustain meaningful links between impoverished gang neighborhoods and community prosperity. Placing parole offices within gang neighborhoods may be a small first step toward achieving that objective.

Vocational training and substance abuse treatment may have little payoff if former inmates cannot find jobs. But one job for one former inmate, however, will not resolve the problem of neighborhood and family poverty. In poor neighborhoods like those that former prison gang members call home, households are often multigenerational and the household composition may shift from week to week. With a shift in household composition comes a shift in household economy. A job may help one former inmate but that same former inmate may be obligated to then assist his extended family of 6, 8, or 10 family members, all or most of whom may be unemployed. Add to that the fact that former inmates may be poorly skilled and have access only to menial work. Fast-food employment, for instance, embarrasses these men because they and we see those as teenage jobs (Fleisher, 2000). Even if these men accepted such employment, take-home pay is too low to support themselves and their families; if they abandon their families, they feel alone and alienated. Such economic and social pressure may push a former inmate back into lucrative street trades such as drug selling. Thus, the "one-job-per-inmate" strategy may be flawed from its inception when that strategy is tested against real-life social and economic demands in gang neighborhoods.

Former inmates' struggle to stay crime free can be heard on the streets in a gang neighborhood. The consequences of being poor, never having enough money to support themselves and their families, trying to get better paying jobs at low-skill levels are common topics among adult, former prison gang members. These men are aware of their difficulty and know well that if they move toward crime, the local police likely will knock on their door first.

A more difficult approach to integrating prison gang and non-gang members as well requires a long-term strategy to improve local neighborhood economies and strengthen the tie between local neighborhoods and its encompassing dominant community. Decker and Van Winkle (1996), Moore (1991), and Klein (1995) have shown clearly the relationship between community social organization and local economies and the emergence and perpetuation of gangs. However, creating long-term social and economic change in economically disadvantaged communities, such as described by Wilson (1987), has advantages and disadvantages from a communitywide planning perspective.

A major advantage of thinking broadly about community development rather than looking past the social and economic context of gang formation is that such a broad approach tackles head on the context of gang formation and offers a long-term remedy. Community development refers to the nature of the relationship among local residents and between local residents and schools and businesses as well as to the stake local residents have in community government (Bursik & Grasmick, 1993). By reducing the number and severity of risk factors, such as lowering unemployment for adults and reducing school truancy, communities can expect a reduction in gang crime and related problems. Such an approach requires careful planning and the participation of community stakeholders including representatives of the disadvantaged neighborhoods.

A major disadvantage of this approach is that it will not bring a quick, politically efficacious solution to the so-called gang and/or crime problem. Indeed, creating closer ties between residents of gang neighborhoods and the dominant community may be inimical to the wishes of community power brokers, voters, and even elected officials who believe that punishment means long prison terms and that such an approach is the only adequate way to respond to gangs and gang members.

Were a community to consider implementing a community development approach, the opinions of local residents must be included (Spergel, 1995). Fleisher's (2000) research in Champaign's gang neighborhoods has sought in part to understand the nature of local residents' ties to the dominant community, including the federal government. In these predominantly African-American neighborhoods, the prevailing attitude about the link between the neighborhoods and the broader community was expressed by a middle-aged member of the Black Gangsters who has been to state prison seven times and federal prison once: "*Nobody*—let me tell you that again—*nobody* in this here neighborhood wants the white man coming in and telling us what we need or what we should be doing. People in here know what they want, they just don't know how to get it. Sure there are folks up in here who will sell drugs and act stupid [gangbang] no matter what you do, but most folks don't want to do that stuff. If you want to do something around here, ask these people what kinds of jobs they want, what kinds of services they want, and how they want to get them things. But don't let no white man come up in here waving his finger in the black man's face telling him what he should be doing. Slavery days are over" (Fleisher, 2000).

As seen from inside gang neighborhoods, the dominant community is perceived to be criticizing poor persons for not trying harder to improve their lot in life. But with low levels of education and little familiarity with life outside of public housing projects and gang neighborhoods, poor persons are doing as well as they can, especially when they are isolated socially and economically. To be sure, long prison terms increase social and economic isolation within the dominant community by removing employable men who may link local neighborhoods to the dominant community. Prison sentences never improve the economic opportunities for former inmates who carry the label of ex-con.

While a "one-job, one-person" approach is necessary, such an approach is insufficient to prevent and/or intervene on the social and economic context of gang formation. Such an approach even may be insufficient for reasons already noted to reduce the likelihood that former (male and female) gang members will stay out of prison. A more productive approach first should include an assessment of the skills of the former inmates within gang neighborhoods and then should proceed to a realistic communitywide discussion of the best ways to link job skills to jobs. Local neighborhood small-scale businesses, such as car maintenance (tune-ups, oil changes), barbering, beauty parlors, house painting, carpentry, and even cottage industries such as sewing (common in women's prisons) may encourage legal employment while allowing former inmates to remain within neighborhoods where they feel comfortable and are not treated as outsiders.

Linking Corrections and the Community

Facilitating the successful community integration of prison gang members is a difficult process, but it is achievable if community members and law enforcement officials have a clear understanding of the real-life difficulties that former inmates/gang members encounter in the community. On an individual-level, these former inmates have low levels of education, substance addictions, and criminal records. Krienert's and Fleisher's article in this issue shows that gang membership can be seen as a proxy for risk factors of a severity greater than those of non-gang members. This means, among other things, that a community response to gang members must be more intense, prolonged, and targeted to balance the disabilities that former inmates/gang members bring back to the community.

On the neighborhood level, there are likely to be few if any jobs available in the poor neighborhoods. In the larger mainstream community, local employers may not find a gang-affiliated former inmate an attractive potential employee, especially when other potential employees with similar or better job skills without a felon record are easily available. Such an obstacle to employment surely would be the case in the dominant community, especially in the competition for high-paying jobs that require more technical skills than most former inmates have.

While some companies hire ex-cons (Tatge, 2000), such an approach is "one-person, one-job" and is driven by a corporate need to fill jobs rather than a need to develop poor communities. Even though one or even 100 former prison gang members may be helped temporarily, such an approach does little to improve local social and economic conditions in communities where, generation after generation, chronic features of life include joblessness, poverty, and street gangs. Without a communitywide approach to building economic and social capital in poor neighborhoods, the families there would continue to suffer the well-documented deprivations of chronic poverty with little meaningful assistance from mainstream communities (Katz, 1993).

Prison deganging programs have struggled to find a solution to the disorder of prison gangs as communities have struggled to find solutions to the disorder of street gangs. We have argued that a solution to gang-affiliated social disorder must act at multiple levels, offering individuals, neighborhoods, and communities economic support. At the same time, however, a communitywide solution must strengthen the social and economic link between gang neighborhoods and the dominant community. Doing that would require that the dominant community pour job training and employment opportunities into poor neighborhoods the direct participation of residents of those poor areas.

Prison systems can and should take the lead in such activity because they have a major stake in ensuring that former inmates go home and stay home. When inmates walk away from prisons, their supervision is passed to parole officials. Parole officers are likely to be charged with the responsibility of law enforcement officers rather than providers of opportunities to former offenders and their communities. However, even if parole officers want to help, they may not have the time or resources to actively assist former inmates in finding employment and supporting their other needs. In the end, inmates are passed from one agency to another until they are home again—older but with little else having changed for the better.

Correctional officials can develop a bridge between gang neighborhoods and the mainstream community. A telephone call from a state commissioner of corrections to a state attorney general or a governor could initiate a planning commission to establish realistic planning to overcome the obstacles of community integration. We already have suggested that such an approach would be to the long-term advantage of a correctional system and a community. Lower recidivism rates may reflect well on institutional corrections, but at the same time, a lower recidivism rate means less community crime. While recidivism has been a customary measure of the effectiveness of imprisonment as an intervention and a punishment, recidivism also may be a measure of a community's degree of meaningful support of former inmates. A number of steps, which are outlined below, can be taken to improve community support.

First, senior correctional officials should initiate tactical and strategic planning between themselves and local community agencies such as law enforcement, social welfare, community college, mental health and treatment, and small businesses. Correctional officials have inmate release and criminal history data, and such data can be useful to plan the type and level of community services. Data show (see Krienert & Fleisher) that gang-affiliated inmates have lower levels of employment and more serious drug problems than non-gang inmates. Treatment may be delivered in prison, but when these men are back in the community, drug use likely will resume. Knowing, for example, that 150 men will be released to a particular neighborhood during the next 18 months is information necessary to deliver drug treatment services to this specific group of former inmates.

Second, multimodal community-based service delivery systems should be developed, keeping in mind the realistic obstacles faced by former inmates and the realistic behavior we can expect from them. A multimodal system would provide a variety of complementary services, such as drug treatment, education, and vocational training, in one place. We would argue that it would be insufficient for a community to have drug treatment available somewhere in a community, education somewhere else, and vocational training in yet another place. Rather, it is essential to centralize those services in the neighborhoods where former inmates and their families reside. Doing that would enable easy reach to these services and may help to overcome the persistent attitude among gang members that social service agencies are more of an obstacle than an aid (Hagedorn, 1988). It is equally important for those services to be available when former inmates need them most such as late evenings and weekends. Social services, vocational training, and treatment services that operate at a city center Monday to Friday, from eight to five, are not likely to meet the needs of former inmates/gang members.

Accomplishing the task of centralizing drug treatment and other services in poor neighborhoods likely will strain the standard procedures that agencies use to offer such services. However, the realistic limitations on life in a gang neighborhood and the predications of the realistic behavior of gang members demand a change from a conventional approach if we wish to reduce recidivism, improve the future for former inmates, and lower levels of gang-based street crime.

Third, correctional institutions employ experts in the delivery of a wide variety of services to inmates. These staffers may be significant resources in the development of neighborhood-based service delivery in high-crime gang communities. Former inmates are not likely to intimidate prison workers and they may be used to train and support community agency staffers in learning the best practices of dealing with often-aggressive former inmates. Using prison workers as community mentors may strengthen local agencies' abilities to design programs that fit inmates' needs.

Fourth, we should reconfirm publicly our responsibility of ensuring that former inmates find a lawful place in the community. With nearly two million men and women in state and federal prisons in late 2000, overlooking the future needs of millions of currently imprisoned men and women is the equivalent of overlooking the needs of the residents of an area the size of metropolitan Denver. Nearly all of these prisoners will be released and as they serve their sentences, correctional agencies and communities should be planning what will happen to them after release and how they best can prepare for the day they go home. If the community approach is punitive, states will continue to build more prisons for recidivists. The consequences of avoiding a proactive approach to inmate integration are dire: Overlooking millions of today's prisoners has a high opportunity cost that our children will pay with higher taxes and/or less support for public education, higher education, and community-based initiatives.

Correctional institutions' programs in education and vocational training, and work opportunities in small-scale factories, culinary arts, welding, automotive repair, and the like may meet the needs of minimum-wage employment of today's former inmates. But communities change faster than prisons. Imagine returning home in the year 2000 having spent the last 20 years in prison. It may take inmates more than 30 to 60 days in a half-way house to learn how to negotiate in a community significantly different from the one they left in 1980 when there was no Space Shuttle, when computers did not sit on everyone's desks, and when no one held a Palm Pilot in one hand and cellular phone in the other.

A 25-year-old inmate imprisoned in 2000 on a federal drug conspiracy conviction may face 300 months in prison and would not be released until sometime around 2021. What economic opportunities will be available then to former inmates? Will welding and food service be desirable employment in 2021? To realistically prepare inmates for the future, we will have to do more than teach them to read and write, which were useful vocational skills in the early 20th century but are inadequate in the 21st century. Realistic planning for the release of millions of inmates should be done jointly between correctional and community agencies. We must move quickly to narrow the training gap that now prepares former inmates for 1940s-like jobs.

We have reviewed a range of issues that likely would influence the integration of prison gang members into their home communities. These are serious issues, we have argued, that will not be remedied with solutions of remedial education and basic vocational training. The risk factors producing delinquents who became members of street and prison gangs are enormously complex, and simple solutions will not reasonably meet the challenges of overcoming poverty, marginalization, class structure, and education deficits so extreme that research cited here has shown that the only way many gang members can earn a sufficient income is by selling illegal drugs.

Street and prison gang members are different in important ways from non-gang members. Gang members participate in social networks built on crime partnerships that accelerate the rate of crime as well as the severity of the crime committed. Despite the criminal conduct linked to gang groups, gangs do offer members a sense of identity and belonging as well as, paradoxically, a sense of security. Among middle-aged men, research shows that a gang identity is another element in one's distinctiveness in the community and asking men to relinquish such an identity might be the equivalent of asking them to relinquish their ties to family. We have argued that trying to strip men of a gang identity may be possible in prison because prison is a highly controlled, closed community operated by, in a real sense, a law enforcement agency. When on the street, however, a man's gang identity can be used to negotiate a place to reside, a source of income, and a ready-made set of friends.

A central theme in this article has been the critical need of community involvement in the post-release integration of prison gang members. These men were marginal community members before they were imprisoned and surely now that each one has an ex-con tag, their community lives won't get easier. Surely, communities will have many failures, that is, men whose criminal lives dominate their conduct and these men will end up in prison again. On the other hand, research has shown that most men want to live lawful lives but either do not know how or do not have the resources to accomplish it. These men need help. We are the only ones capable of helping them.

We have suggested that such help be a blend of services delivered to them in a way that meets their lifestyle. A pedantic approach requiring former inmates and gang members to meet "our conditions or else" is unreasonable and in the long run will be counterproductive as we repeatedly imprison men who were just released. Helping individual gang offenders is critical but we also must infuse with financial resources and social services the impoverished communities where most were reared. Research has shown that treating the individual and avoiding the more complex problem of community rehabilitation only allows the problem of street gangs to persist. With a concerted effort initiated by correctional officials, who indeed understand offender programming and treatment perhaps better than any other agencies in the criminal justice system, we can plan intervention strategies that work to lower recidivism and improve the lives of former inmates. Accomplishing that mission will improve community life as well.

References

Beck, A. J., & Mumola, C. J. (1998). *Prisoners in 1998.* Bulletin NCJ–175687. Washington, DC: U.S. Department of Justice.

Bossler, A. (1999). *The role of employment in the lives of federal prisoners: An holistic approach.* Master's thesis, Department of Criminal Justice Sciences, Illinois State University, Normal, Illinois 61790.

Bossler, A., Fleisher, M., & Krienert, J. (2000, February). Employment and crime: Revisiting the resiliency effect of work on crime. *Corrections Compendium, 25,* 1(2), 1–3, 16–18.

Bursik, R. J., & Grasmick, H. G. (1993). *Neighborhoods and crime: The dimensions of effective community control.* New York: Lexington Books.

Curry, G. D., Ball, R. A., & Decker, S. H. (1996). *Estimating the national scope of gang crime from law enforcement data.* Washington, DC: National Institute of Justice.

Curry, G. D., & Spergel, I. A. (1992). Gang involvement and delinquency among Hispanic and African American adolescent males. *Journal of Research on Crime and Delinquency, 29,* 273–291.

Decker, S. H., Bynum, T. S., & Weisel, D. L. (1998). Gang as organized crime groups: A tale of two cities. *Justice Quarterly, 15,* 395–423.

Decker, S. H., Pennell, S., & Caldwell, A. (1996). *Arrestees and guns: Monitoring the illegal firearms market.* Washington, DC: National Institute of Justice.

Decker, S. H., & Van Winkle, B. (1995). Slingin' dope: The role of gangs and gang members in drug sales. *Justice Quarterly, 11,* 1001–1022.

Decker, S. H., & Van Winkle, B. (1996). *Life in the Gang: Family, friends, and violence,* New York: Cambridge University Press.

Esbensen, F., & Huizinga, D. (1993). Gangs, drugs and delinquency in a survey of urban youth. *Criminology, 31,* 565–590.

Fagan, J. (1989). The social organization of drug use and drug dealing among urban gangs. *Criminology, 27,* 633–670.

Fleisher, M. S. (1989). *Warehousing violence.* Newbury Park, CA: Sage.

Fleisher, M. S. (1995). *Beggars and thieves: Lives of urban street criminals*. Madison: University of Wisconsin Press.

Fleisher, M. S. (1998). *Dead end kids: Gang girls and the boys they know*. Madison, WI: University of Wisconsin Press.

Fleisher, M. S. (2000–2001). *Adult male gang member residential mobility*. Unpublished field notes.

Fleisher, M. S., & Rison, R. H. (1999). Gang management in corrections. In P. M. Carlson & J. S. Garrett (Eds.), *Prison and jail administration*. Gaithersburg, MD: Aspen Publishers, Inc.

Hagedom, J. M. (1988). *People and folks: Gangs, crime and the underclass in a rustbelt city*. Chicago: Lake View.

Jacobs, J. B. (1974). Street gangs behind bars. *Social Problems, 21*, 395–409.

Katz, M. B. (1993). Reframing the "underclass" debate. In M. B. Katz (Ed.), *The "underclass" debate: Views from history*. Princeton, NJ: Princeton University Press.

Klein, M. W. (1995). *The American street gang*. New York: Oxford University Press.

Moore, J. W. (1991). *Going down to the barrio: Homeboys and homegirls in change*. Philadelphia: Temple University Press.

Spergel, I. (1995). *The youth gang problem*. New York: Oxford University Press.

Tatge, M. (2000). With unemployment low, a new group is in demand: Ex-cons. *The Wall Street Journal, CV*(81), 1, AB.

Thornberry, T. (1998). Membership in youth gangs and involvement in serious and violent offending. In R. Loeber & D. P. Farrington (Eds.), *Serious and violent juvenile offenders: Risk factors and successful interventions*. Thousand Oaks, CA: Sage Publications.

United States Department of Justice (1999, January). *Substance abuse and treatment, state and federal prisoners, 1997*. Special Report NCJ-172871. Washington, DC: U.S. Department of Justice.

Wilson, W. J. (1987). *The truly disadvantaged*. Chicago: University of Chicago Press.

Yablonsky, L. (1997). *Gangsters: Fifty years of madness, drugs, and death on the streets of America*. New York: New York University Press.

CORRECTIONS MANAGEMENT QUARTERLY, 2001, 5(1), 65–77.

34. "Just Like Baking a Cake": Women Describe the Necessary Ingredients for Successful Reentry after Incarceration

by Patricia O'Brien

Eighteen female ex-prison inmates describe the strengths they used to manage their reentry after release from prison. As a group, the women stressed that a mix of personal resiliency, interpersonal capacities, and social resources facilitated their successful transition.

One of the guiding principles of the strengths perspective is the belief that people have the ability to grow and change throughout their lives. This faith in human potential is likewise linked to the idea that people often have untapped and therefore unrealized resources that can serve them in even their darkest times (Saleebey, 1997). Offenders in the criminal justice system find their very selfhood is defined by the crimes they have committed. The related stigma often follows them out to the "streets" where statistics attest, they often fall back into former patterns of behaviors and associations, that then lead them back to prison as recidivists. What the statistics of failure fail to convey are the individual and almost heroic stories of those labeled "bad" who successfully negotiate the journey back to the "free world" regardless of their previous transgressions.

Women in prison on average are over age 30, at least high-school graduates or holders of a General Equivalency Degree (GED), and are disproportionately African American. Women are substantially more likely than men to be serving time for a drug offense and less likely to have been sentenced for a violent crime. Nearly six in 10 female inmates grew up in a household with at least one parent absent, and about half reported that an immediate family member had also served time. More than four in 10 reported prior physical or sexual abuse (Greenfeld & Snell, 1999; Snell, 1994).

Nationally, more than a quarter of a million children have mothers in jail or prison (Greenfeld & Snell, 1999). Most of these women lived with their children before their incarceration; many are single mothers who were their children's sole caretakers. Maternal imprisonment affects future generations because children's psychological health and sense of family is damaged by the separation from their mothers. Increasingly, families are destroyed forever through termination of parental rights. The ripple effects of family fracture are felt in the community when the adult caretaker is no longer available to parent or contribute as a citizen to the social community we share.

Of concern to practitioners is that so many of the families we see in counseling agencies, in public aid offices, and in substance abuse treatment centers have previous or current involvement with the criminal justice system. The research on transition from prison has primarily focused on predicting failure on the basis of demographic and psychological characteristics and has relied mostly on male samples. Recidivism among women is a matter of rising alarm as "we keep on building prisons" (Dressel, 1994) to hold them. The challenge then is how we can support women, consistent with our belief in empowerment practice, who are trying to beat the odds of recidivism to make it out in the communities to which they return after incarceration? Gutiérrez and Lewis (1999) have described empowerment with women of color and other oppressed groups as comprised of consciousness, connection with others, and confidence. The current study sought to answer the question, "What constitutes empowerment for formerly incarcerated women?" (O'Brien, 2001).

The Study

The goal of this exploration was to explicitly identify women who had successfully negotiated the transition from prison to community and through their eyes, understand the strengths and resources they used to manage their reintegration. The study, drawing on interviews with 18 formerly incarcerated women examined how family, friends, intimate partners, parole or supervision officers, and experiences during incarceration promoted the women's progress after release from prison.

Findings and Interpretations

The women's narratives produced the overarching themes of the immediate post-release need to address basic survival issues and the importance of their intrapersonal and interpersonal attitudes about their own identity and functioning. The women provided many examples of these two interwoven and overlapping themes. For example, all discussed the necessity of finding shelter or having "someplace to go" as a crucial start to their transition. They also discussed the need to address the impact of incarceration upon their relationships, their everyday choices, and how they thought and felt about themselves as a consequence. Often women expressed insights about their experiences that they had not been aware of before their articulation in the interviews. They also identified internal strengths that had nourished their sense of survival and hope. These themes were not sequential or hierarchical but rather unique to each woman and her particular psychosocial context. Yet, all the women to some degree identified five categories of markers that signified their success. These included:

1. Finding shelter
2. Obtaining employment/legal income

3. Reconstructing connections with others
4. Developing community membership; and
5. Identifying consciousness and confidence in self

The following sections discuss the themes supported by the women's narratives that fit these categories.

Finding Shelter

Home as both a metaphor and a physical place of being is crucial to human well being. Women coming out of a state facility with limited resources often have to start over to find safe and sufficient housing and so initially stay with family members or a former or current partner. On the other hand, selected federal inmates can serve part of their sentence in a residential setting, as a step back to the community. One of the latter, Deeni, (all of the women used pseudoynms) said that this concrete resource facilitated her reentry because she did not have to depend on others to support her when she was released.

> The halfway house was very helpful for me . . . because I really didn't have any place to go. I'd rather just be there and know what I had to deal with there, and do what I had to do, because I'm a warrior, see. I had to be there for 6 months. One of my goals was to save my money and make sure I had my apartment and everything ready to go when I got out. I set my goals and reached my goals.

The state inmates, who were released from state facilities directly to the streets, tended to move from place-to-place, depending on more temporary supports until they had amassed enough money to move into their own home. Several of the inmates came out of prison with money they had saved while working prison industry jobs. Nan saved $3,500 from the employment that she had while in federal custody; Sadie and Laura also saved money from their private industry jobs in the state system. Sadie came out of prison after 8 years of incarceration with enough of a lump sum that she was able to make a down payment and secure a mortgage loan for a house about 6 months after her release.

Mandi's situation was more typical among the women. She began her reentry by sleeping on the sofa in her brother's crowded two-bedroom apartment. She reported feeling very uncomfortable and left there after a few weeks. She then moved to a friend's house but because she did not want to start a relationship with him, she moved from there as soon as she was able to save enough money from her minimum wage job at a Taco Bell to rent a small apartment.

However, she needed a much larger place in order to regain custody of her four children who had been in her mother's care before and during her incarceration. She describes what she calls a "Christmas present" she received when she called a landlord about a house for rent that she saw as she was walking to her apartment from her job. She went to meet with the landlord and was honest with him about her lack of credit and her prison history. She recalled she told him:

> "You know, I know how to paint and stuff. So, instead of a deposit, I'll just paint the house for you." He ended up giving me the keys. I didn't give him a dime. I remember walking away from there crying. It was my Christmas present from God.

Mandi may have considered this accomplishment divine intervention, but it was also likely that the landlord was impressed with her determination, honesty and nerve.

Securing and Maintaining Employment/Legal Income

While it may be obvious that the savings from in-prison employment enabled the women to manage their immediate and concrete needs after release from prison, employment during incarceration also imparted a normalizing effect for the women. Nan expressed this when she related, "you kinda like still get to be human in a sense." Sadie said that the inmates (who worked at these jobs) "didn't get involved in near as much the everyday life in the prison . . . a pretty good benefit too" meaning these inmates might be less likely to get caught up in potentially negative activities in the institution.

The idea that employment could be meaningful as well as sufficient for support was also important to the women in this group who were working at the time of the interviews. As is true for many women, a lack of education and gender discrimination as well as the specific stigma attached to a drug or criminal background sometimes worked against their success. However, these women discussed how they had managed their circumstances and exploited opportunities to eventually support themselves and in some cases, their children.

Ashley found that she was able to manage her childcare challenge and obtain useful employment when she went to work as an aide at the childcare center her daughter attended. Mandi was sure that acknowledging that she was an ex-felon would prevent her from getting a job. She drew upon personal contacts (as many of us do) to find her initial job:

My parole officer gave me this sheet of paper and said, "When you find a job, your employer has to sign this. That way they know you're on parole." I thought, "I'm never gonna get a job." I ended up gettin' a job at Taco Bell because my brother's wife's sister was the manager there.

Mandi moved from her minimum wage job at the Taco Bell to increased wages as a manager at McDonald's in part due to her personal engagement skills. She recounted that when she would stop in at McDonald's "The manager there would tell me, "You're very friendly." I try to be, you know." And even though she had some hesitation about working at McDonald's since it was every inmate's hope she could do better than get a job at McDonald's she took the job and found that having the title of manager "meant something."

Anita reflected that the controlling prison culture reinforced the lack of planning for future responsibilities that women face when they exit the institution. Yet she used some of what she had learned in maintaining a regular schedule while in prison to manage the routine she developed while working at a dry cleaner. Anita also talked about the connection between her employment and her new identity when she said she had put on "new clothes" for her "new life" since her release from prison.

The women who resided in the community placement facility were expected to obtain employment and pay toward their room and board. They were already identified as ex-inmates due to their residence, and so did not report as much concern with stigma related to finding a job, as did those women who came out to the community directly from a prison facility. Jeanette described her relief when a computer skills class sponsored by a local job training agency provided her an opportunity for employment, and in that setting, the fact that she was a felon provided her with additional currency: "I covered a lot of slots for them in one big hiring."

Although Ashley attributes her employment success to "luck," she was also able to present herself in a manner that attenuated the "ex-con" stigma:

> I had to go in there and tell this lady. "I was in jail for this but I want to do social work." And, I basically sold myself. "I know I can do this. I love kids." And, she hired me. That was a good step in the door.

Sadie's involvement with an in-prison domestic violence program became a support system in multiple ways when she left prison. Sadie used this support system and what she reframed as "7-and-a-half years experience in the criminal justice system" as a bridge in her transition:

> My major support system . . . was the people at [the shelter] who had been coming into the prison for all that time . . . those women were a great support system for me. They were like friends, and being in that group was real good. I certainly learned a lot about domestic violence, which benefited me in getting a job.

Although not all the women worked full-time after their release, almost all in some way drew upon family resources for concrete assistance in the early days of their transition. An exception was Bernie, the oldest member of the group who was 65 when she was released. Instead, she recalled that it was the kindness of strangers in the network of social and church-based services and the assistance of another former inmate that enabled her to both obtain a home and to find the means to support herself. She related that when she got off the bus that deposited her after her final incarceration, she had "nowhere to go." She initially spent several nights with the former inmate while she applied for subsidized housing and other forms of public assistance. She was fearful that her criminal record would nullify her eligibility but apparently her police report sent over by the Sheriff's office indicated "no warrants and no arrests" so she secured an apartment. Out of her recognition of "Who better but we people" to help each other, she later started a thrift store with the help of a local church that not only supplemented her meager fixed income but also enabled her to assist other inmates who were returning to the community.

Soon after Susan's release, she went to work in a family-owned business. Later, she began working in a nursing home where she acquired her certified nursing assistant license. At the time of the interview, her husband had agreed to financially support their family while she returned to school to study for her licensed practical nurse designation.

Connection with Others

Recent developmental models have demonstrated the importance of relationships for enhancing, women's well being throughout the life span (Jordon, Kaplan, Miller, Stiver, & Surrey, 1991). For the women in this study, relationships were crucial both for their management if their incarceration as well as their release.

One of the major ways that family members supported the participants was by caring for their children while the women were incarcerated, and for some of the women who were not yet financially stable, continuing to provide a home for their children after release. Several of the women found themselves in the position of "proving themselves" to their family but also finding that as they did, the response was positive. For example, Nicole related that her mother told her that if "you start working and tryin' to save some money, and we'll go look for a car, and I'll try to help you out and see what I can do about co-signin'." Regina, the youngest participant, returned home on parole after release from prison and found her parents sheltered and supported her (and soon her newborn infant) "as long as I show them I'm a responsible person." Several of the women had the experience of reconstructing their lives after prison with a new partner. Rene, who at the time of the interview had been released from the federal residential facility for only a few months, described the process of building support for her and her two children with the help that her new fiancé provided:

> I started while I was there in prison. It's just like doin' a diagram of a house, and you're gonna have this what's gonna hold it up, and you're gonna do all these things to keep it standin'. And, it's like keeping all the bricks in place. The basic thing is keepin' straight. Keep straight and maintain, and then workin' everything around. That's what I did, because my boyfriend was there. He came to see me. He stuck in there with the kids.

At the time of the interviews, eight of the participants had alternative physical or legal custody arrangements for their children. Most of these children resided in the care of their mothers or other family members. These parents chose a more graduated process of regaining eventual custody that facilitated them developing the financial and emotional means of supporting their children.

The reawakened capacity to care for their children made some participants feel rewarded by their resumption of their mothering role. Nan explained how creating a home for her children enabled her to overcome some of the compulsions that had resulted in her previous convictions:

> Havin' to go to prison, bein' in a matchbox room and only havin' X-amount of dollars and havin' nowhere to go and nobody to turn to. I don't ever want that again, Honey. All them fine fancy clothes and good livin', I don't want that, because I had all of that. I wasn't even happy. Now, I'm so happy bein' right here with my kids. With little money and nothin', because it's real, true love right here in the home with me and my kids.

Many of the women said the necessity of repairing fractured relationships with family members, especially their mothers, was also a priority. This was surprising since their mothers had served as caretakers of the participants' minor children during the time their daughters were in prison. Ten of the 18 study participants described their relationships with their mothers as historically problematic, and sometimes abusive. Working out the difficulties in their relationships with their mothers contributed to the women's sense of growth following incarceration, even if their mother was no longer living. For some women, regaining the ability to parent their children also depended on their mending these relationships.

Ashley indicated that asserting herself to her mother opened the door to having a more healthy relationship:

> My mom and I were never really close, because she did abuse me. I would never open up to her and talk to her. So, about a year ago, I just sat her down one day, and I said, "look, Mom, this is me and this is the way I am. You either deal with it or you don't, because you don't have another daughter. But, I'm not gonna let you downgrade me and talk bad about me. You have to accept me the way I am, because, if not, I can just walk out of your life like I've come back in." You have to make those steps forward sometimes.

In counseling sessions during her incarceration and after her release, Susan reported that she gained insight by examining some of the abuse prior to her incarceration:

> From the time I was 3, my mom was real abusive to me and I grew up with it so all my boyfriends were guys who were abusive and everything's always my fault so I was a very big people-pleaser and I did what ever I had to make them happy and a lot of times it had to do with money so I would steal money to give it to them so I wouldn't get beat or so they wouldn't just fly off and leave me.

Meanwhile, Susan's mother also obtained therapy and began to understand and own some of what she had perpetrated upon her daughter:

> The second time, my mom had started counseling a year before I went in . . . we both worked through a whole bunch of stuff and they came up and talked to me

> a lot; there was no, "I blame you"; they were there to support me and stood behind me, and they helped me when I came out. I'm closer to my mom and dad than I've ever been in my life.

Most of the women discussed the importance of their relationships with their parole or supervision officers as facilitating their success in their transition. Racque, who essentially married out of her life "on the streets" in a west coast city and moved to a small town in the Midwest, recalls that she had an "understanding" parole officer who helped her deal with the paperwork required for moving from one state to another.

Mandy came out of prison for the second time, steered clear of old associations, and settled in a larger city where she knew no one. She faced an overwhelming list of both parole conditions and family court expectations that she had to meet in order to regain custody of her four children in foster care. She recounts the difficulty of her first few months:

> I didn't have a car. I found a house within walking distance of Taco Bell. I couldn't have a phone in my name because of an outstanding bill, so I couldn't get a phone in my house, but I had to report once a month by phone and you get charged for that. So, finances were a real big struggle, getting to work without a vehicle, trying to go see the parole officer without a vehicle.

Mandi met her conditions, but not without some personal cost, and at great risk to her freedom. After a relapse in her use of crack cocaine, it was the understanding assistance of her employer that facilitated Mandi's acquiring the treatment she needed to get clean again. Soon after the interview, she celebrated her first year of sobriety and eventually she regained legal and physical custody of her children and received a discharge from parole supervision. She attributes much of her success to her parole officer who was willing to be flexible and responsive to her individual situation and assist her in managing the conditions despite her massive financial challenges.

Other women also identified positive attributes of their parole officers that facilitated their transition. These included being treated "as a person rather than a number," being "left alone," without intense intrusion into the woman's daily life; willingness to respond to changing circumstances by modifying conditions when appropriate to do so; and providing accurate information about the supervisory process. In several examples, the parole officer facilitated the woman's early discharge from supervision.

Confidence

This section describes what participants identified as internally derived indicators of change since the incarceration. These self-initiated changes include developing a sense of efficacy for managing everyday life, creating relational competence, making decisions to promote physical health, and using internal resources to cultivate hope. For example, Nicole related some of the differences she recognizes that have enabled her to feel more confident and self-assured as a consequence of her experiences in prison.

> I'm pretty much the same person I was before—a little bit older and a little bit wiser—I guess it's just part of growin' up and goin' through hard times and realizin' that things can get better, which they have for me in a lot of ways. I think I still relate to people the way I was before I was in—some people say I'm a little hard—I've been called an evil woman by an old friend. I said, "Well, when you've been where I have and gone through things that I have, I learned to build a wall and it takes a lot to get through it." If I feel that somethin's not right, then I'm goin' the other direction. I woke up and realized had I not went there and went through the things I had, I don't think I'd be where I am today.

Mandi recalled that a correctional officer told her while Mandi was incarcerated that, "the company you keep will determine the trouble you're in," In order to grow the fragile seed of her sobriety, Mandi surrounded herself with what she describes as "positive people," including her self-help group, her church sponsor, and one of her employers who first noticed her potential.

A number of the participants recalled particular ministers, counselors, or other prison staff members who simply treated them as "human beings." Most of the women who had resided at the community placement facility spoke glowingly of the drug counselor who worked with them. For example, Elena found that he encouraged her to "prove 'em all wrong":

> When I came out of prison, I had the same attitude that I was gonna do everything like before. I wasn't gonna change. I just thought, "They made me wiser, you know." I was just gonna be slicker. I had a terrible attitude. My drug counselor was the one that really helped me decide on what I really want out of life. He was like . . . my inspiration, somebody that I really looked up to.

Although these women described major struggles in gaining housing and employment, they reflected an ability to bounce back from adversity by taking advantage of what they could while incarcerated and being strategic in using resources when they exited prison. The women identified some of their strengths that promoted their success as "stubbornness," "problem-solving skills," and "confidence" all of which often relate to competence for handling challenges (Bandura, 1992).

Community Membership

Once the women had met their concrete needs for survival, they recognized the motivational force that membership in the world around them provided. The ability to "give back" or contribute to others was an important marker that many of the women discussed as reflective of their citizenship in the communities to which they had returned.

For example, Nan wrote letters to the friends who were still in prison about what she had learned about managing her freedom and the continuing supervision. Mandi became a volunteer with a prison advocacy organization and returned to the women's prison facility to facilitate an inmate support group. Elena talked about her dream of working with Latina girls to help them avoid some of the troubles she experienced. Bernie gave out bras and bus tokens to newly released women so they can look presentable and get around the city for job interviews. Deeni negotiated with the community placement facility so the residents could attend exercise classes she taught. Sadie helped organize an annual crafts sale that features the work of local women artists as well as led off-road bike trips for novice trail bikers. Elizabeth worked in a substance abuse center with other previously jailed women. Participants expressed pride in the ways in which they felt their giving reflected their inclusion in the free world.

In addition to having some insight about the elements that contributed to their successful reentry, these women expressed aspirations that reflected their sense of hope for transforming their lives. These aspirations included returning to college, better-paying employment and doing meaningful work.

Discussion and Implications

Running through the women's narratives is a sense of both dormancy and growth. The women project wisdom sharpened by experience for how they must function in order to free themselves from correctional involvement. The process of successful integration depends on both the woman's developing a sense of self-efficacy and her strategic use of family, correctional, and community resources. These findings are consistent with what others have identified as necessary for addressing the continuum of service needs for formerly incarcerated women in an empowering process (Zaplin, 1998) and fit with the elements of consciousness, connection, and confidence Gutiérrez and Lewis (1999). A crucial difference is the necessity of addressing the concrete realities of reconstructing families and lives after separation from home and community. As Denni so eloquently stated, "It has to be a combination. It's just like bakin' a cake. You can't leave out the flour. You need all the ingredients to make it come out right."

The study also suggests important policy implications, particularly given the financial and social costs of incarceration (Chesney-Lind, 1992; Dressel, 1994). It is time to look at alternatives to incarceration, especially considering the mix of social and environmental factors that are producing female inmates at an increasing rate and the fact that the largest proportion of the increasing bulge in our state and federal penal institutions consists of inmates convicted on drug charges. Further examination of community-based programs for female (and male) offenders is a crucial area of needed research. We have indications that these alternatives are successful for some women offenders (Devine, 1997; Morash, Bynum, & Koons, 1995). While many questions remain about the most effective ways to respond to relapse and recidivism, it seems crucial to adopt and maintain a rehabilitative and a broad-based perspective to comprehensive treatment as opposed to a single focus approach that targets one risk factor alone.

References

Bandura, A. (1992). Exercise of personal agency through the self-efficacy mechanism. In R. Schwarzer (Ed.). *Self-efficacy: Thought control of action*, (pp. 338). Washington, DC: Hemisphere Publishing.

Bloom, B., & Steinhart, D. (1993). *Why punish the children: A reappraisal of the children of incarcerated mothers in America*. San Francisco: National Council on Crime and Delinquency.

Chesney-Lind, M. (1992). Putting the brakes on the building binge. *Corrections Today*, 30–34.

Daly, K. & Immargeon, R. (1998). The past, present, and future of restorative justice: Some critical reflections. *Contemporary Justice Review*, *1*(1), 21–46.

Devine, K. (1997). *Family unity: The benefits and costs of community-based sentencing programs for women and their children in Illinois*. Chicago: Chicago Legal Advocacy to Incarcerated Mothers.

Dressel, P. L. (1994). . . . and we keep on building prisons: Racism, poverty, and challenges to the welfare state. *Journal of Sociology & Social Welfare, 21(3)*, 7–30.

Federal Bureau of Investigation. (1998). *Crime in the United States—Uniform Crime Reports*. Washington, DC: U.S. Department of Justice.

Glaser, B., & Strauss, A. (1967). *The discovery of grounded theory*. Chicago: Aldine.

Goldstein, H. (1997). Victors or victims. In D. Saleebey (Ed.) *The strengths perspective in social work practice* (2nd ed.) (pp. 21–35). White Plains, NY: Longman.

Greenfeld, L. A. & Snell, T. L. (1999). *Women offenders*. (Bulletin No. NCJ-175688). Washington, DC: Bureau of Justice Statistics.

Gutiérrez, L. M. & Lewis, E. A. (1999). *Empowering women of color*. New York: Columbia University Press.

Hairston, D. F. (1991). Family ties during imprisonment: Important for whom and for what? *Journal of Sociology and Social Welfare, 18*(1), 87–104.

Holquist, S. E. (1999). Nurturing the seeds of restorative justice. *Journal of Community Practice* 6(2), 63–77.

Jordon, J. V., Kaplan, A. G., Miller, J. B., Stiver, I. P., & Surrey, J. L. (1991). *Women's growth in connection: Writings from the Stone Center*. New York: The Guilford Press.

Koons, B. A., Burrow, J. D., Morash, M., & Bynum, T. (1997). Expert and offender perceptions of program elements linked to successful outcomes for incarcerated women. *Crime & Delinquency, 43*, 512–532.

Lincoln, Y. S., & Guba, E. G. (1985). *Naturalist Inquiry*. Beverly Hills, CA: Sage.

O'Brien, P. (2001). *Making it in the "free world": Women in transition from prison*. Albany, NY: State University of New York Press.

Saleebey, D. (1997). Introduction: Power in the people. In D. Saleebey (Ed.), *The strengths perspective in social work practice* (2nd ed.) (pp. 3–19). White Plains, NY: Longman Press.

Snell, T. L. (1994). *Women in prison*. (Special Report No. NCJ-145321). Washington, DC: Bureau of Justice Statistics.

Strauss, A., & Corbin, J. (1990). *Basics of qualitative research: Grounded theory procedures and techniques*. Newbury Park, CA: Sage.

Zaplin, R. T. (Ed.). (1998). *Female offenders: Critical perspectives and effective interventions*. Gaithersburg. MD: Aspen Publications.

Ziedenberg, J., & Schiraldi, V. 1999. *Punishing decade: Prison and jail estimates at the millennium*. Washington, DC: Justice Policy Institute.

FAMILIES IN SOCIETY: THE JOURNAL OF CONTEMPORARY HUMAN SERVICES